哈佛要培养的,是具有雅典人那种高素质的公民,即一个人要不断意识到,活着对社会有意义,才是生活中最有价值的东西。

Franklin D. Roosevelt
——富兰克林·罗斯福

哈佛
毕业典礼
演讲精选

带着激情与梦想上路

Beginning a Journey with
Inspirations and Dreams

刘海翔 甘露 编译

汉英
对照

人民日报出版社

Content

Preface 前言 … 1

1940's
America's Role in the Rehabilitation of Europe
George C. Marshall
美国在欧洲重建中应担当的角色
乔治·马歇尔 … 3

1950's
Novel Experience of a Fraternal Community
Thornton N. Wilder
体验人类大同的境界
桑顿·怀尔德 … 13

Words to the American Intellectual
John F. Kennedy
给美国知识界的建言
约翰·肯尼迪 … 25

United to Fight Poverty
Lady Barbara Ward Jackson
联合起来 消除贫困
杰克逊男爵夫人 … 39

The Disunity of European Countries
Pieter Geyl
欧洲国家的分裂问题
彼得·盖尔 … 51

1960's
Radical Thought as Modern Energy
Lionel Trilling
激进思想是现代动力
莱昂内尔·特里林 … 71

1970's
Global Citizen for World Peace
Theodore M. Hesburgh
做世界公民 实现世界和平
西奥多·赫斯伯 … 89

Conscience and Consciousness, and More Conscientiousness
Ralph Ellison
良心与良知——呼唤更多的自主意识
拉尔夫·埃利森 … 109

Watergate and the Balance of Power
Archibald Cox　水门事件与权力制约　127
　　　　　　　　　　　　阿奇博尔德·考克斯

A World Split Apart
Alexander Solzhenitsyn　分裂的世界　151
　　　　　　　　　　　　亚历山大·索尔仁尼琴

1980's

Understanding Our Brave New World
John H. Finley　认知我们的新奇世界　183
　　　　　　　　　　　　约翰·芬利

Starting Our Journey at Daybreak
Carlos Fuentes　迎着曙光上路　201
　　　　　　　　　　　　卡洛斯·富恩特斯

Embracing the Beginning of a New Morning
Juan Carlos I　迎接新黎明的开始　237
　　　　　　　　　　　　胡安·卡洛斯

Democratic Nations Must Unite
Mohtarma Benazir Bhutto　民主国家　团结一致　255
　　　　　　　　　　　　贝娜齐尔·布托

1990's

The Social Responsibilities of American Universities
Derek Bok　美国大学的社会责任　273
　　　　　　　　　　　　德瑞克·伯克

Sustainability and Our Environment
Gro Harlem Brundtland　可持续发展与我们的环境　285
　　　　　　　　　　　　格罗·布伦特兰

Cynicism Will Take People No Where
Al Gore　玩世不恭于事无补　301
　　　　　　　　　　　　阿尔·戈尔

2000's

Global Culture and Diversity, Mass Communication and Our Fate
Vaclav Havel   全球文明多元文化 大众传播与人类前途   **325**
瓦茨拉夫·哈维尔

Poetic Exploration of Science
Harold Varmus   科学的诗意探索   **351**
哈罗德·瓦尔穆斯

Shaping History as a Pathfinder
Madeleine Albright   勇于做创造历史的人   **369**
玛德琳·奥尔布莱特

All Human Rights for All
Mary Robinson   让所有人享有一切人权   **389**
玛丽·罗宾逊

Education as an Investment in the Information Age
Alan Greenspan   信息时代的教育投资   **401**
艾伦·格林斯潘

Global Doubts
Amartya Sen   对质疑全球化的回应   **417**
阿玛蒂亚·森

The Critical Function of Decision-making
Robert Rubin   决策能力决定命运   **431**
罗伯特·鲁宾

History Summons Us Once More
Daniel Patrick Moynihan   历史的再次召唤   **445**
丹尼尔·莫伊尼汉

The Impact of Multilateralism
Ernesto Zedillo   多边合作的作用和意义   **461**
欧内斯托·塞迪略

Three Crises, and the Need for American Leadership
Kofi Annan 三个危机呼唤美国的领导作用 **477**
  科菲·安南

An Actor's Own Words
John Lithgow 一个演员自己的话 **491**
  约翰·利特高

All Aboard for Your Departing Bus
Jim Lehrer 长途客车的下一站：参与服务 **507**
  吉姆·莱勒

From Those to Whom Much Is Given, Much Is Expected
Bill Gates 得到越多　责任越重 **525**
  比尔·盖茨

The Power of Imagination
J.K. Rowling 想象的力量 **543**
  J.K. 罗琳

Play Your Role in Our Future
Steven Chu 在未来扮演好你的角色 **559**
  朱棣文

2010's

Keeping Hope and Not Giving Up
Ellen Johnson Sirleaf 坚守希望　永不言弃 **577**
  埃伦·约翰逊－瑟利夫

We Live in an Age of Progress
Fareed Zakaria 生活在一个永远进取的时代 **597**
  法瑞德·扎卡利亚

带着激情与梦想上路
——代前言

哈佛作为世界最负盛名的高等学府之一，正如该校 2010 年毕业典礼演讲者、非洲第一位女总统瑟利夫所说：历年来哈佛培养出了总统、首相、联合国秘书长，商界、政界领袖，也培养了各行各业富有才华的领军人物，杰出的律师、医生、商人、公务员、设计师、教育家和思想家等等。

能够成为哈佛学生的人，无疑是学业优良，也是幸运的。在经历数年寒窗苦读终于毕业的时候，除了对自己完成学业充满自豪，对光明前途无限期待，他们是不是还在思考什么？那些被请来在毕业典礼上发表演说的演讲者，对这些幸运的毕业生说了些什么？

翻开这本书的目录，我们会发现，站在哈佛大学毕业典礼演讲台上的演讲者（不少是哈佛的校友），可谓都是事业有成、享誉一方的成功人士。他们当中，既有来自亚非拉、欧美国家的政界人物，如总统、总理、国务卿、部长、联合国秘书长等；有科学界、文化界的诺贝尔奖获得者；有像比尔·盖茨这样的高科技行业的创领者，也有像罗琳这样的畅销书作家，还有新闻主持和优秀的演员兼作家等等。

各行各业的卓越人士，讲述着他们自己曲折丰富的人生故事：他们所经历的大起大落、成功和失败；他们对世界和社会的看法、对理想和信念的追求，还有他们对哈佛学子的殷殷期望和热情鼓励。

不仅如此，随着历史风云的变幻，年复一年的毕业典礼演讲，也实时地反映出当年的国际局势和人们关注的话题。有时，身处决策层的领导者甚至借助这个平台传达出政府将要采取的重要举措。最著名的莫过于1947年的毕业典礼了。当时的美国国务卿乔治·马歇尔就是站在哈佛庭院中，面对1947届的毕业生，宣布了著名的"马歇尔计划（又称欧洲恢复计划）"，美国提供当时价值约131亿美元的援助，帮助被二战摧毁的欧洲国家重建家园。马歇尔说道：

> 毫无疑问，美国应该力所能及地帮助世界经济恢复正常，若非如此，就不会有政治的稳定与和平的保障。我们的政策不只是针对任何国家或是某个教条，而是应对饥饿、贫穷、绝望和动乱。它以世界范围内的经济复苏为目标，进而帮助我们创造能够让自由体制存在的政治和社会条件。

马歇尔计划成为影响战后世界形势的重要政策，对后世产生了深远影响。它不仅奠定了新的世界格局基础，也影响了半个多世纪以来的国际事务和国际关系，对在那之前两年成立的联合国，后来的世界贸易组织都有非常积极正面的影响。这份演讲也成为公共演讲的经典作品，更一再被包括安南、盖茨以及来自欧洲的多位演讲者在哈佛毕业典礼上反复述及。因此，我们把马歇尔的演讲作为本书的开篇，因为马歇尔计划标志着国际关系中一个新时期的开始——世界开始走向一个"深刻的和平"时期,正如2012年的演讲者、新闻评论家法瑞德·扎卡利亚所言:世界上最富有的国家之间,没有地缘政治之争,没有打仗或进行代理战争,甚至没有从事军备竞赛和进行冷战,这在历史上是非常罕见的。

这样的一头一尾,恰好形成了很好的呼应,也让人们看到了二战之后的变迁。

马歇尔在这里所提到的对世界承担的社会责任,也是很多演讲者所强调的重点。比如瑟利夫、罗琳从自己充满挫折的人生,朱棣文从地球资源和能源危机,比尔·盖茨从他所认识的世界不平等……都阐述了这个世界存在着诸多亟待解决的问题,特别强调作为幸运地获得最好教育的哈佛毕业生在"学术卓越,追求真理"的过程中所应当担负的社会职责,为什么那些幸运儿,在得到天赋、权益、机会的同时,也应该承担起更多的社会责任,为世界、为人类作出更多的贡献。

哈佛大学2008届的毕业生们,你们又将对他人的生命产生多大的影响?你们的智慧,你们应对艰难工作的能力,以及你们所受到的教育,都赋予你们独特的地位和责任。(J.K.罗琳)

毕业生们,你们在我们的未来中,要扮演举足轻重的角色。当你们追求个人的志向时,我希望你们也要培育热情、积极发声,以或大或小的方式有助于这个世界。(朱棣文)

  我们能做些什么？当你想想我们现在这个院子里的人，被给予过什么——天赋、特权、机会——因此全世界的人几乎都有无限的权力，要求我们做出贡献。(比尔·盖茨)

  有很多像你们一样有天赋、有雄心壮志的人，却永远不会有你们这样的机会——你应该为你所取得的成绩而骄傲。但我请求你们，要把你们受到的教育，用在最有价值的目标上，这样的目标，应当有助于改善别人的生活。(玛丽·罗宾逊)

  这是品读这些毕业演讲给我们印象最深刻的地方，也是我们把它们介绍给读者的最主要原因。我们无法任意延长生命的长度，但我们可以努力拓展生命的厚度和高度。这就像《哈利·波特》的作者罗琳在2008年哈佛毕业演讲中，引用古罗马哲人塞内加的那句名言："人生犹如故事，关键不在于长短，而在于是否精彩。"

  精彩的人生不仅在于追求个人理想，实现自我价值，更重要的，是同时对人类、对社会有所贡献。开卷有益，愿读者们聆听这些成功人士的肺腑之言，从他们的人生得失中获得启发，把自己的人生故事也尽可能地书写得丰富、精彩！

刘海翔　甘露

1940's

乔治·马歇尔（1880—1959）

二战期间担任美国三军参谋长联席会议主席，直接指挥庞大的军队，为反法西斯战争作出了卓越贡献。1947年至1949年间，担任美国国务卿，1953年获得诺贝尔和平奖，他是迄今为止唯一一位获得诺贝尔和平奖的职业军人。马歇尔在二战结束后曾来中国，参与国共调停，希望中国能够避免内战，他和毛泽东、周恩来、蒋介石等都打过交道，是中国人民较为熟悉的一位美国政治家。

在马歇尔将军的葬礼上，美国前总统杜鲁门这样评价道："他是我们这个时代伟人中的伟人。我衷心希望，当我跨入另一个世界，马歇尔能收留我当他的部下，从而让我得以努力报答他为我们所做的一切。"

在这篇演讲里，时任美国国务卿的马歇尔宣布了美国准备对饱受战争之害的欧洲提供经济援助的项目，这就是后来著名的"马歇尔计划"。他之所以选择在哈佛毕业典礼这样一个特殊场合宣讲这项计划，可谓用意深刻。他的演讲不仅给毕业生们，也给所有的美国人民提出了一系列值得思考的问题。在以后的哈佛毕业演讲中，马歇尔的名字和他的远见卓识，成为许多演讲者必谈的话题。

马歇尔计划（The Marshall Plan）的正式名称为欧洲复兴计划（European Recovery Program），是二战之后美国对被战争破坏的西欧各国进行经济援助、协助重建的计划，对欧洲国家的发展和世界政治格局产生了深远影响。该计划于1947年7月正式启动，并整整持续了四个财政年度。在这段时期内，西欧各国通过参加经济合作发展组织（OECD），总共接受了美国130多亿美元的援助，包括金融、技术、设备等各种形式。

1947

America's Role in the Rehabilitation of Europe
美国在欧洲重建中应担当的角色

George C. Marshall 乔治·马歇尔

Mr. President, Dr. Conant, members of the Board of Overseers, Ladies and Gentlemen:

I'm profoundly grateful and touched by the great distinction and honor and great compliment accorded me by the authorities of Harvard this morning. I'm overwhelmed, as a matter of fact, and I'm rather fearful of my inability to maintain such a high rating as you've been generous enough to accord to me. In these historic and lovely surroundings, this perfect day, and this very wonderful assembly, it is a tremendously impressive thing to an individual in my position. But to speak more seriously, I need not tell you, gentlemen, that the world situation is very serious. That must be apparent to all intelligent people. I think one difficulty is that the problem is one of such enormous complexity that the very mass of facts presented to the public by press and radio make it exceedingly difficult for the man in the street to reach a clear appraisement of the situation. Furthermore, the people of this country are distant from the troubled areas of the earth and it is hard for them to comprehend the **plight** [n. 困境. 苦境] and consequent reactions of the long-suffering peoples, and the effect of those reactions on their governments in connection with our efforts to promote peace in the world.

In considering the requirements for the rehabilitation of Europe, the physical loss of life, the visible destruction of cities, factories, mines and railroads was correctly estimated but it has become obvious during recent months that this visible destruction was probably less serious than the dislocation of the entire fabric of European economy. For the past 10 years conditions have been highly abnormal. The feverish preparation for war and the more feverish maintenance of the war effort engulfed all aspects of national economies. Machinery has fallen into disrepair or is entirely obsolete. Under the **arbitrary** [adj. 专 制 的. 武 断 的] and destructive Nazi rule, virtually every possible enterprise was geared into the German war machine. Long-standing commercial ties, private institutions, banks, insurance companies, and shipping companies disappeared, through loss of capital, absorption through nationalization, or by simple destruction. In many countries, confidence in the local currency has been severely shaken. The breakdown of the business structure of Europe during the war was complete. Recovery has been seriously retarded by the fact that two years after the close of hostilities a peace settlement with Germany and Austria has not been agreed upon. But even given a more prompt solution of these difficult problems the rehabilitation of the economic structure of Europe quite evidently will require a much longer time and greater effort than had been foreseen.

There is a phase of this matter which is both interesting and serious. The farmer has always produced the foodstuffs to exchange with the city dweller for the other

尊敬的校长、科南特博士、哈佛监管会的董事会成员们，女士们、先生们：

对今天上午哈佛请我演讲这一巨大的荣誉和肯定，本人非常感动，并深表谢意！

实际上，我有点不知所措，因为我无法保证达到你们给予我的厚望。在这个历史性的环境下，在阳光明媚的这一天，在嘉宾云集的时刻，站在我这个位置，是件令人印象无比深刻的事情。但我有更重要的话要说，甚至不用我提醒，先生们，当下的世界形势极为严峻，这对所有有识之士来说都是显而易见的。我认为，我们面临的问题是如此庞杂，报纸和电台向公众提供的报道是如此之多，以至于让一个普通人仅靠自己来对这纷繁复杂的情况作出明确的分析判断，非常困难。此外，我们的国家和地球上的动乱地区相距遥远，使得我们很难理解那些长期遭受苦难的人们的窘境，以及与之相应的后果；也较难理解这些后果对他们的政府在与我们进行合作、促进世界和平方面，会有什么样的影响。

在考虑欧洲战后重建的需要时，生命逝去的损失和随处可见的城市、工厂、矿山和铁路的破坏是容易估算的，但这几个月的情况表明，这些肉眼可见的毁灭程度，可能还比不上欧洲经济整个系统发生了错位的严重性。过去10年来的情况是极其异常的。狂热的备战和更狂热的持续战争，笼罩了欧洲国家经济的方方面面。机器失修或者完全过时，在军事独裁和毁灭性的纳粹统治下，几乎每一个企业都卷进了德国的战争机器。因为资金匮乏、民粹主义的狂热或者单纯的破坏，长期以来的商业联系、私人机构、银行、保险公司和船务公司大都消失了。在很多国家，人们对本国货币的信心已严重动摇。战争中，欧洲的商业结构已经完全坍塌。即使在战争结束两年后的今天，德国与奥地利的和平协议仍无法达成，由此导致重建工作的严重滞后。但是，就算这些棘手问题得到很快解决，战后欧洲经济的重建很明显需要一个更长的时间，并且需要人们付出比现有措施更大的努力。

在这个问题中，有一个现象既有趣也很严重。传统上，农民总是生产粮食，用来和城市居民交换他们所需的生活必需品。这种劳动分工是现代文明社会的基础，现如今，它却濒临崩溃。城市和城镇工业不能生

necessities of life. This division of labor is the basis of modern civilization. At the present time it is threatened with breakdown. The town and city industries are not producing adequate goods to exchange with the food producing farmer. Raw materials and fuel are in short supply. Machinery is lacking or worn out. The farmer or the peasant cannot find the goods for sale which he desires to purchase. So the sale of his farm produce for money which he cannot use seems to him an unprofitable transaction. He, therefore, has withdrawn many fields from crop cultivation and is using them for grazing. He feeds more grain to stock and finds for himself and his family an ample supply of food, however short he may be on clothing and the other ordinary gadgets of civilization. Meanwhile people in the cities are short of food and fuel. So the governments are forced to use their foreign money and credits to procure these necessities abroad. This process exhausts funds which are urgently needed for reconstruction. Thus a very serious situation is rapidly developing which bodes no good for the world. The modern system of the division of labor upon which the exchange of products is based is in danger of breaking down.

The truth of the matter is that Europe's requirements for the next three or four years of foreign food and other essential products – principally from America – are so much greater than her present ability to pay that she must have substantial additional help or face economic, social, and political deterioration of a very grave character.

The remedy lies in breaking the vicious circle and restoring the confidence of the European people in the economic future of their own countries and of Europe as a whole. The manufacturer and the farmer throughout wide areas must be able and willing to exchange their products for currencies the continuing value of which is not open to question.

Aside from the demoralizing effect on the world at large and the possibilities of disturbances arising as a result of the desperation of the people concerned, the consequences to the economy of the United States should be apparent to all. It is logical that the United States should do whatever it is able to do to assist in the return of normal economic health in the world, without which there can be no political stability and no assured peace. Our policy is directed not against any country or doctrine [n.学说，主义] but against hunger, poverty, desperation and chaos. Its purpose should be the revival of a working economy in the world so as to permit the emergence of political and social conditions in which free institutions can exist. Such assistance, I am convinced, must not be on a piecemeal basis as various crises develop. Any assistance that this Government may render in the future should provide a cure rather than a mere palliative [n.缓和剂]. Any government that is willing to assist in the task of recovery will find full co-operation I am sure, on the part of the United States

产足够的产品,去与生产粮食的农民交换。原材料和燃料供应不足,机器缺乏或者是报废。乡村农民无法找到所需的物品,靠出卖农产品获得的钱币无处使用,这对他们来说无异于一个无利的交易。因此,农民只好缩小粮食种植面积而改为放牧。他的粮食用来喂牲口,从而使自己的家庭有足够的食物补给,但在衣着和其他日常城市生活物品上却所缺多多。与此同时,城里的人们缺少粮食和燃料,政府不得不动用他们的外汇储备和信用从国外购买这些必需品。这个过程耗尽了本来急需用于重建的资金。于是,这个越来越严重的情况加速恶化,这无利于世界。建立在劳动分工基础上的现代体系正面临垮塌的危险。

事实的真相是这样的:欧洲在今后3年到4年时间内,对于国外食品和其他生活必需品的需求——主要依赖于美国——非常之大,以其现有的能力根本无法负担,欧洲将面临一种非常可怕的后果,经济、社会和政治方面将持续恶化。

解决问题的关键,是打破这个恶性循环,并且重建欧洲人民对于自己国家、乃至整个欧洲的经济前景的信心。广袤土地上的制造业者和农民,必须能够并愿意交换他们的产品来获取货币,而且不用担心货币贬值。

且不说相关国家的人民在绝望中可能产生动乱,并由此给全世界带来消极影响,这些后果对美国经济的影响也是显而易见的。所以毫无疑问,美国应该力所能及地帮助世界经济恢复正常,若非如此,就不会有政治的稳定与和平的保障。我们的政策不是针对任何国家或是某个教条的,而是应对饥饿、贫穷、绝望和动乱。它以世界范围内的经济复苏为目标,进而帮助我们创造能够让自由体制存在的政治和社会条件。

我相信,这样的帮助不是只针对不同危机的出现而采取的临时措施。本届政府以后提供的任何帮助,都必须是治根而不仅仅治标。我相信,任何愿意在这个复兴过程中提供帮助的政府,都将从美国政府这里获得完全的合作,任何试图阻止其他国家复兴的政府将不能从美国获得帮助。并且,任何政府、政党或团体,如果为了获得自己的政治或其他利益,而不惜试图延长人类的灾难,也必将遭到美国的严重反对。

很明显,在美国政府能够进一步努力改变这种状况、并帮助欧洲走

Government. Any government which maneuvers to block the recovery of other countries cannot expect help from us. Furthermore, governments, political parties, or groups which seek to perpetuate [vt.使永存，使不朽] human misery in order to profit therefrom [adv. 由此，从此] politically or otherwise will encounter the opposition of the United States.

It is already evident that, before the United States Government can proceed much further in its efforts to alleviate the situation and help start the European world on its way to recovery, there must be some agreement among the countries of Europe as to the requirements of the situation and the part those countries themselves will take in order to give proper effect to whatever action might be undertaken by this Government. It would be neither fitting nor **efficacious** [adj. 有效的，灵验的] for this Government to undertake to draw up unilaterally a program designed to place Europe on its feet economically. This is the business of the Europeans. The initiative, I think, must come from Europe. The role of this country should consist of friendly aid in the drafting of a European program and of later support of such a program so far as it may be practical for us to do so. The program should be a joint one, agreed to by a number, if not all European nations.

An essential part of any successful action on the part of the United States is an understanding on the part of the people of America of the character of the problem and the remedies to be applied. Political passion and prejudice should have no part. With foresight, and a willingness on the part of our people to face up to the vast responsibility which history has clearly placed upon our country, the difficulties I have outlined can and will be overcome.

I am sorry that on each occasion I have said something publicly in regard to our international situation, I've been forced by the necessities of the case to enter into rather technical discussions. But to my mind, it is of vast importance that our people reach some general understanding of what the complications really are, rather than react from a passion or a prejudice or an emotion of the moment. As I said more formally a moment ago, we are remote from the scene of these troubles. It is virtually impossible at this distance merely by reading, or listening, or even seeing photographs or motion pictures, to grasp at all the real significance of the situation. And yet the whole world of the future hangs on a proper judgment. It hangs, I think, to a large extent on the realization of the American people, of just what are the various dominant factors. What are the reactions of the people? What are the justifications of those reactions? What are the sufferings? What is needed? What can best be done? What must be done?

Thank you very much.

向复兴之路之前，欧洲国家之间必须达成一些共识，了解现实的需要，知道这些国家自己需要采取什么行动，来配合美国政府的努力。制定一个让欧洲在经济上重新站立起来的计划，如果只是由美国政府单方面做主的话，既不合适也不会有成效，这是欧洲的事情。这个主动权，必须来自欧洲。我们国家的角色，应该包括起草一个针对欧洲的友好援助项目，以及对这个项目的后续支持，只要这个项目对我们而言是可行的。这个项目应当得到最大多数欧洲国家的赞同。

在美国方面，任何措施成功的关键，就是代表美国人民关注这个问题，并研究解决办法。政治热情和偏见不能牵涉其中。有了这种远见，加上我们的人民愿意面对历史已经十分清楚地赋予我们的重大责任，我所列举的种种困难，都将能够而且必将得到克服。

很抱歉，在每一个我公开阐述国际局势的场合里，我都不得不因情况的需要而进行这种技术层面上的探讨。但是在我看来，与其仅仅因为热情或者偏见，或是一时的冲动而作出反应，我们的人民还应当对这些情况的复杂性有一个基本的了解，这一点至关重要。正像我刚才用较正式的方式所表述的，我们远离那些麻烦的现场，仅仅靠远观，或道听途说，或者看照片和纪录片，远远无法理解这个现状的真正重要性。但是，整个世界的未来将取决于我们作出的正确判断。我认为，世界的未来在很大程度上将取决于美国人民的认识，即什么才是主要因素。这些认识包括：人民的反应是什么？什么理由可以解释这些反应？什么是苦难？我们需要做什么？怎样做才能最好？什么是我们必须做的？

非常感谢各位！

1950's

桑顿·怀尔德（1897—1975）

美国小说家和剧作家，与尤金·奥尼尔、阿瑟·米勒和田纳西·威廉斯并称为美国现代四大剧作家。怀尔德是美国文学史上唯一一位戏剧和小说都获得过普利策奖的作家。

怀尔德1897年出生于美国威斯康辛州的麦迪逊市。其父任职于美国驻中国领事馆，因此他的大部分童年时光是在中国度过的。怀尔德于1920年从耶鲁大学毕业获得文学学士学位，1926年获普林斯顿大学法国文学硕士学位，曾到意大利罗马的美国学科学院学习两年考古学。1930年至1936年和1950年至1951年间，他分别在芝加哥大学和哈佛大学执教，这篇毕业演讲就是他在哈佛任教期间发表的。

怀尔德于1926年发表第一部小说《卡巴拉》，紧接着他的第二部小说《圣路易斯雷伊的桥》(The Bridge of San Luis Rey)就获得了广泛赞誉，摘得1927年普利策文学奖的桂冠。小说讲述了一位牧师试图在秘鲁的一座桥垮塌后揭示五位遇难者生与死的意义。他的剧本《我们的城市》(Our Town, 1938年获普利策奖)，是美国话剧史上最受欢迎的剧作之一。他的另一个剧本《我们牙齿的外壳》(The Skin of Our Teeth)是一部描绘人类历史的寓言性剧本，同样大获成功，并于1942年再度夺得普利策奖。他排除了自然和风景，还放弃道具，故意使用一些弄错年代的东西，让演员直接面对观众讲话。他的滑稽剧《红娘》(The Matchmaker)在1964年被改编成音乐剧《你好，多莉！》。怀尔德晚期的小说包括《初八》(The Eighth Day, 1967年获国家图书奖)和《北西奥菲勒斯》(Theophilus North, 1973年)等。

1951

Novel Experience of a Fraternal Community
体验人类大同的境界

Thornton N. Wilder 桑顿·怀尔德

Mr. Larsen, Mr. Conant, alumni and friends of Harvard:

Mr. Larson, this is not the moment to remind me that I am a Yale man. It took me six months to break myself of the habit of referring to this area as the Harvard campus. I have now broken myself of it.

Harvard has been **sovereignly** [adj. 具有主权的，至高无上的，极好的] kind, not only today but through the years to its guest at its gates, and Harvard, visible and invisible, has been increasingly impressive to one who comes to it anew.

I have been an intermittent teacher all my life and when, as this year, I return to university community, I find myself continually drawing comparisons, not comparisons between institutions but comparisons between something far more striking and instructive, comparisons between attitudes, tacit assumptions, the thought-world of students that I have known throughout the decades of my teachings; attitudes that we held in 1917, 1918, 1919 and 1920, attitudes that my students in the University of Chicago held in the '30s, and the attitudes which I see in the students around me this year. What a difference! What a difference!

Now the students today have been told sufficiently that they are living in an age which has variously been called by Professor Toynbee, Mr. Auden and others, the Age of Upheaval and the Age of Anxiety. And indeed it seems so to the seniors whom we graduated this morning, who were 12 years old at the time of the attack on Pearl Harbor. They have spent their lives then in our view in stormy or in threatening weather. They never knew, as we who were born about the turn of the century, they never knew that evenly-running world to which one of our Presidents gave the name of **Normalcy** [n. 常态].

When I go about my occupation of drawing comparisons, I become aware that those who live in troubled weather build or discover resources that we in 1920 felt no need to call upon. Like species among the order of the animal kingdom, they develop adaptations. These resources, of course, are not of their manufacture but they find what they need from the currents of thought and literature that are about us all, and it is how they assimilate it that is Interesting to us. I am talking about **tacit** [adj. 心照不宣的，默示的] assumptions, basic attitudes of so deep a level that they themselves are often not aware. But what they are aware of is that many of the concepts to which we older persons clung are to them irrelevant, irrelevant and irritating.

The twentieth century is shifting its foundations and it is altering its emphases

拉森先生、科南特先生、哈佛的校友及朋友们：

拉森先生，这不是提醒我、说我是个"雅礼"（耶鲁人）的时候¹。我花了6个月的时间才把自己的习惯改过来，把这个地方称作哈佛校园。我现在终于改过来了。

哈佛对到访的客人一直非常友善，不仅是在今天，而是多年如此。对来到这里的人而言，无论于有形的方面还是无形的方面，哈佛都令人印象深刻。

我一直断断续续地当教师，今年，我又回到大学环境，发觉自己会不断地去做些比较，不是去比较学校，而是一些更突出和更有启发性的东西，比如比较我在过去数十年间教过的学生，他们的态度、他们心照不宣的想法、他们的思想世界等等之间的不同；比较我们在1917年、1918年、1919年和1920年时持有的态度；比较我于1930年代在芝加哥大学所教过的学生的态度，以及我在今年所看到的学生的态度。这是多大的不同！这是多大的不同啊！

现在的学生已经听到足够多的说法，说他们生活在汤因比教授、奥登先生和其他人用不同形式形容的"动荡不安的年代"和"焦虑的年代"。的确，对今天上午毕业的学生来说，情况就是如此，日本袭击珍珠港时，他们年仅12岁。当时的生活，在我们看来，也是处在暴风骤雨般令人恐惧的气候之下。他们从来不曾知道，像我们这些在世纪之交出生的人经历过的，那种被我们国家的一位总统形容为"太平盛世"的平稳世界。

当我专心致志地做着比较的时候，我意识到，那些生活在动乱环境里的人所构建或发现的资源，是我们在1920年时认为没有必要的东西。就像生存在动物王国里的物种一样，适者生存。当然，这些资源并不是他们自己生造出来的，而是从所有人的思想潮流和文学中找出他们需要的部分，他们如何吸收消化这些东西，很令我们感兴趣。我说的是心照不宣的认同，那些扎根于深处的基本态度，是连他们本身都常常没有意识到的。但他们意识到，我们这些年长者所抱持的许多观念，对他们来说无关紧要，既不相干又令人反感。

20世纪的根基正在移动，其重心的变化异常迅速。科学家、诗人和

with striking rapidity. The scientists and the poets and the writers have described this new mentality which is moving into place. The man on the street is beginning to be aware of it. **But to teach the young today is to put one's self in the way of learning from the superior student the new description of man in his relation. And that is what supports and sustains those who have only known troubled weather.**

  I teach literature. I teach the **consecrated** [*adj.* 神圣的，被视为神圣的] classics but I am attentive also to the masters of modern literature and if I were not so my students would have waked me up to them. About five years ago a professor who was a friend of mine in a university far from here once said to me, "You know, when a student in my classes has written a brilliant paper on the Scarlet Letter or on Tom Jones, I invite him into my office to compliment him and to make his acquaintance, and we talk for a while. Often, too often, the young man or woman on leaving my office turns and says to me, 'Well, Professor X, of course, we like these books we read for you, but what we are really interested in is T. S. Eliot, James Joyce, Franz Kafka, Gertrude Stein, Ezra Pound.'"

  And the professor said to me, "Now, what's the matter? I spent my life studying great literature. These books are purportedly in the English language, yet I cannot read five pages of them with any pleasure, to say nothing of intelligibly. I have no choice but to think that my most gifted students are either hypocrites, imitative snobs, or else just **incult** [*adj.* 未开垦的，无教养的] barbarians who don't know beauty and clarity when they see it."

  Well, that is the gulf between the generations and it is up to us to be very attentive to it. Now, freshmen and sophomores stop me on the street and visit me in my room to ask me about these very writers. And that shows us that these writers are fulfilling a profound need for those who live in stormy weather. And I find three tacit assumptions within their work that are reflected in the best young twentieth century minds, assumptions that we could not have grasped in 1920. First, the young person today in the light of science sees himself not as one of many hundred thousands, not as one of many millions, but as one of billions.

  Secondly, a whole new tacit assumption in relation to responsibility. And, thirdly, a realization that the things that separate men from one another are less important than the things that they have in common. Now, the multiplicity of the human creation. Kierkegaard, the great Dane, the greatest of the Danes, wrote in his journal

作家都描述了这种正在流行的全新心态，连街头的普通人也开始意识到这种心态。但如果想要教导今天的青年，就有必要让自己用优秀学生的那种方法来学习，用新的视野来了解人和他所处的环境。而这正是那些经过动荡年代的人，得到支持和得以延续的方式。

我教的是文学，是被奉为经典的古典文学，但我也关注现代文学的大师，因为如果不这样做，我的学生会提醒我去注意他们。大约5年前，一个在很远的一所大学里当教授的朋友对我说："你知道吗，当我班上的学生就《红字》[2]或《汤姆·琼斯》[3]写了精彩的评论时，我会请他到我的办公室，表示欣赏，与他结识，我们会聊一会儿天。很多时候，学生在离开我的办公室时往往会说：'教授，我们当然喜欢这些你布置的阅读书籍，但我们真正感兴趣的是艾略特、詹姆斯·乔伊斯、弗朗茨·卡夫卡、格特鲁德·施泰因，还有艾兹拉·庞德这些先锋作家。'"

这位教授说："嗨，这叫什么事儿？我毕生研究文学作品。这些新锐作家的书，据说是用英语写的，可是我觉得不堪卒读，更不用说从中得益了。我不得不想到，这些最聪明的学生要么是伪君子，要么是人云亦云的势利小人，否则就是一些毫无教养的野蛮人，看到那些美而简洁的作品，却不懂欣赏。"

哦，这就是代沟，我们对此应当十分留意。现在，一二年级的学生会在街头喊住我，或来找我，向我询问这些作家。这就表明，这些作家适应了那些生活在动荡年代里的人们的深层需要。而且，我在这些作家的作品中，看到三种心领神会的设想，这些设想都反映在20世纪最优秀的年轻人的头脑中，这些设想是我们在20年代无法领会的。第一，今天经受了科学洗礼的年轻人，看自己时，不仅把自己看做成千上万人中的一分子，也不仅把自己看做是数百万人中的一分子，而是把自己视为数十亿茫茫人海中的一分子。

第二，他们对责任有一种全新的理解。第三，他们意识到，那些使人们隔离的东西，与他们的共同点相比微不足道。让我们来看看人类的庞大。伟大的丹麦人，我认为是最伟大的丹麦人克尔凯郭尔[4]，曾在1844年写道，一位人类学家告诉他说，从古到今，世界上共生活过大约340

in 1844 that he had an anthropologist tell him that 34 billion men and women were living or had lived and died, men and women above the level of the aborigine. He put it in his journal and his reflection follows: "I carried that to an anthropologist friend of mine and he said, 'How childish! How childish! Three and four times that many fully responsible human beings have lived and died.'"

Now it is a matter of fact that we have learned to count. Anybody can make figures, but since archaeologists, historians, scientists, physicists have poured numerals and numerals across us, this generation does not theoretically think in large numbers. The power of the mind to grasp ever larger quantities of units is a thing which the young have and we in middle age still do not have and really cannot have to the same degree. And one thing that follows from that is that they realize this **multiplicity** [n. 重复，多样] of the souls that have lived and the presumable billions and billions yet to live and die.

Now I see that we of the twentieth century, of the Class of 1920, were appallingly provincial and **parochial** [adj. 地方性的，狭隘的]. We were one of lots of Americans and across certain oceans were lots of other people, and that lots was a vague term with no resonance of any kind.

French literature is a very glorious and splendid treasury, but really it is about 60 million Frenchmen, isn't it? The masters of modern literature are engaged in describing **multitudinous** [adj. 无数的，包括许多部分的，人口稠密的] man, and at once we see a violent shift of values taking place. **In one sense the individual shrinks in this vast cousinage and in another sense his assertion of his validity takes on a new urgency and seeks a new authority.**

When we now say, "I love," "I believe," "I suffer," or "I mean to be a success," and hear it fall into the human universe of billions, it is, of course, threatened with absurdity. And yet the young know this to the very **marrow** [n. 骨髓，精华] of their bones in a way we did not used to know it. It arouses anxiety when one feels one is only one example among so many, but it is a new kind of anxiety. It is a **metaphysical** [adj. 形而上学的，抽象的] unease; it is not a nervousness. And it drives them to find a new basis for their individual assertion. And can't you see how easily bored they would be with many consolations which we older ones found sustaining? No wonder that Shelley is unfashionable to them and Carlyle unreadable. They are full of this kind of assertion and the assertion to them is on the wrong ground.

亿人。他在日记中这样记到："我把这个说法告诉我的人类学家朋友，他说，'幼稚！这太幼稚了！在这世上活过和死亡的人数，少说有这个数字的三四倍以上。'"

我们现在都学会了计算。任何人都可以说出一些数字，但因为考古学家、历史学家、科学家、物理学家等等，都在我们面前列出了一大堆数字，这一代人从理论上来说，不去想那些大数目。年轻人有这种心智的力量，去领会庞大的数量单位，而我们这些中年人，还没有这种能力，而且能力的确不在同一程度上。与之相关的，是他们意识到过往人类数量的庞大，也知道今后还会有数以亿万计的人不断地出生或死去。

我现在明白了，我们这些20世纪的人，毕业于1920年的人，视野是如何有限和狭隘。我们是许多美国人中的一分子，知道在大洋彼岸还有很多其他人，但那个"很多"只是一个含糊的概念，不会掀起什么心中的波澜。

法国文学灿烂辉煌，是一座文化宝库，但它描绘的，其实只是有关大约六千万的法国人，不是吗？现代文学大师们描写了人的多样性，我们立刻看到其中价值观的剧变。**在某种意义上，个人在这巨大的人群中缩小了；而在另一种意义上，作为一个个体，我们更迫切地想要证明自己，寻求新的自信。**

如果我们把"我爱"、"我相信"、"我难受"或"我想要成功"等语词放在十亿人中时，这些话会显得荒谬。年轻人懂得这个道理，犹如鱼儿熟悉水性，而我们不知道。当感觉自己只是沧海一粟时，很容易引起内心的焦虑。但这种焦虑是全新的，它是形而上的不安，而非一般的紧张。这也促使人们为个性去寻找新的基础。你没看到年轻人对自我安慰是如此厌烦吗？而我们对这些安慰却觉得很受用。难怪在他们眼里，英国诗人雪莱已经过时，卡莱尔[5]也不堪卒读。那些作品充满了主张，他们认为这些主张是错误的。

这第二种心领神会的设想涉及责任。今天的年轻人已不再被"黄金时代"的概念所困扰。我们生于1900年前后的人，都记得那段时间的安宁。20年代后期和30年代初期，我们曾经历过自由运动，我们脑子里充

The second tacit assumption is this matter of responsibility. The young of today are not haunted by the notion of a Golden Age. We who were born about 1900 remember that span of security. We who lived through the late '20s and early '30s, the liberal movements, were filled with a notion that if we strained and strained and strained we would pretty soon usher in a Utopia. These young have not that impatience. They have not that regret. It is not a matter of disillusion nor does it mean that they are indifferent to social betterment. It is that for them it is self-evident that human beings contain large elements of cruelty and of ignorance, themselves included. Think what they have lived through and think what they have not lived through! We in the '20s would never quite have grasped that. We mistook our good intentions for good performances, and we mistook the good intentions of Christian civilization for irreversible achievement.

Now the modern student is all alive to the complexity of man in himself and others. He is profoundly interested not only in good but in evil, and he assumes that life is difficult, morally difficult.

In the '20s we used to talk about our expectation of happiness. You can't imagine how seldom you hear the word "happiness" today, except colored by derision, and with this has come a whole shift in the concept of responsibility. His last responsibility is to himself and not to systems. He is engaged in responsibly exploring himself as we never were. I am astonished, for example, at the rapidity with which the terminology of the new psychology is heard in all the classes of my students. And no wonder. No wonder the masters of modern literature speak to them as they do not to my friend, Professor X -- Kafka about the sense of guilty; T. S. Eliot about the sources of conviction and authority. James Joyce has given two extended portraits of a young man's relation to his parents and cultural history in their terms.

Thirdly, science has made one more contribution to the 20th century thought-world. It has broken down the barriers between race and color and environment and cultural background. To the great surgeon with the patient on the operating table it is of secondary importance whether it is a cousin of his wife or the sister of an Oriental **potentate** [n. 统治者，君主] or the **derelict** [n. 被遗弃的人或物] found by the police the night before. To the engineer in telegraphy it is a matter of indifference who sends that cable which goes half about the world in a few seconds. To the historian of culture, the myths of the creation of Eskimos or the Tahitians are now side by side with those of

满了一种观念,那就是,如果我们努力、努力、再努力,很快就会迎来一个乌托邦似的理想境界。这些年轻人可没有那种焦虑,也没有那种遗憾。这不是幻灭,也不意味着他们不关心社会进步。对他们来说,人性中有不少冷酷的因素,也包含了许多无知,这是不言而喻的,因为他们本身就这样。想想看,他们经历了多少,他们又错过了多少!我们在20年代绝不会理解这些。我们把我们的良好意愿误解为良好表现,也把基督教文明的善意误解为不可逆转的进步。

现在的学生对自己和他人的复杂性都很了解。他们不但对善深感兴趣,对恶也颇想了解,他们也知道,生活是困难的,从道义上来说会是困难的。

20年代,我们习惯于谈论对幸福的期盼。你无法想象,现在竟难得听到"幸福"这个词,除非你想揶揄什么人。而随着这种变化,责任的概念也发生了转变。人的责任只是为了自己,而不是为了社会。人要用负责任的态度来探索自己,而这是我们从未做过的。例如,在我所有的班上,都能听到学生们谈论心理学的最新术语,这令我倍感惊讶。这不奇怪。难怪现代文学大师很对他们的胃口,而不合我那位某某教授朋友的口味:卡夫卡的作品表现了罪恶感;艾略特深入探讨有关信念和权力的来源;詹姆斯·乔伊斯详细描绘了一个年轻人和他父母,以及他父母所习惯的文化之间的关系。

第三,科学对20世纪的思潮有着很大的贡献。它打破了不同种族和人群、环境和文化背景之间的壁垒。对一位优秀的外科医生来说,手术台上的患者不论是他妻子的表弟,还是东方君主的姐妹,或是警察前一天晚上收容的流浪汉,都是次要问题。对一位电报工程师来说,谁来发一份在几秒钟内就能抵达地球另半边的电报,也全无所谓。而对文化史学家来说,爱斯基摩人或大溪地人所创造的神话,与基督教的《创世记》同样值得研究。

人类这些共有的东西,其比重开始大大超过那些使他们隔离开的东西。对歌德、帕斯卡尔或伯克等人而言,这样的想法并不新颖,但是,从这个角度看问题,在很多我这一代人眼里都觉得颇为新奇。我在哈佛

the Book of Genesis.

These things which all men hold in common are beginning to outweigh enormously -- those things which separate them. That was not new to Goethe or Pascal or Burke; but in this sense it is astonishingly new to many of my own generation. My young friends in Cambridge have shown me over and over again that to them it is as simple as breathing that all societies are but variants of one another, that somehow all wars from now on are civil wars and the human adventure is much the same in all times and all places.

Now, my friends, it is disturbing to have lost the feeling of belonging to one reassuring community, to New England or the United States, or to Western civilization, to be sustained and supported by one of these localizations. But they are gone, they are going and they are gone in that sense of being a psychic nest, and the scientist and poet took them away.

Yes, when T. S. Eliot **juxtaposes** [v. 并置，并列] a line from Dante with a cry from the Sanskrit epic poems, it annoys my friend, Professor X. But the students understand very well that what he means is that all literature is one expression of one human life experience. And when James Joyce plays upon 24 languages as upon a **clavier** [n. 键盘乐器（尤指钢琴），乐器键盘] they don't find it preposterous. All the languages in the world are but local differentiations of one planetary tongue.

These concepts are very full of something frightening but they are also full of promise. Oh, it is a lonely and alarming business to feel one's self one in the creation of billions and billions, and especially lonely if your parents seem never to have felt that sensation at all, but is exciting and inspiring to be among the first to hail and accept the only fraternal community that finally can be valid, -- that emerging, painfully emerging unity of those who live on the one inhabited star.

Best of luck to today's graduates. Thank you!

的青年朋友一次又一次向我显示，所有的社会只是彼此稍有不同，从现在起，所有的战争在某种程度上都是内战，人类在所有时间和所有地方的冒险，很多其实是一样的。年轻人觉得，这些观点就像呼吸一样，是简单自然的事情。

朋友们，失去那种可以让自己放松的社会归属感，比如认为自己属于美国的新英格兰地区，或者美国，或觉得自己属于西方文明，从而在认同中找到精神支柱，这种失落是令人不安的。如果想把它们当做自己精神归宿的话，这些东西已经消失了，认同感正在成为过往，科学家和诗人已使它们不复存在。

是的，当艾略特把但丁的一行诗和梵文史诗里的一句呐喊并列在一起时，这样的做法惹恼了我的朋友——那位教授。但学生们很明白，诗人的意思是，一切文学都是人的生命体验的一种表达。当詹姆斯·乔伊斯使用24种语言，就像他在敲击乐器的键盘时，学生们也并不觉得荒谬。世界上所有的语言，其实不过是我们这个星球上的共同语言的不同方言而已。

这些概念充满了令人惧怕的东西，但同时又充满希望。哦，认识到自己只是数十亿人当中的一员，特别是，如果你的父辈从来没有感受过那样的体验，那会是一种让人觉得孤独又害怕的事。但作为第一批人去欢迎并接受这种共识，即人类大同，四海之内终于可以皆为兄弟——居住在这个星球上的人类，好不容易才努力得来了团结，这是多么令人振奋、鼓舞人心的事啊！

祝福今天的毕业生们！谢谢大家！

---

1 演讲者毕业自耶鲁本科，哈佛、耶鲁两校常常互相竞争，故有此说。

2 《红字》(The Scarlet Letter)，美国作家纳撒尼尔·霍桑 (Nathaniel Hawthorne, 1804—1864) 所写的一本名著。

3 《汤姆·琼斯》(Tom Jones)，英国作家亨利·菲尔丁 (Henry Fielding, 1707—1754) 的小说。

4 克尔凯郭尔 (Soren Kierkegaard, 1813—1855)，丹麦思想家，早年在哥本哈根大学学习神学，因对理性哲学，特别是黑格尔主义的批评而著称，极端推崇"个体性"，对20世纪的哲学走向产生了深远的影响，又被称为"存在主义之父"。

5 卡莱尔 (Thomas Carlyle, 1795—1881)，苏格兰作家、历史学家、哲学家。

约翰·肯尼迪（1917—1963）

约翰·肯尼迪1917年出生于马萨诸塞州的一个爱尔兰移民家庭，从他的爷爷起，肯尼迪家族就开始涉足政坛。肯尼迪的父亲约瑟夫从哈佛毕业后从事银行工作，很快成为当时全美最年轻的银行董事长。在积累了几亿美元资产后，约瑟夫也开始从政，并于1937年被罗斯福总统任命为美国驻英大使。

约瑟夫对几个儿子从小就朝着将来要当总统的方向培养。肯尼迪18岁时赴英国伦敦政治经济学院学习，1936年进入哈佛大学，毕业后加入美国海军，在二战中参加过很多战役。肯尼迪自己曾说，如果不是因为他的哥哥阵亡于二战，他会继续当作家写作。长子的遇难，使家族的希望落在了次子肯尼迪身上。

肯尼迪于29岁时竞选众议员获胜并连任3届，36岁进入参议院也获得连任。1960年1月，他击败了共和党候选人尼克松，成为美国历史上最年轻的总统。肯尼迪脍炙人口的一句名言就是在他的总统就职演说上说的："我的美国同胞们，不要问你的国家能为你做什么，而要问你能为你的国家做什么！"

作为美国历史上最年轻的总统，肯尼迪短暂的一生给后人留下很多难忘的印象。因为制定阿波罗计划，他被列入"影响人类历史进程的100位名人"之一；他同时还是一位作家，因出版《勇敢者传略》一书获得普利策奖，被列为"美国十大文化偶像"。肯尼迪遇刺后，人们为了纪念他，许多事物以他的名字命名，在美国各地随处可见。2010年的民意调查显示，肯尼迪在美国近50年历届总统中位居榜首，受到高达85%的民众的肯定，这在美国是不多见的。

1956

Words to the American Intellectual
给美国知识界的建言

John F. Kennedy 约翰·肯尼迪

Mr. President, today's graduates and our alumni:

It is a pleasure to join with my fellow alumni in this pilgrimage to the second home of our youth.

Prince Bismarck once remarked that one-third of the students of German universities broke down from overwork; another third broke down from **dissipation** [n. 损耗]; and the other third ruled Germany. As I look about this campus today, I would hesitate to predict which third attends reunions (although I have some suspicion) but, I am confident I am looking at rulers of America in the sense that all active, informed citizens rule.

I can think of nothing more reassuring for all of us than to come again to this institution whose whole purpose is dedicated to the advancement of knowledge and the dissemination of truth.

I belong to a profession where the emphasis is somewhat different. Our political parties, our politicians are interested, of necessity, in winning popular support - a majority; and only indirectly truth is the object of our controversy. From this **polemic** [n. 争论. 论战] of contending factions, the general public is expected to make a discriminating judgment. As the problems have become more complex, as our role as a chief defender of Western civilization has become enlarged, the responsibility of the **electorate** [n.(全体)选民] as a court of last resort has become almost too great. The people desperately seek objectivity and a university such as this fulfills that function.

And the political profession needs to have its temperature lowered in the cooling waters of the scholastic pool. We need both the technical judgment and the disinterested viewpoint of the scholar, to prevent us from becoming imprisoned by our own slogans.

Therefore, it is regrettable that the gap between the intellectual and the politician seems to be growing. Instead of synthesis, clash and discord now characterize the relations between the two groups much of the time. Authors, scholars, and intellectuals can praise every aspect of American society but the political. My desk is flooded with books, articles, and pamphlets criticizing Congress. But, rarely if ever, have I seen any intellectual **bestow** [vt. 授予. 利用] praise on either the political profession or any political body for its accomplishments, its ability, or its integrity - much less for its intelligence. To many universities and scholars we reap nothing but censure, investigators and perpetrators of what has been called the swinish cult of anti-intellectualism.

尊敬的校长、各位毕业生和校友们：

今天能和各位校友一起回到我们青春年代的第二家园，心情真是无比愉快！

俾斯麦[1]曾经说过，德国大学里三分之一的学生因为过度操劳而垮掉；三分之一的学生因为自然损耗而销声匿迹；剩下的三分之一则统治着德国。当我今天看着这个校园，很难预测哪三分之一的人能重返校园团聚（虽然我有些预感），但我赞同所有活跃而见多识广的公民参与领导，因此我现在所面对的，是美国的领导人。

我们大家再次聚集在以探索知识和传播真理为己任的学府，我感到无比宽慰。

在我从事的行业里，其重点有所不同。我们的政党、我们的政客，出于争取选民，特别是赢得多数选民的需要，不可避免地带有偏见，真理变成了我们争论中并非直接的目标。在这不同派系的互相论战中，普通民众必须作出区别和评判。由于问题变得更加复杂，由于我们——作为西方文明的主要捍卫者——的作用已经扩大，所有选民作为最后的裁决者的责任已经变得不能承受之重。人们迫切需要能够提供客观见解的来源，像我们这样的大学，就刚好满足了这个职能。

政治这个行业需要有学术的清净池水来帮着降温。我们需要学者公正的观点和技术性的判断，来防止我们被自己的宣传口号固步自封。

令人遗憾的是，知识分子和政治家之间的距离似乎越来越大。二者非但没有相辅相成，在很多时间里，这两个群体之间更多的是冲突与不和谐。作家、学者和知识分子可以赞扬美国社会的任何一个方面，但政治方面除外。我的办公桌上堆满了批评美国国会的书籍、文章和小册子。而我很少，甚至可说几乎从未看到过来自知识界对政治行业或政治团体的成就、能力，或其正直性这些方面的好评，更不用说知识界看不上政治行业或政治团体的智力了。从许多大学和学者那里，我们得到的名声，只是审查者、调查员和作恶之人，是蠢猪一般的反智力集团。

詹姆斯·罗素·洛厄尔[2]100多年前对迦勒·库欣，当时一位著名的

James Russell Lowell's satiric attack more than 100 years ago on Caleb Cushing, a celebrated Attorney General and Member of Congress, sets the tone, "Gineral C is a dreffle smart man, he's ben on all sides that give places or pelt but consistency still wuz a part of his plan - he's ben true to one party, that is himself."

But in fairness, the way of the intellectual is not altogether **serene** [adj. 安详的，宁静的]; in fact, so great has become popular suspicion that a recent survey of American intellectuals by a national magazine elicited from one of our foremost literary figures the guarded response, "I ain't no intellectual."

Both sides in this battle, it seems to me, are motivated by largely unfounded feelings of distrust. The politician, whose authority rests upon the mandate of the popular will, is resentful of the scholar who can, with **dexterity** [n. 灵巧，机敏], slip from position to position without dragging the anchor of public opinion. It was this skill that caused Lord Melbourne to say of the youthful historian Macauley that he wished he was as sure of anything as Macauley was of everything. The intellectual, on the other hand, finds it difficult to accept the differences between the laboratory and the legislature. In the former, the goal is truth, pure and simple, without regard to changing currents of public opinion; in the latter, compromises and majorities and procedural customs and rights affect the ultimate decision as to what is right or just or good. And even when they realize this difference, most intellectuals consider their chief functions that of the critic - and politicians are sensitive to critics - (possibly because we have so many of them). "Many intellectuals," Sidney Hook has said, "would rather die than agree with the majority, even on the rare occasions when the majority is right."

It seems to me that the time has come for intellectuals and politicians alike to put aside those horrible weapons of modern internecine [adj.两败俱伤的，内讧的] **warfare, the barbed thrust, the acid pen, and, most sinister of all, the rhetorical blast. Let us not emphasize all on which we differ but all we have in common. Let us consider not what we fear separately but what we share together.**

First, I would ask both groups to recall that the American politician of today and the American intellectual of today are descended from a common ancestry. Our Nation's first great politicians were also among the Nation's first great writers and scholars. The founders of the American Constitution were also the founders of American scholarship. The works of Jefferson, Madison, Hamilton, Franklin, Paine,

司法部长和国会议员的讽刺攻击，很能代表这类观点："库欣部长是个绝顶聪明的人，他左右逢迎、上下通吃，但从未偏离自己的观点，他永远忠于一方，那就是他自己。"

但是，公平地说，知识界也不是一片恬静宜人，事实上，对知识界的怀疑也在不断增多，以致最近一份全国性杂志对美国知识界的一项调查中，我们文学界的一位重要人物就做出了谨慎的回答："我可不是什么知识分子。"

在我看来，双方在这场斗争中很大程度上是出于毫无根据的互不信任。政治家掌握权力是源于民意的授权，他们讨厌学者能够在不引起公众舆论非议的情况下，在一个又一个观点间游刃有余。就是这种技能，导致墨尔本勋爵在评论充满朝气的历史学家麦考利时说，他希望自己对某件事的把握，能够达到麦考利对世上一切的把握程度。

而在另一方面，知识界觉得难以接受实验室和立法机关之间有什么不同。在实验室里，目的是找到真理，就是如此简单，而不必考虑民意变化的潮流。而到了立法机关那里，达成妥协，达到多数通过规定的程序，以及尊重权利等等考虑，会影响到什么才是对的、公正的、或好的等方面的最终决定。即使认识到了这种差异，大多数知识分子还会认为，他们的主要作用是作为批评者和评论家。而政治家们对批评很敏感，可能是因为我们有太多的批评者了，就像西德尼·胡克[3]所说："许多知识分子宁死也不愿意去附和多数人，甚至在多数人是正确的时候依然如此。"

我认为，知识分子和政治家们都应当抛开那些造成我们两败俱伤的可怕武器、带钩的匕首、讽刺的文笔，还有最可怕的修辞上的攻击，这个时机已经到来。让我们不再强调我们何处不同，而是强调我们何处相同；让我们考虑的不是各自阵营担心害怕的东西，而是我们能共同分享的东西。[4]

首先，我想请这两个群体回想一下，当今美国政治家和美国知识分子，都是源于一个共同的祖先。我们国家第一批伟大的政治家们，同时也是我们国家第一批伟大的作家和学者。美国宪法的缔造者们，也是美

and John Adams - to name but a few - influenced the literature of the world as well as its geography. Books were their tools, not their enemies. Locke, Milton, Sydney, Montesquieu, Coke, and Bollingbroke were among those widely read in political circles and frequently quoted in political pamphlets. Our political leaders traded in the free commerce of ideas with lasting results both here and abroad.

In those golden years, our political leaders moved from one field to another with amazing versatility and vitality. Jefferson and Franklin still throw long shadows over many fields of learning. A contemporary described Jefferson, "A gentleman of 32, who could calculate an eclipse, survey an estate, tie an artery, plan an edifice, try a cause, break a horse, dance a minuet, and play the violin."

Daniel Webster could throw thunderbolts at Hayne on the Senate floor and then stroll a few steps down the corridor and dominate the Supreme Court as the foremost lawyer of his time. John Quincy Adams, after being summarily dismissed from the Senate for a notable display of independence, could become Boylston professor rhetoric and oratory at Harvard and then become a great Secretary of State. (Those were the happy days when Harvard professors had no difficulty getting Senate confirmation.)

The versatility also existed on the frontier. In an obituary of Missouri's first Senator, Thomas Hart Benton, the man whose **tavern** [n. 酒馆. 客栈] brawl with Jackson in Tennessee caused him to flee the State, said, "With a readiness that was often surprising, he could quote from a Roman law or a Greek philosopher, from Virgil's Georgics, the Arabian Nights, Herodotus, or Sancho Panza, from the Sacred Carpets, the German reformers or Adam Smith; from Fenelon or Hudibras, from the financial reports of Necca or the doings of the Council of Trent, from the debates on the adoption of the Constitution or intrigues of the kitchen cabinet or from some forgotten speech of a deceased Member of Congress."

This link between the American scholar and the American politician remained for more than a century. Just 100 years ago in the presidential campaign of 1856, the Republicans sent three brilliant orators around the campaign circuit: William Cullen Bryant, Henry Wadsworth Longfellow, and Ralph Waldo Emerson. Those were the carefree days when the eggheads were all Republicans.

I would hope that both groups, recalling their common heritage, might once again forge a link between the intellectual and political professions. I know that

国学术的创始者。随手举几个例子：杰弗逊、麦迪逊、汉密尔顿、富兰克林、潘恩和约翰·亚当斯，他们的作品不但影响了世界文学，也改变了世界的版图。书是他们的工具，而不是他们的敌人。洛克、弥尔顿、悉尼、孟德斯鸠、科克和博林布鲁克等人的作品，为政界人物广泛阅读，并经常在政见小册子里被援引。我们的政治领袖们自由地交流观点，在美国和国外，都产生了深远的影响。

在那些黄金岁月里，我们的政治领袖们从一个领域到另一个领域，都展现了惊人的能力和活力。杰弗逊和富兰克林仍然是许多领域绕不开的身影。有个同代人这样描述杰弗逊："君子年方三十二，擅长测算日食，丈量地产，医治动脉，规划大厦，裁决法案，掌控奔马，跳小步舞，拉小提琴……"

丹尼尔·韦伯斯特[5]可以在参议院对海恩议员发出雷霆般的质问，然后沿着走廊漫步几步，在称霸最高法院时又成了当时最好的律师。约翰·昆西·亚当斯[6]，因为桀骜不驯的独立精神而被参议院清除之后，却可以成为哈佛大学的博伊尔斯顿客座教授，教修辞学和演讲，后来又成为一个出色的国务卿。（那可是快乐的时光，哈佛大学教授在得到参议院认可后，就可担当任何要职。）

在美国当时的边疆地带，同样也涌现出多才之士。密苏里州的第一位参议员托马斯·哈特·本顿[7]，因为在田纳西州的小酒馆里与杰克逊斗殴而不得不逃离该州，他的讣告里说："常常令人惊讶的是，他可以随时引用古罗马法律的某个条款、希腊哲学家的句子、维吉尔的农事诗集、阿拉伯的一千零一夜故事、希罗多德的哲学，或《堂·吉诃德》里的桑丘·潘沙轶事，从神圣地毯、德国的宗教改革者到亚当·斯密；从如何通过宪法时的辩论，或影子内阁的趣事，到某个已故的美国国会议员已被人遗忘的讲话，他都能如数家珍。"

美国学者和美国政治家之间的这种联系持续了一个多世纪。就在100年前的1856年的总统竞选中，共和党派出三名出色的演说家四处游说：威廉·卡伦·布莱恩[8]、亨利·沃兹沃斯·朗费罗[9]、拉尔夫·沃尔多·爱默生[10]。那时的理论家们都属于共和党人。

scholars may prefer the mysteries of pure scholarship or the delights of abstract discourse. But, "Would you have counted him a friend of ancient Greece," as George William Curtis asked a century ago during the Kansas-Nebraska controversy, "who quietly discussed patriotism on that Greek summer day through whose hopeless and immortal hours Leonidas and his 300 stood at Thermopylae for liberty? Was John Milton to conjugate Greek verbs in his library or talk of the liberty of the ancient Shunamites when the liberty of Englishmen was imperiled?" No, the duty of the scholar, particularly in a republic such as ours, is to contribute his objective views and his sense of liberty to the affairs of his State and Nation.

Secondly, I would remind both groups that the American politician and the American intellectual operate within a common framework - a framework we call liberty. Freedom of expression is not divisible into political expression and intellectual expression. The lock on the door of the legislature, the Parliament, or the assembly hall - by order of the King, the **Commissar** [n. 代表. 苏俄人民委员], or the **Fuehrer** [n.(德) 元首, 德国独裁者] - has historically been followed or preceded by a lock on the door of the university, the library, or the print shop. And if the first blow for freedom in any subjugated land is struck by a political leader, the second is struck by a book, a newspaper, or a pamphlet.

Unfortunately, in more recent times, politicians and intellectuals have quarreled bitterly, too bitterly in some cases, over how each group has met the modern challenge to freedom both at home and abroad. Politicians have questioned the discernment with which intellectuals have reacted to the siren call of the extreme left; and intellectuals have tended to accuse politicians of not always being aware, especially here at home, of the toxic effects of freedom restrained.

While differences in judgment where freedom is endangered are perhaps inevitable, there should, nevertheless, be more basic agreement on fundamentals. In this field we should be natural allies, working more closely together for the common cause against the common enemy.

Third and finally, I would stress the great potential gain for both groups resulting from increased political cooperation.

The American intellectual and scholar today must decide, as Goethe put

我希望，这两个群体在回顾他们的共同遗产时，可以再次把知识界和政治界联系起来。我知道学者们可能更喜欢探索纯学术或抽象演绎的奥秘，但是，一个世纪前乔治·威廉·柯蒂斯[11]曾在一场有关堪萨斯和内布拉斯加的争论中说过："如果当列奥尼达斯[12]和他的三百爱国志士在塞莫皮莱为希腊的自由而浴血奋战时[13]，某人却在那儿静悄悄地讨论爱国主义的概念，你会认为这样的人算是古希腊的朋友吗？当英国人的自由岌岌可危时，约翰·弥尔顿[14]会在书房里研究希腊动词，或高谈阔论古人的自由吗？"不！特别是在像我们这样的一个共和政体里，学者有责任为我们的国家和民族，奉献出他的客观看法和他对自由的理解。

其次，我想提醒这两个群体，也就是美国的政治家和美国的知识分子，都在一个共同的框架内运作，这个框架我们称之为自由。言论自由是不可以区分成政治的表达和思想的表达两部分的。不管是国王君主、苏俄的人民委员或是德国的独裁者，他们在下令封锁议会机构或群众团体之前或之后，总是同时要封闭大学、图书馆，或印刷店之门。而如果一个政治领导者在其操控的领地内限制自由的话，他们接下来要做的就是控制书籍、报纸或小册子的出版。

不幸的是，近期以来政治家和知识分子们只是愤恨地争吵，有时甚至是过于愤恨地争吵，挑剔对方无法应对国内和国外出现的对自由的新挑战。政治家们质疑知识分子对极左势力苗头的洞察力；而知识分子往往指责政治家通常认识不到，特别是在美国国内，对自由采取限制所带来的恶性后果。

虽然判断我们的自由在哪个方面受到威胁，不可避免地会出现不同的评判标准，但我们应该在根本点上有基本的一致。在这方面，我们应该是天然的盟友，为我们的共同目标，为反对我们共同的敌人，而更加紧密地协同合作。

第三，也是最后，我想强调这两个方面加强政治合作，会给各自带来怎样的巨大收获。

it, whether he is to be an anvil - or a hammer. Today, for many, the stage of the anvil, at least in its formal phase, is complete. The question he faces is whether he is to be a hammer - whether he is to give to the world in which he was reared and educated the broadest possible benefits of his learning. As one who is familiar with the political world, I can testify that we need it.

For example: The password for all legislation, promoted by either party, is progress. But how well do we tell what is progress and what is retreat? Those of us who may be too close to the issue, or too politically or emotionally involved in it, look for the objective word of the scholar. Indeed, the operation of our political life is such that we may not even be debating the real issues.

In foreign affairs, for example, the parties dispute over which is best fitted to implement the long-accepted policies of collective security and Soviet containment. But perhaps these policies are no longer adequate, perhaps these goals are no longer meaningful - the debate goes on nevertheless, for neither party is in a position to undertake the reappraisal necessary, particularly if the solutions presented are more complex to, and less popular with, the electorate.

Or take our agricultural program, for another example. Republicans and Democrats debate long over whether flexible or rigid price supports should be in effect. But this may not be the real issue at all - and in fact I am convinced that it is not, that neither program offers any long-range solution to our many real farm problems. The scholars and the universities might reexamine this whole area and come up with some real answers - the political parties and their conventions rarely will.

Other examples could be given indefinitely - where do we draw the line between free trade and protection, when does taxation become prohibitive, what is the most effective use we can make of our present nuclear potential? The intellectuals who can draw upon their rational disinterested approach and their fund of learning to help reshape our political life can make a tremendous contribution to their society while gaining new respect for their own group.

I do not say that our political and public life should be turned over to experts who ignore public opinion. Nor would I adopt from the Belgian constitution of 1893 the provision giving 3 votes instead of 1 to college graduates; or give Harvard a seat in the Congress as William and Mary was

就像歌德所说的那样，作为一个美国的知识分子和学者，现在必须决定他是要做铁砧，还是做个铁锤主动出击。对于许多人来说，今天作为铁砧的阶段，至少在其表面意义上已经做好了。他所面临的问题是，他是否要做一个铁锤，他是否准备把他所学的知识尽可能地回馈社会。作为一个熟悉政界的人，我可以作证说，我们需要这个铁锤。

例如，任何一方想推行法律，是否有利进步是其决定因素。但我们怎样区分何为进步、何为后退？对这个问题，我们那些当局者迷的人，就需要学者的客观话语。事实上，我们政治生活中的某些操作方式，可能使我们进行文不对题的辩论。

例如，在外交事务上，有关方面为如何最好地实施共同安全、遏制苏联等长期政策而辩论不休。或许这些政策已不够用，也或许这些目标已经失去意义，但这些辩论会继续进行下去，因为任何一方尚未准备好对这些政策作出重新评估，特别是如果某方提出的解决方案对选民来说过于复杂和不受欢迎。

我们的农业计划是另一个例子。共和党人和民主党人一直在争论，对农产品价格的支持应当是固定的还是浮动的。但是，这未必是真正的问题所在，事实上，我相信这不是问题的关键，两个方案都无法为美国农业的真正问题提供具有远见意义的解答。我们的学者和大学，可以重新审视这一整个问题，并拿出一些真正的答案，而各政党和他们的聚会，却很难拿出这种答案。

我还可以举出无数的例子：我们如何区分自由贸易和自我保护？什么时候税收过高？我们如何最有效地利用目前的核潜能？知识分子可以采用他们理性的、不带偏见的分析，重塑我们的政治生活，在给他们的团体带来新的声望的同时，为我们的社会作出贡献。

我不是说我们的政治和公共生活应当交给忽视民意的专家手中。我不会采用1893年的比利时宪法，他们当时规定大学毕业生的1票算作3票；也不会像弗吉尼亚州的众议院曾经给威廉和玛丽学院一

once represented in the Virginia House of Burgesses.

But, I would urge that our political parties and our universities recognize the need for greater cooperation and understanding between politicians and intellectuals. We do not need scholars or politicians like Lord John Russell, of whom Queen Victoria remarked, he would be a better man if he knew a third subject - but he was interested in nothing but the constitution of 1688 and himself. What we need are men who can ride easily over broad fields of knowledge and recognize the mutual dependence of our two worlds.

"Don't teach my boy poetry," an English mother recently wrote the Provost of Harrow. "Don't teach my boy poetry; he is going to stand for Parliament." Well, perhaps she was right - but if more politicians knew poetry and more poets knew politics, I am convinced the world would be a little better place in which to live on this commencement day of 1956.

Thank you!

个固定席位那样，在美国国会给哈佛大学提供一个位子。

但是，**我呼吁我们的政党和我们的大学，应当认识到政治家和知识分子之间加强合作和理解的需要**。我们不需要像约翰·罗素勋爵[15]那样的学者或政治家，维多利亚女王在评论罗素勋爵时这样说过，如果还有第三个话题可以引起他的兴趣的话，他会是一个更好的人，可惜他只对1688年的宪法和自己本人这两方面感兴趣。**我们需要的人，应该可以轻松驾驭广泛的知识领域，并承认这两个领域应当相互依存。**

"不用教我孩子诗歌。"英国有位母亲最近写信给哈罗公学的教务长，说："不用教我孩子诗歌，因为他以后的志向是当议员。"好吧，也许她是对的，但是，如果更多的政治家都懂得诗歌，而更多的诗人懂得政治，那么，我相信今后的世界，会比我们1956年毕业典礼的今天，变得稍微美好一点。

谢谢各位！

Words to the American Intellectual　John F. Kennedy
给美国知识界的建言　约翰·肯尼迪

1　与清朝李鸿章相同时期的德国首相

2　詹姆斯·罗素·洛厄尔（James Russell Lowell, 1819—1891），美国诗人与政论家。

3　西德尼·胡克（Sidney Hook, 1902—1989），美国实用主义哲学家。

4　这段发言让人想起肯尼迪后来在其1961年1月的美国总统就职典礼上的演讲中那段经典的话："Ask not what your country can do for you; ask what you can do for your country."——不要问国家能为你做什么，而要问你能为国家做些什么。

5　丹尼尔·韦伯斯特（Daniel Webster, 1782—1852），美国参议员，当时有影响的政治家。

6　约翰·昆西·亚当斯（John Quincy Adams, 1767—1848），曾任美国国务卿，后于1925—1829任美国第六任总统。

7　托马斯·哈特·本顿（Thomas Hart Benton, 1782—1858），美国参议员，积极主张美国向西部扩张。

8　威廉·卡伦·布莱恩（William Cullen Bryant, 1894—1878），美国诗人与著名记者。

9　亨利·沃兹沃斯·朗费罗（Henry Wadsworth Longfellow, 1807—1882），美国诗人与教育家。

10　拉尔夫·沃尔多·爱默生（Ralph Waldo Emerson, 1803—1882），美国作家、诗人。

11　乔治·威廉·柯蒂斯（George William Curtis, 1824—1892），美国作家、演说家。

12　列奥尼达斯（Leonidas），古希腊英雄，于公元前480年8月带领300名斯巴达将士，为保卫希腊不受波斯人入侵而全部战死。

13　塞莫皮莱，希腊东部的一个多岩石平原，古时曾是一处山口。

14　约翰·弥尔顿（John Milton, 1608—1674），英国诗人，代表作为《失乐园》。

15　约翰·罗素（John Russell, 1792—1878），英国政治家，曾在19世纪中期两度担任英国首相。

芭芭拉·玛丽·沃德（1914—1981）

英国经济学家和作家，也是最早倡导"可持续发展"理念的经济学家，并以倡导环境保护、敦促西方发达国家援助发展中国家而著称。在沃德后半生中，因其澳籍丈夫杰克逊将军被英国授予男爵爵位，而被称为杰克逊男爵夫人。

芭芭拉·沃德于1935年毕业于牛津大学。毕业之后，在奥地利研究政治和经济。在那里她目睹了纳粹德国的反犹太主义，开始帮助犹太难民。二战期间，沃德曾在英国的新闻部工作，后来成为英国著名的《经济学家》杂志的记者。战争结束后，沃德积极支持马歇尔计划的实行，推崇建立一个强大的欧洲，实行欧洲自由贸易区。

芭芭拉·沃德于1950年与在联合国任职的罗伯特·杰克逊结婚。在那之后的几年里，他们居住在西非，并多次访问印度等国。这些经验强化了沃德的观点，即西方国家必须帮助促进经济贫困国家的发展，因为除了道德意义上的关怀之外，这种援助也有利于世界的稳定与和平，她由此被有些人称为"分配主义者"（"distributist"）。

沃德专注于研究发展中国家的问题，敦促西方国家与世界其他国家和地区分享其繁荣成果。她强调贫富国家之间合理的财富分配与资源保护两者之间的密切联系，并用了"内在约束"和"外部限制"的概念，认为人类的生活标准和地球能够维持的物质供应之间，应该有一个平衡。

1972年，沃德于与杜博斯共同为联合国人类环境会议撰写了《只有一个地球》（Only One Earth）的报告。她认为保护环境和关注全人类的福祉，是人们的"双重责任"。

1957

United to Fight Poverty
联合起来 消除贫困

Lady Barbara Ward Jackson 杰克逊男爵夫人

Mr. President, members of the Harvard Corporation and the Board of Overseers, faculty, parents, and especially, the graduates:

No one coming from Europe to take part in Harvard's Commencement ceremonies in 1957 can fail to recall that just ten years have passed since one of America's most distinguished sons, General George Marshall, chose Commencement at Harvard for his first public proposal of a vast and imaginative American plan to help restore the war-shattered economies of Europe. The European Recovery Program -- or rather the Marshall Plan -- marked an entirely new departure in the history of nations. Its importance can in part be measured by its physical results. Europe, after the Second World War, recovered its pre-war standards within five years and continued to expand its economy in every direction thereafter. Whereas after 1919, full recovery took a decade and was then shattered by world wide depression.

But its chief significance lay surely in the fact that on the **morrow** [n. 翌日．特殊事件后紧接的时期] of a devastating war, it expanded the political possibilities and the social vision of free men. **Hitherto** [adv. 到目前为止．迄今], all Western Europe had been threatened by the combination of external Soviet pressure and internal extremist subversion. It restored production but, even more, restored hope. Men felt they were working with friends for a common purpose. They did not feel they were being bribed to take sides in a quarrel they did not want to share.

The Plan proved that, given the larger framework of a joint enterprise, local difficulties, sensitivities and acerbities could be left behind. The war, after all, registered an enormous advance in the United States' position as an international trader. Markets once supplied by Europe were now dominated by American commercial interests. America's share in world trade had sharply increased, Europe's had declined -- and all the while, Totalitarian propaganda was repeating the **refrain** [n. 副歌．重复] that "imperialist" America was out to kill competition and to establish its own trade monopoly. But all grievances and difficulties were overlaid by the more powerful sense of working together, within the framework of the Plan, to achieve a common end, the revival of Europe. Who could accuse America of 'selfish exploitation' when it was engaged, at heavy cost to itself, in restoring its competitors?

尊敬的校长、哈佛集团和监管理事会的各位理事、各位老师、家长，特别是今天毕业的同学们：

从欧洲来参加 1957 年哈佛大学毕业典礼的人都无法忘记，就在 10 年前，美国一个杰出的儿子、乔治·马歇尔将军，选择了哈佛毕业演讲这样一个场合，首次公开提议，要推行一个宏大而富有想象力的美国计划，去帮助恢复受到战争破坏的欧洲经济。"欧洲复兴方案"也就是马歇尔计划，标志着在国与国之间关系历史上一个崭新的开始，其重要性，从其部分结果即可见一斑。第二次世界大战后，欧洲在 5 年之内就恢复到了二战前的水平，并在各方面持续发展。而在 1919 年第一次世界大战结束之后，欧洲的全面恢复用了整整 10 年时间，随后便受到世界性经济衰退的摧残。

但这个计划的伟大意义，在于经过了一场损失惨重的战争后，为自由世界的人们拓展了政治空间和社会远见。迄今为止，整个西欧受到双重威胁，外有苏联的压力，内有激进主义的威胁。该计划恢复生产，但更重要的是重建希望。欧洲人觉得自己是在与朋友一道，为了一个共同的目标而努力。他们不觉得自己是受到了贿赂，要在他们不想参与的争吵中，站到某一方。

马歇尔计划证明，在一个共同事业的大框架下，各方都可以抛开各自的困难、顾虑和恩怨。 说起来，二战使美国在国际贸易中的地位处于强势。过去曾经是欧洲的市场，现在已被美国商界占据。美国在世界贸易中所占的份额急剧增加，而欧洲的则有所下降。与此同时，极权主义的宣传不断在说"美帝国主义"的目的是扼杀竞争、建立自己的贸易垄断。在该计划的框架内，人们有了一个共同工作的强大愿望，从而能够抛开恩怨、克服困难，为了实现那个共同的目标——重振欧洲。当美国以付出重大代价来帮助竞争对手重建家园时，还有谁能指责美国是为了"自私的利益"呢？

马歇尔计划还为人们的政治思想和行动开辟了一个新的视野。它表明，在这个有着原子能、超音速、空间消失、地球人都要抱团在一起的时代里，不可能说一切都变了，而政治理念却还会保持不

The Marshall Plan also opened up a new dimension of political thought and action. It showed that, in an age of atomic power, supersonic flight, the annihilation [n. 歼 灭；消 灭] of space and the huddling together of the earth's peoples, man was not to be condemned to changing everything except his political ideas. By reaching across frontiers, by moving beyond narrow national interest, by establishing new cooperative agencies between free nations, by proving that men of different loyalties could combine in a wider dedication -- in all these ways the Plan pointed beyond the political limitations of unmixed sovereignty----just as hydrogen power and **strontium** [n.[化] 锶 （元素符号为 Sr）] 90- ---"raining on the just and the unjust" ---- make nonsense of the myth of **inviolable** [adj. 不可侵犯的；不可亵渎的] frontiers.

Last of all, the Marshall Plan proved that men need not be, as Marx proposed, prisoners of their own most narrow material interests. It showed that no limits need be set to the imaginative generosity of free men.

This was ten years ago. How, after a decade, shall we read the profit and loss account?   Some of the effects have been enduring----the upward physical surge of Europe goes on. It Is Western Europe that has grown and prospered while Eastern Europe is in **penury** [n. 贫穷；拮据] and despair. The hope of a wider political unity in Europe, first sparked by the Marshall Plan, has not flickered out, and this year could bring the first foundations of a Common Market. The United States has sustained the practice of foreign aid and Congress now seems likely to accept the salutary principle of aid planned on a sustained basis and linked to long-term purposes. All this is a great gain and to measure how great it is we can recall the end of the decade after the First World War, when with depression, unemployment and despair, the world was already preparing for Hitler, for Japanese militarism and for renewed conflict.

But in spite of these real and sustained gains, I would not say that today, ten years after General Marshall's great speech, the alliance of free men stood in as hopeful a posture. No great enterprise unites us now. We maintain a defensive alliance within NATO, but as history always shown, nothing dissolves so quickly as defensive coalitions----and at this moment, while Khrushchev steals the headlines over disarmament, NATO is in fact disarming itself with little mutual consultation and certainly no quid pro quo from the Russian side.

变。该计划跨越国界，超越了狭隘的国家利益，在民主国家之间建立起新的合作机构。它证明，目标不同的人可以集合在一个更大的目标之下。该计划在这些不同的方面，跨越了不同主权带来的政治局限，正如氢和锶的结合，"使得公正和不公正的，都受其雨露滋润"，它使界限森严的做法变得不合时宜。

最后，"马歇尔计划"还证明人们不一定会像马克思说的那样，受自己狭窄的物质利益的束缚。它表明，自由人在慷慨方面的想象力是没有极限的。

这是10年前的事了。现在，我们是否可以回过头来评价一下利弊得失？该计划所产生的一些影响意义深远，比如欧洲在物质上的不断进步。西欧正在繁荣发展，而东欧国家则陷入赤贫和绝望之中。由马歇尔计划所引发的有关建立一个广泛的欧洲政治同盟的希望，仍在闪烁，今年可能为建立一个欧洲共同市场而打下第一批基础。美国继续为外国提供援助，美国国会现在似乎会接受这样一个有益的原则，即有计划的援助，并把援助和长远目标挂钩。所有这些都带来非常大的好处，要想衡量这个益处到底有多大，我们只需回顾一下第一次世界大战结束之后的那10年，在经济衰退、普遍失业和一片绝望之中，全世界做好准备要对付希特勒、日本的军国主义和新的冲突。

然而，尽管我们取得了这些实实在在的可持续的成果，我还不敢说，今天在马歇尔将军发表那篇伟大演讲的10年之后，我们自由人的联盟达到了所希望的高度。现在没有什么大目标能把我们团结在一起。我们的北约组织只是一个防御性的联盟，但正如历史所表明的那样，防御性的联盟最容易解散。而在这个时刻，赫鲁晓夫靠着讨论裁军吸引了话题关注。北约的确在没什么相互协商，甚至在没有得到俄罗斯方面投桃报李的情况下，就自解武装。

在政治上，该联盟于去年秋季裂痕加深，成员间的信任和谅解大大降低，以致出现了苏伊士危机[1]这样的悲剧。任何来自欧洲的人都会坦率地说，人们普遍变得不喜欢大西洋联盟了。

Politically, the alliance had by last autumn drifted so far apart and confidence and understanding had dwindled to such a pitch that the tragedy of Suez became possible. Anyone coming from Europe must candidly report that distaste for the Atlantis association is widely expressed.

In fact, one distinguished American statesman, questioned about the alliance on his recent return from Europe, replied: "There isn't any." While this may be too extreme, what is certain is that the distrust, the envy, the fear of American power and competition -- which are inevitable given the nations relative strengths -- are now unchecked by any opposite sense of working with America to achieve any larger purpose and of experiencing first hand the energy, the vitality and the imagination which America can bring to any high task it proposes to itself.

The trend, therefore, is now towards a disintegration of the Atlantic Community. The work begun by General Marshall still persists. But it is growing weaker and unless it is renewed, the political cooperation of free men -- that vision of a new method and a new purpose in world diplomacy -- will vanish as surely as did the union between the Greek states before Persia or the Italian cities before the Spaniard. The drift in human affairs is against cooperation and we are in those dangerous waters now.

But at least we are not as badly off as we might have been ten years ago. Then one could have despaired of free coalition of nations ever uniting in time of peace to achieve some great and constructive aim. Today at least we know it is possible and we know, from the Marshall Plan, some of the preconditions of success. If we wish to restore our alliance, we know what we have to do. The lessons of the last ten years are not lost. The book is open, if only we will read.

In the first place, our aim should be our own, not dictated by external pressure, not evolved as a counter measure, but springing from the positive needs of our society and taking the initiative in meeting them. Ten years ago, General Marshall declared that the policy of free men was not directed against any country or any doctrine but "against poverty, despair and chaos." They were the international enemies then---- they are the enemies now. But we are no longer fighting them together.

Secondly, the enterprise should not be the monopoly of any one nation.

事实的确存在。有一位著名的美国政治家最近从欧洲回来，有人问及大西洋公约组织的联盟，他回答说："没有什么联盟。"虽然这个回答可能太过偏激，但可以肯定的是，西欧对美国的不信任、嫉妒，对美国势力和竞争力的恐惧（由于美国相比其他国家有太大的优势，这是无可避免的），现在完全盖过了另一种可能，那就是为了一个更大的目标而与美国合作，以实现更高的追求，并亲身感受美国在为它自己制定更高追求时所带来的活力和想象力。

因此，现在大西洋组织正朝着解体的方向发展。马歇尔将军开创的工作虽仍然幸存，但它正变得越来越弱。除非它得到更新，否则人们之间的政治合作——在世界外交中创立一种新的办法和建立一个新的目标的设想——将会消失，就像希腊城邦国家之间的联盟，却在波斯人进攻时解体；或像意大利城市之间的联盟，在西班牙人进攻的时候便消失一样。人事间的倾轧不利于合作，我们现在就游荡于这样的危险水域。

但至少我们不比10年前差。在那个时候，人们失去信心，没有认识到和平时期国家之间能够在自由联盟下团结起来，共同追求一个宏大而有建设意义的目标。今天，至少我们知道这是可能的，由于有了马歇尔计划，我们知道想要成功，需要什么先决条件。如果想要恢复我们的联盟，就应当知道我们要做的事情。过去10年的教训不会白费。书本是打开的，就看我们是否去读。

第一，我们的目标应该由自己制定，而不应随着外界的压力而变化，不应作为一种反制措施而展开。我们的目标应着眼于社会积极的需要，并采取主动措施去满足这些需要。10年前，马歇尔将军宣布说，自由人的政策不必针对任何国家或任何理论，而是为了"对付贫困、绝望和混乱状态"。这些弊病是那时国际社会的敌人，现在我们仍然面对这样的敌人，但我们没有团结起来一起投入战斗。

第二，我们的目标不应该由任何一个国家垄断。那些具有最大财富和最大力量的国家，要担负起领导责任。马歇尔计划的精华部分是，美国提供援助给一些互相合作的国家，并要求它们自己也做

Those with most wealth and strength cannot abdicate the duty of leadership but the essence of the Marshall Plan was that American aid, given to a cooperative group of powers, called out their efforts and energies in equal measure. Today, when these economies are largely restored, they can participate as givers as well as receivers. The cooperation could thus be more complete. But the essential point is joint, not unilateral, action.

Last of all, our joint work as free nations ought to aim, as the Marshall Plan aimed and succeeded, in going beyond the conventional, national limits of our traditional economy and diplomacy. In 1947 the crisis facing Europe could only be solved by America's disregarding the conventional limits set to international buying, selling, trading and lending and by Europe setting aside the narrow, bilateral political inhibitions under which each nation separately had been trying to drag itself up from the **morass** [n. 沼泽，陷阱，困境].

If we look for the preservation of our alliance in these terms, I do not think we need look far for the kind of concrete constructive programs which would meet what one might call the Marshall criteria. Take, for instance, the issue of the Common Market in Europe. Valuable as it can be, it could also become a means of division, setting up that political **chimera** [n.[希神]奇美拉（喷火女怪），神话怪物，嵌合体] -- a "Third Force" -- and splitting the free world straight down the Atlantic Ocean. But why should not Europe's efforts develop a low tariff area -- if not a free trade area -- for the Atlantic Community as a whole? Such an effort would need a new attack upon the problem of convertibility and would require a high, progressive overseas investment program to ensure that lowered tariffs and wider competition could be eased by expanding markets elsewhere. But again, there is no shortage of such possible areas of investment.

All West Africa is within sight of independence and this area, bulging out into the Atlantic, may be the first arena where Africa's unforced allegiances are tested. France is urging its fellow-Europeans to invest there. Such new states as Ghana are in search of capital. Wide international schemes for Saharan development could be one factor in pacifying North Africa. No, it is not shortage of potential areas for imaginative investment that is impeding Western plans. It is the fading away of all idea that exceptional policies are still necessary in our continuously exceptional, revolutionary, and indeed catastrophic world.

出同样的努力、付出相同的精力。今天，当这些国家的经济基本上恢复的时候，他们可以既接受援助，也对外提供帮助，这样的合作就更加圆满。最重要的一点是联合行动，而不是单方面的作为。

最后，我们作为自由国家的联合工作，正如马歇尔计划所瞄准并成功做到的那样，应该着眼于超越我们的传统经济和外交那种通俗的、以国家来划分的限制。在1947年，只有通过美国打破国际采购、销售、交易和贷款方面的传统局限，通过欧洲国家消除狭隘的双边政治的禁忌（当时每个国家都各自想让自己脱离泥沼），欧洲的危机才能够得到解决。

如果我们想按照这些条件来维护我们的联盟，我想我们就不用上下寻觅，去找到那些具体的建设性方案，而那些方案要满足可称为马歇尔标准的要求。例如，在欧洲建立一个共同市场就是一个问题。虽然建立这样的市场会有价值，它也可能成为造成分裂的手段，并带来一个政治怪物——"第三种力量"，从而让自由世界从大西洋一分两半。但欧洲为什么不努力发展成一个低关税地区——如果不是一个自由贸易区的话——并让大西洋联盟形成一个整体？这样的努力，需要人们处理货币可兑换问题，需要逐步进行大量的海外投资，以确保降低关税和更多的竞争能够通过扩大其他市场来加以缓解。而这类需要进行投资的领域还有很多。

非洲西部的所有国家都即将独立，这片延伸到大西洋的地方，可能会是非洲想要自主和与谁结盟的第一个场所。法国正在敦促其他欧洲人向那里投资。像加纳这样新独立的国家正在寻求资本。国际社会为撒哈拉地区的发展提供广泛援助，这可以是安抚北非洲的一个因素。不，我们不缺少需要富有想象力的投资的潜在地区，不是这种缺少阻碍了西方推出计划。我们缺少的，是能够启发出色政策的那些主意，在我们这个不断出新、不断革命，而且确实充满灾难的世界上，我们需要更多这样的思想。

在马歇尔计划实行10年后，这显然是我们麻烦的根源。我们一直生活在蘑菇云的阴影下，看到受压迫人民的痛苦，经历死亡和灾

For this surely is the root of our trouble, ten years after the Marshall Plan. We have lived with the mushroom cloud and the falling strontium, the agony of subject peoples, with death and disaster, until, in some way, we have managed almost to accept our universe in these terms. While the gates of hell swing ajar, we turn away our eyes and conduct our affairs almost as though the **staid** [adj. 固定的; (指人、外表、行为、爱好等) 古板的; 一本正经的] patterns of limited eighteenth century diplomacy and sovereignty were still relevant. In the Marshall Plan for once, the Western world had a concept and achieved a program which in some measure met the extreme challenge, the extreme strangeness and newness of our atomic age. But since that time, we have done little but coast along on its declining momentum and that momentum is nearly spent. Today our world is no less revolutionary but we have almost created -- as we did between 1919 and 1929 -- the illusion of normalcy.

The illusion is as deadly now as it was then -- indeed, more deadly now than the stake is literally the annihilation of the human race. The old days lead to the old disasters. Today we need for very survival to revive the vision of the Marshall period and think, work and plan together in enterprises adequate to our revolutionary world and worthy of the energies of free men.

Thank you!

难,直到我们在某种程度上,几乎把这些东西接受为理所当然。当地狱之门大开,我们却移开双眼,在处理事务时,仍旧使用18世纪那种古板而有局限的外交和主权概念,理所当然地认为它们与今是相关的。马歇尔计划是个例外,西方世界有了这样一个概念,取得了这样一个方案,可以在一定程度上应付极端的挑战,应付我们这个极其陌生和新颖的原子时代。但从那以后,我们无所事事,只是吃老本,那老本现在几乎被吃光了。我们今天的世界充满变化,但我们几乎创造了——犹如我们在1919年到1929年间沉迷其中的那样一种——平安无事的幻想。

现在,这种幻想就像过去一样致命,事实上,它比过去更加致命,因为我们面对的是人类存亡的问题。过往的时日造成了过去的灾难。今天,我们出于生存的需要,必须重启马歇尔时期的远见,为了适应不断变化的世界,为了自由人值得去付出的精力,而共同思考、协力合作。

谢谢大家!

---

1 苏伊士危机(The Suez Crisis),指1956年下半年,围绕着苏伊士运河的管理权而展开的外交和军事冲突,在埃及总统纳赛尔宣布要将苏伊士运河收归国有后,为了控制苏伊士运河,以及把纳赛尔赶下台,英国、法国和以色列对埃及发起了军事攻击,后在美、苏和联合国的斡旋下停火。

彼得·盖尔（1887—1966）

　　荷兰历史学家。从莱登大学获得博士学位后，曾在英国伦敦大学任教，自1935年起，任荷兰乌特勒支大学历史教授。乌特勒支大学是荷兰最古老的大学之一，至今已有近400百年的历史。

　　盖尔曾在1940年被德国纳粹关进集中营，到1944年才获得自由。1947年时，盖尔曾与著名的英国历史学家阿诺德·汤恩比（Arnold Toynbee）进行过激烈的论战，说汤恩比的著作虚浮，认为汤恩比自认为发现了文明兴起与衰亡的历史"规律"是缺少实证，没有做到"论从史出"，且受宗教影响太深。

　　盖尔的主要著作有：1955年出版的《与历史学家的辩论》、《历史的应用与滥用》和1961年出版的《与历史的不期而遇》。盖尔认为，所有的历史学家在写历史时，都会受到自己所处时代的影响，所以每个时代对过去的历史都会有不同的看法，因此，"历史是一场永无休止的辩论"，在盖尔看来，历史学家所能做的，就是认真审视自己的观点，并敦促读者也这样做。

1959

The Disunity of European Countries
欧洲国家的分裂问题

Pieter Geyl 彼得·盖尔

Mr. President, faculty, family and friends, and today's graduates:

I am going to offer you some reflections on one of the most vital problems by which we Europeans find ourselves faced: the problem of, I shall not say how to achieve unity, but of how to remedy the worst drawbacks inherent in our old, historic multiplicity of nationalities and of sovereign states, of how to achieve at least some measure of unity, some method to ensure united action.

The two wars that occurred in the first half of our century revealed in frightful flashes, the dangers inseparable from the System, or rather the lack of system, presented by the existence of a number of unrelated and completely sovereign states. There is in fact more than this purely political problem of the prevention of any more **internecine** [*adj.* 两败俱伤的；内讧的] wars and of the setting up of a common defense against the menace from the East. There is the economic aspect. The modern world has developed in a way which puts a premium on vastness. A national economy **cooped** [coop; *n.* 笼子；*v.* 把……关起来] up within the frontiers of even a relatively large European State, is bound to fall behind the restless expansion we are witnessing in countries like the U. S. and Russia.

Ever since the war, then, the European countries have been struggling with this problem of our inherited disunity.

Let me remind you of what has been done so far. There is first of all the North-Atlantic Treaty Organization, of which of course the distinguishing feature is that the U. S. is a member and plays a leading part. Then there is the Organization for European Economic Co-operation (O.E.E.C.), set up in 1943 to administer the distribution of Marshall aid among its seventeen members. Along with it, and now to some extent fused with it, there was soon created the Council of Europe, and the Consultative Assembly of Europe. All based on the principle of co-operation between sovereign and equal governments. The Council is composed of ministers of the various countries; the Consultative Assembly, which meets at Strasburg, of delegations from their parliaments. These institutions have done useful work in gradually and partially freeing trade from the shackles of national restrictions and in accustoming their seventeen members to consultation and working out common lines of action not only on economic but on political questions.

However, there has been from the beginning a school of thought which regarded this method as irremediably insufficient. The tenderness towards national sovereignty

尊敬的校长、各位老师、各位家长、各位朋友,各位毕业生们:

我想跟你们谈的,是对我们欧洲人面临的一个最重要的问题发表一点感想。我不谈如何实现步调一致,而是对国家众多、主权分散的这种古老的多元历史所造成的固有缺陷,如何能够有所补救,以及如何实现至少某种程度上的团结一致,找到一些联合行动的方法。

我们这个世纪前半叶发生的两场战争,以可怕的方式显示了与这种体制不无关系的危险,或者说,一些互不关联的主权国家之间,由于没有一个统一体系而带来的危险。问题不仅仅在于如何预防再次发生自相残杀的战争和面对来自东方的威胁,而建立起一个共同防御同盟,还有经济方面的问题。现代世界看重规模庞大、幅员辽阔。哪怕欧洲能成为联邦,作为一个国家经济来经营,相比美国和俄罗斯的不断发展,欧洲经济也都显得是"憋"在相对小的范围之内。

自二战以来,欧洲国家都受困于这种分裂所带来的固有问题。

让我来回顾一下迄今已做过的事情。首先,我们有北大西洋公约组织[1],其显著特点,当然是因为美国是其中一员,并发挥了主导作用。此外还有欧洲经济合作组织[2],该组织成立于1943年,目的是负责管理马歇尔计划所提供的援助,如何在17个成员国之间分配。当时还很快设立了欧洲委员会和欧洲协商大会,这些组织现在在某种程度上与经合组织密不可分。这些组织都倡导主权国家之间的合作与平等。欧洲委员会由各成员国的部长组成,在奥地利的斯特拉斯堡举办的协商大会,由各国的议会派代表参加。这些机构已做了不少有益的工作,逐步解除成员国之间限制贸易的桎梏,并使它的17个成员国不仅在经济问题上,而且在政治问题上,逐步适应以协商的方式来处理。

不过,从一开始就有人说这一方法有着无可弥补的缺憾。他们认为,对国家主权的迷恋,让人们很难办成什么有实质性的事情。不久前,人们在探讨设立一个超国家的主权管理机构,可以

would, so these men think, prevent any really worthwhile effects. It was not long before a contrast was becoming manifest between Great Britain on the one hand, immovably opposed to any federalist arrangements, that is arrangements setting up a supra-national authority by which the sovereign power to decide participating national governments would in any way be interfered with; and some of the leading Western European countries which favored tackling the problem in that fashion. No responsible person, certainly, advocated suddenly merging national sovereignties over the entire field of the State's action, but a powerful clamor was raised in favor of a piecemeal subtracting from it one important subject after another.

Great Britain remaining unwilling, the other countries decided to proceed by themselves, and so, in 1951/2, the European Steel and Coal Community was set up, with a High Authority seated at Luxemburg between France, Germany, Italy and the three Benelux countries. I have always regarded this nomenclature European as usurpation. The Europe of the Six, Little Europe, as it is sometimes called, is not Europe. It seemed to me paradoxical that the enthusiasts who were always indulging in big talk about Europe should, in their eagerness for supra-national arrangements, overlook the danger that the constitution of a closer community within Europe, far from advancing the cause of European union, might lead to a permanent splitting up of Europe.

The steel and Coal Community was not in itself so very dangerous. But when in 1953/4 the Six contemplated the European Defense community, by which their armies were to be merged and a parliament directly elected by their peoples to be set up, the danger seemed to me very real indeed.

Nothing came of this scheme in the end because France, which had been the prime mover, suddenly swung over to the other side and the French Chamber rejected the proposal. This was in 1954. However, the European Federalists soon plucked up courage and so there was created, last year, the European Economic Community, again consisting of the Six only, and intended to do away with tariff barriers, and to equalize all kinds of economic and social provisions, within the territory of the Six.

The danger to which I alluded now suddenly manifested itself in a somewhat alarming manner. The Six had professed all along that their association was not intended to be exclusive, that on the contrary they hoped that other members of the O.E.E.C. would join in. The supra-national institutions provided for in the

干预会员国的事情，西欧一些主要国家也赞成以这种方式来处理问题，但英国坚定地反对这种带有联邦性质的安排。当然，没有什么负责的人，会主张在整个欧盟之间突然合并国家主权。一个重要议题接一个重要议题，就这样零敲碎打地，在这种设想中不了了之。

由于英国不情愿参加，其他国家决定它们自己先行一步，因此，在1951至1952年间，法国、西德、意大利和比、荷、卢三国，建立了设在卢森堡的最高机构"欧洲钢铁和煤炭共同体"。我一向认为这一做法是对欧洲权力的一种篡夺。这种"6国欧洲"，或像人们有时称呼的"小欧洲"，并不代表欧洲。在我看来这是自相矛盾的，喜欢奢谈欧洲一统的人，在热衷于做出超国家的安排时，却忽视了潜在的危险，即推行所谓的欧洲内部更紧密的联盟，这不是在促进欧盟的事业，反而会造成欧洲永远的分裂。

该钢铁和煤炭共同体本身并没什么危险，但在1953年至1954年间，这6个国家探讨成立"欧洲防务共同体"，将其军队合并，成立由该6国人民直接选举的议会，我认为，这样的危险已经摆到面前了。

这项计划后来无疾而终，因为法国一直是该计划的主要推动者，后来突然转向，法国议会也否定了该项建议。这是发生在1954年的事。但是，欧洲联邦主义者很快又鼓起勇气，所以，这6个国家去年又成立了"欧洲经济共同体"，要在这6个国家之间消除关税壁垒，并在各种经济和社会方面达成统一。

我刚才提到的危险，现在突然以有些令人担忧的方式出现了。这6个国家一直声称，该组织没有排他性，相反，他们希望欧洲经济合作组织的其他成员国加入。该条约里规定议会直接选举这样的超国家机构（虽然如何做还要在实践中摸索），实际上是绝对限制了英国的参与。今年1月1日生效的该项协议，隐含了对协议外国家的歧视，于是，其他国家想要建立一个广泛的自由贸易区域，以便减少这种歧视，但这些谈判由于受到法国的反对而

treaty, however - again a directly elected parliament (plans for which have still to be worked out in practice) -, amounted in effect to an absolute bar to the participation of England. Negotiations for a wide free trade area, which would have softened the discrimination implicit in the arrangement as it came into being on January 1st of this year, failed owing to French obstruction, to the very great regret especially of the Dutch, but also of the Belgians.

The Coal and Steel Community, too, is going through a crisis of first magnitude, and here it is especially Belgian interests which have been treated with scant regard. The curious part is that both the French and the Germans are now openly impatient at the supra-national tendencies of both the Coal and Steel Community and of the Economic Community, and there are in the treaties enough provisions to safeguard national sovereignty for them to be able to whittle these down as soon as it suits their interests to do so. In fact, the whole of this development of a especially close association of the Six, which seemed to the European federalists in Holland and Belgium so glorious a victory, is at the moment beginning to be regarded with grave misgivings in both those countries.

About a month ago, for instance, Mr. Van der Beugel, who was until lately sub-minister for European affairs in the Dutch government, said in a speech that it was time to **bethink** [vt. 使思考；想起] ourselves very seriously. In becoming a partner in the Common Market of the Six, Holland had proceeded on three suppositions. One, that this Common Market would be completed by a Free Trade Area embracing the rest of Western Europe. This had been prevented by the stubborn protectionism of France. Secondly, that German economic liberalism would prove a **counterpoise** [n. 平衡；砝码] to French protectionism. We are, however, faced by a close Franco-German co-operation, inspired by political motives. Thirdly, it had been thought that the interests of the smaller partners would receive a fair deal at the hands of the new European organs; the crisis in the Coal and Steel Community has taught us that there too the powerful Franco-German combination sweeps all before it. "The time of sweet dreams of European unity is past", the speaker exclaimed, "we shall have to put up a fight for our interests."

Of course I noted with satisfaction in this utterance the return to common sense, although at the same time I was amazed at the naive confession that the entire policy by which we had become entangled with the Six had been based on a threefold

失败，荷兰对此特别遗憾，比利时人也不愿这样。

"钢铁和煤炭共同体"也正经历着第一场较大规模的危机，在这里，特别是比利时的利益极少受到顾及。奇怪的是，现在法国和西德对"钢铁和煤炭共同体"以及"经济共同体"中出现的超国家倾向，公开表示出了不耐烦，这些协议中，有足够多的关于维护国家主权的条款，使这些国家在保护其自身利益时能从中脱身。事实上，在这6国间建立起特别密切的联系，荷兰和比利时的欧洲联邦主义者对此曾显得如此光荣，但眼下，这两个国家开始有了严重的顾虑。

例如，大约一个月前，荷兰政府负责欧洲事务的副部长范德伯格尔先生在一次讲话中说，现在是我们认真思考的时候了。在成为"6国共同市场"的一个伙伴时，荷兰抱着三个假设。第一，这一共同市场最后将会成为一个包括其他西欧国家的自由贸易区，但法国顽固的保护主义阻碍了这一点；第二，西德的自由主义经济能够抗衡法国的保护主义力量，然而，我们却看到法、德出于政治动机，紧密合作；第三，人们曾经以为，在新的欧洲机构中，较小伙伴的利益会得到公平的对待，但"钢铁和煤炭共同体"最近出现的危机告诉我们，强大的法德组合，横扫它面前的一切。"欧洲统一的甜美梦想已经过时了"，这位发言者声称"我们必须为了我们的利益而抗争"。

这种说法代表着回到常识，我当然对此感到满意，但与此同时，我很惊讶地注意到这种天真的想法，我们纠缠于6国共同体的所有政策依据，竟然会建立在对欧洲情况的这样三重误解之上。我们的政治家们直至现在才承认自己一直陶醉于欧洲一统的甜美梦想，这让人有点吃惊。让他们从乐观的幻想中惊醒的是，他们发现《罗马条约》（即"欧洲经济合作组织"）没能将西德与法国变成欧洲人，西德人与法国人还是老样子。

其实我们一直都应该持这样的怀疑。在1953年和1954年，当"欧洲防务共同体"（当然是"小欧洲"的构想）还在讨论桌

misconception of the European situation. The confession, too, that our statesmen had until now been indulging in sweet dreams about European unity was a little startling; and no less the admission that what had shocked them out of their illusionist optimism was the discovery that the treaty of Rome (the E.E.C. treaty) had failed to turn the Germans and the French into Europeans, that they still were Germans and French.

Really we might have suspected this all along. In 1953/4 already when the European Defense Community (Little European really, of course) was on the **tapis** [n. 桌毯], I tried to shake the complacency with which our public opinion was allowing that policy to be pushed through. I wrote that the mentality in which the enthusiasts approached the European problem was in the profoundest sense unhistorical and that the disregard of history could only lead to disappointments if not worse. No doubt my opponents in that debate at times referred to history themselves. They recalled, for instance, the unification of Germany, and especially the Philadelphia Congress of the Founding Fathers. But there is no more unhistorical way of proceeding than to **adduce** [v. 引证; 举出] parallels which may help you to make a debating point, but only you succeed in making your audience overlook the fundamental difference.

That the American case does not apply has been pointed out hundreds of times. The American states had in common language and traditions of law and government; they had in fact already been united under the English crown. Similar observations could be made about the German states in the mid-nineteenth century, when the great movement for unity roused an enthusiasm by the side of which the European movement, for all the devotion and fervour of its local leaders, makes but an artificial and shallow appearance. But even so the German parliament assembled at Frankfort in 1848, proved a miserable failure and the great work had in the end to be achieved - to use Bismarck's words - "by blood and iron". But even in America, did the constitution established in peaceful debate and by democratic methods settle the problem of union or state rights once and for all? I seem to remember that a terrible Civil War had to be fought a generation or two later before there was an end of the matter.

"Blood and iron". Nearly always the great territorial and constitutional changes in history have had to be brought about by war or by revolution: by violence. In a cynical mood one might exclaim: what a pity that Napoleon was overthrown; what a pity that Hitler was not allowed to finish his work; what a pity that we banded together to stop

上时，我就曾试图唤醒人们不要沉浸在自满情绪中，我们公众舆论中的这种倾向，使得那个政策得以通过。我写道，那些热衷于此的人，处理欧洲问题的方法是置历史于不顾，这只会导致失望，如果不说比失望更糟的话。不用说，我的反对者在辩论时也提到历史本身。例如，他们举出德国能够统一，特别是美国的缔造者们的费城集会的例子。但一个人引经据典来证明他要辩论的论点，却使听众忽视了两种情况间的根本性分歧，那就是不顾历史事实了。

人们已经无数次指出，美国的例子不适用于这种讨论。美国各州之间有共同的语言和在法律、政府上的相同传统，事实上，它们已经在英王室的旗帜下联合起来了。19世纪中期的德国各州，情况也颇为类似。当时德国呼吁统一的热情是如此之高，现在欧盟化运动虽然有各地领导人的热情支持，相比之下就显得人为和浅薄多了。但即使这样，当德国议会于1848年在法兰克福聚集时，仍然遭遇了悲惨的失败。最后，德国统一的工作，用俾斯麦的话来说，仍然要用"铁与血"来达成。就是在美国，以和平辩论和通过民主方式制定的宪法，一劳永逸地解决了合众国体制或各州权力之间的问题了吗？我似乎记得在一两代人之后，通过一场可怕的内战，美国才让这一问题告一段落。

"血与铁"。历史上，领土和制宪方式的重大变化，几乎都要诉诸以革命或战争等暴力的方式。玩世不恭的人可能感叹说：拿破仑被推翻了，这多可惜啊；希特勒不能做完他的工作，这多可惜啊；我们联合起来，制止斯大林往西方扩张，这多可惜啊。征服者可不会介意保存那些现在明显阻碍统一进程的国家的传统和利益，而在我们看来，欧洲一统似乎是如此可取、如此必要。

我要赶紧向你们保证，在这一严重问题上，我绝不会抱有任何玩世不恭的态度。**如果欧洲一统的代价是牺牲我们的自由和我们的国家特性，就像我们前辈最优秀的人在面对拿破仑专制，或我们这一代人面对希特勒和斯大林的专制时的那样，我也要说：**

Stalin before he got going in the West. A conqueror would not have bothered about all these national traditions and national interests which now so obviously impede the process of unification that seems to us so desirable, so necessary.

Let me hasten to assure you that I am not in the least inclined to be cynical about this grave matter. **If union could only be bought at the price of the surrender of our liberties and of our national individualities, I should say, as said the best men of an earlier generation when faced with the despotism of Napoleon, and as our own generation said when faced with the despotism of Hitler and of Stalin: never! The variety, so closely bound up with national independence, with language, with historic reminiscences - this variety is the very life blood of Western civilization, and a merciless unity imposed from above would be the death of it.** This does not mean that we must close our eyes to the need for a greater measure of unity. Only, the forces of tradition have so strong a life of their own, such vital interests are bound up with the existing forms of organization on the lines of national states, that any interference dictated by a dogmatic preference for supra-national institutions, may well give rise to dangerous reactions. Why, for instance, am I so skeptical about this scheme for a directly chosen parliament for Little Europe that found a place in the E.D.C. treaty of 1953/4 and that now again figures in the E.E.C. treaty? Simply because I cannot believe that it will work.

"Parliaments on a basis of democracy", as I wrote in 1954, "can succeed only where there exists a strong feeling of community", an understanding for each other's problems, a willingness to give and take. That condition is lacking in Europe. One may reply: it ought not to be. But it is. One might observe: history should no longer count. But history does count."

Some of the advocates of E.D.C. at that juncture prophesied the most wonderful effects if only we had a parliament entitled solemnly to assert that it represented the European peoples. I pointed (I am still talking about 1954) to the instability characteristic especially of the French and Italian domestic situations, an instability by which the Chamber in Paris or the Chamber in Rome, far from being able to restrain it, was on the contrary thrown into hopeless confusion. It seemed to me incomprehensible at the time that a stable country like Holland was of its own free will going to enter into so close an association with - as I put it - "the most problematic countries" of Europe, and I included, on other grounds, Germany in the

妄想！这种多样性，由于民族独立、不同语言、不同历史记忆所带来的多样性，是西方文明之所以具有生命力的血脉，如果自上而下地强调大一统，则只会让西方文化消亡。 这并不意味着我们对欧洲在更大程度上需要统一的情况视而不见，只是，传统的力量具有强大的生命力，很多至关重要的利益，都取决于现有的民族国家那种组织形式，以致任何出于教条式的超国家机构的设立，都有可能引起危险的反应。例如，为什么我对在1953年和1954年的"欧洲防务共同体"所说的，现在又在"欧洲经济合作组织"所构想的在"小欧洲"直接选举议会，感到如此怀疑，就因为我不认为这会有效。

正如我在1954年所写到的，"在民主基础的议会制，只有在人们具有一种强烈的群体感时，才可能成功"，人们要互相理解对方的问题，要有取有舍。这个条件在欧洲尚未达到。有人会说：不应该是这样的。但它确实如此。有人可能说：不应再去纠缠历史。但历史的确在起作用。

"欧洲防务共同体"的一些倡导者曾预言说，如果我们有一个议会能够庄严地承诺代表欧洲各国人民，那会是多么美妙。我曾指出，（我仍然是在说1954年的事），特别是在法国和意大利国内情况有着不稳定的特点这个情况下，在巴黎或在罗马的议会，不能控制这种不稳定的局面，反而让自己陷入无望的混乱之中。我当时觉得无法理解，为什么像荷兰这样一个稳定的国家，要出于自愿地与如我所说的欧洲"问题最多的国家"（我把西德也包括在内），建立如此紧密的联系，而把英国排除在外！

"欧洲经济合作组织"今天的情况与此相似，尽管它在一些方面表现出非常的不同。当然，我想到了法国，该国的国民议会有气无力，其组成部分遭到篡改，而且在议会中出现了一种顽固的民粹主义。真是不可理解，为什么荷兰和比利时会选择与这样不负责任的国家建立那么密切的关系？我前面说过，虽然人们开

description; and this without England!

The situation with respect to E.E.C. is today similar, although in some ways showing a very different appearance. I am thinking, of course, of France, where the national parliament has been reduced to impotence and its composition doctored, where, moreover, a spirit of **unregenerate** [adj. 不能再生的；顽固不化的；死不悔改的] nationalism has come to the fore. It seems hardly less incomprehensible that Holland and Belgium have chosen to associate themselves so intimately with that unaccountable country. Well, as I told you, second thoughts are beginning to stir, but I must not leave you under the impression that the views which I am expressing are, even now, representative for my country. While I was composing these remarks, Mr. De Quay, speaking for the new Dutch Cabinet of which he is Premier, expressly confirmed the policy of E.E.C. and of the institutionalizing of the association of the Six, with directly elected parliament and all. The estrangement from England which has begun to develop may in that way well grow to alarming dimensions.

I said, incomprehensible, - but I have an explanation, which I offered in 1954, and gave great offence in doing so, but in which I still believe.

It is not that there is any deep-seated feeling for European federation in a supra-national sense among the public at large. A former Dutch Foreign Minister, Mr. Beyen, who may be regarded as one of the architects of the federalist policy which has led to the Community of the Six---- he is now Dutch Ambassador in Paris---- Mr. Beyen wrote not long ago that "the readiness to enter into a close association of the Six is more alive among the populations than among the Governments, the politicians and especially the intellectuals." Now this seem to me (but you will realize that I belong to the class of men who come in for Mr. Beyen's severest disapproval) - to me it seems completely fanciful. No doubt to the average Dutchman the word Europe has, after the catastrophic events of 1940, an attractive sound. He will not look too closely at the modalities that are concocted by the men who are engaged in those mysterious confabulations in Brussels, in Paris, in Strassburg, in Luxemburg, the results of which are presented to him under the patronage of that magic word. But as soon as unpleasant consequences make themselves felt, as they are doing at this moment, I don't think that Mr. Beyon can count on the public at large for standing their ground, or his ground.

What has happened so far is that he and the small number of diplomats,

始有了怀疑,但即使现在,我也不能给你们留下这样一个印象,以为我在这里表达的观点在我的国家有什么代表性。就在我撰写这篇演讲稿时,德奎先生作为总理代表荷兰新内阁发言,他明确肯定了"欧洲经济合作组织"的政策、"6国集团"的制度化和直接选举议会等做法。英国不愿搅和其中的态度,可能会达到令人震惊的程度。

我说"令人不可理解",但我在1954年就曾提出过一个解释,我的说法得罪了很多人,但我仍然相信自己所说的话。

对广大公众而言,他们对建立一个超国家的欧洲联邦并没有什么浓厚兴趣。荷兰前外交部长拜恩先生可以被视为这种联邦政策设计者之一,该政策导致了"6国集团"的建立,他现在是荷兰驻巴黎的大使。拜恩先生不久前写道:"民众对在这6个国家间建立一个紧密的组织,其热情比各国政府、政界人士的热情,特别是知识分子的热情要高。"在我看来,这完全是天方夜谭,你们当然会意识到我属于拜恩先生特别反感的那类人。在经历过1940年的灾难性事件后,对普通荷兰人来说,"欧洲"这个词很有吸引力。政客们在布鲁塞尔、巴黎、施特拉斯堡和卢森堡等地方,神神秘秘地弄出一些名堂,打着"欧洲"这个神奇字眼的幌子,显示给普通人,他们是不会想太多的。而一旦感觉到什么不愉快的后果,比如像他们现在感受到的那样,我不认为拜恩先生会指望得到广大公众的支持,他自己可能也说服不了自己。

迄今为止,他和一小批专长于炮制这些欧洲"神秘妙方"的外交官、政治家和其他官员们,总是能天马行空随心所欲。不仅是公共大众,就是一般的政治家,甚至内阁部长,都把这些事交给他们去做,我用略带讽刺的说法,称这一小批人为"我们的专职欧洲人士"、"施特拉斯堡的常客"、"我们的欧洲爱好者"和"我们的专家"。这些欧洲组织的事务,已变得如此复杂,匪夷所思。这些问题已成为一种传说,不仅普通读者完全无法掌握,就是多

politicians and officials who have made their specialty of these European **arcana** [n. 秘密; 神秘事物] have had it all their own way. Not only the public, but the general run of politicians, even Cabinet ministers, have left these matters to what I am used with an under-tone of sarcasm to call our professional Europeans, our Strassburg travellers, our enthusiasts and our experts. For these European organization affairs have grown so unbelievably complicated. They have come to constitute a lore which is entirely beyond the grasp, not only of the average newspaper reader, but of the majority of politicians and Cabinet ministers who are too much immersed in national affairs to give them more than passing attention. It is this that has made it so difficult for the doubters to make their influence felt. Many people felt uneasy at every step in the direction of supra-national arrangements, but in arguing with the men who have made Europe their special field of action, and who have acquired a kind of vested interest in Europe, they were at a disadvantage. I assure you that when in 1954 I sounded my warning, I had to take my courage in both hands. Now, all of a sudden, unpleasant facts are making themselves felt, and, to quote Mr. Van der Beugel once more, there is an end of sweet dreaming.

I shall not try to predict how matters will now develop in practice, what, in particular, will be the future of the European Economic Community of the Six. But this I will say, and say with some emphasis. Whatever comes of the disagreements and complications of the moment, I do not expect, and I certainly do not wish, the idea of a closer European unity to vanish from the scene of practical politics. It will still, I trust, be brought nearer to reality by the methods of gradualness; ultimately these may even succeed in creating a solid basis for federation in the true sense of the word, a basis which is still lacking in the situation such as we observe it today.

Some of you may have wondered, at moments, why on a day when I am being honored as a historian (and let me assure you that I consider a Harvard degree to be an honor indeed!) I should have chosen to speak on a subject of contemporary politics. I hope that I have made it clear as I went along that the value of my contribution to the great debate that is going on in Europe (if it has any value at all) is in that it is the contribution of a historian.

The constant reference to history is apt to irritate the enthusiasts. As they see it, all that it means is that we want the living generation to remain enslaved to the past, that we are the advocates of a policy of immobility, of no-change. Now that is an

数政界人士和内阁部长，由于他们更多地耽于国家事务，对此也无法去更多关注。所以，持怀疑态度的人很难产生影响。很多人对超国家设想的每一步都感到不安，但要同把欧洲问题当做专注的领域、并在欧洲问题上已经取得某种既得利益的人去辩论，还是处于不利的地位。我向你们保证，1954年我是拿出全部的勇气来提出警告的，现在，让人不愉快的事实一一呈现出来。让我再次引用范德伯格尔的话：甜美的梦想终结了。

我不想去预料事情将怎样发展，特别是由6国组成的"欧洲经济合作组织"的未来，但是我还要说，而且是作为重点要强调的，无论有何分歧以及时下的症状如何，我并不预计，当然也不希望，在现实政治中欧洲更加团结统一的想法会销声匿迹。我相信，随着时间的推移，这将会更加接近现实。等有了稳固的基础，真正意义上的联邦最终会有可能实现。但依照今天我们所看到的情况，这种基础尚未出现。

在座的诸位中，可能有一部分人会想，为什么在我作为一个历史学家接受荣誉的这一天，（我向各位保证，哈佛学位于我确实是一种荣幸！）会选择讨论当代政治。我希望我前面已经讲清，对欧洲正在进行的重大讨论，（如果这种讨论有任何价值的话），我的贡献就在于发表一个历史学家的观点。

经常提到历史，很容易刺激到那些"欧洲爱好者们"。在他们看来，这一切都意味着我们想让活着的这代人接受过去的束缚，意味着我们主张政策僵化、没有变化。这完全是误解。历史学家都很清楚，变化一直是、今天依然是生命的法则。他不会说，历史已然停滞不前，每一个时代都有各自的变化。如果说我们现在必须绝对听从于以前的那些条条框框，那真是发疯了。相反，发生在我们这个世纪的两次世界大战，如同宗教改革、法国革命或美国内战一样，都已经属于历史，两次世界大战取代了这之前发生的很多事件的重要性，给我们出了一套难题，哪怕这些问题并不完全是新的，都需要我们用新的办法赶

entire misconception. The historian knows very well that change has always been, and still is, the law of life; he does not imagine that history has come to a stop. In the past, every age has had a principle of change of its own. It would be madness to pretend that we must now be absolutely governed by conditions that belong to an earlier state of affairs. On the contrary, the two great wars of our century, which belong to history just as much as do the Reformation or the French Revolution or the American Civil War, have superseded much of what went before and have presented us with a set of problems which, if not entirely new, have a novel and compelling urgency. But to think that therefore the burden of our remoter past has just simply dropped from us, is an illusion.

We are, as all previous generations have been, faced by a challenge to act, and acting means choosing. But we are not free, no more than they were, to act or to choose according to the dictates of our fancy. **The past is still with us to set limits to our freedom. To neglect these, to try to transgress them and to set out on an adventurous course traced by our imagination or our dreams and enthusiasms, is to invite disaster.** I am not suggesting that history will provide us with the one and only answer to our questionings. No historian can speak positively in the name of an all-knowing Goddess, History.

The historian remains a fallible human being, and you have heard in me, I am sure, not only the historian' but the Dutchman, the liberal, in short the individual specimen of the **genus** [n. [生物学] 属; 类; 种; 型] European that I am and do not for a moment wish to renounce. But for all that, I do believe that there is such thing as the historical way of looking at the world's affairs, and I often deplore the neglect of it by the practical politicians.

Thank you very much!

紧解决。但因此认为，那些更久远的历史已经跟我们无关，则是痴人说梦。

就像前人一样，我们也面临挑战，要采取行动，行动就意味着做出选择。但我们不能随意地根据幻想行事，前人也是如此。**历史仍然在我们当中，仍在限定着我们的自由。**忽视这些，试图绕开历史，全凭我们的想象力、我们的梦想和热情，去踏上一条冒险的征途，只会带来灾难。这并不是说，历史会给我们提供唯一的正确答案。没有任何一个历史学家，可以凭借"历史"这个全知女神的名字来乱说话。

历史学家也会犯错误，我相信，而且你们也已经听到，我发言的角度不仅是作为历史学家，也是作为一个荷兰人，一个自由派，简言之，是作为一个"欧洲人"的个体，我一点儿也不想放弃"欧洲人"的称号。但尽管如此，我仍然相信，应该用历史的眼光来看世界，那些抱着实用态度的政治家却对此视之不见，这让我常常感到痛心疾首。

谢谢各位！

---

1 北大西洋公约组织（the North-Atlantic Treaty Organization,），即北约（NATO）

2 欧洲经济合作组织（the Organization for European Economic Co-operation）简称 O.E.E.C.

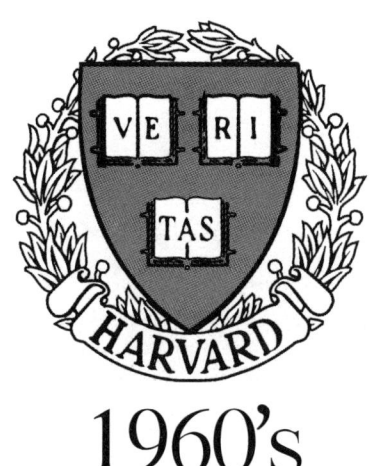

1960's

莱昂内尔·特里林（1905—1975）

美国哥伦比亚大学著名教授，也是活跃于20世纪30至70年代的美国著名文学评论家和作家，曾被英美文化界、知识界誉为"文化良心"。

莱昂内尔·特里林1905年出生于纽约一个犹太家庭，从出生到去世，他一生中的大部分时间是在纽约度过的，是一个地道的"New Yorker（纽约客）"。特里林16岁进入哥伦比亚大学，先后获得哥伦比亚大学文学学士、硕士和博士学位，并成为哥伦比亚大学英语系的第一个犹太裔教授。据他的同事回忆，特里林对教学充满热情并极其负责。在30多年的教学生涯中，他开设的文学、文学与文化历史的关系等课程大受欢迎。

特里林的博士论文《马修·阿诺德》发表的时候就引起过很大反响。当时英美等地的文学批评家们把他与阿诺德相提并论，认为他们都是富有智慧的作家，直面当代社会议题、激励和引导广大读者。特里林曾出版过三部小说《在旅行中》、《此时、彼地和其他故事》及《未完成的旅行》，但影响力更大的是他的教学，大量的文学批评、文化评论书籍和论文对英语国家的文化界影响深刻。他继承阿诺德和利维斯的批评传统，侧重从社会历史和道德心理的角度评论文学和社会文化，被称为20世纪中期美国年轻一代的思想导师，英语世界最伟大的批评家之一。

特里林也曾获得过多次国家人文科学奖，在50多年的写作和教学生涯中，他以自己的作品展示了文化批评的目的和知识分子的责任。因其巨大的成就和在文化界的地位，当他于1975年去世时，美国媒体叹息"一个时代结束了"，因为同时代没有人能够达到他的高度：教育一代人去信仰文学的力量。

1962

Radical Thought as Modern Energy
激进思想是现代动力

Lionel Trilling 莱昂内尔·特里林

Ladies and Gentlemen, Dear Friends, and Today's Graduates:

An anniversary such as you have been celebrating is charged with many emotions, of which some are grave and even sad. But no one will doubt that what you have chiefly been feeling during these last few days of your reunion is an emotion which is only happy -- your pleasure and pride in your college, a pleasure and pride which I am now privileged to share with you. The manifest virtues of your college are, indeed, so present in your minds that you will scarcely be disposed to remember that there once was a very distinguished and intelligent alumnus of the College who found it possible to say that Harvard had done almost nothing for him intellectually. Yet there actually was such a person, and inevitably he was Henry Adams.

Adams devotes the fourth chapter of his Education to his undergraduate days at Harvard College, and you will recall that, although he speaks in affectionate gratitude of the personal good the College did him, he is very severe on the quality of instruction he received. He tells us that in mathematics he learned nothing at all. The course in chemistry taught him a number of theories which, as he says "befogged his mind for a lifetime." His work in the ancient languages gave him only an acquaintance with two or three Greek plays. Political economy consisted of some incoherent theories of free trade and protection, and he goes on to say that "he could not afterwards remember to have heard the name of Karl Marx mentioned, or the title of Capital." From the general condemnation he exempts only a simple course -- he did find some intellectual satisfaction in Louis Agassiz's lectures on the Glacial Period.

I should like to take special notice of Adams' remark that "he could not afterwards remember to have heard the name of Karl Marx mentioned, or the title of Capital." Adams' memory was not in the least at fault -- we can be perfectly sure that he never did hear the title of Capital mentioned in his college. For Adams was graduated in 1858 and the first volume of Capital was not published until 9 years later, in 1867. Nor is there any likelihood that Adams could have heard Marx's name mentioned by his professor of political economy, for even the Critique of Political Economy was not to appear until after Adams had left college. So no blame attaches to Harvard, for not even Harvard can fairly be expected to teach books that have not been written. The instance of Henry Adams clearly demonstrates that alumni who criticize their college educations are merely **captious** [adj. 吹毛求疵的; 强词夺理的].

But that odd historical error of a great historian doesn't entirely rob his

女士们、先生们、朋友们,今天毕业的同学们:

你们正在举办的周年庆祝,一定令人百感交集,心中伤感。但没有人会怀疑,你们过去的几天里,返校团聚的感觉主要是快乐——为你们的母校感到高兴和骄傲。而现在,我也有幸得以与你们共享。在你们心目中,母校的优点明摆在那儿,你们甚至可能不知道,有一位校友、著名并机智的哈佛校友曾经说:说起来,哈佛大学几乎没给他什么知识上的益处。然而,确有其人,他就是亨利·亚当斯[1]!

亚当斯在他的《教育》一书中,专门用第四章来写他在哈佛受到的本科教育。你们也许会记得,虽然他深情回忆了在学校里结下的个人情谊,但他对学校的教学质量批评有加。他告诉我们,在数学课上他什么也没学到;化学课只是教给了他一些理论,而如他所说,这些理论"让他一辈子都搞不清";他所学的古代语言,只是让他略微知道了几出希腊戏剧;而政治经济学课只罗列了一些有关自由贸易和贸易保护等支离破碎的理论。他接着说,他"事后都想不起来,是否曾听到人们提及卡尔·马克思的名字,也没听说过《资本论》的书名"。在一通批评声中,他只对一门简单的课程手下留情——路易·阿格西有关冰川时期的课程,使他稍稍满足了一些求知的欲望。

我想特别提一下亚当斯的这句话,他"事后都想不起来,是否曾听到人们提及卡尔·马克思的名字,也没听说过《资本论》的书名",亚当斯的记忆一点都没错——我们完全可以肯定,他在上学时不可能听到过《资本论》的书名,因为亚当斯毕业于1858年,而《资本论》第一卷在他毕业9年后的1867年才出版。亚当斯也不可能在政治经济学课上听到教授提马克思的名字,因为《政治经济学批判》这本书也是在他离开大学后才面世的。所以不该怪罪哈佛,就算是哈佛,也无法教那本还没写出来的书。亨利·亚当斯的例子清楚表明了,那些批评他们的大学教育的人,都只是在吹毛求疵。

但是这位伟大的历史学家所犯的史料错误,并不能完全否定他

observation of **cogency** [n. 说服力；中肯]. For the point that Adams was making was that his college education gave him no sense of the world as it then was, that it left him ignorant of all that he needed to know if ever he was to have a hand in controlling the world, in shaping the course that modern life was to take. It was a criticism that became central to our thought about college educations in the twentieth century. Any man of spirited intellect who had any **tincture** [n. 气息；染料；色泽] of Adams' interest in power, who shared his desire to take part in the intelligent rule of the world, was sure to say, if he considered the substance of American college education, that it had no connection with modern life.

The same adverse characterization cannot fairly be made today. Whatever else is to be said in criticism of American colleges, they cannot be called indifferent to the modern. Among our almost **innumerable** [adj. 无数的；数不清的] undergraduate schools there is, of course, the widest variety in the quality and substance of instruction. But I think we can say that there is nowadays a direct relation between the intellectual force and prestige of any particular college and the degree of its responsiveness to modern life. I don't mean that the student can count upon his college to introduce him to all the important intellectual figures of our period, but in our best colleges he can be reasonably sure that such figures will not be excluded from his curriculum just because they are not yet traditional or because they disturb the tradition. For it is now the prevailing assumption of our colleges that a study is best justified by its relevance to contemporary life, that the true purpose of all study is to help the young person to be at home in and in control of the modern world.

This is now taken for granted as the intention of the modern college, whatever the degree of success with which it is carried out and -- it seems so natural and right that we can scarcely imagine that anyone might bring it into question.

And there can be no doubt that it deserves our respect and praise. It has made a new demand on the American college which on the whole has been beneficial. The academic life is never as good as it could be, it never lives up to its own notion of itself, and its scholars never have enough courage, or simplicity, or wit. But in my opinion our colleges are notably better than they used to be ---- they are both rather more serious and more **vivacious** [adj. 活泼的] ever since they came to believe that the modern world had issued to them some sort of challenge which they feel in honor bound to meet. Our faculties are the better for this new demand and our students are less bored

的观点的说服力。亚当斯想要阐明的是，他的大学教育没有让他认识到当时的世界，没有让他知道足够多的事物，从而使他在有朝一日有能力影响世界时，能够引导现代生活的走向。这是我们思考20世纪大学教育如何做好时很重要的一点批评意见。任何天赋聪明的人，如果像亚当斯那样对权力感兴趣，和他一样渴望用知识来管理世界，从这样的角度看美国大学教育的实质，都会认为我们的大学教育与现代生活脱节。

而在今天，人们是不会做出类似的负面评价的。不管你对美国的大学如何批评，都不能说它们对现代社会漠不关心。我们的本科院校几乎数不胜数，其教学质量和教学内容当然也差异甚大。但我认为，现在任何一所大学的知识影响力及名声，都和它关注现代生活的紧密程度有直接关系。这并不是说，学生们可以指望学校向他们介绍我们这个时代中知识界所有重要的人物，但基本可以肯定，在最好的院校里，这样的人物不会因为他们不够传统，或脱离了传统，就被排除在课程讨论之外。因为我们的院校时下流行的观点是，教学要贴近当代生活。所有教学的真正目的，是要帮助年轻人熟悉并掌握现代世界。

不同院校在这方面做的有好有差，但人们现在已经理所当然地把这当做现代大学的目标，它显得如此自然和正确，我们简直不能想象，有任何人会来挑战、否认这一点。

而且毫无疑问，这是值得我们尊重和赞美的事，它对美国的院校提出了新的要求，并从整体而言益处多多。学术生活永远都不可能如我们想象的那么好，它永远无法达到完美，学者的勇气、简约或机智，也永远不会嫌多。但在我看来，我们的院校明显地超过以往任何时候——学校比过去更严肃，也更活泼，这是因为学校认识到，面对现代世界的挑战，它们责无旁贷。由于有了这种新要求，我们的师资得到改善，学生也不像过去那样，厌烦和疏远他们的老师。

学术界现在的趋势，是面向外界、走向全球，没有人会想去扭

by and alienated from their teachers than they used to be.

No one can possibly want to reverse the tendency to move outward toward the world which the academic life now shows. But sometimes some of us will feel a touch of uneasiness about the effects of the new and developing **entente** [n. （国家间的）谅解，协定；协约国] between the academy and the contemporary world.

To speak by way of example of my own subject of literature, I have the growing sense that those of us who teach literature in its modern phase must sometimes wonder what we are up in our enterprise, even to the point of to questioning its **pedagogic** [adj. 教学法的] legitimacy. I need scarcely say that what uncertainties we may have imply no doubt of the literature we deal with. A canon that includes Yeats, Eliot, Lawrence, Joyce, Proust, Kafka, Mann, and Gide, and which, if it is conceived in the full **catholicity** [n. 普遍性；大量] of its tradition, also includes Flaubert, Baudelaire, Rimbaud as well as the later Tolstoy and Dostoyevsky, is obviously to be judged one of the very greatest in history. The uneasiness arises exactly from the particular nature of the greatness. For this is a literature whose force may be said to derive from its preoccupation with spiritual salvation. It is a literature which has taken to itself the dark power which certain aspects of religion once exercised over the human mind. Its purpose is to trouble and upset us, to make us doubt the value of those things which our parents, and all of respectable society, taught us we were to be most sure of. More than the secular literature of any other time, it seems to me, modern literature reaches into our most private selves. It is relentless in the questions it puts to us, questions of a shocking intimacy. The questions it puts to society are no less fierce ----its moral radicalism can be so extreme as to come to the point of rejecting society itself, not merely the anomalies and injustices of some particular society, but the very idea of society.

The spiritual intensity and the fierce personal intimacy of the classic literature of our period being what they are, the teacher must sometimes wonder if he is dealing with a subject that is appropriate to the classroom. There is, of course, one aspect of the subject which makes an obviously appropriate matter for collegiate instruction -- the aesthetic of modern literature is sometimes difficult and the teacher must deal with quite complex considerations of form and technique.

Yet he knows that, important as such considerations are, they are after all ancillary to the doctrinal intentions of the works he is discussing. And eventually he

转这种趋势。但有时候，我们当中的一些人会为学校与当今世界之间日益紧密的联系所产生的影响而感到一丝不安。

拿我自己熟悉的文学领域来说，我越来越感觉到，我们这些现在教文学的人，有时会怀疑自己到底在做什么，甚至会质疑是否有开设这门课的必要。我几乎不需要点明，我们碰到的这些不确定因素，毫无疑问地跟我们接触的文学有关。我们读的作品包括叶芝、艾略特、劳伦斯、乔伊斯、普鲁斯特、卡夫卡、曼[2]和纪德[3]，而且如果按照传统的范畴来看，还包括福楼拜、波德莱尔、兰波[4]，以及托尔斯泰和陀思妥耶夫斯基，这些作家，显然都是文学史上的巨匠。我们的不安正是来自于这些作品的伟大特质，因为它们的文学感染力，源于它们关注精神救赎。这样的文学，对人类的心灵有一种魔力，就像宗教的某些方面曾经对我们有过的影响一样。其目的是刺激我们、让我们不安，使我们对自己的父母和主流社会所教给我们的那些东西，那些我们最为相信的东西，都产生怀疑。在我看来，现代文学似乎比以往任何时候的世俗文学，都更加深入地触及我们内心最私密的自我。它不断地向我们提出问题，而且问得那么犀利，触及灵魂。它向社会提出的问题也同样尖刻，其道德上的激进观点是那样极端，它排斥社会本身，不仅仅是抛弃一些特定社会的异常和不公正之处，而是要抛弃"社会"这个概念。

我们这个时代的文学经典，有着强烈的精神张力和个人体验，作为教师，有时会怀疑这样的东西是否适用于课堂教学。当然，这些文学作品的某个方面，显然适用于高校教学。现代文学的审美有时是很难说清的，作为教师，必须面对相当复杂的文学形式和技巧。

不过他（作为教师）也知道，这些（文学形式和技巧）东西虽然重要，但相对于所讨论的文学作品的主观意图来说，还只是次要的附加的东西，最终他还得面对作品的观点。这样做也许会感到很不舒服，因为讨论起观念来，一个人就必须验证自己有关真假对错的看法，他必须根据自己对生活的态度来做出反应。要想不让学生受到老师的人格个性的影响，还真不是一件容易的事。但老师在处

must face into the doctrine. He does so, perhaps, at no small cost of comfort, for the doctrine is of a kind which requires that whoever deals with it must testify to his own sense of its truth or falsity; he must respond to it out of his own personal sense of life. It is not easy to find a way to do this which does not bring the student further into the **ambience** [n. 气氛] of the teacher's personality than it is right for them to be. But he does find a way and he deals with his momentous subject as directly and honestly as he knows how. And when the semester has come to its end, he reads his examination books and term papers; and his heart sinks at what he finds there.

If his students are as able and serious as I know students can be, he will find no lack of commitment and enthusiasm. He will be aware of that quick perceptivity which yields the kind of remark we have learned to call an insight. But he will find very little coherence, very little intellectual order, and most of the essays will puzzle him as to their intention -- with the best will in the world, he will not know what these students are trying to say. He will have the sense that the writers have not been concerned with any actuality he knows, neither an actuality in the world nor an actuality in literature.

The seriousness and enthusiasm of the papers will make it plain to him that the writers of them must have had the experience of something real and momentous, and if that is so he will be led to conclude that they have not been provided with the intellectual categories which can actualize experience by communicating it, by relating the strange and new to what is already familiar. No reader will be able to guess that these very gifted students are writing about books which, however far gone they are in what I have called spirituality, however far gone in moral radicalism, are nevertheless concerned with man's life here on earth, and in terms that really are susceptible of comprehension and exposition.

Nor is the failure to realize the actuality of the object being dealt with, the inability -- in Matthew Arnold's phrase -- to see the object as in itself it really is, special only to students of literature, as I discovered when I recently gave a senior seminar in collaboration with a colleague of the sociology department in which at least half of our students were sociology majors.

The subject we were teaching was not a modern one; we were investigating the assumptions of the society of Victorian England, and the first thing that struck us was the uneasiness of our students in dealing with a historical subject.

Despite the **vivacity** [n. 活泼; 精神充沛] of their minds, they found it almost impossible

理这样一个重大题目的时候,还是要找到他自己知道的直接和诚实的方法。

当学期结束,老师批改试卷和学期论文时,他会为自己看到的东西而感到沮丧。如果学生既能干又认真,就像我见过的学生那样,老师会发现学生有干劲、有热情。他会意识到学生的悟性,以及他们由此发出的、我们称之为"洞察力"的言语。但他很难看到连贯性,也很难看到知识的累积,大部分作业会让他摸不着头脑。老师哪怕尽了最大的努力,他可能还是无法知道这些学生想说什么。他会感觉到,学生们并不关心他们知道的现状,既无关世界,也无关文学。

那些论文中表现出的严肃和热情让老师看到,写论文的学生们肯定有过不同寻常的经历和训练。如果情况的确如此,老师就会认为,学生们还没有学会运用知识分类的方法,通过把新奇的感受与已经熟悉的经历结合起来,从而传达个人的体会。读者无法猜测,这些很有天赋的学生所讨论的著作,无论它们离我所说的灵性层面多么遥远、无论在道德方面多么激进,其实都还是在关注人们的世间生活,而且是容易感知和表达明白的。

这种无法把研究对象放在现实场景中的问题,照马修·阿诺德[5]的说法,是不能透过现象看本质,并不仅限于文学专业的学生才有,我最近在和社会学系的一位同事共同举办的一门为高年级学生开设的讨论课中,也发现了这个问题,上那门讨论课的学生中,至少有一半是社会学专业的学生。

我们教的内容不是一个现代的话题,而是要去探究维多利亚时代的英国社会。让我们吃惊的第一件事,是我们的学生在涉及历史课题时,表现得手足无措。

尽管他们头脑活跃,却几乎无法想象发生在不算久远的年代里的个人和社会的情况。年代遥远的事,对他们来说可能还更好理解,因为那些东西几近想象,而且也可以按照想象来理解。事实上,很多学生把这些当做宗教研究来学习,他们在了解神学的神秘性和精神危机的微妙之处的确很有才华,但如果我们提出问题,问及"39

to imagine the actuality of personal and social situations in the fairly recent past. The distant past might perhaps have given them less trouble, as being nearly in the realm of fantasy and comprehensible as such. Many of them as it happened, had concerned themselves with the study of religion, and they were surely most gifted in their understanding of the more arcane aspects of theology and the subtleties of the spiritual crisis; but if we raised questions about the 39 Articles, or the disabilities of Dissenters, or the functions of a bishop, they were not merely impatient of such **philistine** [*adj.* 市侩的] considerations; we had the distinct impression that, whatever religion was for them, it clearly had nothing to do with a religious community, a church, or prayer.

Apart from the physical sciences, most subjects that are studied in college whatever their particular concerns, bear upon ethics, and we may say that, in their totality, they constitute our way of thinking about ethics. Aristotle says that a very young man is not fit to discuss ethics, and it has occurred to me to think that the elaborate abstractness, the principled resistance to the concrete, which some of us nowadays note in our students might be the result of our permitting or requiring them to study subjects inappropriate to their years. And yet I do not really believe this to be true. I am rather of the opinion that their intellectual procedures are in large part proposed to them by the theory of education to which they are being exposed -- an education which puts its emphasis so strongly on the modern.

When Henry Adams described the inadequacy of his Harvard training, his reference to Karl Marx was not casual; the very anachronism he fell into suggests that it was not. Although Adams never became a Marxist, Marx was standing for **subversion** [*n.* 颠覆；破坏]. Adams, for all his social respectability, was a very subversive man. "By rights," he says of himself, "he should have been... a Marxist, but some narrow trait of the New England nature seemed to **blight** [*v.*(使) 枯萎；摧毁] socialism and he tried in vain to make himself a convert. He did the next best thing; he became a Comteist ... He was ready to become anything but quiet. As though the world had not been enough upset in his time, he was eager to upset it more." One could not have a better clue to modern thought and art than this statement of Adams' -- in the degree that the world is upset, upset it more: this is the only way we shall get things straight.

It is uncomfortable, a dismaying program, but it is not to be evaded. **The energy of the radical and the subversive is likely to be the chief energy in the world today.**

条宗法说明"⁶，问及在宗教上持不同意见者的沉默，或问及主教的职能等问题，我们得到的印象是：他们不仅会因这类庸俗问题而感到不耐烦，而且无论宗教在他们眼里如何，它都显然与宗教社区、教堂或祈祷无关。

除了物理科学，在大学里学习的其他大多数课程，其特别关注的问题可能不同，但都会涉及道德，我们可以说，这些学科从总体上构成了我们有关伦理的思考方式。亚里斯多德说，年轻人不适合于讨论道德，我也曾认为，我们当中的一些人都看到的，现在的学生有精巧的抽象能力，从原则上抵制具体问题，这些可能都是由于我们过早地允许或要求学生修读与他们年龄不相称的科目。但我并不真的相信事实如此。我倒是认为，他们的智力进度，在很大程度上取决于他们接受的教育，而这种教育强烈地注重于现代。

当亨利·亚当斯描述他哈佛教育的不足之处时，他提到卡尔·马克思的名字不是偶然的，他弄错年代这件事也许并非无意。虽然亚当斯从未成为一个马克思主义者，马克思却代表着颠覆性。亚当斯的社会声望很高，但他却是一个很有颠覆性的人。他说自己"理应成为一名马克思主义者，但有些新英格兰人狭隘的特性似乎使社会主义难以扎根，使他想成为信徒的尝试徒劳无用。他只好退而求其次，成了一名'无产无神论者'——他就是不想静默以待。仿佛五洲震荡得还不够似的，他急着要让它更加动荡"。从亚当斯的这番话里，人们会找到理解现代思想与艺术的一条最佳线索，如果世界动荡，就让动荡来得更猛烈一些，大乱才有大治，这是唯一的方法。

这听起来很不舒服，且令人失望，但我们无法回避。**激进和颠覆的能量，很可能是当今世界的主要动力。艺术作品或思想，如果没有在某种形式上显得激进和有颠覆性，就不容易唤起我们的兴趣。今后一段时间里，我们无法安静歇息了。**

现代社会既激进又有颠覆性的一个表现，就是人们已给欲望、意志和特定的喜好，赋予更多的道德和智力权威性。马修·阿诺德

No work of art or thought which is not in some way radical and subversive establishes itself in our interest. We are not going to be allowed to rest for some time to come.

One aspect of the radical, subversive energy of the modern period is the increased moral and intellectual authority that has been given to desire, to will, to particular tastes and preferences. When Matthew Arnold said that the function of criticism was to see the object as in itself it really is, he meant that the ideal critic should suppress all the impulses of his desire, will and particular taste and preference which might mislead him as to the true nature of the object. This he called being disinterested, and we can see what has happened to Arnold's no doubt primitive theory of knowledge by taking note of what has happened to the word itself. Scarcely anyone nowadays -- and certainly not Webster's Third International Dictionary -- supposes that a "disinterested third party" is anything but a bored person, and most people would reprobate a disinterested judge as one given to paying no attention to the argument. And even if the modern world can manage to conceive of disinterestedness as a virtue, it takes it to be but a dull virtue -- we like a passionate subjectivity, we respond warmly to a display of desire, will and particular preference.

It is what Henry Adams wanted -- all through the Education we see him reaching out for the intellectual justification of a mode of thought and life that would not be controlled by a strict rationality but that would spring from the personal will and desire. **And if I were to describe the present-day student at his most gifted, I should say that he too is motivated chiefly by the impulse toward free subjectivity.** But it is surely not a passionate subjectivity that we see in even our best students. For reality can be mastered by a passionate subjectivity: that is what art does. But surely what must trouble the college teacher today is that his students are not mastering subjects, they are experiencing them.

If we speak of a modern energy of radicalism and subversion, the radicalism of our students turns out, that is, to be at a very low point on the general curve. Yet we must remember that the modern radical subjectivity first put forth its strength in opposition to a very strong antagonist, the old idea of mind, detached from the passions and all uncircumstanced. The effectual resistance to the traditional idea of Mind was an assertion of life itself. It

说，批判的功能就是要把评判对象当做它本身来看。他的意思是，理想的评论家应当压制自己的欲望、意志和特定的喜好，因为这些可能会干扰他客观真实地评估对象的性质。他把这叫做"不带个人色彩"，看看这个单词本身含义的变化，我们就可以看到阿诺德有关知识的理论，有了何种遭遇。现在人们都把"不带个人色彩的第三方"当做一个毫无趣味的人，韦氏国际词典第三版就是这样定义的，大多数人也会把一个不带个人色彩的法官，当做不听辩护解释的人。就算现代世界可以努力把不带个人色彩当做一种美德，它也把这种态度当成一种沉闷的美德——我们喜欢充满激情的主观性，在看到欲望、意志和特定的喜好时，我们给以热烈的响应。

这就是亨利·亚当斯所希望的。在《教育》这本书里，我们看到他通篇都在试图找到理论根据，倡导不受严格的合理性限制，而是发自个人意愿和欲望的那种思想和生活模式。**如果要我描述当代最有天赋的学生是怎样的，我应该说，驱动他的动力，主要也是追求自由的主体意识的那种冲动**。但即使是在最好的学生身上，我们也看不到那种充满激情的主观意识。充满激情的主观意识可以帮助我们把握现实，这就是艺术所做的事。但让今天的大学老师焦虑的是，他的学生不是去掌握主观，而只是浅尝辄止。

如果我们说激进主义和颠覆性是当代的动力，我们学生的激进程度现在其实是在非常低的一个点上。然而，我们必须记住，现代的激进主体意识，是针对一个很强的对手而提出来的，那个对手就是有关心智的旧思想，那种心智与激情无关，与环境分离。对心智这种传统观念的有效抵抗，就是要证明生命本身的意义。这是必要和有益的，而且现在依然必要和有益。但是，如果要保留激进冲动的创造性潜力，我们就必须为它提供制约性的力量。我们必须用这样一种思想来和它针锋相对，即事实是如此这般，世界不可逆转，但却有可塑性。我相信，我们必须专门向我们的学生，在他们产生激进和颠覆性的冲动时，向他们提供这种制约性的力量，否则他们永远无法发展他们掌握知识的能力，他们会坠入由常规性而带来的

was necessary, it was **salutary** [*adj.* 有益的; 有用的]. And it is still necessary and salutary. But if the radical impulse is to be maintained in all its potentiality of creativeness, it must be met with a countervailing force. It must be confronted with the mind that insists that things are so and not otherwise, that the object is as it really is, that the world is intractable as well as **malleable** [*adj.* 可塑的; 有延展性]. And such a countervailing force must, I believe, be specifically offered to the radical and subversive impulses of our students, else they will never develop their powers of intellectual mastery, they will fall into inertness and the weariest of all conventionalities, the conventionality of an outworn radical mode.

I do not know how this is to be done, by what intellectual disciplines, techniques, or attitudes. But I am sure that if we are to develop in this country an intellectual class of the kind that we deserve and need, our colleges must complicate -- complicate, not retract -- their commitment to the modern. **If, as I believe, the modern energy of radical thought is essentially good, then we as teachers, we as colleges, shall have to guard against subverting it by mere bland tolerance, or by a philistine delight in its intent of outrageousness.** It is best for us, it is best for the state of the general culture, it is best for the poet himself, that we do not establish William Blake as the Poet in Residence. That is the way to destroy William Blake. **When it comes to dealing with the subversive energy of modernity, the right way is to keep our doors hospitably open to a powerful and unpredictable guest, but not, by our household familiarity with him, rob him of his frightening strangeness.**

Thank you!

反应迟钝和疲惫，这种常规性是由抱残守缺的激进模式所造成的。

我不知道如何才能做到这些，有什么知识学科、技术，或态度能有助于此。但我相信，如果我们想在这个国家，培养出我们需要、并应该具有的知识阶层，我们的高校就必须加强贴近现代——加强，而不是减弱。**如果像我所愿，激进思想这种现代动力在本质上是好的话，我们作为老师、我们的院校，就不能仅仅是待之以宽容，或让其不拘一格的风格备受冷落，因为这样会使之失去锐气。**对我们来说、对文化的普遍状况，甚至对诗人自己来说，我们都最好不要把威廉·布莱克捧做住校诗人，这会毁了他。**在面对现代性的颠覆性能量时，正确的方法是敞开大门，热情欢迎强大和不可预知的客人，而不是取决于我们对他是否熟悉，这样才会使他不再显得陌生和可怕。**

谢谢大家!

---

1 亨利·亚当斯（Henry Adams，1838—1918），美国著名历史学家、作家，著有《美国通史》等。出身世家，其祖父约翰·昆西·亚当斯（John Quincy Adams）和曾祖父约翰·亚当斯（John Adams）都曾担任过美国总统。

2 托马斯·曼（Thomas Mann，1875—1955），德国作家，1929年因长篇小说《布登勃洛克一家》获诺贝尔文学奖。

3 安德烈·纪德（André Paul Guillaume Gide，1869—1951），法国著名作家。1947年获诺贝尔文学奖，"为了他广泛包容性的、有艺术质地的著作，在这些著作中，他以无所畏惧的对真理的热爱，并以敏锐的心理学洞察力，呈现了人性的种种问题与处境"。

4 阿尔蒂尔·兰波（Arthur Rimbaud，1854—1891），法国诗人，早期象征主义诗人的代表之一，开启了超现实主义的诗歌流派。

5 马修·阿诺德（Matthew Arnold，1822—1888），英国诗人、评论家。

6 "39条宗法说明"（The Thirty-Nine Articles of Religion），是英国教会在1563年制定的神学教条。

1970's

西奥多·赫斯伯

本届毕业典礼的演讲者是美国圣母诺特丹大学的在任校长西奥多·赫斯伯。圣母诺特丹大学（University of Notre Dame），又称"诺特丹大学"，建于19世纪中期，坐落在芝加哥远郊。

赫斯伯1917年出生于纽约州，从小就希望将来做一位牧师。中学毕业后进入圣母诺特丹大学神学院，后被神学院送往意大利罗马深造，二战爆发，被迫中断学业回到美国，1945年获美国天主教大学神学博士学位。1949年出任圣母诺特丹大学副校长，3年后升任校长，并在这个位置上做了35年，直到1987年70岁时退休，是该校历史上校长任期最长的一位。

在担任校长期间，赫斯特致力于扩大学校规模和学校教育的多样性，从单一的神学教育到综合性的教学与研究，期间，学校规模扩大了一倍多，成立了多种研究机构。

赫斯伯曾于1957年担任美国"公民权利委员会"委员，并于1967年担任该委员会主席，后因他经常反对尼克松总统的政策而离职。

赫斯伯有一个著名的主张：完整的教育应该同时包括"学会做事"和"学会做人"，即学校教育不仅要教给学生知识，还应包括道德的培养。这一理念可说与传统的中国"教书育人"理念不谋而合。

在这篇演讲中，赫斯伯从美国宇航员拍摄的地球照片说起，批评了发达国家对地球资源的过度使用和日益增大的贫富差距，呼吁全人类团结起来，发达国家应当帮助发展中国家和地区，强调环境保护的重要性。赫斯伯甚至提出了"双重国籍"，其中之一为"世界公民"这样近乎乌托邦式的概念，表达了他对公平与正义的理想的追求。

1973

Global Citizen for World Peace
做世界公民 实现世界和平

Theodore M. Hesburgh 西奥多·赫斯伯

Mr. President, dear guests, and especially students who graduate today,

It is a strange paradox that the most striking photograph brought back from the moon by the astronauts was no a close-up picture of the moon itself, but a far away picture of the earth. There it shines as no earth dweller had ever seen it before: blue, green, flecked with white cloud patterns, a beautiful small globe set against the blackness of space's void through which it is whirling at incredible speed.

Harvard's own Archibald McLeish caught the poetry of the vision. It is up to all of us to make the new vision come true. The sad reality is that the earth is much more beautiful from afar than it is up close. Not that physical beauty does not exist on earth. I have been awed by the majesty of the soaring snowy, windswept heights of the Himalayas seen against the jade green uplands of Nepal. The pastel colored sweep of the Britannica Range in Antarctica seen from McMurdo base camp almost two hundred miles away is enough to thrill the soul of any observer. A sunset following a storm at sea, a sunrise on the bushed African game-filled **caldera** [n. 火山口] of Ngorongoro Crater, the **cordillera** [n. 山脉] blanca of Peru and Chile viewed from a high flying jet on a bright winter afternoon, these are unforgettably beautiful earthly visions. Note, however, that in most of them, man, apart from the viewer, is almost completely absent, and where man is present in large numbers on earth, one can almost always expect a **diminution** [n. 减少；缩小；减少量；缩小量] of beauty, both physical beauty diminished through pollution and spiritual beauty marred by violence and injustice.

It is a singular blessing for our age that we have been able to see the earth from the moon, to see it as it really is, in Barbara Ward's words: Spaceship Earth, a beautiful, small space vehicle, providing a viable ecosystem for human beings with quite limited resources. As Heilbroner has said so well: "Life on this planet is a fragile affair, the kind of miraculous microbial activity that flourished on the thin film of air and water and decomposed rock which separates the uninhabitable core of the earth from the void of space."

We, the passengers of spaceship earth, have the capability of creating by our intelligence and freedom, a whole series of man-made systems that will enhance the inherent beauty of our planet, and make it even more humanly viable and physically beautiful, or we can turn spaceship earth into an ugly wasteland where human beings barely survive and hardly live in any human sense.

If you have any doubt that we are doing the latter rather than the former, walk

尊敬的校长、各位来宾、特别是今天毕业的同学们：

说来也奇怪，宇航员从月球带回的照片中，最引人注目的并不是月球本身的特写照片，而是遥望地球的景象。地球上的居民还从来没有见过这样的光景：地球呈现出澄蓝、碧绿的颜色，白云缭绕，在太空的黑暗背景中，小小寰球如此美丽，并以超乎想象的速度在旋转着。

哈佛大学的阿奇博尔德·麦克利什从这个景象中看出了诗意，我们每个人都有责任，让这种新的远见成为现实。但不幸的现实是，地球远看很美，却不能近观——这并不是说地球上没有实实在在的美景。我曾怀着敬畏之心，欣赏喜马拉雅山高耸入云、饱经风袭的雪峰，衬托在尼泊尔翡翠般的高地上。在南极洲上色彩斑斓的大不列颠山脉，从近两百英里以外的麦克默多基站[1]看去，那景观足以让任何人激动不已。暴风雨后的海上日落；在非洲恩戈罗恩戈罗火山口，初升的阳光照着野生动物在长满灌木的林间游荡；在某个冬季明亮的下午，乘坐飞机从高空俯瞰蜿蜒于秘鲁和智利之间的布兰卡山脉——这些都是令人难忘的世间美景。

不过请注意，在这些景象中，除了观景者之外，几乎都没有人的存在。而地球上人口集中的地方，完全可以想见，美景就会相应减少：自然美景被污染，人的精神面貌遭受暴力和不公正的摧毁。

我们生活在这个时代真是有福，因为我们能够从月球上看地球，看到地球的真实面貌。就像芭芭拉·沃德[2]所说的：地球飞船是一个美丽但狭小的载体，为人类提供了资源相当有限的一个生态系统。海尔布伦纳[3]说得好："生命在这个星球上是很脆弱的，薄薄的一层空气和水，加上风化的岩石，奇迹般地为微生物的活动提供生活环境，使广袤的空间和没有生命的地球核心之间，充满了生机"。

我们作为地球飞船的乘客，有智力和自由去创造各种人为的东西，使我们的星球更加完美，在外观上更美丽，内部更人性化；另一方面，我们也可能把地球飞船变成一片荒地，人类在其中很难生存，甚至生不如死。

遗憾的是，我们正在做的却是后者而不是前者。如果你们对此有任何疑问，就去加尔各答的街道上走走，看看围绕着拉丁美洲国家首都城

through the streets of Calcutta, visit the **favellas** [n. 棚屋; 简陋小屋], **barriadas** [城市贫民区], villas miserias, and callampas surrounding the Latin American capital cities, step aboard the floating junks adjacent to Hong Kong's harbor, or look at the native locations north of Johannesburg in South Africa, or inspect some of our own inner city slums or Chicano colonies in the Southwest, or miners' rotting villages in Appalachia, or almost any American Indian reservation in the West. It isn't just what you see that will sicken you. It is that it is all so unnecessary, that it is man-made, and man-kept, and that it is in startling contrast to the way other humans are living in luxury only a few miles away from each of these human sewers and garbage heaps.

An easy answer would be to say that there is just not enough of the world's resources to house and feed everyone -- but then remember that last year, and for most of the years that we can remember, the governments of this planet have spent about $200 billion dollars on armaments, and that is more than the total annual income of the poorest half of the earth's population. We do it because the Russians do it, and they do it because we do it, and so the foolishness goes on, and on, and on, all around the world. Meanwhile, the poor go to bed hungry, if they have a bed.

To put the case for the poor most simply, imagine our spaceship earth with only five people aboard instead of more than three billion. Imagine that one of those five crew members represents those of us earth passengers who live in the Western world of North America and Europe, one fifth of humanity on earth, mainly white and Christian. The person representing us has the use and control of 80% of the total life sustaining resources available aboard our spacecraft. The other four crewmen, representing the other four-fifths of humanity -- better than 2 1/2 billion people -- have to get along on the 20% of the resources that are left, leaving them each about 5% to our man's 80%. To make it worse, our man is in the process of increasing his use of these limited resources to 90%.

Now if this sound piggish to you, it is! If you put resources just in terms of energy, we in the United States, with 6% of the world's population, used last year about 40% of the total world's available energy. While we complained about a trade deficit, we made two billion dollars excess from the less developed countries, depending on our less favored **brethren** [n.＜古＞同胞; 同党] in Latin America to provide us with one billion of these dollars in surplus trade balances, while we provided them with the least aid ever, since aid began.

市的棚屋区、城市贫民区，登上香港港口附近的舢板船体验船民的生活，看看南非约翰内斯堡以北的原住民聚居地，或观察一下我们国家里，某些内城的贫民区或在西南部的奇卡诺人[4]生活区，或去阿巴拉契亚山区衰败的矿工村庄，或去美国西部的几乎任何一个印第安人保留区。你所看到的东西会让你愤慨，因为这都是些可以避免的现象，都是人为的，也被人为地维持着。当你看到就在这些污水沟及垃圾堆几英里外的地方，却有人过着豪华的生活时，这样强烈的对比真是令人吃惊。

一个简单的答案是，世界上没有足够的资源来满足每个人的衣食住行之需。但是请记住，去年，而且在我们能够记起的大多数年头里，这个星球上，各国政府的军备开支大约是2000亿美元，这个数字超过了世界上最贫困的那一半人口的全年总收入。我们扩充军备，是因为俄罗斯人这样做，而他们这样做，是因为我们做了。在世界各地，这种蠢事就这样循环往复地发生着。与此同时，穷人睡觉时饿着肚子，即使他们侥幸有一个地方暂时安身。

如果用最简单的方式来形容穷人的情况，不妨让我们想象一下，我们的地球飞船上，只有5个船员，而不是30多亿人。这5个船员中的一个，代表着居住在北美和欧洲这个西方世界里的人，这是地球人类的五分之一，主要是白种人，信基督教。这个代表着我们的人，使用并控制着飞船上赖以维持生命的总资源的80%。另外4个船员代表着其他五分之四的人类——总共有25亿多人——他们只能靠剩下的20%的资源过活。也就是说，相对于我们这个船员的80%，他们每个人只有约5%的资源。更为糟糕的是，我们这个船员还在拼命占有，近90%的有限资源将归他一人所有。

如果这让你听起来觉得肮脏不堪的话，它的确如此！如果从能源方面来谈资源，我们美国人仅占世界总人口的6%，去年使用的能源却占全世界的40%。尽管我们抱怨贸易逆差，我们从较不发达的国家那里获得了20亿美元的贸易顺差，其中10亿美元的顺差来自过得没我们好的拉丁美洲兄弟，而我们向他们提供的援助，是自从我们开始援助以来，给的最少的。

当我们的飞船上，有限的资源是如此不公正地分配，特别是每年情

How much human peace can you visualize or expect aboard our spacecraft when its limited resources are so unjustly shared, especially when the situation is worsening each year? **Peace is not gained by armaments, but by justice. If four-fifths of the world's people live in misery while the other fifth in the United States and Europe enjoy ever greater luxury, then we can expect no peace aboard spaceship earth, only frustration, despair, and, ultimately, violence.**

The tragedy is that this is the world that man has made and is making. The general human condition is very bad indeed aboard our spacecraft.

Is there any hope for man? Is our spacecraft really hurtling towards massive human disaster, cataclysmic human upheaval and ultimately the reduction of this beautiful globe to a burned-out **cinder** [n. 煤渣; 灰烬] in space? One can be optimistic, I believe only if this generation -- and I address the young particularly -- can shuck off the madness of the nightmare that man for centuries, and increasingly of late, has been creating aboard our planet. A new global vision is needed if man is to create on earth the beauty that this planet manifests and seems to promise from afar. The vision must be one of social justice, of the interdependence of all mankind on this small spacecraft. Unless the equality, and the oneness, and the common dignity of mankind pervades the vision -- the only future of this planet is violence and destruction on an ever increasing scale, a **crescendo** [n. 声音渐增; 高潮; 顶峰] of man's inhumanity to man that can only result globally in the extermination of mankind by man.

As one of our graduates in the Peace Corps in Malawi, Africa, put it: "While our leaders have their power battles and ego trips, countless millions of unknowns are in need of a bit more food, a year or two more of education, another pot or pan, a sensible way of controlling family size, a book or a bicycle. These people aren't asking for much; they would only like to be a bit more free to be a bit more human."

I believe that none but the young ---or the young in heart -- can dream this vision or pursue this ideal. Why? Because it means leaving behind the conventional wisdom that pervades the old and aging bones of the Western World. The vision of one peaceful community of mankind on earth, dedicated to justice, equity and human dignity for all is contrary to most of the modern American myths -- unlimited growth for us at the expense of almost everyone else; the absoluteness of our Declaration of Independence; patriotism isolated from every other moral value my country right or wrong; security only by force of arms, however unjustly used; material wealth as the

况还在恶化，你如何能够想象或指望人类还有多少和平可言呢？**和平无法通过军备竞赛获得，而是要靠公正。如果世界上五分之四的人生活在痛苦中，而美国和欧洲的那五分之一的人却享受着越来越多的繁荣，那么我们不能期望地球飞船上会有和平，它只会有失望、绝望，并最终带来暴力。**

这是个悲剧。这样的世界是人类过去造成的，而且现在还在造孽。我们飞船上的人类环境，可以说非常恶劣。

人类还有希望吗？我们的飞船，真的就要飞往巨大的人类灾难，万劫不复，最后把这个美丽的星球变成飘荡在空间的一片灰烬？我相信只有当我们这一代——尤其是我今天面对的年轻人——摒弃那些千百年来人们在这个地球上制造的人间噩梦，人类才有希望。如果人们想要创造这个地球上客观显现的、并且从远处就能看到的那般美丽的景象，就需要一种新的全球视野。这个远景必须体现社会公义，体现在这个小型航天器上，全人类的相互依存。除非这个远景体现平等、开放，以及所有人的尊严，否则这个星球的未来就是规模日益增大的暴力和破坏，人对人的非人道做法，最终只会导致人类在全球范围内的毁灭。

正如一位到非洲的马拉维去参与和平团队的毕业生所说："就在我们的领导人争权夺利，顾影自怜的时候，有千百万个不为我们所知的人，迫切地需要多一点粮食，多接受一两年的教育，多一个锅或烤盘，能有可行的节育方法去控制家庭规模，有一本书或一辆自行车。这些人所求不多，只是想要多一些自由，活得有点人样。"

我认为，只有年轻人，或内心保持年轻的人，才会产生这样的梦想或追求这一理想。为什么这么说呢？因为这意味着要抛开旧的传统观念，而这种传统观念已经渗透到西方世界正在变得老旧的骨头里去了。盼望在地球上人类大同，让所有人都能享受公正、平等和人的尊严，这样的愿景和大多数的美国现代神话是背道而驰的。我们追求的是自己无限的欲望，而让所有其他人都为此付出代价；我们的《独立宣言》绝对是不可触碰的；不管我的国家是对还是错，都要把爱国主义凌驾于其他道德准则之上；为了我们的安全而使用武力，不管使用武力是否恰当；把追求物

greatest goal of all, since it guarantees pleasure, power and status -- everything but compassionate, unselfish **rectitude** [*n.* 诚实；正直；操行端正].

Who but the young or young in heart can say, I will march to another drum beat; I will seek another vision for my country and my world. Not a vision of might makes right, but **noblesse** [*n.* 贵族阶级；贵族地位；地位高责任重者] oblige. Not a vision of power, but of honor. Not just honor proclaimed as we hear it proclaimed so loosely today, but honor lived. As Robert Frost said:

Two roads diverged in a wood, and I --
I took the one less travelled by,
And that has made all the difference.

What is mainly needed today to make the difference is a vision of justice to which we commit ourselves anew at home, to demonstrate that if justice is possible here in America, between different races, different religions, different socio-economic classes, it might just be possible all around the world. America's leadership must be demonstrated at home while it is proclaimed abroad, and lastly, **our leadership must be inspired by the same kind of vision that first inspired the birth of this country, a vision of human equality and dignity needed today to create the rebirth of one whole world, a new planet where human beings aspire to be humane, where beautiful human beings begin to replace the past creations of human ugliness with new creations born of compassion, concern, and competence, too.**

Is all this an empty dream, a naive vision? Not if young people take it seriously, joining intelligence to their idealism, competence to their vision, and the courage to dare to be different in how they view the world they are going to make, or better, remake. I am often asked, "How can we possibly turn the world over to them?" My answer is both simple and obvious. "What other choice do you have? Tomorrow is theirs, not ours."

We might all begin by a declaration of the interdependence of mankind today. The evidence is totally on the side of such a declaration -- even as regards this country which was founded almost two centuries ago by a Declaration of Independence. There is no serious problem facing our country, and indeed the world today, that is not global in its sweep, as well as in its solution. You can make a whole list: pollution, the

质财富当做最大的目标，因为它会给人带来快感、权力和地位——总之，一切皆可，就是把富有同情心与正直无私这样的品德遗忘了。

除了年轻人，还有谁会说：我不用随着别人的鼓点起舞，我要为我的国家和我的世界探寻另一种前景？不再有强权即公理这种现象，而是以德服人。追求荣耀，不仅仅是像我们今天所宣称的那种荣耀，而是如罗伯特·弗罗斯特所说的：

一片林中分出两条岔道——
我偏选择人迹更少的那条，
从而决定了我一生的道路。

要想有所不同，今天我们首先需要的，是在国内实行公平正义的信念。向世人展示，如果美国能够做到在不同种族、不同宗教、不同社会经济阶层之间取得公正，那么全世界范围内也都可能做到。美国的领导作用不是靠在国外鼓吹的，而是必须先在国内做到。最后一点是，**激励我们领导层的，应该是引导人们创建这个国家的那种远见，这种远见倡导人类平等和尊严，今天我们需要这样的远见来创造一个新世界，在这样的崭新天地里，人类追求的是人道，有着美丽的心灵，消除过去的丑恶，代之以同情、关切和富有能力。**

这一切只是一场空洞的梦想、一个天真的理想吗？如果年轻人认真加以对待，把他们的理想和智慧结合起来，把他们的远见和能力结合起来，并展现出敢于与众不同的勇气，去创造（或重新建造）他们的世界，这样的梦想就不会落空。常常有人问我："我们怎么能将世界交给他们这样的人呢？"我的回答既简单又明确："难道还有其他选择吗？明天是他们的，而不属于我们。"

我们首先要做的，可以宣告当今人类都有着一种相互依存的关系。所有证据都表明我们可以发布这样一个宣言——我们的国家诞生于近两个世纪前的《独立宣言》。我们国家、甚至整个世界所面临的所有严重问题，都是世界性的，其解决方案也要从世界的角度来寻找。你可以举出

dollar, population, trade, peace, human rights, human development, security, health, education, communication, drugs, crime, energy, space, raw materials, food, freedom, and so forth. Try solving any one of these problems in any adequate way without involving the whole world. Try even thinking about the philosophical implications of a true solution without reference to the inherent unity, equality, fraternity, and dignity of mankind and what that dignity demands and requires of human persons everywhere, but more especially those who live where the power, the wealth, and the leverage lie.

I was brought up in an America visualized as completely separated from the rest of the world, proud of its independence and oceanic-insured isolation. Now we learn that the energy that makes all of America run, or be lighted, heated, mechanized, and mobile, will depend mainly on sources outside the United States in another dozen years, and that the fourteen basic metal resources we need for our manufacturing and industrial process will come mainly from other less developed countries by the turn of the century. The almighty dollar my contemporaries idolized has been devalued twice in less than two years.

It would appear quite obvious at this point that the winds of unity are blowing, that many are working to bridge the many chasms that have separated man-kind aboard spacecraft earth. Diplomacy is happily bridging the chasm of ideology. All mankind need no longer visualize society exactly as we do. **Ecumenism** [n. 泛基督教主义] is bringing the Christian and non-Christian religions together in understanding at last, thank God.

Cultural exchange is finding new and mutual values in the East and the West, while mercantilism in the modern dress of the multi-national corporation is pioneering some unusual ways of economic development between the Northern and Southern parts of our spacecraft. The energy crisis is pushing for a solution to the Middle Eastern dilemma. Racial prejudice stands convicted worldwide of idiocy when Africans in Uganda expel Asians who were born there and have adopted that country long ago, or when the citizens of Bangladesh cannot forgive their fellow Bihari. Male Chauvinism is on the way out in the Western World, belatedly since in the East and Middle East, India and Israel already have female Prime Ministers. The unity of mankind must be the wave of the future if we are not to divide ourselves unnecessarily according to race, religion, color, sex, and age, and thereby make human life impossibly complicated aboard our shrinking space-craft.

好多例子：环境污染、美元汇率、人口增加、贸易平衡、和平维护、人权保障、人类发展、安全、保健、教育、通讯、毒品、犯罪、能源、航天、原材料供应、食品卫生和自由，等等。如果没有全世界的参与，很难有效解决这些问题的任何一个。你也可以想想，如果真有一个解决办法，却没有考虑到人类的团结、平等、友爱、尊严，以及世界各地的人们所要求的尊严，特别是如果这个解决办法没有对那些有权力、财富和能力的人提出更高的要求，那在哲理上意味着什么呢？

在我成长的环境中，觉得美国好像和世界的其余部分完全分割开来，它为自己的独立而自豪，又因为有海洋的隔离而颇觉安稳。现在我们知道，驱动美国的能源，我们的照明、取暖、机械化和人员流动的活动，在十几年后都将主要依靠境外的提供，而到本世纪末，我们的制造业和工业所需要的14种基本金属，将主要依靠来自其他较不发达国家的进口。我们这代人推崇的万能的美元，在过去不到两年的时间里，已经两次贬值。

此刻，团结之风很显然正在吹起，很多人正在为弥补地球飞船上的人为鸿沟而工作。外交努力正在跨越意识形态的鸿沟，人类不再需要像我们那样看待社会。真要感谢上帝，普世教会总算为基督教和非基督教宗教之间，搭建起了理解的桥梁。

文化的交流在东西方之间找到了新的共同价值观，表现为跨国公司的重商主义，在我们飞船的北部地区和南部地区之间，开拓出了一些不同寻常的经济发展方式。能源危机的出现，促使人们去应对中东面临的两难境地。当乌干达的非洲人驱逐早就在那个国家土生土长的亚洲人，或当孟加拉国的公民不能容纳比哈尔人时，全世界都觉得这样的种族偏见是一种白痴的表现。在中东和东方，以色列和印度早就有了女总理，而西方世界的大男子主义也迟早要式微。只要我们不再根据种族、宗教、肤色、性别、年龄来分裂自己，不使我们这个日渐缩小的飞船上的生活变得格外复杂，人类的统一就必定是未来的潮流。

这样的话，使人类分裂的东西，可能也是最易导致分裂的，就剩下主权国家的划分了。让我们假想一下，如果从另一个太阳系来了个有知识、有文化的客人，就像宇航员从月球上看到我们这个地球那样，除了

This leaves the one great remaining divider of human kind, perhaps the worst of all, national sovereignty. Suppose that an intelligent and cultured visitor from another solar system were to be informed, on seeing our planet earth as the astronauts saw it from the moon, that in addition to all the inequities, injustices and alienations already mentioned, mankind on earth insisted on governing our spaceship by dividing it into 150 different nationalities, some very large, some very small, and quite a few in between. Our inter-planetary visitor would also learn that there was no reasonable rationale for these national divisions, that they often represented people of the same language, religion, race, and culture, and were, in fact, often separated only by historical accidents. Now that the political separation is a fact, they are ready to fight to the death to maintain their national identities and territorial prerogatives.

Since this is a factual description of how things mainly are on spaceship earth, how difficult it will be to achieve human unity, decency, and oneness of purpose aboard our spaceship. We must find some new way of transcending this **inane** [*adj.* 愚蠢的； 无意义的] block of nationality that pits human against human because by an accident of birth they happen to be American or Canadian, East or West German, Venezuelan or Colombian, Kenyan or Ugandan, North or South Vietnamese.

I would like to propose a solution that would by-pass, rather than cut the Gordian know of nationality. It is likewise a solution which is bound to be misunderstood unless someone stands in spirit on the moon and views the world from there, with all its promise of beauty, unity, and a common home for mankind united. As McLeish said: "To see the earth as it truly is, small and blue and beautiful in that eternal silence where it floats, is to see ourselves as riders on the earth together, brothers on that bright loveliness in the eternal cold -- brothers who know now they are truly brothers."

What I would suggest is that everyone in the world would be allowed to hold dual citizenship -- to be a citizen of the nation in which he or she happens to be born and, in addition, to be able to qualify for world citizenship.

The application to be a citizen of the world, of spaceship earth, would involve certain commitments:

1. One would have to certify his or her belief in the unity of mankind, in the equal dignity of every human being, whatever his or her nationality, race, religion, sex, or color.

我前面已经提到的那些不公平、不公正和冷漠隔绝以外，人类在管理我们的飞船时，还坚持要把它分为150多个不同的国家，有些国家很大，有些很小，还有一大批大小不等的夹杂在其中。我们的天外来客还会了解到，这些国家的划分毫无章法可言，他们往往有相同的语言、宗教、种族和文化，而事实上，国界的划分，常常是由于历史上的一些意外原因。而现在因为这种政治上的分离已经既成事实，人们为了保持其民族特征和领土所有权，时刻准备着做殊死搏斗。

这是对地球飞船情况的一个现实描述，那么，在我们的飞船上，争取人类团结、良知和目标一致，会有多么困难！我们必须找到某种新的方式，来超越这种毫无意义的国界划分，它使人们对立。一个人生为何国人，是很偶然的，他们偶然生为美国人或加拿大人，东德人或西德人，委内瑞拉人或哥伦比亚人，肯尼亚人或乌干达人，北越人或南越人。

我想提出一个解决方案，来快刀斩乱麻地解决国籍问题。这样的一个解决方案，要带着从月球上看地球的态度来理解，把地球当做一个美丽的、人类团结的共同家园，才不会误解这个方案。正如麦克利什所说："看到地球的真切模样，一个小小的蓝色星球，美丽而永远沉默地漂浮在那里，就会把我们自己看做是在地球上同舟共济的乘客，在永恒的寒冷中，可爱的星球在闪烁，四海之内皆兄弟。人们应该知道，他们是真兄弟。"

我要建议的是，世界上每一个人都将被允许拥有双重国籍，既是他碰巧出生的那个国家的公民，此外，还能申请成为世界公民。

要想成为世界公民、成为地球飞船的公民，这个人将要做出特定的承诺：

1. 无论其国籍、种族、宗教、性别或肤色如何，他或她必须表明坚信人类的统一和每个人有平等的尊严。

2. 他或她必须表明，愿意在本国及国外，通过促进并实践正义而为世界和平努力。

3. 他或她必须做出具体的事情，表明对这些信仰的诚意，在本国及国外，以具体的行动去促进全人类的和平与福祉。

2. One would have to certify his or her willingness to work for world peace through the promotion and practice of justice at home and abroad.

3. One would have to do something to prove the sincerity of these beliefs, something to promote justice for all, something to promote the peace and well-being of his or her fellow humans at home and abroad.

The growing number of human beings on spaceship earth who would freely opt for world, in addition to national citizenship might begin to prove that **men and women are ready to regard each other truly as brothers and sisters, to seek justice for all, to live in peace, to commit one's idealism to practice, to transcend nationalistic chauvinism, and to seek to realize a new vision of a spaceship earth with liberty and justice for all -- the only true road to world peace.**

One would hope that whatever international agency would certify this additional world citizenship might also grant to its world citizens some benefits befitting their commitment, such as free passage without visas anywhere in the world, a small concession, but one symbolic of what one free world might be for all its citizens as more of them apply for world passports.

One would like to hope that our country, with its rich transnational, multi-racial, and poly-religious population base, might be the first to propose and allow this new idea of dual citizenship for all who would desire to give leadership and meaning to this new concept of a more beautiful, more human spaceship earth.

I would like to say for myself, and I would hope for many of you, that I would welcome this kind of opportunity to declare myself interested in the welfare of mankind everywhere in the world, concerned for the justice due all who suffer injustice anywhere in the world. I would like to believe that being a citizen of the world would enlarge me as a person, would declare my fraternity with every other man, woman, and child in the world. I would take world citizenship to be a firm commitment to work for a new vision of spaceship earth and all its passengers, to be a harbinger of hope for all who are close to despair because of their dismal human condition, finally, to be a beacon of light for humanity beleaguered by darkness in so many parts of our world today.

Again, one of Notre Dame's Peace Corps volunteers, now studying at Harvard, puts it well: "One comes away from an experience like the Peace Corps with a sense of real international brotherhood. The fact that a fellow who had never been out of

当地球飞船上越来越多的人除了自己国家的公民身份，也自由地选择成为世界公民的时候，就证明大家准备好了。**要把对方当做兄弟姐妹来看待，要为所有人寻求正义，要在和平中生活，要致力于超越民族沙文主义的实际，并努力为飞船上所有人都能有自由和正义而努力奋斗——这才是实现世界和平的唯一正道。**

人们可以希望，会有某个国际机构来证明世界公民的身份，让世界公民们做出承诺的同时，也享有一些利益，比如到世界上任何地方都不用签证。这只是一个小小的让步，但却是一种象征，当越来越多的人申请世界护照时，一个自由的世界会是什么样子？

人们可以希望，我们的国家由于有着丰富的跨国籍、多种族和多宗教的人口基础，能够首先倡议并践行拥有双重国籍的新理念，让能为一个更加美丽、更加人道的飞船带来领导能力和意义的人，都能拥有这样的双重国籍。

我想说，并希望你们中的很多人也这样想，我想有机会宣布：希望维护世界各地所有人的福祉，世界任何地方遭受不公的人，正义能够得到伸张。我要宣布我对世界上每个男女老少的博爱。我希望拥有世界公民的身份，就是一种坚定的承诺，我愿为地球飞船以及所有乘客拥有新的愿景而工作；给那些因为生存条件极为糟糕而快要绝望的人，送去希望。最后，我愿为今天这个很多地方仍然黑暗的世界，起到一个照亮人性的灯塔作用。

圣母诺特丹大学一位参加过和平志愿队、现在就读于哈佛的学生说得很好："参与和平自愿队的收获，是真正意识到四海之内皆兄弟。我从来没有离开过美国中西部，只会讲英语，却到亚洲南部和东部边沿的两个国家生活，和当地的人民建立了深厚而持久的友谊，在斯里兰卡和韩国学会了那里的语言、了解了当地的文化，这让我感觉到，自己和世上所有的人是同呼吸共命运的。"

我并不认为大家都做世界公民就能很快消除世界上所有的灾难和罪恶。它对我们每一个人来说是一种机会，可以宣告我们是相互依存的。我们同为人类，我们对地球飞船抱有相同的希望，我们作为飞船乘员患

the Midwest and could speak only English could then live in two countries on the South and Eastern fringes of Asia, form deep and lasting friendships with the native people, learn a language and a culture in both Ceylon and Korea and function well in them -- it makes one feel a sense of oneness with people all over the world."

I do not see the possibility of world citizenship as a panacea or an immediate answer to all the world's ills and evils. Rather, it would be for each of us a chance to declare our interdependence with one another, our common humanity, our shared hopes for our spaceship earth, our brotherhood as members of the crew, our common vision of the task facing humanity -- to achieve human dignity and the good life together.

Once more, Barbara Ward has elucidated the new vision best:

One of the fundamental moral insights of the Western culture which has now swept over the whole globe is that, against all historical evidence, man-kind is not a group of warring tribes, but a single, equal and fraternal community. Hitherto, distances have held men apart. Scarcity has driven them to competition and enmity. It has required great vision, great holiness, great wisdom to keep alive and vivid the sense of the unity of man. It is precisely the saints, the poets, the philosophers, and the great men of science who have borne witness to the underlying unity which daily life has denied. But now the distances are abolished. It is at least possible that our new technological resources, properly deployed, will conquer ancient shortage. Can we not at such a time realize the moral unity of our human experience and make it the basis of a patriotism for the world itself?

It will be easy to scoff at this vision of our humanity, our oneness, our common task as fellow passengers on a small planet. The great and powerful of this earth, and indeed of our country and Europe, can easily sniff cynically and return to their game of power politics, national jealousies, mountains of armaments, millions of graves of men mourned by widows and orphans, ravaged oceans, and unverdant plains and hungry homeless people who despair of the good life.

Somehow I believe that there is enough good will in our country and in

难与共，我们对人类抱有共同的愿望——实现人类尊严，一起过上好日子。

针对这种新的设想，巴巴拉·沃德再次为我们作了深刻的阐述：

西方文化中一个根本的道德观念，现在已经风行整个世界。不同于以往所有的历史证据，这个观念认为，人类不是一群互相打仗的部落，而是一个单一且平等的兄弟集体。到目前为止，地理距离把人们隔开，人们因为物质缺乏而竞争和敌对。想要让人们团结，就需要极大的远见、伟大的神圣感和巨大的智慧。正是由于这种潜在的统一性在我们的日常生活中难得一见，我们的圣徒、诗人、哲学家以及科学家们，才努力为此作出见证。但现在，距离已经不成问题了。我们有了新的科学技术，如果使用得当的话，可能克服这些自古存在的问题。我们在这种时候，在人类经验的基础上，不能实现道德上的一致吗？难道不能把热爱世界本身，当做一种爱国主义吗？

把我们人类当做是在一个很小的星球上同行的乘客，我们同属一体、任务相同。要嘲笑这种愿景，是一件很容易的事。这个地球上，甚至在我们这个国家和欧洲有权有势的人，都可以轻易地对这种愿望嗤之以鼻，然后回到他们的游戏中去，继续争权夺利，制造国家间的争端，造出堆积如山的军备，让千百万寡妇和孤儿在坟前哭泣，让海洋不宁、山河涂炭，忍饥挨饿的人们无家可归，无缘于美好的生活。

但我总觉得，在我们国家和整个世界上，会有无数的善良的人民，他们会宣告说，这些腐败政客们的你争我斗，对这艘飞船来说简直就是胡闹。他们会宣告说，我们希望所有男男女女都是兄弟姐妹，我们仍然相信正义与和平，我们认为拥有祥和的家园、随风摇曳的稻田、朗朗书声的学校，远远强于把数以万亿计的钱花在枪炮、坦克、潜艇和反弹道导弹这类东西上。可惜的是，当政客们故作姿

the world to expect millions of people to declare all of this powerful posturing of corrupt politicians to be **arrant** [*adj.* 彻头彻尾的；极端的；臭名昭著的；声名狼藉的] nonsense on a common spaceship, to say that we do want all men and women to be brothers and sisters, that we do believe in justice and peace, and that we think homes, and swaying fields of grain, and schools and medicine are better than billions spent for guns, tanks, submarines, and ABM's. The trouble is that the millions of little people, the ones who really man spaceship earth, the ones who really work, and suffer, and die while the politicians posture and play, these little ones have never been given a chance to declare themselves. And this is wrong, globally wrong.

It is, I believe, a most important, urgent, and timely part of the new world a-borning that everyone in the world should be able to declare his or her broader citizenship in adopting a wider vision for spaceship earth, a vision that transcends nationality and anything else that separates man from man. Having traveled across the face of our beautiful planet, having traversed all its oceans and its continents, having shared deep human hopes with my human brothers and sisters of every nationality, religion, color, and race, having broken bread and found loving friendship and brotherhood everywhere on earth, I am prepared this day to declare myself a citizen of the world, and to invite all of you, and everyone everywhere to embrace this broader vision of our interdependent world, our common humanity, our noblest hopes and our common quest for justice in our times and, ultimately, for peace on earth. **Lest** [*conj.* 惟恐；以免；担心] I sound too Utopian, or even too secularistic, since I am first and foremost a priest, may I also now pray that the good Lord Jesus who lived and died for us may also bless these living efforts of ours to be truly followers of Him who blessed both the peacemakers and all who hunger for justice.

Congratulations to you and good luck.

态、玩弄手法时，那些千千万万的小人物，那些真正操作着地球飞船的、正在努力工作、受苦并牺牲的人，却从来没有机会发声。这实在是错误的，可谓大错特错！

  我认为，世上每一个人，都应该能够申明他们的世界公民身份，为地球飞船展现更宽广的远见，这种愿景超越国籍和其他任何使人分离的东西，这样做对我们拥有一个新世界来说是最重要、最紧迫和最及时的。我在我们这个美丽的星球上广泛游历过，跨过了所有的海洋、走遍了每一个大陆，和我有着不同国籍、宗教、肤色、种族的兄弟姐妹，分享过共同的深切希望。我在地球各地，都和人们共享食物、得到友爱和兄弟情谊，今天，我准备宣布自己是一位世界公民，并请所有的朋友不管身在何方，都接受这种更加开阔的视野，看到我们在这个相互依存的世界，我们同为人类，畅想我们这个时代应有的崇高理想和共同的对正义的追求，最终实现世界和平。因为我的身份首先是个牧师，为了避免让我的讲话显得太理想化，甚至太世俗化，现在请允许我祈祷，祈求为我们生也为我们死的我主耶稣，保佑我们这些人的努力，保佑和平缔造者和所有追求正义的人。

  祝贺各位，并祝你们好运！

---

1 南极洲最大的科学研究中心

2 英国作家和著名环保倡导者，曾在 1957 年哈佛毕业典礼上发表演讲。

3 罗伯特·海尔布伦纳（Robert Heilbroner，1919—2005），美国经济学家和哲学史家。

4 奇卡诺人，指墨西哥裔美国人或在美国的讲西班牙语的拉丁美洲人后裔。

拉尔夫·埃利森（1914—1994）

美国著名的黑人作家、文学评论家和学者，也是20世纪最有影响的美国作家之一。他的代表作长篇小说《隐形人》("The Invisible Man")于1952年一经出版，立即在文学界和美国社会引起巨大反响，次年获得美国国家图书奖和普利策文学奖，1965年又被评为二战以来美国最重要、最有影响的小说之一。

埃利森出生于美国俄克拉荷马州的俄克拉荷马市。他的父亲希望他成为诗人，因而给他起了与美国19世纪著名作家诗人拉尔夫·沃尔多·爱默生（Ralph Waldo Emerson）一样的名字，他在演讲中也提到了这一点。

埃利森从小喜欢爵士乐，中学毕业后获得奖学金进入塔斯克基学院主修音乐。学业期间他花了大量时间泡在图书馆阅读，他曾说美国作家T.S.艾略特的《荒原》一书对他的触动最大。

3年后埃利森来到纽约学习视觉艺术，在这里结识了黑人作家理查德·莱特。在莱特的影响和鼓励下，埃利森走上了文学之路。早期他主要写评论和短文，发表其对文学音乐以及美国黑人政治社会生活方面的观点。从1945年开始，他用了7年时间创作长篇小说《隐形人》，该书主要描写一个黑人青年在充满种族歧视与隔离的社会中寻找自我的心路历程，通过看似简单的故事情节表达了深刻的主题。小说的发表和获奖，使埃利森在美国文坛获得重要的一席之位。

埃利森主张种族融合、文化多元，他致力于改变传统的黑人公式化形象。他的著名观点之一是："你的写作与你的肤色无关，而要源于你的思想和智慧。"（"You do not write out of your skin. You write out of your ideas and the quality of your mind."）

1974

Conscience and Consciousness, and More Conscientiousness
良心与良知——呼唤更多的自主意识

Ralph Ellison 拉尔夫·埃利森

Messrs. Presidents, members of the illustrious class of 1949, honored guests, fellow students, ladies and gentlemen:

To have been invited to say a few words on this grand ceremonial occasion is a high honor indeed -- and yet, I must confess to having accepted your invitation with certain grave apprehensions. For not only was I aware that words uttered here in the past have launched lofty visionary programs that helped to reshape the world -- a feat no words of mine could hope to equal -- but I also recalled having read that once some one-hundred-and-thirty-eight years ago another writer whose first and middle names I happen to share, gave a talk here at Harvard that was so rankling and ill-received that it got him banished from this campus for close to thirty years! Indeed, before he was allowed to return, the Civil War had been fought and terminated by an uneasy peace, Abraham Lincoln had been assassinated, and American society had been so utterly transformed that my paternal grandfather, a recently freed slave, had become actively involved in South Carolina politics.

Now let me hasten to say that I drew no conclusions from all this -- other than that Harvard audiences were capable of reacting to the spoken word with an awesome sensitivity and an intimidating power. Therefore my first impulse was to say thanks for considering me worthy for such an honor and then to excuse myself in the name of that discretion which is prudence.

Nevertheless, such was the graciousness and power of persuasion of those who extended your invitation that my apprehensions were somewhat stilled, and I found myself slipping in the direction of acceptance. I began to view your request as a call to adventure, as an opportunity to partake of a new and rare experience. Then I was nudged even closer by a question of personal consistency. "How," I asked myself, "could you who have protested against policies of social exclusion and denials of opportunity now refuse one of the rarest opportunities of all?" To this I had no easy answer; for as I see it, protest is not an end in itself, but an effort in the direction of responsible and creative participation. And although I was still a bit uneasy and perhaps overly mindful of the glamour of the occasion and of the mystique with which words spoken here have inspired this platform, I reassured myself that such uneasiness was only normal; and that like any young black freshman entering an Ivy League college for the first time I was reacting to the presence of a mystery -- Please! Not that of race, but of the mystery of social hierarchy; that mystery which arises from strangeness and from

校长先生、1949届的优秀毕业生们、各位嘉宾、同学们、女士们、先生们：

获邀到这个盛大的仪式上说几句话，对我来说真是极高的荣誉。但我必须承认，在接受你们的邀请时，我带着相当惶恐的心情。因为我不仅知道，前人过去在这里说过的话，曾经推动了崇高的富有远见的计划，从而帮助改变了世界——这样的壮举，我的话是不可能与之相比的。而且我还读到过，138年前，有另一个我的名字碰巧和他一样的作家[1]，在哈佛大学发表演讲，结果引起众怒，不受欢迎，以致他在那之后的近30年里，都不能再进哈佛校园！事实上，等他被允许再次返回校园时，美国内战已经打完，并在一个不稳定的和平氛围里结束，亚伯拉罕·林肯已经被人暗杀，美国社会发生了彻底的改变，我的祖父、一个被解放不久的奴隶，已经开始积极地参与南卡罗来纳州的政治活动。

现在我要赶快补上一句，我并没有从这些事件中得出什么结论，只想表达一个意思，哈佛的听众在听演讲方面，有着令人敬畏的敏感性和威慑力。所以，我的第一个冲动就是要对你们说声"谢谢"，感谢你们认为我配得上这样的荣誉，然后我要借用行事须谨慎的名义，给我自己找个借口。

不过，你们邀请的那些人大多亲切和蔼，很有说服能力，让我稍稍减少了些顾虑，我倾向于接受这个邀请了。我开始把你们的邀请当做冒险的召唤，当做体验一种新的难得经历的一个机会。然后我问自己是否能够做到始终如一，这更促使我要接受邀请。我问自己："如果你曾抗议社会不公、机会不等，那么，现在怎么能拒绝这样一个少有的机会？"对此，我无法简单地回答，在我看来，抗议本身不是目的，而是要朝着能够负责并灵活地参与社会活动那个方向做出努力。虽然我还是有点惴惴不安，而且对这个场合是那么高调、前人讲过的言语那么激动人心等这些问题，可能过于在意了，我安慰自己：紧张是正常的，就像任何一位黑人新生平生第一次跨入常春藤盟校校园一样，我感觉到有一个谜在那里。不过拜托，我可不是在说这是由于种族歧视，而是出于一种社会阶层的神秘感。神秘的产生，是因为对来自不同地区、社群和社会层次的个人和团体之间，那些不同的生活方式和经验感到陌生。神秘感的存

the differences in life-style and experience existing between individuals and groups occupying different regions, neighborhoods and levels of the social pyramid. Such mysteries arise out of the difficulty of communicating across the hierarchal divisions of American society, and a great deal of our misunderstanding springs from our failures of communication. Such mystery is a product of psychological distance, and of our ignorance of one another, and it is so persistent that even our great improvements in communications technology only make it easier for Americans to misunderstand one another.

Should a writer be balked by such a mystery? Surely not if he has the curiosity characteristic of novelists, and certainly not when he realizes that he has not only been asked to communicate but also to break bread and take part in nothing less than a Cantabrigian pageant rite of spring! Obviously, I could not.

Therefore, like any young initiate, I could do nothing less than confront whatever mystery might lurk within this symbolic occasion, take my chances, and hope that at the least I wouldn't be banished. Then something happened that almost changed my mind: I received a letter from Harvard addressed to Ralph Waldo Emerson!

Lord, but what tenacious memories you Harvards have!

And now that I stand before you, how fortunate for me that my unmistakable pigmentation shines forth no less as sign than as symbol! I assure you that even though I've insisted for years that our American obsession with practical joking was originally not intentional but arose out of the incongruities abounding in a man-and-mammy-made society that was set up within an unexplored and alien land, it was still somewhat shocking when under the most **decorous** [adj. 合宜的；高雅的；端庄的] of circumstances one finds the image of a Negro American novelist being made to show forth through the ghostly (and I hope benign) **lineaments** [n. (常复) 线性构造；轮廓；特征；容貌] of a white philosopher and poet.

But then, this was not the first time that my contact with Harvard was productive of shock. During the summer of 1953, a few short years after you gentlemen set forth upon the journey which you celebrate by your presence here today, I found myself in Memorial Hall taking part in a conference on the contemporary novel. There had been an impassioned exchange of ideas, and after the session had ended I was approached by a lady who complimented me on some of the remarks I had made - and then without pause or transition, she informed me that she was in communication with

在，是由于美国社会不同层次之间很难沟通而造成的，而我们很多误解，便源于沟通的失败。这种神秘感是心理距离和互相不了解所形成的产物，这个结果是如此顽固，以致通信技术的大大改善，反而使美国人相互之间的误解更容易产生了。

一个作家应该被这样的谜吓倒吗？如果他有着小说家对凡事都感到好奇的特点，他当然不会。特别是当他认识到，人们邀请他去，不仅是发表讲话，而且还能共同进餐，并参加一个名校的盛会，显然——我不能错过这样的机会。

因此，像所有的年轻新人一样，在这样一个富有象征意义的场合内，无论有什么样的神秘存在，我都必须勇敢地尝试，同时希望至少我不会被禁止再来校园。然后发生了一件让我几乎改变主意的事情：我收到了哈佛寄给拉尔夫·沃尔多·爱默生的信！

天哪！哈佛人的记忆可真强！

而现在我真的就站在你们面前，我真是幸运，我明显的肤色既是象征也是标志！我向你们保证，虽然多年来我一直坚持认为，我们美国对实用玩笑的痴迷，本来并不是故意的，而是由于人们对这个人造社会中出现的许多不协调的东西难以适应所产生的反应，因为这个社会是建立在未知而陌生的土地上的。但在这样一个高雅庄重的场合下，人们发现一个白人哲学家和诗人[2]的幽灵，（我希望是友好的幽灵），以一个黑人小说家的形象出现的时候，还是有点令人震惊。

但是，在我与哈佛的接触中，这并不是第一次让我吃惊的事。1953年夏天，在你们今天庆祝毕业的人出生没几年，我曾来到哈佛的纪念礼堂参加一个当代小说研讨会。我们慷慨激昂地交流了思想，在会议结束后，我遇到一位女士，她称赞了我的一些发言，然后没有经过任何暂停或过渡，她就告诉我说，她像是与在火星的智能生命有了沟通。

那时候，人类甚至还没有踏上月球，所以不用说，我大为惊讶。她显然是一个上流社会的女性，她声调不高，但讲话带着令人印象深刻的自信，以致听她说话的时候，我都呆立在那儿。直到她转身与其他与会者交谈，我才昏头昏脑地走到大厅，试图把我所形容的关于小说和美国

intelligent beings on the planet Mars!

Now at the time man hadn't even set foot on the moon, so I needn't tell you how surprised I was. But this was obviously a genteel and learned lady and she spoke quietly but with an impressive ring of conviction. So much so, that I stood fascinated, hearing her out; and only when she had excused herself to exchange ideas with others of the participants did I stumble out into the hall with my head **awhirl** [adj. 旋转着的] as I tried to tie what I'd been saying about the relationship between the novel and American experience together with what she'd said about communicating with Marsmen. And it was then it happened.

As I stumbled along, my attention was drawn upward and I was aware of the marble walls, somber and carved with names. And then came a moment in which perception leaped dizzily ahead of the processes of normal thought. Up to that time no history book that I had read had told me anything of what I stood before, but I knew its significance almost without knowing and the shock of recognition filled me with a kind of anguish.

Something within me cried out, "Not" against that painful knowledge, for I knew that I stood within the presence of Harvard men who had given their young lives to set me free. But no, not for me personally, because I didn't exist, nor perhaps for any slave they'd ever seen. They had sacrificed their lives, had paid what Abraham Lincoln termed the last full measure of devotion, for an ideal of freedom. And what filled me with anguish was that I had been ignorant of their sacrifice, had been unaware of my indebtedness. And standing there I was ashamed of my ignorance and of the circumstance that had assigned these young men to the shadows of our historical knowledge. Upon them a discontinuity had been imposed by the living, and their heroic gestures had been repressed along with the details of the shameful abandonment of those goals for which they had given up their lives. Without question, the consequences of that imposed discontinuity, of that betrayal of ideal and memory, are still with us today.

That shock of recognition, that **epiphany** [n. 顿悟;（神灵）显现], occurred, as I say, back in 1953. A few weeks ago I had an occasion for suggesting to the graduating class of a great state university that they were among the first American generations to have grown up under the full impact of the malignant forces that had been generated by the suppression of such heroic details no less than by the more shameful details of

经验之间的关系，和她所说的与火星人有了沟通这事联系起来。就在那时，一件事情发生了。

我一边慢慢踱着方步，一边把目光投向大理石墙壁，我看到灰暗的墙上刻有名字。然后一种感觉突然打断了我的正常思绪。直到那时，我读过的历史书里从来没有一本告诉过我眼前看见的事，但我马上意识到了它的重大意义，而这种认识让我充满了痛楚。

伴随着痛苦的认识，我的心底有一个声音在呐喊："不！"，因为我知道我站在那些为了让我自由而献出年轻生命的哈佛人面前。不！他们的牺牲不是为了我个人，因为那时还没有我，也不是为了与他们未曾见过面的黑人奴隶。他们牺牲自己的生命，付出亚伯拉罕·林肯所说的"最后的奉献"，是为了一个自由的理想。而使我痛苦的，是我并不知道他们做出的牺牲，不知道我欠着这份债。站在那堵牺牲校友的墙壁前，我为自己的无知和这些年轻人被我们的历史知识所淡忘而感到羞愧。我们的所作所为无法与这些先烈的行动相衔接，他们的英勇作为被遗忘，他们牺牲生命所捍卫的那些目标，也随着后人令人羞愧的举止而蒙垢。毫无疑问，后人没能跟随先烈的足迹，那些对他们理想和记忆的背叛，在今天仍然存在。

正如我所言，我那次震撼的感觉、那种顿悟发生在1953年。几个星期前，我有机会向一所著名州立大学的毕业班同学发表演讲，我说他们是在压制这种英雄行为的恶性势力的影响下成长起来的第一代美国人，他们也受到了我们国家那些更为可耻的行为的影响。我认为其结果就是，他们不再能轻易地谈论"美国的本真"，而这一点，则是从爱默生到福克纳这些美国作家都很关注的，也是激发亨利·詹姆斯[3]艺术动力的重要因素。

在这里，"本真"是指我们忽略了良好的意愿也可能产生邪恶，和美国人在发现完全积极的行为却造成了负面的、而且是令人震惊的结果后，所表现出的一片惊讶。用悲剧的术语来说，这种"本真"是人们性格的一个侧面，而当把这种情况放在评价英雄的心理时，本真则被称为"悲剧性缺陷"。希腊人把这种性格和感知方面的缺陷

our national conduct. The results of this, I suggested, was to deny them an easy access to that convenient posture of "American innocence" that had been the concern of American writers from Emerson to Faulkner and which engaged much of the artistic energy of Henry James.

Here "innocence" refers to our tendency to ignore the evil which can spring from our good intentions as well as to the **consternation** [n. 惊愕; 惊惶失措] with which Americans are given to reacting upon discovering the negative, often appalling, results that can erupt from actions conceived as totally positive. In the terminology of tragic drama such "innocence" is viewed as an aspect of human character, and when operative in the psychology of the Hero it is termed a tragic flaw. The Greeks termed this flaw in character and perception hybris, and to the force which springs up from the enactment of such tragic flaws, and which clings to tragic action like the clicks of erasure to magnetic recording tape, the Greeks termed **nemesis** [n. [希神] 复仇女神].

I find it interesting that such American failures of perception were termed "innocence", because hybris is usually accompanied by some form of arrogance and **insolence** [n. 傲慢; 无礼]; by some form of overbearing pride. Perhaps this because in the drama of American society one of the most damaging forms of insolence and pride is racism.

Now lest I appear about to take off on a **tirade** [n. 长篇的攻击性演说] of indictment -- of which we've had quite enough -- let me hasten to add that neither tragic arrogance nor insolence are limited to Americans; they arise from the nature of the human animal and from the limitations encountered by human consciousness when asserting itself against the vast multiplicity of the universe.

As for nemesis, well here I think it best to reject the definitions of literary critics as perhaps too moralistic in favor of that offered by a mathematician and philosopher who once taught here at Harvard, namely, Scott Buchanan. Buchanan defines nemesis as "the eventual consequence of that blindness and arrogance/ produced by hybris, and as/ the vengeance that the ignored factor in a situation takes on man and his virtues/." Note that he speaks of man's pride as an aspect of his virtues, for I'd not have you miss the fact that I see Americans as motivated, even in their failures, by the virtues embodied in the American creed. And I'd even go so far as to give the pride of racism its due by reminding you that when Faust asked Mephistopheles what he was, the reply was "A part of that force which always seeks evil and always does good."

称为"hybris",而对这种悲剧性的缺陷所产生的力量,以及它如何与悲剧性行为如影相随的特性,希腊人称之为"不可避免的报应"。

美国人在这种认知上的失败被称为"本真",我觉得挺有意思,因为"hybris"通常伴随着某种形式的傲慢和无礼,表现出某种形式的傲气。这或许是由于在美国社会中,傲慢和骄傲所造成的最有害的现实,就是种族主义。

为了避免我好像要发表一个长篇大论式的控诉——这方面已有很多人说过了——我要赶紧补充说明一下,悲剧性的傲慢或无礼并不仅限于发生在美国人身上,它是人类天性的产物,也是人类在认知广阔多样的宇宙时,囿于认识的局限所造成的。

至于"不可避免的报应",我认为最好不要去理会文学评论家们提出的那些也许带有太多说教性的定义,而是引用一位在哈佛任教过的数学家和哲学家,即史葛·布坎南的解释。布坎南把"不可避免的报应"定义为"由hybris所造成的／盲目自大所带来的最终后果／被忽视的因素,会导致个人和他的德行遭到报复"。请注意,他在提到人的骄傲时,是当做美德来说的,因为我也不想让你们忽略这个事实,即我认为,哪怕是在失败的时候,美国人也受到美国信条的激励。我甚至可以认同,种族主义里包含着种族优越感,就像浮士德问梅菲斯特他是谁时,得到的回答是:"我属于追求邪恶,却总是做了好事的那股力量。"

这是很难让人接受的一个答案,但它表明我们需要仔细地审视自己的动机。**无论如何,种族自豪感本身并不是什么邪恶的东西,甚至黑人也为自己骄傲,但邪恶在于以种族自豪感的名义犯下的那些暴行。**同样的道理,也表现在一系列我们为之自豪的东西上:我们的生产能力、我国国民生产总值的大小、我们的宏大规模、我们的创造力、我们有能力创造并满足不管是真的还是假的需求,以及我们在利用这片伟大土地上的自然资源方面所表现出的聪明才智。但是,所有这些领域最近开始有了惊人的逆转。我们经过认真设想的机构,就像带有恶意动机的一个恶作剧。就连我们管理自己的能

It is a tough answer to accept, but it suggests that we look carefully into our own motives. At any rate, pride of race is not an evil in itself - even black men possess such pride - the evil lies in the brutalities committed in its name. The same goes for our pride in production, in the size of our gross national product, in sheer bigness, in our inventiveness, in our ability to create and fulfill needs both false and real, and in our ingenuity in exploiting the natural resources of this great land. Yes, but in all of these areas we have recently begun to suffer startling reversals. Our most seriously considered enterprises have taken on the character of maliciously motivated practical jokes. Even our ability to govern ourselves appears to have gotten out of hand. So if I speak here at length of nemesis it is because I suspect that whatever else the times in which we live turn out to be, they are our days of nemesis.

Hence my suggestion to those students that the society in which they were about to enter as adults would be quite unlike the society of their parents. Nor could they ignore its tragic realities by adopting a posture of innocence. Since 1954, say, events both negative and positive have rendered such innocence impossible. American society and the world alike have changed more drastically than at any time during our relatively short history and this generation of students has observed and been a part of that change. Fundamental to that change has been the broadening of our dispensing of justice, an action that has solved many crucial problems and created still others. But with the legal supports of racism giving way there has come a broadening of access to our institutions, the individuality and talent, the potential, of those once assigned to the anonymity of the racial stereotype is now being recognized, and a wavering struggle toward an equalizing of opportunity is under way. Further, the patterns of political alliances have been changing, bringing new chaos and indecision as well as a rectification of past inequities. Regional antagonisms have receded along with the smug hypocrisies used to justify them. In brief, chaos has come with order and some good things have been exchanged for other good things; some bad things for other bad things, and some, Thank God, for good.

Yes, but before such experience, such knowledge, what innocence? This generation of students has, like ourselves, observed vast changes in the direction of the American social drama and felt the shock and trauma of acts that have deprived us of a President, a senator and a great spiritual leader. We have witnessed startling reversals of attitudes and alliances in the field of politics; with southern politicians, following the lead of a

力，似乎也已经失控。所以，如果我在这里大谈"不可避免的报应"，是因为我在猜测，我们生活的时代不管变得怎样，都会是我们的"报应"。

因此我提醒那些学生们，他们作为成人即将步入的社会，与他们父辈的社会是不一样的。他们也不能采取天真的姿态去忽略社会的悲惨现实。自从1954年以来，消极事件和积极事件的发展，让人们再难有这种天真。美国社会和整个世界，都在这个历史阶段发生了前所未有的巨大变化，这代学生见证了这些变化，他们自己也是其中的一部分。这些变化当中最根本的改变，是我们比过去有了更为广泛的公正，这解决了许多关键问题，当然也带来了其他问题。种族主义失去了法律支持，过去忍受种族偏见的人，现在比较有机会接触我们的机构，展现个性、才华和潜能，人们还在争取机会均等。此外，政治联盟的形式也在改变，这让人们产生了新的混乱和优柔寡断，也让人们纠正过去的不平等。那些带着自鸣得意的伪善所造成的区域对立，也已经消失。总之，混沌之中有了秩序，有些好的东西被类似的好事物代替；有些不好的东西则变成其他不好的事物，还有一些，谢天谢地，由坏变好。

是的，在这样的经历和知识面前，还有什么本真可言呢？和我们一样，这代学生看到美国社会如同一出大戏的巨大变化，那些给我们带来创伤的行为，夺走了我们的一位总统、一位参议员和一个伟大的精神领袖[4]。在政治领域，我们目睹了在态度和结盟方面出现的惊人逆转。南部的政界人士追随得克萨斯州的一位本地人[5]，很多人开始时相当鄙视他的自由派倾向，但这位得州佬有着政客那种让人扑朔迷离的动机和经常变换的政治立场，他越来越多地显示出愿意遵守法律，并与南方黑人同事分享权力。这让人不由得相信，种族歧视和隔离，不折不扣地只是一个战术、一种象征性的姿态。如果一个人能忘记最近刚发生的事，或那些刻在哈佛墙上的名字的话，人们可以这样相信。

但伴随这些态度改变和习惯逆转的，是另一种变化，北方黑人

native Texan whom many despised for his liberalism at first grudgingly and then with that bewildering mixture of motives and shift of position characteristic of politicians, showing a growing willingness to obey the law and share the common power with their black fellow southerners. One could almost believe that racial discrimination and disenfranchisement were nothing more than a tactic, a symbolic gesture. One could, that is, if he could forget either the recent past or the names engraved on the wall.

But accompanying these reversals in attitudes and customs is yet still another, wherein northern whites have reacted to the pressures of black northerners for more equality as vehemently and in some cases as violently and irrationally as their southern counterparts. And this accompanied by reams of pseudo-scientific justification, double-talk and **diversionary** [adj. 使转换注意；牵制的] tactics. So the tensions and contentions continue, but for the first time in our history the social drama that is American Society is beginning to proceed according to the original acting script -- by which I mean the Constitution and Bill of Rights; virtue and nemesis exert their tensions, yes. But for the first time we appear to be **facing up to the reality of the Americanness of American diversity and to the past which made us what we are**. For the first time we are facing up to the tragic cost paid by some for the achievements of our form of government without recognition or **recompense** [v. 补偿；赔偿].

T.S. Eliot's reminder that: *What we have inherited from the fortunate/ We have taken from the defeated*, must not be forgotten, for such forgetfulness leaves us vulnerable to nemesis.

Because today nemesis exerts its force in forms and places we least expect. In areas of society thought safe from chaos; in the form of criminal acts, including murder, proclaimed as being committed in the name of human freedom; in the corruption of art and the **perversion** [n. 误用；反常；性变态] of fashion, in drug cults and satan worship; in superstition and false science and in the distortion of the communicative function of language. None of this is new, I know, only its extent and the malignity which it embodies. And what is the **antidote** [n. 解毒剂；解药；对抗手段]?

Here I can only fall back upon the teaching of that earlier Ralph Waldo and suggest, conscience and consciousness, more consciousness and more conscientiousness! This achieved, and it will take time, perhaps we can then say truly of the 1960's what Henry James had to say mistakenly of the late 1860's, that they mark "an era in the history of the American mind/ in which there was/ introduced into the

要求更多的平等，而北方白人对此的反应像南方白人一样强烈，在某些情况下，还更具暴力和非理性。由此而生的，是大量的被伪科学证明的理由、空话连篇和牵制战术。因此，关系紧张和争论不断的情况还在继续，但在我们的历史上，美国社会这部大戏第一次开始按照原始剧本开演了——我指的是按宪法和权利法案来行事。美德和报应依然造成紧张，是的，但我们好像是第一次正视美国的多样性就是美国的特性这个事实。**正视什么样的历史，我们今天就成了什么样的人**。我们也第一次面对这样的现实，即为了建立我们的政府模式，有的人付出了悲惨的代价，却从没有得到过承认或补偿。

T.S. 艾略特提醒过我们："我们从幸运者那里继承来的，其实是我们从失败者那里夺来的。"我们不能忘记这一点，因为这种健忘症会使我们易受"不可避免的报应"的伤害。

因为今天，报应以我们最想不到的形式和在我们最想不到的地方显现，出现在那些被我们认为是安全的领域里，包括在人类自由的名义下进行杀戮的犯罪行为；艺术堕落、时装变成奇装异服；人们沉迷于毒品，崇拜撒旦邪教；盲目迷信、相信伪科学，语言的交际功能也被扭曲。我知道，这些都不是什么新的事物，只是其程度和它所表现出来的毒性更厉害。我们能找到什么解药吗？

在这里，我只能借用那位拉尔夫·沃尔多前辈的教诲，要有良心和良知，要有更多的良知和更多的自主意识！想要做到这一点，当然需要时间，也许到那时才可以真正描述我们的1960年代，就像亨利·詹姆斯曾经错误地描述了1860年代后期，他说那标志着"美国思想史的一个年代／在那段时间里／人们在国家意识中开始运用纵向和横向对比，认识到世界比人们所知道的要更复杂，未来更充满未知，要成功则需付出更多的艰辛"。

按事情的进展速度来看，很明显，美国人中的好人会越来越多，但在未来的日子里，一位正直的美国人比起他自满且自信的祖辈来说，将会带有更多的批评眼光，他像亚当一样吃了智慧之树的果实。我想他不会是一个怀疑论者，当然更不会是一个玩世不恭的人，但

national consciousness a certain sense of proportion and relation, of the world being a more complicated place than it had hitherto seemed, the future more treacherous, success more difficult."

At the rate at which things are going, it is obvious that good Americans will be more numerous than ever; but the good American, in days to come, will be a more critical person than his complacent and confident grandfather. He will have eaten of the tree of knowledge. He will not, I think, be a skeptic, and still less, of course, a cynic; but he will be, without discredit to his well known capacity for action, an observer. He will remember that the ways of the Lord are **inscrutable** [adj. 难以了解的; 不能预测的], and that this is a world in which everything happens; and eventualities, as the late Emperor of the French used to say, "will not find him intellectually unprepared."

What a glorious **exhortation** [n. 劝告; 训词; 讲道词]! For exhortation it was -- Yes, but when taken at short range, what a flawed act of prophesy! But then, if I may say so, James' imagination was always ahead of his times. And besides, his experience, class identity and refinement of taste placed him at a distance which made knowledge of the **recalcitrant** [adj. 反抗的; 顽强的] complexity of much of the humanity for which he had such bright hopes difficult to come by. What is more, he had no idea of the great potential for chaos and order that was embodied in those who had been liberated by the forces that made for and decided the outcome of the Civil War -- if indeed the outcome of that war has yet been decided. Quite frankly, it is my opinion that it is still in the balance and only our enchantment by the spell of the possible, our endless optimism, has led us to assume that it ever really ended. Instead, it would seem that while the military phase of that war ended in 1865, there actually occurred a reversal of Clausewitz's famous formula through which the Civil War -- upper case; continued on as civil war, -- lower case, and in which that war of arms was replaced by a war of politics, racial and ethnic violence, ritual sacrifice based on race and color, and by economic and judicial repression.

Our general awareness of this **metamorphosis** [n. 变质; 变形; [生、医] 变态] of that ongoing conflict was obscured for all but its victims by the burgeoning growth our industrial capacity and technological potential -- all made possible by the defeat of a rival slavery-based economic system. Yes, and by the assertion of that American innocence of which I spoke earlier. Yes, I know, viewed in this light that "innocence" took the basic form of a flaunting disregard for the principles upon which this nation was

他会是一个观察家,当然这不是说他会失去众所周知的行动能力。他会记住接近上帝之路是神秘莫测的,并且记住,这个世界上一切都有可能发生,正如一位已故的法国国王说过的,一个人不论如何准备,不测之事"都会令他措手不及"。

这是多么好的告诫啊!是的,这是真心实意的告诫,但是,当放在短时间的范围内来看时,这种预言却有缺陷。当然,我也可以说詹姆斯的想象力总是领先于时代。此外,虽然他对人性抱着美好的愿望,但他的经验、阶级认同和优雅的品位,都使他只能远观,而难以真正了解人性中顽强的复杂性。更重要的是,他对那些推动并决定了美国内战结果的力量,以及由此而获得解放的奴隶所具有的带来混乱与秩序的潜力并不了解,如果说那场战争的结果尚待决定的话。坦率地说,我的看法是,其结果如何仍待衡量,只是我们对可能做到的事无限向往,抱着无限的乐观,才让我们以为内战是真的结束了。相反,现在看来,虽然那场战争的军事行动早在1865年就结束了,现实却发生了改变,按照克劳塞维茨的著名公式来讲,那场内战其实没有结束,没有硝烟的战争还在继续,取而代之的是政治上的争斗、种族和族群的暴力,以种族和肤色来决定成败的习俗,以及在经济上和司法上的压迫。

我们对这种以变异形态出现的持续不断的冲突,一般都是认识不清的,除非是迅速增长的工业生产能力和技术潜力所造成的受害者,而这种工业生产能力和技术潜力,只有在打败了以奴隶制为基础的经济体系才可能出现。是的,还是要提到我前面说过的美国本真论。我知道,从这个角度而言,那种"本真"根本就不顾这个国家赖以建立的那些原则。所以,我想我的意思现在该清楚了:不管是积极的还是消极的,所有的迹象似乎都表明,我们的国家已经认识到美国经验的悲剧性质,我们历史的黑暗部分已经形成了一个多头的报应克星。但如果这一切让人听了太悲观的话,请记住,对"hybris"和太过自负的骄傲,有效的解药是讽刺,是那种发现和整理清晰思路的能力。或像爱默生所坚持的那样,要培养意识、意识、

founded. So, I think that by now my meaning is clear: All of the signs, both positive and negative, seem to indicate that the nation has been pushed toward an awareness of the tragic nature of the American experience, the dark underside of our history has taken on the form of a many-headed nemesis. But if all this seems too pessimistic, remember that the antidote to hybris, to **overweening** [adj. 自负的; 过分的] pride, is irony; that capacity to discover and systemize clear ideas. Or, as Emerson insisted, the development of consciousness, consciousness, Consciousness. **And with consciousness, a more refined conscientiousness, and most of all, that tolerance which takes the form of humor.**

Gentlemen of the Class of 1949, you have been termed fortune's darlings by no less an authority than Fortune Magazine. That alone suggests that the many forms of nemesis that threaten the nation haven't completely overwhelmed us. We admire your achievements and are well aware that many of the rectifications of past failures are the results of your willingness to deal with change.

If I have sounded pessimistic, your involvement with the complexities of American society allows you to know where to say amen and to say nay. All American society, since 1954, has undergone a profound change. Let us not be dismayed, let us not lose faith, simply because the correctives which we have set in motion, and you have set into motion, took a long time. It took strong stomachs, it took strong arms, it took our capacity for violence and for humor to get us to this point. I say this to you, as one who believes that the difficulties which we face today are indeed minor. What seems to be called for is an honest confrontation with our mistakes, as any scientist or scholar would say, and a willingness to confront the chaos, the nemesis, which is about us. After all, nemesis is but another word for peril.

Thank you!

更多的意识。**我们要有更多的意识，更完善的自觉性，以及最重要的，要有以幽默的形式表现出来的宽容。**

1949届毕业的前辈们，你们被《财富》杂志这样的权威刊物称为命运的宠儿。这本身就表明，以各种形式威胁我们国家的报应，还没有完全压倒我们。我们钦佩你们的成就，也意识到对过去许多失败进行纠正，是由于你们愿意面对变化的结果。

如果我的演讲听起来有些悲观，待你们亲身体验了美国社会的复杂性后，就会知道我对在哪里，错在哪里。自从1954年以来，整个美国社会都发生了深刻变化。让我们不要惊惶，不要失去信心，不要担心我们立志要改变的东西和你们立志要改变的东西，会耗用很长的时间。我们忍受了很多、做了很多，我们经受了暴力，我们带着幽默感才走到这一步。我对你们这样说，是因为我认为我们今天面对的困难其实很小。我们需要的，就像科学家和学者会说的那样，是要诚实地面对我们的过错，并愿意面对混乱和报应，就是说面对我们自己。毕竟，报应是危险的另一种说法。

谢谢大家！

---

1 这里指拉尔夫·沃尔多·爱默生（Ralph Waldo Emerson，1803—1882），美国思想家，诗人。

2 演讲者这里是在拿哈佛给他的邀请信上，把名字拼错成"爱默生"一事来说事。

3 亨利·詹姆斯（Henry James，1843—1916），从英国移民到美国的作家。他擅长小说，也写过许多文学评论和传记。

4 指美国总统肯尼迪、他的弟弟肯尼迪参议员和美国黑人领袖马丁·路德·金皆被刺杀的事件。

5 这里指继任肯尼迪的美国总统林登·约翰逊，他来自得克萨斯州。

阿奇博尔德·考克斯（1912—2004）

考克斯出生于美国新泽西州，他的舅舅麦克斯维尔·柏金斯（也毕业于哈佛大学），是美国出版史上的一位传奇人物，许多后来成就斐然的著名作家如海明威、托马斯·伍尔夫、斯考特·菲兹杰罗等都是由柏金斯发现并提携的。

1937年，考克斯毕业于哈佛大学法学院，获硕士学位。二战期间，他被分配到美国国防委员会，后来担任律师工作。战争结束后，考克斯回到哈佛大学任教，先后教授宪法、行政法、劳工法等课程。1955年，他入选美国人文与科学学院院士。1950年代约翰·肯尼迪担任马萨诸塞州参议员时，考克斯是肯尼迪的非正式顾问，经常为肯尼迪撰写演说文稿，并于1960年协助支持肯尼迪的总统竞选活动。1961年肯尼迪入主白宫，考克斯也成为肯尼迪的内阁成员，担任白宫首席检察官。

1965年，考克斯回到哈佛法学院继续担任法学教授，他仍然是非常受欢迎的律师和法律顾问。在1973年著名的水门事件中，考克斯担任首席特别检查官，他发现尼克松总统涉嫌非法窃听政治对手后，要求白宫交出那些录音带，尼克松以"总统行政特权"为由拒绝，提出可以交出文字记录摘要，但考克斯表示不能接受，并就此召开记者招待会。后来美国最高法院以8比0的投票结果，要求尼克松交出录音带。百般无奈的尼克松被迫宣布辞职，从而成为美国历史上首位辞职的总统。考克斯在这篇演讲中多次提到此事。

考克斯还撰写了许多法律专著，其中包括《法律与劳工政策》《民权、宪法与法院》《美国政府中的最高法院》《表达自由》，最后一本为《法院与宪法》。

1975

Watergate and the Balance of Power
水门事件与权力制约

Archibald Cox 阿奇博尔德·考克斯

Dear friends, and especially today's graduates:

It would be pleasant to stand on the eve of the Bicentennial comfortably assured of the continued success of the great American adventure in self-government. But there is no assurance now, as indeed there was none then. The war and collapse of U.S. policy in Indo-China, the practice and tendencies revealed by the disclosures labeled Watergate, the divisiveness and drift throughout the Nation have shaken self-confidence and even produced cynicism, despair and distrust. Was the vision of our fore-fathers a bubble destined sooner or later to burst? When they came later to form a government, were there basic defects in the structure which now stand revealed because the fissures widened and deepened under stress?

In my view Watergate provided more evidence of strength in the American system of government than of defects. The wrongs disclosed by Watergate and the agonies of Viet Nam were produced not by defects in the constitutional plan but by departures from it. The adventure will go forward if we have the will-- silly if we have the will for in Sir Thomas More's oft quoted words, "We may not look at our pleasure to go to heaven in featherbeds."

Let me begin by ticking off some of the things revealed by Watergate:

It proved that high public officials can abuse their trust, but it may also be worth noting that with one exception they were not politicians but outsiders playing at politics who were silly enough to credit the **canard** [n. 谣言；误传] that in politics you must surrender your principles.

Given the wrongdoing, our political institutions worked.

There was no cover-up of the abuses of offices or of the widespread illegalities in the conduct of electoral campaigns--partly because of the freedom of the press guaranteed by the First Amendment; partly because the separation of powers provides an independent Congress with oversight over the Executive Branch; and partly because there were men of honor, even within the Administration, who insisted that the truth be uncovered and any wrongs dealt with according to due process of law.

The machinery of justice proved adequate to the vigorous, thorough, but fair investigation and prosecution of charges of pervasive abuse of power in the highest official circles---no mean accomplishment. Except for the pardon of former President Nixon and inescapable room for argument over sentencing, the country learned that powerful political figures receive no favored treatment under law.

朋友们，特别是今天毕业的同学们：

在即将迎来美国 200 周年 [1] 国庆的前夕，如果我们对美国在实行自治方面获得长久的成功而信心百倍，这将是很愉快的事。但可惜现在我们没有这种保证，过去也没有。美国在印度支那的战争和政策的崩溃、水门事件的发生，以及人们对此作出的不同解释，该事件在全国各地造成的分裂和震荡，动摇了我们的信心，甚至让人产生愤世嫉俗、绝望和失去信任的情绪。我们先辈的梦想，注定要像泡沫一样破灭吗？当他们后来构建政府的时候，政府的结构形式有什么根本的缺陷，导致它一遇到压力，裂痕就会加宽加深？

在我看来，水门事件更多地证明了美国政府体制的长处，而不是缺陷。水门事件所暴露出来的问题和越南战争带来的痛苦，不是由于我们宪法的设计有错，而是因为我们偏离了它。假如我们有这种意志，这个探索就将继续下去，正如被经常引用的托马斯·莫尔爵士的那段话："哪怕能躺在羽绒床垫上，我们都不想去天堂享受快乐。"

首先让我谈谈水门事件揭露出来的一些事情。

水门事件表明高级公职人员会滥用人们对他们的信任，但也有一点值得注意，除了一个人以外，涉案人员并不是政界人士，而是玩弄政治的外行，他们愚蠢地相信了这样的谣传，即如果想从事政治，就必须放弃自己的原则。

当不法行为发生时，我们的政治机构发挥了应有的作用。

滥用权力，还有在竞选活动中广泛存在的非法行为，都被一一揭露出来，这一部分归功于我们宪法的"第一修正案"，保证了新闻自由；另一部分原因是我们独立的国会能够监督行政部门，使权力不至于太集中；还有一部分原因是我们有正义之人，哪怕在政府机构里，他们坚持把事实搞清楚，并根据适当的法律程序处理问题。

我们的司法机构证明，它能够有效、彻底并公平地对最高权力圈子里普遍存在的滥用权力的行为进行调查和起诉，这可不是简单的事情。除了对前总统尼克松进行赦免和对其他人的量刑有不可避免的争论之外，我们的国民了解到，再有权势的政治人物，在法律面前也和其他人一样。

Even the largely untried, formless mixture of politics and quasi-judicial inquiry called impeachment seemed to work pretty well in the end, so far as there was need to pursue it. In the House Judiciary Committee we saw the strength of self-government at work -- citizens chosen by ordinary men and women wrestling, each after his own fashion, with a novel and awesome responsibility. It is sometimes said that the process took too long. The delay protracted the agony and caused neglect of substantive issues, but it also served the extraordinary purpose of enabling an entire people to sit in judgment upon its highest political leaders, to deliberate upon the proper standards of conduct in public office and not merely to upon innocence or guilt. Being convinced of the authenticity of this exercise in self-government, I am also persuaded that its value far outweighed the costs.

Watergate reinforced the constitutional tradition protects liberty by subjecting all government officials to constitutional restraints end other legal obligations as interpreted by an independent judiciary. The rule had never been applied to a President personally. Jurists from other countries find it shocking that a judicial order should be directed to a Chief of State. There was also doubt whether, if a President proved **obdurate** [adj. 固执的; 冷酷的], a judicial ruling could be enforced. But when the claim of personal immunity was asserted on behalf of President Nixon, the courts did not hesitate to extend the traditional principle. When he announced the intent to disobey the first court order to turn over Watergate Tapes, a firestone of opinion compelled obedience. The people demonstrated their determination--and their moral and political power--to require the highest officials to meet their obligations under law.

Watergate proved the conscience of America. That wrongs were committed in a world characterized by human propensity [n. 倾向; 习性] **for evil seems less significant than that they demonstrated that Americans still have the moral sense and idealism associated with their past.**

The most serious worries raised by Watergate or Vietnam concerning the political system focus about the Presidency and the relationship between the Executive and Legislative Branches.

For 40 years the size and power of the Executive Branch have been increasing at an extraordinary rate. The growth results chiefly from the revolutionary decision, made during the 1930's, to use government to meet the social and economic problems of industrial and urban society. Putting broad aspirations into concrete government

虽然对总统进行弹劾在很大程度上从未有人尝试过，但最后看来，这种出于政治和带有司法性质的调查，只要有必要去做，结果还算不错。在众议院的司法委员会，我们看到公民自治的力量。由普通民众选出的公民，带着全新的重大责任，用自己的方式来做判断。有些人说这个过程花的时间太长，该委员会对水门事件的判决拖了太长时间，让人们等得心焦，并使很多实质性问题被忽视了。但它也起到了不同寻常的作用，那就是使人们能够评判最高政治领导人。对公职人员来说，评判他们作为的标准不只是有罪或无罪，还应该有适当的行为准则。我对这种公民自治的做法深以为然，也相信它的价值远远超过了它的成本。

水门事件令所有政府官员必须受到由独立的司法机构来执行的宪法限制，并承担其他法律义务，从而加强了受到宪政传统保护的自由。该规则过去还从来没有用到过一个总统身上。其他国家的法学家会发现，美国的司法命令竟然直接指向国家元首，这令他们震惊。也有人怀疑说，如果一个总统顽固抵抗的话，司法裁决如何能够执行？但当尼克松总统的代表要求给总统个人豁免时，法院毫不犹豫地运用了传统的原则。当尼克松宣布他不愿意按照法院的第一个命令交出水门事件的录音带时，群众奋起的呼声使他不得不服从。人们表明了决心以及他们在道德上和政治上的力量，他们要求最高官员也要依法办事。

水门事件证明了美国的良心。在这样一个人们容易滑向邪恶的世界上，美国人民仍然持有道德感和理想主义的优良传统，相形之下，有人犯错这件事本身反而没那么重要了。

水门事件或越南战争，给我们在政府机制方面带来的最严重忧虑，是有关总统以及行政和立法部门之间的关系。

过去40年来，行政部门的规模和权力都以惊人的速度增加。这主要是由于在1930年代时，人们想用政府管理的方式来应对工业化与城市化所面临的社会和经济问题。把宏大的愿望变成政府的具体方案，需要无数部门配合，提供数据和技能，而国会做不了这些，只有行政机构才能去做。

美国在国际事务中起到的领导作用，让美国总统成了令世界瞩目的

programs requires masses of fact and skills from numerous disciplines which Congress lacks and only an Executive bureaucracy can provide.

The United States' assumption of a leading role in world affairs built up the Presidency by focusing world attention upon the President. The Constitution, combined with necessity, gives the President greater personal authority in foreign affairs than domestic matters. A succession of Presidents pushed these powers to, and sometimes beyond, their limits. The personal manner in which they conducted international relations doubtless influenced their style in domestic affairs.

Radio and television give a President unique ability to focus attention upon his acts and words, and thus to choose the subjects and frame the terms of political debate. Neither Senator nor Congressman, nor all Senators and Congressmen together, can approach this source of presidential power.

By the 1960's Presidents were exercising law-making power with little or no Congressional authority, on a scale unthinkable 30 years earlier. Often the pressures were great and the results commendable, even though in retrospect one has doubts about the method. President Kennedy, for example, issued an executive order prohibiting racial discrimination in housing affected by federal loans or guarantees at a time when Congress would have rejected such legislation. President Johnson regulated large segments of industry by executive orders prohibiting discrimination among employees on grounds of race, sex or age by government contractors. In some cases even the results seem questionable. Presidents Johnson and Nixon asserted the inherent executive power to conduct electronic "bugging" and other secret domestic intelligence operations without specific statutory authority or even general congressional authorization. President Nixon asserted an executive right to seek judicial aid to suppress publication of the Pentagon Papers, again without even a vague legislative foundation. Presidents Johnson and Nixon asserted the constitutional right to carry on large-scale military operations in Indo-China without a declaration of war or any other clear-cut authorization from the Congress.

The growth of Presidential power has usually been a matter of concern to Congress, partly because of political rivalry, partly from a growing sense of frustration, but also because of fear of the threat to self-government and individual liberty inherent in executive aggrandizement. Even President Eisenhower had sharp tussles with Congress over claims of executive privilege. Watergate was a major engagement

总统。美国的宪法加上现实的需要，赋予了总统在外交事务上比在国内事务上更大的权力。一任接一任的总统，把这些权力推到了极限，有时甚至越过了界限。每个人处理国际关系的方式，无疑影响了他们处理国内事务的风格。

电视和电台的传播，使总统具有一种独特的能力，让人们关注他的行为和言语，从而让他能够选择想要谈的话题，并给政治辩论定调。任何一位参议员或众议员，甚至所有的参议员和众议员加在一块，都比不上总统的这种特权。

到了 1960 年代，美国总统很少经过国会授权，有时根本不用寻求授权，就去行使立法权，这些事在那之前的 30 年是不可想象的。总统们这样做，是因为当时压力很大，而且取得的结果令人称道。哪怕在事后看来，人们对具体的办事方法会有所保留。例如，肯尼迪总统在国会肯定拒绝这项立法的时候，就直接发布行政命令：禁止在提供联邦住房贷款或担保时，有种族歧视行为。约翰逊总统则通过行政命令，禁止政府承包商在种族、性别或年龄等方面歧视员工，从而影响了大部分行业。

某些情况下，甚至这样做的结果本身都让人怀疑。约翰逊总统和尼克松总统在没有具体的法规许可，也没有得到国会授权，就利用行政权力进行电子"窃听"，以及在国内进行其他秘密情报搜集活动。尼克松总统利用行政职权寻求司法援助，来限制"五角大楼内部文件"[2]的出版，这在法律上都是说不通的。同样，在没有宣战或取得国会任何明确授权的情况下，约翰逊总统和尼克松总统就越权在印度支那展开了大规模的军事行动。

总统权力的增长，是国会一直关注的一个问题，部分原因是两者在政治上存在竞争，另一部分原因是国会有越来越多的挫败感。还有，国会担心如果总统权力太强，领袖自我膨胀，而不可避免地会威胁到人民自治和个人自由。就连艾森豪威尔总统都与国会就总统有什么样的行政特权，产生过尖锐的冲突。水门事件是这种长期角力中的一场重要战役，立法部门这次取得了胜利，是由于行政部门犯下了太多过错。这次立法部门的胜利扩大到外交政策层面，是因为国民不认同总统在越南问题上

in the long war in which temporary victory went to the Legislative Branch because of pervasive wrongdoing within the Executive Offices. The Legislative victory was the more complete and extended to foreign policy because of the country's **repudiation** [n. 拒绝；否认] of presidential involvement in Viet Nam. For the moment the balance of power has shifted violently toward Congress.

In my view it is quite wrong to draw from these events a general, vaguely worded conclusion that the power of the President should be lessened. The practice of committing the country to major policies by executive action without the effective participation of the people or their representatives may not--indeed, should not -- survive; but I do not expect our Presidents to lose the power of strong leadership nor would I wish them to cease to exercise it. The forces that I mentioned will continue to operate. The times require novel policies, energetic programs and a voice capable of restating our common aspirations and restoring our self-confidence. These are tasks which the Chief Executive can perform much better than Congress.

For a legislative body to initiate and formulate policies and programs successfully, if at all possible, requires a degree of party discipline and cohesiveness which is unthinkable without Presidential leadership in a country as large and comprising as many diverse local interests as the United States.

I use the word "leadership" advisedly. For the adventure in self-government to go forward we need Presidents and Presidential aides who identify themselves with the people, cherish and consider them as the most honest and safe, and therefore admit them to, and share with them, the making of decisions. For the President to lead in common adventure is one thing; to command is another. To help a people make its own decisions, to persuade yet trust their judgment, is the essence of the self-government bequeathed to us; to say, "leave it to me," even to do for the people what is best for them, is to embrace the form of government rejected in 1776.

At worst, the shift leads to secrecy, manipulation, lies and cheating. At best, it erodes the sense of sharing the mutual trust which holds a free society together. Trust in government is not to be had for the asking. It begins with trust which those who govern repose [v. 休息；将（信赖等）寄托于] **in the people.**

A bit of history may clarify the difference. For 40 years nearly all our Presidents have been strong Chief Executives, but there were marked and decisively important differences in the degree of their dedication to the ideals of 1776. Franklin Roosevelt,

的干涉政策。目前的权力平衡已向国会大幅度倾斜。

在我看来，如果仅从这些事件中得出一个措辞含糊的结论，说总统的权力应当缩小，这是非常错误的。没有人民或者他们的代表的有效参与，就由总统的行政命令来实行国家的重大政策，这种做法不能，实际上也不应该存在。但是我不希望我们的总统失去实行强有力的领导的权力，也不希望他们从此就不再使用这种权力。我提到过的这些力量将继续产生效力。我们的时代需要有新的政策、充满活力的项目和能够重振我们的共同愿望，以及恢复我们自信的那种声音，这些任务，总统会比国会做得更好。

光靠立法机构发起和制定政策方案，先不说是否成功，就算可能的话，也需要一定的党派规则和凝聚力，而在这么大、有这么多不同地方利益的美国，如果没有总统的领导，真是不可想象的事！

我是特意使用"领导"这个词的。要想让我们在自治的探索历程中前进，就需要有把自己当做人民的一员、把人民当做最诚实和可靠的人，并由此让人民参与和分享决策的总统及其助手。因为总统在我们的共同探索中，起到带头作用是一回事，发号施令却是另一回事。帮助人们作出自己的决定，去说服他们，但同时也相信他们的判断能力，这是我们所继承的自治传统。不能只说"让我来做吧"，哪怕是为人民做了最好的事，也是想倒退到我们在 1776 年就摈弃了的那种政府形式。

在最坏的情况下，这种做法会导致暗箱操作，人为操纵，说谎欺骗；在最好的情况下，它也会侵蚀一个自由社会凝聚在一起的彼此信任。对政府的信任，不是你想要就会有的，它首先要求那些领导者建立诚信。

简单回顾一下历史就可以看出区别。过去 40 年来，几乎所有的总统都是很强有力的执行领导，但在奉行我们 1776 年的立国思想方面，他们有着明显而重要的差别。富兰克林·罗斯福深刻领会我们独立革命的历史，信任人民，也受到人民的特别信任。因为他理解并正视人民面对的问题，他恢复了我们国家的自信，重新阐明了我们在当下的愿望，并激起我们往最好处努力。塞缪尔·莫里森记载了一位农村妇女对罗斯福第一次总统就职演说的反应："我们觉得他把国家还给了人民。"约翰逊总统

steeped in our revolutionary history, gave the people trust and received trust from them in a unique degree. Because he understood and faced up squarely to the problems of the people, he was also able to restore the nation's self-confidence, to restate its aspirations in contemporary conditions and to evoke its highest efforts. Remember Samuel Morison's account of the farm woman who said of Roosevelt's first inaugural address, "We felt that he had given the country back to the people." President Johnson never succeeded in convincing the public of his faith in self-government; his years in the Senate bred a manipulative style that concealed what may well have been his true philosophy. At the end of one of the briefs filed in the litigation over the Watergate Tapes in support of the claim of executive privilege, President Nixon's attorneys wrote:

*The right of Presidential confidentiality is not a mystical **prerogative*** [n. 特权; 显著的优点]. *It is, rather, the raw essence of the Presidential process, the institutionalized recognition of the crucial role played by human personality in the negotiation, manipulation and disposition of human affairs.*

It seems to me now, as it did during the litigation, that the plea for power to engage in Presidential manipulation revealed the fatal flaw. The growing concentration of power in the White House had led its occupants to forget that the people must be trusted not only to elect officials but to make with them the big decisions. The fundamental mistake then joined with an increasing passion for secrecy to produce the self-defeating view that it is the function of the President, not to join in the great adventure of self-government, but to circumvent or fight the Congress, and to manipulate the people. American involvement in Viet Nam --whatever the wisdom or folly of the substantive policy --epitomized the fault from the beginning because it attempted to commit the Nation upon questions even of life and death without ever putting the issue fairly before either the people or their representatives. The source of recent tensions between the Executive and Congress, I suspect, is not opposition to strong Presidential leadership nor friction resulting from the separation of powers so much as uncertainty over whether the philosophy of manipulation -- of secrecy, circumvention and "leave it to me" -- has been supplanted by true Executive willingness to govern with the Congress and the people.

The defect is chiefly one of attitude, but political philosophy and political

从来就没有成功地说服过公众，让人们相信他对人民自治的信念。他通过在参议院的多年经历，练成了很能隐藏自己真实思想的政客手腕。在就水门事件录音带诉讼案提出的辩护状中，为支持行政部门享有一定特权的论点，尼克松总统的律师们写道：

> 总统有权保密，并不是什么神秘的特权。相反，这只是行使总统职责过程中基本的要素，是为制度所认可的，是对在处理事务的一系列商谈、操控当中，总统所起关键作用的承认。

在我现在看来，就像在（对水门事件的）诉讼期间我感觉的一样，这种让总统有权进行操控的请求表现出致命的缺陷。白宫的权力越来越大，让领导者全然忘记了，不仅选举官员，而且在让人民参与重大决定方面，都必须要相信人民。其根本的错误在于涉事人员越来越多地热衷于暗箱操作，他们弄巧成拙地认为这就是总统的职能，不是去参与人民自治的伟大探索，而是绕过国会，或与国会争斗，并操控人民。

美国介入越南这件事——无论这项政策在实质上是聪明的还是愚蠢的——从一开始就漏洞百出，因为它在涉及生死攸关的问题上，甚至没有把这个问题公正让人民或他们的代表进行讨论。我认为，行政部门和国会之间最近出现的紧张关系，不是人们认为总统太强势，也不是因为权力分立而带来的摩擦，而是因为人们担心，行政部门是否把操控的手法——那些暗箱操作、规避制约和"都让我来吧"的想法——替代了真正同国会与人民一起施政的意愿。

这里主要是态度问题，但政治哲学和政治结构是一种共生关系。其结构缺陷体现在总统办公室职能的强化，特别是这种强化导致其他制度化部门和机构的弱化。在最近几任总统领导下，白宫工作人员的数量快速增长，权力不断加大。出任白宫预算和管理办公室主任这类职位，权力很大，但政治地位并不显赫，也不需要经过国会批准，即可声称豁免而不需要去国会专门委员会听证，而国会专门委员会则是国会实行监督的主要手段。艾森豪威尔总统和尼克松总统基于行政特权，以前所未有

structure have a symbiotic relation. The structural fault is the **aggrandizement** [n. 增大；扩大；强化] of the Presidential establishment, especially at the expense of the institutionalized departments and agencies. Under recent presidents the White House staff grew rapidly in size and power. Increasing control passed to men like the Director of the Office of Budget and Management who lack political status, who are not subject to senatorial confirmation, and who claim immunity from testifying before the congressional committees which are the principal means of congressional oversight. Presidents Eisenhower and Nixon advanced claims to secrecy, based upon executive privilege, with unprecedented frequency and for novel reasons. Presidential aides under President Nixon began to expect and obtain unquestioning obedience even from Cabinet members denied access to the President.

At first glance the growth seems natural enough. It began with need to extend the President's eyes and ears. It spread in the effort to rationalize and energize an increasingly unwieldly bureaucracy; and still later, in the belief that a presidential establishment was needed to overcome the hostility of established departments with vested attitudes and interests. But other means dealing with departments and agencies are available and the cost of this means is excessive. The power of Presidential aides is like that of royal courtiers. They are responsive, and responsible, to only one man. Unlike many Cabinet officers and agency heads, White House aides usually have no independent source of support, no constituency or other group whose response, being of concern to them, limits their behavior. Unlike Cabinet officers and agency heads, they are subject to almost none of the checks of regularized procedure, of speaking for an organization, and of having to respond to it. If the President exposes himself, directly and often, to all the ideas and pressures which can be brought to bear by other centers of power and responsibility, then his aides may be a useful way of extending the President's eyes and ears. But if the President's own style is monarchical or if the Palace Guard succeeds in isolating the President because of excessive protectiveness towards him or concern for their own influence, then the power of White House aides breeds an obsessive concern for secrecy and an arrogant sense not only that the King but that they, can do no wrong.

George Reedy, a long-time friend and press secretary, drew a chilling picture of these tendencies as he observed them in President Johnson's White House. The tendencies intensified under President Nixon. We have from Jeb Magruder

的频率和新的理由,经常要求保密。尼克松总统的幕僚甚至居中传话,让那些没有机会接近总统的内阁成员,对总统助手也要无条件服从。

乍看之下,总统权力的增长似乎相当自然。它始于加强总统的耳目(视听能力)之需。后来因为官僚机构越来越难以操控,需要使那些机构合理化和效率化,而这就需要总统更为有权。再后来,人们认为只有从总统的角度来协调,才能克服不同部门之间因为既得利益和固有态度而造成的敌意。虽然有其他手段可以处理部门和机构之间的问题,但这样做成本过高。总统的幕僚们就像皇宫里的朝臣一样,他们只听一人的话,也只对一人负责。和很多内阁官员及机构负责人不同,白宫幕僚通常没有独立的支持力量,也没有任何选民区或其他组织能让他们关心这些方面的反应,从而限制他们的行为。与内阁官员以及各机构负责人不同,他们几乎不必受到规范化程序的审查,不需要为某个组织代言,从而必须对那个组织的需求做出反应。

在这种情况下,如果总统能够经常亲自接触所有的思想及其他权力中心和职能部门带来的需求,那么他的幕僚们可能起到扩大总统耳目功能的作用。但如果总统自己的领导风格是君主式的,或如果这类"皇宫护卫者"出于对总统的过度保护,或想维护他们自己的影响力,而将总统与外界隔离开来,那么白宫幕僚就会特别重视保守秘密,并产生一种傲慢感,以为不仅国王本身,就是他们自己,也不会做错任何事情。

白宫新闻秘书乔治·里迪是我一位多年的朋友,他描述自己在约翰逊总统任内所观察到的情况使人寒心。这些趋势在尼克松总统执政时期更加强了。杰布·马格鲁德承认,尼克松总统执政团队的核心成员认为,只要达到目的,做任何事情都不应该被认为是错的。罗伯特·海德曼的电视采访让全世界看到,白宫弄臣们不仅在遵守道德方面近乎麻木,而且近乎偏执地把国会和其他外人当做对抗的敌人,有可能的话,还要将之摧毁。

如果这些说法是准确的,我们可能必须对两个机构做出改变,以光大我们开国者的思想。

一个办法是缩小白宫工作人员的人数并削减他们的权力,指定有自

the acknowledgment that those close to the center of the Nixon Administration came to believe that nothing done in pursuit of their objectives could ever be found wrong. Robert Haideman's television interview displayed before all the world not only chilling moral insensibility but the almost-paranoid sense of the White House courtiers that Congress and all other outsiders are enemies to be fought and destroyed if possible.

If these impressions are right, two institutional charges might help to restore the Founders' philosophy.

One step would be to reduce the size and power of the White House staff, to appoint stronger public figures with their own sources of political support to head the Executive Departments, and to make substantial use of them as a Cabinet to the members of which the President would owe and who would owe each other a duty of candid consultation. In theory, Congress can limit the size of the White House staff by curtailing appropriation; it can require senatorial confirmation for men named to positions of authority; and it can put an end to the practice of giving more and more power to formulate executive policy to men and woman who claim immunity from testifying before congressional committees. Practically speaking, only the President-- a succession of individual Presidents --can determine the pattern for the organization and style of the Administration. They may find it easier to work with courtiers and manipulate levers of power without consulting strong, independent individuals and established agencies, but perhaps they too will read recent history and conclude that the solid accomplishment is likely to be less, just as the danger to liberty is greater.

Second, we should deal with executive privilege. John Dickinson advised the Pennsylvania Ratification Convention: "The executive is better to be trusted when it has no screen." Executive confidentiality is too often too important to give every congressional committee power to compel information from the President, but surely a statute should be enacted laying upon him a legally enforceable duty to provide whatever either the Senate or House of Representatives requires upon a vote taken after full debate upon the particular instance.

Given even a perfect structure, the adventure in self-rule cannot succeed without a basic confidence in government and mutual trust among people. Without confidence in the enterprise the spirit of toleration and cooperation vanishes, and warring factions press to achieve their goals not through general progress but by

己政治基础的较强的公众人物来执掌行政部门，并且把他们当做总统要经常进行坦率咨询的内阁成员。从理论上说，国会可以通过削减拨款来限制白宫工作人员规模的大小，可以要求总统任命重要岗位时必须经过参议院确认，它也可以不让那些豁免到国会专门委员会作证的人有越来越大的制定行政政策的权力。

实际上，只有总统——不同任期的总统——才可以确定他们执政当局的组织模式和风格。他们可能会觉得通过朝臣和操纵手中的权力，办起事来会更得心应手，而不需要与独立的个人和现有的机构进行协商。但他们从最近的历史中也应该得出这样的结论：如果那样做的话，取得稳固成就的可能就会减少，而自由面对的危险会加大。

其次，我们应该修正行政特权。约翰·狄金森在《批准宾夕法尼亚公约》中建议："官员在没有掩盖时才值得信赖。"行政上要有保密，这往往是很重要的，不能让每一个国会委员会都有权力强迫总统公开信息。但在某一个特定事例上，参议院或众议院代表在经过充分辩论后，如果表决同意，就应该在法律上有办法要求总统提供必要的信息。

即使有了一个完美的结构，如果人民对于政府以及人与人之间没有基本的互信，人民自治的探索就不可能成功。如果对这项事业没有信心，宽容与合作的精神就会消失，不同派别就会相互敌对，不再是共谋发展，而是靠占取他人的便宜来实现一己之利。

有位高中学生这样写道："水门事件让人们无法相信任何公众人物，它让我们远离社会体系。"从狭隘的意义上来解释这个问题，人们可以说，在公共生活中还有人在维持着我们的体系，比如艾略特·理查德森、山姆·欧文、彼得·罗迪诺和约翰·杜尔等，这些人坚持着基本的理想主义和美国人民的品德。此外，用政客来做替罪羊是没有用的，因为你我这样的人可以造就和毁掉政客。他们和我们自己比起来，既不算好，也不能说坏。但这种狭义的回答是不够的。早在水门事件被揭露前，人们对政治程序就有了越来越多的怀疑，对政治家玩世不恭的态度，个人的作为于事无补，这些迹象都表明了人们普遍感受到的嘲讽、怀疑和绝望的体验。

taking away from others.

A high school student writes: "Watergate makes it impossible to trust anyone in public life; it turned us from the system." Taking his point narrowly, one might reply that it was other men in public life--the Elliot Richardson, Sam Erving, Peter Rodinos and John Doars--who made the system work; that the upshot revealed the basic idealism and morality of the American people' and further it is no good using the politicians as scapegoats, for you and I make and unmake the politicians, and they are neither better nor worse than ourselves. But the narrow answer is not enough. Long before Watergate there were growing doubts about the political process, cynicism toward politicians, a sense of individual helplessness, and other signs of a long slide into general cynicism, distrust and despair.

In some ways it is harder than it sometimes was to have faith in the common adventure.

Confidence cannot be built by those who find the "essence of the Presidential process" in "manipulation"; nor by Administrations which lie and snoop [vi. 窥探；打听] **or conceal their acts in the name of security, whether it is Democrat or Republican. By eroding our trust in each other they do more harm than any enemy, foreign or domestic. Nor can trust be gained by the politics of image. No consumer supposes that he and the advertising agencies are engaged in a joint adventure.**

Even without these faults confidence in our politics would come harder. For one thing, we ask much more of government.

Society is bigger and infinitely more complex. We yearn for simplicity, but the complexity yields gains against three of the four horsemen of the Apocalypse, ignorance, poverty and disease, not likely to be traded for a nostalgic illusion.

We have assigned a new and larger role to the political system. It was never the human lot that every man or woman may have at once all he or she desires, even though what each desires may, viewed by itself, be wholly commendable. Once the inescapable adjustments were left largely to individual **prowess** [n. 英勇；非凡的能力], to the vagaries of nature, and to supposedly impersonal economic forces. Now, because of the revolutionary decision taken in the 1930's, very many more of the adjustments are mediated through government. Government has become the forum in which men and women, business corporations and other organized groups contend for their own interests with all the selfishness and ambition, and sometimes the ruthlessness

从某些方面来说，想要激发人们对我们共同事业的信心，现在要比过去困难。

如果有人认为，"总统行使职责的要素"是要靠"操控"，或者政府（无论是民主党还是共和党的政府）以安全为名，做出欺骗、窥探或掩盖自己行为这样一些事，人们是不可能有信心的。这种行为侵蚀我们彼此的信任，比任何敌人都更加伤害我们，无论那些敌人来自国内或国外。通过塑造形象等政治手法，也不可能赢得人们的信任。没有任何一个消费者认为，他会和广告商站在同一条战线上。

即使没有这些问题，想让人们对政治有信心都会很难，因为人们对政府的要求比过去更高了。

社会变得比过去更大，也更复杂。我们渴望简单，但社会需要有这种复杂性，来对付《启示录》里提到的四个骑手，其中的三个分别是无知、贫困和疾病。社会也不可能为了怀旧幻想而放弃复杂性。

我们赋予政治制度一个新的和更大的作用。人类的命运就是这样，一个人的所有欲望从来不会同时得到满足，哪怕单个欲望可能是非常值得追求的。对不同欲望做出不可避免的调整，主要是靠个人实力，靠变幻莫测的大自然和所谓的客观经济规律。

现在，由于我们在 1930 年代做出的那些革命性决定，越来越多的调整是通过政府的调控来完成的。政府已成为一种论坛，各色男女、商业企业和其他组织团体，出于自己利益的私心和野心，有时甚至可以说是残酷和欺骗，在此争论，就像在市场上的尔虞我诈一样。政客的输赢，取决于他们是否能够满足那些有优势力量的人，弱者有时对他们是否能拥有信任而信心不足。

你能把权力转移回来吗？人们在政治论坛上，是否会比在市场里表现得更高尚、更诚实，不那么贪得无厌？对我来说，我并不指望看到这种事情发生，我对不受管制的经济力量是不抱希望的，就像联邦对武力实行垄断前，武装团伙可以无法无天一样。我倒是觉

and deceit, that once characterized the market. Politicians win or lose according to their ability to satisfy those with **preponderant** [adj. 占优势的; 压倒性的] power. The weak are sometimes faithless to the trust reposed in them.

Would you transfer the power back? Would men be nobler, more honest, or less **avaricious** [adj. 贪财的; 贪婪的] in the markets than in political forums? For my part I have no expectation of seeing the millennium either way, but having no greater trust in unregulated economic power than in the armed bands which dominated society before the State achieved its monopoly of force, I can see some gain in putting the contest in a forum which is relatively open to public scrutiny, where voices, somewhat less interested and charged with the general view may exercise some influence, and where every now and then something lifts the public spirit to meet a great occasion.

Confidence also comes harder today than a generation ago because time has destroyed some illusions. The quick conquest of a continent, the industrial and technological revolutions, and our might in two wars bred a folk lore of endless resources and easy success. Now we know that our power is limited. We have lost our innocence and learned our capacity for evil, witness the conspiracies to conduct foreign policy by assassination and the discrepancy that still exists between our pretenses and our practices in the treatment of blacks, chicanos and native Americans. It takes honesty and courage to face these facts; and we should not shrink from them.

Our mistake is to suppose that we are the first to face these perceptions. Our danger is that we become obsessed by human failings, lose perspective, and forget the true nature of the enterprise bequeathed to us. Contemporary literature and the arts tell of man the absurd, the **pervert** [n. 变态; 色狼], and the drop-out, but rarely of man the hero or even the tragic, for the tragic requires a degree of nobility and it is the fashion to forget Prometheus' reach and see only the chains.

But we are not the first. The Founders had no illusions about human weakness. Their experience showed them government's power of evil. They did not use Pogo's words "We have met the enemy and he is us,' but their religion taught them the same truth in the language of original sin. They faced both, yet they also had the insight to perceive the nobler potential of man and the courage to commit themselves to the shared pursuit of that vision. They believed, and ask us to believe, that man is by nature a rational and social being; that each may grow in nobility and strength through the freedom and responsibility of each to choose the best he can discern and further, that

得，应当让各种势力在有公众监督的论坛里自由辩论，让不带有偏见、且代表公众观点的声音发挥一些影响力，而且偶尔在某个精彩时刻提升一下公众的精神。

我们现在也比前一代人难有信心，因为时间已经摧毁了一些幻想。我们快速征服北美大陆，工业革命和技术革命成就喜人，我们赢得了两次世界大战，这些都造就了资源丰富和容易成功的传说。现在我们知道，我们的力量是有限的。我们失去了曾经的纯真，发现自己也有作恶的能力，见证了通过暗杀来实行我们的外交政策，并在对待黑人、墨西哥裔美国人和土著美国人方面言行不一。我们应该诚实并勇敢地面对这些事实，不要回避这些问题。

我们总以为自己是最先碰到这些情况的人，这是我们的错误所在。我们的危险在于过多地纠缠于他人的过失，失去了方向感，从而忘记了我们事业的真正性质。当代文学和艺术只展示人的荒谬、变态和半途而废，却很少表现作为英雄或悲剧的人物，因为悲剧其实显示着一种崇高，而眼下的时尚是忘记普罗米修斯[3]的奋斗，只看到他被缚了锁链。

但我们并非这样的人，我们的建国者对人性的弱点就不抱幻想。经验告诉他们，政府是有可能作恶的。他们并不套用俗话，说"我们遇到的敌人，其实就是我们自己"，他们的宗教教给他们同样的有关原罪的道理。这两种情况他们都遇到了，但他们也有洞察力，能够感知到人能够变得更高尚些，并且勇于共同追求这个目标。他们认为，并要求我们相信，人在本质上是理性的社会化的存在。每个人都有自由和责任，能够根据自认为最好的方法去提升自身的性格和力量，而且这种信念最适合于帮助我们去做该做的事情。他们知道，我们必须共担此任，哪怕个人自由和责任的思想前提就是要有目标和意见的多样性。

共担此任，意味着甚至那些我们最强烈反对的人，也不是"敌人"，（比如尼克松的白宫所认为的敌人那样），而应该是一条船上的伙伴，任何一个人受到伤害或忽视，对其他人来说也是一种伤害。

there is an ideal fitness of things suited to this belief that we ought to do what we can to make prevail in human affairs. They knew it must be a joint adventure even though the very ideas of personal liberty and responsibility presuppose diversity of goals and opinion:

Joint in the sense that even those with whom we most bitterly disagree are not "enemies" as the Nixon White House supposed but fellow voyagers in the same boat, where the injury or neglect of any one is a wound to every other. Joint in the sense that the use of force, lying, cheating and other breaches of the ways of reason and civility which destroy our mutual trust by whomever used, cannot be justified by citing the sure righteousness of one's objectives.

Joint, too, in the sense that none can move very far toward his personal goals unless the vessel moves, and the vessel cannot move while some voyagers pull ahead, some backwater, others demand a new boat, and more and more drop out to go fishing.

Now we must ask whether this adventure is too difficult for us. Those who bequeathed it held out no assurance of the millennium, not for themselves, nor for us, nor for our children nor our children's children. They promised no ease along the way. Jefferson responded to bleak reality in 1790 by paraphrasing Sir Thomas More: "We are not to be translated…to liberty in a featherbed."

Forty-one years ago I stood in this Yard at my Commencement. Hitler's storm troopers were moving toward their zenith with brutality and oppression for all but the master race. The **scourge** [n. 灾难；祸患] of infantile paralysis still killed tens of thousands of children and doomed more to lives with crippled limbs. The minimum factory wage was not yet 25 cents an hour. There was no social security, no Medicare. Men were supposed to be independent and self-reliant, but 20 percent of the work force, one out of five, were unemployed.

During the past 40 years we have accomplished two social and political revolutions peacefully within the existing frame of government.

One was the New Deal. The practice and theory of government were revolutionized. Laissez-faire yielded to social responsibility. Industry and labor were brought under a measure of control. Industrial workers gained new opportunities and new protection. A vast transfer of economic and political power was accomplished. Some of the power has slipped back, I fear, but the transfer was nonetheless

共担此任，意味着无论谁使用武力、说谎、欺骗和其他违反理性和文明的手段，都会破坏我们的互信，不能因为相信自己目标的正确，就违规利用。

共担此任，还意味着除非我们同舟共济，否则没有人可以接近自己的目标，如果有些人向前划，有些人向后划，有些人要求换一艘新船，还有越来越多的人弃船去钓鱼了，这样的船是前进不了的。

现在我们必须要问，这项事业是否太难了？我们的前人没有这样的保证，他们自己没有，也没有给我们，甚至我们的子孙后辈提供这样的保证。他们知道路途不易。1790年杰弗逊在回答所面临的暗淡现实时，借用了托马斯·莫尔爵士的话："我们不可能舒适地躺在羽绒床垫上……就想得到自由。"

41年前，我参加我的毕业典礼时也是站在这个院子。希特勒的冲锋队正走向残暴的巅峰，他们迫害除了所谓"优等民族"以外所有的人。小儿麻痹这一灾难让成千上万的儿童致死，并使更多的人注定终生残疾。工厂的最低工资每小时还不到25美分。没有任何社会保障，也没有医疗保险。人们全靠独立与自立，但还是有百分之二十的劳动力，也就是每五人中就有一人失业。

在过去40年里，我们在现有的政府框架内，以和平的方式完成了两场社会和政治的革命。

一个是"罗斯福新政"[4]。政府的实践和理论都发生了革命性的变化。提倡社会责任取代了自由放任政策；劳资关系都被控制在一定的程度内；工人获得了新的机会和新的保障；经济和政治权力发生了巨大的转移。我担心有些权力又退回原步了，但这种权力转移真是相当巨大，而且还有很大部分仍待转移。

接下来，在各方面的协助下，我们击败了希特勒，并重建欧洲。

然后是民权革命——这是在法治范围内进行的。去年我们庆祝了"布朗诉教育委员会案"[5]20周年。在这项裁决发布后，各州法律中，基于种族的隔离制度被宣布无效，种族隔离也逐渐停止。有关"平等保护条款"的新理论得到发展。新的联邦法规得以颁布，

tremendous, and much of the transfer remains.

Next with the help of others, came the defeat of Hitler and the reconstruction of Europe.

Then came the civil rights revolution--again within the rule of law. Last year we celebrated the 20th anniversary of Brown v. Board of Education. After the decision, state laws enforcing a caste system based upon race were invalidated, and their enforcement gradually stopped. New doctrines were developed to extend the reach of the Equal Protection Clause. New federal statutes were enacted curtailing practices restricting equal voting rights, denying equal accommodations, denying equal employment opportunities, and assuring equal housing.

The application of the equal protection clause to the black people revived concern with other inequalities in our national life, especially sex discrimination.

Granted that the tasks are unfinished. Granted too that resulting bureaucracy seems remote and hard to manage. Still, I think that people can have confidence in a system that can peacefully produce two great libertarian and egalitarian revolutions within 40 years and also within a framework of constitutionalism.

If you know a better 'ole, go to it. But before you leave, remember that the greatest wrongs in history were done by those who dealt in certitudes. Look sharply, too, before you leave. You may see the vessel though almost imperceptibly move ahead; and does not the mist lift a little, revealing in dim outline a distant shore? Can the shore be won? Perhaps not ever; it is most assuredly beyond our reach. But there is always a chance to row another stroke as each age that is past surrenders to the age that is waiting before.

Thank you!

消除了限制平等选举权的做法，清除了平等待遇、平等就业机会方面的限制，并确保住房平等。

应用平等保护条款来保护黑人，这也唤醒了人们关注在我们国家生活中存在的其他不平等现象，特别是性别方面的歧视。

应该说，任务尚未完成。应该说，后来出现的官僚机构似乎很难接近、很难管理。但是我认为，在40年的时间内，能通过和平方式和在宪政框架内促成两场宏大的自由平等革命，对这样一个体系，我们可以给予信任。

如果你知道有更好的掩体，那就去吧[6]。不过，在你离开前请记住，历史上那些最大的错误是由盲目自信的人所犯下的。在你离开之前，也请仔细看看，你可能会觉得船只好像根本没有移动。迷雾难道没有散掉一些，让你看到轮廓模糊的遥远海岸，而感觉能够到达彼岸吗？或许永远也到不了。很明显，彼岸不在我们所能掌控的范围之内。但在一代接一代人的前进历程中，我们总会有机会再划上一桨。

谢谢各位！

---

1 美国于1776年7月4日宣布独立，这篇演讲发表于1975年6月，故有此说。

2 "五角大楼内部文件案"（The Pentagon Papers），是指美国《纽约时报》1971年在头版披露的一批美国国防部文件，显示美国总统约翰逊当局在越战问题上，欺骗了美国国会和公众。文章发表之前，美国政府曾试图通过法院要求报社不要发表，但法院以"第一修正案"允许新闻与言论自由的原则，而未同意美国政府的要求。这已成为一个经典案例。

3 古希腊神话中，为人类盗来火种的人。

4 "罗斯福新政"（The New Deal），是指罗斯福在1930年代为从"大衰退"中振兴经济而推出的政策，主要包括三点，即为失业和贫困者提供援助，努力把经济提升到正常水平，以及改革金融体系，防止大衰退的再次发生。

5 "布朗诉教育委员会案"（Brown v. Board of Education），1954年，美国最高法院全体作出裁决：公立学校的种族隔离违反宪法。这是美国民权史上的重要一页。

6 这个说法来自二战一张有名的漫画，画中两位士兵躲在一个掩体内，其中一个人说："如果你知道有更好的掩体，那就去吧。"（If you know a better 'ole, go to it）

亚历山大·索尔仁尼琴（1918—2008）

索尔仁尼琴出生于俄国北高加索的基斯洛沃茨克。中学毕业后，他就读于罗斯托夫大学的物理数学系。因为酷爱文学，大学期间他也在莫斯科文史哲学院函授班学习文学。

索尔仁尼琴曾应征入伍，服役期间因为在和朋友的通信中批评斯大林而被捕，经过8年劳改刑满后又被流放到哈萨克斯坦，直到1956年解除流放，恢复名誉。

在接下来的15年间，他写下了许多揭露社会阴暗面的作品，成为著名的"持不同政见者"。1970年，"因为他在追求俄罗斯文学不可或缺的传统时所具有的道义力量"，索尔仁尼琴获得该年度的诺贝尔文学奖。但是迫于形势，索尔仁尼琴没有前往瑞典领奖。1974年他被开除苏联国籍并被驱逐出境，开始了流亡西方的生涯。

上世纪80年代末期，索尔仁尼琴被允许回国，原来遭禁的一些作品陆续在国内出版。苏联解体后，索尔仁尼琴于1994年回归祖国俄罗斯。2007年，他获得了2006年度的俄罗斯人文领域最高成就奖——俄罗斯国家奖。2008年8月，89岁的索尔仁尼琴逝世于莫斯科。

这篇在哈佛毕业典礼上的演讲曾经让许多人大跌眼镜，并引起了一场争论。因为其时索尔仁尼琴正流亡西方，经济上依靠西方的支持生活。人们以为他会揭露抨击苏联的专制，没想到他出人意料，着重讲的是西方的实用主义，讽刺西方文明对世界广泛的外侵，批评西方社会对物质的过度追求等等。过去在西方人眼里，索尔仁尼琴是个与苏联当权者作斗争的伟大文学家、民主斗士，可是索尔仁尼琴也抨击所谓的民主派和自由主义者，这使他被看做是难以理解和应对的人。

1978

A World Split Apart
分裂的世界

Alexander Solzhenitsyn 亚历山大·索尔仁尼琴

I am sincerely happy to be here with you on this occasion and to become personally acquainted with this old and most prestigious University. My congratulations and very best wishes to all of today's graduates.

Harvard's motto is "Veritas." Many of you have already found out and others will find out in the course of their lives that truth eludes us if we do not concentrate with total attention on its pursuit. And even while it eludes us, the illusion still lingers of knowing it and leads to many misunderstandings. Also, truth is seldom pleasant; it is almost **invariably** [adv. 不变地，一贯地] bitter. There is some bitterness in my speech today, too. But I want to stress that it comes not from an adversary but from a friend.

Three years ago in the United States I said certain things which at that time appeared unacceptable. Today, however, many people agree with what I then said...

The split in today's world is **perceptible** [adj. 可察觉的，看得见的] even to a hasty glance. Any of our contemporaries readily identifies two world powers, each of them already capable of entirely destroying the other. However, understanding of the split often is limited to this political conception, to the illusion that danger may be abolished through successful diplomatic negotiations or by achieving a balance of armed forces. The truth is that the split is a much profounder and a more alienating one, that the rifts are more than one can see at first glance. This deep **manifold** [adj. 多种的，多方面的] split bears the danger of manifold disaster for all of us, in accordance with the ancient truth that a Kingdom -- in this case, our Earth -- divided against itself cannot stand.

Contemporary Worlds

There is the concept of the Third World: thus, we already have three worlds. Undoubtedly, however, the number is even greater; we are just too far away to see. Any ancient deeply rooted autonomous culture, especially if it is spread on a wide part of the earth's surface, constitutes an autonomous world, full of riddles and surprises to Western thinking. As a minimum, we must include in this category China, India, the Muslim world and Africa, if indeed we accept the approximation of viewing the latter two as compact units. For one thousand years Russia has belonged to such a category, although Western thinking systematically committed the mistake of denying its autonomous character and therefore never understood it, just as today the West does not understand Russia in communist captivity. It may be that in the past years Japan has increasingly become a distant part of the West, I am no judge here; but as to Israel,

在这样的场合里和你们在一起,并能亲身了解这所古老而又最负盛名的大学,我感到由衷的高兴。我要向今天所有的毕业生表示祝贺和最良好的祝愿。

哈佛大学的座右铭是"VERITAS"("真理")。你们中许多人已经发现,其他人也将在他们未来的日子里发现,假如我们不全神贯注地追求真理,真理是不会自己找上门来的。而且即使真理遥不可及,我们也时有以为自己知道真理的幻觉,这将会导致许多误解。此外,真理很少让人愉快,它几乎总是苦涩的。我今天的发言里也会有这样的苦涩。但我想强调的是,这样的苦口婆心不是来自对手,而是出于一个朋友之口。

3年前我在美国说过一些话,在当时曾被认为是不合时宜的。然而今天,许多人都认可我当时的说法……

当今世界的分裂随处可见。大家都知道当下有两个超级大国,都拥有将对方完全摧毁的能力。然而,人们对这种分裂的理解往往仅限于政治概念上,局限于幻想通过成功的外交谈判,或取得武力上的平衡就能消除危险。实际上,这个分裂比我们知道的更深,而且更加让人疏远,其裂痕比乍看之下要多得多。这种多方面的分裂给我们大家都带来了发生各种灾难的危险,因为根据那个古老道理的说法,一个王国——在这里指的是我们的地球——合则立,分则败。

当代世界

现在还有一个第三世界的概念,因此,我们有了三个世界。但是毫无疑问,还有比这更多的世界,只是我们离得太远无法看见。任何根深蒂固的、古老的、独立的文化,特别是当它广布于地球一大部分地区时,就构成一个自治的世界。这个世界,以西方思维方式来看充满未知与惊奇。从最低限度来说,可以归于这个类别中的有中国、印度、穆斯林世界和非洲,如果我们确实可以把最后两者视为紧凑的单位的话。在过去一千年里,俄罗斯也属于这样一个单独的世界,虽然西方思想一直犯了否定其自主性的错误,并因此永远无法理解它,就像今天的西方不能理解在共产主义思想下的俄罗斯。在过去的一些年里,日本可能也与西方

for instance, it seems to me that it stands apart from the Western world in that its state system is fundamentally linked to religion.

How short a time ago, relatively, the small new European world was easily seizing colonies everywhere, not only without anticipating any real resistance, but also usually despising any possible values in the conquered peoples' approach to life. On the face of it, it was an overwhelming success, there were no geographic frontiers to it. Western society expanded in a triumph of human independence and power. And all of a sudden in the twentieth century came the discovery of its fragility and **friability** [n. 脆弱, 易碎性]. We now see that the conquests proved to be short lived and precarious, and this in turn points to defects in the Western view of the world which led to these conquests. Relations with the former colonial world now have turned into their opposite and the Western world often goes to extremes of **obsequiousness** [n. 奉承, 谄媚], but it is difficult yet to estimate the total size of the bill which former colonial countries will present to the West, and it is difficult to predict whether the surrender not only of its last colonies, but of everything it owns will be sufficient for the West to foot the bill.

Convergence

But the blindness of superiority continues in spite of all and upholds the belief that vast regions everywhere on our planet should develop and mature to the level of present day Western systems which in theory are the best and in practice the most attractive. There is this belief that all those other worlds are only being temporarily prevented by wicked governments or by heavy crises or by their own barbarity or incomprehension from taking the way of Western pluralistic democracy and from adopting the Western way of life. Countries are judged on the merit of their progress in this direction. However, it is a conception which developed out of Western incomprehension of the essence of other worlds, out of the mistake of measuring them all with a Western yardstick. The real picture of our planet's development is quite different.

Anguish [n. 苦闷, 痛苦] about our divided world gave birth to the theory of convergence between leading Western countries and the Soviet Union. It is a soothing theory which overlooks the fact that these worlds are not at all developing into similarity; neither one can be transformed into the other without the use of violence. Besides, convergence inevitably means acceptance of the other side's defects, too, and this is hardly desirable.

If I were today addressing an audience in my country, examining the overall

渐行渐远，我这里无法判断，但是在我看来，以色列也独立于西方世界，因为它的国家制度与宗教紧密相关。在一段相对来说不算久远的时间以前，小小的新欧洲世界轻而易举地到处征服殖民地，不仅长驱直入没有遇到任何真正的阻力，而且通常也蔑视被征服地区的人民，不认为他们（当地人）的生活方式有任何价值。

从表面上看来，这是一个巨大的成功，这种成功不受地理疆界的限制。西方社会因为人类独立和意志的胜利而扩张。但猛然间，人们在20世纪时发现其脆弱性和易碎性。我们现在看到，西方文明对其他文明的征服被证明是短暂的和不稳定的，这反过来证明了，推动这些征服世界行为的西方观点本身就有缺陷。西方与前殖民地的关系，现在已经到了相反的地步，西方世界往往表现出极端的媚态，但现在还很难估计，那些前殖民地国家会如何与西方国家算账，不仅要放弃最后的殖民地，西方世界就算放弃它所拥有的一切，都还不知道能否足以为之买单。

融合

尽管这样，人们依然盲目相信西方文明高人一等，而且坚持着这样的信念，即我们这个星球上的所有地区，都应当发展和成熟到当今西方制度的水平，因为西方体系从理论上来说是最好的，在实践中是最有吸引力的。人们认为世界上其他地方，但凡还没有采取西方多元化的民主和接受西方的生活方式，都是由于邪恶政府的控制，或遭受沉重的危机，或由于他们自己不开化，或本身无能等暂时的原因。国家是否进步，全凭他们在这一西化方向取得的进展如何来评判。但是，这个衡量标准脱胎于西方对其他世界的不了解，它们与西方所有的错误，都是犯了用西方的标准来衡量他人的错误。我们这个星球的发展，真实状况与此很不相同。

有感于我们世界分裂的痛苦，催生了倡导西方主要国家和苏联之间进行互融的理论。这是一个足以安慰人的理论，但它忽略了一个事实，那就是，这些不同的世界不是变得更加相似，除非使用武力，任何一方都不会转化成和对方一样。此外，趋同必然意味着接受对方的缺陷，这也几乎是不可取的。

pattern of the world's rifts I would have concentrated on the East's **calamities** [n. 灾难，不幸事件]. But since my forced exile in the West has now lasted four years and since my audience is a Western one, I think it may be of greater interest to concentrate on certain aspects of the West in our days, such as I see them.

A Decline in Courage

may be the most striking feature which an outside observer notices in the West in our days. The Western world has lost its civil courage, both as a whole and separately, in each country, each government, each political party and of course in the United Nations. Such a decline in courage is particularly noticeable among the ruling groups and the intellectual elite, causing an impression of loss of courage by the entire society. Of course there are many courageous individuals but they have no determining influence on public life. Political and intellectual bureaucrats show depression, passivity and perplexity in their actions and in their statements and even more so in theoretical reflections to explain how realistic, reasonable as well as intellectually and even morally warranted it is to base state policies on weakness and cowardice. And decline in courage is ironically emphasized by occasional explosions of anger and inflexibility on the part of the same bureaucrats when dealing with weak governments and weak countries, not supported by anyone, or with currents which cannot offer any resistance. But they get tongue-tied and paralyzed when they deal with powerful governments and threatening forces, with aggressors and international terrorists.

Should one point out that from ancient times decline in courage has been considered the beginning of the end?

Well-Being

When the modern Western States were created, the following principle was proclaimed: governments are meant to serve man, and man lives to be free to pursue happiness. (See, for example, the American Declaration). Now at last during past decades technical and social progress has permitted the realization of such aspirations: the welfare state. Every citizen has been granted the desired freedom and material goods in such quantity and of such quality as to guarantee in theory the achievement of happiness, in the morally inferior sense which has come into being during those same decades. In the process, however, one psychological detail has been overlooked:

如果我今天是在对我自己国家的听众演讲，探讨世界裂痕的总体格局，我会集中讨论出现在东方的灾难。但是，因为我被迫流亡到西方已有 4 年，而且我的听众来自西方，我认为着重讨论就我所见的当今西方社会的某些方面，会更有意思一些。

勇气的沦丧

在我们这个时代，一个外来者观察西方时，可能觉得这一点是最为突出的。西方世界已经失去了其社会的勇气，无论是作为一个整体还是个体，在每个国家、每个政府、每个政党，以及当然的，在联合国里，都是这样。这种勇气的缺失，在统治阶层和知识精英当中尤为明显，以至给人以整个社会都失去勇气的印象。当然也有很多有勇气的人，但他们对公众的生活无法产生决定性的影响。政治和知识官僚们在行动和言语上都表现出低沉、被动和困惑的情绪，当他们辩解基于软弱和怯懦而制定的国家政策，是如何实用、合理、明智，甚至符合道义时，显得更加如此。

具有讽刺意味的是，这些官僚在与没人支持的软弱政府和弱势国家，或没有能力进行抵抗的机构打交道时，偶尔会爆发出愤怒和表现出僵化，这更显出他们勇气的缺失。当他们跟强大的政府或有威慑力的势力交手，或者与侵略者和国际恐怖分子交手时，却噤若寒蝉，软弱无力。

还需要我们指出，从远古时代起，勇气的缺失就一直被认为是灭亡的开始。

康乐安宁

现代西方国家的创建是依据以下原则为基准的：政府的目的是服务于人，人类生而自由，从而追求幸福（可以参见美国的《独立宣言》）。现在，技术和社会的进步使得这种愿望成为可能，我们进入了福利社会。每个公民都获得了他们所需的自由和物质产品，其数量和质量都足以在理论上保证人们实现幸福。不过与此同时，人们却在道义上不断堕落。在这个进程中，人们忽视了一个心理细节，那就是人们对物质的需求越来越大，希望生活越来越好，这种需求是永无止境的，而对这些东西的追求，

the constant desire to have still more things and a still better life and the struggle to obtain them imprints many Western faces with worry and even depression, though it is customary to conceal such feelings. Active and tense competition **permeates** [v. 弥漫，渗透] all human thoughts without opening a way to free spiritual development. The individual's independence from many types of state pressure has been guaranteed; the majority of people have been granted well-being to an extent their fathers and grandfathers could not even dream about; it has become possible to raise young people according to these ideals, leading them to physical splendor, happiness, possession of material goods, money and leisure, to an almost unlimited freedom of enjoyment. So who should now renounce all this, why and for what should one risk one's precious life in defense of common values, and particularly in such nebulous cases when the security of one's nation must be defended in a distant country?

Even biology knows that habitual extreme safety and well-being are not advantageous for a living organism. Today, well-being in the life of Western society has begun to reveal its **pernicious** [adj. 有害的，恶性的] mask.

Legalistic Life

Western society has given itself the organization best suited to its purposes, based, I would say, on the letter of the law. The limits of human rights and righteousness are determined by a system of laws; such limits are very broad. People in the West have acquired considerable skill in using, interpreting and manipulating law, even though laws tend to be too complicated for an average person to understand without the help of an expert. Any conflict is solved according to the letter of the law and this is considered to be the supreme solution. If one is right from a legal point of view, nothing more is required, nobody may mention that one could still not be entirely right, and urge self-restraint, a willingness to renounce such legal rights, sacrifice and selfless risk: it would sound simply absurd. One almost never sees voluntary self-restraint. Everybody operates at the extreme limit of those legal frames. An oil company is legally blameless when it purchases an invention of a new type of energy in order to prevent its use. A food product manufacturer is legally blameless when he poisons his produce to make it last longer: after all, people are free not to buy it.

I have spent all my life under a communist regime and I will tell you that a society without any objective legal scale is a terrible one indeed. But **a society with no other scale**

让许多西方人的脸上印满了担忧,甚至是抑郁症的表情,虽然人们习惯于隐瞒这种情绪。主动和激烈的竞争贯穿了人类全部的思想,而没有给精神的自由发展留下任何余地。个体可以不受来自国家的多种类型的压力,这种独立性已有保证。大多数人得到的福祉,是他们的父辈和祖父辈所不敢想象的。依据这些理想来培养下一代,已经成为可能,这让年轻人体力充沛、幸福美满、物质丰富、有钱有闲,享乐几乎是无限的。那么,现在谁还会放弃这一切,为什么、而且为了什么目标,要牺牲宝贵的生命去捍卫共同的价值观,特别是必须到一个遥远的国家去保卫自己国家的安全?

在生物学里,我们知道长期的过度安全和舒适,对一个活的有机体来说,其实是不利的。今天,西方社会舒适的生活,已经开始显露其有害的一面。

墨守成规的生活

西方社会为自己找到了最适合其目的的组织方式,其基础,我应该说,是建立在法律条文上的。人权和正义的范围由法律制度限定,这种限定范围是非常宽广的。在西方,人们使用、解释和操作法律已有相当的技巧,虽然法律往往过于复杂,一般人没有专家的帮助很难了解。根据法律条文来解决任何冲突,这被认为是至高无上的解决之道。如果一个人从法律的角度来看是对的话,其他什么都不重要了。没有人能多句嘴,说某人可能不一定全对;也没有人敦促人们进行自我克制,自愿放弃这种合法权益,作出牺牲和做到无私。

这样做是有风险的,它会被看做无稽之谈。我们几乎从来没有看到出于自愿的自我约束,每个人都在那些法律框架的极限处行事。石油公司购买某种新型能源的一项发明,目的却是为了防止它使用,而在法律上无法指责。当食品制造商毒化他的产品,为的是让产品有效期更长,在法律上也是无可指责的,因为你可以不去买他的东西。

我过去所有的日子都是在公有制下度过的,所以我可以告诉你,一个没有任何客观的法律制度的社会,确实是可怕的。但**一个除了法律制**

but the legal one is not quite worthy of man either. A society which is based on the letter of the law and never reaches any higher is taking very scarce advantage of the high level of human possibilities. The letter of the law is too cold and formal to have a beneficial influence on society. Whenever the tissue of life is woven of legalistic relations, there is an atmosphere of moral mediocrity, paralyzing man's noblest impulses.

And it will be simply impossible to stand through the trials of this threatening century with only the support of a legalistic structure.

The Direction of Freedom

In today's Western society, the inequality has been revealed of freedom for good deeds and freedom for evil deeds. A statesman who wants to achieve something important and highly constructive for his country has to move cautiously and even timidly; there are thousands of hasty and irresponsible critics around him, parliament and the press keep rebuffing him. As he moves ahead, he has to prove that every single step of his is well-founded and absolutely flawless. Actually an outstanding and particularly gifted person who has unusual and unexpected initiatives in mind hardly gets a chance to assert himself; from the very beginning, dozens of traps will be set out for him. Thus **mediocrity** [n. 平凡. 平庸之才] triumphs with the excuse of restrictions imposed by democracy.

It is feasible and easy everywhere to undermine administrative power and, in fact, it has been drastically weakened in all Western countries. The defense of individual rights has reached such extremes as to make society as a whole defenseless against certain individuals. It is time, in the West, to defend not so much human rights as human obligations.

Destructive and irresponsible freedom has been granted boundless space. Society appears to have little defense against the abyss of human decadence, such as, for example, misuse of liberty for moral violence against young people, motion pictures full of pornography, crime and horror. It is considered to be part of freedom and theoretically counter-balanced by the young people's right not to look or not to accept. Life organized legalistically has thus shown its inability to defend itself against the corrosion of evil.

And what shall we say about the dark realm of criminality as such? Legal frames (especially in the United States) are broad enough to encourage not only individual freedom but also certain individual crimes. The culprit can go unpunished or obtain undeserved **leniency** [n. 宽大. 仁慈] with the support of thousands of public defenders. When a government starts an earnest fight against terrorism, public opinion immediately

度以外，没有其他衡量准则的社会，同样不值得人们骄傲。只是基于法律条文，并永远不想设定任何更高标准的社会，就会疏远人类可能达到的崇高情怀。法律条文冰冷教条，对社会难以产生有益的影响。每当人们生活中的关系和法律交织时，就会出现道德平庸的状况，使人无法产生更崇高的冲动。

我们要应对这个充满威胁的世纪的考验，光靠法律结构的支撑，是根本不可能的。

自由的走向

在今天的西方社会中，选择善行或劣迹都有自由，但选择做什么的自由其实是不平等的。一个政治家要为他的国家做出重要的富有建设性的事，都必须缩手缩脚甚至是谨言慎行。在他周围，有成千上万的草率的、且不负责任的批评者，议会和媒体也不断给他使绊。当他向前迈进时，他必须证明他的每一步都是有根有据，是绝对完美无瑕的。一个出色的、极有天赋的人，如果脑子里装着非同寻常的想法，实际上很难得到证明自己的机会，从一开始诸多陷阱就已经在等着他了。因此，以民主为借口造成的限制，使平庸大行其道。

削弱行政权力，这是可行并且容易做到的，事实上，行政权力在所有西方国家已被大大削弱。对个人权利的保护已经达到相当程度，以致社会对某些人基本上毫无办法。在西方，要强调人类义务多于捍卫人权，现在是时候了。

破坏性的和不负责任的行为自由，已经有了无限的空间。社会似乎对人间丑恶毫无办法。比如，对年轻人海淫海盗，制作充满色情、犯罪和恐怖的电影，这些就是对自由的滥用，但这却被认为是自由的一部分。而且，年轻人有不看或者不接受的权利，所以从理论上来说达成了平衡。这就说明了用法律方法来构建我们的生活，无法抵御邪恶的腐蚀。

面对如此黑暗的犯罪，我们还有什么可说的？法律框架（尤其是在美国）是如此的宽大，不仅促进了个人的自由，而且也鼓励了某些犯罪行为。有数以千计的辩护人的支持，坏人可以逍遥法外或获得没道理的

accuses it of violating the terrorists' civil rights. There are many such cases.

Such a tilt of freedom in the direction of evil has come about gradually but it was evidently born primarily out of a humanistic and benevolent concept according to which there is no evil inherent to human nature; the world belongs to mankind and all the defects of life are caused by wrong social systems which must be corrected. Strangely enough, though the best social conditions have been achieved in the West, there still is criminality and there even is considerably more of it than in the **pauper** [n. 贫民. 穷人] and lawless Soviet society. (There is a huge number of prisoners in our camps which are termed criminals, but most of them never committed any crime; they merely tried to defend themselves against a lawless state resorting to means outside of a legal framework).

The Direction of the Press

The press too, of course, enjoys the widest freedom. (I shall be using the word press to include all media). But what sort of use does it make of this freedom?

Here again, the main concern is not to infringe the letter of the law. There is no moral responsibility for deformation or disproportion. What sort of responsibility does a journalist have to his readers, or to history? If they have misled public opinion or the government by inaccurate information or wrong conclusions, do we know of any cases of public recognition and **rectification** [n. 改正. 矫正] of such mistakes by the same journalist or the same newspaper? No, it does not happen, because it would damage sales. A nation may be the victim of such a mistake, but the journalist always gets away with it. One may safely assume that he will start writing the opposite with renewed self-assurance.

Because instant and credible information has to be given, it becomes necessary to resort to guesswork, rumors and suppositions to fill in the voids, and none of them will ever be rectified, they will stay on in the readers' memory. How many hasty, immature, superficial and misleading judgments are expressed every day, confusing readers, without any verification. The press can both simulate public opinion and miseducate it. Thus we may see terrorists heroized, or secret matters, pertaining to one's nation's defense, publicly revealed, or we may witness shameless intrusion on the privacy of well-known people under the slogan: "everyone is entitled to know everything." But this is a false slogan, characteristic of a false era: people also have the right not to know, and it is a much more valuable one. The right not to have their divine souls stuffed with gossip, nonsense, vain talk. A person who works and leads a meaningful

从宽处理。当一个政府开始切实打击恐怖主义时,公众舆论立即指责政府侵犯了恐怖分子的公民权利。这样的例子有很多。

这种把自由向邪恶立场倾斜的趋势是逐步形成的,但它显然主要来源于这样一种人的观念和仁慈的概念,即人性本来是没有邪恶的。世界是属于全人类的,我们生活中所有的缺陷,都是错的社会制度造成的,而这些社会制度必须纠正。

奇怪的是,虽然西方已经有了最佳的社会条件,但仍然有犯罪出现,而且这些犯罪甚至大大超过贫困和无法无天的苏联社会。(在我们的囚禁地里,关押着数量庞大的囚犯,但其中大多数人从来没有犯下任何罪行,他们只是试图在一个没有法制的国家,当国家采用法律框架之外的办法行事时,试图保卫自己而已。)

新闻界的导向

新闻界理所当然地享有最广泛的自由(我将使用这个词来指所有的媒体),但新闻界是如何使用这种自由的呢?

这个行业主要关注的是不去触犯法律条文,歪曲和不全面的报道在道义上是没有责任的。记者对读者或历史负有什么样的责任?如果他们不准确的信息或错误的结论误导了公众舆论或政府决策,我们何曾听过同一位记者或同一家报纸就这类错误公开认错并作出更正?不,这不会发生,因为这会影响销售量。一个国家可能成为这种错误报道的受害者,但记者总是能够逃避责任。我们完全可以假设,记者又会用全新的自信来阐述跟原来完全相反的观点。

由于新闻界必须即时提供可信的消息,为了填补空隙,采用猜测、传言和推测在所难免,而这些都不会得到纠正,从而将留在读者的记忆中。每天都会有许许多多草率的、不成熟的、肤浅的和误导性的判断来混淆读者视听,而不经过任何验证。媒体既可以模拟公众舆论,又可以加以误导。因此,我们会看到恐怖分子被英雄化,或有关自己国家国防的机密消息被公开披露,我们也在"每个人都有权知道一切"的口号下看到名人的隐私被无端骚扰。但是,这是一个不实的口号,突显了一个

life does not need this excessive burdening flow of information.

Hastiness and superficiality are the psychic disease of the 20th century and more than anywhere else this disease is reflected in the press. In-depth analysis of a problem is anathema to the press. It stops at sensational formulas.

Such as it is, however, the press has become the greatest power within the Western countries, more powerful than the legislature, the executive and the judiciary. One would then like to ask: by what law has it been elected and to whom is it responsible? In the communist East a journalist is frankly appointed as a state official. But who has granted Western journalists their power, for how long a time and with what prerogatives?

There is yet another surprise for someone coming from the East where the press is rigorously unified: one gradually discovers a common trend of preferences within the Western press as a whole. It is a fashion; there are generally accepted patterns of judgment and there may be common corporate interests, the sum effect being not competition but unification. Enormous freedom exists for the press, but not for the readership because newspapers mostly give enough stress and emphasis to those opinions which do not too openly contradict their own and the general trend.

A Fashion in Thinking

Without any censorship, in the West fashionable trends of thought and ideas are carefully separated from those which are not fashionable; nothing is forbidden, but what is not fashionable will hardly ever find its way into periodicals or books or be heard in colleges. Legally your researchers are free, but they are conditioned by the fashion of the day. There is no open violence such as in the East; however, a selection dictated by fashion and the need to match mass standards frequently prevent independent-minded people from giving their contribution to public life. There is a dangerous tendency to form a herd, shutting off successful development. I have received letters in America from highly intelligent persons, maybe a teacher in a faraway small college who could do much for the renewal and salvation of his country, but his country cannot hear him because the media are not interested in him. This gives birth to strong mass prejudices, blindness, which is most dangerous in our dynamic era. There is, for instance, a self-deluding interpretation of the contemporary world situation. It works as a sort of **petrified** [adj. 惊呆的，石化的] armor around people's minds. Human voices from 17 countries of Eastern Europe and Eastern Asia cannot

虚假时代的特点：我们有权利不去知道，而这是一个更有价值的选择。我们有权不让自己神圣的灵魂充塞着闲话、废话、无用之谈这类东西。一个工作着并过着有意义生活的人，并不需要这类信息的额外负担。

匆忙和肤浅是20世纪的精神疾病，这种疾病大多显示在报刊上。深入分析问题是新闻界极不愿做的事，它仅限于耸人听闻的套路。

但是，即使有这些问题，媒体已成为西方国家最有权势的机构，比立法机关、行政机关和司法机关都更强大。人们有必要发问：它依据哪条法律当选，又对谁负责呢？在东方社会主义国家，坦白地说，记者像一个国家官员一样，是被任命的。但谁给了西方记者这样的权力？他们的权力应有多长的时间限制？又应当有什么样的赦免权？

作为一位从舆论统一的东方国家走出来的人，还会看到另一种惊奇，他会逐步发现整个西方媒体也有一个共同偏好的趋势。这是一种时尚；媒体有普遍接受的判断模式，也可能代表共同的企业利益，所以出现的结果就不是竞争，而是声音一致。新闻界有着巨大的自由，但这种自由不是给读者的，因为报纸给予足够关注和聚焦的意见，一般都是他们自己的观点，以及大形势大同小异的看法。

思考的时尚

虽然没有任何审查，在西方，流行的思想和理念被仔细地从那些不时髦的思想和理念分离出来，没有什么是会被禁止的，但不入时的东西很难刊登在期刊或书籍上，很难在高校听到。在法律上，你们的研究人员是自由的，但他们受限于当下的时尚。这里没有东方式的公开暴力，然而，由时尚控制的筛选过程，以及迎合多数人标准的需要，经常会阻止有独立思想的人为公共生活作出他们的贡献。危险的从众倾向阻止了成功的发展。我在美国收到过非常聪明的人给我写的信件，比如一位来自一个边远小学院教书的老师，他也许可以为他的国家重建和救赎做很多事，但他的国家听不到他的声音，因为媒体对他没有兴趣。这就产生了深厚的群体偏见和盲目，而这在我们充满活力的时代正是最危险的。比如，眼下对当代世界形势就有一个自欺欺人的认识，它像坚硬的盔甲

pierce it. It will only be broken by the pitiless **crowbar** [n. 撬棍] of events.

I have mentioned a few trends of Western life which surprise and shock a new arrival to this world. The purpose and scope of this speech will not allow me to continue such a review, to look into the influence of these Western characteristics on important aspects on [the] nation's life, such as elementary education, advanced education in [?...]

Not a Model

But should someone ask me whether I would indicate the West such as it is today as a model to my country, frankly I would have to answer negatively. No, I could not recommend your society in its present state as an ideal for the transformation of ours. Through intense suffering our country has now achieved a spiritual development of such intensity that the Western system in its present state of spiritual exhaustion does not look attractive. Even those characteristics of your life which I have just mentioned are extremely saddening.

A fact which cannot be disputed is the weakening of human beings in the West while in the East they are becoming firmer and stronger. Six decades for our people and three decades for the people of Eastern Europe; during that time we have been through a spiritual training far in advance of Western experience. Life's complexity and mortal weight have produced stronger, deeper and more interesting characters than those produced by standardized Western well-being. Therefore if our society were to be transformed into yours, it would mean an improvement in certain aspects, but also a change for the worse on some particularly significant scores. It is true, no doubt, that a society cannot remain in an abyss of lawlessness, as is the case in our country. But it is also demeaning for it to elect such mechanical legalistic smoothness as you have. After the suffering of decades of violence and oppression, the human soul longs for things higher, warmer and purer than those offered by today's mass living habits, introduced by the revolting invasion of publicity, by TV **stupor** [n. 麻木. 不省人事] and by intolerable music.

All this is visible to observers from all the worlds of our planet. The Western way of life is less and less likely to become the leading model.

There are meaningful warnings that history gives a threatened or perishing society. Such are, for instance, the decadence of art, or a lack of great statesmen. There are open and evident warnings, too. The center of your democracy and of your culture is left without electric power for a few hours only, and all of a sudden crowds of American citizens start looting and creating havoc. The smooth surface film must be

一样，禁锢着人们的头脑。从东欧和东亚17个国家人民发出的声音无法将它穿透，只有当无情事件发生时，才能像撬棍一样将它打破。

我刚才所说的几个西方生活中的趋势，给一个新到这个世界的人以惊讶和震撼。这次讲话的目的和范围，不允许我继续检讨，比如西方的这些特征对一个国家生活的重要方面，像基础教育、高等教育等等，会有哪些影响？

称不上模式

但是，如果有人问我，是否会认为今天的西方社会可以作为我的祖国发展的模式，坦白地说，我将不得不作出否定的回答。不，我不会把你们目前状态下的社会作为改造我们社会的理想模式。我的国家经过剧痛，目前在精神层面已经达到了这样的强度，以致对我们来说，现在呈现出精神疲惫状态的西方制度已经不那么吸引人了。还有我刚才提到的你们生活中的那些特点，都是让人望而生悲的。

一个不争的事实是，在西方，人类在弱化；而在东方，人们正变得更加坚定、更加强大。我们的人民在过去60年里，东欧人民则在过去30年里，经受的精神考验比西方人的体验要严峻得多。生活的复杂性和难以承受的重量，造就了更强、更深、更有趣的人格，而这些是西方普遍性的福利社会下人们所无法企及的。因此，如果我们的社会转变成像你们的社会，那意味着在某些方面会有改善，但在一些特别重要的方面，则意味着变得更糟。毫无疑问，一个社会不会停留在无法无天的深渊中，就像我的祖国目前的情况，但要它去选择你们现有的这种机械化的、墨守成规中的平静，也不是完美的。经受过几十年的暴力和压迫的苦难，人类灵魂渴望有一些更高、更温暖和更纯洁的东西，而不是像今天普罗大众所习惯的充斥着令人作呕的广告宣传、浑浑噩噩的电视节目，还有让人难以忍受的音乐。

所有这一切，都是我们这个星球所有的观察家可以看到的，西方生活方式已越来越不可能成为世界的主导模式。

历史总是会给一个受到威胁或正在消亡的社会以意味深长的警告，

very thin, then, the social system quite unstable and unhealthy.

But the fight for our planet, physical and spiritual, a fight of cosmic proportions, is not a vague matter of the future; it has already started. The forces of Evil have begun their decisive offensive, you can feel their pressure, and yet your screens and publications are full of prescribed smiles and raised glasses. What is the joy about?

Shortsightedness

Very well known representatives of your society, such as George Kennan, say: we cannot apply moral criteria to politics. Thus we mix good and evil, right and wrong and make space for the absolute triumph of absolute evil in the world.

On the contrary, only moral criteria can help the West against communism's well planned world strategy. There are no other criteria. Practical or occasional considerations of any kind will inevitably be swept away by strategy. After a certain level of the problem has been reached, legalistic thinking induces paralysis; it prevents one from seeing the size and meaning of events.

In spite of the abundance of information, or maybe because of it, the West has difficulties in understanding reality such as it is. There have been naive predictions by some American experts who believed that Angola would become the Soviet Union's Vietnam or that Cuban expeditions in Africa would best be stopped by special U.S. courtesy to Cuba. Kennan's advice to his own country -- to begin unilateral disarmament -- belongs to the same category. If you only knew how the youngest of the Moscow Old Square officials laugh at your political wizards! As to Fidel Castro, he frankly scorns the United States, sending his troops to distant adventures from his country right next to yours.

However, the most cruel mistake occurred with the failure to understand the Vietnam war. Some people sincerely wanted all wars to stop just as soon as possible; others believed that there should be room for national, or communist, self-determination in Vietnam, or in Cambodia, as we see today with particular clarity. But members of the U.S. anti-war movement wound up being involved in the betrayal of Far Eastern nations, **in a genocide and in the suffering today** imposed on 30 million people there. [指東共波尔布特对柬埔寨人民的大屠杀] Do those convinced pacifists hear the moans coming from there? Do they understand their responsibility today? Or do they prefer not to hear? The American Intelligentsia lost its [nerve] and as a consequence thereof

这些警告信号包括艺术的颓废，或缺少伟大的政治家。也有公开和明显的警告。你们的民主和文化中心仅仅因为发生了几小时断电[1]，有些美国民众就突然间开始抢劫，制造混乱。那么，这层光滑表面的薄膜一定非常薄弱，这个社会制度是相当不稳定和不健康的。

但我们在物质和精神方面为这个星球而进行的伟大战斗已经打响。邪恶势力也已经开始了决定性的进攻，你们可以感受到他们的压力，但你们的屏幕和出版物还是充满了格式化的笑容和酒杯频举这样歌舞升平的画面。有什么值得高兴的呢？

鼠目寸光

西方社会非常有名的代表人物乔治·凯南说："我们不能把道德的标准套在政治上。这样的话，我们就会混淆善恶，是非不分，并让绝对的邪恶有了在世界上获得绝对胜利的空间。"

正好相反，只有道德标准能够帮助西方应对共产主义国家精心策划的世界战略。除此之外，没有其他标准。任何形式的实用考虑或偶然计划，都将不可避免地被对方的战略打败。在这个问题发展到一定程度后，墨守成规的思想会导致麻痹，它使人无法看到事件的规模和意义。

尽管信息丰富，或许正因为信息太丰富，西方难以准确了解现实的状况。一些美国专家作出天真的预测，认为安哥拉将成为苏联的越南，而如果美国对古巴表现得彬彬有礼，才是制止古巴在非洲远征的最好办法。凯南给自己国家提出的建议——单方面裁军——就属于同一类别。你们真应当知道莫斯科老广场[2]最年轻的官员是如何嘲笑你们的政界大拿的！至于菲德尔·卡斯特罗，坦率地说，他蔑视美国，把他的部队从他的国家派送到遥远的地方冒险征战，也派到你们的邻国。

然而，最残酷的错误在于人们没能了解越南战争的意义。有些人真诚地希望所有的战争都能尽快停止，另一些人则认为在越南、柬埔寨，应该有他们自己选择国家自主、或选择共产主义的空间，我们今天特别清晰地看到了这样的情况。但是，美国反战运动的成员们，最后却造成了对远东国家的背叛，造成了今天那里三千万人民正在经受种族灭绝的

danger has come much closer to the United States. But there is no awareness of this. Your shortsighted politicians who signed the hasty Vietnam capitulation seemingly gave America a carefree breathing pause; however, a hundredfold Vietnam now looms over you. That small Vietnam had been a warning and an occasion to mobilize the nation's courage. But if a full-fledged America suffered a real defeat from a small communist half-country, how can the West hope to stand firm in the future?

I have had occasion already to say that in the 20th century democracy has not won any major war without help and protection from a powerful continental ally whose philosophy and ideology it did not question. In World War II against Hitler, instead of winning that war with its own forces, which would certainly have been sufficient, Western democracy grew and cultivated another enemy who would prove worse and more powerful yet, as Hitler never had so many resources and so many people, nor did he offer any attractive ideas, or have such a large number of supporters in the West -- a potential fifth column -- as the Soviet Union. At present, some Western voices already have spoken of obtaining protection from a third power against aggression in the next world conflict, if there is one; in this case the shield would be China. But I would not wish such an outcome to any country in the world.

Loss of Willpower

And yet -- no weapons, no matter how powerful, can help the West until it overcomes its loss of willpower. In a state of psychological weakness, weapons become a burden for the **capitulating** [capitulate, vi. 有条件投降] side. To defend oneself, one must also be ready to die; there is little such readiness in a society raised in the cult of material well-being. Nothing is left, then, but concessions, attempts to gain time and betrayal. Thus at the shameful Belgrade conference free Western diplomats in their weakness surrendered the line where enslaved members of Helsinki Watchgroups are sacrificing their lives.

Western thinking has become conservative: the world situation should stay as it is at any cost, there should be no changes. This debilitating dream of a status quo is the symptom of a society which has come to the end of its development. But one must be blind in order not to see that oceans no longer belong to the West, while land under its domination keeps shrinking. The two so-called world wars (they were by far not on a world scale, not yet) have meant internal self-destruction of the small, progressive West which has thus prepared its own end. The next war (which does not have to be

苦难。那些坚信和平主义的人,听到了那里发出的哀鸣吗?他们明白自己今天所负的责任吗?还是他们不想去听?美国知识界失去了它的胆量,其后果是危险更加接近美国。但目前人们还没有意识到这一点。你们目光短浅的政客急急忙忙地签署了越战投降书,这似乎让美国有了一个不用操心的短休期,但现在一个大了一百倍的越南盘旋在你们头上。那个小小的越南曾经是一种预警,也是一个调动全美国勇气的机会。但是,如果连羽毛丰满的美国都在一个只有半边国家是共产主义的小国遭到真正的失败,那么西方今后如何还有立场强硬的希望?

我曾在不同场合说过,在 20 世纪,民主国家如果不是获得了一个强大的欧洲大陆盟友的帮助,那就还没有在任何重大战争中取得过胜利。这些盟友的理念和意识形态,民主国家不一定认同。在反对希特勒的第二次世界大战中,西方民主国家依靠自己的力量,就无疑能够赢得那场战争,但却培养了另一个后来被证明是更坏且更强大的敌人。因为希特勒从来没有像苏联那样,有这么多的资源,这么多的人口,希特勒没有提供过任何有吸引力的观念,在西方也没有这样大量的支持者,这些支持者是一个潜在的第五纵队。目前,西方有些人已经在讨论,如何在下一次的世界冲突中,借助第三股力量来反对侵略,如果有那么一种可能的话。在这种构想里,能够起这个保护作用的会是中国。

意志力的丧失

但是,没有任何一种武器——哪怕那种武器再强大——可以救助西方,除非它能克服其意志力丧失这种局面。当心理软弱的时候,拥有武器其实成了投降一方的负担。要自卫,就必须做好牺牲的准备。但在一个崇尚物质福利的社会里,很少有人有这样的准备。所以,除了退让、苟延残喘和背叛,其他什么也没剩下。因此,在可耻的贝尔格莱德会议上,自由西方的外交官们软弱无力,把赫尔辛基观察组织[3]在枷锁中的成员们不惜牺牲自己生命换来的坚持,轻易放弃。

西方思想已变得保守,它要不惜任何代价,让世界形势有如现在,不要变化。这种维持现状、削弱人心智的状况,是一个已经发展到了最终阶

an atomic one and I do not believe it will) may well bury Western civilization forever.

Facing such a danger, with such historical values in your past, at such a high level of realization of freedom and apparently of devotion to freedom, how is it possible to lose to such an extent the will to defend oneself?

Humanism and Its Consequences

How has this unfavorable relation of forces come about? How did the West decline from its triumphal march to its present sickness? Have there been fatal turns and losses of direction in its development? It does not seem so. The West kept advancing socially in accordance with its proclaimed intentions, with the help of brilliant technological progress. And all of a sudden it found itself in its present state of weakness.

This means that the mistake must be at the root, at the very basis of human thinking in the past centuries. I refer to the prevailing Western view of the world which was first born during the Renaissance and found its political expression from the period of the Enlightenment. It became the basis for government and social science and could be defined as rationalistic humanism or humanistic autonomy: the proclaimed and enforced autonomy of man from any higher force above him. It could also be called anthropocentricity, with man seen as the center of everything that exists.

The turn introduced by the Renaissance evidently was inevitable historically. The Middle Ages had come to a natural end by exhaustion, becoming an intolerable despotic repression of man's physical nature in favor of the spiritual one. Then, however, we turned our backs upon the Spirit and embraced all that is material with excessive and unwarranted zeal. **This new way of thinking, which had imposed on us its guidance, did not admit the existence of intrinsic evil in man nor did it see any higher task than the attainment of happiness on earth. It based modern Western civilization on the dangerous trend to worship man and his material needs. Everything beyond physical well-being and accumulation of material goods, all other human requirements and characteristics of a subtler and higher nature, were left outside the area of attention of state and social systems, as if human life did not have any superior sense.** That provided access for evil, of which in our days there is a free and constant flow. Merely freedom does not in the least solve all the problems of human life and it even adds a number of new ones.

However, in early democracies, as in American democracy at the time of its

段的社会才有的症状。但一个人除非瞎了眼,否则就会看到海洋控制权已经不再属于西方,而其统治下的领土也在不断缩小。两次所谓的世界战争(其实这两次大战远非是世界的),意味着小而进步的西方在从内部自我毁灭,从而导致了自己的最终结束。下一场战争(不一定是一场原子战,而且我也不相信会是原子战)很可能就会将西方文明永远埋葬。

面临这样的威胁,拥有你们过去那样的历史价值观,在这样高的一个水平上实现了自由,而且人们显然热爱自由,那种自卫的意愿,怎么会输到这种地步呢?

人文精神与它的后果

这种力量的不利对比是如何造成的?西方是如何从胜利高歌衰落到目前状况的呢?在其发展中,有过致命的转变和挫折吗?似乎并非如此。西方国家按照其宣布的意愿,在辉煌的技术进步的帮助下,不断推动社会的发展。然而,突然间,却发现自己处在目前的软弱状态中。

这意味着,错误必定是在根源处发生的,即错误的根源在于过去的几个世纪里人类思维的基础。我指的是当下流行的西方世界的观点,它始于文艺复兴时期,并从启蒙运动中找到其政治观点。它成为政府组建和社会科学研究的基础,我们可以称之为理性的人文主义或人文自治:人可以不用受制于任何比他更高的力量,这种自治是经过正式宣布并得到实施的。它也可以被称为人类中心学,把人类看做是一切存在的中心。

文艺复兴时期所带来的转变显然是历史上不可避免的规律。中世纪已经毫无活力,到了其自然结束的时候,它压抑人的自然天性,倡导精神属性,成了一种让人无法忍受的专制。但是,我们随后却抛弃了精神追求,以过度和不必要的热情去追求一切物质的东西。**这种新的思维方式,强加在我们头上成为我们的指导,却不承认人都有内在的邪恶,也没有看到除了追求尘世的幸福之外,人还有什么更高的任务。它把现代西方文明的基础,危险地建立在崇拜人和他的物质需求之上。除了身体享受和物质的积累,人的所有其他需求,以及人类所具有的较微妙的和更高的品质,都不在国家和社会制度关注的范围之内,犹如人的生命不**

birth, all individual human rights were granted because man is God's creature. That is, freedom was given to the individual conditionally, in the assumption of his constant religious responsibility. Such was the heritage of the preceding thousand years. Two hundred or even fifty years ago, it would have seemed quite impossible, in America, that an individual could be granted boundless freedom simply for the satisfaction of his instincts or whims. Subsequently, however, all such limitations were discarded everywhere in the West; a total liberation occurred from the moral heritage of Christian centuries with their great reserves of mercy and sacrifice. State systems were becoming increasingly and totally materialistic. The West ended up by truly enforcing human rights, sometimes even excessively, but man's sense of responsibility to God and society grew dimmer and dimmer. In the past decades, the legalistically selfish aspect of Western approach and thinking has reached its final dimension and the world wound up in a harsh spiritual crisis and a political impasse. All the glorified technological achievements of Progress, including the conquest of outer space, do not redeem the Twentieth century's moral poverty which no one could imagine even as late as in the Nineteenth Century.

An Unexpected Kinship [n. 血缘关系，亲属关系]

As humanism in its development became more and more materialistic, it made itself increasingly accessible to speculation and manipulation at first by socialism and then by communism. So that Karl Marx was able to say in 1844 that "communism is naturalized humanism."

This statement turned out not to be entirely senseless. One does see the same stones in the foundations of a despiritualized humanism and of any type of socialism: endless materialism; freedom from religion and religious responsibility, concentration on social structures with a seemingly scientific approach. (This is typical of the Enlightenment in the Eighteenth Century and of Marxism). Not by coincidence all of communism's meaningless pledges and oaths are about Man, with a capital M, and his earthly happiness. At first glance it seems an ugly parallel: common traits in the thinking and way of life of today's West and today's East? But such is the logic of materialistic development.

The interrelationship is such, too, that the current of materialism which is most to the left always ends up by being stronger, more attractive and victorious, because

再有任何更高意义似的。 这使邪恶乘虚而入，而邪恶在我们这个时代是四处泛滥的。自由本身并不能解决人类生活的所有问题，它甚至给我们带来了一些新的问题。

然而，在早期的民主体制里，比如在美国民主制度诞生之初，人之所以能够获得属于自己的权利，因为人是神的造物。也就是说，个人得到自由是有条件的，其前提是他要不断地遵守自己的宗教信仰。这也是那之前千百年间的习惯。200年前，甚至50年前，在美国似乎都不太可能只为了人的本能或率性，就给予某人以无限的自由。然而随后，所有这些限制在西方每个地方都被抛弃了，人们彻底抛弃了基督教数百年间积累下来的有关怜悯和自我牺牲的道德遗产。国家制度日益变得彻底唯物论。西方真正落实了人权，有时甚至做得过分，但人对神和社会的责任感却越来越弱。

在过去几十年里，西方模式在法律上只照顾自私的一面，以致到了它的极限，而世界也面临着严重的精神危机和政治僵局。所有号称"进步"带来的辉煌的科技成果，包括对外层空间的征服，都不足以赎回20世纪的道德贫困，这种道德贫困，就连19世纪的人都无法想象。

意想不到的血缘关系

由于人文主义在其发展过程中变得越来越物质化，使得它本身越来越容易受到先是社会主义、后来是共产主义的操控，所以，马克思在1844年时说，"共产主义是归化了的人文主义"。

这种说法并非毫无道理。人们可以看到，在丧失了精神的人文主义以及任何类型的社会主义两者那里，它们的基础都有着同样的部分：无尽的唯物主义；不相信宗教，也不承担宗教道义，还有注重社会结构的一种看似科学的做法。（这在18世纪的启蒙运动与马克思主义理论中，相当典型。）不无巧合的是，共产主义所有毫无意义的承诺和宣誓都是有关人的，一个大写的人，以及他的尘世幸福。乍一看，似乎可以看到这样一个丑陋的并列现象：今天的西方和东方，在思维模式和生活方式上，怎么有这么多的共同点？但这就是物质发展的逻辑。

it is more consistent. Humanism without its Christian heritage cannot resist such competition. We watch this process in the past centuries and especially in the past decades, on a world scale as the situation becomes increasingly dramatic. Liberalism was inevitably displaced by radicalism, radicalism had to surrender to socialism and socialism could never resist communism. The communist regime in the East could stand and grow due to the enthusiastic support from an enormous number of Western intellectuals who felt a kinship and refused to see communism's crimes. When they no longer could do so, they tried to justify them. In our Eastern countries, communism has suffered a complete ideological defeat; it is zero and less than zero. But Western intellectuals still look at it with interest and with empathy, and this is precisely what makes it so immensely difficult for the West to withstand the East.

Before the Turn

I am not examining here the case of a world war disaster and the changes which it would produce in society. As long as we wake up every morning under a peaceful sun, we have to lead an everyday life. There is a disaster, however, which has already been under way for quite some time. I am referring to the calamity of a despiritualized and irreligious humanistic consciousness.

To such consciousness, man is the touchstone in judging and evaluating everything on earth. **Imperfect man, who is never free of pride, self-interest, envy, vanity, and dozens of other defects. We are now experiencing the consequences of mistakes which had not been noticed at the beginning of the journey. On the way from the Renaissance to our days we have enriched our experience, but we have lost the concept of a Supreme Complete Entity which used to restrain our passions and our irresponsibility. We have placed too much hope in political and social reforms, only to find out that we were being deprived of our most precious possession: our spiritual life.** In the East, it is destroyed by the dealings and machinations of the ruling party. In the West, commercial interests tend to suffocate it. This is the real crisis. The split in the world is less terrible than the similarity of the disease plaguing its main sections.

If humanism were right in declaring that man is born to be happy, he would not be born to die. **Since his body is doomed to die, his task on earth evidently must be of a more spiritual nature. It cannot be unrestrained enjoyment of everyday life. It**

这种互连关系使得最激进的物质论的潮流总是会变得更强大、更具吸引力和更能得胜，因为它比较有连续性。没有基督教传统的人文精神无法抗拒这样的竞争。在过去几个世纪，特别是过去几十年的过程中，我们在世界范围内看到这种形势变得越来越富有戏剧性。自由主义不可避免地会被激进主义所取代，激进主义肯定会屈服于社会主义，而社会主义不可能抗拒共产主义。在东方的共产主义政权能够建立和成长，要归功于众多的西方知识分子的热情支持，他们对共产主义感到有一种血肉关系，并拒绝去了解共产主义的特性。当他们不能再这样做时，他们试图找到解释。在东欧国家，共产主义在意识形态上已经是一个完全的失败，它得零分，甚至要小于零。但是，西方知识分子仍然对它心向往之，这恰恰是为什么西方难以对付东方的原因。

转变之前

我在此不是研究世界战争的灾难，以及它会给社会带来什么样的变化。只要我们每天在和平的阳光下醒来，我们就要过一天的日子。但是，有一场灾难已经发生好一段时间了。我指的是人文意识中失去精神和宗教信仰的灾难。

在这种意识里，人是判断和评价地球上一切事物的试金石。但**人是不完美的，他从来摆脱不了骄傲、自私、嫉妒、虚荣和其他诸多缺陷。这是我们正在经历这个旅程的开始时，没有注意到的错误所带来的后果。从文艺复兴到现在，我们丰富了经验，但我们失去了这个概念，即用一个"至高无上的主宰"来约束我们的滥情和我们不负责任的做法。我们在政治和社会改革上寄托了太多的希望，结果发现，我们失去了最宝贵的财产：自己的精神生活。**在东方，它受到执政党的蓄意破坏；而在西方，它受到商业利益的窒息。这是真正的危机。世界上的分裂，其可怕程度远比不上这种普遍困扰世界的疾病。

如果人文主义宣告说人生来就要幸福的话，他就不会生来想死。**由于人的躯体注定要消亡，他在地球上的任务显然必须带有更多的精神性。他不能总是无拘无束地享受日常生活，不能总是孜孜不倦地寻找获取物**

cannot be the search for the best ways to obtain material goods and then cheerfully get the most out of them. It has to be the fulfillment of a permanent, earnest duty so that one's life journey may become an experience of moral growth, so that one may leave life a better human being than one started it. It is imperative to review the table of widespread human values. Its present incorrectness is astounding. It is not possible that assessment of the President's performance be reduced to the question of how much money one makes or of unlimited availability of gasoline. Only voluntary, inspired self-restraint can raise man above the world stream of materialism.

It would be **retrogression** [n. 倒退，退步] to attach oneself today to the **ossified** [adj. 已骨化的，守旧的] formulas of the Enlightenment. Social dogmatism leaves us completely helpless in front of the trials of our times.

Even if we are spared destruction by war, our lives will have to change if we want to save life from self-destruction. We cannot avoid revising the fundamental definitions of human life and human society. Is it true that man is above everything? Is there no Superior Spirit above him? Is it right that man's life and society's activities have to be determined by material expansion in the first place? Is it permissible to promote such expansion to the detriment of our spiritual integrity?

If the world has not come to its end, it has approached a major turn in history, equal in importance to the turn from the Middle Ages to the Renaissance. It will exact from us a spiritual upsurge, we shall have to rise to a new height of vision, to a new level of life where our physical nature will not be cursed as in the Middle Ages, but, even more importantly, our spiritual being will not be trampled upon as in the Modern era.

This ascension will be similar to climbing onto the next anthropologic stage. No one on earth has any other way left but -- upward.

质的最佳途径，然后乐呵呵地从中尽可能地索取。他必须永久地、认真地履行一个责任，这样，人生的旅途才会成为道德成长的经历，才能做到在离开人世时，比自己的生命开始时更为美好。现在，当务之急是检讨人类价值的总体得失。人类目前的错误之多令人咋舌。把评价一个总统的表现简化到只问他能让你挣多少钱，或汽油是否可无限提供这些问题，这是远远不够的。只有自觉自愿的约束，才能把人提高到不再局限于物质主义的世界潮流之上。

把自己限制在启蒙运动的僵化公式里，这将是一种倒退。社会教条主义使我们在时代考验面前束手无策。

即使我们幸免于战争的毁灭，如果我们想从自我毁灭中拯救生命，也必须改变我们的生活。我们必须修改对人类生命和人类社会的基本定义，这是不可逃避的。人真的是高于一切吗？他上面有没有"精神主宰"？人类的生活和社会活动，首先取决于物质的发展，这是正确的吗？损害我们的精神完整性来促进这种物质发展，这能被允许吗？

如果世界还没有毁灭，那它已经接近了一个重大转折关口，其重要性有如从中世纪到文艺复兴的转变。它将要求我们精神上的提升，我们将要上升到一个新的视野、新的水平，在那里，我们的物质属性不会受到像在中世纪那样的打压，但更重要的是，我们的精神不会像今天一样被践踏。

这种提升将与我们攀登到人类下一个阶段的努力相似。地球上的每个人只有一条路可走——向上。

---

1 索氏这里指的是 1977 年 7 月 13 日至 14 日间纽约市发生了大规模断电，在一片黑暗中，全市出现了抢劫和骚乱现象，而且在 10 个月后，婴儿出生率大增。

2 这里是苏共中央政治局的总部所在地，也就是西方人通称的"克里姆林宫"。

3 赫尔辛基观察组织（Helsinki Watch）是一个设在美国的非政府组织，旨在跟踪苏联和东欧国家人权状况，该组织在 1988 年改名为"人权观察"（Human Rights Watch）。

1980's

约翰·芬利（1904—1995）

1982年哈佛毕业典礼的演讲者约翰·哈斯顿·芬利（John H. Finley），是在哈佛任教多年的希腊文学教授，也是通识教育理论的主要创始人之一。

约翰·芬利于1904年11月出生于纽约市，他的父亲曾是《纽约时报》的资深编辑，后来担任纽约城市学院院长。芬利于1921年进入哈佛大学学习，1925年获得本科学位，1933年获得博士学位，同年留校任教，直到退休。

1945年，哈佛大学出版了著名的《哈佛通识教育红皮书》，这本书来源于一份研究报告。由包括当时的哈佛校长柯南特和芬利教授在内的12名来自不同学科的著名教授组成的委员会，经过两年多的研究，发表了题为"自由社会的通识教育"的报告，因为是红色装帧，俗称"红皮书"。芬利教授担任该委员会的副主席，并主笔写了其中重要的篇章。

红皮书一经发表，就在美国社会各界引起了强烈反响，并为战后的美国高等教育制定了蓝图。报告认为通识教育不仅是一般意义上的知识教育，它还肩负特殊使命，即将学生塑造成有责任感的公民，同时培养学生完善的人格和对自我及世界的认识。红皮书对高等教育的地位与作用、通识教育和专业教育之间的关系等论述，得到了高教界的普遍认同，是过去70多年来美国高等教育研究领域的最重要的文献之一。芬利教授在哈佛大学开设有关通识教育的课程"人文科学入门"，年复一年，吸引了无数学生。

芬利教授不仅是一位充满激情的人文和文学教授，还是一位对学生关心备至的慈祥的学监，学生们对芬利教授本人的敬重，甚至超过了他的著作和他杰出的教学成就。

1982

Understanding Our Brave New World
认知我们的新奇世界

John H. Finley 约翰·芬利

Mr. Bok, Mother Teresa, Mr. Appell, Mr. Burr, on this the last of his twenty-eight eminent years on this high platform, Mr. Smith, Mr. Deland, classmates of 1925, our youthful reunioning successors of 1932 and 1957, fellow alumni, new alumni, proud parents, ladies and gentlemen, how have we foreseen long ago one's fortune in Harvard?

Shafts of gratitude will keep opening to today's new graduates. Life has three stages: youth, middle years, and how well you look. May today's young reach in their many ways such a **consummation** [n. 终 结; 圆 满] as mine both in this afternoon and in the equally undeserved fortune of June 10th, our 49th wedding anniversary.

What luck. Life is a kind of mountain-climbing. You reach a perspicuous ridge only to spy farther ridges ahead, each with wider views. Kind parents inspired the climb, as did our remoter parentage, in Lincoln, Washington and the settlers of this new world, but Harvard opened the path.

To contemporaries here today let me invoke Odysseus at home at last with his Penelope. The horizons of his wide and sometimes dangerous journeys are now his in memory. To be sure, he, as a mortal, failed to hear to the end the Sirens' interminable song of all knowledge. Had he kept listening, he would never have reached home----would have ended, so to speak, on the bottommost sub-floor of the Widener Library under a mound composed of the Encyclopedia Britannica. Today is not that, nor is Harvard. It is at once home and travel, the dearly possessed and the continually beyond, forever intermixed.

These afternoons have commonly looked to the world's vast problems, to diminish which is education's task. **The final purpose of education is not to teach people to get ahead, though in youth they may think so, but to improve themselves in order to improve life on earth.** Aristotle held that we do not **impute** [v. 归 罪 于; 嫁 祸] order and beauty to the world, we draw them from it. Yet I am hardly Secretary Marshall, Mr. Solzhenitsyn, Chancellor Schmidt, Ambassador Watson, or our silently blessing Mother Teresa, am still less president Roosevelt, in 1936 suspect in some circles, seated on this platform in the downpour of the last day of the **Tercentennial** [n. 三百年纪念日] Celebration.

Mr. Angell of Yale then charmingly noted Harvard's way of soaking the rich, an art that Mr. Bok, like Mr. Pusey before him has well understood, and

伯克校长¹、特蕾莎修女²、阿培尔先生、伯尔先生（他在这个主席台上站了28年，今年是最后一次了），史密斯先生、戴兰先生，1925届的校友们，我们充满朝气的参加1932届和1957届返校聚会的校友们、各位校友、新校友、自豪的学生家长，女士们、先生们，我们是不是早就预见了自己能幸运地在哈佛度过时光？

今天新毕业的学生，心中将会涌起一种感激之情。人生有三个阶段：青年、中年，以及你看上去会是多大年纪。祝愿今天的青年人，也能达到像我今天下午这样的圆满人生。巧合的是，（今年）6月10日是我结婚49年的纪念日。

多好的运气啊。生活就像爬山，你攀上一座山岭，却又看到更远处的山峰，远近高低各不同。慈祥的父母鼓励我们攀登，激励我们的还有像林肯、华盛顿这样的先辈、筚路蓝缕开创我们这个新世界的开拓者，哈佛为我们打开了一片天地。

对今天在这里的同仁，我想用奥德赛最终回到家和妻子佩内洛普团聚的情景来形容。奥德赛历经万险，征途已成追忆。当然，作为一个凡人，他在最后也未能听从海上女妖带有先知先觉的歌。如果他仔细倾听，他永远也回不到家，但他还是会沉到怀德纳图书馆³最底层的故纸中，沉淀在大英百科全书的书堆里。但今天不是那样的时候，哈佛也今非昔比。我们的聚会既是回家又是出门，令人难以忘怀，五味杂陈。

过去的毕业典礼通常都要谈谈世界面临的诸多问题，改善世界当然是教育的任务。**教育的最终目的，不是教人出人头地，虽然在年轻的时候，人们可能会有这样的想法。教育的最终目的是改善自己，从而改善人类的生命。**亚里士多德认为，不是我们赋予世界秩序和美感，而是我们从中获取灵感。我自然无法和这些人相提并论，比如马歇尔国务卿、索尔仁尼琴先生、德国总理施密特、沃森大使，或默默地在给我们以祝福的特蕾莎修女，我更比不上罗斯福总统，1936年哈佛庆祝建校300周年时，在庆祝活动的最后一天，他就冒着大雨坐在这个台上。

even extends to the non-rich. It is only one more sign, a minor sign, of his noble equity of mind. In Mrs. Bok he, of course, enhances his native truthfulness at home; they jointly embody Veritas. We are proud of them. The goal has been an ever more shared, more generous, more outreaching enlightenment.

Mr. Eliot created here the new model of the American university-college. The European universities lacked colleges; Oxford and Cambridge lacked graduate schools. By superimposing the continental higher learning on the transplanted Anglo-Saxon college he gave rise to Harvard's glory and endless demand. We run with the hares and hunt with the hounds, forever seek to combine the best of colleges with the best of graduate schools. Ancient seaboard Athens invented in democracy an outward-looking culture given to skill and self-reliance. Land-based Sparta relied on conformity; the distant contrast still holds. Settlers of this continent went west by what they called prairie-schooners with the stars as guide. Opportunity, skill, and communication now make the country, huge as it once seemed, a kind of island relatively to the emergent land-powers. The call of self-improvement that had begotten Harvard took on far-reaching scope in Mr. Eliot's great changes.

His reform of the previously simple medical school may serve as example. Local practitioners whom he wished, against heavy objection, to replace by expert, full-time professors had taught there. His biographer the younger Henry James, William James's eldest son, describes how prospective graduates then filed before their teachers, who were each provided with a card, clear on one side, with a black dot on the other. When the firm-minded secretary rang a bell, the examiners flashed their cards, and a candidate who got no more than two black dots received the M.D. Mr. Adams, our Civil War ambassador in London and later an Overseer, had returned to a mysterious plague in his native Quincy, where a recent medical graduate had settled. The young man turned out to have had a back dot in pharmacology and was poisoning the town. Mr. Adams's testimony, needless to say, sped Mr. Eliot's proposed change.

Boston lawyers had similarly driven to Cambridge----possibly by one of the new horse-cars after, I think, 1860----to lecture large-mindedly in

耶鲁大学的安吉尔先生当时饶有兴趣地提到，哈佛很有办法从富人那里拉到赞助，伯克校长，就像他的前任帕塞先生一样，很精通这门艺术，他们甚至让并非大富大贵的人，也热心捐助。这是伯克校长思维高超的一个表现。有了伯克夫人，他在家里自然更是本性流露，他们共同体现了哈佛"真理"的校训。我们为他们感到骄傲。我们面前共享的目标更大，得到的启示会更多。

艾略特校长[4]在这里为美国大学的学院制创立了一个新的模式。欧洲（大陆）的大学没有本科学院制度，（英国的）牛津和剑桥则没有研究生院。他把盎格鲁－撒克逊的学院体系和欧洲大陆的高校制度综合起来，从而给哈佛带来了声誉，学子们纷至沓来。我们追逐野兔，带上猎犬去打猎[5]，不断寻求把最好的本科学院与最好的研究生院结合起来的办法。古代过着讨海生活的雅典人，创造了民主制度和注重技能与自力更生的外向型文化；守着乡土的斯巴达人，则注重群体。这个很久以前的对比，现在仍然成立。美洲大陆的定居者们，靠着星辰指路，往西部去寻找机会。机会、技术与通讯这些因素，现在使这个一度显得很大的国家，相比欧洲大陆的强国来说，显得像个小岛。在艾略特校长倡导的巨大变化影响下，哈佛声名鹊起，那种自我完善的精神影响深远。

艾略特校长对曾经要求松散的医学院进行改革，就是这样一个例子。他希望聘请全职教授来替代授课的本地行医者，但这受到了强烈的反对。为他写传记的作家小亨利·詹姆斯（威廉·詹姆斯的长子）这样描述准备毕业的学生：他们站在老师面前，每个老师都有一张卡片，卡片的一面是白的，另一面有一个黑点。当刻板的秘书敲响铃声后，考官们亮出他们的卡，得到黑点少于两个的候选人，就可以获得医学博士证书。亚当斯先生在美国内战时期曾担任美国驻英国大使，后来成为哈佛监事，他在回到家乡昆西时，发现那里好像发生了神秘的鼠疫，一位新近从哈佛医学院毕业的人到这里行医。这位年轻人在药理学那门课上得过一个黑点，他给镇里的人都开错了药。不用说，亚当斯先生的这一发现，加快了艾略特先生改

their subject; a new student might encounter an advanced course. But Mr. Christopher Columbus Langdell's novel case method soon guided the Law School toward its present height; the Graduate School of Arts and Sciences in 1878 instituted the Ph.D. long familiar in Europe. Whether Thoreau would have approved those widening steps may be questionable; his early American graduate school was Walden Pond, with thrushes and trout for professors. But teaching now looked **vernally** [adv. 春天地（清新地）] outward: by, among older men, the Swiss-born Louis Agassiz in whom rocks of the White Mountains bred theories of glaciations, the sail maker's far-sailing son James Francis Child, whose zeal for early ballads effectually founded literary scholarship, and Charles Eliot Norton, the gifted pioneer of the study of fine arts; also newly rising men, the inspired and inspiring William James and Santayana, Theodore Richards, who charted the table of chemical elements, and the historians Henry Adams, Channing, and Haskins.

This new part of the Yard kept pace; **yonder** [adj. 那边的；远处的] lone pine may be the sole token of President Kirkland's wish to conceal the wood piles once stored here. Opposite the federalist clarity of Bulfinch's University Hall, with windows wide enough for the scent of lilacs, Richardson's medievally enclosed Sever enhanced the new gothic of Memorial Hall. Both matched the spreading curriculum. To look ahead, the Widener Library's ranged pillars hinting of the card catalogue indoors analytically complement the Memorial Church's sky-pointing spire. The four buildings, with Emerson's **oversoul** [n. 大灵；超灵] hovering beyond, come near stating our inheritance. This week's solemnities once took place in the First Church opposite the Johnston Gate. The beloved Professor Bliss Perry long ago described to us young Thoreau from outside in the graveyard hearing through a window the clarion call of Emerson's Phi Beta Kappa oration of 1837, "The American Scholar." Its summons to a loftier sweep of mind echoed in Mr. Eliot's epochal innovations, not for Harvard only but soon throughout the nation.

Mr. Lowell went on to reshape the ever-growing college; he was of the generation that had felt in youth its emergent scope. Mr. Eliot may have taken the old college for granted. He had rowed on the famous crew of 1858 which, to mark itself in a **regatta** [n. 赛舟会], had first worn the crimson, in the form of

革建议的实行。

同样的,波士顿的律师开车去剑桥市——我想,在1860年以后,很可能是开着当时人称的"新马车"——就他们的科目高谈阔论,一个新生可能会面对高年级的课程。但克里斯托弗·哥伦布·朗德尔先生倡导新型的用案例讲解的方法,很快就引导哈佛法学院达到了目前这样的高度;文理学院在1878年实行了在欧洲早已为人们熟悉的博士学位制度。梭罗[6]是否会认可这些日益加快的步骤,可能有待争论,瓦尔登湖才是他的美式研究生院,画眉和鳟鱼是开导他的教授。不过,哈佛的教学开始具有了外向性:年长男子中,出生于瑞士的路易斯·阿加西斯,从白色山脉的岩石中总结出冰川作用的理论;帆船建造商的儿子詹姆斯·弗朗西斯·查尔德,对早期歌谣情有独钟,创立了文学学派;查尔斯·艾略特·诺顿是天才的美术研究的开拓者。此外还有不少后起之秀,比如很能激励人心的威廉·詹姆斯和桑塔亚纳,研究化学成分表的西奥多·理查兹,以及历史学家亨利·亚当斯、切宁和哈斯金斯等等。

哈佛的校园同样发生了很大变化。老校长柯克兰曾想用一棵孤松来遮挡住堆放在这边的柴火木块。布尔芬奇设计的大学礼堂窗口宽大,让丁香花爬满窗口,在这座线条清晰的建筑对面,是理查森设计的富有中世纪情调的新哥特式的大学纪念楼。这两座建筑,就像哈佛日益扩充的课程。朝前看,怀德纳图书馆排列整齐的石柱,暗示着楼里有条不紊的卡片目录,并与大学纪念教堂指向天空的尖顶相映成辉。这四座建筑,加上爱默生树立在校园里的雕像,默默地述说着我们的传承。本周的这类毕业仪式,以前是在庄士敦门对面的第一教堂里面举办的。广受尊重的布利斯·佩里教授很早以前曾经描述说,年轻时的梭罗,曾在窗口外聆听了爱默生1837年在哈佛一个学生兄弟会发表的致词《论美国学者》。这篇演说志存高远,与艾略特校长划时代的创新异曲同工,不只是为哈佛,而且很快就为全国各地所传颂。

洛厄尔校长接着改变了这所不断扩大的大学,他们那一代人在

bandana handkerchiefs somewhat accidentally bought at Hovey's store. After a football victory over Yale he later emerged at his door to inform the cheering procession that rowing is morally superior to football as involving no deception, only strength, skill, and endurance. Through the free elective system his risen sky of teachers was simply to lure the young, as it doubtless did.

Mr. Kittredge as firmly held classes in Shakespeare as, with lifted cane, he arrested the traffic of Harvard Square. The erudite editor of the *Divine Comedy*, Charles Grandgent, a Boston school teacher's son, had returned from years abroad to expound Dante as feelingly as had Longfellow and James Russell Lowell, but from immense knowledge. Centuries of history unrolled before young Roger Merriman; the still younger Harlow Shapley, the discoverer in youth of the flattish galaxy near the edge of which our solar system turns, lived on to the astonishment of innumerable galaxies beyond; Samuel Eliot Morison, an undergraduate in Mr. Eliot's last years, magisterially moved from the history of Harvard, to that of the nation, the Second World War navy, and the discovery of the new world. Just of late, William Bentinck-Smith's *The Harvard Book* admirably carries forward in Morison's spirit.

This was the memory that drew Mr. Lowell to college. He had other concerns----the Widener Library and the Business School rose in his time----but in the system of concentration and tutorial he both strengthened undergraduate work and made guidance more personal; above all, founded the freshman dormitories by the river and in his last years victoriously the houses. The old intimacy had faded as classes grew. A member of 1900 once told me that a classmate who later fell on hard times was never helpless; the class would rally to him. Memory of that loyalty actuated Mr. Lowell.

The visionary Professor Edward Forbes, that touchingly practical Yankee saint, had after college felt the beauty of the Oxford gardens and wanted something similar for Harvard. With the projected damming of the Charles River, finished in 1911, he foresaw that the formerly quaking, by no means fragrant river banks would turn green and solid, and with friends began acquiring them. Mr. Eliot expressed doubt that Harvard would ever stretch so far----even he was not infallible----but soon changed his mind.

年轻的时候就感觉到了学校的宽广前景,而艾略特校长则可能更认可古老的学院。洛厄尔是1858年那场著名划船竞赛的队员之一。为了在划船比赛中便于辨认,他们第一次采用了深红的颜色,他们用来绑头的头巾,是偶然在附近商店买来的。一次,在和耶鲁大学比赛橄榄球获胜后,人们欢呼游行,他却走出大门,告诉大家说赛艇比橄榄球更棒,因为它没有弄虚作假,只能靠力量、技能和耐力。他倡导的自由选课体系,使老师要设法吸引学生,这一点无疑是做到了。

基特里奇先生讲莎士比亚的课十分引人入胜,他在哈佛广场举着拐杖讲话,同样引来围观而影响了交通。《神曲》的编者查尔斯·格兰金特十分博学,是波士顿一位教师的儿子,他在国外住了多年后返美,在阐释但丁方面,比朗费罗和洛威尔更显得知识丰厚。几个世纪的历史画卷,在年轻的罗杰·梅里曼面前展开,年纪更轻的哈洛·夏普利在青年时代就发现,在我们太阳系的边缘,星系是扁平的,他还在世时,人们又发现了无数星系;塞缪尔·艾略特·莫里森读本科时是老校长艾略特在任的最后几年,后来成为研究哈佛校史、美国历史、第二次世界大战时期的海军史,以及美洲发现史等方面的权威。近年来,威廉·本廷克-史密斯编辑的《哈佛校书》令人钦佩地发扬光大了莫里森的精神。

就是这种记忆,把洛厄尔引回到大学。他还改进了其他一些事情。怀德纳图书馆和商学院在他的任期内声誉上升,在选课和讲解方面,他加强了本科教学,并让辅导更个性化。更重要的是,他在沿河一带建了大一新生宿舍,并在最后几年建起了学院宿舍楼。此前班级规模的增大,一度淡化了人们的紧密关系。1900届的一个毕业生曾经告诉我说,在以后岁月里遇到困难的同学,绝对不会孤立无助,同学们都会帮助他。那种同窗情谊是洛厄尔校长办好学校的动力。

爱德华·福布斯教授很有远见,堪称扬基圣人,他毕业之后感受到牛津大学那花园般的美丽,觉得哈佛也应该如此。查尔斯河当

The freshman dormitories crowned Mr. Forbes's and Lowell's hopes; college classes now entered together. President Wilson had left Princeton on failing to bring there some version of the Oxford and Cambridge colleges, and Mr. Edward Harkness's similar proposal to his former Yale had languished, as such things do, in a faculty committee. But when he brought his great offer here, Mr. Lowell bothered with no committee; he legendarily drew from a drawer and showed Mr. Harkness ideal plans for just this change. The Harvard Houses have been called a Princeton hope done with Yale funds.

Mr. Lowell extended to the college Mr. Eliot's epochal innovations in the graduate schools. When Mr. Conant's national scholarships brought students here from the whole country, a lone youth from a distant school soon made friends in the Yard and moved with them to a House. The Houses replaced the long-lost intimacy of the early Yard. We celebrate today the Harvard-invented, wholly American bond, now carried to the nation and **nascently** [adj. 新生的；尚不成熟的] to the world, between college and university.

What conclusions to draw? A former master of a Harvard House, if hardly a prophet, learned something in those bright years. Entering sophomores tended to comprise two groups: the studious and, to put it mildly, the less studious. The ones had come with university motives, the others with college motives. The former haunted scientific laboratories and got A's (some were reputed to sleep occasionally in the waste baskets of the Mallinckrodt Laboratory); the latter got C's, if that. But friendship and the talk of the dining hall soon wove their spell. Former A-getters started lingering so long over luncheon that they sank to B's; genial souls began to find more in college than sport and friends, and rose to B's. Only God, one concluded, awards life's ultimate A's.

Girls were lacking to the Houses in those days. In my college years we welcomed girls on only three occasions: the freshman jubilee, the junior dance, and the senior spread. But the more fetching sex, among its many superior gifts, heeds life's enticing summons. In this pre-medical era, a girl of course takes chemistry and biology but, life being beautiful, does some fine arts and acquires a picture or two. She reads, and her bookcase shows Shakespeare and Emily Dickinson. In deference to modernity, she

时正在筑坝，计划于1911年完成，他预见到那些气味闻起来并不佳的河岸可以变成绿地，于是便和朋友们一起收购河滩土地。艾略特校长曾表示怀疑，说哈佛大学不会发展到那儿，但即使是他，有时也难免会判断失误，所以他很快就改变了主意。

建立大一新生宿舍，代表了福布斯先生和洛厄尔校长最大的希望——从那时起，每届学生都可以一起进入大学课堂。威尔逊校长因为无法在普林斯顿大学实施牛津和剑桥大学的学院制而离开了那里。爱德华·哈克尼斯[7]也提出过类似的建议，但当时在他的母校耶鲁大学没有取得进展，很多事就这样被拖延下来，因为教师委员会对他的提议争辩不休。但当他把该项建议带到哈佛时，洛厄尔校长没有麻烦任何委员会，据说他从抽屉里取出正合哈克尼斯先生之意的计划，来推行这一方案。这些哈佛校舍，后来被人们戏称是用了耶鲁大学的钱来实现了普林斯顿的希望。

如果说艾略特在研究生院的设计上有着划时代创新的话，洛厄尔校长的功绩在于把这种创新扩展到了本科学院。当科南特先生推行全国性的奖学金制度之后，从某所遥远的中学来到这里的学生，很快就会在校园里交上朋友，并与他们同住在学院楼里。学院楼给哈佛带回了那种久违的亲密关系。今天，我们欣喜地看到，哈佛开始的那种学院和大学之间的紧密联系，现在全美流行，而且在全世界都开始时兴。

我们能得出什么结论呢？虽然我不是先知，但我做过哈佛宿舍院的学监，在那些快乐的时光里也学到一些东西。升入大学二年级的学生往往包括两种人：好学的，还有（用婉转的话来说）不那么勤奋好学的。有些学生一心向学，也有的学生就想混混。前一种学生整天待在实验室里，总是拿A（据说有些人偶尔还会睡在马林克罗特实验室的废物筐里），后一种学生会勉强得C。但学生之间的友谊和他们在餐厅的谈话很快就产生魔力。原来得A的学生，开始在午餐桌边闲聊，以致成绩降到B；喜欢交往的学生不再仅仅想着体育和朋友，学业上升到B的水平。人们得出的结论是，只有上帝才

even does some sociology. Then when a member of my obsessive sex who simple-heartedly looks to the Business School via economics seeks to make headway with her, she starts educating him----needless to say, a lifelong process.

More seriously, only a few people----one in a hundred may be high----will advance to crucial futures as specialists, and fewer will become Conants or Oppenheimers; fewer still will become a Roosevelt or Kennedy. But intelligence and human understanding are asked of everyone. We humans lack the marvelous powers that take the Canada geese to their far ranges; mental perception is our gift. It is not confined to college graduates. A simple older woman at this moment working in some hospital knows the difference between idleness and dedication, selfishness and altruism. The gains are partly self-taught; children learn from their parents but shine toward another child.

A glory of college is freshness of feeling. The world sparkles to friends but suddenly to ideas and hopes. Someone whom you did not know well says something that you never forget. The task is to keep that freshness even through widening experience. Every day is in fact new; the memory of youth that draws us here is still our guide. **Invaluable as teachers are, they do not exist to set forth pre-marked paths but to spur the young themselves to discover the forward steps. Good teachers rather inspire than command.** Undergraduates overrate, even this year, the problem of finding and rising in a job; at twenty they fail to foresee that everyone now forty-five will be seventy when they are forty-five. Someone must inherit the jobs, and they of course will.

Work and purpose remain essential, but ultimately for more than the job itself. Early stages of work are a kind of pencil sharpener looking to the farther, wider message. The good lawyer, the good architect, the good practitioner of any field, have more in common than each has with **desultory** [adj. 散漫的；断断续续的；不连贯的] associates. Professions resemble portholes on the world's ship, set at different angles but all giving on the immense sea beyond. **The goal of education, temporarily hidden to the young but ever emerging, is to reach the porthole and look out—to the nation, to the world, to one's fellow human beings, to try to repay as best one can the privilege of living.** Comprehension is redemptive; understanding is the endless call, not in

能发给人们生命的最好成绩。

那时候，宿舍院里没什么女孩。我上大学时，仅三次有女孩来到我们宿舍院：新生入学纪念会、三年级舞会和毕业班交际会。但女生们更有才华，懂得听从生命的召唤。在读医学预科的时候，女生当然要上化学和生物课程，但生活是美丽的，她还会上上美术课，画上几张画。她喜欢阅读，书架上有莎士比亚和艾米莉·狄金森的书。为了显示尊重现代，她甚至会选一些社会学的课。当痴迷的男生选修经济学课程，一心想着上商学院，还跟她套近乎时，她开始对他进行教育。不用说，这是他们一辈子都讲不通的事。

严肃地说，只有少数人——可能百里挑一都不到——能做到专科医生，成为科南特那样的教育家或奥本海默那样的科学家，就更少了。而成为罗斯福或肯尼迪，几乎是凤毛麟角。但每个人都应该有智力和基本的理解力。我们人类缺乏像加拿大大雁的那种奇妙能力，能长途来回迁徙，我们有的是心理的感知，这种能力并不局限于大学毕业生中。在某个医院工作的年长妇女，知道什么是懒惰什么是奉献，知道什么是利己什么是利人。这种认识，部分原因是自学的，孩子们从父母身上学习，但和同龄人在一起的时候才更有特色。

大学的妙处是让人有新鲜感。这里点缀着友谊，也会突然之间激起见解和希望。你不那么熟悉的人说的一句话，可能让你永生难忘。我们要做的事，就是把那种新鲜感保持下去。每天的确都是新的，年轻时将我们引到这里来的记忆，依然是我们前进的指南。**教师是可贵的，但他们的作用不是给学生指出已经标好记号的路径，而是激励年轻人去自己探索前进的步骤。好的教师激发人而不是约束人。**即使是在今年，大学生们也总是过分强调找工作和职场升迁的问题。20岁时他们无法想到，当他们到了45岁时，现在45岁的人将是70开外了。一个人的工作必须得有人来接替，年轻人当然有机会。

在一份职业中，努力工作和认准目标仍然是很重要的。入职初始，人们难免四处探索。不管是任何职业，比如好的律师、建筑师、

mental isolation but in deepening human sympathy, companion to the advancing years.

Shakespeare's last play, *The Tempest* of 1611, from three years after the Virginia colony, ten years before the Mayflower, twenty-five years before the founding of Harvard, first lifts to poetry the hope of the new world. Old Prospero's life-renewing western island is as mysterious as its denizens, lyric Ariel and rude Caliban. Deposed as Duke of Milan by his treacherous brother, he had reached the island with his daughter Miranda; now years later magically evokes a second storm that brings his brother and the latter's allies at Naples, the frail old king, his equally treacherous brother, and his young son, Miranda's destined beloved.

But unlike the early *As You Like It*, in which another unjustly deposed duke inhabits the Forest of Arden ("Blow, blow thou winter wind. Thou art not so unkind as man's ingratitude"), but in which the young lovers are central, The Tempest is old Prospero's play; the time, the hope, the promise, the renewal breathe of Shakespeare's last years. Treachery continues; Ariel saves the king of Naples from his equally jealous brother and as easily saves Prospero from Caliban and a pair of drunken seamen. The magic pageant that celebrates Miranda's and Ferdinand's love rises to the visionary lines: "Our revels now are ended. These our actors, / As I foretold you, were all spirits, and / Are melted into air, into thin air; / And like the baseless fabric of this vision, / The cloud-capp'd towers, the gorgeous palaces, / the solemn temples, the great globe itself, / Yea, all which it inherit, shall dissolve / And, like this insubstantial pageant faded, / Leave not a rack behind. We are such stuff / As dreams are made on, and our little life / Is rounded with a sleep."

But later lines more express Prospero's change of heart; his magic falls away; the width of his new world and of his onward year finally describes him. How shall he treat, he asks Ariel, the guilty people who had once deposed him and had now plotted murder? Forgive them, Ariel answers. "Your charms so strongly works 'em, / That if you now beheld them, your affections / Would become tender."

"Dost thou think so, spirit?" Prospero asks, and Ariel replies, "Mine would, sir, were I human." Prospero decides, "And mine shall. / Hast thou which art but air a touch, a feeling / Of their afflictions, and shall not myself be kindlier moved than

医生,他们之间的共同点是要超过业内的同事。不同的职业就像世界之船的舷窗,角度尽管不同,但都面向大海,可以看到无尽的风光。年轻人也许暂时看不到,但会渐渐领悟到,**教育的目的就是引导你从舷窗往外看——关注国家、放眼世界、关心人类,在有生年华尽力回报社会。这一点是至高目标**。随着年龄的增长,不要在心理上孤立自己,而要对人世充满同情。

莎士比亚的最后一个剧本《暴风雨》写于1611年,那正是弗吉尼亚出现殖民地3年之后,"五月花号"[8]抵达美洲10年之前,而哈佛在这之后的25年才建校。该剧第一次用诗歌的形式表现人们对新世界的向往:老普罗斯佩罗的西方小岛令人的生命焕然一新,有着神秘的居民、淘气的精灵和粗鲁的妖怪。他曾是米兰公爵,但被他奸诈的兄弟废黜,只好和女儿米兰达来到岛上。多年后来了一次神奇的风暴,把他在那不勒斯的哥哥和同伙、体弱的老国王、奸诈的弟弟和弟弟年轻的儿子也带到岛上,弟弟的儿子成了米兰达的心上人。

莎翁早些时候的剧本《皆大欢喜》也写了一个公爵,在被人用计废黜后逃避到阿登森林,("吹啊,冬季的风在吹。比起人间的忘恩负义,汝尚不那么刻薄。")但那个剧本主要描写的是年轻恋人,而《暴风雨》则是以写老普罗斯佩罗为主,表现了莎翁晚年的希望、承诺和枯木逢春。背叛的事情还在发生。淘气的精灵把那不勒斯国王从嫉妒他的哥哥那里解救出来,并轻而易举地从妖怪和喝醉了的水手那里救出普罗斯佩罗。米兰达与费迪南德的爱情引出了庆祝盛会上这样的诗句:"我们的狂欢到此为止。我们这些演员,/就像我预先说的,是一些精灵,/都化成了空气,飘入高空;/所见皆为虚幻,/耸入云端的高塔,华丽的宫殿,/庄严的寺庙,宏大的地球本身,/是啊,芸芸众生,命将归土,/如此欢歌过眼消散,/留不下踪迹。我等在世,/有如梦中,渺小生命/一觉终结。"

但后面的台词表明普罗斯佩罗改变主意了。他的魔力消失,他的年龄增长、眼界扩展。他问精灵,该如何对待推翻他、而且想要谋害他的人?"原谅他们。"精灵答道,"你的魔法在他们身上生效,如果你现在看见他们,你的感情/将不再有恨。"

thou art? / Though with their high wrongs I am struck to the quick, / Yet with my nobler reason 'gainst my fury / Do I take part: the rarer action is / In virtue than in vengeance [n. 报复；报仇]: they being penitent, / The sole drift of my purpose doth extend / Not a frown further. Go release them, Ariel; / My charms I'll break, their senses I'll restore, / And they shall be themselves."

Miranda and Ferdinand have found their love, and at sight of the others she exclaims, "O wonder. / How many goodly creatures are there here. / How **beauteous** [adj. [诗]美的；美丽的] mankind is. O brave new world / That has such people in't."

This is our today, our forever new Harvard. It keeps telling us that clarity and charity are one. **That life is not a career (privileged though such onward scope is) but a journey. Widening comprehension is both the heart's and the mind's goal. Solution to the world's problems will come with more Harvards far and wide, the jointly mental and spiritual answer to division, bigotry, and hatred. This is the faith for which we give thanks today, "O brave new world that has such people in't."

Thank you all!

"精灵啊，你真这么认为吗？"普罗斯佩罗问道，精灵回答说："先生，如果我是人，会这样做的。"普罗斯佩罗于是决定，"我就饶了他们吧。/ 你只是一股空气，尚且有情 / 对人宽容爱惜，让我又怎能不为之心软？/ 他们虽然罪大恶极 / 但我用理智权衡愤怒 / 愤怒容易；但难得的是 / 我要以德服人，不再光想报仇，让他们自己忏悔，/ 我的目的于是明确 / 不再皱眉头。放了他们吧，我的精灵；/ 我要消除魔法，让他们恢复知觉 / 他们又会活灵活现。"

米兰达和费迪南德找到了爱情，在看到其他人时，她叹道："神奇啊，神奇。/ 这里有多少美丽的生命。/ 人类是美的。啊，在这个英勇的新世界里，如此豪杰在此生息！"

这就是我们的今天，我们日新月异的哈佛大学。它不断告诉我们，要与人为善。**生活不只是职业的升迁（虽然这样的前景对你们来说看起来应该不成问题），生活也是一个旅程。心与智的目的地，应该是扩展我们的理解**。哈佛的毕业生散向四方，就更能从思想和精神上帮助解决世界存在的问题，比如分裂、偏见和仇恨。我们今天胸怀这样的信心，表示我们的感谢："啊，在这个英勇的新世界里，如此豪杰在此生息！"

谢谢各位！

Understanding Our Brave New World John H. Finley
认知我们的新奇世界 约翰·芬利

1 德瑞克·伯克（Derek Curtis Bok），为当时在任的哈佛校长。

2 特蕾莎修女，（Mother Teresa，1910—1997），是世界著名的天主教慈善修女。

3 怀德纳图书馆（Widener Library），哈佛大学主要的图书馆之一。

4 查尔斯·艾略特（Charles Eliot），1869年至1909年任哈佛大学校长，是哈佛历史上在任时间最长的校长。

5 这两项活动是英国绅士热衷的运动。

6 亨利·梭罗（Henry Thoreau），从哈佛毕业的美国自然主义者，文学名著《瓦尔登湖》的作者。

7 毕业于耶鲁大学的著名慈善家，耶鲁校园内的最高建筑钟楼（Harkness Tower）即为哈克尼斯家庭捐赠。

8 五月花号（Mayflower）是1620年从英格兰的普利茅斯港搭载清教徒开往美洲新大陆马萨诸塞的航船，它标志着欧洲（主要是英国）向美洲移民的开始，在美国历史上是必提的一页。

卡洛斯·富恩特斯（1928—2012）

　　墨西哥著名作家，也是当今西班牙语世界最负盛名的小说家、剧作家、散文家和文学评论家。从上世纪50年代中期开始，富恩特斯深刻影响了当代拉丁美洲文学，他的作品被翻译成多种文字。

　　卡洛斯·富恩特斯出生于巴拿马城的一个墨西哥家庭，祖籍德国。由于父亲是外交官，富恩特斯自幼随父母在南、北美洲大陆上不同的国家生活学习。16岁时，富恩特斯回到墨西哥，进入墨西哥自治大学攻读法律，获法律硕士学位。以后他前往日内瓦，曾在国际高等学院学习。1965年始，富恩特斯也开始了他的外交官生涯，先后在英国、瑞士、西班牙和法国等国的首都工作。

　　富恩特斯很小就爱好文学并显露才华。13岁就在智利的国立学院校刊上发表短篇小说。担任外交官后，他仍然坚持写作。1954年发表的短篇小说集《假面具的日子》在文坛上引起关注，1959年发表的《最明净的地区》使他一举成名，1962年的《阿尔特米奥·克罗斯之死》则奠定了其在拉美文坛乃至世界文坛的地位。

　　富恩特斯对西方古代和现代文明有比较深入的了解，对拉丁美洲的落后原因有深刻的研究。他总是用自己的作品来抨击墨西哥社会的弊端，发掘墨西哥民族之根，弘扬墨西哥民族的传统文化。

　　在这篇演讲中，富恩特斯用他富有激情和诗歌般的语言表达了他对自己的祖国墨西哥及南美洲国家的认识。在赞扬西方科学文明的同时，也尖锐地批评了美国社会存在的偏见与傲慢，不平等对待甚至干预他国的行为，呼吁国家间的相互理解，建议发达国家应该对周边地区负起责任。

1983

Starting Our Journey at Daybreak
迎着曙光上路

Carlos Fuentes 卡洛斯·富恩特斯

Mr. President,

Members of the Corporation,

Members of the Harvard alumni association,

Ladies and Gentlemen:

Some time ago, I was travelling in the state of Morelos in Central Mexico, looking for the birthplace of Emiliano Zapata, the village of Anenecuilco.

I stopped on the way and asked a *campesino* [n. 〈西〉 农夫], a laborer of the fields, how far it was to that village.

He answered me: "If you had left at daybreak, you would be there now."

This man had an internal clock which marked the time of his own personality and of his own culture.

For the clocks of all men and women, of all civilizations, of all histories, are not set at the same hour.

One of the wonders of our menaced globe is the variety of its experiences, its memories and its desires.

Any attempt to impose a uniform politics on this diversity is like a prelude to death.

Lech Walesa is a man who started out at daybreak, at the hour when the history of Poland demanded that the people of Poland act to solve the problems that a repressive government and a hollow party no longer knew how to solve.

We in Latin America who have practiced solidarity with Solidarity salute Lech Walesa today.

The honor done to me by this great center of learning, Harvard University, is augmented by the circumstances in which I receive it.

I accept this honor as a citizen of Mexico, and as a writer from Latin America.

Let me speak to you as such.

As a Mexican first:

The daybreak of a movement of social and political renewal cannot be aset by calendars other than those of the people involved.

With Walesa and Solidarity, it was the internal clock of the people of Poland that struck the morning hour.

So it has always been: with the people of my country during our revolutionary experience; with the people of Central America in the hour we are all living; and with

迎着曙光上路 卡洛斯·富恩特斯

校长先生、哈佛监管会的委员们、哈佛校友会的校友们、女士们、先生们：

不久前，我在墨西哥中部的莫雷洛斯州旅行，想去找埃米利亚诺·萨帕塔[1]的诞生地安内内库尔科村。

我在路上停下来问一位农夫，到那个村庄还有多远？

他回答说："如果你在天亮时上路，现在就该到了"。

这位农夫有着自己的时间规律，这个时钟带着他的个性，标志着他的文化。

因为不同的男女之间、不同的文化之间、不同的历史之间，时间的标度并不一样。

我们这个饱受威胁的世界有着许多奇妙的东西，其中之一就是，人们可以拥有不同的经历、记忆和不同的追求。

任何想把一种单一的政治形式强加于这种多样性之上的企图，注定是死亡的前奏。

瓦文萨就是一位在黎明时分开始赶路的人，他在波兰的专制性政府和空洞的政党不知道如何解决问题时，在历史的关键时刻引领了波兰人民。

我们拉丁美洲曾经声援瓦文萨的团结工会，今天再次向他致敬。

哈佛大学这样一所著名的学府给了我如此巨大的荣誉，我因为自己的身份，而感到特别的荣幸。

我以墨西哥公民的身份，并以拉丁美洲作家的身份，接受这个荣誉。

请让我以这些身份来讲话。

首先从身为一个墨西哥人的角度来说，社会和政治的重建，如果没有身处其中的人民去参与，那就是无源之水。

对瓦文萨和团结工会来说，是波兰人民自己的时钟在黎明时分敲响了。

历史规律就是这样的，在我的国家，人民推动了革命；在现在这个时刻，中美洲人民揭竿而起；在1776年时，马萨诸塞州的人民推动了美国独立。

革命的曙光预示着整个社会的历史。

一个社会的这种自我认识不可剥夺，否则会有严重的后果。

the people of Massachsetts in 1776.

The dawn of revolution reveals the total history of a community.

This is a self-knowledge that a society cannot be deprived of without grave consequences.

The Experience of Mexico

The Mexican revolution was the object of constant harassment, pressures, menaces, boycotts and even a couple of armed interventions between 1910 and 1932.

It was extremely difficult for the United States Administrations of the time to deal with violent and rapid change on the southern border of your country.

Calvin Coolidge convened both Houses of Congress in 1927 and – talkative for once----denounced Mexico as the source of "Bolshevik" subversion in Central America.

We were the first domino.

But precisely because of its revolutionary policies favoring agrarian reform, secular education, collective bargaining and recovery of natural resources----all of them opposed by the successive governments in Washington, from Taft to Hoover----Mexico became a modern, contradictory self-knowing and self-questioning nation.

The Revolution did not make an instant democracy out of my country. But the first revolutionary government, that of Francisco I. Madero, was the most democratic regime we have ever had: Madero respected free elections, a free press and an uncontrollable Congress. Significantly, he was promptly overthrown by a conspiracy of the American Ambassador, Henry Lane Wilson, and a group of reactionary generals.

So, before becoming a democracy, Mexico first had to become a nation.

What the revolution gave us all was the totality of our history and the possibility of a culture. "The Revolution----wrote my compatriot, the great poet Octavio Paz—the Revolution is a sudden immersion of Mexico in its own being. In the revolutionary explosion…each Mexican …finally recognizes, in a mortal embrace, the other Mexican."

Paz himself, Diego Rivera and Carlos Chavez, Mariano Azuela Azuela and Jose Clemento Orozco, Juan Rulfo and Rufino Tamayo: we all exist and work because of the revolutionary experience of our country. How can we stand by as this experience is denied, through ignorance and arrogance, to other people, our brothers, in Central

墨西哥的经验

墨西哥的革命不断受到干扰、打压、威胁和抵制,甚至在1910年至1932年间,经历过几次武装干涉。

对于当时的美国政府来说,应付你们国家边界以南的地方发生的暴力且快速变化,是一件非常难的事情。

卡尔文·柯立芝[2]在1927年召集了参众两院国会,他滔滔不绝地谴责墨西哥为颠覆中美洲的"布尔什维克"之根源。

我们是多米诺骨牌的第一张。

但正是因为墨西哥革命性的政策,支持土地改革,提倡世俗教育,允许工会集体谈判,并收回天然资源的所有权,这些政策遭到了华盛顿从塔夫脱总统到胡佛总统历届政府的反对,从塔夫脱总统到胡佛总统。墨西哥成了一个国家,既充满自信、又时时自我反省。

那场革命没有让我的国家立刻获得民主,但以弗朗西斯科·马德罗为首的第一届革命政府,是我们有史以来最为民主的一届。马德罗尊重民主选举、新闻自由和独立的国会。然而,他很快就被美国大使亨利·威尔逊和一批反动将领搞的阴谋推翻了。

因此,在成为一个民主国家之前,墨西哥首先必须成为一个国家。

革命给我们所有人带来的,是让我们的历史变得完整,文化成为可能。我的同胞、伟大的诗人奥克塔维奥·帕斯写道:"革命使墨西哥突然真正沉浸在自己的本质中。在轰轰烈烈的革命中,每一个墨西哥人终于认识到,要在尘世中拥抱其他墨西哥人。"

帕斯他自己,此外还有迭戈·里维拉、卡洛斯·查韦斯、马里亚诺·阿苏埃拉·阿苏埃拉和何塞·克莱蒙托·奥罗斯科、胡安·卢佛和鲁菲诺·塔马约等[3]:我们都是为我们国家的革命经验而生存和工作的。我们怎么能容忍这种经验被无知且傲慢地否定,让其他人,让那些我们在中美洲和加勒比地区的兄弟无法分享体验?

一个伟大的政治家,必须是一个务实的理想主义者。当墨西哥在任总统拉萨罗·卡德纳斯于1938年将国家的石油资源收归国有,把墨西哥

America and the Caribbean?

A great statesman is a pragmatical idealist. Franklin D. Roosevelt had the political imagination and the diplomatic will to respect Mexico when President Lazaro Cardenas, in the culminating act of the Mexican Revolution, expropriated the nation's oil resources in 1938.

Instead of menacing, sanctioning or invading, Roosevelt negotiated.

He did not try to beat history. He joined it.

Will no one in this country imitate him today?

The lessons applicable to the current situation in Latin America are inscribed in the history----the very difficult history----of Mexican-American relations.

Why have they not been learnt?

Against Intervention

In today's world, intervention evokes a fearful symmetry.

As the United States feels itself authorized to intervene in Central American to put out a fire in your front yard----I'm delighted that we have been promoted from the traditional status of back yard----then the Soviet Union also feels authorized to play the fireman in all of its front and back yards.

Intervention damages the fabric of a nation, the chance of its resurrected history, the wholeness of its cultural identity.

I have witnessed two such examples of wholesale corruption by intervention in my lifetime.

One was in Czechoslovakia in the fall of 1968. I was there then to support my friends the writers, the students and statesmen of the Prague Spring. I heard them give thanks, at least, for their few months of freedom as night fell once more upon them: the night of Kafka, where nothing is remembered but nothing is forgiven.

The other time was in Guatemala in 1964, when the democratically elected government was overthrown by a mercenary invasion openly backed by the C.I.A. The political process of reform and self-recognition in Guatemala was brutally interrupted to no one's benefit: Guatemala was condemned to a vicious circle of repression, that continues to this day.

Intervention is defined as the action of the paramount regional power against a smaller state within its so-called "sphere of influence."

革命推向高潮时，富有政治想象力和外交能力的美国总统富兰克林·罗斯福，对此表示了尊重。

罗斯福没有采取威胁、制裁或入侵等手段，而是进行谈判。

他没有逆历史潮流而动，他顺之而昌。

在这个国家，今天就再无人能效仿他了吗？

适用于当今拉丁美洲现状的教训，早就刻写在我们的历史上了，那就是墨西哥与美国之间那段艰难的历史。

这些教训，为什么没人去研究？

反对干涉

在今天的世界中，干预会导致一种可怕的反应。

如果美国感到自己有责任在中美洲，这个你们认为是自己前院的地方四处灭火——我很高兴我们不再被你们当做后院，那么苏联也会因此觉得自己有权利在其前院和后院的地方发挥消防队员的作用了。

干预一个国家，会破坏其机体，剥夺它重振历史、恢复其文化整体性的机会。

在我此生中，我已经目睹过两个这样由于外界干预而带来全面溃败的例子。

一次是在1968年秋天的捷克。我当时在那里，声援我那些参与布拉格之春的作家、学生和政治家朋友们。我听见他们表示感谢，在夜幕再一次降临到他们身上之前，他们至少有过几个月的自由，就像卡夫卡笔下的夜晚，人们什么都没去想，但也什么都没忘。

另一次是1964年的危地马拉，它的民选政府被美国中央情报局公开支持的雇佣军入侵而推翻。危地马拉改革和自我认识的政治进程被无情打断，这对所有人都没好处。危地马拉陷入了残酷镇压的恶性循环中，至今未能停止。

干预的定义，是一个区域里最强大的国家，针对在它所谓的"势力范围"内较小的国家所采取的行动。

受害者的遭遇，定义着什么是干预。

Intervention is defined by its victims.

But the difference between Soviet actions in their "sphere of influence" and United States actions in theirs is that the Soviet regime is a tyranny and you are a democracy.

Yet more and more, over the past two years, I have heard North Americans in responsible positions speak of not caring whether the United States is loved, but whether it is feared; not whether it is admired for its cultural and political accomplishments, but respected for its material power; not whether the rights of others are respected, but its own strategic interests are defended.

These are inclinations that we have come to associate with the brutal diplomacy of the Soviet Union.

But we, the true friends of your great nation in Latin America, we the admirers of your extraordinary achievements in literature, science and the arts and of your democratic institutions, of your Congress and your Courts, your Universities and publishing houses and your free press—we your true friends, because we are your friends, will not permit you to conduct yourselves in Latin American affairs as the Soviet Union conducts itself in Central European and Central Asian affairs.

You are not the Soviet Union.

We shall be the custodians of your own true interests by helping you to avoid these mistakes.

We have memory on our side.

You suffer too much from historical amnesia.

You seem to have forgotten that your own Republic was born out of the barrel of a gun: the American Revolutionaries also shot their way to power.

We hope to have persuasion on our side, but also the body of international and inter-American law to help us.

We also have our own growing strategic preoccupations as to whether, under the guise of defending us from remote Soviet menaces and **delirious** [adj. 神志昏迷的; 精神错乱的; 发狂的] domino effects, the United States would create one vast Latin American protectorate.

Meeting at Cancun on April 29, the presidents of Mexico and Brazil, Miguel de la Madrid and Joao Figueiredo, agreed that "the Central American crisis has its origin in the economic and social structures prevalent in the region and that the efforts

但苏联在他们的"势力范围"内的所作所为,和美国在它"势力范围"内所采取的行动,这两者之间的区别是,苏维埃是一个专制政权,而你们是一个民主国家。

然而,在过去的两年里,我越来越多地听到在北美位高权重的人说,他们不在乎别人是否喜欢美国,只要怕就够了;不在乎别人是否敬佩美国在文化和政治上的成就,只要尊重美国强大的能力就够了;不在乎其他人的权利是否得到尊重,只要美国自己的战略利益得到维护就够了。

而这些倾向,是我们通常用来形容苏联弱肉强食的外交做派的东西。

但我们是你们这个伟大的国家在拉丁美洲真正的朋友,我们仰慕你们在文学、科学和艺术领域的非凡成就,仰慕你们的民主机构、国会和法院,仰慕你们的大学、出版社和自由的新闻,作为你们真正的朋友,也正因为我们是你们的朋友,所以我们才不想让你们在处理拉丁美洲事务的做法,沦为像苏联在中欧和中亚的所作所为那样。

你们不是苏联。

通过帮助你们避免这些错误,我们才是真正保护了你们的利益。

我们有历史记忆的帮助。

而你们患了历史失忆症。

你们似乎已经忘记了,自己是从枪杆子里诞生的,美国的革命家也是从炮火中夺取权力的。

我们希望我们会有说服力,但也希望有国际法和适应于美洲国家之间的法律来帮助我们。

我们也有我们自己日益增长的战略考量,那就是,美国是否会用帮助我们防止来自苏联这种遥远的威胁,和阻止胡说有什么多米诺骨牌效应等这类幌子,来把拉丁美洲变成一个地域广阔的保护国。

墨西哥总统米格尔·德拉马德里和巴西总统若昂·菲格雷多4月29日在坎昆举行了会议,他们一致认为,"中美洲的危机,源于在该地区到处可见的经济和社会结构,解决这个问题的办法,必须……避免把这个问题看做是东西方对峙的这种倾向"。

西班牙首相费利佩·冈萨雷斯在访问华盛顿前夕说,美国卷入中美

to overcome it must ...avoid the tendency to define it as a chapter in East-West confrontation."

And the Prime Minister of Spain, Felipe Gonzalez, on the eve of his visit to Washington, defined U.S. involvements in Central America as "fundamentally harmful" to the nations of the region and damaging to the international standing of the United States.

Yes, your alliances will crumble and your security will be endangered if you do not demonstrate that you are an enlightened, responsible power in your dealings with Latin America.

Yes, you must demonstrate your humanity and your intelligence here, in this house we share, our Hemisphere, or nowhere shall you be democratically credible.

Where are the Franklin Roosevelt's, the Sumner Welles, the George Marshalls, and the Dean Achesons demanded by the times?

Friends and Satellites

The great weakness of the Soviet Union is that it is surrounded by satellites, not by friends.

Sooner or later, the rebellion of the outlying nations in the Soviet sphere will eat, more and more deeply, into the **innards** [n. 〈口〉内部结构; 内脏] of what Lord Carrington recently called "a decaying Byzantium."

The United States has the great strength of having friends, not satellites, on its borders.

Canada and Mexico are two independent nations that disagree on many issues with the United States.

We know that in public, as in personal life, nothing is more destructive of the self than being surrounded by sycophants.

But the same way as there are "yes men" in this world, there are "yes nations."

A "yes nation" harms itself as much as it harms its powerful protector: it deprives both of dignity, foresight and the sense of reality.

Nevertheless, Mexico has been chosen as a target of "diplomatic isolation" by the National Security Council Document on Policy in Central America and Cuba through Fiscal Year 84.

We know in Latin America that "isolation" can be a euphemism for

洲事务的做法，对该地区的国家"从根本上来说是有害的"，也对美国的国际地位不利。

是的，如果在与拉丁美洲的交往中不能展现出你们是一个负责任的大国，你们的联盟便会崩溃，你们的安全会受到危害。

是的，在我们共享的这个空间、在我们这个半球，你们必须在这里展现你们的人道和智慧，否则你们的民主就很难得到世人的相信。

我们时代所要求的巨人，像富兰克林·罗斯福、萨姆纳·韦尔斯、乔治·马歇尔和迪安·艾奇逊这样的美国政界人物，他们而今安在？

朋友和卫星国

苏联最大的弱点是，围绕着它的只是卫星国，而非朋友。

苏联势力范围内，处于外围的国家迟早会反抗，这样就会逐渐破坏苏联这个卡灵顿勋爵最近将之形容为"腐烂的拜占庭"的结构。

美国的强处则在于，靠着它边界的是朋友，而不是卫星国。

加拿大和墨西哥是两个独立的国家，在许多问题上都与美国意见不同。

我们知道，在公开场合，就像在个人的生活中一样，身边围着的都是些谄媚者的话，是有害无益的。

同样的，在这个世界上，有当"应声虫"的人，也有当"应声虫"的国家。

当"应声虫"的国家既害了自己，也害了它强大的保护者，这会让双方都失去尊严、远见和对现实的把握。

尽管如此，在（美国）国家安全事务委员会推出的"1984财政年度有关中美洲和古巴政策文件"中，墨西哥已被列为"要在外交上孤立"的目标。

在拉丁美洲，我们知道"孤立"可以是准备加以颠覆的委婉说法。

事实上，每当华盛顿政府里的重要官员提到墨西哥是最后一块多米诺骨牌时，在墨西哥城的政府当局，就必须有一位重要官员放下手边的事对之提出反驳，并调动民族主义对墨西哥政府的支持：墨西哥能够在不受外界干扰的情况下，管好自己。

但如果墨西哥真是一块多米诺骨牌的话，它要担心的是有人从北方

destabilization.

Indeed, every time a prominent member of the Administration in Washington refers to Mexico as the ultimate domino, a prominent member of the Administration in Mexico City must stop in his tracks, offer a rebuttal and consolidate the nationalist legitimating of the Mexican government: Mexico is capable of governing itself without outside interference.

But if Mexico is a domino, then it fears being pushed from the North rather than from the South; such has been our historical experience.

This would be the ultimate accomplishment of Washington's penchant for the self-fulfilling prophecy: A Mexico destabilized by American nightmares about Mexico. We should all be warned about this.

Far from being "blind" or "complacent", Mexico is offering its friendly hand to the United States to help it avoid the repetion of costly historical mistakes which have deeply hurt us all, North Americans and Latin Americans.

Public opinion in this country shall judge whether Mexico's obvious good faith in this matter is spurned as the United States is driven into a deepening involvement in the Central American swamp.

A Vietnam all the more dangerous because of its nearness to your national territory, indeed, but not for the reasons officially invoked. The turmoil of revolution, if permitted to run its course, promptly finds its institutional channels.

But if thwarted by intervention it will plague the United States for decades to come: Central America and the Caribbean will become the Banquet of the United States: an endemic drain on your human and material resources.

The source of change in Latin America is not in Moscow or Havana: it is in history.

So, let me turn to ourselves, as Latin Americans.

Four Failures of Identification

The failure of your present hemispheric policies is due to a fourfold failure of identification.

The first is the failure to identify change in Latin America in its cultural context.

The second is the failure to identify nationalism as the historical bearer of change in Latin America.

来推它,而不是从南来的捣乱,这是我们的历史经验。

这将是华盛顿喜欢自作自受的最终后果:美国将墨西哥妖魔化,却真的破坏了墨西哥的稳定。我们都应当听到这个警告。

墨西哥绝对没有"盲从"或"自满",而是向美国伸出友好之手,要帮助它避免重复那些代价高昂的历史错误,那些历史错误给我们所有人——北美人和拉丁美洲人——都造成了很深的伤害。

美国的公众舆论应该判断一下,看看墨西哥明显的善意是否被拒之门外,而美国却逐渐陷入中美洲的泥沼。

由于与你们国家的领土接壤,墨西哥变成越南那样情况的话,的确对你们会更危险,但其原因却不会是官方所提的那些。革命风暴吹到足够多的时候,就会很快回到正常的渠道。

但如果革命受阻于美国的干预,它就会在今后的几十年里困扰美国,中美洲和加勒比地区将成为美国的麻烦,你们的人力和物质资源会一耗而空。

拉丁美洲人心思变的根源不是来自莫斯科或哈瓦那,它来源于历史。

因此,作为拉丁美洲人,让我来谈谈我们自己。

四种认识上的失败

你们针对这半球政策目前的失败,源于四种认识上的失败。

第一是没能从其文化语境中来认识拉丁美洲的变化。

第二是没能认识到,民族主义情绪在拉丁美洲历史上就是变革的带动者。

第三是没能认识到国际权力再分配所带来的问题,对拉丁美洲的影响。

第四是没能认识到,在美国和拉丁美洲之间,这些问题引起冲突时,要设法找到能够进行谈判的空间。

拉丁美洲的文化语境

首先,让我来谈谈引起拉丁美洲变化的文化背景。

我们的社会有着文化的连贯性和政治上的非连贯性这样的特点。

我们是一个个分开的政体,但共同的文化体验又把我们紧紧地团结

The third is the failure to identify the problems of international redistribution of power as they affect Latin America.

The fourth is the failure to identify the grounds for negotiations as these issues create conflict between the United States and Latin America.

The Cultural Context of Latin America

First, the cultural context of change in Latin America.

Our societies are marked by cultural continuity and political discontinuity.

We are a Balkanized polity, yet we are deeply united by a common cultural experience.

We are and we are not of the West.

We are Indian, Black and Mediterranean.

We received the legacy of the West in an incomplete fashion, deformed by the Spanish monarchy's decision to outlaw unorthodox strains, to defeat the democratic yearnings of its own middle class and to superimpose the vertical structures of the Medieval imperium [n. 绝对统治；最高权力；[律]司法权] on the equally pyramidal configuration of power in the Indian civilizations of the Americas.

As it embarked on its imperial dealings with men and women of different cultures----if they had left at daybreak, they would be there now----Spanish absolutism mutilated the Iberian tree of its Arab and Jewish branches, heavy with fruit.

The United States is the only major power of the West that was born beyond the Middle ages, modern at birth.

As part of the fortress of the Counter-Reformation, Latin America has had to do constant battle with the past. We did not acquired freedom of speech, freedom of belief, freedom of enterprise as our birthrights, as you did.

We have had to fight desperately for them.

The complexity of the cultural struggles underlying our political and economic struggles has to do with unresolved tensions, sometimes as old as the conflict between pantheism and monotheism; or as recent as the conflict between tradition and modernity.

This is our cultural baggage, both heavy and rich.

The issues we are dealing with, behind the headlines, are very old.

在一起。

我们既可谓西方,又不是西方。

我们是印第安人、黑人和地中海人。

我们继承的西方遗产很不完整,西班牙的君主曾决定取缔非正统的宗教观念,打击中产阶级对民主的渴望,并将中世纪的宗法结构,叠加到美洲的印第安文明那种金字塔形的权力架构上。

如果他们在天亮时上路,现在应该已经走到了。但西班牙的专制主义在和其他文化的人打交道时,帝国味十足,它砍掉了伊比利亚[4]之树上的阿拉伯和犹太人树枝,哪怕这些枝头结满果实。

美国是在中世纪以后,西方出现的唯一大国,从诞生之时就带有现代性。

作为反对宗教改革的堡垒的一部分,拉丁美洲常常不得不与过去做斗争。我们不像你们,生来就有言论自由、信仰自由、创业自由的权力。

我们不得不努力为之奋斗。

我们的政治和经济斗争,都包含着文化斗争的复杂性,并与那些尚未解决的紧张关系有关,这些紧张关系中,老的有泛神论和一神论之争,新的有传统与现代之间的冲突。

这是我们的文化继承,它既沉重又丰富。

在我们看到的头条新闻后面,我们要处理的问题其实是很古老的。

虽然这些问题今天才上了新闻,但它们起源于殖民地时期,有的甚至起源于欧洲殖民之前的问题中,而且还包含了伊比利亚天主教注重教条和层次结构这样的文化因素,这种知识上的倾向,有时会促使我们从一个教堂转到另一个教堂,去寻找避难所和归宿。

这些问题掺杂了私人和公共权利世袭的混淆,以及各种令人习以为常的陋习,这些陋习包括裙带关系、心血来潮,以及群体头领在经济方面做出的非理性决定,这种决定没有人能够制约。

这些问题还涉及我们盲从于元首的传统,不顾事实而坚信观念的信仰、精英主义与人格主义的长处和公民社会的弱点;涉及神权和政治机构之间,还有权力集中制与地方政府之间的斗争。

They are finally being aired today, but they originated in colonial, sometimes in pre-Conquest situations and are embedded in the culture of Iberian Catholicism and its emphasis on dogma and hierarchy, an intellectual inclination that sometimes drives us from one church to another in search of refuge and certitude.

They are bedeviled by **patrimonial** [adj. 祖传的; 世袭的] confusions between private and public rights and forms of sanctified corruption that include nepotism, whim and the irrational economic decision made by the head of the clan, **untrammeled** [adj. 自由自在的; 无阻碍的] by checks and balances.

They have to do with the traditions of paternalistic surrender to the **Caudillo** [n.【西】(西班牙语系国家之)元首], the profound faith in ideas over facts, the strength of elitism and personalism and the weakness of the civil societies; the struggles between theocracy and political institutions, and between centralism and local government.

Since Independence in the 1820's we have been obsessed with catching up with the joneses: the West.

We created legal countries which disguised the real countries abiding---or festering----behind the constitutional facades.

Latin America has tried to find solutions to its old problems by exhausting the successive ideologies of the West: Liberalism, Positivism and Marxism.

Today, we are on the verge of transcending this dilemma by recasting it as an opportunity, at last, to be ourselves----societies neither new nor old, but, simply, authentically, Latin American as we sort out, in the excessive glare of instant communications or in the eternal dusk of our isolated villages, the benefits and the disadvantages of a tradition that now seems richer and more acceptable than it did one hundred years of solitude ago.

But we are also forced to contemplate the benefits and disadvantages of a modernity that now seems less promising than it did before economic crisis, the tragic ambiguity of science and that barbarism of nations and philosophies that were once supposed to represent "progress," all drive us to search for the time and space of culture in ourselves.

We are true children of Spain and Portugal. We have compensated for the failures of history with the successes of art.

We are now moving to what our best novels and poems and paintings and films and dances and thoughts have announced for so long: the compensation for the

自从 1820 年代独立以来,我们一直想着如何跟别人攀比——追上西方。

我们创建了法治国家,却在宪法的表象后面,掩饰了维系我们,或使我们没落的那些真正的国家形态。

拉丁美洲曾先后尝试了用西方的意识形态来解决它的旧问题,这些意识形态包括自由主义、实证主义与马克思主义。

今天,我们就要超越这一困境,把它当做总算能做回自己的一个机遇,我们的社会不再只是或新或旧,而只是正宗的拉丁美洲社会。不论是在过度耀眼的传播里,还是在我们孤独村庄永恒的暮色中,我们整理着自己传统的优缺点,现在才发现,我们的传统比"百年孤独"[5]前其实更丰富,更能让人接受。

但我们也不得不思考现代性的优缺点,在经济危机发生后,现代性看起来似乎没以前那么好,思考科学的模糊性,以及一度被认为代表"进步"的国家和哲学所表现出来的野蛮性,这些都迫使我们为自己的文化寻找时间和空间。

我们是西班牙和葡萄牙真正的子孙。我们用艺术方面的成就来弥补在历史方面的失败。

我们现在做的,就像我们最好的小说、诗歌、绘画、电影、歌舞和思想等早已经就宣布的:在历史方面的失败,我们用政治方面的成功来弥补。

那么,就像过去那样,拉丁美洲的真正斗争,始终是在与自我做斗争。

我们必须自己去解决。

其他人无法真正知道的是,我们正在经历家庭式的争吵。

我们必须消解过去的矛盾。

有时我们不得不通过暴力手段来消除过去的矛盾,就像发生在墨西哥、古巴、萨尔瓦多和尼加拉瓜的情况那样。

我们需要时间和文化。

我们也需要耐心。

需要我们和你们的耐心。

failures of history with the successes of politics.

The real struggle for Latin America is then, as always, a struggle with ourselves, within ourselves.

We must solve it by ourselves.

Nobody else can truly know it: we are living through our family quarrels.

We must assimilate this conflicted past.

Sometimes we must do it----as has occurred in Mexico, Cuba, El Salvador and Nicaragua----through violent means.

We need time and culture.

We also need patience.

Both ours and yours.

Nationalism in Latin America

Second, the identification of nationalism as the legitimate bearer of change in Latin America.

The cultural conflict I have evoked includes the stubbornness of the minimal popular demands, after all these centuries, which equate freedom with bread, schools, hospitals, national independence and a sense of dignity.

If left to ourselves, we will try to solve these problems by creating national institutions to deal with them.

All we ask from you is cooperation, trade and normal diplomatic relations.

Not your absence, but your civilized presence.

We must grow with our own mistakes.

Are we to be considered your true friends, only if we are ruled by right-wing, anti-Communist despotisms?

Instability in Latin America----or anywhere in the world, for that matter----comes when societies cannot see themselves reflected in their institutions.

Democracy in Latin America

Change in our societies shall be radical in two dimensions.

Externally, it will be more radical the more the United States intervenes against it or helps to postpone it.

Internally, it will of necessity be radical in that it must one day face up to the

拉丁美洲的民族主义

第二，认识到民族主义在拉丁美洲历史上就是变革的推动者。

我提到过的文化冲突，包括人们在经过这些世纪后，要求已经变得很低，他们把自由等同于有饭吃、有学上、有医院可以看病，民族能够独立，以及有尊严感。

如果让我们自己来处理，我们将会尝试通过建立国家机构来解决这些问题。

我们所要求你们的，是给予合作、贸易和正常的外交关系。

不是要你们别出现，而是以文明的方式出现。

我们必须在自己的错误中成长。

难道只有右翼、反共的独裁专制统治我们，你们才会把我们当做真正的朋友吗？

在拉丁美洲的不稳定，或者说，**在世界上任何地方的不稳定，都是由于社会大众在他们的政府机构中无法看到自己的反映。**

拉丁美洲的民主

我们社会的变化在两个层面是激进的。

从外部来看，如果美国介入干预或去推迟它，这个变化就会来得更加激烈。

从内部来看，由于我们迄今无法正视这些挑战，变革总有一天会不可避免地激进。我们必须在改革的同时面对民主；我们必须在改革的同时面对文化的完整性；我们所有人，古巴人、萨尔瓦多人、尼加拉瓜人和阿根廷人、墨西哥人和哥伦比亚人等，都必须最终正视在我们历史上真正紧要关头出现的问题：在我们文明的所有基础上，我们是否有能力建立起自由的社会，满足人们对保健、教育和劳动这些基本的社会需要，同时又保证人们对辩论、批判以及政治上、文化上的表达等等，这些同样基本的需求？

我知道，毫无例外地，我们所有人都还没有在拉丁美洲真正得到这些需求的满足。

我也知道，把我们社会变革的国家运动，化为东西方对弈中的小卒子，这使得我们更加无法回答这一问题：我们能够建立自由的社会吗？

challenges we have so far been unable to meet squarely: we must face democracy along with reform; we must face cultural integrity along with change; we must all finally face, Cubans, Salvadorans, Nicaraguans and Argentinians, Mexicans and Columbians, the questions that awaits us on the threshold of our true history: are we capable, with all the instruments of our civilization, of creating free societies, societies that take care of the basic needs of health, education and labor, but without sacrificing the equally basic needs of debate, criticism and political and cultural expression?

I know that all of us, without exception, have not truly fulfilled these needs in Latin America.

I also know that the transformation of our national movements into pawns of the East-West conflict makes it impossible for us to answer this question: Are we capable of creating free national societies?

This is perhaps our severest historical test.

Rightly or wrongly, many Latin Americans have come to identify the United States with opposition to our national independence.

Some perceive in United States policies the proof that the real menace to a great power is not really the other great power, but the independence of the national states: how else to understand U.S. actions that seem meaninglessly obsessed with discrediting the national revolutions in Latin Amercia?

Some are thankful that another great power exists, and appeal to it.

All of this also escalates and denaturalizes the issues at hand and avoids considering the third failure I want to deal with today: the failure to understand redistribution of power in the Western hemisphere.

Latin America and the Re-Distribution of Power

It could be debated whether the explosiveness of many Latin American societies is due less to stagnation than to growth, the quickest growth of any region in the world since 1945.

But this has been rapid growth without equally rapid distribution of the benefits of growth.

The contrast has become as explosive and understandable as it was in 1810 against Spanish colonial rule.

And it has coincided, internationally, with rapidly expanding relations between

这也许是我们最严峻的历史考验。

无论是对还是错,许多拉丁美洲人认为美国反对我们的国家独立。

有些人从美国的政策中解读出这样的证据,那就是说,对一个大国真正的威胁,其实并不是另一个大国,而是民族国家要独立,否则,你如何解释美国对在拉丁美洲发生的革命,坚持一种看起来似乎是毫无意义的怀疑?

有些人庆幸还有苏联这样另一个大国存在,并寻求它的支援。

所有这一切,都加剧了我们手头的问题,并让人们无法考虑到我今天要想谈的第三种失败:没能了解西半球权力的重新分配。

拉丁美洲和权力的重新分配

拉丁美洲许多社会的爆发性,更多的是出于增长而不是由于停滞,这种说法还是有待讨论的,拉美地区的增长,自1945年以来在世界上是最快的。

不过,这种快速增长,并没有给人们带来同样迅速的利益分配。

这种对比,和1810年人们反对西班牙殖民统治一样,既强烈,也可以理解。

在国际上,拉丁美洲也正好和新的欧洲及亚洲合作伙伴,在贸易、财政、科技和政治支持方面,迅速扩大关系。

拉丁美洲也因此成为国际间大趋势的一部分,即由两极关系向多极化或多元化结构的国际关系发展。

鉴于这一趋势,一个超级大国的衰落,反映了另一超级大国的衰落。

这就势必会造成许多冲突。正如德国总理赫尔穆特·施密特在这同一个讲坛上曾雄辩地说过的:

我们生活在一个在经济上相互依存的世界里,这个世界有150多个国家,但我们却没有足够的经验来处理这一相互依存的关系。

这两个超级大国,都越来越多地面临一个完全符合逻辑的趋势,即每个国家都要坚持自己的观点,同时也在大国影响日渐衰减的领域之外,越来越多地发展自己的多边关系。

Latin America and new European and Asian partners in trade, financing, technology and political support.

Latin American is thus part and parcel of the universal trend away from bipolar to multipolar or pluralistic structures in international relations.

Given this trend, the decline of one superpower mirrors the decline of the other superpower.

This is bound to create numerous areas of conflict. As Chancellor Helmut Schmidt eloquently expressed it from this same **rostrum** [n. 演讲坛],

"We are living in an economically interdependent world of more than 150 countries----without having enough experience in managing this interdependence."

Both superpowers increasingly face a perfectly logical movement towards national self-assertion accompanied by growing multilateral relationships beyond the decaying spheres of influence.

No change comes about without tension and in Latin America this tension arises as we strive for greater wealth and independence, but also as we immediately start losing both because of internal economic injustice and external economic crisis.

The middle classes we have spawned over the past fifty years are shaken by a revolution of diminishing expectations ----of Balzacian "lost illusions."

Modernity and its values are coming under critical fire while the values of nationalism are discovered to be perfectly identifiable with traditionalist, even conservative considerations.

The mistaken identification of change in Latin America as somehow manipulated by a Soviet conspiracy not only irritates the nationalism of the left. It also resurrects the nationalist fervors of the right----

Where, after all, Latin American nationalism was born in the early 19th century.

You have yet to feel the full force of this backlash, which reappeared in Argentina and the South Atlantic crisis last year, in places such as El Salvador and Panama, Peru and Chile, Mexico and Brazil.

A whole continent, in the name of cultural identity, nationalism and international independence, is capable of uniting against you.

This should not happen.

所有的变革都会带来紧张。在拉丁美洲,当我们努力争取更多的财富和更大的独立性时,这种紧张局势会出现;由于内部的经济不公和外部的经济危机,我们的财富和独立性也立即开始流失时,这种紧张局势同样也会出现。

我们在过去 50 年里发展起来的中产阶级,被这场期望值日益减小的革命所震撼,正如巴尔扎克小说里所写的,"产生了幻灭"。

现代性及其价值大受批评,而人们发现,民族主义的价值观和传统的,甚至是保守的想法不谋而合。

有人错误地把拉丁美洲发生的变化说成在某种程度上是受了苏联阴谋的操纵,这不仅惹恼了左派的民族主义情绪,也重振了右派的民族主义热情。

毕竟,拉丁美洲的民族主义早在 19 世纪初期就已经诞生了。

你们还没有充分感受到这份反作用力,它在阿根廷和去年的南大西洋危机中又重新出现,也重新出现在诸如萨尔瓦多和巴拿马、秘鲁和智利、墨西哥和巴西等地方。

这一整个大陆,可能会在文化认同、民族主义和国际独立的名义下,团结起来一致对付你们。

这种情况,本来是不应该出现的。

找到机会,避免这种同属一洲的国家之间发生冲突,要靠我今天要谈的第四和最后一点:谈判才是正道。

在为时太晚之前进行谈判

美国在与本半球的遥远国家(比如智利和阿根廷)、与最大的国家(巴西)、与地理上靠得最近的国家(墨西哥)等,在文化、民族诉求上和国际主义的压力方面分别同左、右两派进行谈判前,美国应当迅速地同中美洲和加勒比地区举行谈判,这符合你们的利益,也符合我们的利益。

我们在墨西哥的人认为,该地区的每一个冲突点,在为时太晚之前,都可以通过谈判,靠外交的方法寻求解决。

这样说并不意味着政治上的灭亡——不管在该地区的任何国家发生了革命运动,这并不能说,它不可避免地就成为苏联的基地。

在一个边缘国家发生革命的黎明,到假想它成为苏联基地的结局之间,

The chance of avoiding this continental confrontation is in the fourth and final opening I wish to deal with today: that of negotiations.

Negotiations Before It Is Too Late

Before the United States has to negotiate with extreme cultural, nationalistic and internationalist pressures of both the left and the right in the remotest nations of this hemisphere----Chile and Argentina----, in the largest nation----Brazil----and in the closest one----Mexico----it should rapidly, in its own interest as well as ours, negotiate in Central America and the Caribbean.

We consider in Mexico that each and every one of the points of conflict in the region can be solved diplomatically, through negotiations, before it is too late.

There is not fatality in politics that says: given a revolutionary movement in any country in the region, it will inevitably end up providing bases for the Soviet Union.

What happens between the daybreak of revolution in a marginal country and its imagined destiny as a Soviet base?

If nothing happens but harassment, blockades, propaganda, pressures and invasions against the revolutionary country, then that prophecy will become self-fulfilling.

But if power with historical memory and diplomacy with historical imagination come into play, we, the United States and Latin America, might end up with something very different:

A Latin America of independent states building institutions of stability, renewing the culture of national identity, diversifying our economic interdependence and wearing down the dogmas of two **musty** [adj. 发霉的；落伍的] 19th century philosophies.

And a United States giving the example of a tone in relations which is present, active, co-operative, respectful, aware of cultural differences and truly proper for a great power unafraid of ideological labels, capable of coexisting with diversity in Latin America as it has learnt to coexist with diversity in Black Africa.

Precisely twenty years ago, John F. Kennedy said at another Commencement ceremony:

If we cannot end now our differences, at least we can help make the world safe for diversity.

会有什么事情发生？

如果人们看到，这个发生革命的国家面临的只是骚扰、封锁、宣传、施压和入侵，那么，那样的预言就会不幸成为现实。

但是，如果人们能够记住历史，外交努力能够富有历史想象力，那么，美国和拉丁美洲就有可能最终获得一些非常不同的结果：

让拉丁美洲的独立国家，建立起稳定的机构，更新其文化的民族特性，把我们经济上的相互依存向多样化发展，并且消除 19 世纪哲学思想里的两个落伍的信条。

而美国则能起到一个表率作用，把双边关系的调子，定位为及时的、积极的、寻求合作、尊重他人、了解文化差异，并且真正像一个大国的样子，不怕意识形态的标签，能够与拉丁美洲的多元文化共存，就像美国已经学会了与黑非洲的多元文化共存那样。

整整 20 年前，约翰·肯尼迪在哈佛的毕业典礼上这样说道：

如果我们现在还不能消除彼此之间的差异，我们至少可以让世界的多样性更安全一些。

这一点，我认为是这位让我们大家共同悼念的政治家，给我们留下的最大遗产。

让我们理解这种遗产，肯尼迪的死亡不再是一个谜，不再为他未能办成什么事而感伤，而是化为我们能做什么事的希望。

这是可以办到的。

在中美洲和加勒比地区发生的战争，时间拖得越长，从政治上获得解决方案的机会就越难。

桑德内思特[6]政权由于受到（美国的）外界压力而宣布国家进入紧急状态，让它越来越难以显示诚意、着手处理内部的民主问题。

萨尔瓦多反叛力量里的平民部分，就将更难以让武装派别接受他们提出的政治倡议。

把巴拿马当做发起北美战争的一块跳板，让它的局势越来越紧张，发生

This, I think, is the greatest legacy of the sacrificed statesman whose death we all mourned.

Let us understand that legacy, by which death ceased to be an enigma and became, not a lament for what might have been, but a hope for what can be.

This can be.

The longer the situation of war lasts in Central America and the Caribbean, the more difficult it shall be to assure a political solution.

The more difficult it will be for the Sandinistas to demonstrate good faith in their dealings with the issues of internal democracy, now brutally interrupted by a state of emergency imposed as a response to foreign pressures.

The more difficult it will be for the civilian arm of the Salvadoran rebellion to maintain political initiative over the armed factions.

The greater the irritation of Panama as it is used as a springboard for a North American war.

The greater the danger of a generalized conflict, dragging into Costa Rica and Honduras.

Everything can be negotiated in Central America and the Caribbean, before it is too late.

Non-aggression pacts between each and every state.

Border patrols.

The **interdiction** [n. 封锁; 禁止] of passage of arms, wherever they may come from, and the interdiction of foreign military advisers, wherever they may come from.

The reduction of all the armies in the region.

The interdiction, now or ever, of Soviet bases or Soviet offensive capabilities in the area.

What would be the quid pro quo?

Simply this: the respect of the United States, respect for the integrity and autonomy of all the states in the region, including normalization of relations with all of them.

The countries in the region should not be forced to seek solutions to their problems outside themselves.

The problems of Cuba are Cuban and shall be so once more when the United

更大冲突的危险就越大，会把哥斯达黎加和洪都拉斯都拖进这个冲突。

只要不是太晚，中美洲和加勒比地区的所有事情都可以协商。

每一个国家之间都应订立互不侵犯条约。

进行边境巡逻。

禁止输入武器、无论武器来自何方；也禁止外国军事顾问参与，无论他们来自任何地方。

裁减该地区的所有军队。

现在不允许，以后也禁止苏联在这个地区建立基地或纠集发动进攻的能力。

作为交换的条件该是些什么呢？

那就是：美国尊重该地区所有国家的领土完整和自治，包括与所有这些国家都实现关系正常化。

该地区的国家不应当被迫从外界寻求方案，来解决他们自己的问题。

古巴的问题应当由古巴人自己去解决，当美国认识到，如果拒绝和古巴谈古巴问题，这不仅对古巴和美国没好处，反而让苏联得势。有了这样的认识，古巴问题就更应当由古巴人自己去解决了。

古巴不断提出，愿意同美国就任何问题进行谈判，但都遭到了拒绝。这使在古巴内部，希望有更大的内部灵活性和国际独立性的力量倍感失望。

菲德尔·卡斯特罗是像马基雅维里[7]那样高明的政治家，以致没有哪位美国谈判代表可以在谈判桌上和他交手，而不被他算计吗？我不相信这一点。

尼加拉瓜

尼加拉瓜的问题属于尼加拉瓜人，但如果那个国家被剥夺了正常存在下去的一切可能，那问题就大了。

为什么美国对仅出现4年的桑地诺主义[8]如此不耐烦，而对长达45年的索摩查统治，却是如此宽容？

为什么美国如此担心在尼加拉瓜举行的自由选举，但却平淡地对待智利的自由选举？

还有，如果美国那么尊重民主，为什么当智利的民选总统萨尔瓦多·阿连德被人们称为"南方的雅鲁泽尔斯基"[9]的奥古斯托·皮诺切特将军推翻

States understands that by refusing to talk to Cuba on Cuba, it not only weakens Cuba and the United States, but strengthens the Soviet Union.

The mistake of spurning Cuba's constant offers to negotiate whatever the United States wants to discuss frustrates the forces in Cuba desiring greater internal flexibility and international independence.

Is Fidel Castro some sort of superior Machiavelli whom no **gringo** [n. 外国佬（拉美人对英美等外国人的蔑称）] negotiator can meet at a bargaining table without being bamboozled by him? I don't believe it.

Nicaragua

The problems of Nicaragua are Nicaraguan but they will cease to be so if that country is deprived of all possibility for normal survival.

Why is the United States so impatient with four years of Sandinismo, when it was so tolerant of forty-five years of Somocismo?

Why is it so worried about free elections in Nicaragua, but so indifferent to free elections in Chile?

And why, if it respects democracy so much, did the United States not rush to the defence of the democratically elected President of Chile, Salvador Allende, when he was overthrown by the Southern Jaruzelski, General Augusto Pinochet?

How can we live and grow together on the basis of such hypocrisy?

Nicaragua is being attacked and invaded by forces sponsored by the United States.

It is being invaded by counter-revolutionary bands led by former commanders of Somoza's National Guard who are out to overthrow the Revolutionary government and re-instate the old tyranny.

Who will stop them from doing so if they win?

These are not freedom fighters. They are Benedict Arnolds.

El Salvador

The problems of El Salvador, finally, are Salvadoran.

The Salvadoran rebellion did not originate and is not manipulated from outside El Salvador. To believe this is akin to crediting Soviet accusations that the Solidarity Movement in Poland is somehow the creature of the United States. The passage

时，美国不赶去捍卫？

在这种虚伪的基础上，我们怎能和平共处，一道成长？

尼加拉瓜正在受到由美国所赞助势力的攻击和入侵。

由索摩查国民卫队的前指挥官带领的反革命集团，想要推翻尼加拉瓜的革命政府，恢复过去的暴政。

如果他们赢了，有谁能制止他们这样做？

这些人不是自由战士。他们是些乌合之众。

萨尔瓦多

说到底，萨尔瓦多的问题，要由萨尔瓦多人自己去解决。

萨尔瓦多发生的反叛活动，并不是起源于萨尔瓦多之外，也没有受到外界的操纵。相信"外界操纵"之说，就像相信苏联指责波兰团结工会运动在某种程度上是美国操纵出来的指控一样。从尼加拉瓜向萨尔瓦多运送武器一说也还无法证明，人们还没有查到过武器运输。

萨尔瓦多冲突的起因，是由于当地人民看到政治上的腐败和民主的不可能，从1931年军队操纵选举结果开始，到1972年由于选举舞弊达到高潮，1972年的选举舞弊，剥夺了基督教民主党和社会民主本应赢得的选举，迫使中产阶层的子弟拿起武装进行反抗。该国的军队已用尽了通过选举的可能得出的各种解决方案。

这支军队继续愚弄萨尔瓦多（包括美国）的每一个人。它在暗杀了反对派的政治领袖后宣布选举，然后邀请反动派参与这些仓促组织的选举，也许死魂灵才能当选？

这种果戈理[10]小说里写过的场景，意味着只要由美元资助的军队和死刑执行队还在大行其道，萨尔瓦多就无法举行真正的自由选举。

现在，没有什么力量能向萨尔瓦多人民保证，该国的军队和死刑执行队能够打败叛军，或能由政治机构来对它们进行约束。

恰恰是由于该国军队的性质，萨尔瓦多必须迅速找到政治解决的办法，不仅是为了制止可怕的死亡人数继续增加，不仅是为了制约军队和武装叛乱分子的活动，不仅是为了保证你们美国的年轻人不用再去重复发生在越南的

of arms from Nicaragua to El Salvador has not been proved: no arms have been intercepted.

The conflict in El Salvador is the indigenous result of a process of political corruption and democratic impossibility that began in 1931 with the electoral results by the Army, and culminated in the electoral fraud of 1972, which deprived the Christian Democrats and the Social Democrats of their victory and forced the sons of the middle class into armed insurrection. The Army had exhausted the electoral solution.

This Army continues to outwit everyone in El Salvador -- including the United States. It announces elections after assassinating the political leadership of the opposition, then asks the opposition to come back and participate in these same hastily organized elections as dead souls, perhaps?

This Gogolian scenario means that truly free elections cannot be held in El Salvador as long as the Army and the death squads are unrestrained and fueled by American dollars.

Nothing now assures Salvadorans that the Army and the squads can either defeat the rebals or be controlled by political institutions.

It is precisely because of the nature of the Army that a political settlement must be reached in El Salvador promptly, not only to stop the horrendous death count, not only to restrain both the Army and the armed rebels, not only to assure your young people in the United States that they will not be doomed to repeat the horror and futility of Vietnam, but to reconstruct a political initiative of the center-left majority that must now reflect, nevertheless, the need for a restructured Army. El Salvador cannot be governed with such a heavy burden of crime.

The only other option is to transform the war in El Salvador into an American war.

But why should a bad foreign policy be bipartisan?

Without the rebels in El Salvador, the United States would never have worried about "democracy" in El Salvador. If the rebels are denied political participation in El Salvador, how long will it be before El Salvador is totally forgotten once more?

Let us remember, let us imagine, let us reflect.

The United States can no longer go it alone in Central America and the Caribbean. It cannot, in today's world, practice the anachronistic policies of the "Big

那种徒劳无益,而是重建反映大多数人愿望的中间偏左的政治形式。不过,这种政治形式也必须代表经过重组后的军队的需要。萨尔瓦多不能再由犯过这么多罪行的势力来管辖。

如果不这样,其他的唯一选择,就是把在萨尔瓦多发生的战争变成一场美国的战争。

但为什么一项坏的外交政策,要由两党来支持?

如果在萨尔瓦多没有叛乱分子,美国永远也不会担心萨尔瓦多的"民主"。如果反叛分子在萨尔瓦多的政治上没有一席之地,要过多久,美国才会再一次把萨尔瓦多完全遗忘?

让我们记住这点,让我们想象一下,让我们进行反思。

在中美洲和加勒比地区,美国不再可以独立行事。在当今世界,美国不能再不合时宜地推行"挥舞大棒"的政策。

如果美国挥舞大棒,它得到的将会是它正好不想要的东西。

我们许多国家都在努力,不想再作"香蕉共和国"[11]。

他们也不想成为俄式共和国。

不要强迫他们不是向苏联献媚,就是屈从于美国。

我的呼吁是:

不要在我们这个半球搞唯我独尊。

实行积极的领导。加入拉丁美洲推动变化、保持耐心和延续认同的力量。

美国应当把握这种世界权力重新分配的现实,乘势而上。我前面所谈论的所有途径,现在都各就其位,可能带来和谐。美国在西半球有真正的朋友。这些朋友必须进行谈判,而这种谈判如果只是美国自己参加,那是谈不成的。这些参与谈判的国家有对其中涉及的文化问题了如指掌,这些国家包括墨西哥、委内瑞拉、巴拿马和哥伦比亚,或许明天还会有我们讲葡萄牙语的伟大姊妹国巴西,或许也有新的民主化了的西班牙,(它能帮助我们重建伊比利亚的遗产),并扩大孔塔多拉集团[12]的结构。

这些国家也会有足够的想象力,保证离开了美国的势力范围,不是要进入苏联的势力范围,而是在一个多元化的世界中,形成我们自己的拉丁美洲一角。

Stick."

It will only achieve, if it does so, what it cannot truly want.

Many of our countries are struggling to cease being banana republics.

They do not want to become **balalaika** [n. 俄式三弦琴] republics.

Do not force them to choose between appealing to the Soviet Union or capitulating to the United States.

My plea is this one:

Do not practice negative **overlordship** [n. 封建君主的权位] in this hemisphere.

Practice positive leadership. Join the forces of change and patience and identity in Latin America.

The United States should use the new realities of re-distributed world power to its advantage. All the avenues I have been dealing with come together now to form a circle of possible harmony: the United States has true friends in this hemisphere; these friends must negotiate the situations that the United States, while participating in them, cannot possibly negotiate for itself, and the negotiating parties -- from Mexico and Venezuela, Panama and Colombia, tomorrow perhaps our great Portuguese speaking sister, Brazil, perhaps the new Spanish democracy, re-establishing the **continuum** [n. 【哲】连续] of our Iberian heritage, and expanding the Contadora group -- have the intimate knowledge of the underlying cultural problems.

And they have the imagination for assuring the inevitable passage from the American sphere of influence, not to the Soviet sphere, but to our own Latin American authenticity in a pluralistic world.

President Bok, Ladies and Gentlemen:

My friend Milan Kundera, the Czech novelist, makes a plea for "the small cultures" from the wounded heart of Central Europe.

I have tried to echo it today from the convulsed heart of Latin America.

Politicians will disappear.

The United States and Latin America will remain.

What sort of neighbors will you have?

What sort of neighbors will we have?

That will depend on the quality of our memory and also of our imagination.

"If we had started out at daybreak, we would be there now."

伯克校长、女士们、先生们：

我的朋友，捷克小说家米兰·昆德拉在中欧那个伤心的地方，请求人们为"弱小文化"保存一席之地。

今天，拉丁美洲的心脏在抽搐，我要做出类似的呼吁。

政客们将会烟消云散。

美国和拉丁美洲将青山常在。

你们会有怎样的邻国？

我们会有怎样的邻国？

这将取决于我们是否记住过去，也取决于我们的想象力。

"如果我们黎明时就上路，我们现在应该已经到了。"

我们的时间未能趋于一致。

你们的黎明很快就要来到。

我们的夜还长。

但如果我们都认识到，人心一念在于当下，在眼下这个我们既能记住又有期望的时刻，我们要克服时代的距离：我们的过去与我们的未来，在当下融为一体。

现实不是意识幽灵的产物，

它是历史的产物。

历史是我们自己创造的东西，

因此，我们要对我们的历史负责。

没有人能穿越到过去，

已经逝去的，无法在今天复活。

没有人能活在未来，

但如果我们无法想象一个更好的世界，那我们就白活了。

我们共同创造了这个半球的历史，

我们必须一起牢记，

我们必须共同畅想。

我们需要有你们的记忆、你们的想象力，否则我们的记忆和想象力永远也不会完整。

Our times have not coincided.

Your daybreak came quickly.

Our night has been long.

But we can overcome the distance between our times if we can both recognize that the true duration of the human heart is in the present, this present in which we remember and we desire: this present where our past and our future are one.

Reality is not the product of an ideological phantasm [n. 幻像；幻影；幽灵].

It is the result of history.

And history is something we have created ourselves.

We are thus responsible for our history.

No one was present in the past.

But there is no living present with a dead past.

No one has been present in the future.

But there is no living present without the imagination of a better world.

We both made the history of this Hemisphere.

We must both remember it.

We must both imagine it.

We need your memory and your imagination or ours shall never be complete.

We need our memory to redeem your past, and our imagination to complete your future.

We may be here on this hemisphere for a long time.

Let us remember one another.

Let us respect one another.

Let us walk together outside the night of repression and hunger and intervention, even if for you the sun is at high noon and for us at a quarter to twelve.

我们需要用我们的记忆来弥补你们的过去,用我们的想象力来支持你们的未来。

我们可能要在这个半球上共处很长时间。

让我们记住彼此。

让我们互相尊重。

让我们一起走出压迫、饥饿和干涉的黑夜,哪怕对你们来说,正是艳阳高照,而对我们来说,仍是长夜未央。

---

1 埃米利亚诺·萨帕塔(Emiliano Zapata),墨西哥革命的领袖,他所领导的墨西哥南方农民武装是墨西哥1910年革命的重要组成力量。1879年8月8日生于安内内库尔科(莫雷洛斯州),1919年4月10日在莫雷洛斯州遭伏击身亡。萨帕塔以"土地与自由"为革命的目标,他在1911年公布的《阿亚拉计划》(Plan Ayala)中,提出革命要解决农民问题,要求实行土地改革。

2 卡尔文·柯立芝(Calvin Coolidge,1872—1933),曾于1923年至1929年任美国总统。

3 这里提到的人都是墨西哥著名的文学家、艺术家。

4 伊比利亚(Iberia),南欧的伊比利亚半岛上有西班牙、葡萄牙、英属直布罗陀等国家和地区。

5 这里借用了"百年孤独"的说法,《百年孤独》(One Hundred Years of Solitude)是哥伦比亚作家加西亚·马尔克斯的代表作。

6 尼加拉瓜的一个政党

7 马基雅维里(Machiavelli,1469—1527),文艺复兴时期意大利著名的政治思想家。

8 桑地诺主义(Sandinismo)是指尼加拉瓜民族英雄桑地诺(1893—1934)倡导的抗美爱国的民族革命。

9 雅鲁泽尔斯基(Wojciech Jaruzelski),曾于1980年代任波兰共产党的领导人。

10 果戈理,俄罗斯著名作家,代表作有发表于1842年的长篇小说《死魂灵》。

11 香蕉共和国(banana republic),政治专有名词,是指经济体系属于单一经济(通常是经济作物如香蕉、可可、咖啡等)、拥有不民主或不稳定的政府,特别是那些拥有广泛贪污和强大外国势力介入的国家的贬称,通常用来指中美洲和加勒比海的小国家。

12 孔塔多拉集团(Contadora Group),1980年代初,中美洲多国的内战严重影响了拉美的政治稳定和安全,史称"中美洲危机"。1983年1月,墨西哥、哥伦比亚、委内瑞拉、巴拿马在孔塔多拉举行会议,形成孔塔多拉集团,试图化解危机。

胡安·卡洛斯一世（1938— ）

　　胡安·卡洛斯一世是西班牙的国家元首，也是西班牙武装部队的最高统帅。不同于当今世界上现存的大多数只有着某种象征性作用的君主，胡安·卡洛斯在本国的政治生活中起着举足轻重的决定性作用。

　　胡安·卡洛斯出生于意大利罗马，当时他的祖父、西班牙波旁王朝的最后一位国王阿方索十三世已经流亡海外。幼年时的胡安·卡洛斯随父母旅居意大利、瑞士和葡萄牙等国，从小接受严格的王室教育，在8岁时就被送进了纪律严格的寄宿学校。1947年西班牙军阀佛朗哥宣布恢复君主政体，选择胡安·卡洛斯为未来的国王，并把他召回西班牙接受教育。因为父亲不能回到西班牙，1948年10岁的胡安·卡洛斯就告别父母，独自前往马德里。中学毕业后，胡安·卡洛斯接受了全面的军事训练，先后在陆、海、空三军军事学院学习。1960年，胡安·卡洛斯进入马德里大学学习政治、法律、哲学、历史、文学和国际法等课程。大学毕业后，他到政府各部门开始从政实践，了解国家的行政管理情况。1975年11月胡安·卡洛斯正式登基，王号为胡安·卡洛斯一世。

　　胡安·卡洛斯执政开明，对内主张民主与改革，他于1981年1月粉碎了那些企图终止西班牙民主进程的佛朗哥旧势力暗中发动的一次军事政变。他对外主张与所有国家保持友好，重视西班牙与中国的关系，曾先后两度访华。

　　胡安·卡洛斯在位期间推行了西班牙从专制到民主的改革，后来他更主动放弃权力，使西班牙实现了从君主专制制度到君主立宪制的过渡，因此胡安·卡洛斯在世界范围内赢得了广泛的认可和赞赏。

1984

Embracing the Beginning of a New Morning
迎接新黎明的开始

Juan Carlos I 胡安·卡洛斯

Ladies and Gentlemen, Dear Friends, and Especially Today's Graduates:

On the **Plateresque** [n. 带复杂花叶形装饰的] front of Salamanca University, beside a **medallion** [n. 圆形浮雕，圆形装饰] of King Ferdinand and Queen Isabella, there is a Greek inscription which reads, "The Monarchs for the University and the University for the Monarchs". These words express the deep ties which for many centuries in Spain linked the Crown to the University.

They also explain my feelings of profound satisfaction on being awarded this Doctorate Honoris Causa and thus being welcomed into Harvard, a university of great distinction for so many reasons.

As the Spanish philosopher Jose Ortega y Gasset reminded us, the development of the University is **indissolubly** [adj. 不能溶解的，牢不可破的] associated with the origins of our Western history.

I come from an old country, whose University tradition is deeply rooted in history. Our first university, the "Estudio General" of Palencia, was founded in 1212 by Tello Tellez de Meneses.

His life was short, but long enough for him to have as a student Santo Domingo de Guzman, founder of the Order of Preachers, and to compose the "Gaudeamus Igitur". You sing it on all solemn occasions, and it still retains its original freshness, after nearly nine centuries.

Three years later, in 1215, King Alfonso the Ninth of Leon founded the University of Salamanca, whose fame transcended all national borders, and whose masters in the law of nations laid the foundations of modern international law.

The Universities of Sevilla, Valladolid and Lerida were founded in the XIIIth century, and those of Huesca, Valencia, Gerona, Barcelona and Alcala de Henares in the XIVth and XVth centuries. In the XVIth century, about twenty new names – some as distinguished as Santiago de Compostela—were scattered over the Peninsula in a **veritable** [adj. 确实的，真正的] explosion of cultural vitality that provided an accurate measure of Spain's contribution to the progress of learning of the age.

Then, only fifty-nine years were to **elapse** [v. 逝去，过去] from the moment that Christopher Columbus first set foot on the soil of Hispaniola until the founding in Lima and Mexico of the first two universities of the American continent.

The powerful impulse of the universities on this side of the Atlantic has followed in the wake of the prestige of the Mediaeval and Renaissance universities of Spain and

女士们、先生们、朋友们,特别是今天毕业的同学们:

在萨拉曼卡大学[1]带有雕花装饰的正面,在费迪南德国王和伊莎贝拉女王的圆形浮雕旁边,有一句希腊铭文,它这样写道:"君主爱大学,大学爱君主。"这些话表达了许多世纪以来,西班牙的君主与大学的深厚渊源。

这些话也能解释为什么我对获得哈佛授予荣誉博士学位,并在这里得到礼遇而深感高兴,因为有太多的原因让这所大学独享盛名。

正如西班牙哲学家何塞·奥尔特加·加塞特[2]所提醒我们的,大学的发展与我们西方的历史起源有着不可分割的紧密联系。

我来自一个古老的国度,大学的传统深深地植根于其历史。我们的第一所大学,帕伦西亚的"开放学院",是在1212年由特洛·特勒兹·德·蒙内西斯创立的。

德·蒙内西斯的一生是短暂的,但他在有生之年培养出了传教士使团的创始人圣多明哥·德·古斯曼,并谱写了《让我们同欢乐》("Gaudeamus Igitur")的歌词[3]。我们在所有隆重的场合唱这首歌,哪怕时间过了将近9个世纪,这首歌词仍然清新无比。

3年后,莱昂国王阿方索九世在1215年创立了萨拉曼卡大学,该校的名气超越所有国界,学校里研究国家法律的大师们奠定了现代国际法的基础。

塞维利亚、瓦拉多利德和莱里达大学成立于13世纪,韦斯卡、瓦伦西亚、赫罗纳、巴塞罗那和阿尔卡拉-埃纳雷斯大学成立于14和15世纪。到了16世纪,约有20所新的学校出现,比如圣地亚哥著名的孔波斯特拉,散布于西班牙半岛上。这种文化活力的爆炸,准确反映了西班牙在那个时代对学术进步的贡献。

然后,就在克里斯托弗·哥伦布首次踏足伊斯帕尼奥拉土地,之后仅仅过了59年,在利马和墨西哥就出现了美洲大陆最早的两所大学。

在大西洋此岸的大学,其强大的发展动力来自于追寻西班牙和欧洲故土上中世纪和文艺复兴时期那些大学的声望。其中,哈佛大学以思想的先行及赋予科学以最高的价值,在发挥重大影响方面成为一个范例。

这所大学成立于1636年,也是美国最古老的大学。它的学堂里闪耀

old Europe. Among them, Harvard University constitutes a **paradigm** [n. 范例，典范] of their great influence in the vanguard of thought, and of their supreme scientific values.

This University, founded in 1636, is also the oldest seat of learning in the United States. Its halls are hallowed by a **pleiad** [n. (人或物的) 一批精华] of famous names: Robert Frost, T.S. Eliot, William James and so many others who have contributed to the universal prestige in which Harvard's name is held today.

Its humanistic tradition has been upheld throughout the years, reflecting the spirit of each century, while its rigorous devotion to scientific disciplines has made it one of the campuses to receive the greatest number of Nobel Prizes.

It is therefore not difficult to understand the prestige acquired by graduating from Harvard, a prestige won during centuries of tenacious effort, ever since the Reverend John Harvard gave his name and left his books and his estate to the future University.

For obvious reasons, it is particularly gratifying for me to mention one aspect of your activities: the special attention that has always been given by Harvard to the study of Hispanic culture.

Indeed, ever since the 1800's, Harvard University has been one of the world's leading institutions in its concern for Hispanic culture. The first scholarly History of Spanish Literature was written by a pioneering Harvard professor: George Ticknor. It was translated into Spanish two years after its publication in English in 1849, and for many years it was one of the principal textbooks in Spanish universities for students of literature.

This **propitious** [adj. 有利的，吉利的] atmosphere enabled Harvard to produce Hispanic specialists of the caliber of George Ticknor, Francis Sales, J.M.D. Ford, Henry Wadsworth Longfellow, James Russell Lowell, Bennet Hubbard Nash and Stephen Gilman, and many Spanish professors to come and work here fruitfully.

Men as distinguished as Jorge Santayana, Americo Castro, Rafael Lapesa and Damaso Alonso have been here, as well as many others.

But I shall not review the whole history of Hispanic studies at Harvard: it would require much more time than I have, and many of you know far more about it than I do. I shall not refrain, however, from expressing the gratitude of the Spanish people to Harvard university (as well as to many other American universities and colleges) for what they did after the ending of the Spanish Civil War to help maintain the

着一大批不朽的名字：罗伯特·弗罗斯特、T.S.艾略特、威廉·詹姆斯以及其他许多人物，让哈佛的名字在今天受到普遍的尊敬。

多年来哈佛一直坚持了体现每个世纪独特精神的人文传统，而且严谨地致力于科学探索，使这个校园产生了众多的诺贝尔奖得主。

因此，不难理解，自从约翰·哈佛牧师把自己的名字和他的藏书留给了未来的这所大学后，通过几个世纪的顽强努力，毕业于哈佛本身，就已经足以赢得人们的尊敬。

不用说，我最愿意提及的是哈佛一向对研究西班牙文化特别重视这个方面。

事实上，自从1800年代以来，哈佛大学就一直是世界上研究西班牙文化的重镇之一。第一本学术著作"西班牙文学史"就是由哈佛教授乔治·提科诺撰写的。这本书于1849年在英国出版，两年后被翻译成西班牙文，多年来一直是西班牙大学里文学学生的主要教科书之一。

这种有利的气氛，使乔治·提科诺、弗朗西斯·萨里斯、J.M.D.福特、亨利·沃兹沃斯·朗费罗、詹姆斯·罗素·洛厄尔、班纳特·哈伯德·纳什和斯蒂芬·吉尔曼这样水准的西班牙专家，以及许多西班牙教授，来到这里进行卓有成效的工作。

杰出人物如乔治·桑塔亚纳、阿梅利科·卡斯特罗、拉斐尔·拉培萨和达马索·阿隆索，以及其他许多人，也曾经到过这里。

不过，我不会回顾哈佛西班牙学研究的通篇历史，这会需要太多的时间，你们当中许多人对此也比我知道的多得多。然而，我要毫无保留地表达西班牙人民对哈佛大学（还有许多其他美国大学和学院）的感谢，因为在西班牙内战结束后，这些美国院校帮助保持了西班牙文化的连续性和完整性。在这里以及这个国家的其他地方，西班牙的流亡学者和作家们找到了一个欢迎他们前来生活和工作的避风港。本世纪西班牙文化史上，有整整一个篇章涉及那些在这个国家继续创造性活动的西班牙人。

我想向两位在这个地方去世的人表达哀思：他们是文学家阿马多·阿隆索和医学家霍尔迪·福尔克·拜。

另外两位曾在哈佛任教的伟大的西班牙人，最近在西班牙去世，他

continuity and the integrity of Hispanic culture. Here and elsewhere in this country, exiled Spanish scholars and writers found a welcome haven for their lives and work. An entire chapter in the history of Spanish culture of this century concerns those who continued their creative activity in this country.

I would like to pay tribute to the memory of two who died here: the literary scholar Amado Alonso, and the medical scientist Jordi Folch Pi.

Two other great Spaniards who taught at Harvard have recently died in Spain: the poet Jorge Guillen, and the architect Josep Lluis Sert. Some of you no doubt attended lectures by Jorge Guillen when he was the Charles Eliot Norton Professor in 1957-58, and others among you must have heard him read his poetry during his many years of residence in Cambridge. Nor can we fail to notices Sert's enduring presence here, in the architectural landscape of the University.

I also wish to convey a special message of thanks and encouragement to Professors Juan Marichal and Francisco Marquez Villanueva, who continue to bear aloft the torch of Hispanic studies.

Ladies and Gentlemen,

On this day that is so memorable for me and for Spain, I feel deep humility and great pride. My humility, of course, is due to the scholarly distinction conferred upon me by Harvard, an honor that I did not earn after years of study in its halls, as did all of you Harvard graduates who received your degrees this morning. But this feeling of personal humility cannot be separated from my sense of great national pride, because Harvard university has honored through me the people of Spain, and as their representative I wish above all to express our gratitude to Harvard University for the significance of this day as a historic recognition of the exemplary manner in which the Spaish people have restored democratic institutions in our country.

The driving force behind this historic accomplishment has been the strong aspirations of the Spanish people as a whole to reconstruct institutions that would offer Spain freedom and peaceful coexistence, equality and political stability, and at the same time—having learned the lessons of history—to avoid **recriminations** [n. 反控告, 反责] and revenge.

This may be surprising to those who think of Spain as Metternich did in the 1830's when he wrote, "Spain is a country of extremes and it will be either an absolutist monarchy or a radical republic". Metternich justified his view of Spain by

们是诗人乔治·吉兰、建筑师何塞普·路易斯·瑟特。毫无疑问，当他1957年至1958年担任查尔斯·艾略特·诺顿讲座教授时，你们中的一些人一定听过乔治·吉兰的讲课，其他人则肯定在他多年居住在坎布里奇期间，听过他朗诵自己写的诗。我们也不能不注意到瑟特在这里的持久影响，因为我们大学校园里，就有他设计的建筑景观。

我也想向在这里继续高举西班牙研究火炬的教授胡安·马利查尔和弗朗西斯科·马尔克斯·维拉纽瓦教授，表达特别的感谢和鼓励。

女士们先生们，

在对我和西班牙来说是如此令人难忘的这一天里，我深感谦卑，也感到非常自豪。当然，我感到谦卑是因为哈佛授予我的荣誉学位，不是我在这里的学堂经过多年学习而得来的，而今天上午获得学位的所有哈佛毕业生，都经历了这样的历程。但这种个人谦卑的感觉，不能与我感受到的一种伟大的民族骄傲感分开，因为哈佛大学通过我，给了西班牙人民荣誉，作为他们的代表，我想首先感谢哈佛大学，把这当做历史性的一天，来肯定西班牙人民在我们国家恢复民主体制方面，起到的模范表率。

这一历史性成就背后的推动力，是全体西班牙人民重建家园的强烈愿望，他们希望西班牙能有自由与和平共处、有平等和政治稳定，与此同时，他们吸取了历史的教训，要避免互相指责和报复。

梅特涅[4]在1830年代时写道："西班牙是一个极端的国家，它不是专制君主制，就是一个激进的共和国。"那些和他一样看待西班牙的人，可能会对此感到惊奇。毕竟，梅特涅这样解释他对西班牙的看法（这里我引述一下）："全欧洲最单一构成的国家。"他这第二个观察，今天可适用于自1976年以来西班牙人民已经做到的事情：我们从一个独裁的过去，和平过渡到现在的民主体制，这的确是一个绝无仅有的例子。

西班牙再度成为国际社会的一部分，它的名字可以激发人们的信心，那就是一个国家有能力自我管理。

这就是为什么在拉美西班牙语区，西班牙这个名字已不再仅仅是殖民历史的象征，它也代表一个民主未来的承诺。让我补充一下，对王后

saying that, after all, it was (I quote) "The most singularly constituted country of all Europe". This second observation could be applied today to what the Spanish people have accomplished since 1976: we are indeed a singular example of peaceful transition from an authoritarian past to a democratic present.

Spain has once more become a part of the international community, and its name can inspire confidence in the capacity of a nation to govern itself.

This is why the name of Spain in Hispanic America is no longer merely the symbol of a colonial past, but also the promise of a democratic future. Let me add that my visits to Hispanic American countries have been deeply moving experiences for the Queen and myself: we sensed, in all the countries that we visited, that a new era has begun in the history of that vast continent, that magna patria, as a Spanish-speaking poet once called it: the community of Hispanic peoples and nations. In that community, Spain is now rightly regarded as a sister nation, committed to the ideal of all the Spanish-speaking peoples: the establishment of free societies ruled by justice and progress for all their citizens.

Unfortunately, the burden of a past filled with oppression of all kinds still lies heavily on this vast group of nations of Spanish-speaking peoples. We all suffer on seeing the present tragedy of Central America, about which the great Mexican writer Carlos Fuentes delivered a most eloquent speech here, exactly a year ago. Nevertheless, the Hispanic peoples can also look back to their great legacy from the past of civilized life and culture.

Indeed, there is no question that the people of Spain have a cultural heritage of transnational significance. It is not necessary to go back to the age of Cervantes to find it. During the initial decades of our century, from the first essays of Unamuno to the last tragedies of Garcia Lorca, the literature of Spain reached levels of artistic universality as high—and at times higher—than those of the Golden Age of Cervantes. Moreover, during those years where were achievements unrivalled in the past, and here I refer to the scientific discoveries marking what a great Hispanic American poet, Ruben Dario, called "the universalization of the Spanish mind" and intellectual movement that received its first international recognition in 1906, when Dr. Ramon y Cajal was awarded the Nobel Prize for his work on man's nervous system.

The following years saw one of the most extraordinary flowerings of national

和我自己来说，我们对拉美西班牙语区的访问，是很让人感动的经历，在我们参观的所有国家里，我们感觉到，在这片辽阔的土地上，一个新的时代已经开始，就像一个讲西班牙语的诗人曾说的那样，magna patria 就是所有讲西班牙语的民族和国家的共同体。在那个团体里，西班牙现在被视为一个姐妹国家，致力于建立这样的理想社会：所有讲西班牙语的人民能生活在自由社会里，并享受进步。

不幸的是，过去各种压迫所造成的负担，在很大程度上还压在这个庞大的讲西班牙语的国家群体身上。我们都不情愿地看到中美洲目前遭受的悲剧，对此，伟大的墨西哥作家卡洛斯·富恩特斯[5]整整一年前，就在这里发表了一个颇为雄辩的讲话。尽管如此，西班牙语系的人民也可以回顾他们伟大的历史，看看自己过去的文明生活和文化。

的确，西班牙人民毫无疑问地拥有一个跨越国度的文化遗产。我们都不用回到塞万提斯的年代去找到这种遗产。在本世纪的最初几十年，从乌纳穆诺写的第一批散文，到加西亚·洛尔卡创作的最后的悲剧，西班牙文学总体的艺术水准达到、有时甚至超过了塞万提斯所处的"黄金时代"。此外，在那些年里，西班牙还取得了其他一些过去无与伦比的成就，我这里指的是科学上的发现，犹如伟大的西班牙语系美洲诗人鲁本·达里奥所描述的，它标志着"西班牙心灵的普及化"，这种知识运动在 1906 年，当拉蒙·卡哈尔博士因为对人的神经系统所做的研究而被授予诺贝尔奖时，第一次得到了国际性的承认。

在随后的岁月里，西班牙文化在 20 世纪的欧洲绽放出了奇异的艺术、文学和科学之花，后来虽然中断了一段时间，其他杰出的人士把这个势头保持并延续了下去。

其中，我想特别提到同卡哈尔一样，被授予诺贝尔奖的人有：1956 年诗人胡安·拉蒙·希门尼斯获文学奖，3 年后，在美国的洛克菲勒大学任教的塞韦罗·奥乔亚博士获奖。最近一个获得诺贝尔奖的西班牙人是伟大的诗人维森特·亚历山大。当瑞典文学院在 1977 年秋天选中他时，大多数西班牙人认为这是瑞典这样一个拥有长期自由和幸福历史的国家，对西班牙新恢复的民主做出认可的一个象征。

culture, in art, literature and science in 20th century Europe, which —although interrupted for a time—was later maintained alive and extended by other distinguished men.

Among them, I wish only to mention those who, like Cajal, were awarded the Nobel Prize: the poet Juan Ramon Jimenez, in 1956, and three years later, Dr. Severo Ochoa of Rockefeller University. The last Spaniard to be distinguished with the Nobel Prize was the great poet Vicente Aleixandre. When the Swedish Academy chose him in the fall of 1977, most Spaniards felt that their newly-restored democracy had been given symbolic recognition by a country with a long and happy history of freedom.

I do not think it would be a patriotic exaggeration to say that today Spainards enjoy more freedom than ever before in the history of their country. At the same time, never before have so many of my compatriots had so many opportunities for education and cultural activity. I venture to predict that towards the end of our century Spanish creativity will again reach levels of international significance. My prediction is based on the creative activity of the great writers of Hispanic America, because another characteristic of present-day Spain is what could be termed the new encounter with America.

Here, I refer, of course, to the literature and thought of the great Hispanic American authors of our time—Borges, Octavio Paz, Vargas Llosa, Garcia Marquez, Fuentes and so many more. You know some of them quite well, since Borges and Octavia Paz have taught here as Charles Eliot Norton Professors and have also been honored by Harvard with doctoral degrees. And, on behalf of Spain, I have had the privilege of awarding them the most important prize for literature in the Spanish language: the Cervantes Prize.

However, I wish to emphasize that all these great writers are not regarded by Spaniards today as voices of alien lands; they are truly our own voices, that is, the voices of the vast community of the Spanish-speaking peoples and nations.

For the first time in the history of this community there is not only a fraternal transatlantic dialogue; there is also a new consciousness of everything that links us, a new consciousness of our own historic identity as a world community. Thus, I consider the distinction that Harvard has conferred upon me today as an honor for all my compatriots of the magna patria constituted by Spanish-speaking peoples and nations. On their behalf, I now wish to convey to you some of our present concerns.

如果说今天的西班牙人比以往任何时候都享有更多的自由，我不会认为这是一种出于爱国的夸张说法。与此同时，我的这么多同胞，以前从未享有过这么多的教育和文化活动机会。我斗胆预测，到本世纪末，西班牙的创造力将再次达到具有国际影响的水平。我的预测是基于西班牙语系美洲作家杰出的创造性活动，因为现今西班牙的另一个特点，就是可以称为重新与美洲相遇。

当然，在这里，我指的是当代那些伟大的西班牙语系美洲作家的作品和思想，他们包括博尔赫斯[6]、奥克塔维奥·帕斯[7]、巴尔加斯·略萨[8]、加西亚·马尔克斯[9]、富恩特斯等许多人。你们对其中某些人会相当熟悉，因为博尔赫斯和奥克塔维奥·帕斯曾在这里担任过查尔斯·艾略特·诺顿讲座教授，也曾被哈佛授予过荣誉博士学位。我也曾有机会代表西班牙，授予他们西班牙语系中最重要的文学奖项——塞万提斯奖。

不过，我想强调，今天的西班牙人不把这些伟大的作家视为来自异国土地的声音，他们发出的真正是我们自己的声音，也就是说，他们代表了讲西班牙语的民族和国家的广大社会的声音。

在这个社群的历史上，第一次不仅有了兄弟般的跨大西洋对话，也形成了一个新的意识，这种源于我们自己的历史认同的新意识，把我们作为一个国际社会而连接在一起。因此，我把哈佛今天授予我的荣誉，作为是给我所有的讲西班牙语的民族和国家的同胞的荣誉。现在，作为他们的代表，我想和你们谈一些我们目前关注的问题。

我们都很清楚地意识到，我们这个时代所面临的危机，严重地影响到了西班牙语系美洲人民，他们在政治、经济和社会动乱的多重痛苦中挣扎。

拉美外债的规模、社会不公和动荡、有时最起码的人格尊严都受到侵犯，还有武装冲突等等，这些都是现实的存在，我们无法对此无动于衷。我们也决不能逃避责任，而要对拉美人民为寻求一个更美好的未来而做的努力，给予尽可能的帮助。

西班牙希望将我们和这块大陆上的人民数百年来的深厚关系，朝着寻求解决问题的方向，转化成积极务实的团结：共同保护人权，把每一件

We are all too well aware of the severity with which the crisis of our times affects the peoples of Hispanic America, and of the gravity of the political, economic and social **convulsions** [n. 震动. 动乱] from which they are suffering.

The size of their foreign debt, the inequalities and social upheavals, the violation at times of the most elementary human dignity, as well as the armed conflicts, constitute realities to which we cannot remain indifferent. Nor must we escape from responsibility in contributing to any efforts that may enable them to find the way to a better future.

Spain hopes that its centuries' old deep ties with the peoples of this Continent will be transformed into active and practical solidarity with them with a view to seeking solutions to their problems: solidarity in the protection of human rights, each violation of which is as unjustifiable as any other; solidarity in the efforts to re-establish democracy in those countries in which people are still deprived of the full exercise of freedom; solidarity in the search for peaceful solutions for armed conflicts, while acknowledging the advisability of a solution to the region's problems by the countries of the area themselves.

Those in the United States who are concerned by these problems have an important responsibility, precisely on account of the immense influence of your great nation in the affairs of this hemisphere. At the same time, they are in a privileged position to understand them well, one reason being that there are about twenty million people living in the United States whose mother tongue is Spanish.

I should like to say a few words to the Hispanic community of the United States, whose numbers give this country one of the largest Spanish-speaking communities in the world.

We are aware of the efforts and will for self –betterment of the Hispanic community of this nation, that have enabled it over the past few years to make spectacular advances in all areas of American life. Spain wishes to become better acquainted with their situation, their concerns and their problems, and to strengthen the ties of all kinds that link us together.

Spain, together with all the American peoples, is now preparing to celebrate an outstanding event. 1992 will be the five-hundredth anniversary of one of the most important happenings in human history: the arrival in America of the three Castillian **caravels** [n. 轻快帆船] chartered by my ancestors, the Catholic Monarchs, and commanded

违反人权的事,都看成是不可饶恕的;共同努力,在那些人民仍然无法充分得到自由的国家里,重新建立起民主;共同寻求用和平方式解决武装冲突,同时也要看到,解决该地区的问题,最终还是要靠当地人民自己的努力。

正因为你们伟大的国家在西半球的事务中发挥着巨大影响,那些在美国关心这些问题的人担负着一种重要的责任。同时,他们也处于一个有利的地位,能够较好地了解问题,原因之一是,居住在美国的人中,有大约两千万人的母语是西班牙语。

我想对美国的西班牙族裔人民说几句话,他们在这个国家人数众多,是世界上最大的西班牙语系群体之一。

我们知道,在这个国家的西班牙语系人民努力地追求上进,并在过去几年里,在美国社会的各个领域取得了卓越的成就。西班牙希望更好地了解他们的情况、他们关注的事情和他们的问题,并加强各种把我们联系在一起的关系。

西班牙和全体美国人民一起,现在正准备庆祝一个美好事件。1992年将是人类历史上最重要的事件之一的500周年纪念,当年由我的祖先、天主教的君主所指派的三艘轻便帆船,在哥伦布的指挥下来到了美洲。

西班牙当时已经成为第一个现代化的欧洲国家,在随后的几个世纪里,为发现和探索地球上的大片区域作出了极大的努力,从而使那些地区成为已知世界的一部分。其他具有历史意义的里程碑事件,包括了世界上第一次环球航行。

现在,为发现美洲500周年而举办的庆祝活动正在积极筹备中,其意义是非常深刻的,西班牙连同其他美洲人民在为此做准备的同时,也在思考着未来。与其说这是为一个历史事件而做的纪念,不如说我们必须共同把视线集中到这个地平线上,为实现更美好、更公正的未来而付出我们全部的努力。

谁也不能否认,西班牙语美洲地区面临着巨大的和非常复杂的问题,但今天,我们有新的领导人决心要解决那些最棘手的问题。在这方面取得重要成就的一个例子,就是在阿根廷恢复了民主体制,这对所有讲西班牙语的国家来说是一件大喜事。

总之,我确信西班牙语系美洲现在正进入一个新的历史时期,我也很有信心地预测,对这块大陆上讲西班牙语的国家来说,1992年将是一个决定

by Christopher Columbus.

Spain, which at that time had become the first modern European state, made vigorous efforts during the following centuries in the exploration and discovery of vast areas, thus making them part of the known world. Among other symbolic milestones of historic significance was the first circumnavigation of the globe.

The significance of these celebrations that are now being prepared in connection with the fifth centenary of the Discovery and Encounter with America is very profound, and Spain—together with the other American peoples—is getting ready for them while thinking of the future. It is not so much a historic commemoration as a horizon on which together we must fix our sights, concentrating all our efforts in order to achieve a better and more just future.

Nobody can deny that there are enormous and highly complex problems in Hispanic America, but there are new leaders today who are determined to tackle the most intractable of them. An example of an important achievement in this respect is the restoration of democratic institutions in Argentina, which has been a cause for rejoicing among all the Hispanic nations.

In short, I am certain that Hispanic America is now entering a new period in its history, and it is with confidence that I predict that 1992 will mark a decisive turning point for the Spanish-speaking countries of this continent. But there is an obvious need for dialogue between the two Americas, a dialogue that would be beneficial for both of them and, in fact, for the entire world.

Octavio Paz, the former Harvard teacher and one of the great minds of our times, has often observed that in order to survive our civilization must preserve its cultural diversity and this means the preservation of traditional societies, or as Octavio Paz put it, "with the disappearance of a traditional society—destroyed or absorbed by industrial civilization—we lose variety of mankind, not only a past variety, but also a future variety."

To this, Octavio Paz added, "To preserve our diversity is to preserve the varieties of our future, the very life of mankind". That respect for traditional societies obviously does not mean that nothing should be changed in them.

We all know that reforms are indispensable in many countries of the world, and particularly in Hispanic America. But, as our great Spaniard Miguel de Unamuno said again and again, "**tradition and progress are inseparable because tradition always**

性的转折点。但很明显的是，南北美洲之间需要对话，而且这种对话不仅对他们有利，对整个世界也有利。

曾在哈佛任教的、我们这个时代的伟大思想家之一奥克塔维奥·帕斯经常说，我们的文明如果要存在下去的话，就必须保持文化的多样性，而这就意味着保护传统的社会。就像帕斯所说的那样，"随着某个传统社会的消失，不管它是被工业文明破坏抑或吸收，我们也就随之失去了人类的多样性，失去的不仅是过去的多样性，而且也使我们的未来少了一种多样性"。

对此，奥克塔维奥·帕斯补充说："保存我们的多样性就是保护我们未来的多样性，这正是人类的生命线。"当然，对传统社会的尊重并不意味着所有东西都要一成不变。

我们都知道，世界上许多国家，特别是在西班牙语系美洲地区，改革是必不可少的。但是，正如我们伟大的西班牙人米格尔·德·乌纳穆诺[10]所说，"**传统与进步是分不开的，因为传统在开始时，总是一种创新、一种进步。**"

传统与进步，用这些词来形容我的国家今天的主要优势，也许是最合适的说法。因为1978年西班牙宪法的指导原则，就是要保存西班牙社会的历史多样性和区域特色。因此，我们现在建立了一个很新的体制，叫做基于传统自治机构的"多自治区组成的国家"，但它也具有相当的创新。简而言之，西班牙在宁静和平地重建传统，同时也在开启社会改革和文明进步的新途径。

我恐怕已经超出了给我的时间，也让你们在这个毕业典礼的下午失去了耐心。然而，我无法在还没有表达西班牙人民今天的主要关注就结束我的讲话。这种关注可以归纳为一个字：和平。也就是说，不仅是国家或区域内部的和平，而是要世界和平。

我知道，在座的各位，在世界历史的这个困难时期，共享着西班牙人民对和平的关注，你们和我们一样，决心把庆祝发现美洲500周年的时机，当做在人类历史上创造全球和平奇迹的崭新的一年。让我们继续坚信我们的未来：

"Mientras haya

Alguna ventana abierta

began as innovation, as progress".

Tradition and progress: these terms are perhaps the most appropriate to describe the chief strength of my country today. Because the guiding principle of the 1978 Spanish Constitution is to preserve the historic diversity of Spanish society and its regional features. Thus we now have a very new institutional structure called " a State of Autonomies" based on the traditional bodies of self-government but with considerable innovations. In brief, Spain, quietly and peacefully, is reconstructing its traditions as well as opening up new ways to social reform and civilized progress.

I am afraid that I have exceeded my allotted time and taxed your patience on this Commencement afternoon. I cannot, however, conclude without expressing the chief concern of the Spanish people today. That concern can be summarized in just one word: peace. That is, world peace, and not only national or internal peace.

I know that all of you here, in this difficult period of world history, share the concern of the Spanish people for peace, and that you are resolved, as we are, to celebrate the Fifth Centennial of the Americas as miraculous new year in the history of mankind: the miracle of global peace. Let us keep out faith in the certainty of our future,

"Mientras haya
Alguna ventana abierta
Ojos que vuelven dell sueno,
Otra manana que empieza ..."
As long as there is
an open window,
and eyes coming back from sleep,
at the beginning of a new morning...

That farewell to life by a Spanish poet who died here in 1951 is my own message to all of you on this memorable day of peace and faith.

Thank you very much!

Ojos que vuelven dell sueno,

Otra manana que empieza..."

只要还有一扇开着的窗,

昏睡中的眼睛就会迎接新的黎明……

那位于1951年在这里去世的西班牙诗人告别人生的话语,就是今天这个期盼和平的难忘日子里,我想对你们说的话。

非常感谢各位!

---

1 西班牙一所历史悠久的大学

2 何塞·奥尔特加·加塞特 (Jose Ortega y Gasset, 1883—1955年),西班牙哲学家,他最著名的观点就是"我是我本人和我的环境的组合",("Yo soy yo y mi circunstancia",英文:"I am I and my circumstance")。

3 "让我们同欢乐"(拉丁语:Gaudeamus igitur),又译"同欢",是一首18世纪的拉丁文歌曲,歌词取材于德·蒙内西斯1287年的一份手稿,因国际大学生体育联合会选用这首歌在世界大学生运动会开幕式播放,升起国际大运会会旗,该歌曲有时也被称为"国际大学生体育联合会会歌"。

4 克莱门特·梅特涅 (Clement Metternich),19世纪奥匈帝国的外交大臣和首相,美国政治家基辛格非常崇拜此人。

5 卡洛斯·富恩特斯 (Carlos Fuentes,生于1928年),墨西哥作家,当代西班牙语系最重要的作家之一。

6 豪·路·博尔赫斯 (Jorge Luis Borges, 1899—1986),阿根廷作家、诗人,倡导根据自己的兴趣阅读,被称为"作家中的作家",但一生无缘诺贝尔奖。有人评论说,他的作品"为一代西班牙语美洲作家打开了道路"。

7 奥克塔维奥·帕斯 (Octavio Paz, 1914—1998),墨西哥著名诗人、作家,1981年获西班牙塞万提斯文学奖,1990年由于"他的作品充满激情,视野开阔,渗透着感悟的智慧并体现了完美的人道主义"而获得诺贝尔文学奖。

8 巴尔加斯·略萨 (Vargas Llosa,生于1936年),当代拉美最重要的作家之一,拥有秘鲁与西班牙双重国籍,因他"对权力结构的描绘,以及他作品中那反抗、起义、失败的犀利印象"而获得2010年诺贝尔文学奖。

9 加西亚·马尔克斯 (Garcia Marquez,生于1927年),哥伦比亚作家,于1982年获诺贝尔文学奖,其1967年出版的小说《百年孤独》以"魔幻现实主义"的写法而影响深远。

10 米格尔·德·乌纳穆诺 (Miguel de Unamuno, 1864—1936),西班牙著名作家、诗人、哲学家,长期任教于萨拉曼卡大学并出任该校校长。乌纳穆诺曾因反对西班牙独裁统治于1924年被流放,后逃亡法国。1931年共和国成立后,他当选为立宪议会议员、科学院院士。

贝娜齐尔·布托（1953—2007）

巴基斯坦前总理、人民党主席，她是穆斯林国家第一位民选女总理，也是迄今为止巴基斯坦唯一的一位女总理。

被誉为"铁蝴蝶"的贝·布托生于巴基斯坦南部港口城市新德省的卡拉奇市，是巴基斯坦已故前总理阿里·布托的长女。贝·布托从小受到良好教育，16岁进入哈佛大学主修比较政治学，在这里度过了她自称是"生命中最快乐的四年时光"。1973年本科毕业后，贝·布托进入英国牛津大学学习哲学、政治与经济学，并完成了国际法与外交的课程。在牛津她积极投身学生活动，曾被选为牛津大学学生会主席。

1976年贝·布托学成回国开始了她的政治生涯，在政治上深受她父亲的影响。1977年其父（时任巴基斯坦总理）因齐亚·哈克发动军事政变而被罢黜，并于1979年被处以绞刑。

贝·布托曾两度就任巴基斯坦总理，第一次是在1988年她年仅35岁的时候。20个月后，贝·布托因被控贪污而免职。1993年她重新当选总理，1996年再次被出身于人民党的总统莱加里免职。1998年她被迫流亡迪拜，直至2007年获得时任总统穆沙拉夫大赦，所有针对她的腐败指控被撤销，才重返巴基斯坦。

2007年12月27日，在巴基斯坦首都伊斯兰堡邻近的拉瓦尔品第市举行的竞选集会上，贝·布托遭遇自杀式袭击受伤，在送往医院后不治身亡。2008年贝·布托被授予联合国人权奖，是七个获奖者之一。

1989

Democratic Nations Must Unite
民主国家 团结一致

Mohtarma Benazir Bhutto 贝娜齐尔·布托

Mr. President, faculty, family and friends, and today's graduates:

I feel honored to have been asked to make this commencement address to the Class of 1989. But I would like to begin by first of all congratulating all those who have been awarded degrees today.

Not too long ago, I sat where you now sit. I can vividly recall the effort your degrees represent-tramping to class in sub-arctic temperatures, fighting for books at Hilles library, cramming for exams, and at times staying awake all night to complete a term paper.

Today is a day of celebration and I am privileged to share it with you. But while I am greatly honoured by the degree you have conferred on me and grateful, President Bok, for the words in your citation, you will understand that I regard this honour as more than a personal recognition. I consider it an affirmation of the universality of the principles of democracy, liberty and human rights. It was here that the first successful struggle against European imperialism began. It was here--under the banner "no taxation without representation" -- that the idea of government by the consent of the governed first gained currency.

Cambridge and Harvard were my cradle of liberty too. I arrived here from a country, that in my lifetime, had not known democracy or political freedom. As an under-graduate, I was constantly reminded of the value of democracy by the history of freedom that permeates this place. It was not just the history of democracy that inspired me. It was above all, the concrete expression of it.

My Harvard years, 1969 to 1973, coincided with growing frustration over U.S: policy in South East Asia. This was particularly true in the campuses where students were in the forefront of those protesting the Vietnam War. For me, there were demonstrations on Boston Commons and in Washington; mass meetings in Harvard Stadium.

Some American commentators argued that the division over Vietnam signalled American weakness. I saw it as a measure of America's greatness-a reflection of democracy in action, of an open society, which because it was open, had the means of regeneration and revitalisation.

In the Pakistan of those days, the press did not criticize the government. Because the government controlled the press.

While I was a junior at Harvard, Pakistan initiated an experiment in democracy.

尊敬的校长、各位老师、各位家长、各位朋友，今天毕业的同学们：

能够应邀为1989届毕业生作毕业演讲，我深感荣幸。我首先想向所有在今天获得学位的同学们表示祝贺。

就在不久以前，我也曾坐在你们现在坐着的地方。我清楚地知道你们为获得学位所付出的努力：在严寒的天气里徒步走到教室、在希里斯图书馆里争着借书、为考试而挑灯夜战，有时还通宵达旦赶写一篇学期论文。

今天是一个值得庆祝的日子，我有幸能与大家共享。伯克校长，在你授予我荣誉学位时提到的所有美誉，令我非常荣幸与感激。同时你知道，我认为这个荣誉不止是对我个人的肯定，这是对民主、自由和人权的原则具有普世价值的肯定。第一个反对欧洲帝国主义的成功斗争，就是从这里开始的[1]。正是在这里，人们举起"不给代表权，就别来收税"的义旗，使得"政府必须获得选民认同"这一认识，第一次深入人心。

对我来说，剑桥[2]和哈佛也是自由的摇篮。我最初来到这里时，我生活的国家还不知道民主或政治自由为何物。作为一个本科生，我接触到这个弥漫着民主气氛和具有自由历史的地方，不仅民主的历史，更重要的是民主的具体表现不断给我以启发。

我的哈佛岁月是从1969年到1973年，正值美国在东南亚的政策遭受到越来越多的挫折。尤其是在校园里，学生们走在抗议越南战争的最前沿。在波士顿市区和首都华盛顿都有游行示威，学生们也在哈佛体育场举行群众集会。

有些美国评论家认为，在越南问题上的分歧表现了美国的弱点。我则认为这正是美国的伟大之处：它代表了民主的运行、社会的开放，正因为社会是开放的，使它得以再生和复兴。

在那些年代里，巴基斯坦的报刊不会批评政府，因为政府控制了新闻界。

当我还是哈佛大三学生的时候，巴基斯坦进行了一个民主的实

That experience is instructive.

As 1971 ended, Pakistan was in ruins. A third of the territory and one half of the population was gone, the result of a military defeat precipitated by military repression in what was then known as East Pakistan. War and mismanagement had left our treasury empty and our economy in shambles. Ninety-three thousand prisoners-of-war were threatened by their captors with trial and punishment. Internal discord in West Pakistan threatened the survival of what was left of my country.

A protracted period of military rule produced this catastrophe. It was a disaster resulting from rule without accountability, brought about by the arrogance of a self imposed mission to save the country from its own people.

In the face of this catastrophe, what did our leaders do? They turned power over to the civilians, to an elected Prime Minister. In a pattern repeated by the Greek colonels and the Argentine junta, our military said, in essence: "we have created a hopeless situation; now we wash our hands of it and of the responsibility to resolve it".

But resolve it, we did. The elected Prime Minister negotiated an honourable peace with the victor; he secured the return of the prisoners-of war; and put the economy back on its feet; he initiated a programme of social and economic reform to benefit the poor and dispossessed, who are the majority in our land. All this was done, I might add, at a time of global economic recession brought about by the oil shocks of the 70's.

But what then happened? As is the case in democracies, the political process again became **rambunctious** [adj. 粗暴的，放纵的]. Opposition politicians challenged the elected government. They challenged it in the press, at the polls and in the streets. The military whose dignity was restored by the elected government moved in "to end the squabbling amongst politicians". The new dictatorship proved more brutal; more determined to stay in power than any of its predecessors. Elections were promised and cancelled. The elected Prime Minister was arrested and then, under the cloak of judicial proceedings, murdered. Floggings, imprisonment, and execution became the staple of political life in our land.

Under circumstances that were as remarkable as they were unexpected, Pakistan got a second chance at democracy at the last polls. It is an opportunity that we must not now lose.

In our first act, I am happy to say, our government freed all political prisoners and commuted all death sentences. We restored the freedom of speech, freedom of

验。那个经验是有益的。

随着1971年的结束,巴基斯坦成了一片废墟。因为在当时的东巴基斯坦进行军事镇压的行动失败,它丧失了三分之一的领土和一半的人口。战争和管理不善使我们的国库空虚,我们的经济满目疮痍。我们有九万三千人被俘,对方威胁说要对他们进行审判和惩罚。西巴基斯坦内部的不和谐,更是威胁着我们国家的生存。

长期的军事统治导致了这场灾难。这场灾难的产生,要归结于那种自以为是地要把国家从本国人民那里挽救出来的不负责任的统治。

在面临这场灾难时,我们的领导人做了什么?他们把权力移交给平民,移交给一位民选总理。就像希腊的军官和阿根廷军政府一再重复的那样,我国军队实际上在说:"我们搞得一团糟,现在我们洗手不干了,也不再负责任解决问题。"

但问题要解决,我们做到了。当选的总理[3]与胜利的敌方[4]斡旋,谈成了一个体面的和平,他使战俘得以回国,经济开始复苏;他发起了一项社会和经济改革方案,旨在为我们国家占大多数的穷人和被剥削者造福。我要补充强调的是,所有这一切,都是在上世纪70年代的石油危机所带来的全球经济衰退时期做到的。

但是,随后发生了什么呢?就像在民主制度下常见的那样,政治再次变得粗暴。反对派的政治家们挑战民选政府,他们在报刊上、在投票站和街头发出挑战。由民选政府帮助恢复了尊严的军队接着出动,号称来"结束政治家之间的争吵"。新的专政结果更加残酷,比它前面的专治更加牢固地控制着政权。它承诺举行选举,但却食言。民选的总理被逮捕,然后,在司法审判的外衣下被谋杀[5]。鞭笞惩罚、监禁关押和处死成为我们国家政治生活中的家常便饭。

在既特殊又出人意料的情况下,巴基斯坦在最近的选举中又让民主有了第二次机会。这个机会我们现在绝不能失去。

在我们的第一个回合里,我很高兴地说,我国政府释放了所有政治犯并赦免了所有死刑。我们恢复了言论自由、结社自由以及新闻自由的权利。在国民议会中有一个活跃的反对派,在我国历史上,

association. and freedom of the press. In the National Assembly there is a lively opposition and, for the first time in our history, the State-owned television provides full coverage of their activities.

Senator Daniel Patrick Moynihan, who recently visited me in Islamabad, once wrote that "If you are in a country where the newspapers are filled with good news, you can be sure that the jails are filled with good men". Even a casual review of our press would serve to confirm the opposite of the Senator's statement.

Around the world, democracy is on the march. In the last decade, Pakistan is only the most recent country to change course and return to democracy. But we must be realistic. We must recognize that democracy, particularly emerging democracy can be fragile. I have already cited the experience of our last democratic government. But the example is not confined to Pakistan alone. In the Philippines, Mrs. Aquino's three-year-old democracy has already survived several coup attempts; in Argentina, there have been half a dozen military rebellions; in Peru, narcotics and terrorism threaten a fifteen-year-old experiment in democracy.

Democracy needs support and the best support for democracy comes from other democracies. Already, there is an informal network to support democracy. Annually, the United States prepares a report on human rights in every country. In prison I was heartened to learn that the Congress had linked U.S. assistance to Pakistan in the Pell Amendment, to the "restoration of full civil liberties and representative government in Pakistan". Friends of democracy in other countries, including Britain, Canada, and Germany, sent delegations to investigate human right abuses in Pakistan. Our elections last November were made easier by the presence of observers sponsored by the United States, Britain, and the South Asian Association for Regional Cooperation.

This informal network for democracy can and should be strengthened. Democratic nations should forge a consensus around the most powerful political idea in the world today: the right of people to freely choose their government. Having created a bond through evolving such a consensus, democratic nations should then come together in an association designed to help each other and promote what is a universal value---democracy.

国营电视台第一次对反对派做了全面报道。

参议员丹尼尔·帕特里克·莫伊尼汉[6]最近在伊斯兰堡访问过我，他曾经这样写道："如果你在一个国家里看到报纸上都充斥着好消息，你可以肯定那里的监狱会关满好人。"即使是随便翻阅我们的报刊，也能证明我们的情况是和参议员的说法正好相反。

放眼世界各地，民主风云正起。在过去10年中，巴基斯坦是新兴的改弦更张恢复民主的国家。但是，我们必须认清现实。我们必须认识到民主，尤其是新兴民主是脆弱的，我已经列举了我们上届民主政府的经验。但这种情况并不仅限于巴基斯坦。在菲律宾，阿基诺夫人过去3年的民主政府已经经历过几次政变考验；在阿根廷，有好几次军事叛乱；在秘鲁，毒品和恐怖主义威胁着那个国家已有15年的民主实验。

民主需要支持，而对民主最好的支持，来自其他民主国家。目前，有一个非正式的网络在支持着民主。每年，美国针对每一个国家的人权状况做出报告。我在监狱里时高兴地获悉，在佩尔修订案中，美国国会把对巴基斯坦的援助和"恢复公民全面自由，以及人们选举巴基斯坦政府"相联系起来。其他国家的民主之友，包括英国、加拿大和德国，都派代表团到巴基斯坦调查侵犯人权的情况。我们去年11月举行的大选，由于有美国、英国和南亚区域合作联盟派出的观察员监督，而变得简单有序。

这种民主的非正式网络，可以而且应该得到加强。民主国家应建立一个共识，认同今天在世界各地都会是最强大的政治思想：人民有权自由选择他们的政府。通过围绕这样一个共识不断发展关系，民主国家应该互相帮助，共同促进一个普世价值——民主。

并不是每一个民主国家的组织方式都是一样的，每个民主国家表现的方式也不尽相同。但我认为，所有民主国家都必须考虑两个要素：一、定期举行选举，让每个有规模的政党参选，选举程序公正，并有选民广泛的或普遍的参与；二、尊重包括言论自由、良心自由和结社自由的基本人权。

Not every democracy organizes itself in the same way; nor does every democracy express itself the same way. But there are two elements I consider essential to all democracies. These are:

(1) the holding of elections at regular intervals, open to the participation of all significant political parties, that are fairly administered and where the franchise is broad or universal; and

(2) respect for fundamental human rights including freedom of expression, freedom of conscience, and freedom of association.

There are several ways in which members of an Association of Democratic Nations can help each other. One way is to ensure the impartiality of elections. After all, democracy as a system of government can only work when all participants in the political process accept the verdict of the people. For the verdict to be accepted as legitimate, elections must not only be fair, but they must also be seen to be fair.

International observer missions have already played critical roles in ensuring fair outcomes to elections in several countries including mine. The presence of observers is a deterrent to fraud. The observers' report can help legitimize an election in an emerging democracy where popular skepticism can be rife, as in South Korea, or it can validate local perceptions of fraud, as in the Philippines and Panama.

Observers also bring television cameras with them. It is much harder to steal an election if the whole world is watching, and. As the experience of the Philippines suggests, attempted fraud under the glare of television lights can help galvanise a popular uprising.

There are other ways in which an Association of Democratic Nations can provide some protection for democratic governments in the Association. In countries without established traditions of representative government, democracy is always at risk. All too often, there is the overly ambitious general, the all too determined fanatic, or the all too **avaricious** [adj. 贪财的, 贪婪的] politician. The Association of Democratic Nations can help change the calculus for each of these potential coup plotters by adding the element of international **opprobrium** [n. 耻辱, 咒骂]. The Association can mobilize international opinion against leaders of any coup. Ultimately, I believe, the door should be open to

"民主国家协会"的成员有几种方法可以互相帮助。一种方法是确保选举的公正性。毕竟作为一个政府系统的民主，只有在政治进程中的所有参与者都接受人民的决定时，才能运行。只有当选举是公平的，而且还必须被认为是公平的情况下，选举结果才会被接受为合法。

在包括我国在内的几个国家的选举中，国际观察团已经为保证结果公平发挥了重要作用。观察员的存在，对欺诈行为起一种阻吓作用。在一个新兴的民主国家的选举中，比如在韩国，观察员的报告可以帮助消除人们对选举公平的普遍怀疑，而在菲律宾和巴拿马这些国家，它则可以证实当地人们对选举中有欺诈行为的怀疑。

观察员也带来了电视摄像机。如果整个世界都在注视着，就更难在选举中靠作弊取胜。菲律宾的经验表明，在电视照明灯的强光下，如果试图作弊，只会激发人民抗议。

这种"民主国家协会"，还可以有其他方法来为协会里的民主政府提供一些保护。在没有代议体制传统的国家里，民主总是岌岌可危。很多时候，总会有某个过于雄心勃勃的将军、某个执著的狂热分子，或者某个过于贪婪的政客，出来捣乱。"民主国家协会"所做出的国际谴责，会让这些潜在的政变策划者们有所顾忌。该协会可以动员国际舆论，反对发动政变的领导人。最后，我相信，国际社会还应该采取更强硬的包括经济制裁在内的措施。

民主依赖于我们给人民带来实惠的能力。 许多新兴的民主国家发现，因为不顾后果的支出，独裁使他们的国库空虚。像在其他洲的新兴民主国家一样，比如阿根廷和巴西，我们在巴基斯坦也发现独裁者花空了国库。我们的情况不是唯一的。其他的新兴民主国家也在执政时发现无米下锅。这个"民主国家协会"就应该促进给予民主政体外援的做法。捐助者想倡导某个观点，这没什么错。民主的前景可能依赖于这种倡导。

有些人可能会认为，我建议成立的这种协会将只有道德力量。我承认这一点，但我也督促大家要认识到，在国际关系中，道德有

stronger steps including economic sanctions.

Democracy depends on our ability to deliver goods to the people. Many new democracies find that dictatorship has left them with empty treasuries-because of reckless spending. As was true for new democracies in other lands notably Argentina and Brazil, we, in Pakistan, also found that dictatorship had left the state coffers empty. Our situation is not unique. Other new democracies also come to power to find the cupboard bare. This Association of Democratic Nations could promote the idea that foreign aid should be channelled to democracies. There is nothing wrong in rewarding an idea in which the donors believe. The prospects for democracy may depend on it.

Some may object that the Association I am proposing will have primarily moral force. I acknowledge this but I would urge that morality has a larger power in international relations than is commonly recognized.

Democratic nations can also cooperate in building an international machinery to protect human rights and principles of justice and due process of law. National efforts to strengthen institutions that protect people from human rights abuses and guarantee their political freedoms needs to be reinforced at the international level. For, dictatorship will always seek ways and means to clothe its crime in the garb of legality-always seek to settle political scores and eliminate opponents in the name of justice, law and due process. The instrument that they use is as old as political history, as old as the trial of Socrates. It is the instrument of the political trial-a most pernicious and destructive weapon, which in the hands of skilful manipulators is extremely effective in suppressing dissent and in destroying opponents. I believe it is time that the international community makes a concerted effort to put an end to such practices.

In my country, many of those who resisted dictatorship the heroes of our democratic struggle-were young men and women of your age. Many of them endured long periods of **incarceration** [n. 监禁. 幽闭], and faced charges on political trials that were a **travesty** [n. 滑稽模仿. 歪曲] of truth and justice. Many suffered the worst forms of torture and humiliation of the physical punishment of flogging. Indeed, many had to make the supreme sacrifice of their lives. I can never forget what they endured. I can only strive with all my strength to

比人们的意识更大的力量。

民主国家也可以合作，建立一个国际机制，以保护人权、正义和正当法律程序这些原则。需要在国际间加强努力，以促进各国建立国内机构，防止侵犯人权、保障人民政治自由。因为独裁者总是会想方设法，为其罪行披上合法的外衣，总是会设法利用公正、法律和正当程序等名义，来解决政治分歧和消除对手。他们所运用的工具和政治史一样有历史，犹如苏格拉底受审判那么久远。在老辣的操控者手里，政治审判是最有害的和最具破坏性的武器，他们可以非常有效地用来压制不同政见者，用来摧毁对手。我认为国际社会应当共同努力制止这种做法，现在是时候了。

在我的祖国，那些抵制独裁的人，那些我们民主斗争的英雄，有许多都是与你们年龄相仿的青年男女。其中许多人遭受长期的监禁，并面临政治审判，而那些政治审判是对真理和正义的嘲弄。许多人遭受形式极端的酷刑，还有鞭打体罚的羞辱。事实上，许多人还不得不做出最大的牺牲，献出自己的生命。我永远不能忘记他们所忍受的一切。我只能努力，用尽我所有的力量，让他们的追求变得有意义，即为了那些看起来简单却是无价之宝的自由。那些自由，当你们身在此地，也许会认为是理所当然的。信心鼓舞着我们，让我们的民主斗争有了动力，我们的信心在于相信我们的事业是正义的，在于我们相信伊斯兰关于"暴政不可能持久"的教义。

常常有一种说法，认为巴基斯坦作为一个穆斯林国家不可能实现民主，这是非常错误的。我经常听到这样的论调，说穆斯林国家不能有民主，或有了民主也做不好。但站在你们面前的我，是一名穆斯林妇女，是由一亿穆斯林人民选出来的总理，就活生生地驳斥了这种说法。

这样的事情能够发生，是因为巴基斯坦人民一次又一次证明他们想要拥有自由的根本权利，这样的信念是阻挡不住的。这种对自由和人权的热爱，在相当程度上要归功于殖民地的传统和西方民主体制的以身作则。

give meaning to what they sought -- those simple but priceless freedoms that you here, perhaps, take for granted. But it is faith that inspired and provided sustenance to our democratic struggle -- faith in the righteousness of our cause, faith in the Islamic teaching that "tyranny cannot long endure".

How wrong, therefore, is the picture that is often painted about Pakistan as a country that cannot be democratic because it is Muslim. I have often heard the argument that a Muslim country as such cannot have or work democracy. But I stand before you, a Muslim woman, the elected Prime Minister of one hundred million Muslims, a living **refutation** [n. 辩驳. 反驳] of such arguments.

This has happened because the people of Pakistan have demonstrated, time and again, that their faith in their inherent right to fundamental freedoms is irrepressible. This love for freedom and human rights owes a considerable degree to the colonial legacy and to the example of Western democratic institutions.

But it arises fundamentally from the strong egalitarian spirit that pervades Islamic traditions. The Holy Book calls upon Muslims to resist tyranny. Dictatorships in Pakistan, however long, have, therefore, always collapsed in the face of this spirit.

Islam, in fact, has a strong democratic ethos. With its emphasis on justice, on equality and brotherhood of men and women, on government by consultation, its essence is democratic.

Pakistan is heir to an intellectual tradition of which the illustrious exponent was the poet and philosopher Mohammad Iqbal. He saw the future course for Islamic societies in a synthesis between adherence to the faith and adjustment to the modern age. It is this tradition which continues to inspire the people of Pakistan in their search for their own way of life amidst competing ideologies and doctrines. Tolerance, open-mindedness, pursuit of social justice, emphasis on the values of equality and social concord and encouragement of scientific inquiry are some of its hallmarks. These are the hallmarks that the founder of Pakistan, Quaid-i-Azam Mohammad Ali Jinnah propounded. These are the hallmarks Pakistan's first democratic Prime Minister, Shaheed Zulfikar Ali Bhutto, tried to live up to. Intensely devoted as the pioneers of this tradition were to the Islamic spirit, they were also strongly opposed to bigotry

但从根本上来说，这起源于渗透伊斯兰传统的那种强烈的平等精神。圣书里呼吁穆斯林要抵制暴政。在巴基斯坦的独裁统治不管掌权多久，总是会在这样的精神面前垮台。

事实上，伊斯兰教具有很强的民主精神。它强调注重司法、借助协商，倡导男女平等、四海之内皆兄弟的精神，注重政府要有协商，所以其实质是民主的。

巴基斯坦有自己的文化传统，其杰出代表是诗人和哲学家穆罕默德·伊克巴尔[7]。他认为伊斯兰社会的未来，在于坚持信仰和向现代调整这两者之间的结合。就是这一传统，仍然不断激发巴基斯坦人民，在各种互相竞争的思想和学说中，探索属于自己的生活道路。宽容、开放的态度、追求社会公正、强调平等与社会和谐、鼓励科学探索，这些都是这个传统的特点，也正是巴基斯坦的创始人、卡伊德·阿扎姆·穆罕默德·阿里·真纳[8]所倡导的目标。这些也都是巴基斯坦第一个民选总理沙希德·佐勒菲卡尔·阿里·布托[9]所努力奋斗的方向。全身心地投入这一传统的开拓者们，无限忠于伊斯兰的教义，他们也强烈反对一切形式的偏见。仇外心理或对其他文明的偏见，不管是针对西方或非西方的偏见，都不容于他们的远见中。

正是这份遗产，使我能够承担起出任我国总理的巨大责任。

正当我的祖国走向更大的自由，并确立我们在21世纪要达到的目标之际，我们从诗人和哲学家伊克巴尔的话语中获得启示，他的话同样具有普世价值：

生命在专治下会萎缩成小溪，但在自由的国度里，就会蔚然成为大海。

在巴基斯坦和地球上的每一块大陆，都是这样的。让所有相信自由的人，加入我们的行列，共同维护自由。我想说：民主国家，团结起来！

in all their forms. Xenophobia or prejudice against other civilizations, western or non-western, was repugnant to their outlook.

It is this heritage that has enabled me to take on the awesome responsibilities of the Prime Ministership of my country.

As my country stands on the threshold of greater freedom and sets the priorities that it will take into the 21st century, we draw our inspiration from what the poet-philosopher Iqbal said -- and what is universally applicable:

Life is reduced to a **rivulet** [n. 小河，小溪] *under dictatorship. But in freedom it becomes a boundless ocean.*

This is true in Pakistan and on every continent on earth. Let all of us who believe in freedom join together for the preservation of liberty. My message is: `Democratic nations unite'.

Before I take your leave, Mr. President, Mr. Governor and other distinguished guests, I know that there are students who are graduating today and there is something that I would like to say specially for them. When I was an under-graduate at Harvard I used to conduct Crimson Key tours for newcomers and we Crimson Key tour guides had our own special lines. One of them related to the institute of fine arts, and it went: a famous architect.

L.E. Corbusier, designed this building but the constructors got the plan upside down. As you go out in the world perhaps you will sometimes find things a little upside down. In the words of the Latin scholars of today I can only repeat. **You will go, you will see, and you will reform, and in so doing you will live up to the Harvard motto: Veritas.**

Thank you and best wishes!

在我要离开之前，尊敬的校长、州长先生和其他嘉宾，我知道今天有我们要毕业的学生，我想对他们说几句话。当我还在哈佛读本科时，我曾为新同学做校园导游，我们这些校园导游有自己的专用词，其中有一句说到美术学院，是这样讲的：著名建筑师。

建筑师勒柯布西耶设计了这座大楼，但大楼的承包商在盖楼的时候把图纸上下搞反了。当你走向世界，也许你有时也会发现有些事情被搞颠倒了。用今天拉丁学者的语言，我来重复这句话：**你走去，你将看到，你必须改变** [10]。只有这样做时，你才没有辜负哈佛的座右铭：**真理**！

祝福各位！谢谢大家！

---

1 指美国反对英国统治的独立战争，起源于波士顿的抗税。

2 或译坎布里奇（Cambridge），在波士顿市郊，是哈佛所在地。

3 这里指贝·布托的父亲阿里·布托。

4 指当时为获胜一方的印度。

5 指阿里·布托被齐亚·哈克军政权绞死。

6 丹尼尔·帕特里克·莫伊尼汉（Daniel Patrick Moynihan，1927—2003），美国社会学家、政治家，美国民主党成员，曾任美国驻印度大使，美国驻联合国大使和美国参议员。

7 穆罕默德·伊克巴尔（Mohammad Iqbal，1877—1938），巴基斯坦著名诗人、哲学家和历史学家。他用乌尔都和波斯语写的诗歌，被认为是当代最伟大的诗篇，在穆斯林世界里被尊称为"学者伊克巴尔"。他和被称为"巴基斯坦之父"的阿里·真纳一道，倡导建立巴基斯坦，被称为"巴基斯坦的思想家"和"东方诗人"，其诞辰日 11 月 9 日成为巴基斯坦的一个纪念日。

8 卡伊德·阿扎姆（尊称，意为"伟大领袖"）·穆罕默德·阿里·真纳（Quaid-i-Azam Mohammad Ali Jinnah，1876—1948），巴基斯坦立国运动领袖，巴基斯坦国的创建者，被巴基斯坦人民尊为"巴基斯坦之父"。

9 佐勒菲卡尔·阿里·布托（1928—1979，简译为阿里·布托），巴基斯坦政治家、总理。齐亚·哈克 1977 年 7 月发动政变推翻布托政府，并以下令杀害政敌的罪名将其处以绞刑。

10 贝·布托这里引用拉丁文"Veni, Vidi, Vici"，（I came, I saw, I conquered.）"我来了，我看见，我征服！"据载是古罗马恺撒大帝在公元前 47 年的一次征战时发出的豪言壮语，为西方广为人知的名言。

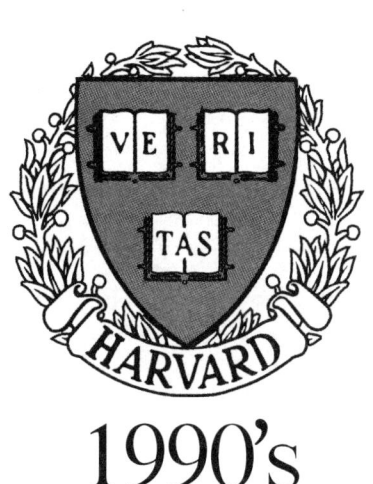

1990's

德瑞克·伯克（1930— ）

在哈佛大学毕业典礼的历史上，由本校校长发表演讲的先例很少，德瑞克·伯克是其中之一，他是美国著名的教育家和律师。

1930年3月，德瑞克·伯克出生于宾夕法尼亚州的一个书香世家，其父是宾州著名法学家，祖父是出版社主编，曾获得普利策奖；祖母是费城柯蒂斯音乐学院（建于1924年）的创始人，曾祖父则是柯蒂斯出版社的创始人，早在1896年前后，柯蒂斯的出版物就拥有上百万的读者，是当时美国最大的出版公司之一。

伯克1951年毕业于斯坦福大学，获文学学士学位，后进入哈佛大学法学院学习。博士毕业后，伯克于1958年开始在哈佛大学教授法律，曾担任3年的法学院院长。从1971年起伯克出任哈佛大学校长，任期长达20年，直至1991年，这次毕业典礼上的演讲，可算是他卸任前的告别演讲。

离开校长职位后，伯克继续在哈佛教育学院和肯尼迪学院任教，并领导一个非营利机构。2006年7月至2007年7月，伯克又担任过一年的哈佛代理校长。

伯克的妻子西舍拉是一位出生于瑞典的哲学家，也同样家世显赫：她的父母都是诺贝尔奖的获得者。她的父亲贡纳尔·默达尔（Gunnar Myrdal）是瑞典著名的经济学家、政治家，曾任瑞典商业部部长、斯德哥尔摩大学教授，于1974年获诺贝尔经济学奖。西舍拉的母亲艾尔娃·默达尔（Alva Myrdal）是瑞典著名的政治家，因为积极推进裁军活动，而于1982年获得诺贝尔和平奖。

除了教学和校长的行政工作，伯克还出版了十多本有关高等教育、社会政论等方面的书籍。

1991

The Social Responsibilities of American Universities
美国大学的社会责任

Derek Bok 德瑞克·伯克

Members of the Harvard Corporation and the Board of Overseers, faculty, parents, dear friends and today's graduates:

In this, my last speech to all of you, I would like to share some very personal thoughts about the direction in which I have tried to take the University and the reasons why I chose to do so. This is not a simple task, for Harvard is hardly a simple institution. It is not merely a university but a universe of many separate galaxies and solar systems----a vast collection of stars and planets, some growing hotter and more luminous, others giving off a paler glow, some shining only with reflected light, and a few, like meteors, bursting across the heavens in an **incandescent** [adj. 光亮的，白热化的] moment of glory.

To find in this great cosmos a single pattern or theme requires a desperate oversimplification. But since I have no choice, I thought that I would spend these last few minutes pondering a question that has worried me throughout these past two decades. What social purpose can an American university claim to have at the end of the twentieth century? What contributions can we make to society that will justify the benefits we receive and inspire the students who come with us here to learn?

Forty years ago, when I first came to Cambridge to study here in the Law school, the answer was obvious. America and it's universities were united in a common **revolve** [v. 旋转，围绕] to build a system of scientific research preeminent in the world and to expand our colleges to embrace our returning veterans. In less than two decades, we achieved these goals, and we created the strongest universities of any country on the face of this earth.

By the time I took office, that unity of purpose had all but disappeared. Our students were alienated from a society in which they saw their heroes assassinated, their government engaged in a cruel war, their leaders embroiled at the highest level in scandal and deceit. Undergraduates no longer showed much interest in careers of public service. Some turned to political protest and cried out loudly for grandiose reforms. Others quietly prepared themselves for lucrative callings: "If you find yourself on the Titanic," one Harvard senior explained, "why not grab a comfortable chair and go first class?"

Meanwhile, government officials and the general public had little patience with the violence and intolerance on university campuses. After the demise of

美国大学的社会责任   The Social Responsibilities of American Universities   德瑞克·伯克 Derek Bok

哈佛集团和监管理事会的各位理事、各位老师、家长、朋友们,今天毕业的同学们:

  这是我最后一次向各位发表演说了,我想就自己尝试把我们的大学引向何方,以及我为什么选择这样做的原因,跟大家谈一些很个人的看法。这可不容易做到,因为哈佛不是一所简单的大学。哈佛不只是一所大学,而是由许多单独的星系和太阳系组成的一个宇宙——是许多恒星和行星的组合,这些星座里,有的越来越热,越来越亮;有的光亮较为苍白;有的只是借光返照;也有的就像流星一样,耀眼地划过天空,转瞬即逝。

  在这个巨大的宇宙中,要找到一种单一模式或主题,未免过于简单。但由于我别无选择,我想在我最后不多的时间里,再思考一下过去 20 年我一直担心的一个问题。在 20 世纪结束之际,美国的大学何以履行其使命,报效社会?我们做出什么贡献,来向社会证明我们得到的好处适得其所,并激励前来这里求学的学生?

  40 年前,当我第一次来到这里,在法学院学习时,答案是显而易见的。美国和它的大学目标一致,要构建一个领先于世界的科学研究体系,并扩大院校以迎接我们的退伍军人重返校园。在不到 20 年里,我们实现了这些目标,创建了一批这个地球上最强的大学。

  当我上任的时候,那种万众一心的景象都消失了。我们的学生疏离社会,因为他们看到自己心目中的英雄被暗杀[1],政府正忙于进行一场残酷战争[2],最高领导人则深陷丑闻和欺骗之中[3]。大学生们对从事公共服务事业缺乏兴趣。有些学生则转向政治抗争,大声呼吁彻底改革。还有的人则不动声色地学习能够给自己带来丰厚收入的本事,"如果你身在泰坦尼克号上,"哈佛的一个高年级学生说,"为什么不抢到一把舒适的椅子,暂时享受一下头等舱的快乐呢?"

  与此同时,政府官员和一般公众对大学校园里发生的暴力和歧视事件也失去了耐心。在"伟大社会"[4]措施的失败和"聪明精英"们黯然失色之后,很多美国人甚至丧失信心,不再把先进知识当做社会进步的关键,也不再相信专家们能帮助解决我们的问题。在这样消沉的环境中,

the Great Society, after the misadventures of the Best and the Brightest, many Americans even lost confidence in advanced knowledge as a key to progress or in experts as guides to help resolve our problems. In this demoralized environment, the social purposes of the university seemed very much in doubt.

As I end my term of office, the campuses are quieter. The angry **tumult** [n. 骚 乱. 烦 乱] of the late 1960s is all but forgotten. But even so, the bonds of understanding between our universities and the nation have not grown stronger. While universities are as dependent as they've ever been on public support, neither educators nor community leaders share a clear and compelling view of what universities can do for our society. Instead of common efforts toward common goals, there is a buzzing confusion of complaints over tuition, over financial aid practices, over reading lists, over affirmative action, even over modern literary theory. Although these are all legitimate issues, the fact that they should dominate the debate about American higher education only shows how muddled we have become about why universities truly matter to society.

This confusion is rather new for Harvard. Those who founded the College had little doubt about its social mission. In President Eliot's words, "Teachers and students alike are profoundly moved by the desire to serve the democratic community." As late as 1936, at our **Tercentenary** [n. 三 百 年 纪 念 日], Franklin Roosevelt repeated this theme when he said: "**Harvard trains men to be citizens in that high Athenian sense which compels a man to live his life unceasingly aware that its civic significance is its most abiding.**"

It is no longer clear what civic significance still inspires our work and justifies the subsidies, benefits, and protections that society grants us to help us carry on our labors.

Are we simply training an elite with the skills they need to move on into the professions and achieve worldly success? No, you will say. We have become an instrument for achieving America's ideals of social mobility and equal opportunity. It has taken great effort, and great generosity from alumni like yourselves, to make it possible to admit every deserving student, regardless of family income, and I hope and pray we will always cling to that ideal.

And yet, we have to face some hard truths. Admitting the ablest students in America is a noble practice, but in today's society, children from working-

美国大学的社会责任 德瑞克·伯克

大学有什么社会功能好像还真难说。

在我结束任期之际,我们的校园安静下来了。1960年代后期的那种愤怒喧嚣早已被人遗忘。但即便如此,我们的大学和整个国家之间互相理解的纽带并未加强。虽然大学仍然依赖于社会的支持,教育工作者和社区领袖们仍然无法达成清晰和令人信服的共识,看看大学到底能为我们的社会做些什么。人们不是向着共同目标一起努力,而是一片乱哄哄地抱怨大学学费、如何给学生提供财政援助的做法、什么可以放在指定阅读书单上、平权行动是否有效,甚至现代文学理论是否正确,等等。尽管这些都是应该讨论的问题,但这些话题主导了美国高等教育的争论本身,就表明我们对大学如何才能真正有益于社会还是没想清楚。

这种混乱对哈佛来说是相当新鲜的事。创建哈佛的那些人毫不怀疑学校的社会使命。用艾略特校长[5]的话来说,"哈佛的教师和学生都有一种为民主社会服务的渴望。"即便到了1936年,当我们庆祝300周年校庆的时候,富兰克林·罗斯福总统也重提了这一主题,他说:**"哈佛要培养的,是具有雅典人那种高素质的公民,即一个人要不断意识到,活着对社会有意义,才是生活中最有价值的东西。"**

什么样的社会影响还能激励我们的工作,并且证明社会应该给予我们补贴、优惠和保障,从而让我们从事自己的事业?这一点已经不太明确了。

我们只培训精英的技能,让他们能进入专业并取得世俗的成功吗?你们会说:不。我们已成为实现社会流动和机会平等这些美国理念的工具。通过像你们这样的校友所付出的巨大努力和给予的慷慨资助,我们可以让每一个适合录取的学生入学,而不用顾虑其家庭收入,我希望并祈祷我们会始终坚持这个理想。

不过,我们必须直面一些严酷的事实。录取美国最好的学生,这是一种很好的做法,但在当今社会里,从劳动阶层的家庭、从城市里的贫民区、从乡下的村庄出来的孩子们,常常受限于较差的学校、破碎的家庭、治安不好的街区,他们很难在激烈的竞争中胜出,

class families, from urban ghettos, from country villages, are much too often handicapped by poor schools, by broken homes, by troubled neighborhoods, to fare well in the stiff competition to enter Harvard College. Despite the thirty million dollars in undergraduate scholarships that we award each year, the fact is that we enroll fewer students from farm communities or blue-collar families than we did 75 or even one hundred years ago.

We must also ask ourselves whether it is enough to offer a Harvard education to the brightest applicants without asking how their talents will be used. A Harvard education must serve a larger social purpose if it is to justify our existence and inspirit our students.

During my twenty years in office, conditions have actually grown worse for many of our citizens. One need not stray very far from Harvard Yard to witness sights I never saw as a student in the 1950s. Yet an eerie indifference hangs over the land. It is the peculiar misfortune of our age that those who are fortunately placed in our society often seem the least exposed to the suffering around them and the least inclined to help. Instead of a popular outcry to end the urban violence, the poverty, the homelessness, the hunger of children, the loudest clamor we hear from the public today is No New Taxes—and this in a country where the total tax burden—state, local, and federal—is lower than in any industrial country in the world.

Against this rising tide of insensitivity and neglect, is it enough for Harvard to attract the brightest students if we do not excel in making them caring, active, enlightened citizens and civic leaders? In asking this question, I do not mean in anyway to suggest that we should press upon our students any particular social policy or economic doctrine. There is no proper place at Harvard for Political Correctness. But neither should we accept the view, so prevalent now in our society, that it is politically correct to tolerate our domestic problems and stand by idly when there is so much work to be done to revitalize our nation. At Harvard, surely, we must teach our students to appreciate the Biblical **admonition** [n. 警 告. 劝 告]: "Much has been given and much will be expected."

The traditional view has been that great universities should promote discovery and the growth of knowledge, not by trying to solve the world's

从而进入哈佛。尽管我们每年给本科生的奖学金高达 3000 万美元，一个事实是，在我们入校的学生里，来自农村或者蓝领家庭的学生，比 75 年前甚至 100 年前，还要少。

我们还必须问问自己，光给最聪明的申请人提供哈佛大学教育，而不问他们将来会如何使用自己的才华，这是否就够了？如果要证明我们存在的理由并激励我们的学生，哈佛大学的教育就必须要有更大的社会目标。

在我担任校长的这 20 年里，对我们的许多民众来说，情况其实变得越来越差。人们不需要从哈佛校园走出多远，就能看到我在 1950 年代当学生时从未见过的景象。然而一种怪异的冷漠笼罩着这片土地。很不幸的是，在我们这个时代，那些社会的宠儿们常常好像最少感触到他们身边发生的不幸，也最不想提供帮助。让人们群情哗然的，不是呼吁制止城市暴力、消除贫困、无家可归、儿童饥饿这些问题，我们今天听到公众闹得最欢的，是"不要加税"，而在我们这个国家里，州税、地方税、联邦税等等税收加起来，在世界上所有工业国家中，其实是最低的。

在这股冷漠与忽视的浪潮泛起之际，哈佛仅仅招徕最聪明的学生，而没能更好地培养他们成为有爱心的、积极的、开明的公民和民众领袖，这就足够了吗？我提出这个问题，并不是说我们应该强迫学生接受任何特定的社会政策或经济理论，哈佛大学不是一个要讲"政治正确"的地方。那么，容忍我们国内所见的问题，在振兴国家方面有这么多工作该做时还袖手旁观，觉得这样做也是政治上正确的，现在社会上所流行的这个观点，我们是不能苟同的。在哈佛，理所当然地，我们必须教导学生领会这句《圣经》箴言："所得多者，其责亦重。"

传统的观点认为，优秀的大学应当鼓励学者们根据自己的兴趣探索真理，从而推动知识的发现和增加，而不是试图解决世界的问题。

这种观点仍然是非常重要的。**我们必须尽力吸引最有创意的、**

problems, but by encouraging scholars to pursue the truth wherever their curiosity leads them.

That view remains extraordinarily important. **We must always do our best to attract the most creative, powerful minds to Harvard and give them the freedom and support they need to make their profound and lasting contributions. The scholars who succeed most grandly in this enterprise are the brightest stars in our firmament** [n. 苍穹, 天空]. If their achievements do not solve immediate problems, they endure nonetheless as monuments of our civilization to enlarge our understanding of our culture, our past, our environment, and, not least, ourselves.

But contributions of this stature are not the only work of a great university. Much of our research, especially in our professional schools, has a more practical thrust, so much so that universities have become the nation's principal resource for helping our society to comprehend its problems. University investigators who do such work can also claim a respected place in our firmament.

The contributions we need to pursue our social mission come from every part of the scholarly universe—from academic disciplines and from professional schools, from the humanities as well as from the sciences. If any single thread connects many of the initiatives I have tried to take at Harvard, it is the effort to strengthen our work along these lines. It is our social mission that animates much of the Core Curriculum and the emphasis placed on moral reasoning, ethics, and community service in the College and professional schools. It was this mission that inspired the building of a Kennedy School that could attract able people to public service and train them to govern wisely. It was this mission that spurred our efforts to strengthen the schools of Education, of Public Health, of Divinity—each of them faculties weak in material resources but strong in their orientation toward serving human needs. And it was this mission, finally, that led to the creation of active centers of research to work on poverty, arms control, Third World development, AIDS, housing, public education, delivery of health care, and soon, I hope, the environment as well.

I know all too well that no social problem will ever be solved by universities alone. But lawmakers and officials will never solve the world's

最有思考能力的人才来到哈佛，给他们以自由和支持，以便他们作出影响深远的贡献。在这种探索中，取得最大成功的学者是我们苍穹中最亮的明星。哪怕他们的成就不能解决眼前的问题，但因为拓展了我们对自己的文化、我们的环境的认识，以及很重要的，加深了我们对自己的了解，他们因而成为我们文化上的丰碑。

但这种重要的贡献不是一所优秀大学唯一的工作。我们很多研究，特别是在我们行业性学院的研究，都有更实际的作用，这方面的作用是如此之大，以至于在我们国家，大学已成为帮助我们理解社会问题的主要渠道。做这样工作的大学研究人员，在我们这片天地里也同样受到尊重。

我们追求社会使命而需要做出的贡献，来自学术界的每一部分，从每一个学科和每一个专业，从人文科学到自然科学。如果有哪条线索能够贯穿我曾尝试在哈佛采取过的许多措施的话，那就是我为加强我们在这些方面的工作而做的努力。正是社会使命，才激励着我们的"核心课程"强调道德理念和情操，在本科和专业学院里强调社区服务。正是这种使命感，才激发了我们建立肯尼迪政府管理学院，以吸引人才从事公共服务，并培训他们明智的管理能力；正是这种使命感，才激励我们加强教育学院、公共卫生学院和神学院的发展，这些学院在物质方面可能贫乏，但在服务人类需求方面做得可一点都不差。也正是这种使命感，才导致哈佛创建活跃的研究中心，研究贫困、军备控制、第三世界的发展、艾滋病、住房、公共教育、保健方面的问题，以及在不久的将来，我希望，会有涉及环境方面的研究中心。

我很清楚地知道，仅靠大学本身不可能解决任何社会问题。但如果没有高校所提供的新发现、专业化的知识、高学历的人才，国会议员和政府官员们将永远无法解决世界上的问题。这就是为什么大学对我们的社会而言已经非常重要。而且随着时间的推移，随着我们的问题日益复杂化，随着我们面对越来越繁琐和大量的数据，随着技术设备变得日益复杂和精细，高校的重要作用会更加突显。

problems without the new discoveries, the specialized knowledge, the highly educated people that universities can uniquely supply. That is why universities are already so essential to our society. As time goes on and as our problems grow increasingly complex, our data increasingly cumbersome and **voluminous** [adj. 卷数多的，大量的], our technical **apparatus** [n. 装置，机构，仪器] increasingly elaborate and sophisticated, the role of these institutions can only become more critical.

Unless society appreciates the contributions of its universities, it will continue to reduce them to the status of another interest group by gradually stripping away the protections and support they need to stay preeminent in the world. Unless universities take their social responsibilities seriously, they will never inspire their students with a purpose large enough to fill their lives with meaning. And more important still, unless universities discharge their duties to the society fully, they will fail to do everything they can to make this troubled planet a better, happier place.

Because of its good fortune, Harvard has a special obligation to give generously of its abilities and imagination to the society that sustains it. I am more grateful than words can say for all that so many of my colleagues have done to carry out this responsibility vigorously and well. Because of these efforts, I can leave you now, secure in the faith that at a critical time in our nation's history, Harvard will do its best to lend its talents to the cause of justice, compassion, and enlightenment in a world in urgent need of those blessings.

Thank you!

除非社会赏识大学做出的贡献，否则它将继续看轻高校，把高校看做是另一类利益集团，并逐步减少对高校的保护和支持，而这些是高校想要在世界上保持领先地位而必不可少的。除非大学认真对待自己的社会责任，否则它们永远无法激发学生，让他们的生活充满意义。更重要的是，除非大学充分履行其社会职责，否则它们将无法尽自己所能，让这个烦恼多多的星球变成一个较好、较快乐的地方。

由于幸运的机缘，哈佛有特别的义务，对这个社会慷慨地献出自己的能力和想象力，并因此而使哈佛得以维系。我这么多的同事尽力地承担这个责任，而且做得这么好，对此我无法用言辞来表达自己的谢意。因为有了你们这些努力，我现在可以放心离开，并深信在我国历史上的这个关键时刻，哈佛会倾其全力，应世界所需，支持正义、表达同情，并为世人提供启示。

谢谢！

---

1 指肯尼迪和马丁·路德·金等在公众中享有威望的人物被暗杀事件

2 指越南战争

3 指尼克松的水门事件

4 "伟大社会"（the Great Society）指美国总统林登·约翰逊在1960年代推行的旨在消除贫困和种族歧视，从而建设繁荣社会的一系列社会措施。

5 查尔斯·艾略特（Charles Eliot, 1834—1926），美国教育家，从1869年起担任哈佛校长，直到1909年，是哈佛校史上任期最长的校长。

格罗·哈莱姆·布伦特兰（1939— ）

　　布伦特兰夫人是挪威杰出的政治家。1939年生于挪威奥斯陆市，1963年毕业于奥斯陆大学医学系，1965年毕业于哈佛大学，获公共卫生硕士学位。1981年出任工党政府首相，是挪威历史上第一位女首相。以后又多次受命组阁，先后担任首相达10年之久。布伦特兰夫人也是国际上著名的妇女活动家，曾于1984年被联合国秘书长任命为联合国环境和发展委员会主席，1998年5月又出任世界卫生组织总干事。

　　布伦特兰夫人早在1974年担任挪威环保大臣以后，就一直重视国内环保工作，并取得了举世瞩目的成绩。由于挪威的东、南、西三面邻国的工业污染所导致的酸雨对挪威树木、鱼类生长等造成严重危害，特别是北方邻国俄国的污染和核泄漏，直接威胁着挪威人，布伦特兰夫人由此深切感到，保护环境是全球性的事业，只靠少数国家努力不可能完成。

　　特别值得一提的是，布伦特兰夫人对挪中环保领域的合作一直十分关心。1995年11月，她在访华时，向中国领导人提出建议："一些工业化国家对环境问题抓晚了，不仅环境遭到污染，而且整治花的钱更多，希望中国能注意这个教训。"在布伦特兰夫人的支持下，挪威政府向中国方面提供了相当可观的用于环保项目的赠款和优惠贷款。挪威一些公司积极参与了中国不少城市和地区的污水处理、大气监测、古城保护等项目，双方在环境保护领域里进行了广泛而深入的合作。

1992

Sustainability and Our Environment
可持续发展与我们的环境

Gro Harlem Brundtland 格罗·布伦特兰

Mr. President, faculty, family and friends, and today's graduates:

It has been an honor to be invited to address you here today, and in particular the young students and graduates of Harvard in whom so much hope for the future is reposed.

In the course of the less than 400 weeks left of the twentieth century you will enter professional life with promising chances of influencing the future course of this country, a future which is of so decisive importance to the whole world.

In the final decade of the second millennium, 2500 years since the birth of democracy in ancient Greece, humanity – and nature of which it depends, finds itself at a cross-roads.

Technological and scientific advances have created a world economy of staggering dimensions, but it has left more than half of the world's people in poverty. Through over exploitation of our natural resources, we have brought life on earth even closer to the brink of disaster.

The **predicament** [n. 困境] is new to present generations, the first ones to face the formidable moral challenge: Not only one of responsibility to the needs and rights of others, but of those not yet born – and of the future life of nature itself.

At this point in our evolution, we can not hope that the environmental and development crisis will go away as a passing fad. Technological trends, patterns of production and consumption – and pure human numbers – call for radical changes in order to reconcile human activities with the laws of nature.

The 1990s will be a decade of destiny, in which we must summon our human resources, our knowledge, and our moral conviction to seriously face the real challenge of the future.

53 years of life experience and 18 years of political work in Government and the parliament of my country has brought me to the following view of the most fundamental challenge of our time:

The forces of technology, of finance and of electronic communication have increasingly taken over the powers which were vested in democracy to shape our future.

What should be our global village is threatening to turn into a global jungle. We need to replace international anarchy by international governance.

The challenge of the 1990s is to deepen and widen the forces of democracy and

尊敬的校长、各位老师、各位家长、各位朋友，今天毕业的各位同学：

很荣幸受到邀请在这里发表演讲，特别是面对哈佛的青年学子和毕业生，因为在你们身上寄托着未来的厚望。

从现在到 20 世纪结束，只有不到 400 周的时间了，你们也将进入职业生涯，大展宏图，从而很有可能影响这个国家的未来进展，这种未来，对整个世界来说，将会有决定性的重要意义。

在公元 2000 年的最后一个 10 年，当民主在古希腊诞生 2500 年后——人类，包括人类赖以生存的大自然，都处在一个十字路口上。

技术和科学的进步，创造了世界经济的惊人规模，但世界上一半以上的人口，仍然生活在贫困之中。由于对自然资源的过度开发，地球上的生命越来越近地走向灾难的边缘。

当代人面临全新的困境，他们首当其冲地面对这样巨大的道德挑战：我们不仅要对其他人的需求和权利负责，而且要对那些尚未出生的人负责，还需要对未来大自然的生命负责。

在进化过程的这个时间点上，我们不能幻想（环境与发展的）危机会像昙花一现般消失。技术的发展，生产和消费的趋势，乃至人口的庞大数字，都要求人们改弦易辙，以便让人类活动与自然法则相协调。

20 世纪 90 年代将是决定命运的 10 年，我们必须集中人力资源、集思广益、坚定信念，严肃面对未来的真正挑战。

我的 53 年生活经验，和在我国议会及政府中任职的 18 年政治生涯，让我意识到我们这个时代面临着下面这些最基本的挑战：

技术、金融和电子通信的力量，已经越来越多地接手民主体制本来固有的权力，从而塑造我们的未来。

原本应该是地球村的社会，正有可能成为一个弱肉强食的全球丛林。我们需要通过国际社会共同治理，来取代国际无政府状态。

1990 年代的挑战是要扩大和深化民主的力量，并把民主决策运用到国际事务中。

我们从小接受的教导，就是在一个民主国家里，政府是代表人民来进行治理的，而每个国家的人民，可以通过他们对民主进程中的参与，

to lift democratic decision-making also to the international level.

We are brought up being taught that democracy allows us to govern on behalf of the people, and that people, through their participation in democratic processes in each country, can make decisions and choices about their own future.

We elect our leaders on their programs, our elected representatives, in turn, pursue the objectives of society by means of legislation, rules, and taxation.

The idea of democracy – 2500 years old – has a stronghold here near Boston. All of you, and those who are fortunate to get higher education, are familiar with the account of the Tea Party.

Today, the ideas summed up in Gettysburg: "government of the people by the people for the people", while formally in good order, are, when applied at the level of the nation state not alone able to lead us to a future which is more safe, more just and more secure.

The nation state, even the most powerful, is too small a scene for addressing regional and global challenges. It will become increasingly contradictory to promise remedy through national measures alone to challenges which are of an international nature and origin.

I can give you an example from my own country. People expect that the government sees to it that the general interest rate is such that they can repay the mortgages without too much hardship - reasonable interest rates are good for investments and for jobs. The last time the Federal Bank of Germany raised the prime lending rate, however, it took 17 seconds until the Norwegian National Bank had to raise its interest rate.

Another example: In Norway, we have cut our sulphur emission by more than 50 percent since the seventies, still rain as sour as vinegar keeps falling down destroying our lakes and soil, and 90 percent of this acid rain originates in other countries.

If we maintain the illusion that nations can act in isolation we not only risk postponing critical decisions which can only be made effective when states act in cooperation: We risk an increase in the growing skepticism and lack of respect democracy, politics and politicians because they seemingly can't do what is in reality beyond the reach of their present powers.

We are used to holding politicians accountable and to measure their results and how they are able to improve our lives. If their results do not meet our expectations,

来决定和选择自己的未来。

我们根据候选人的提案选出我们的领导人，我们选出的代表反过来又通过法案、规则和税收的方式来满足社会的意愿。

已经有2500年历史的民主观念，就在波士顿附近扎了根。你们和那些有幸获得高等教育的人，都熟悉茶党的故事。

今天，林肯在盖底茨堡所总结的理念"民有、民治、民享的政府"，虽然总的来说是好想法，但应用到独立国家之间的关系时，还不能够完全把我们带向一个更安全、更公正、更稳定的未来。

单一国家，哪怕是最强大的国度，想要应对区域和全球挑战，还是显得势单力薄。通过单个国家制定的措施，就想解决国际性的挑战和源于境外的问题，结果将会是南辕北辙。

我可以把我自己的国家当做一个例子。人们一般都期望政府维持利率稳定，这样的话他们在偿还按揭贷款时不会太难，合理的利率也有利于投资和创造就业机会。但是，当德国联邦银行最近一次提高利率时，挪威国家银行在17秒内也不得不提高其利率。

另一个例子是，自70年代以来，挪威已把硫排放降低了50%以上，但像酸醋一样的酸雨，还是照样落下来，侵蚀我们的湖泊和土壤，而这种酸雨的90%来自其他国家。

如果我们依旧持有这样的幻想，希望一个国家可以单独行事，我们不仅要冒拖延关键决策的风险——这些关键决策只有当不同国家协调行动时才可能有效，我们还可能看到人们对民主、对政治和政治家怀疑增多、尊重减少，因为政治家们似乎一事无成，而实际上靠他们现有的权力，是心有余而力不足的。

我们习惯于要求政治家敢做敢当，衡量他们的政绩，并看他们是否能够改善我们的生活。如果其结果没有达到先前的期望，我们会很快速地反对他们，同时也不再支持这个政治制度。

如果这种对政治离心离德的倾向继续下去，我们传统的政治体制也有逐步解体的危险。有些国家新出现的反民主趋势和呼吁强人统治的趋势，就是我们必须认真对待的危险现象。

we are quick both to turn against them and against the political system.

If this alienation towards political life is allowed to continue, we risk a gradual disintegration also of traditional political institutions. The new and dangerous anti-democratic trends in some countries and calls for the strong man are dangerous symptoms which we must take seriously.

We must not forget that it is we ourselves, not somebody else, who are responsible for how our democracies work. We cannot wait for someone else to do the job or put all our faith in an illusion of omnipotence [n. 全能，万能] **at the top political level. All segments of our societies must become more deeply involved in the real issues of our time.**

Democracy cannot be achieved by top-down processes. It must have its base in our communities, in the minds and priorities of the individual citizen and voter, in political parties and in the network of interest groups and non-governmental organizations which are an essential part of our pluralistic societies.

I have come here directly from the United Nations Conference on Environment and Development in Rio de Janeiro which opened yesterday. That conference is about survival of the human race and about its reconciliation with the biosphere.

Cynics are often quick to dismiss international conferences as futile, costly, and substantively contrary to what they see as national privileges and vested interests. Such attitudes are dangerous. "Cynics know the price of anything and the value of nothing", said Oscar Wilde.

Presently, the vast majority who are poor make only a minimal claim to our natural resources, while the more **voracious** [adj. 狼吞虎咽的，贪婪的] North is consuming in a few decades what has taken the planet billions of year to accumulate.

This growing difference between the fortunate few and the powerless impoverished majority is a destabilizing trend. It is dangerous as well as morally unacceptable.

Achieving or approaching sustainability demands a profound understanding of a series of the challenges facing societies between now and the year 2050. Can a doubled world population be adequately fed in an environmentally sustainable way? How can they be educated and become our partners when today only 8 percent, in some very poor countries only 2 percent have access to higher education?

How can we find the energy needed to fuel a world economy perhaps five times

我们不应忘记，是我们自己而不是其他人，才是必须对民主制度负责的人。我们不能等待别人来做这项工作，或把我们所有的希望寄托在政治高层的某个万能的人物身上。我们社会的各个阶层，都必须更深入地参与解决这个时代的真正问题。

民主不能自上而下地推进。它必须扎根于我们的社区里、扎根于每个公民和选民的头脑里，并成为他们优先考虑的东西；它必须扎根于政党中、扎根于利益团体和非政府组织的网络里，这些都是我们多元社会的重要组成部分。

我从昨日在里约热内卢才开幕的联合国环境与发展会议上直接来到这里。这次会议讨论的主题，是人类的生存及与我们生存环境的和谐。

愤世嫉俗者们往往随便就说，国际会议不过是些徒劳无用、成本高昂的活动，而且从本质上违背他们国家的权益和既得利益。这种态度是危险的。正如奥斯卡·王尔德所说："愤世嫉俗者知道所有东西的价格，但对其价值却一无所知。"

目前，绝大多数身处贫困的人只享用了我们天然资源的极小一部分，而胃口大开的北方发达国家，却在短短几十年里，消耗掉了地球亿万年才积累起来的资源。

这种少数幸运儿和贫困无力的大多数人之间不断扩大的差距，形成一种不稳定的趋势。这种差距是危险的，也是在道义上让人不能接受的。

达到或接近可持续发展，就需要我们深刻认识到，从现在起到2050年我们的社会将面临的一系列挑战。世界人口将翻倍，我们能有在环境上可持续的方法来让人们吃饱吗？他们将得到何种教育，从而成为我们的伙伴？而事实是，今天只有8%、在一些非常贫穷的国家只有2%的人，能够接受到高等教育。

我们如何能找到足够的能源，以满足也许会5倍于当今世界经济规模所需要的燃料，而不损害环境并严重扰乱气候？

除非我们协助发展中国家绕过在他们发展过程中造成最严重污染的阶段，并激发那些国家人们的潜能，否则我们自己也可能成为受害者。我们不能对发展中国家说："对不起，我们已经把垃圾箱装满，没有地方

larger than today's without spoiling the environment and significantly disrupt climate?

Unless we assist developing countries in bypassing the most polluting stages of development and in developing the potential of their people, we ourselves may be the victims. We can not say to the developing world: "Sorry, we have filled the wastebasket, there is no room left for you."

Developing countries require environmental space for their development. For them, the future is essentially about the development and justice. For them, the environment is vital, as it is for us. But they will not accept the unequal burden that seems to be asked of them – to be the caretakers of our common responsibilities for future generations, while we who have been destroying nature and raised our standard of living, through unsustainable patterns of growth, are not ready to take our share – the bill of repair.

I have been stunned to see how the Rio Conference seems to fail to make workable decisions on how to curb population growth. States which do not have a population problem, in one particular case even no births at all, are doing their utmost to prevent the world from making sensible decisions regarding family planning.

Family planning services must be made universally available. The status of women must be raised, and they must receive better education. Women have been patronized long enough.

We are faced with a watered down climate convention. It fails to set firm targets. It fails to recognize that the longer we wait the greater the bill.

Many countries have already made deep cuts in their emissions, and pledged further reductions. And still, their economies are among the primary forces on the global scale. Germany is a case in point. The energy-efficiency of Japan is well known. We can not be surprised when these countries increase their edge in the future because the forced their industry to become more effective.

Carbon taxes have been introduced in some countries including my own. They may not be popular but they are accepted as necessary. But all such measures in small and medium sized countries will not make a decisive difference unless they are matched by similar strong measures in major countries.

Faced with these challenges and ever dwindling natural resources, I see the Rio Earth Summit as steps in the staircase leading to what will have to come: A better organized world community where we pool resources as well as formal sovereignty in

留给你们了。"

  发展中国家的发展，需要有相应的环境空间。对他们来说，未来关注的主要是发展和公正的问题。对他们来说，如同对我们一样，保护环境是至关重要的。但他们不会接受外界强加于他们的看来不太平等的负担。比如说，我们要求大家一起为子孙后代负责，虽然我们自己靠破坏大自然、通过不可持续的增长模式提高了生活水平，我们却不想承担义务：为治理环境买单。

  看到里约会议似乎无法就如何遏止人口增长问题作出可行的决定，我感到震惊。那些没有人口问题的国家（有一个国家甚至没有新增人口），竭尽全力地阻止世界做出倡导计划生育的明智决策。

  计划生育的措施必须到处都能够提供。必须提高妇女的地位，她们必须得到更好的教育。女性被当做垂怜眷顾的对象已经够长时间的了。

  我们看到的是一个走了样的讨论气候会议。这次会议未能设置明确的目标，它未能认识到，我们等待的时间越长，要花的钱就越多。

  许多国家已经大幅削减它们的排放量，并承诺进一步削减。然而它们的经济仍在全球范围内举足轻重。德国是一个典型的例子，日本的能源效率也是众所周知的。当这些国家今后的竞争优势增加时，我们不应感到惊讶，因为它们迫使自己国内的行业变得更为有效。

  一些国家，包括我自己的国家，已经开始征收碳排放税。这些税可能不受欢迎，但人们知道这是必要的。除非那些主要国家也实施类似的强有力的行动，否则中小国家的所有此类措施，都无法产生决定性的作用。

  面对这些挑战和不断减少的天然资源，我认为里约保护地球首脑会议像是楼梯上的台阶，想要通往将来，一定要做的事情是：更好地组织国际社会，集中资源以及主权权力，以便给我们的未来带来更多真正的主权和选择，而不是让后人无从选择。

  我们需要更仔细、更有效地使用地表资源这一馈赠。我们对之应该更加珍惜、准确定价，并尽可能多地留给后人。

  时间本身就是一种稀缺资源，正如"罗马俱乐部"发布的"增长的限制"这份报告用一个法国童话谜语所表述的那样：

order to obtain more real sovereignty and choices for the future, not foreclosing the choices of future generations.

We need to use the gifts of the world's **crust** [n. 外壳] more thoughtfully and efficiently. We should treasure them more, price them properly and keep more of them available for future generations.

Time itself is a scarce resource as the Club of Rome's report "Limits to growth" illustrates by a French children's riddle:

You own a pond with a water lily. The lily plant doubles in size each day. If the plant was allowed to grow unchecked, it would completely cover the pond in 30 days, ruining all other forms of life in the pond completely. Imagine that you decide not to worry until the water lily covers half the pond. On which day will that be? Only one day to go!

It shows how little time we have and why **derisory** [adj. 嘲笑的，可笑的] attitudes will be self-destructive.

If we signal that the task is almost hopeless, we will foster environmental **nihilism** [n. (否认一切宗教信仰和道德观念的) 虚无主义，无政府主义，(精神病学) 虚无幻觉], rather than stimulate a new global ethic. The World Commission on Environment and Development, which I had the honor to chair, concluded that the situation is far from hopeless. Instead, the Commission expressed the hope and the firm belief that humankind has the capacity to change the dangerous course we have been travelling.

We need new policies at local, national and international levels based on sustainable patterns of development.

We do not have global institutions strong enough to determine new directions or to implement effective global policies. We must develop an international public sector based on the United Nations and existing institutions.

Countries have sovereignty over their national resources, but decisions leading to sustainable development will be illusionary if we can only move forwards at snail's pace decided by the most reluctant movers.

It is difficult to see how decision-making in international institutions can become effective unless we introduce new elements of **supranational** [adj. 超国家的] rule. We need elements of global governance that can serve our real interests, across national barriers.

We have come to a watershed in human history. Political leaders will have to lead into unchartered land, where familiar concepts of purpose and interests fail to match reality. But democratically elected leaders cannot do the job alone. They need

如果有一个长了睡莲的池塘，睡莲的数量每天加倍。如果让这种植物任意生长，池塘将在30天内被完全覆盖，这样就会完全毁灭池塘里的所有其他植物和生物。想象一下，如果你不去管它，直到睡莲覆盖了半个池塘，你还有多少天可以等着而不用管呢？只剩一天了！

这表明我们已经没有多少时间了，那些冷嘲热讽的态度只会带来自我毁灭。

如果我们说，这项任务几乎是没有希望完成的，我们就会助长环境的虚无主义，而不是倡导一种新的全球理念。我有幸主持的"世界环境保护与发展委员会"的结论是，情况还远没到毫无指望的地步。相反，该委员会表达了一个希望和坚定的信念，那就是，人类有能力改变我们一直走的危险道路。

我们需要在各地区、各国和国际社会，都推行基于可持续发展模式的新政策。

我们还没有强有力的全球机构，来确定新的方向或实施有效的全球政策。我们必须在联合国和现有机构的基础上，建立起一个国际管理部门。

每个国家都对自己的国土资源享有主权，但如果我们按着那些最消极怠惰的人所采取的蜗牛速度前进，对可持续发展的问题做出决断只会是一个幻想。

除非我们制定一些新的超国家的管理规则，否则在国际机构中做出有效的决策将会是很难的事。我们需要全球性的管理，从而在跨国家的情况下，保护大家的实际利益。

我们正处在人类历史的一个分水岭上。政治领导人将不得不把人们带入一个陌生的领域，在这个新的领域里，人们过去所熟悉的有关目的和利益的概念，都已经脱离现实。但是，民选的领导人无法独自做这项工作。他们需要千千万万负责任的公民给予支持，特别是从短期来看，那些必要措施显得成本高昂的时候。

我们过去在武器上已经花费数万亿美元，现在我们这项新的共同努力，同样需要巨大的花销。

由于有美国的领导和联合国的参与，我们对伊拉克入侵科威特斩钉截铁地说"不行"。我们必须以同样的方式，对全球环境和社会秩序崩溃这种更严重的威胁，斩钉截铁地说"不行"，并调动一切手段来促成这件事。北方国家需要做出榜样[1]。我们必须搞好自己的事，并为发展中国家和前共产主

to be supported by increasing millions of responsible citizens, in particular when the necessary measures seem costly in a short-term perspective.

Trillions of dollars have been spent on arms in the past, now comparable gigantic efforts are needed in a new and common struggle.

Thanks to US leadership and the United Nations, we said effectively no to the Iraqi invasion of Kuwait. In a similar manner we must say effectively no and deploy the resources needed to repel the much more serious threat of global environmental and social collapse. Leadership will have to come from the North. We must set our own house in order, and assist both the developing countries and the former communist countries. The West has won the Cold War. Now the West must again resume real leadership.

In my view there are compelling political reasons for ensuring that Europe and the US will be walking together, breaking new ground. Political innovation must come from those countries which derive their values and form of government from the same sources of free, democratic thinking. We must use our cultural, political and humanitarian capital to undertake an even greater responsibility for those who are less fortunate than we are.

Then we can hope to build the truly global democracy which will comprise also those parts of the world, where today the seeds of our values are growing on the thinnest soil.

We need a collective engagement which goes beyond building a new East-West relationship. We need a new era of internationalism where peace, environment and development are linked, and placed in the epicenter [n. 震中. 中心] **of national and international affairs.**

You stand here today – as I once did – as a highly privileged group. You have been gifted with talent, opportunity, knowledge and access to the best education the world has to offer. You have hopes and may also have doubts about the future. But most of all each of you has a great opportunity to make a difference and to play a role in the establishment of the primacy of global democracy.

As generations before you have experienced, the world – and life itself has changed during the couple of decades of your childhood and youth. That pace of change is likely to increase.

When I myself left Harvard, in 1965, before most of you were born, there was a war in Vietnam. A reformist wave was under way. President Johnson was announcing

义国家提供帮助。西方国家赢得了冷战，现在西方国家必须再次承担起真正的领导作用。

在我看来，确保欧洲和美国步调一致、共同开拓新天地，这在政治上是很有必要的。政治上的创新，必须来自那些倡导自由和民主的价值观、并以自由和民主的形式来管理的国家。我们必须利用我们的文化、政治和人道主义方面的资本，为那些没有我们那么幸运的人，承担起更大的责任。

这样，我们才能有希望真正在全球建立起民主社会，把今天我们价值观的种子正生长于稀薄贫瘠土壤上的那些国度，都包括进来。

我们不仅需要建立起一个新的东西方关系，还要比这做得更多。我们需要开拓一个国际主义的新时代，把和平、环境保护与发展关联起来，并在国家和国际事务中，把这些关注当做中心。

你们今天站在这里，正如我作为毕业生时曾经站在这里一样，属于非常幸运的一群人。你们天资聪明、生逢其时、知识丰富，得到了这个世界所能够提供的最好的教育。你们对未来满怀希望，可能也有疑虑。但最重要的是，你们每个人都有一个难得的机会，可以在全球建立起民主的事业中，起到推动和关键的作用。

正如你们前人所经历过的那样，我们的世界和生活本身，在你们童年和青少年时代的这些年里发生了改观。这种改变的速度以后还可能会加快。

当我在 1965 年离开哈佛的时候，你们中的大部分人都还没有出生，越南战争正在进行，改革浪潮风起云涌。约翰逊总统公布了"伟大社会"的计划[2]，瑞秋·卡森在《寂静的春天》中[3]，发出了有关生态的警告，逐渐地，世界准备第一次举办有关保护环境的联合国会议。

你们生活过的这 20 年里，从 1972 年到 1992 年，新的右翼思潮不断涌现。但是让我们记住：不管市场机制如何能够充分、有效地分配资源，它们都无法树立起我们共同的目标，或培养社会责任感，也无法构建一个有关公正和可持续未来的宏伟远景，而只有人，才能做到这些。

事实是，要想做出影响深远的决定，政府依赖于选民的支持，从而能做出哪怕是最困难的决定。只有这样，才可能获得真正有效的改变。

通过卫星和有线电视，我们一天 24 小时都能收到来自世界各地的支离破

the Great Society, Rachel Carson gave us her warning, in "Silent Spring" – and gradually the world was preparing for the first UN conference on the Environment.

Your two decades from 1972 to 1992 have seen the new radical right movement evolving. But let us remember: however good the markets are at allocating resources efficiently and effectively, they cannot build community purpose or instill social responsibility, or assert the larger vision only people can have of a just and sustainable future.

The truth is that in order to make far reaching decisions governments depend upon a population that will support even the most difficult decisions. Only then can truly effective change come about.

Through satellites and cables we receive fragmented images from all over the world, 24 hours a day. Complexity is reduced to disconnected simplicity. One day of multimedia information comes close to what Umberto Eco calls a journey in hyper-reality.

We must not be blinded by the immediate. We must all take a longer term view. We need to expand and share knowledge and we must get much more people engaged in the overriding issues of our time.

Luckily, at the beginning of the 1990s, democracy is gaining ground worldwide, now that we need it so urgently. These changes could have been slower had it not been for the information revolution and the global media. We will have to rely on the gift of information technology for spreading knowledge and for developing those common perspectives and those common attitudes which our human predicament now requires.

We are compelled to manage the most important global transition since the agricultural and industrial revolutions – the transition to sustainable development – how to reconcile human activities and human numbers with the long-term carrying capacity of his finite earth.

If we succeed as we must we may with greater confidence teach generations yet unborn the Gettysburg ideals and how they were made to work at a time when people and countries realized that they had to move towards more mature stages of civilization.

My own faith is in the youth of the world – custodians of the present the trustees of the future. We, and you should see to it that the day will come when people look back on your generation and say: Faced with the challenge they managed to upgrade human civilization.

Congratulations and thank you!

碎的影像画面。很多复杂的问题被简化为互不关联的东西。我们一天之内接触到的多媒体信息，相当于安伯托·艾柯[4]所说的一个"超现实旅程"。

我们不应该只着眼于当下，必须重视长远的目标。我们需要扩大和分享知识，必须让更多人来参与解决我们这个时代里最首要的问题。

幸运的是，在1990年代初，正当我们迫切需要它的时候，民主在全世界范围内风起云涌。如果没有信息革命和全球媒体，这些变化可能会来得较慢。我们还将依靠信息技术传播知识、促进人们达成共识和形成相同的态度，这些都是我们改善人类处境所必需的。

我们必须处理好自从农业革命和工业革命以来最重要的全球性过渡，即向可持续发展方向的过渡，学会如何协调人类活动和人口数量，以及地球有限承载能力之间的问题。

当我们取得成功时——我们必须成功，我们就能有更大的信心，向后人传授林肯在盖底茨堡所倡导的理想，向后人解释说，当人们和不同的国家都认识到我们的文明必须走向更成熟的阶段时，林肯的理念在这个决策中又如何得到了运用。

我的希望寄托在全世界的青年身上，他们保管着我们的今天，肩负着我们的未来。我们，还有你们，应该做到，当有一天后人回顾这一代人时，会说：面对挑战，他们奋力提升了人类的文明！

祝贺各位并谢谢大家！

---

1 "南北国家"，是从地理上划分的南北半球，从经济角度看，刚好发达国家大部分分布在北半球，发展中国家大都分布在南半球，所以南北国家实际上说的就是发达国家和发展中国家。

2 美国总统约翰逊（Lyndon B. Johnson）在1960年代推行的"伟大社会"（"the Great Society"）计划，包括倡导民权、环境保护、资助教育，以及为低收入和老年人提供医疗保健和帮助等措施。

3 瑞秋·卡森（Rachel Carson），美国生物学家、倡导自然保护的作家，其发表于1962年的代表作《寂静的春天》（"Silent Spring"），指出滥用杀虫剂严重影响了自然生态，如果再不改变，春天将不再有鸟语花香，也将波及人类健康。

4 安伯托·艾柯（Umberto Eco, 1932— ），意大利著名哲学家、符号学家、历史学家、文学批评家和小说家。

阿尔·戈尔（1948— ）

与许多哈佛毕业典礼的演讲者一样，戈尔也是哈佛校友，在发表这个演讲的时候，他正担任着美国副总统。

戈尔是美国前总统克林顿的搭档，任期为1993年至2001年。执政期间，戈尔是互联网产业的积极推动者，著名的"信息高速公路"和"数字地球"的概念就是他参与提出的。

戈尔出身于美国首都华盛顿，一个来自田纳西州的政治世家。他的父亲是美国国会的众议员，后来曾出任代表田纳西州的参议员。戈尔1969年毕业于哈佛大学的政治学专业，同年参加美国陆军，担任航空兵学校的情报军官，曾以军队记者身份进入越南战场。从战场回来后，戈尔就读于范德堡大学的神学院和法学院，并获得洛克菲勒基金会奖学金。随后戈尔开始了他的政治生涯，28岁时当选田纳西州众议员，1984年成为该州参议员。1992年作为克林顿的竞选伙伴参选，成功当选副总统。他后来还在2000年竞选美国总统，但以微弱劣势输给了乔治·布什（通称小布什）。

戈尔卸任后主要致力于环保事业，他2006年参与制作和演出的纪录片《难以忽视的真相》（同时出版同名书籍），讲述工业化对全球气候变暖和人类生存的影响，在西方国家影响很大。该片获得第79届奥斯卡最佳纪录片奖，戈尔本人也因为对环保事业的努力和贡献获得了2007年的诺贝尔和平奖。

1994

Cynicism Will Take People No Where
玩世不恭于事无补

Al Gore 阿尔·戈尔

Mr. President, members of the Harvard Corporation and the Board of Overseers, faculty, parents, and especially, the graduates:

A Harvard commencement is a special occasion. How could anyone not have been thrilled by this morning's assembly -- 25,000 people packed into Harvard Yard to celebrate one of the great occasions of life. I loved it all. And I have especially enjoyed my 25th reunion. I'm so proud of my class. It has been wonderful to have an opportunity to visit with so many friends.

I remember the 25th reunion class when they came in 1969 walking around the Yard with their children. They seemed like ordinary people. I remember that they seemed older then than we do now. But in fact they were responsible for one of the saving triumphs of modern civilization.

That was the class of 1944. They were part of the generation President Clinton commemorated this week in Normandy, the group that went from Harvard to boot camp and basic training and from there were transfused into the weary divisions battling across Europe. Only 11 members of the class were present at graduation; all the rest had by then already left to enlist. Some did not come back to their reunion. Their names are carved in stone in Memorial Church just behind me. Many did come back and some of them are here again today for their 50th reunion. We salute you.

Back in 1969 our graduating class was in no mood to salute or to celebrate your sacrifice your achievement. But we understood then and understand now ever more clearly that without any question because of your service, the world changed in 1944. Indeed, our world a half century later is still shaped by the events of that tumultuous and triumphant year.

I want to describe today the reasons why I believe the world also changed in important and enduring ways because of the events of 1969, a year of contradiction and contrasts, of glory and bitterness.

In July 1969 one-quarter of the population of the world watched on live television while Neil Armstrong brought his space module Eagle down to the Sea of Tranquility, slowly climbed down a ladder and pressed his left boot into the untrod surface of the moon.

But 1969 was also the year Charles Manson and his followers made the innocent words Helter Skelter symbols of a bloodbath. It was the year of music in the rain at Woodstock and the year of the My Lai Massacre in Vietnam.

尊敬的校长、哈佛集团和监管理事会的各位理事、各位老师、家长，特别是今天毕业的同学们：

哈佛毕业典礼是一个特殊的场合。今天上午，两万五千人聚集在哈佛校园，共同庆祝我们生命中最重要的日子之一。有谁能不激动万分？我喜欢这一切，而且我特别享受我的毕业25周年团聚，我为我的年级自豪。有机会与这么多朋友见面，真是一件美好的事情。

我还记得1969年毕业的时候，看到校友回来参加他们的25周年团聚，带着自己的家人孩子，流连在校园内。他们显得很普通，看上去好像比我们现在要显得老一些。但事实上正是他们的奋勇作战，拯救了现代文明。

那是1944届的毕业班，他们属于克林顿总统本周在诺曼底所要纪念的那一代人。他们离开哈佛，去新兵训练营接受基本训练，并从那里被派到战火纷飞的欧洲战场。当时还能够参加毕业典礼的只有11名学生，其余所有的人那时已经身在部队了。有些人再没有机会重返校园，他们的名字就刻在我身后这个纪念教堂里的石头上。许多人回来了，其中一些校友今天重返母校，参加他们的50周年聚首。我们向你们致敬！

回头看1969年，当时的毕业班还没有意识到应该向你们的奉献、你们的牺牲致敬。我们知道，现在也越来越清楚地明白，是你们在1944年的奋斗改变了世界。事实上，直到半个世纪后的今天，那个动荡而又辉煌的一年里所发生的事件，仍然决定着今天世界的格局。

我今天想描述一下，为什么我认为1969年发生的事件，给世界带来了重大而深远的变化，那一年充满矛盾和反差、光荣与痛苦。

1969年7月，世界上有四分之一的人观看了电视直播，美国宇航员尼尔·阿姆斯特朗[1]驾驭着"老鹰"号宇宙飞船，降落在月球表面的"静海"地带，慢慢爬下梯子，成为第一个踏上月球的人。

但1969年也是查尔斯·曼森[2]和他的追随者屠杀无辜的一年。那年，伍德斯托克音乐节[3]在雨中上演，而在越南的美莱村则发生了屠杀事件[4]。

当我们去课堂听讲、写论文、听音乐、谈论体育、从事运动以及在谈恋爱时，越南战争炸翻了那个小小的国家，而美国则在精神上被撕裂。由战争而引起的莫名的黑暗感觉，每天都笼罩在我们心头。

While we went to class and heard lectures and wrote papers and listened to music and talked and played sports and fell in love, the war in Vietnam was blasting that small country apart physically and ripping America apart emotionally. A dark mood of uncertainty from that tragic conflict clouded every single day we were here.

The year 1969 began with the inauguration of Richard Nixon, a ceremony that seemed to confirm for many of us the finality of a change in our national mood and **ratify** [v. 批准, 认可] the results of a downward spiral that had begun with the assassination of President Kennedy five years, two months, and two days earlier.

Throughout our four years at Harvard the nation's spirits steadily sank. The race riot in Watts was fresh in our minds when we registered as freshmen. Though our hopes were briefly raised by the passage of civil rights legislation and the promise of a war on poverty, the war in Vietnam grew steadily more ominous and consumed the resources that were needed to make good on the extravagant promises for dramatic progress here at home.

The year before our graduation, our hopes were once again briefly raised by the political insurgency we helped inspire and that we hoped might somehow end our national nightmare. Then, months later, those hopes were cruelly crushed by the assassinations of Martin Luther King, Jr., renewed race riots --this time nationwide -- and then the assassination of Robert Kennedy, and what seemed like the death of any hope that we might find our way back to the entrance of the dark tunnel into which our country had wandered. All of this cast a shadow over each of our personal futures.

My personal attitudes toward the career I have chosen changed dramatically during that time. I left Harvard in 1969 disillusioned by what I saw happening in our country and certain of only one thing about my future: I would never, ever go into politics.

After returning from Vietnam and after seven years as a journalist, I rekindled my interest in public service. Yet I believe the same disillusioning forces that for a time drove me away from politics have continued for the country as a whole.

After all, the war raged on for five more years and the downward spiral in our national mood reached a new low when the Watergate scandal led to the growing belief that our government was telling lies to our people.

The resignation of President Nixon, his subsequent pardon, the Oil shocks, 21% interest rates, hostages held seemingly **interminably** [adv. 没完没了地] and then swapped

1969年理查德·尼克松总统宣誓就职,他的当政使我们许多人感到,这种低沉的民族情绪该有所转变,而这种呈螺旋式下降的士气,从那之前的5年两个月零两天里,肯尼迪被暗杀的日子便已经开始了。

　　我们在哈佛的4年里,民族精神一直都在下降。我们新生报到时,瓦茨种族骚乱[5]犹在眼前。虽然公民权利法案的通过和政府宣布要消除贫困,使我们暂时燃起了希望,但越南战争越来越残酷,战争消耗了本来可以用于国内发展、实现宏伟目标的资源。

　　在毕业的前一年,我们投身政治活动,希望民族噩梦早点结束。然而,几个月后,这些希望又破灭了——马丁·路德·金遭暗杀,种族冲突再度兴起,这次是全国性的。接着,罗伯特·肯尼迪[6]遇刺,让我们感到前途渺茫,好像我们国家徘徊在无尽黑暗的隧道里。这一切,让每个人都不知道自己路在何方。

　　我个人对职业选择的态度,也在那个时候发生了巨大转变。1969年我离开哈佛时,对我们国家发生的事大失所望,只有一件事是明确的:我以后决不从政。

　　从越南回来后,我当了7年记者,这使我重新燃起了对公共服务的兴趣。尽管我仍认为,曾经让我对政治失望的那些令人幻灭的东西,依然影响着全国。

　　毕竟,战争又拖了5年多,水门事件的发生,使民族情绪下跌到新的最低点,它使得民众更加坚定地认为政府在欺骗人民。

　　尼克松总统的辞职,以及后来对他的赦免,石油危机的发生、(由于通货膨胀)高达21%的利率、(在伊朗的)人质看似遥遥无期地被扣押,然后我们以武器换人质,那些恐怖分子却称我们为"大魔头"。在十几年里,国债增加了4倍,贫富差距进一步加大,人民的实际收入在下降,所有这些,都增加了美国的负面形象,使我们看待政府的态度发生了根本的改变。

　　当我们还在哈佛学习的那几年,有个民意测验表明,美国的民族精神在逐步发生着变化。1965年秋刚入校时,基本上相信政府想把事情办好的人数超过60%,今天这个数字只有10%;那时认为政府会偏向有钱人和有权人的比例是29%,今天这个数字高达80%。应该指出的是,持这种看法

in return for weapons provided to terrorists who called us "the Great Satan", a quadrupling of our national debt in only a dozen years, a growing gap between rich and poor, and steadily declining real incomes -- all of these continued an avalanche of negative self-images which have profoundly changed the way Americans view their government.

A recent analysis of public opinion polling data covering the years since my class came to Harvard demonstrates the cumulative change in our national mood. When my class entered as freshmen in the fall of 1965, the percentage of people who believed that government generally tries to do the right thing was over 60%. Today it is only 10%. The percentage believing that government favors the rich and the powerful was then 29%. Today it is 80%. And it is important to note that these trends hold true for Democrats and Republicans, conservatives and liberals.

In fact, this may be an **apocrayphal** [adj. 伪的，不足凭信的] story, but someone actually claimed the other day the situation has gotten so bad that when they conducted a new poll and asked people about their current level of cynicism, 18% said they were more cynical than five years ago, 9% thought they were less cynical, and 72% suspected the question was some kind of government ploy, and refused to answer.

Democracy stands or falls on a mutual trust -- government's trust of the people and the people's trust of the governments they elect. And yet at the same time democratic culture and politics have always existed in a strange blend of **credulity** [n. 轻信，易信] and skepticism. Indeed, a certain degree of enduring skepticism about human nature lies at the foundation of our representative democracy. James Madison argued successfully in the Federalist Papers that the United States Constitution should create a protective balance of power among the factions that were bound to rise in any society.

Democracy did not mean unity in the body politic. People do have reasonable differences. Human ignorance, pride, and selfishness would always be with us, prompting inevitable divisions and conflicting ambitions.

Yet, freedom and order could be protected with safeguards insuring that no one branch of government and no one group or faction would be able to dictate to all the rest. We were the first large republic to build a nation on the revolutionary premise that the people are sovereign and that the freedom to dispute, debate, disagree and quarrel with each other created a fervent love of country that could hold us

的人里，既有民主党人，也有共和党人；既有保守派，也有自由派。

这听起来像是一个虚构的故事，但有人声称说，现在情况已变得更加糟糕，当他们进行一项新的民意调查，研究美国人现在玩世不恭的程度时，有18%的人认为自己比5年前态度更消极，9%的人认为他们不那么冷嘲热讽了，但有72%的人怀疑这是政府的某种花招，所以拒绝回答问卷。

民主体制要建立在相互信任的基础上，政府信任人民，而人民信任他们选出的政府。但同时，民主文化和政治一直以一种奇怪的方式结合在一起——既轻信又怀疑。事实上，我们以选举代表为机制的民主体制的基础，就是对人性一定程度上的怀疑。詹姆斯·麦迪逊在他写的"联邦党人文集"中，就精辟地阐明，美国的宪法应该在任何社会都会出现的派别集团之间，创造出一种保护性的力量平衡。

民主并不意味着政治上的团结一致。人与人之间存在着不难理解的区别。人类的无知、傲慢以及自私等毛病，一直都伴随着我们，从而使人们不可避免地分出派别，各有所求。

因此，**要建立措施，防止政府的任何一个部门、任何一个团体或派别去支配其他所有的人，这样自由和秩序才能得到保护**。我们的国家，是第一个建立在革命性设想之上的共和体，那就是：人民做主。可以自由地互相质疑、争执、持有异议和进行争吵，这样反而会激励人们的爱国情感，从而使我们团结对外。这仍是一项革命性的设想，它仍然建立在对人性怀疑的基础上，认为任何人都不可能达到智力、逻辑、知识或道德情操的完美。

所以，美国人对美好生活的不懈追求，总是会磕磕碰碰地交织着他们对政党和领导人的不断疑虑，怀疑他们自称有智慧、有能力来带领人民支配自己命运的说法。我们一方面尊重我们的国家机构，同时又像老鹰一样盘旋在上空，监视领导者的一举一动，准备用自己张开的利爪，抓住我们见到的任何不足或失败。

就连我们最受爱戴的乔治·华盛顿总统，在1796年7月6日写给托马斯·杰弗逊的最后一封信上也写道："我没料到，我治下政府的每一个行动都受到责难，而责难形式的夸张和手段的下流，就算针对古罗马暴

together against the world. It is still a revolutionary premise. And it is still built on a skeptical view of human nature that refuses to believe in perfection in intellect, logic, knowledge, or morals in any human being.

And so the ceaseless American yearning for the ideal life has always stumbled uneasily over a persistent American skepticism about the parties and leaders who claim to have the wisdom and ability to guide us to our destiny. We revere our institutions, and at the same time we watch our leaders as though we were hawks circling overhead, eager to dive with claws extended onto any flaw or failure that we see.

Even our most beloved president, George Washington, wrote in his last letter to Thomas Jefferson, on July 6, 1796: "I had no conception...that every act of my administration would be tortured...in such exaggerated form and indecent terms as could scarcely be applied to a Nero, a notorious defaulter or even a common pickpocket."

Our feelings about ourselves as a people are mixed. We Americans have often beenproud to the point of cocky arrogance. But we have never been able to hide indefinitely from what we do wrong. Our failures eat at our conscience, and our sins itch under the showy garb of our achievements and prevent us from being complacent.

Faith in the future, and skepticism about every person or group who offers to lead us there. These conflicting forces work together to shape the American character.

And yet these forces must remain in a rough balance of emotional power. If we receive too heavy a dose of concentrated self-doubt and too many repetitive injuries to our confidence in self-government, then our normal healthy skepticism can fall into a **mire** [n. 泥沼，困境] of **cynicism** [n. 愤世嫉俗，犬儒主义，犬儒哲学] and we start to question the ability of any human community to live up to the democratic ideals that we proclaim.

Once it is widely accepted, cynicism -- the stubborn, unwavering disbelief in the possibility of good -- can become a malignant habit in democracy. The skeptic may finally be persuaded by the facts, but the cynic never, for he is so deeply invested in the conviction that virtue cannot prevail over the deep and essential evil in all things and all people.

The last time public cynicism sank to its present depth may have been exactly 100 years ago, when Mark Twain said, "There is no distinctly native American criminal class except Congress." That was a time when Americans felt the earth moving under their feet. Debt and depression forced farmers off the land and into cities that they

君尼禄、恶贯满盈的坏人，甚或小偷这样的人，都不适合使用。"

我们对自己的感受是喜忧参半。我们美国人经常自我感觉良好，有时甚至到了趾高气昂的地步。但我们从来无法掩饰所犯的错误。失败困扰着我们的良心，罪恶感潜藏在成功所带来的浮华中，但也使得我们不敢迷醉于自满。

相信未来，但对每个想要带领我们走向未来的个人或团体表示怀疑，这些相互矛盾的力量，塑造了美国人的性格。

然而，这些情感必须在大体上保持平衡。如果我们得到的都是强烈的自我怀疑意见，我们自治的信心受到的都是反复打击和伤害，那么我们正常而健康的怀疑态度就会陷入玩世不恭主义的泥潭。我们会开始怀疑，不相信有任何人类社团能够达到我们倡导的民主理想高度。

玩世不恭的犬儒哲学，顽固不化地怀疑人类习性本善，这种玩世不恭主义一旦被广泛接受，就可能成为民主体制的一个恶习。怀疑者最终可能会被事实说服，但玩世不恭主义者则永远不会，因为他的信念根深蒂固，认为善无法战胜万物中固有的邪和人性中天生的恶。

上一次公众的玩世不恭思想达到目前这样的程度，大约刚好是在100年前，马克·吐温当时说："美国本土的犯罪集团，以国会为最。"在那个年代里，美国人民觉得身无立足之处。债务和萧条的双重压力，迫使农民离乡背井，到了他们觉得冰冷陌生的城市，进入人和机器没有多大区别的工厂。玩世不恭主义因此很快盛行。

我们现在正处于另一个历史性的经济转型的动荡中。随着计算机和自动化装置取代人力劳动，信息革命导致了许多工人失业。

二次大战后，美国有35%的就业是在工厂里，如今，从事制造业的劳动力不到17%。正如那些100年前失去农场工作的大多数人，后来在工厂里就业一样，今天，信息革命创造了新的职业，但这个变革更加迅速，对许多人来说，这种经济调整也更加复杂和令人迷茫。

在这一点上，我们其实做得比其他国家要好。世界上的每一个工业国家都面临创造足够多的就业机会的困难，哪怕在经济发展火热时也无法做到。所以毫不奇怪，世界上每个工业化国家的公众谈起他们的领导

found cold and strange and into factories where human beings became scarcely more than the extensions of machines. Cynicism was soon abroad in the land.

We are now in the midst of another historic and unsettling economic transformation. Now the information revolution is leading to a loss of jobs in many factories, as computers and automation replace human labor.

After World War II, 35% of America's employment was on the factory floor. Today fewer than 17% of our labor force works in manufacturing. Just as most of those who lost their jobs on the farm a hundred years ago eventually found new work in factories, so today new jobs are opening up in new occupations created by the information revolution -- but this time the transition is taking place more swiftly and the economic adjustment is, for many, more difficult and disorienting.

In this respect we are actually doing better than most other nations. Every industrial society in the world is having enormous difficulty in creating a sufficient number of new jobs --even when their economies heat up. So, not surprisingly, public cynicism about leadership has soared in almost every industrial country in the world.

History is a precarious source of lessons. Nevertheless, I am reminded that similar serious economic problems prevailed in Athens in the 4th century B.C., when the philosophical school we now know as Cynicism was born. The Cynics were fed up with their society and its social conventions and wanted everybody to know it. The root of the word "cynic" is the same as the Greek word for "dog," and some scholars say the Cynics got their name because they barked at society. Sounds almost like some of our talk radio shows.

In a time of social fragmentation, vulgarity becomes a way of life. To be shocking becomes more important -- and often more profitable -- than to be civil or creative or truly original. Given the vulgarity that fragmentation breeds, cynicism seems almost irresistible. Sometimes it even looks like a refuge of sanity, a rational response to a world seemingly driven by the fast hustle, the pseudo-event, the rage for sensationalism.

In any event, cynicism represented then and represents now a secession from society, a dissolution of the bonds between people and families and communities, an indifference to the fate of anything or anyone beyond the self.

Cynicism is deadly. It bites everything it can reach -- like a dog with a foot caught in a trap. And then it devours itself. It drains us of the will to improve; it

时，都是冷嘲热讽。

历史的教训不一定可靠。不过我知道，公元前4世纪的雅典也曾面临类似的严重经济问题，也就在那个时候，我们现在所知道的玩世不恭主义诞生了。玩世不恭主义者对社会和社会习俗充满厌倦，并想让每个人都知道这一点。"玩世不恭"(cynic)这个字的词根，和希腊的"狗"(dog)字同源，有的学者说，"玩世不恭的犬儒主义者"得到这个名字，是因为他们对社会咆哮。这听起来挺像我们现在的电台谈话节目。

在社会四分五裂的时期，粗俗成为一种生活方式。能炒作制造轰动变得更重要，而且往往更有利可图，这超过了温文有礼、或有创意、或做真正的自己这些品质。面对社会一盘散沙所滋养的一片粗俗，人们忍不住要玩世不恭。这有时看起来像一个理智的避难所，是对世人热衷于混乱喧嚣、伪造事件，对哗众取宠的狂热爱好这类现象的一个理性的反应。

不管怎么说，玩世不恭主义在过去和现在，都代表着逃避社会，代表着人与人之间、人与家庭和社会之间的关系瓦解，代表着除了自己之外，对任何事或任何人的命运都漠不关心的态度。

玩世不恭主义会带来致命的伤害。它就像一只被夹住腿的狗一样，乱咬身边的每个人，最后也毁灭自己。它削弱我们改进的意志，破坏我们的公共意识；它慢慢地侵蚀我们的创造力，使我们的灵魂枯萎。玩世不恭主义者常常认为自己只是厌世。在玩世不恭主义者看来，太阳下没有什么新东西，他们什么都见过，而且什么都看穿了。他们说，他们的厌世态度是一种智慧，但其实这只是摆摆样子而已。他们的厌倦态度，在讨论那些比不上他们，那些既没有权力、影响，也没有财富的人时，显得特别有用。玩世不恭主义者宣称，那些不幸的人无药可救。

对社会抱有希望，基本上被当做是对理智的侮辱，个人对集体负有责任的看法，被当做是危险的激进主义。默默苦干、不图回报地给失败者以关怀的人、去安慰受伤者的人、去保护弱者的人，均被他们称为傻瓜。

归根结底，玩世不恭主义者的生活是孤独和自我毁灭式的。人的天性就是要与他人交往。我们天生的同情心是我们最重要的一种情感。如果没有这种情感，我们就不是人类了。事实上，否定这种情感的玩世不

diminishes our public spirit; it saps our inventiveness; it withers our souls. Cynics often see themselves as merely being world-weary. There is no new thing under the sun, the cynics say. They have not only seen everything; they have seen through everything. They claim that their weariness is wisdom. But it is usually merely posturing. Their weariness seems to be most effective when they consider the aspirations of those beneath them, who have neither power nor influence nor wealth. For these unfortunates, nothing can be done, the cynics declare.

Hope for society as a whole is considered an **affront** [n. 侮辱, 冒犯] to rationality; the notion that the individual has a responsibility for the community is considered a dangerous radicalism. And those who toil in quiet places and for little reward to lift up the fallen, to comfort the afflicted, and to protect the weak are regarded as fools.

Ultimately, however, the life of a cynic is lonely and self-destructive. It is our human nature to make connections with other human beings. The gift of sympathy for one another is one of the most powerful sentiments we ever feel. If we do not have it, we are not human. Indeed it is so powerful that the cynic who denies it goes to war with himself.

A few years ago Shelby Steele wrote about his pain as a child, when he was mistreated by a teacher who called him stupid. He said that the teacher's declaration created a terrible reality for him. If the teacher told him he was stupid, he thought he must be stupid. Let me quote what he says: "I mention this experience as an example of how one's innate capacity for insecurity is expanded and deepened, of how a disbelieving part of the self is brought to life and forever joined to the believing self. As children we are all wounded in some way and to some degree by the wild world we encounter. From these wounds a disbelieving anti-self is born, an internal antagonist and **saboteur** [n. 从事破坏活动者] that embraces the world's negative view of us, that believes our wounds are justified by our own unworthiness, and that entrenches itself as a lifelong voice of doubt."

I believe that in a similar way, our nation's attitude towards itself can be and is shaped by national experiences. For example, the **heady** [adj. 陶醉的, 头晕的] and triumphant victories of 1944 enlarged our confidence and helped us build the postwar world. And by contrast, during the years when my class was here at Harvard, America's capacity for insecurity was expanded and deepened by wounds to our national confidence. For example, an unnamed classmate of mine said in today's Boston Globe, "I lost faith in

恭主义者，也常会觉得自我矛盾。

几年前，谢尔比·斯蒂尔[7]描写了他小时候所经历的痛苦，那时他被老师称为笨蛋。他说，老师的话语把他带入了一种可怕的现实。如果老师说他是蠢才，他想，自己肯定是个笨蛋。让我在这儿引用他的一段话："我提起这段经历，是为了举一个例子，说明一个人的不安全感是如何扩大和加深的，说明一个人不自信的那部分，是如何被唤醒，并永远影响着我们的自信。作为孩子，我们免不了要在这种残酷的世界中受到这样或那样的伤害，这些伤害使我们产生不自信，成为我们潜在的敌人与破坏者，接受外界对我们的负面看法，让我们相信因为我们一文不值，所以受到的伤害事出有因，从而让我们终身没有自信。"

我相信，同样的，我们的国家对自己的态度，也由国民的经历而塑造。例如，1944年令人陶醉的胜利加强了我们的自信心，帮助我们建立了战后的世界格局。与此相反，当我在哈佛求学的岁月里，由于我们的国民自信受损，美国人民的不安全感加大加深。例如，我的一位未署名的同学在今天的《波士顿环球报》上说："我对美国在世界上能否成为一股正义的力量而失去了信心。"

我们仍在试图治疗我们政体上的那些伤口，那些由于暗杀、越南战争、骚乱、文化冲突，以及深信传言——说政客们宣誓要维护宪法却不会告诉我们真相——而带来的创伤。

E·J·迪翁[8]最近写道："就像美国内战影响了后来数十年的美国政治生活一样，1960年代的文化内战也是如此，那充满了矛盾和紧张的氛围影响了我们今天的政治局面。我们仍沉陷在60年代的纷争之中。我们国家仍然面临着由旧的文化冲突所遗留下来的三大主要矛盾：公民权利以及如何让黑人全面融入国家的政治与经济生活中；争取女权运动所带来的价值观的改变，以及对养育孩子和性观念等问题态度的改变；还有便是对越南战争眼下还在继续的争论，这个争论主要不是讨论在那个东南亚国家参与一场战争是否正确，而更多地是讨论美国人该怎样看待自己的国家、我们的领袖及美国在世界上的作用。"

迪翁也认为，保守派和中上层社会里的自由主义者，出于各自不同

the United States as a force for good in the world."

We are still trying to heal those wounds burned into our body politic by assassinations, the Vietnam war, the riots, the cultural conflicts and by the terrible conviction that people sworn to uphold our Constitution were not telling us the truth.

E.J. Dionne, recently wrote, "Just as the Civil War dominated American political life for decades after it ended, so is the cultural civil war of the 1960s, with all its tensions and contradictions, shaping our politics today. We are still trapped in the 1960s. The country still faces three major sets of questions, left over from the old cultural battles: civil rights and the full integration of blacks into the country's political and economic life; the revolution in values involving feminism and changed attitudes toward child-rearing and sexuality; and the ongoing debate over the meaning of the Vietnam War, which is less a fight over whether it was right to do battle in that Southeast Asian country than an argument over how Americans see their nation, its leaders, and its role in the world."

Dionne also argues that both conservatives and upper middle-class liberals have -- for separate reasons -- kept this cultural civil war alive. Partly for this reason, our national political conversation has been dominated by increasingly mean-spirited efforts to attack our leaders' motives, character and reputation.

As the public's willingness to believe the worst increases -- that is to say -- as cynicism increases -- the only political messages that seem to affect the outcome of elections are those that seek to paint the opposition as a gang of bandits and fools who couldn't be trusted to pour water out of a boot if the directions were written on the heel.

This fixation on character assassination rather than on defining issues feeds the voracious appetite of tabloid journalism for scandal. And now wets the growing appetite of other journalistic organizations for the same sort of fare.

A few years ago, the Czech leader Vaclav Havel wrote these **prescient** [adj. 预知的，有先见之明的] words, "They say a nation has the politicians it deserves. In some sense that is true: Politicians are truly a mirror of the society and a kind of embodiment of its potential. At the same time, paradoxically, the opposite is also true. Society is a mirror of its politicians. It is largely up to the politicians which social forces they choose to liberate and which they choose to suppress, whether they choose to rely on the good in each citizen, or on the bad."

的原因，使这种文化内战依然延续。在某种程度上，由于这个原因，在我们国家的政治对话中一直占主导地位的，是那种对我们的领导人的动机、品德和声誉进行日益刻薄的攻击。

由于公众愿意相信丑事的发生，也就是说，玩世不恭主义大行其道，所以，能够影响到我们选举结果的政治消息，就只是那些把对手描绘成一帮土匪和傻瓜的说法，说那些人绝对不可信任。

这种热衷于人格中伤，而不是讨论问题的做法，吊起了小报新闻记者对丑闻的贪婪胃口。其他报社组织也在津津有味地捕捉这些信息。

几年前，捷克领导人瓦茨拉夫·哈维尔说过这样有先见之明的话："人们说，什么样的国家就会出什么样的政治家，在某种意义上的确如此。政治家真是社会的一面镜子，也是其潜能的一种体现。与此同时，很矛盾的是，相反的说法也说得通，社会也是政治家的一面镜子。这在很大程度上取决于政治家们是选择提倡还是选择压制某种社会力量，取决于他们是选择依靠每一个公民的优点，还是利用他们的缺点。"

但对我们，尤其是我们这些为公众服务的人来说，至关重要的是要知道，如果政界领导人豪言壮志地许下诺言，然后却做不到，玩世不恭主义的思潮就会增加。如果不能实现自己在诸如教育、种族关系和犯罪等方面的夸夸其谈和浮夸承诺，美国人民那种令人不安的怀疑就会更加强化，不相信我们有掌握自己命运的能力。

从长远来看，长久的信任对健康的自治能力的健康来说，就像持续发展对生态环境的重要意义一样；希望破灭对我们政治热情的毒害，亦如同化学废弃物对地下水资源的毒害。

当希望一再被浇灭，一个国家自治的本能一再被伤害时，民族的凝聚力就会减弱。其结果我们大家都看到了。在国内和国外，个人和社会关系的削弱造成的真空，很快就会被其他组织的认同所填满，而这种认同则基于种族、部落、派别或帮派。外在的常常是体貌上的区别，成为人群认同划分的标准。这些差异被当做某个群体的准则，用来对付与他们只是略有不同的群体。然而奇怪的是，差异越小的派别，彼此间的仇恨也就越多，随之而来的杀戮也越残酷。

But it is crucial for us, especially those of us in public service, to understand that cynicism also can arise when political leaders cavalierly promise to do good things and then fail to deliver. The inability to redeem **glib** [*adj.* 能说善道的，圆滑的] and reckless promises about issues like education, race relations, and crime can add to the disturbing and growing doubts among the American people about our ability to shape our destiny.

Over the long haul sustainable hope is as important to the health of self-government as sustainable development is for ecological health. Dashed hopes poison our political will just as surely as chemical waste can poison drinking water aquifers deep in the ground.

When hopes are repeatedly dashed and a nation's instinct for self-government is repeatedly injured, national cohesion can dissipate. The results are for all to see. At home and abroad the weakening of bonds between the individual and the larger society creates a vacuum quickly filled by other group identities--based on race, or clan, or sect, or tribe, or gang. Some distinguishing quality, often physical, is used to demarcate group identity. These differences become standards raised to summon the group to war against others slightly different from themselves. It is one of the strange perversities of this process that the smaller the difference, the more ferocious the hatred and the more hideous the massacres that follow.

Look at our bleeding world! Hutus versus Tutsis, Bosnian Serbs versus Bosnian Croats and Bosnian Muslims, all of whom seem often to others indistinguishable, but who themselves are driven to mindless ferocity by what Freud called "the narcissism of slight difference," what St. Augustine called pride, the mother of all sins, and about which William Butler Yeats said in a famous poem:

> *Things fall apart, the centre cannot hold;*
> *Mere anarchy is loosed upon the world,*
> *The blood-dimmed tide is loosed, and everywhere*
> *The ceremony of innocence is drowned;*
> *The best lack all conviction, while the worst*
> *Are full of passionate intensity.*

Make no mistake: just as repeated injuries to our national esteem can seriously

看看我们这个充满血腥的世界吧！胡图族敌视图西族[9]、波斯尼亚的塞尔维亚人敌视生活在同一块土地上的克罗地亚人和穆斯林[10]，他们在外人看起来没有区别，但他们被弗洛伊德所称"出于细微差别的自恋"所驱使，由此而头脑发昏地互相残杀。圣奥古斯汀[11]称之为"尊严"的东西，成为一切罪恶之源，而威廉·巴特勒·叶芝[12]则在一首著名的诗里这样写道：

世界四分五裂，中心难存在：
无政府主义遍布全球，
鲜血染红的潮流冲来
无辜生命水中挣扎；
善者少了信仰，
恶者信心满满。

可别产生误会，正如我们民族尊严一次又一次地被伤害，肯定会危及我们解决问题的能力，世界上过多的混乱和恐怖事件，太多像波斯尼亚和卢旺达这样的惨案，会严重破坏我们纠正错误的这种重要的能力，以及我们作为一个种类能否重新控制自己命运的能力。

那么，我们何处寻求治疗？我们何以谋划未来？我们又何以构想不灭的希望？

我认为，我们可以从人际关系中得到安慰，并在逆境中，共同团结在崇高的目标之下。

在1992年的民主党全国代表大会上，我谈到了我的一次亲身经历，它从根本上改变了我的世界观。我的儿子差点死于一次事故。今天在这儿我不想重复整个过程，我只想说，我最大的感触便是，许多与我素不相识的人向我和我的家庭伸出援手，用感人的同情心使我们振作，那些关爱的心灵给予我们安慰，有如圣灵笼罩着我们。

从那以后，我珍惜自己与他人之间的联系，并深信作为人类，我们生存于世，息息相关。

我不知道在我的灵魂中，是什么妨碍了我从感情上去理解人际间的

jeopardize our ability to solve the problems which confront us, so the convergence of too much chaos and horror in the world -- of too many Bosnias and Rwandas -- can seriously damage the ability of our global civilization to get a grip on the essential task of righting itself and regaining a measure of control over our destiny as a species.

Where then do we search for healing? What is our strategy for reconciliation with our future and where is our vision for sustainable hope?

I have come to believe that our healing can be found in our relationships to one another and in a shared commitment to higher purposes in the face of adversity.

At the 1992 Democratic Convention, I talked about a personal event that fundamentally changed the way I viewed the world: an accident that almost killed our son. I will not repeat the story here today except to say that the most important lesson for me was that people I didn't even know reached out to me and to my family to lift us up in their hearts and in their prayers with compassion of such intensity that I felt it as a palpable force, a healing reaching out of those multitudes of caring souls and falling on us like a mantle of divine grace.

Since then I have dwelled on our connections to one another and on the fact that as human beings, we are astonishingly similar in the most important parts of our existence.

I don't know what barriers in my soul had prevented me from understanding emotionally that basic connection to others until after they reached out to me in the dark of my family's sorrow. But I suppose it was a form of cynicism on my part. If cynicism is based on alienation and fragmentation, I believe that the brokenness that separates the cynic from others is the outward sign of an inner division between the head and the heart. There is something icily and unnaturally intellectual about the cynic. This isolation of intellect from feelings and emotions is the essence of his condition. For the cynic, feelings are as easily separated from the reality others see as ethics are separated from behavior, and as life is cut off from any higher purpose.

Having felt their power in my own life, I believe that sympathy and compassion are revolutionary forces in the world at large and that they are working now.

A year after the accident, when our family's healing process was far advanced, I awoke early one Sunday morning in 1990, turned on the television set and watched in amazement as another healing process began, when Nelson Mandela was released from prison. Last month, I attended his inauguration when he was sworn as President

这种基本联系，直到别人在我的家庭处于悲哀的黑暗中向我伸出了援手。但我想这是因为我也曾抱有玩世不恭的心态。如果玩世不恭主义以疏远和分裂为根基，我认为，玩世不恭主义者与他人疏远的外在现象，是只他们自己内在的心智分离的一种表现。玩世不恭主义者外表冰冷，表现出不正常的只凭借理智做事。这种与感觉和情感分离的理性，是其问题的实质。对于玩世不恭主义者来说，把感觉与现实区别开来，就像别人把行为和道德区别开来一样，生命也不应和更高的追求有什么关系。

我在自己的生命中感受过这些力量，所以我相信，同情和怜悯是放之四海而皆准的革命性力量，而且现在这些力量正在起着作用。

那件事故发生后的一年，我们家庭的伤痛已经基本痊愈，我在1990年的一个周日的清晨醒来后，打开电视，惊奇地看到纳尔逊·曼德拉从监狱中被释放出来，另一个伤痛开始痊愈。上个月，我参加了曼德拉的就职仪式，他成了新南非的总统，这件事对我们时代里的玩世不恭主义思想是一个巨大的打击。当曼德拉向别人介绍他的三位贵宾——曾经看守他的狱卒，并讲述他们怎样跨越曾经阻碍他们进行人际交往的鸿沟，从而成为朋友时，许多人都感动得流下热泪。

9个月前，在白宫南草坪上，我目睹了握手的疗伤之效，依扎克·拉宾[13]和亚西尔·阿拉法特[14]开始尝试和解与和平，而在这之前，巴以关系只有仇恨与战争。

不到5年前，全世界的人都惊奇地看着柏林墙被拆除，东欧和中欧各地独裁者的塑像被推翻，独裁政府被关注本国人民需要的市场经济主导的民主政体所取代。

不到3周前，几乎是50年来第一次不再有核导弹瞄准美国的城市。这是扭转核武器竞赛势头的一小步，但也是重要的一步，而核武器竞赛问题长期以来是玩世不恭主义者手里的王牌。现在，换句话说，我们可以有理由反驳玩世不恭主义者，他们一直大声狂叫，其实是错误的。

对我来说，从哈佛毕业的25年间，我用希望代替了绝望，用奋斗取代了颓废，用信心打败了玩世不恭主义。

我相信知识的力量，可以让世界变得更好。玩世不恭主义者可能会

of the new South Africa in what was a **stupendous** [*adj.* 惊人的，巨大的] defeat for cynicism in our time. Many were moved to tears as he introduced three men who had come as his personal guests -- three of his former jailers -- and described how they had reached across the chasm that had separated them as human beings and had become personal friends.

Nine months ago, I witnessed the healing power of a handshake on the South Lawn of the White House as Yitzhak Rabin and Yassir Arafat began the tentative process of reconciliation and peace in a relationship hitherto characterized by only hatred and war.

Less than five years ago, the world watched in amazement as the Berlin Wall was dismantled and statues of dictators were toppled throughout East and Central Europe and as authoritarian governments were replaced by market democracies alert to the needs of their people.

Less than three weeks ago, for the first time in almost fifty years, nuclear missiles were no longer targeted on American cities -- a small but important step in the continuing reversal of the nuclear arms race that long served as the cynics' ace in the hole. There is, in other words, a respectable argument that the cynics who are barking so loudly are simply wrong.

For my part, in the 25 years since my Harvard graduation, I have come to believe in hope over despair, striving over resignation, faith over cynicism.

I believe in the power of knowledge to make the world a better place. Cynics may say: Human beings have never learned anything from history. All that is truly useful about knowledge is that it can provide you with advantages over the pack. But the cynics are wrong: we have the capacity to learn from our mistakes and transcend our past. Indeed, in this very place we have been taught that truth -- Veritas -- can set us free.

I believe in finding fulfillment in family, for the family is the true center of a meaningful life. Cynics may say: All families are confining and ultimately dysfunctional. The very idea of family is outdated and unworkable. But the cynics are wrong: it is in our families that we learn to love.

I believe in serving God and trying to understand and obey God's will for our lives. Cynics may wave the idea away, saying God is a myth, useful in providing comfort to the ignorant and in keeping them obedient. I know in my heart -- beyond

说：人类从来没有从历史中学到什么。知识的真正作用，只是能让你出人头地。但玩世不恭主义者们错了，我们有从错误中吸取教训的能力，能够超越过去。的确，就在这个地方，我们学到：真理——哈佛的校训Veritas——会让我们获得自由。

我相信从家庭中找到满足，因为有意义的生活应该围绕家庭这个真正的中心。玩世不恭主义者会说：所有家庭都让人感到束缚，最终都是得不偿失的。家庭的观念已经过时，纯属无用。但玩世不恭主义者们错了，是家庭让我们学会了爱。

我相信为上帝服务，并试着理解和服从上帝对我们生命的旨意。玩世不恭主义者可能会对此一笑置之，说上帝是个神话，只适用于给无知的人带来安慰，并让他们驯服。然而我打心底里认为——不用争辩也毫无疑问，玩世不恭主义者们错了。

我相信为社会的公正和人类的自由而奋斗。玩世不恭主义者可能会嘲笑此观点实在幼稚，他们认为，我们为公平、为正义、为自由所做的努力，不过又制造了一片充满破灭希望的荒地。但玩世不恭主义者们又错了。自由是我们的目标，公正是我们的向导，我们一定能够克服一切困难。

我相信我们必须保护地球环境，对付史无前例的污染。玩世不恭主义者会笑出声来，说千年老树、柔和清风，或一泓山泉，都是毫无实际用处。但玩世不恭主义者们还是错了。我们是上帝所赐的土地的一部分，无法与之分离。

我对你们每个人有信心！相信你们每一个人、你们这个群体。玩世不恭主义者会说，你们受贪欲驱动，最终除了自己以外，其他什么都不会关心。但玩世不恭主义者们错了。你们会互相关心，珍惜自由，重视正义，寻找真理。

最后，我对美国有信心。玩世不恭主义者会说，我们已经迷失方向，美国人的世纪就要结束了。但玩世不恭主义者们错了。美国仍然是世界竞相效仿的榜样。几乎在世界各地，美国一直倡导、捍卫并努力实行的价值观，都深入人心。

说到底，我们面临着一个根本的选择：是冷嘲热讽还是满腔热情。这

all arguing and beyond any doubt -- that the cynics are wrong.

I believe in working to achieve social justice and freedom for all. Cynics may scorn this notion as naive, claiming that all our efforts for equal opportunity, for justice, for freedom have created only a wasteland of failed hopes. But the cynics are wrong: freedom is our destiny; justice is our guide; we shall overcome.

I believe in protecting the Earth's environment against an unprecedented onslaught. Cynics may laugh out loud and say there is no utility in a stand of thousand year old trees, a fresh breeze, or a mountain stream. But the cynics are wrong: we are part of God's earth not separate from it.

I believe in you. Each of you individually. And all of you here as a group. The cynics say you are motivated principally by greed and that ultimately you will care for nothing other than yourselves. But the cynics are wrong. You care about each other, you cherish freedom, you treasure justice, you seek truth.

And finally, I believe in America. Cynics will say we have lost our way, that the American century is at its end. But the cynics are wrong. America is still the model to which the world aspires. Almost everywhere in the world the values that the United States has proclaimed, defended, and tried to live are now rising.

In the end, we face a fundamental choice: cynicism or faith. Each equally capable of taking root in our souls and shaping our lives as self-fulfilling prophecies. We must open ourhearts to one another and build on all the vast and creative possibilities of America. This is a task for a confident people which is what we have been throughout our history and what we still are now in our deepest character.

I believe in our future.

Thank you!

两种选择，都可能在我们的灵魂中扎根，从而会像自我应验的预言那样影响我们的生命。我们必须打开心扉，创造美国无限宽广的未来。对有自信的人们来说，这是一项任务，而自立国以来，我们就充满自信，而且自信扎根于我们个性的最深处。

我相信我们的未来！

谢谢大家！

---

1 尼尔·阿姆斯特朗（Neil Armstrong，1930—2012）是第一个登上月球的宇航员。

2 查尔斯·曼森（Charles Manson），美国加州的一个邪教组织头领，曾在1960年代和下属一起杀害许多人。

3 伍德斯托克音乐节"Woodstock Rock Festival"，也有译作"胡士托音乐节"，是著名的摇滚音乐节，最早在1969年举办于美国纽约州东南部城镇伍德斯托克，主题是"和平、反战、博爱、平等"。

4 美莱村（My Lai），越南的一个村庄。越战期间，美军曾在这个地方屠杀妇女及老少村民，成为影响重大的事件。

5 瓦茨种族骚乱（Watts Riots）是指1965年8月间，发生在美国加州洛杉矶的瓦茨街区的种族骚乱。事发原因是白人警察逮捕了酒后驾车的黑人，持续5天的骚乱共造成34人死亡，逾千人受伤。

6 美国遇刺总统约翰·肯尼迪的弟弟，时为美国参议员。他在哥哥遇刺后出面竞选总统，1968年6月5日在加州洛杉矶遇刺身亡。

7 谢尔比·斯蒂尔（Shelby Steele）生于1946年，美国当代黑人学者，从事种族关系、多种文化间交流以及平权法案等问题研究。

8 E·J·迪翁（E.J. Dionne）生于1952年，美国记者与政论家，长期担任《华盛顿邮报》评论版专栏作家。

9 1994年发生的卢旺达大屠杀，是胡图族的政府军与图西族的卢旺达爱国阵线之间所发生的武装冲突，有大批图西人被杀。

10 南联盟解体后，于1992年至1995年间发生的领土和种族纠纷及战争。

11 圣奥古斯汀（St. Augustine，354—430），罗马帝国早期基督教教父及哲学家。著有自传体作品《忏悔录》及长篇著作《神之城市》，阐述了"原罪"和"正义战争"的概念，其著作对西方基督教有着深远影响。

12 威廉·巴特勒·叶芝（William Butler Yeats，1865—1939），爱尔兰诗人、剧作家，著名的神秘主义者，是"爱尔兰文艺复兴运动"的领袖，被诗人艾略特誉为"当代最伟大的诗人"。

13 伊扎克·拉宾（Yitzhak Rabin，1922—1995），以色列政治家、军事家。1974年至1977年出任以色列总理；1992年起再次出任总理，直至1995年被刺身亡。

14 亚西尔·阿拉法特（Yasser-Arafat，1929—2004），曾长期任巴勒斯坦解放组织执委会主席，并于1994年获诺贝尔和平奖。

瓦茨拉夫·哈维尔（1936—2011）

　　从实验室的助理到工科学生，从戏剧家到持不同政见者，从多次入狱的囚徒到一国之总统，很少有人一生经历如哈维尔这般曲折多变。瓦茨拉夫·哈维尔曾经是捷克著名的剧作家与持不同政见者，于1993年到2002年间担任捷克共和国总统，1995年哈佛毕业典礼上发表这个演讲，正值他担任捷克总统期间。

　　哈维尔于1936年10月5日出生在布拉格一个工程师家庭，1951年高中毕业后因为家庭出身原因，他不能继续升学深造，只好到一个化学实验室做了4年助理，同时进入夜校学习。哈维尔年轻时就喜爱文学，19岁时开始在文学和戏剧杂志上发表文章，1959年，哈维尔开始在布拉格的一家剧院当舞台管理员，从此和戏剧结下不解之缘。

　　1977年，哈维尔参与发起了"七七宪章运动"等一系列活动，先后两次入狱。1983年因病出狱后，他继续积极参与文学和社会活动，成为著名的公众人物。1990年哈维尔出任捷克斯洛伐克联邦总统，1992年斯洛伐克独立，他辞去联邦总统职位。1993年哈维尔担任独立后的捷克共和国总统，并于1998年连任。

　　哈维尔在担任总统期间广泛接触国际社会，先后出访了很多国家，对许多国际事务作出发言。他总是试图将政治与道德结合起来，并提出"生活在真实中"的观点。在他任职的13年间，他的国家发生了很大变化，每次转变他都能理性面对，正确领导，并积极倡导议会民主机制，这与他主张的"公民社会"理念密不可分。

1995

Global Culture and Diversity, Mass Communication and Our Fate
全球文明多元文化
大众传播与人类前途

Vaclav Havel 瓦茨拉夫·哈维尔

Mr. President, Mr. Vice-President, Ladies and gentlemen,

One evening not long ago I was sitting in an outdoor restaurant by the water. My chair was almost identical to the chairs they have in restaurants by the Vltava River in Prague. They were playing the same rock music they play in most Czech restaurants. I saw advertisements I'm familiar with back home. Above all, I was surrounded by young people who were similarly dressed, who drank familiar-looking drinks, and who behaved as casually as their contemporaries in Prague. Only their complexion and their facial features were different for I was in Singapore.

I sat there thinking about this and again for the **umpteenth** [adj. 经过无数次后又一次的] time I realized an almost **banal** [adj. 陈腐的，平庸的] truth: that we now live in a single global civilization. The identity of this civilization does not lie merely in similar forms of dress, or similar drinks, or in the constant buzz of the same commercial music all around the world, or even in international advertising. It lies in something deeper: thanks to the modern idea of constant progress, with its inherent expansionism, and to the rapid evolution of science that comes directly from it, our planet has, for the first time in the long history of the human race, been covered in the space of a very few decades by a single civilization one that is essentially technological. The world is now enmeshed in webs of telecommunication networks consisting of millions of tiny threads or **capillaries** [n. 毛细管] that not only transmit information of all kinds at lightning speed, but also convey integrated models of social, political and economic behaviour. They are **conduits** [n. 导管，沟渠] for legal norms, as well as for billions and billions of dollars crisscrossing the world while remaining invisible even to those who deal directly with them. The life of the human race is completely interconnected not only in the informational sense, but in the causal sense as well. Anecdotally, I could illustrate this by reminding you since I've already mentioned Singapore that today all it takes is a single shady transaction initiated by a single devious bank clerk in Singapore to bring down a bank on the other side of the world. Thanks to the accomplishments of this civilization, practically all of us know what cheques, bonds, bills of exchange, and stocks are. We are familiar with CNN and Chernobyl, and we know who the Rolling Stones, or Nelson Mandela, or Salman Rushdie are. More than that, the capillaries that have so radically integrated this civilization also convey information about certain modes of human co-existence that have proven their worth, like democracy, respect for human rights, the rule of law, the laws of the market-

尊敬的校长、副校长,女士们、先生们:

不久前的一个傍晚,我去了一个水边的户外餐馆。我坐的椅子和布拉格的沃尔塔瓦河边那些餐馆中的椅子非常相似,耳边听到的是在捷克餐馆经常播放的相同摇滚乐,眼睛看到的也是在家里常看到的那些广告。更令人称绝的是,我周围的那些年轻人,穿着打扮、喝的饮料,以及轻松随意的举止,都和他们在布拉格的同龄人一样。只不过,他们的肤色和长相不同,因为我是在新加坡。

我坐在那里思考着一个问题,这个问题我想过无数次了。然后我明白了这样一个其实很显见的道理,那就是,我们现在生活在一个全球性的文明里。这个文明的特性,并不是简单地表现在全球到处都相似的服装、饮料或不断喧嚣的商业性音乐,甚至也不表现于国际化的广告里。其根源是一些更深层的东西:由于不断进步的现代观念,以及它特定的广泛影响,加上直接来源于这种文明的迅速演变的科学。

在人类漫长的历史上,我们的星球在短短几十年内,第一次被一种单一的文明所覆盖,而这种文明基本上是基于科技的。我们的世界现在笼罩在一个电讯网络里,这个网络包括数以百万计的像毛细血管那样的光纤,它们不仅以闪电般的速度传递各种各样的信息,而且还传播着一体化的社会、政治和经济行为模式。它们是法律规范和世界上千百亿美元得以在全球自由流通的渠道,但即便是对那些直接运用它们的人来说,这些管道仍然是隐藏不见的。

人类的生活不仅是在信息的意义上已经完全互相联系在一起了,而且在因果关系上也是如此。有趣的是,既然我已经提到了新加坡,我不妨再给你们举个例子来说明这种联系。也就是说,今天,哪怕是在新加坡,一个不法的银行职员进行一次不法交易,就可以使远在世界另一头的一家银行一夜之间破产[1]。多亏了这个文明的成就,我们知道什么是支票、债券、汇票和股票。我们都熟悉CNN[2]和切尔诺贝利核电站,都知道谁是"滚石"乐队,谁是曼德拉,谁是拉什迪。不仅如此,那些把这种文明彻底地整合在一起的毛细血管,也传递着有关人类某些特定的共存模式的信息,例如民主体制、尊重人权、法治以及市场规律等。这类信息

place. Such information flows around the world and, in varying degrees, takes root in different places.

In modern times this global civilization emerged in the territory occupied by European and ultimately by Euro-American culture. Historically, it evolved from a combination of traditions classical, Judaic and Christian. In theory, at least, it gives people not only the capacity for worldwide communication, but also a coordinated means of defending themselves against many common dangers. It can also, in an unprecedented way, make our life on this earth easier and open up to us hitherto unexplored horizons in our knowledge of ourselves and the world we live in.

And yet there is something not quite right about it.

Allow me to use this ceremonial gathering for a brief meditation on a subject which I have dwelt upon a great deal, and which I often bring up on occasions resembling this one. I want to focus today on the source of the dangers that threaten humanity in spite of this global civilization, and often directly because of it. Above all, I would like to speak about the ways in which these dangers can be confronted.

Many of the great problems we face today, as far as I understand them, have their origin in the fact that this global civilization, though in evidence everywhere, is no more than a thin veneer over the sum total of human awareness, if I may put it that way. This civilization is immensely fresh, young, new, and fragile, and the human spirit has accepted it with dizzying **alacrity** [n. 乐意. 欣然], without itself changing in any essential way. Humanity has evolved over long millennia in all manner of civilizations and cultures that gradually, and in very diverse ways, shaped our habits of mind, our relationship to the world, our models of behaviour and the values we accept and recognize. In essence, this new, single epidermis of world civilization merely covers or conceals the immense variety of cultures, of peoples, of religious worlds, of historical traditions and historically formed attitudes, all of which in a sense lie "beneath" it. At the same time, even as the veneer of world civilization expands, this "underside" of humanity, this hidden dimension of it, demands more and more clearly to be heard and to be granted a right to life.

And thus, while the world as a whole increasingly accepts the new habits of global civilization, another contradictory process is taking place: ancient traditions are reviving, different religions and cultures are awakening to new ways of being, seeking new room to exist, and struggling with growing fervour to realize what is unique to

传播于世，并在不同程度上四处扎根。

在现代社会，这一全球性的文明首先源于欧洲人活动的领地，最后以欧美文明为主导。从历史上看，它演变于古典的、犹太教和基督教的这些传统之间的结合。从理论上说，至少，这种文明不仅给予人们全球性沟通的能力，而且也让人们面对许多共同的危险时，通过协调来进行自卫。它也能够以前所未有的方式，使我们在这个地球上生活得更容易，并为我们了解自己以及我们所处的这个世界，打开迄今尚未开启的领域。

然而，有些地方好像不大对头。

请允许我利用这个典礼性的场合，就一个我花了很多心思去探究的问题进行短暂的沉思，我也经常在类似的场合提起这个话题。今天，我想集中谈谈在全球性文明的背景下，威胁我们人类的危险源于何处，而这些危险又常常是由这种全球性文明直接引发的。我想特别谈谈如何对付这些危险。

在我看来，我们今天面对的很多重大问题，其根源就在于，这种全球性文明虽然无所不在，但恕我直言，它只不过是在人类意识集大成之上、披着的一层薄薄的外衣。这种文明无比新鲜、年轻、脆弱，而人类精神则在基本没有改变的情况下，欣欣然地接受了它。人类走过了千千万万年的漫长阶段，随着各种各样的文明和文化演变，这些文明和文化以多种多样的方式，逐渐塑造了我们的思想习惯、我们与世界的关系、我们的行为方式，以及我们接受和承认的价值观。从本质上说，世界文明这种新鲜、单一的表皮仅仅是覆盖或掩藏了无比繁杂的文化、民族、宗教世界、历史传统及在历史过程中形成的各种态度。所有这些，在某种程度上都是被这个表皮"覆盖"了。与此同时，随着世界文明外延的扩张，这种"深层"的人性，它藏而不见的宽广度，需要人们越来越清楚地去倾听，并给予它生存的权利。

因此，尽管从整体上来说，这个世界日益接受新的全球文明习惯，另一种矛盾进程也在发生：古老的传统正在复兴，不同的宗教和文化由于人们有了新的存在方式而觉醒，寻求新的生存空间，并带着不断高涨的热情，努力要实现它们的目标，而这些目标使它们与众不同。最终，它

them and what makes them different from others. Ultimately they seek to give their individuality a political expression.

It is often said that in our time, every valley cries out for its own independence or will even fight for it. Many nations, or parts of them at least, are struggling against modern civilization or its main proponents for the right to worship their ancient gods and obey the ancient divine injunctions. They carry on their struggle using weapons provided by the very civilization they oppose. They employ radar, computers, lasers, nerve gases, and perhaps, in the future, even nuclear weapons all products of the world they challenge to help defend their ancient heritage against the erosions of modern civilization. In contrast with these technological inventions, other products of this civilization like democracy or the idea of human rights are not accepted in many places in the world because they are deemed to be hostile to local traditions.

In other words: the Euro-American world has equipped other parts of the globe with instruments that not only could effectively destroy the enlightened values which, among other things, made possible the invention of precisely these instruments, but which could well cripple the capacity of people to live together on this earth.

What follows from all of this?

It is my belief that this state of affairs contains a clear challenge not only to the Euro-American world but to our present-day civilization as a whole. It is a challenge to this civilization to start understanding itself as a multicultural and a multipolar civilization, **whose meaning lies not in undermining the individuality of different spheres of culture and civilization but in allowing them to be more completely themselves. This will only be possible, even conceivable, if we all accept a basic code of mutual co-existence, a kind of common minimum we can all share, one that will enable us to go on living side by side.** Yet such a code won't stand a chance if it is merely the product of a few who then proceed to force it on the rest. It must be an expression of the authentic will of everyone, growing out of the genuine spiritual roots hidden beneath the skin of our common, global civilization. If it is merely disseminated through the **capillaries** [n. 毛细管] of this skin, the way Coca-cola ads are as a commodity offered by some to others such a code can hardly be expected to take hold in any profound or universal way.

But is humanity capable of such an undertaking? Is it not a hopelessly utopian idea? Haven't we so lost control of our destiny that we are condemned to gradual

们会为自己的个性寻求在政治上的表达。

　　人们常说，在我们这个时代，每一个山谷都在呼唤它自身的独立，甚至不惜为此决战。很多国家，或至少是这些国家的部分地区，都在与现代文明或其主要维护者作斗争，要求获得崇拜自己古老神灵和遵循他们古老的神圣禁令的权利。他们使用从自己所反对的文明那里得来的武器进行斗争。他们使用雷达、电脑、激光、神经毒气，甚至有朝一日可能使用核武器——这些东西全都是他们反对的世界性产品——来帮助保卫自己的古老传统，对抗现代文明的侵蚀。相对于这些技术发明，世界文明的其他产品，例如民主或人权观念，在世界很多地方却不被接受，因为这些观念被视为与当地传统不符。

　　换言之，欧美世界为地球的其他地方提供了这样一些装备，它们不仅可以有效地摧毁文明的价值观——正是这些价值观使装备的发明得以实现——而且还可以损害人们在地球上一起生活的能力。

　　在这一切之后，结果会是什么？

　　我相信，这一事态不仅对欧美世界，而且也对当今整个文明，提出了一个清楚的挑战。它要求这个文明把自己当成多元文化和多极文明来加以理解，**这种文明的意义不是要削弱不同领域的文化个性，而是要让那些文化更加彻底地呈现自己。要做到这一点，甚至在构想这一点时，我们都必须接受一种相互共存的基本准则，一种我们都能够共享的最低共识，这种共识至少让我们可以继续生活在一起。**然而，这样的准则如果仅仅是由少数人制定出来，并将之强加在其他人身上的话，那它就丝毫没有站得住脚的机会。这个准则必须是每个人真实意愿的体现，必须来自深藏在我们共同的全球文明表皮下的那些真实的精神根源。如果这个准则仅仅是通过这一表皮的毛细血管来传播，就像可口可乐广告那样，作为一种商品由某些人提供给其他人的话，那么人们就很难期望这个准则能以任何根本的、或普遍性的方式维持下去。

　　但是，人类有能力推进这项事业吗？难道这不是一个毫无希望的乌托邦幻想吗？难道我们不是已经丧失了对自己命运的控制，以至于注定要在各种文化之间进行着的越来越激烈的高科技冲突中逐渐走向灭

extinction in ever harsher high-tech clashes between cultures, because of our fatal inability to co-operate in the face of impending catastrophes, be they ecological, social, or demographic, or of dangers generated by the state of our civilization as such?

I don't know.

But I have not lost hope.

I have not lost hope because I am persuaded again and again that, lying dormant in the deepest roots of most, if not all, cultures there is an essential similarity, something that could be made if the will to do so existed a genuinely unifying starting point for that new code of human co-existence that would be firmly anchored in the great diversity of human traditions.

Don't we find somewhere in the foundations of most religions and cultures, though they may take a thousand and one distinct forms, common elements such as respect for what transcends us, whether we mean the mystery of Being, or a moral order that stands above us; certain imperatives that come to us from heaven, or from nature, or from our own hearts; a belief that our deeds will live after us; respect for our neighbours, for our families, for certain natural authorities; respect for human dignity and for nature; a sense of solidarity and benevolence towards guests who come with good intentions?

Isn't the common, ancient origin or human roots of our diverse spiritualities, each of which is merely another kind of human understanding of the same reality, the thing that can genuinely bring people of different cultures together?

And aren't the basic commandments of this archetypal spirituality in harmony with what even an unreligious person without knowing exactly why may consider proper and meaningful?

Naturally, I am not suggesting that modern people be compelled to worship ancient **deities** [Deity; n. 神, 神性] and accept rituals they have long since abandoned. I am suggesting something quite different: we must come to understand the deep mutual connection or kinship between the various forms of our spirituality. We must recollect our original spiritual and moral substance, which grew out of the same essential experience of humanity. I believe that this is the only way to achieve a genuine renewal of our sense of responsibility for ourselves and for the world. And at the same time, it is the only way to achieve a deeper understanding among cultures that will enable them to work together in a truly ecumenical way to create a new order for the world.

亡吗？这不是在灾难面前——不论生态灾难、社会灾难还是人口灾难，或者由文明本身所引发的各种危险——我们表现出来的无法合作的致命弱点吗？

我不知道。

但我没有放弃希望。

我没有失去希望，是因为我一而再地获得过这样的信念，即在我们大部分（如果不是全部）文化的最深处，都有一种本质上的相似性，它是可以由人创造的，如果人们确实有把它创造出来的意志，这种相似性是团结的真正起点，可以成为人类共存的新准则，而这个准则将要牢牢维系于人类各种传统的伟大多样性之中。

即使存在着一千零一种不同形式，难道我们在大部分宗教和文化的基础中找不出一些共同因素？例如尊重那些超越我们的事物，这里指的是生命的奥秘、引导我们的道德秩序，或者某些来自天堂、大自然及内心的训令。我们相信自己的行为将在死后长存；我们尊重我们的家庭和邻居，也尊重某种大自然的权威；我们尊重人的尊严和大自然，对带着善意来访的客人，都给予认同和款待。

人类古老的共同来源，或我们不同的精神属性之根，不都是人类对同一个现实的不同理解吗？这正是可以使具有不同文化的民族聚集在一起的东西。

对典型的清规戒律，哪怕是没有宗教信仰的人，也可能下意识地同意它是恰当而有意义的准则，这不也体现了和谐吗？

当然，我不是说现代人非得要崇拜古代神灵和接受那些早已被抛弃了的仪式，我说的完全是另一码事。我们必须理解人类精神属性的各种形式之间那种深层的关连和纽带，必须重新发掘我们精神和道德的根源性的本质，而这是从人类共同的基本经验中得来的。我认为，这是真正恢复我们对自身和世界的责任感的唯一途径，也是各种文化进一步相互理解的唯一途径，应该让它们以一种通行的方式通力协作，为世界创造出一个新秩序。

我们都知道，笼罩着现代世界和人类意识的全球文明，其外表

The **veneer** [n. 薄片镶饰，虚饰或虚伪的外表] of global civilization that envelops the modern world and the consciousness of humanity, as we all know, has a dual nature, bringing into question, at every step of the way, the very values it is based upon, or which it propagates. The thousands of marvellous achievements of this civilization that work for us so well and enrich us can equally impoverish, diminish, and destroy our lives, and frequently do. Instead of serving people, many of these creations enslave them. Instead of helping people to develop their identities, they take them away. Almost every invention or discovery from the splitting of the atom and the discovery of DNA to television and the computer can be turned against us and used to our detriment. How much easier it is today than it was during the First World War to destroy an entire metropolis in a single air-raid. And how much easier would it be today, in the era of television, for a madman like Hitler to **pervert** [vt. 歪曲，败坏] the spirit of a whole nation. When have people ever had the power we now possess to alter the climate of the planet or deplete its mineral resources or the wealth of its fauna and flora in the space of a few short decades? And how much more destructive potential do terrorists have at their disposal today than at the beginning of this century.

In our era, it would seem that one part of the human brain, the rational part which has made all these morally neutral discoveries, has undergone exceptional development, while the other part, which should be alert to ensure that these discoveries really serve humanity and will not destroy it, has lagged behind catastrophically.

Yes, regardless of where I begin my thinking about the problems facing our civilization, I always return to the theme of human responsibility, which seems incapable of keeping pace with civilization and preventing it from turning against the human race. It's as though the world has simply become too much for us to deal with.

There is no way back. Only a dreamer can believe that the solution lies in curtailing the progress of civilization in some way or other. The main task in the coming era is something else: a radical renewal of our sense of responsibility. Our conscience must catch up to our reason, otherwise we are lost.

It is my profound belief that there is only one way to achieve this: we must divest ourselves of our egoistical anthropocentrism, our habit of seeing ourselves as masters of the universe who can do whatever occurs to us. We must discover a new respect for what transcends us: for the universe, for the earth, for nature, for life, and for reality.

具有一种双重特质，使人们在它的每一步前进过程中，都对它本身的基础，或它所宣传的价值观产生疑问。这种文明所创造出来的成千上万的辉煌成果，一方面正为我们所用，并造福于我们，但同样它也可以损耗、削弱和摧毁我们的生活，并且已经这样发生了。这些发明创造，很多不但没有服务于人类，反而奴役人类；不但没有帮助人们开发个性，反而让他们丧失了身份。几乎每一项发明或发现——从原子的分裂到DNA[3]的发现，以及电视和电脑的发明——都可以反过来对付并伤害我们。如今用一次空袭来全面摧毁一座大都市，要比第一次世界大战时容易得多。在当今这个电视时代，像希特勒这类疯子要扭曲整个民族精神，也比以前轻易得多。人类历史上，可曾像我们现在这样拥有这种能力：在短短几十年间，改变地球气候、耗尽地矿资源以及丰富的动植物？现在恐怖分子手中拥有的摧毁能力，比本世纪初增大了多少？

在我们这个纪元，似乎人类头脑中那理性的一半，也就是创造出所有这些在道德上并无好坏之分的发明——理性的那一部分，已经有了特别的发展；而另一半，那原应该用来确保发明能够真正为人类服务，而不是用来毁灭人类的那一半头脑，却灾难性地远没跟上相应的发展。

是的，不管我从哪里开始思考我们文明所面临的问题，我总会回到探讨人类责任的主题上，后者似乎跟不上文明的速度，也无法阻止它掉过头来贻害人类。世界仿佛变得让我们太难以应付。

我们没有回头路。只有做梦的人才会相信，可以通过这样或那样的方式来限制文明的进程，以找到解决之道。我们在今后岁月里的主要任务会有所不同：必须全面振兴我们的责任感。我们的良心必须跟上我们的理性，否则我们就会迷失方向。

我深切地相信，只有一条途径可以走到这里：我们必须抛开自大的人类中心论，抛开把自己视为宇宙的主宰、能够为所欲为的那种习惯。对那些超越我们的事物，我们必须有一种新的尊敬，对宇宙、地球、大自然、生命和现实，都必须有所尊敬。我们对其他民族、

Our respect for other people, for other nations, and for other cultures, can only grow from a humble respect for the cosmic order and from an awareness that we are a part of it, that we share in it and that nothing of what we do is lost, but rather becomes part of the eternal memory of Being, where it is judged.

A better alternative for the future of humanity, therefore, clearly lies in imbuing our civilization with a spiritual dimension. It's not just a matter of understanding its multicultural nature and finding inspiration for the creation of a new world order in the common roots of all cultures. It is also essential that the Euro-American cultural sphere the one which created this civilization and taught humanity its destructive pride now return to its own spiritual roots and become an example to the rest of the world in the search for a new humility.

General observations of this type are certainly not difficult to make, nor are they new or revolutionary. Modern people are masters at describing the crises and the misery of the world which we shape, and for which we are responsible. We are much less adept at putting things right.

So what specifically is to be done?

I do not believe in some universal key or **panacea** [n. 万灵药. 灵丹妙药]. I am not an advocate of what Karl Popper called "holistic social engineering", particularly because I had to live most of my adult life in circumstances that resulted from an attempt to create a holistic Marxist utopia. I know more than enough, therefore, about efforts of this kind.

This does not relieve me, however, of the responsibility to think of ways to make the world better.

It will certainly not be easy to awaken in people a new sense of responsibility for the world, an ability to conduct themselves as if they were to live on this earth forever, and to be held answerable for its condition one day. Who knows how many horrific cataclysms humanity may have to go through before such a sense of responsibility is generally accepted. But this does not mean that those who wish to work for it cannot begin at once. It is a great task for teachers, educators, intellectuals, the clergy, artists, entrepreneurs, journalists, people active in all forms of public life.

Above all it is a task for politicians.

Even in the most democratic of conditions, politicians have immense influence, perhaps more than they themselves realize. This influence does not lie in their actual

其他国家和其他文化的尊敬，只能产生于对宇宙秩序的谦卑的尊敬，我们必须意识到我们是宇宙的一部分，且从中得到享受，我们所做的一切都不会白做，而是会变成永恒的记忆，并最终要接受审判。

因此，人类未来另一条更好的出路在于为我们的文明塑造一个精神的层面。这不仅仅需要我们理解其多元文化的本质，也不仅仅要求我们寻找灵感，去开创一个容纳各种文化共性的世界新秩序。 不仅如此，我们还需要欧美文化（它创造出了这一文明并教会人类毁灭性的自傲）回到它自身的精神根源，并在探索新的谦逊精神的过程中，为世界其他地区树立榜样。

作出这样的观察显然不难，而且也不具有新意或革命性。现代人善于描述危机，以及我们对世界所造成的苦难，这些都是我们必须负责的，但我们却远无法把事情做对、做好。

那么，具体来说，有哪些事情是必须做的呢？

我不相信有什么万能钥匙或灵丹妙药。我并不主张卡尔·波普尔[4]所说的"一体化的社会工程"，主要是因为，我个人大部分的成人阶段，都生活在试图创造一个整体化的马克思主义的乌托邦环境里。对于这类努力我知道得足够多。

然而，这并不能使我放下责任，不去思考如何才能让世界变得更美好。

显然，要唤醒人们对世界有一种新的责任感，让他们在为人处世时做到好像他们会永远生活在这个地球上，而且有一天要对地球的状况负责，这可不是一件容易的事。有谁能知道，到底人类要再经历多少可怕的灾难后，这种责任感才会被普遍接受？但这并不意味着那些希望为此而努力的人不能立即行动起来。这是教师、教育者、知识分子、神职人员、艺术家、企业家、记者，以及活跃在各种公共领域中的人们，所应当从事的伟大工作。

首先，这是政治家的任务。

即便是在最民主的环境里，政治家的影响力也是巨大的，也许比他们自己意识到的更大。这种影响力不一定来自他们的实际职位，

mandates, which in any case are considerably limited. It lies in something else: in the spontaneous impact their charisma has on the public.

The main task of the present generation of politicians is not, I think, to **ingratiate** [vt. 逢迎，讨好] themselves with the public through the decisions they take or their smiles on television. It is not to go on winning elections and ensuring themselves a place in the sun till the end of their days. Their role is something quite different: to assume their share of responsibility for the long-range prospects of our world and thus to set an example for the public in whose sight they work. Their responsibility is to think ahead boldly, not to fear the disfavour of the crowd, to imbue their actions with a spiritual dimension (which of course is not the same thing as **ostentatious** [adj. 装饰表面的，浮夸的] attendance at religious services), to explain again and again both to the public and to their colleagues that politics must do far more than reflect the interests of particular groups or lobbies. **After all, politics is a matter of serving the community, which means that it is morality in practice. And how better to serve the community and practise morality than by seeking in the midst of the global (and globally threatened) civilization their own global political responsibility: that is, their responsibility for the very survival of the human race?**

I don't believe that a politician who sets out on this risky path will inevitably jeopardize his or her political survival. This is a wrongheaded notion which assumes that the citizen is a fool and that political success depends on playing to this folly. That is not the way it is. A conscience slumbers in every human being, something divine. And that is what we have to put our trust in.

Ladies and gentlemen,

I find myself at perhaps the most famous university in the most powerful country in the world. With your permission, I will say a few words on the subject of the politics of a great power.

It is obvious that those who have the greatest power and influence also bear the greatest responsibility. Like it or not, the United States of America now bears probably the greatest responsibility for the direction our world will take. The United States, therefore, should reflect most deeply on this responsibility.

Isolationism has never paid off for the United States. Had it entered the First World War earlier, perhaps it would not have had to pay with anything like the casualties it actually incurred.

因为他们的实际职位无论怎么说都是相当有限的。它来自别处，即他们的魅力对公众产生的自然影响。

我想，眼下这一代政治家的主要任务，不是通过他们所做的决定或在电视上的笑容来讨得公众欢心，不是通过赢得选举，来确保他们在阳光下的显赫地位稳定到最后一天。他们的角色应该有所不同，那就是，他们应当履行自己对我们这个世界的长远前景所负的责任，从而在注视着他们的公众心目中，树立起一个榜样。他们的责任是勇敢地进行前瞻性的思考，不怕失宠于众，让他们的行动充满着一种精神品质（这当然与出席宗教活动时的那种炫耀夸张不是一回事）。并向公众和自己的同事不断解释，让人们知道，为什么政治绝不仅仅是反映特定的团体或游说集团的利益，而必须做得更多。**说到底，政治就是一种为社群服务的事业，这就意味着它是实践中的道德。而政治家们服务社群和实践道德的最好方式，就是探索在全球（以及全球范围内都受到威胁的）文明中，自己的全球政治责任何在？也就是说，他们为人类生存这个问题，肩负有何种责任？**

我不相信一个政治家走上这条风险之路，就不可避免地会危及他的政治前途。这是一种错误观念，它把公民当成傻瓜，而政治家必须作出同样愚蠢的事才能成功。实际并非如此。每个人都有良知，带有某种神圣的东西，而那就是我们的信任赖以托付之处。

女士们、先生们！

我现在置身于世界上最强大的国家之中，也或许是最著名的大学，请允许我就大国政治这个题目说几句话。

不言而喻，那些拥有最强大的权力和影响力的人，同时也担负着最大的责任。不管喜欢与否，美国现在担负着影响我们世界走向何方这样一个重大的责任。因此，美国应当对这种责任作出最深刻的反省。

孤立主义从来就没有给美国带来好处。要是美国早点介入第一次世界大战，也许它就可以避免后来实际上遭受的伤亡，可以不必付出那样大的代价。

The same is true of the Second World War: when Hitler was getting ready to invade Czechoslovakia, and in so doing finally expose the lack of courage on the part of the western democracies, your President wrote a letter to the Czechoslovak President imploring him to come to some agreement with Hitler. Had he not deceived himself and the whole world into believing that an agreement could be made with this madman, had he instead shown a few teeth, perhaps the Second World War need not have happened, and tens of thousands of young Americans need not have died fighting in it.

Likewise, just before the end of that war, had your President, who was otherwise an outstanding man, said a clear "no" to Stalin's decision to divide the world, perhaps the Cold War, which cost the United States hundreds of billions of dollars, need not have happened either.

I beg you: do not repeat these mistakes! You yourselves have always paid a heavy price for them! There is simply no escaping the responsibility you have as the most powerful country in the world.

There is far more at stake here than simply standing up to those who would like once again to divide the world into spheres of interest, or **subjugate** [vt. 征服．使服从] others who are different from them, and weaker. What is now at stake is saving the human race. In other words, it's a question of what I've already talked about: of understanding modern civilization as a multicultural and multipolar civilization, of turning our attention to the original spiritual sources of human culture and above all, of our own culture, of drawing from these sources the strength for a courageous and magnanimous creation of a new order for the world.

Not long ago I was at a gala dinner to mark an important anniversary. There were fifty Heads of State present, perhaps more, who came to honour the heroes and victims of the greatest war in human history. This was not a political conference, but the kind of social event that is meant principally to show hospitality and respect to the invited guests. When the seating plan was given out, I discovered to my surprise that those sitting at the table next to mine were not identified simply as representatives of a particular state, as was the case with all the other tables; they were referred to as "permanent members of the UN Security Council and the G7." I had mixed feelings about this. On the one hand, I thought how marvellous that the richest and most powerful of this world see each other often and even at this dinner, can

第二次世界大战的情况也是如此。当希特勒准备入侵捷克的时候，这一行径终于揭开了西方民主国家缺乏勇气的真相，而你们的总统却致函捷克总统，要求他与希特勒达成某种协议。如果你们的总统不是哄骗自己和整个世界，盲目地相信可以与这个狂人达成协议；如果他展示出了准备以牙还牙的姿态，也许第二次世界大战就不会发生，千千万万的美国青年也就不会战死沙场。

同样的，就在那场战争结束之前，如果你们那位其实也算是一位杰出人物的总统，能够向斯大林准备瓜分世界的决定，斩钉截铁地说一声"不"，也许耗费了美国千百亿美元的冷战也不会发生。

我恳请你们，不要让这些错误再次发生！你们自己为这类错误付出过惨重的代价！作为世界上最强大的国家，你们根本无法逃避这个责任。

现在的问题还不只是简单地反对有人想再次瓜分世界，想征服与他们不同的人、征服比他们弱小的人，而是要拯救人类。换句话说，这是我刚才已经谈到的问题，也就是要把现代文明当成多元文化和多极文明来理解，要把我们的注意力转移到人类文化，尤其是我们自己文化的精神本源，并从这些根源中吸取力量，勇敢而高尚地创造一个新的世界秩序。

不久前，我参加了为纪念一个重要周年而举办的晚宴。有 50 位（也许更多）国家元首参与出席，纪念人类历史上那场最大战争中的英雄和受害者。这不是一场政治会议，而是一次社交活动，主要是想向受邀请的贵宾表示欢迎和敬意。当席位安排的计划公布时，我惊讶地发现，与我相邻那张桌子的贵宾，并不像所有其他桌子上所写的那样，只表明某人代表某个国家那么简单，他们的称呼是"联合国安理会常任理事国和七国集团"。我对此感受复杂。一方面，我觉得世界上最富裕、最强大的国家的元首们，能够经常见面，尤其是可以在这次晚宴上非正式地交谈，并增进彼此的了解，真是件好事；另一方面，我不禁有点毛骨悚然。因为我不能不感觉到，某张桌子被挑选出来，当做特殊的和特别重要的来对待。那是一张给大

talk informally and get to know each other better. On the other hand, a slight chill went down my spine, for I could not help observing that one table had been singled out as being special and particularly important. It was a table for the big powers. Somewhat perversely, I began to imagine that the people sitting at it were, along with their Russian caviar, dividing the rest of us up among themselves, without asking our opinion. Perhaps all this is merely the **whimsy** [n. 怪念头．心情浮动] of a former and perhaps future playwright. But I wanted to express it here. For one simple reason: to emphasize the terrible gap that exists between the responsibility of the great powers and their **hubris**. [n. 傲慢．骄傲] The architect of that seating arrangement I should think it was none of the attending Presidents was not guided by a sense of responsibility for the world, but by the banal pride of the powerful.

But pride is precisely what will lead the world to hell. I am suggesting an alternative: humbly accepting our responsibility for the world.

There is one great opportunity in the matter of co-existence between nations and spheres of civilization, culture and religion that should be grasped and exploited to the limit. This is the appearance of supranational or regional communities. By now, there are many such communities in the world, with diverse characteristics and differing degrees of integration. I believe in this approach. I believe in the importance of organisms that lie somewhere between nation states and a world community, organisms that can be an important medium of global communication and co-operation. I believe that this trend towards integration in a world where as I've said every valley longs for independence, must be given the greatest possible support. These organisms, however, must not be an expression of integration merely for the sake of integration. They must be one of the many instruments enabling each region, each nation, to be both itself and capable of co-operation with others. That is, they must be one of the instruments enabling countries and peoples who are close to each other geographically, ethnically, culturally and economically and who have common security interests, to form associations and better communicate with each other and with the rest of the world. At the same time, all such regional communities must rid themselves of fear that other like communities are directed against them. Regional groupings in areas that have common traditions and a common political culture ought to be a natural part of the complex political architecture of the world. Co-operation between such regions ought to be a natural component of co-operation on a world-wide scale.

国坐的桌子。我固执地想象，坐在那张桌子上的人，一边品尝着俄国鱼子酱，一边把我们这些人在他们之间进行瓜分，而不用征求我们的意见。也许这只是一位像我这样曾经当过戏剧家，甚或以后还会再做戏剧家的人才有的怪念头。但我想在这里说出来，只有一个简单的理由：这些大国的责任与它们展示的傲慢之间，有着可怕的差距。座次的设计——我想这不是那天出席的总统们的主意——没有表现出对世界的责任感，而只是展示了强权的陈腐骄傲。

但是，正是自傲会把世界引向地狱。我在此给出一个选择：谦卑地接受我们对世界的责任。

在各个国家和各种文明、文化及宗教之间共存的问题上，有一个很好的机会是我们应当把握并充分利用的，这就是超民族或跨宗教社群的出现。到现在，世界上已经出现了很多这类社群，它们具有多样化的特色和不同程度的融合。我相信这个办法可行。我认为这种介于民族国家与世界社会之间的机体很重要，因为这些机体可以作为全球沟通和合作的重要媒介。我相信，在一个我说过的每一个山谷都会渴望独立的世界里，这种迈向一体化的趋势应当得到最有力的支持。但是，这些机体绝不能仅仅成为为一体化而一体化的表现，它们应当使每一个地区和每一个国家，既可以成为自己，又可以与外界合作的多种工具之一。也就是说，它们的作用之一，是使那些在地理上、种族上、文化上和经济上相近，并且有着共同安全利益的国家和人民能够形成联盟，并在他们自己之间以及与世界其他地方进行更好的沟通。

与此同时，所有这类区域性组织必须克服这种恐惧，即以为其他类似的组织是针对它们的。有着共同传统和共同政治文化的地区形成区域性的集团，应当被看做是复杂的世界政治架构中很自然的组成部分。这些区域的合作，应当是在全世界范围内进行的自然合作。例如，在北约成员国组织扩大时，那些在文化上和政治上属于该联盟保护范围的国家，在加入这个组织时，却被俄罗斯看做是一种反俄罗斯的举动。那么，这就表明俄罗斯还不了解这个时代的挑

As long as the broadening of NATO membership to include countries who feel culturally and politically a part of the region the Alliance was created to defend is seen by Russia, for example, as an anti-Russian undertaking, it will be a sign that Russia has not yet understood the challenge of this era.

The most important world organization is the United Nations. I think that the fiftieth anniversary of its birth could be an occasion to reflect on how to infuse it with a new ethos, a new strength, and a new meaning, and make it the truly most important arena of good co-operation among all cultures that make up our planetary civilization.

But neither the strengthening of regional structures nor the strengthening of the UN will save the world if both processes are not informed by that renewed spiritual charge which I see as the only hope that the human race will survive another millennium.

I have touched on what I think politicians should do.

There is, however, one more force that has at least as much, if not more, influence on the general state of mind as politicians do.

That force is the mass media.

Only when fate sent me into the realm of high politics did I become fully aware of the media's double-edged power. Their dual impact is not a specialty of the media. It is merely a part, or an expression of the dual nature of today's civilization of which I have already spoken.

Thanks to television the whole world discovered, in the course of an evening, that there is a country called Rwanda where people are suffering beyond belief. Thanks to television it is possible to do at least a little to help those who are suffering. Thanks to television the whole world, in the course of a few seconds, was shocked and horrified about what happened in Oklahoma City and, at the same time, understood it as a great warning for all. Thanks to television the whole world knows that there exists an internationally recognized country called Bosnia and Herzegovina and that from the moment it recognized this country, the international community has tried unsuccessfully to divide it into grotesque mini-states according to the wishes of warlords who have never been recognized by anyone as anyone's legitimate representatives.

That is the wonderful side of today's mass media, or rather, of those who gather the news. Humanity's thanks belong to all those courageous reporters who voluntarily

战到底是什么。

联合国是最重要的世界性组织。我想，应当利用联合国成立50周年的时机，来考虑如何赋予这个组织以新的道德风貌、新的力量和新的意义，使它真正成为构成我们这个地球文明的所有文化之间，展开良好合作的最重要的机构。

不管是强化地区性的组织，还是加强联合国的力量，如果这些过程不是在崭新的精神力量启发下，便都难以拯救世界，而我把这种精神力量视为决定人类能否在下一个千年继续生存下去的唯一希望。

我已经谈过我认为政治家们应该做些什么。

然而，还有另一种力量与政治家一样，甚至比政治家更能够影响人们的思想状态。

这种力量就是大众传播。

只有到了命运把我推到政治的高层之后，我才充分认识到媒体的双重威力。这种双重影响力并非媒体特有，它只是我前面谈过的当今文明双重属性的一个组成部分，或是它的一种体现。

由于有了电视，全世界在一夜之间就知道有个叫做卢旺达的国家，那里的人民正在遭受着令人难以置信的苦难；由于有了电视，人们才可能向那些受苦受难的人提供一些帮助；由于有了电视，全世界在数秒之内，就被发生在俄克拉荷马城的爆炸事件所震惊，同时也认识到，那对所有人来说是一次严重警告；由于有了电视，全世界都知道有一个获得国际承认的叫做波斯尼亚—黑塞哥维那的国家，但从这个国家被承认的那一刻起，国际社会就开始徒劳地试图按照一些军阀们的意愿，来将这个国家分裂成一些奇形怪状的袖珍小国，而那些军阀们从未被任何人承认是谁的合法代表。

这是今天的大众传播，或者说，那些采集新闻的人，具有的神奇的一面。人类应当感谢那些勇敢的记者，不管哪里发生了什么坏事，他们都甘愿冒着生命危险，从而唤醒世界的良心。

不过，电视也有它不那么光彩的一面，它仅仅热衷于报道世界的各种恐怖事件，或不可饶恕地让这些恐怖事件变成家常便饭，或

risk their lives wherever something evil is happening, in order to arouse the conscience of the world.

There is, however, another, less wonderful, aspect of television, one that merely revels in the horrors of the world or, unforgivably, makes them commonplace, or compels politicians to become first of all television stars. But where is it written that someone who is good on television is necessarily also a good politician? I never fail to be astonished at how much I am at the mercy of television directors and editors, at how my public image depends far more on them than it does on myself, at how important it is to smile appropriately on television, or choose the right tie, at how television forces me to express my thoughts as sparely as possible, in witticisms, slogans or sound bites, at how easily my television image can be made to seem different from the real me. I am astonished by this and at the same time, I fear it serves no good purpose. I know politicians who have learned to see themselves only as the television camera does. Television has thus expropriated their personalities, and made them into something like television shadows of their former selves. I sometimes wonder whether they even sleep in a way that will look good on television.

I am not outraged with television or the press for distorting what I say, or ignoring it, or editing me to appear like some strange monster. I am not angry with the media when I see that a politician's rise or fall often depends more on them than on the politician concerned. What interests me is something else: the responsibility of those who have the mass media in their hands. They too bear responsibility for the world, and for the future of humanity. Just as the splitting of the atom can immensely enrich humanity in a thousand and one ways and, at the same time, can also threaten it with destruction, so television can have both good and evil consequences. Quickly, suggestively, and to an unprecedented degree, it can disseminate the spirit of understanding, humanity, human solidarity and spirituality, or it can stupefy whole nations and continents. And just as our use of atomic energy depends solely on our sense of responsibility, so the proper use of television's power to enter practically every household and every human mind depends on our sense of responsibility as well.

Whether our world is to be saved from everything that threatens it today depends above all on whether human beings come to their senses, whether they understand the degree of their responsibility and discover a new relationship to the very miracle of Being. The world is in the hands of us all. And yet some have a greater influence on

迫使政治家们首先充当电视明星。但是有什么地方写过,说某人在电视上表现出色,就意味着他会是个好的政治家?我一直都惊异我是那么的受电视导演和编辑的摆布,我的公众形象怎么竟然依赖于他们,而不是取决于我自己?我惊异于在电视上得体地微笑,或选择一条合适的领带,会是多么重要;惊异于电视怎样迫使我尽量少表达自己的思想,而多套用调侃、口号或是简短好记的句子来说话;惊异于我的电视形象,轻而易举地就可以变得和我本人毫不相像。

我为之震惊,同时也担心这不会有什么好处。我知道有的政治家只晓得通过电视镜头来看自己。电视就这样剥夺了他们的个性,使他们失去自我,成了电视中的一个影子。我有时候甚至怀疑,他们睡觉时是不是也要摆出一副能在电视里显得好看的姿态。

我并不是因为电视或报刊扭曲或忽略了我的话,或把我编辑得看起来像一只怪物,而感到愤怒。当我看到一个政治家的浮沉,常常更多地依赖于媒体、而不是政治家自己时,我并不对它们感到愤怒。我感兴趣的是其他事情,即那些掌握大众媒体的人所负的责任。他们也承担着对世界和对人类未来的责任。就像原子的分裂能够以一千零一种方式极大地造福人类,但同时也能够给人类以毁灭的威胁一样,电视也可以有善恶两种后果。它能够快速地、暗示性地,并且以一种前所未有的程度,来传播理解人性、人类团结和灵性的精神,它也可以误导整个民族以至整个大洲。就像我们对原子能的利用,端赖于我们的责任感一样,如何恰当地利用电视对每个家庭和每个头脑的影响力,也有赖于我们的责任感。

我们能否把我们的世界从今天所有的威胁中拯救出来,首先要依赖于我们人类是否诉诸理性,是否理解他们责任的重要性,以及找到和"存在"这个神奇认识的新关系。世界就掌握在我们所有人手中。但有些人对世界命运的影响,要比其他人来得大。一个人的影响力越大,不管他们是政治家还是电视主持人,他们所要承担的责任也就越大,他们也应当较少地考虑个人的利益。

女士们、先生们!

its fate than others. The more influence a person has be they politician or television announcer the greater the demands placed on their sense of responsibility and the less they should think merely about personal interests.

Ladies and gentlemen,

In conclusion allow me a brief personal remark. I was born in Prague and I lived there for decades without being allowed to study properly or visit other countries. Nevertheless, my mother never abandoned one of her secret and quite extravagant dreams: that one day I would study at Harvard. Fate did not permit me to fulfil her dream. But something else happened, something that would never have occurred even to my mother: I have received a doctoral degree at Harvard without even having to study here.

More than that, I have been given to see Singapore, and countless other exotic places. I have been given to understand how small this world is and how it torments itself with countless things it need not torment itself with if people could find within themselves a little more courage, a little more hope, a little more responsibility, a little more mutual understanding and love.

I don't know whether my mother is looking down at me from heaven, but if she is I can guess what she's probably thinking: she's thinking that I'm sticking my nose into matters that only people who have properly studied political science at Harvard have the right to stick their noses into.

I hope that you don't think so.

Thank you for your attention.

最后，请允许我讲一个自己的故事。我出生在布拉格，并在那里生活了几十年，从来没有正规地学习或访问其他国家。不过，我的母亲从未放弃过她的个人的、也是相当宏伟的梦想：有一天我能到哈佛大学学习。

命运不允许我去践行她的梦想，但另一件事情发生了。我的母亲肯定想象不到，不用在这里学习，我也拿到了哈佛大学的博士学位。

更重要的是，我有机会走访新加坡，以及其他无数充满异国情调的地方。我有机会了解到我们这个世界是多么小，而它却充满痛苦。如果人们能找到更多一点勇气，唤醒更多的希望，承担更多的责任，并给予更多的相互理解和关爱，这个世界就能减少一点自我折磨。

我不知道我的母亲是否在天上看着我，如果是的话，我可以猜测到她的想法。她会认为我不请自到地谈论的问题，是只有在哈佛大学认真学过政治学的人才有权利畅谈的。

我希望你们不这么想。

谢谢大家！

---

1 这里指的是英国的巴林银行（Barings Bank，1762—1995），这家有着233年历史的英国著名银行，毁于一个当时年龄只有28岁的毛头小伙子尼克·李森（Nick Leeson）之手。李森未经授权，在该行的新加坡办事处从事期货合约交易失败，致使巴林银行亏损13亿美元，从而破产。

2 美国的有线电视新闻网

3 脱氧核糖核酸

4 卡尔·波普尔（Karl Popper，1902—1994），20世纪最著名的哲学家之一，批判理性主义的创始人。他认为经验观察必须以一定理论为指导，但理论本身又是可证伪的，因此应对之采取批判的态度。

哈罗德·瓦尔穆斯（1939— ）

  1996年哈佛大学毕业典礼的演讲者，是时任美国国家卫生研究院（National Institutes of Health，NIH）院长的哈罗德·瓦尔穆斯。早在1989年，他和自己长期的合作伙伴迈克尔·毕晓普（J. Michael Bishop）就因在癌症研究方面的出色成果而获得诺贝尔医学奖。他们共同提出了一种癌症发生的新理论：癌症的产生是由于我们人体正常基因中的某些基因发生了变异的结果，这些变异或者由外来的致癌因子引起，或者因人体细胞在分裂和DNA复制过程中出现的差错所致。

  瓦尔穆斯的经历颇为传奇，他于1939年出生在纽约一个犹太裔家庭，早期的志向并不是科学，而是文学，他从美国阿默斯特（Amherst）学院获得文学学士学位，后又在哈佛大学获文学硕士学位。在哈佛大学期间，他学的是古典诗词和玄学派诗歌，曾打算将文学作为自己一生的职业，但后来他改学医学，并于1966年获得哥伦比亚大学的医学博士学位。作为病毒研究领域的专家，瓦尔穆斯从上世纪80年代起，投身于发现导致艾滋病的病毒研究，由他担任主任委员的科学顾问委员会于1986年提议，将引起艾滋病的病源命名为人类免疫缺陷病毒（HIV）。

  1993年，瓦尔穆斯经美国总统克林顿提名，成为首位拥有诺贝尔奖头衔的NIH院长。NIH是世界上从事生命科学研究最重要的研究机构之一，在美国联邦政府研发经费中的份额仅次于国防部。目前，从事NIH院外和院内研究项目的雇员有近2万人。

  2000年1月，瓦尔穆斯成为著名的Memorial Sloan-Kettering肿瘤医院的院长。

1996

Poetic Exploration of Science
科学的诗意探索

Harold Varmus 哈罗德·瓦尔穆斯

Mr. President, alumni, graduates, parents, friends:

Many members of today's graduating class reacted to the news that I would give this year's Commencement Address, just as I did: with surprise. The Harvard Crimson recorded some undergraduate responses: "Who is he?" "Wow, that's boring. Everyone else got someone exciting." Editorials criticized the process by which "Dr. Who" was selected. I was featured in entertaining cartoons, something that hasn't happened during three years in Washington. I may never be this famous again.

There is an advantage to starting from low expectations. Agreed, I am not running for President, and I am not a prime minister or a general. But I speak for an element of our culture at least as important as politics or war---an element that has not been at this podium since Alexander Fleming, the discoverer of penicillin, addressed the graduating class of 1945. That element is science.

The products of science shape and **pervade** [vt. 弥漫. 遍及] our lives. Sir Francis Bacon made this point in 1620. "Printing, gunpowder, and the magnet," he wrote, "have changed the whole face and state of things throughout the world....no empire, no sect, no star seems to have exerted greater power and influence in human affairs." Modern equivalents are legion: consider e-mail, nuclear weapons, biotechnology.

I will speak today about the effects of science on our lives. But I will also emphasize science in its most fundamental form, the process by which we make discoveries about the world---like the atom or the gene--- that precede practical inventions. At its core, **science is a way of thinking---making judgments, often creative ones, that are based on evidence, not on desires, received beliefs, or hearsay. Thinking in this way is not unique to the natural sciences; it is important for many disciplines. But the pursuit of evidence, through experiment and observation, is the lifeblood of science.**

My own brand of science is biology---more specifically, biology linked to medicine. I was not born a scientist. In my youth, I preferred tennis and novels to chemistry sets. My father, Harvard Class of '28, was a physician, so medical topics were often at the dinner table. Like my friends, I grew up listening to parental concerns about polio, the crippling illness then common among children and famous for afflicting our family hero, Franklin Delano Roosevelt. In summertime, public swimming pools were forbidden. Neighborhood kids nearly died of the disease. For my generation, the announcement of an effective polio vaccine was a landmark. For

尊敬的校长、各位校友、毕业生、家长们、朋友们：

在听到将由我来发表今年的毕业典礼演讲时，今天在座的许多毕业生的反应和我是一样的——惊讶。《哈佛深红报》**1** 刊载了一些本科生的反应："他是谁啊？""哦，这太没劲了，往届的演讲者可都是让人兴奋的成功人士。"该报发表的社论，批评有关方面选择了我这位"无名先生"来演讲。我的形象出现在讽刺漫画里，这在过去3年我在华盛顿担任公职期间还不曾发生过，我想以后我不可能再像这次一样出名了。

既然期望值这么低，其实也有它的好处。我同意，我没在准备竞选总统，我也不是一位总理或将军。但我的发言，代表我们的文化中与政治或战争至少同样重要的一个因素，这个因素自从发现青霉素的亚历山大·弗莱明**2** 1945年发表毕业演讲以来，一直就没有再出现在这个讲台上，我说的这个因素就是科学。

科学的成果塑造并影响着我们的生活。弗兰西斯·培根爵士**3** 早在1620年时就说过，"印刷术、火药、指南针"，他写道，"彻底改变了全世界一切事物的面貌和状态……从来没有任何一个帝国、任何一个教派、任何一个明星，对人类事务有这样大的影响"。在当代，有相同影响的东西很多，比如电子邮件、核武器、生物技术等等。

我今天会讲到科学对我们生活的影响。但我也要强调最基本形式的科学。科学探索的进程使我们能发现世界的奥秘，比如原子或基因，这些发现会带来实用的发明。说到底，**科学是一种思维方式——往往是有创意的判断，这些判断基于事实根据，而不是基于愿望、别人传输的信仰或道听途说。以这种方式思考并不是从事自然科学才需要的，在其他许多学科中同样重要。但通过实验和观察去寻找证据，则是科学的生命线。**

我自己的主业是生物学，具体来说，是与医学有关的生物学。我并非生来就是一个科学家。年轻时我喜欢网球和小说，而不是化学实验。我父亲1928年从哈佛毕业，是一个医生，所以家里晚餐的饭桌上常常谈到医疗的话题。和我的朋友们一样，我从小就听到父母们对小儿麻痹症的担心，这种能使儿童致残的疾病当时很常见，也因为被我们家视为偶像人物的富兰克林·德拉诺·罗斯福**4** 患过此病而为人所知。到了夏天，

us, the recent eradication of naturally acquired polio from this hemisphere still seems unbelievable.

When I was fourteen, and Jonas Salk had just achieved fame for the first polio vaccine, my parents taught me an important lesson about how progress occurs in medical research. I had intended to describe Salk's triumph in a public speaking contest (a contest, which, incidentally, I did not win). But they persuaded me to talk instead about John Franklin Enders. A member of the Harvard Medical School faculty, Enders and two younger colleagues had been the first to grow the polio virus abundantly, by infecting animal cells in laboratory **flasks** [flask; n. 细颈瓶. 烧瓶]. Previously, virus was prepared with difficulty, mainly from the brains of infected primates. Enders' discovery was pivotal, because Salk needed to inactivate vast amounts of poliovirus for use in a vaccine. Making and testing vaccines ---Salk's and later Sabin's--- came to seem less stirring to me than the more subtle triumph of learning how to grow the virus. And Enders became a heroic figure for me, even before I knew about his long path to science--- studying English literature at your graduate school and converting to microbiology at nearly thirty.

I too had trouble settling on a career. While my fellow pre-meds worked late in their labs, I was editing the Amherst College paper and writing about Charles Dickens. In a prolonged adolescence as a Harvard graduate student, I read Beowulf, Shakespeare, and Sir Thomas Browne, and listened to Bill Alfred, Harry Levin, and Anne Ferry. Finally I went to medical school---in part, because someone once told Gertrude Stein that it "opened all doors," in part because medical students seemed more eager than I was to get out of bed in the morning.

Like many physician-scientists of my generation, I learned to do and to love research while working at the National Institutes of Health, the Federal agency that supports most of the basic medical research in this country. I arrived at the NIH as a twenty-eight year-old doctor seeking two things: the credentials to become a medical school professor and an alternative to service in Vietnam. Then, one day some months later, I was abruptly transformed into a committed scientist, when a method I was developing to detect expression of a gene suddenly worked. The technique was not especially novel, and the questions I was asking were of interest only to a few people in the world. But, at that moment, I knew the intoxicating power of measurement and the sweet anticipation of my own results.

父母不让我们去公共泳池,邻居家也有孩子几乎死于该疾病。对我这一代人来说,研制出有效治疗小儿麻痹症的疫苗,就是一个了不起的里程碑。今天在我们生活的这个半球,自然感染小儿麻痹症的情况已经绝迹,这好像仍然是令人难以置信的事情。

在我14岁的时候,若纳斯·索尔克[5]刚刚因为研制出小儿麻痹疫苗而闻名,我的父母教给我重要的一课,那就是医学研究的进展是如何发生的。我曾经想在一个公开演讲比赛中说说索尔克的成就(顺便说一下,我没有赢得那次演讲比赛),但他们说服我不去讲索尔克,而是谈谈约翰·富兰克林·恩德斯。恩德斯是哈佛医学院的一位教师,他和另外两个比较年轻的同事通过在实验室的试管里感染动物细胞,第一次大量繁殖了小儿麻痹症病毒。在这之前,要获取病毒样品很难,主要是从已被感染的灵长类动物大脑中提取。恩德斯的发现是很关键的,因为索尔克在研制疫苗时,需要用大量的小儿麻痹症病毒。研制和测试疫苗,这是索尔克和后来另一位医学家萨宾所做的工作,相比学会如何培育病毒这种不显山不露水的功夫,让我对索尔克和萨宾的成就不那么崇拜。在我知道恩德斯是如何走上科学道路之前,他就已经成为我眼里的英雄人物——恩德斯先是在哈佛研究生院学习英美文学,快30岁时,才转学微生物学。

我也曾经过一番周折才决定自己的职业。当我的医学预科同学在他们的实验室里开夜车的时候,我还在阿默斯特学院[6]编写校报,还撰写有关狄更斯的文章。直到成了哈佛研究生,我还处于自己的青春期,我读了贝奥伍夫史诗和莎士比亚、托马斯·布朗的作品,听了比尔·阿尔弗雷德、哈里·莱文还有安妮·菲丽的课,最后我却上了医学院。这一部分原因,是像有人曾经告诉格特鲁德·施泰因的那样,因为医学院能"帮你打开所有的门",另一部分原因,是因为医学院的学生似乎每天早上起床时,都比我更有动力。

像我这一代人里的许多医学科学家一样,在NIH(国家卫生研究院)这个支持着我们国家大多数基础医疗研究的地方,我学会并爱上了研究工作。我在28岁时,作为一个医生到NIH,是想要做两件事:拿到成为某所医学院教授的资历,同时也可以不用去越南服兵役。几个月后的某

For more than twenty years afterwards, at the University of California in San Francisco, I enjoyed many measurements and many results. Despite the common myths about science, it was not lonely work. Much of the pleasure came from companionship---with my colleague, Mike Bishop---a newly-minted Harvard Overseer---and our students, post-docs, and technicians. Most of our experiments lacked discernable practical goals. We followed our **hunches** [hunch; n. 预感、直觉], working with cancer viruses from chickens and mice, supported largely by grants from the NIH. Eventually, over many years, patterns emerged. We had learned that cancer genes in viruses are derived from normal cellular genes---some of the genes that guide our growth and development. These genes, now called oncogenes, undergo the **mutation**s [mutation; n. 变化、变异] that are the defining events in cancer. Obscure viruses from experimental animals had in this way allowed us to touch directly the heart of human cancer. A path to understanding had been opened.

Like researchers in all fields, I have also known disappointment, boredom, surprise, and even irony. One example was especially instructive. The painful reality of cancer has always loomed in the background of my work, because my mother and her mother died of breast cancer. For this reason, for many years my lab studied a virus that causes breast cancer in mice, in hopes of finding relatives of human breast cancer genes. Ultimately, we discovered interesting genes that guide formation of the brain and other organs. But, in this case, they don't appear to be involved in human cancer of any kind. There is no simple road map for this kind of research.

In 1989, our discovery of oncogenes was publicly recognized with the award of a Nobel Prize. Four years later, when President Clinton and Secretary Shalala invited me to become the Director of the NIH, I could hardly say no. My indebtedness was deep. The chance to repay it with public service has been gratifying.

This new job has given me a deeper appreciation of the measured pace of progress in medical research. Every morning, on the way to my office, I cross the **portico** [n. 柱廊、门廊] from which Franklin Roosevelt dedicated the first NIH buildings on a late fall day in 1940. His paralyzed legs braced with metal, his energies worn down by his third Presidential campaign, his mind focused on the World War already being waged in Europe, FDR made a powerful statement about medical research:

一天，当我研究的用来发现基因表达方式的一种方法突然奏效时，我顿时全心全意地成了一个科学家。我用的这种技术并不特别新颖，研究的课题在世界也只有寥寥几人会感兴趣。但是那一刻，我知道了能对事物做出衡量是多么令人陶醉，等待结果的时候，会是多么的甜蜜。

从那以后的20多年里，在加州大学旧金山分校，我做了很多测量工作，得到了许多成果。尽管人们对科研普遍抱有神秘感，科学工作其实并不寂寞，其中很多的乐趣来自合作伙伴。我的合作伙伴包括迈克尔·毕晓普（他最近被选为哈佛理事会的监管员），还有我们的学生、博士后和技术人员等。我们大部分的实验并没有显而易见的实用目的，主要靠着NIH科研经费的支持。我们跟着预感走，对从鸡和老鼠身上提取的癌症病毒进行研究。终于，在许多年后，我们发现了一些固定的规律。我们了解到，病毒里的癌症基因其实来自正常细胞基因，这些基因影响着我们的发育和生长。这些基因现在被称为"癌症化基因"，它们发生病变的时候，就是癌症出现的关键时刻。从动物实验中看到的这些病毒表现，让我们能够直接逼近人类癌症的核心点———一条全新之路由此打开。

像所有领域里的研究人员一样，我也经历过失望、无聊、惊讶甚至嘲讽。其中一个例子尤其具有启发性。癌症给人们带来痛苦这个现实，一直笼罩着我的工作，因为我的母亲，还有她的母亲，都是患乳腺癌去世的。由于这一原因，我的实验室多年来一直在研究导致老鼠身上发生乳腺癌的一种病毒，希望能找到导致人类乳腺癌的类似基因。最后，我们发现了引导脑部和其他器官形成的有意思的基因。但是，这些基因好像和人类身上出现的癌症没有什么关联。在这类研究中，没有任何简单的路线图可以参考。

我们在1989年因为发现致癌基因而荣获诺贝尔奖。4年后，当克林顿总统和卫生部长沙拉拉邀请我担任NIH院长一职时，我无法说不。我受过许多恩惠，能通过参与公共服务作为回报，是很令人欣慰的事。

这项新的工作，使我更深刻地了解到医学研究的有序进展。每天早上，在去我办公室的路上，我都要经过一道门廊，1940年深秋的一天，富兰克林·罗斯福就是在那里为NIH的第一批建筑物揭幕。他瘫痪的双

The total defense, which this Nation seeks, [he said] involves a great deal more than building airplanes, ships, guns and bombs. We cannot be a strong Nation unless we are a healthy Nation. And so we must recruit not only men and materials but also knowledge and science in the service of national strength.

Roosevelt's optimism about medical research seems, in retrospect, amazing. Doctors could not prevent or treat the poliovirus infection that had paralyzed him nearly twenty years earlier. John Franklin Enders and vaccines were still in the future; the main therapies were iron lungs and warm baths. Most of the staples of modern medicine were also still unknown. Antibiotics. Hormone replacements. Effective drug therapies for psychotic illnesses. Pre-natal testing. Coronary bypass surgery and artificial joints. Also in the future were medications that could have lowered FDR's blood pressure and perhaps **forestalled** [forestall: v. 占先一步, 先发制人] the stroke that killed him less than five years later, at the now relatively young age of sixty three.

Still, FDR's optimism proved to be justified. Even before the War was over, the chemical synthesis of quinine improved treatment of malaria for soldiers in the Pacific, and the manufacturing of Fleming's penicillin effectively controlled wound infections for the first time in the history of warfare. Following the War, inspired by these successes, the Federal government made unprecedented investments in many fields of science, through the NIH and other agencies. These investments have been essential for the vitality of American science ever since.

Polio vaccines and other early successes that encouraged public enthusiasm for research are now the stuff of legends. Let's consider a more recent and less famous success that gives a different perspective on the pace of progress. About two months ago, as I began to worry about this talk, the senior Senator from Massachusetts, a member of the Harvard Class of 1956 and of our Senate authorizing committee, paid a visit to the NIH. He and I were sitting on a pediatric ward in our research hospital in Bethesda, listening to a 27 year old blind man who looked like a skinny 8 year old boy. The patient was born with a disease called **cystinosis** [n. [医] 胱氨酸病（一种先天性代谢疾患，其特点为胱氨酸尿以及胱氨酸晶体沉积于机体器官内）], having inherited one damaged gene from each parent. In this very rare condition, the amino acid **cystine** [n. [化] 胱安酸] cannot be removed from small sacs within his cells. As a result, cystine accumulates and forms crystals in those sacs, damaging

腿缠着金属板、他的精力在第3任总统选举中耗损很大,他的思绪缠绕于已经在欧洲进行的世界大战。但罗斯福还是就医学研究问题作了强有力的演讲:

这个国家寻求的全面防务,(他说),远不止于制造大量的飞机、军舰、枪支和弹药。除非我们有健康的国民,否则我们不可能成为一个强大的国家。因此,我们必须不仅吸引人员和物力,而且要运用知识和科学,来为增强国力服务。

事后看来,罗斯福对医学研究的乐观态度显得相当惊人。当时医生们还不能预防或治疗大约20年前使他瘫痪的小儿麻痹。约翰·富兰克林·恩德斯和他发明的有效疫苗还没出现,当时的主要疗法是靠人工呼吸器和热水浴。现代医学的大部分常用药品也还未发明。当时没有抗生素、激素替代品,没有治疗精神病患者的有效药物、产前测试、心脏搭桥手术和人工关节这些东西。那时也还没有可以降低血压的药物,否则他也许不至于在那之后的5年就死于中风,罗斯福去世时才63岁,如果放到现在,这还是一个相对年轻的年龄。

但是,事实证明,罗斯福的乐观是有道理的。甚至在二战还未结束之前,用化学综合法制成的奎宁,就为在太平洋作战的士兵改善了疟疾的防治;弗莱明发明的青霉素,在战争史上第一次为伤员的伤口感染提供了有效控制。二战结束后,在这些成就的鼓舞下,通过NIH和其他机构,联邦政府在许多科学领域投入了前所未有的资金。这些投资对美国科学后来展现的活力,起到了不可或缺的作用。

小儿麻痹症疫苗和其他医学研究的成功,激起了公众对研究的热情,这些现在已经快成了某种传说。让我们来看一下一个新近的、但没那么有名的成功事例。大约两个月前,在我开始为今天这个演讲操心的时候,一位来自马萨诸塞州的资深参议员、1956届的哈佛毕业生、同时也是我们参议院授权委员会的一个成员,到NIH来访问。他和我坐在我们在贝塞斯达[7]研究型医院的一个儿科病房里,听一位27岁的盲人讲话,他看

the kidneys, eyes, and other tissues.

The patient told us how he was rescued from death by a kidney transplant at the age of 10, gradually lost his vision, and has lived with chronic pain. Senator Kennedy asked whether he had brothers and sisters. The patient replied, quite matter-of-factly, that two older brothers had died from the disease when he was very young, because kidney transplants were not yet available. So he felt fortunate to have been born recently enough to benefit from a life-saving transplant---the procedure pioneered by the Harvard surgeon, Joseph Murray (who, as it happens, spoke to the Medical School graduates today). The patient was also glad that affected children born yet more recently could avoid the kidney disease altogether; a recently-developed medication prevents formation of the crystals. A few minutes later a normal looking, eleven year old boy who had inherited the same disorder bounded into the room and spoke animatedly about sports, hobbies, school---and about the unpleasant taste of the medicine he had been taking nearly all his life.

This episode embodies many of my messages today: the message that science can improve lives in ways that are elegant in design and moving in practice; that the Federal government, much **maligned** [malign, v. 诽谤. 说坏话] in current politics, can be a powerful force for public benefit; that the government can work productively with universities, where the cellular defect in cystinosis was studied, and with industries, where the new drug was manufactured; and, finally, that progress in medical science occurs at a pace that may seem slow at the time to desperate parents, but astoundingly rapid in retrospect. Just consider: in the space of a generation, this lethal disease was made survivable with transplants, then curable with drugs.

Despite such triumphs, we have a long way to go. Yes, we can treat cystinosis and a few other genetic diseases, but there are thousands of inherited conditions we do not even understand. Yes, we have controlled polio and smallpox, but we are now struggling around the world with a new and intractable virus, HIV, and worried about invasions by exotic viruses, like **Ebola** [n. 伊波拉病毒] and **Lassa Fever** [n. (医) 拉沙热 (由拉沙病毒引起的急性传染病)]. Yes, we can treat most bacterial infections with penicillin and other antibiotics, but many bacteria have now become resistant to what were once our most effective drugs. Yes, we have dramatically reduced the death rates for heart attacks and strokes, but we are still seeking ways to repair the hearts and brains damaged by

上去像个瘦瘦的 8 岁男孩。病人生来就患上一种名叫胱氨酸的疾病，因为他从父母双方身上，各继承了一个受损基因。这种非常罕见的疾病，使病人无法从其细胞内排除氨基酸，因此，胱氨酸在体内积累，并形成水晶状的碎块，从而破坏肾脏、眼睛和其他器官组织。

这位病人告诉我们，他在 10 岁时因为接受了肾脏移植手术而从死亡边缘获救，但逐渐失去视力，并忍受慢性疼痛。参议员肯尼迪[8]问他是否有兄弟姐妹。他实事求是地回答说，还在他很小的时候，他的两个哥哥就死于这种疾病，因为当时还没有肾脏移植技术。因此，他感到非常幸运，因为他赶上了能够拯救生命的器官移植技术，这项技术是哈佛大学外科医生约瑟夫·默里首创的，（很巧的是，今天为哈佛医学院毕业生演讲的，正好是默里先生。）那位病人还为在他之后出生的儿童高兴，因为一种最近才发明的药物，能够阻止水晶结块在病人体内形成，从而让病人完全避免患上肾脏疾病。几分钟后，一个看上去一切正常的 11 岁男孩跑进室内，他也患了同样的遗传疾病，却充满活力地谈起体育、他的爱好、学校，以及他从小就一直在吃的那种药味道如何不好。

这一插曲传达了我今天要讲的许多信息，这就是：科学可以用设计典雅和实践中动人的方式改善人们的生活。在目前的政治环境中备受指责的联邦政府，在谋取公共利益方面可以是一个强大的力量，而政府可以有效地与大学合作，因为大学对胱氨酸病的致残影响进行了研究。政府还可以有效地与工业界合作，因为药厂能制造出新药。最后，医学的进步在绝望的父母眼里，进展可能显得缓慢，但事后来看，其进步的速度令人难以置信。让我们来看一下：就在一代人的时间里，这种致命的疾病因为器官移植技术的出现而不再致命，后来又可通过药物治愈。

尽管取得了这些胜利，我们还有漫长的道路要走。是的，我们可以治好胱氨酸病和其他几种遗传疾病，但还有上千种我们了解不多的遗传病。是的，我们控制了小儿麻痹症和天花，但我们在全世界范围内，正忙于应付艾滋病这种新的棘手病毒，也担心像伊波拉和拉沙热这类外来的病毒。是的，我们可以用青霉素和其他抗生素来治疗大多数细菌感染，但许多细菌现在对曾经是最为有效的药物都形成了抗药性。是的，

poor blood flow. Yes, we know the mutant genes responsible for many cancers, but we haven't transformed that knowledge into better therapies. Yes, we have improved the well-being of most people in the industrialized countries, but **malaria** [n. 疟 疾], childhood diarrhea, and tuberculosis are still common in the developing world. And, yes, we have extended the average life span in this country to nearly eighty years, but we have made little progress against the maladies that make advanced age intolerable for so many people.

Old age and its illnesses are deepening concerns to all of us in this audience---even to youthful graduates. When Alexander Fleming spoke here 51 years ago, only one in seven graduates could expect to reach the age of 85. By conservative estimates, nearly half of you will live past that age. Today, less than four million Americans are over 85; when some of you reach 85, there will be about 20 million. This is not just good news. Today the government spends $25 billion each year on medical care for this group alone. Multiply that by five. Add on the costs of care for the much larger group between 65 and 85. Without more public revenues from taxes, there will be little or no money left for other things the government buys, including the scientific research that might help. Clearly, if science cannot soon relieve the disorders of aging, we will confront some impossible choices.

Of all these disorders, the one we fear most is **Alzheimer's Disease** [n. 阿尔茨海默病、老年痴呆症]. We are right to fear it. It is a modern polio, and more. It destroys the brain and the personality. Its victims become a burden to spouses and children. Unlike polio, once common and now eradicated, or cystinosis, rare and now curable, Alzheimer's Disease is both untreatable and common. Unless things change, nearly half of us who reach the age of 85 will have signs of the disease.

Until recently, all we knew about Alzheimer's Disease was the ugly appearance of brain slices under the microscope and the unremitting deterioration of mental function. Traditional methods --- chemistry and **enzymology** [n. (生化) 酶学], microbiology and immunology, so successful in approaching polio and cystinosis --- provided few clues.

Hope is coming from a new direction. One day about ten years ago, a middle-aged Massachusetts man in the early stages of Alzheimer's Disease sought help from Dr. Daniel Pollen, a neurologist at the University of Massachusetts. His was not the most common form of the disease---the onset was early, and his relatives

我们大大减少了心脏病和中风的死亡率,但我们仍未找到方法去修复因为血流量不足而损坏的心脏和大脑;是的,我们知道不少导致癌症的突变基因,不过我们还没有将那些知识转化为更好的治疗方法;是的,我们改善了工业化国家里大多数人的健康状况,但疟疾、儿童腹泻和肺结核等病,在发展中国家仍很常见;是的,在我们这个国家里,人均寿命已经延长到将近80岁,但我们在治疗让人难受的老年病方面,尚未取得多大进展。

老年及老年病,对今天在座的各位来说,都是令人日益关切的问题——哪怕是年轻的毕业生。当亚历山大·弗莱明51年前在这里发表毕业演讲时,七个毕业生中,只有一人能够指望活到85岁。现在按保守估计,眼下在座的毕业生,有近一半能活到这个年龄。今天,只有不到400万的美国人年龄在85岁以上,当你们活到85岁时,这个数字将达到近2000万。但这并不都是好消息。现在仅在这批人的医疗保健上,政府每年的开支就高达250亿美元。这个数字乘以5,再加上为照顾更加庞大的65岁到85岁之间的人群所需的费用,政府除非增税以带来更多的公众收入,否则除此之外,将很少有钱或根本没有什么钱留作他用,包括可能会于事有益的科学研究。显然,如果科学不能很快减轻老龄化带来的问题,我们将面对一些艰难的选择。

所有这些老年病中,我们最怕的是老年痴呆症。我们怕它是有道理的,这是现代的小儿麻痹症,甚至更糟。它摧毁大脑及人的性格,患者会成为配偶和子女的一个负担。它不像小儿麻痹症——它曾经流行,现在已被消除;或胱氨酸病,得这种病的人很少,而且现在可以治愈,老人痴呆症既常见又无法治愈。除非情况会有变化,否则我们当中有近一半的人活到85岁时,会出现患这种疾病的迹象。

直到最近,我们对老年痴呆症的了解只限于脑部切片在显微镜下看出来的病变,以及由此引起的大脑功能不断恶化。传统的方法——比如化学与酶学、微生物学和免疫学等,在对付小儿麻痹症和胱氨酸病有效的成功方法,对此病症提供不了任何线索。

一个新的研究方向给了我们希望。大约10年前的一天,马萨诸塞州的一位患早期老年痴呆症的中年男子求治于马萨诸塞大学的一位神经学

had been affected early too. With the help of the patient's family, Dr. Pollen reconstructed the family lineage and traced the disease back to one woman, named Hannah, born one hundred and fifty years ago in a Byelorussian village. Scientists here at Harvard, at the NIH, in Canada, and several other places, have tracked several inherited forms of Alzheimer's Disease to abnormal versions of single genes. These genes have been isolated in pure form, and we know the proteins they encode.

So an obvious question: How do we get from Hannah's gene to a remedy for Alzheimer's Disease? This, of course, is precisely what I can't tell you. I can't even tell you how to proceed. All I can do is predict the pace and flavor of the first moments. I imagine a brilliant young neuroscientist, our new Enders, who is trying to understand cell survival---perhaps studying a hormone that keeps nerve cells alive in a dish. One of her students, working late, suggests a novel interaction between the hormone and the protein made from Hannah's gene. The results are surprising, but reproducible. Someone in a lab thousands of miles away learns about this experiment and tries it in a different way, perhaps in a mouse model, and gets an even more interesting result. A young Salk, seeking an anti-Alzheimer drug at a biotechnology company, tries to block the interaction. We are on our way.

What do we need to make these things happen? New talent. Enthusiasm for science. Money. Strong institutions.

In that speech from the NIH steps on the eve of World War Two, FDR knew what we needed:

All of us are grateful [he said] that we in the United States can still turn our thoughts and our attention to those institutions of our country which symbolize peace---institutions whose purpose it is to save life and not to destroy it.

FDR's confidence then underscores the dilemmas that now plague us in the aftermath of the Cold War. The Federal government is broke and under attack by its own citizens. Other countries have recently surpassed our rate of spending for basic research. Universities and colleges are more strapped for funds than ever before. And many industries are turning away from research investments.

Dr. Who is not the person who can solve these problems. Instead I hope to recruit you to my passions. That our institutions must be fit to nurture talent. That new

家丹尼尔·波伦医生。他的症状并不是该病最常见的那种形式,他比较早就得了这种病,他的亲属也在不很老时就受此病影响。在病人家属的帮助下,波伦医生摸清了该家族的族谱,并把病根追溯到一个名叫汉娜的女性身上,汉娜150年前出生在一个白俄罗斯村庄。来自哈佛的科学家和来自NIH,以及加拿大等其他一些地方的科学家一道,把几种遗传性的老年痴呆症归结于某些单个基因发生了不正常的变化。这些基因被提纯出来进行观察,我们得以了解其蛋白质编码。

一个明显的问题摆在了我们面前:我们如何从汉娜的基因中,找到一种治疗老人痴呆症的方法?当然,这正是我无法告诉你们的东西。我甚至无法告诉你们如何向前走。我所能做的,是预测发展的速度和关键时刻的情景。我设想会有一个年轻而优秀的神经科学家,我们时代的恩德斯,试图了解细胞生存的情况,也许其研究的,是看看某种荷尔蒙如何使神经干细胞在实验碟子里存活。而她的一位学生在工作到深夜时,提出一种新方法,使激素和从汉娜那里得来的基因产生反应。其结果是令人吃惊的,但可以复制。在几千英里外的某个人,知道这一试验后,用不同的方式进行尝试,也许是用老鼠实验,从而得到一个更有趣的结果。一个像索尔克一样的年轻人,在某家生物技术公司研制抗老年痴呆的药物,会试图用这些知识来找到阻止病因变化的办法。我们就这样起步了。

我们需要具备什么,才能使这些事情发生呢?新的人才、对科学的热情、资金、强有力的机构。

在二战前夕,罗斯福在NIH的台阶上发表演讲时,他知道我们需要的东西:

> 我们大家都很感激,我们在美国的人,仍然可以把我们的头脑和注意力,放在象征着和平的、我们国家的这些机构上,这些机构的目的是拯救生命,而不是摧毁生命。

罗斯福的信心,点明了我们当前在冷战后面临的困境。联邦政府没钱了,而且受到自己公民的抨击。其他国家最近在为基础研究投入的比

talent is essential to advance science. And that science, a source of beauty and delight, is also our best hope for fighting the threats of Alzheimer's and many other diseases.

Several hundreds of you graduating today have already enlisted to fight these battles, as future scientists or physicians. But the battle does not engage only those on the front lines. It will affect all of you. As worried patients, parents, and caretakers of parents. As taxpayers and good citizens of the world. And as thoughtful Harvard graduates, who know that science---like "no empire, no scct, no star"---can eventually change "the whole face and state of things throughout the world."

Congratulations to you and good luck.

例方面,最近已经超出了我们。各大学和学院比以往任何时候都更捉襟见肘,许多工业界都避开不愿为研发投资。

我这个无名博士,不是可以解决这些问题的人。所以我希望延揽你们加入到我的行列中来,因为我们的机构必须适合于培养人才,因为新的人才是推动科学进步的关键,因为科学是美的源泉、乐趣的所在,同时也是我们治疗老人痴呆症和许多其他疾病的最佳希望。

今天毕业的同学中,已经有几百人作为未来的科学家或医生,要投入这些战斗中。但这场战斗不只是这些战斗在第一线的人的事情。它会影响到你们所有人,不管你们作为病人、家长和照顾老年父母的人,还是作为纳税人和称职的世界公民。而且作为有思想的哈佛毕业生,你们知道,**"没有任何一个帝国、任何一个教派、任何一个明星"**,能像科学那样,最终**"对人类事务有这样大的影响"**。

祝贺你们,祝你们好运!

1 《哈佛深红报》(The Harvard Crimson), 哈佛大学的校报。

2 亚历山大·弗莱明 (Alexander Fleming, 1881—1955), 英国细菌学家, 他首先发现了青霉素。

3 弗朗西斯·培根 (Francis Bacon, 1561—1626), 英国文艺复兴时期最重要的散文家、哲学家。他不但在文学、哲学上多有建树, 在自然科学领域里也取得了重大成就。

4 富兰克林·德拉诺·罗斯福 (Franklin Delano Roosevelt), 常被简称为 FDR, 是二战时的美国总统。

5 若纳斯·索尔克 (Jonas Salk, 1914—1995), 美国科学家和医学家, 他在上世纪 50 年代研制出能有效防疫的小儿麻痹疫苗, 因而蜚声科学界。为验证疫苗有效, 他曾首先在自己身上, 还有他的妻子及三个儿子身上做试验。

6 阿默斯特学院 (Amherst College) 建于 1821 年, 是美国一所著名的私立文科学院。

7 贝塞斯达 (Bethesda), 在美国首都华盛顿郊区, 是 NIH 总部所在地。

8 特德·肯尼迪 (Ted Kennedy), 是来自马萨诸塞州的资深参议员, 美国前总统约翰·肯尼迪的弟弟。

玛德琳·奥尔布赖特（1937— ）

　　玛德琳·奥尔布赖特是美国历史上首位女性国务卿，作为政治家，她在美国和世界政坛广为人知。

　　玛德琳·科贝尔·奥尔布赖特原名玛丽·亚娜·科尔贝洛娃（Marie Jana Korbelová），1937年出生于捷克首都布拉格的犹太家庭。第二次世界大战时，她的祖父母死于纳粹集中营，她和父母家人逃往伦敦，经常在防空洞中躲避空袭。她的父亲科贝尔是外交官兼学者，曾任捷克斯洛伐克驻南斯拉夫大使，流亡到美国后，创办了丹佛大学的国际研究学院，他是美国后来的另一位女性国务卿赖斯的启蒙老师。

　　奥尔布赖特曾在威尔斯利学院学习政治学，后进入哥伦比亚大学并获哲学博士学位。毕业后，奥尔布赖特在乔治敦大学任国际事务学教授兼国家政策中心主任，专门研究美国与东欧国家之间的关系。

　　奥尔布赖特于1976年进入政界，担任吉米·卡特总统的国家安全委员会委员，主管外交立法事务。卡特竞选总统连任失败后，奥尔布赖特重返学术界，回到乔治敦大学教书并著书立说。1992年克林顿担任总统时，奥尔布赖特被任命为美国驻联合国大使。1996年克林顿连任总统后，任命奥尔布赖特为美国国务卿。在克林顿执政的8年时间里，奥尔布赖特参与了一系列重大政治事件，从中东和平会谈到北约维和科索沃战乱，在波黑战争、朝鲜问题、中美关系等国际事务上都有着重要影响。她曲折独特的经历使她特别强调民主自由的意义和国家安全的重要性。在外交事务中，她以尽职尽责、坚定果敢、作风强硬著称。

1997

Shaping History as a Pathfinder
勇于做创造历史的人

Madeleine Albright 玛德琳·奥尔布莱特

Thank you. Thank you, President Pforzheimer. Governor Weld, President Rudenstine, President Wilson, fellow honorands, men and women of Harvard, all those who comprise the Harvard community, guests and friends, thank you.

I'm delighted to be here on this day of celebration and rededication. To those of you who are here from the class of '97, I say congratulations. (Applause.) You may be in debt, but you made it. (Laughter.) And if you're not in debt now, after the alumni association gets through with you, you will be. (Laughter and applause.)

In fact, I would like to solicit the help of this audience for the State Department budget. (Laughter.) It is under $20 billion.

As a former professor and current mother, I confess to loving graduation days - especially when they are accompanied by an honorary degree. I love the ceremony; I love the academic settings; and although it will be difficult for me today - let's be honest - I love to daydream during the commencement speech. (Laughter.)

Graduations are unique among the milestones of our lives, because they celebrate past accomplishments, while also anticipating the future. That is true for each of the graduates today, and it is true for the United States. During the past few years, we seem to have observed the 50th anniversary of everything. Through media and memory, we have again been witness to paratroopers filling the skies over Normandy; the liberation of Buchenwald; a sailor's kiss in Times Square; and Iron Curtain descending; and Jackie Robinson sliding home.

Today, we recall another turning point in that era. For on this day 50 years ago, Secretary of State George Marshall addressed the graduating students of this great university. He spoke to a class enriched by many who had fought for freedom, and deprived of many who had fought for freedom and died. The Secretary's words were plain; but his message reached far beyond the audience assembled in this yard to an American people weary of war and wary of new commitments, and to a Europe where life-giving connections between farm and market, enterprise and capital, hope and future had been severed.

Shaping History as a Pathfinder — Madeleine Albright
勇于做创造历史的人 玛德琳·奥尔布莱特

谢谢！谢谢各位！福兹海默董事长、维尔德州长、鲁登斯坦校长、威尔逊校长，今天接受荣誉学位的同仁们、所有的哈佛男女老少们，各位来宾和朋友，谢谢你们！

我很高兴在这欢庆的日子来到这里。对97届的毕业生们，我要说声祝贺！你们可能为付学费而背上了债务，但是你们扛过来了。如果你们现在无债一身轻，在校友会跟您联系上后，您又要举债了。

事实上，我想向在座的各位，为美国国务院的预算寻求点资助，还不到200亿美元呢！

作为一名曾经的教授，作为一个母亲，我不否认我喜爱毕业日——特别是当我还能捎带拿个荣誉学位的话。我喜欢毕业典礼，喜欢校园的氛围。虽然今天于我而言很难实现，但说句实话，我喜欢在毕业典礼演讲时做做白日梦。

毕业典礼在我们生活的里程碑中是很独特的事，因为在庆祝已取得成就的同时也展望未来，对今天的每一位毕业生来说是这样，对美国来说也是如此。在过去几年中，我们似乎老在庆祝各种50周年。通过媒体报道和人们的记忆，我们再次见证了布满诺曼底[1]天空上的伞兵，布痕瓦尔德集中营[2]的解放，那名水手在时代广场的狂吻[3]；目击了铁幕[4]的降临，还有杰奇·罗宾逊[5]滑回本垒。

今天，我们会回想起那个时代的另一个转折点。就在50年前的今天，乔治·马歇尔国务卿对这所著名大学的毕业生发表演讲。他所面对的毕业班，有许多人曾为自由而战，也有许多人为争取自由而献身。国务卿的话看似平淡，但他发出的信息却远远穿过聚集在这个校园里的听众，传达到美国人民的耳中。美国人民当时厌倦战争，也不想再做出新的承诺。他的话也传递到欧洲，当时那里的农场和市场的供求、企业和资本之间的联系、希望和未来之间的依附关系，都已被生生切断。

马歇尔国务卿没有诉诸于华丽的辞藻，他只是说，帮助世界恢复正常的经济状况，对美国来说是一件自然而然的事，因为如果没有这一点，就没有政治的稳定与和平的保证。他没有为他的计划冠

Secretary Marshall did not adorn his rhetoric with high-flown phrases, saying only that it would be logical for America to help restore normal economic health to the world, without which there could be no political stability and no assured peace. He did not attach to his plan the label, Made in America; but rather invited European ideas and required European countries to do all they could to help themselves. His vision was inclusive, leaving the door open to participation by all, including the Soviet Union - and so there would be no repetition of the punitive peace of Versailles - also to Germany.

British Foreign Secretary Ernest Bevin called the Marshall Plan a "lifeline to sinking men," and it was - although I expect some women in Europe were equally appreciative. (Laughter.)

By extending that lifeline, America helped unify Europe's west around democratic principles, and planted seeds of transatlantic partnership that would soon blossom in the form of NATO and the cooperative institutions of a new Europe. Just as important was the expression of American leadership that the Marshall Plan conveyed.

After World War I, America had withdrawn from the world, shunning responsibility and avoiding risk. Others did the same. The result in the heart of Europe was the rise of great evil. After the devastation of World War II and the soul-withering horror of the Holocaust, it was not enough to say that the enemy had been vanquished, that what we were against had failed.

The generation of Marshall, Truman and Vandenberg was determined to build a lasting peace. And the message that generation conveyed, from the White House, from both parties on Capitol Hill, and from people across our country who donated millions in relief cash, clothing and food was that this time, America would not turn inward; America would lead.

Today, in the wake of the Cold War, we, too, must heed the lessons of the past, accept responsibility and lead. Because we are entering a century in which there will be many interconnected centers of population, power and wealth, we cannot limit our focus, as Marshall did in his speech to the devastated battleground of a prior war. Our vision must encompass not one,

之以"美国制定"的名称,而是包容欧洲提出的观点,并要求欧洲国家付出全力,帮助他们自己。他的设想是富有包容性的,参与的大门对所有国家开放,其中包括前苏联,而且为了防止凡尔赛和约那种惩罚性的条约不再重演,他的计划也帮助战败的德国。

当时的英国外交大臣欧内斯特·贝文把马歇尔计划称为"抛给溺水者的一条救生索",的确是这样,虽然我觉得欧洲的一些女性也会同样心怀感激[6]。

多亏了这条救生索,美国帮助西欧国家统一在民主的原则下,并种下了跨大西洋伙伴关系的种子,这个种子很快就以北约的形式开花,促进了新欧洲的合作。同样重要的,是"马歇尔计划"表达了美国起带头作用的意愿。

第一次世界大战后,美国从世界舞台上撤了回来,回避责任、不愿冒险,其他国家也是如此。结果在欧洲的心脏地带冒出了一个极恶之国。经历过二战的破坏和惨绝人寰的法西斯大屠杀这样的灾难之后,只是说敌人已被消灭,我们反对的东西已经失败,已远远不够。

马歇尔、杜鲁门和范登堡他们那一代人,决心要建设一个持久的和平。从白宫的领袖、国会山上议会的两党,到捐献了亿万救济现金、衣物和食品的美国各地民众,都想表达一个信息:这一次,美国不会再闭关自守,美国要起带头作用。

今天,在冷战之后,我们必须汲取过去的教训,承担重任,起到带头作用。因为在我们正要进入的新世纪中,会出现许多相互紧密关联的人口中心、势力中心和财富中心,正如马歇尔在讲话中对饱受前一场战争蹂躏的世界所说的,我们不能限定自己的重点。我们的愿景,必须包括不仅一个大陆,而是每一个大陆。

不同于马歇尔那一代,我们所面对的不是一个单一的迫在眉睫的威胁。我们面对的危险不再那么显而易见,而是更加多样化:有老的,比如种族冲突;有新的,比如信件炸弹;有些是细微的,比如气候变化;也有一些是致命的,比如担心核武器落入坏人之手。为

but every continent.

Unlike Marshall's generation, we face no single galvanizing threat. The dangers we confront are less visible and more diverse - some as old as ethnic conflict, some as new as letter bombs, some as subtle as climate change, and some as deadly as nuclear weapons falling into the wrong hands. To defend against these threats, we must take advantage of the historic opportunity that now exists to bring the world together in an international system based on democracy, open markets, law and a commitment to peace.

We know that not every nation is yet willing or able to play its full part in this system. One group is still in transition from centralized planning and totalitarian rule. Another has only begun to dip its toes into economic and political reform. Some nations are still too weak to participate in a meaningful way. And a few countries have regimes that actively oppose the premises upon which this system is based.

Because the situation we face today is different from that confronted by Marshall's generation, we cannot always use the same means. But we can summon the same spirit. We can strive for the same sense of bipartisanship that allowed America in Marshall's day to present to both allies and adversaries a united front. We can invest resources needed to keep America strong economically, militarily and diplomatically - recognizing, as did Marshall, that these strengths reinforce each other. We can act with the same knowledge that in our era, American security and prosperity are linked to economic and political health abroad. And we can recognize, even as we pay homage to the heroes of history, that we have our own duty to be authors of history.

Let every nation acknowledge today the opportunity to be part of an international system based on democratic principles is available to all. This was not the case 50 years ago.

Then, my father's boss, Jan Masaryk, foreign minister of what was then Czechoslovakia - was told by Stalin in Moscow that his country must not participate in the Marshall Plan, despite its national interest in doing so. Upon his return to Prague, Masaryk said it was at that moment, he understood he

了抵御这些威胁,我们必须珍惜现有的这样一个历史性的机遇,在依据民主体制、市场开放、法律至上和追求和平为基础的国际体系下,让世界团结在一起。

我们知道,不是每一个国家都愿意或能够充分参与这个体系。有些国家仍处于从集中规划和极权统治中过渡出来的阶段,另一些国家才刚刚开始试行经济和政治改革。有些国家仍然很弱,无法以一种有意义的方式参与。还有几个国家的政体,极力反对民主体系。

我们今天所处的形势也与马歇尔那一代人大不相同,所以我们不能总是采用同样的方式,但是,我们可以拿出同样的精神。我们应当追求马歇尔时代的那种双方合作的政策,让美国同盟友结成一个统一战线,同时也容纳对手。我们要投入足够的资源,以保持美国在经济、军事和外交方面的强大,就像马歇尔一样,认识到这些力量会互相加强、相得益彰。我们采取行动时要认识到,在我们这个时代,美国的安全和繁荣,与世界经济和政治的健康程度是相关的。而且,即使我们在向历史上的英雄们致敬时,还要意识到,我们有自己的责任,我们也是书写历史的人。

要让每一个国家都意识到,今天可以参与以民主原则为基础的国际体系,这个机会对每个国家都是开放的,而 50 年前则不是这样。

那时,斯大林在莫斯科对我父亲的上司、当时的捷克斯洛伐克外交部长扬·马萨里克[7]说,捷克不得参与"马歇尔计划",尽管这样做其实符合捷克的国家利益。回到布拉格后,马萨里克说,在那一刻,他明白了他的政府无法在自己的国土上做主。

今天,没有斯大林这样的人在发号施令,如果一个国家现在还孤立于国际社会,要么是因为这个国家还太弱,无法达到国际标准,要么是因为其领导人故意选择了无视这些标准。

上周在荷兰,克林顿总统说,我们不会把欧洲的任何一个民主国家排斥在跨大西洋共同体之外。今天我要说,世界上所有的国家,都不会被排除在我们正在建设的全球体系之外。每一个国家,只要希望参与,并愿意尽一切可能帮助自己的话,美国就会帮助它们找

was employed by a government no longer sovereign in its own land.

Today, there is no Stalin to give orders. If a nation is isolated from the international community now, it is either because the country is simply too weak to meet international standards, or because its leaders have chosen willfully to disregard those standards.

Last week in the Netherlands, President Clinton said that no democratic nation in Europe would be left out of the transatlantic community. Today I say that no nation in the world need be left out of the global system we are constructing. And every nation that seeks to participate and is willing to do all it can to help itself will have America's help in finding the right path. (Applause.)

In Africa, poverty, disease, disorder and misrule have cut off millions from the international system. But Africa is a continent rich both in human and natural resources. And today, it's best new leaders are pursuing reforms that are helping private enterprise and democratic institutions to gain a foothold. Working with others, we must lend momentum by maintaining our assistance, encouraging investment, lowering the burden of debt and striving to create successful models for others to follow.

In Latin America and the Caribbean, integration is much further advanced. Nations throughout our hemisphere are expanding commercial ties, fighting crime, working to raise living standards and cooperating to ensure that economic and political systems endure.

In Asia and the Pacific, we see a region that has not only joined the international system, but has become a driving force behind it - a region that is home to eight of the ten fastest growing economies in the world.

With our allies, we have worked to ease the threat posed by North Korea's nuclear program, and invited that country to end its self-imposed isolation. We have encouraged China to expand participation in the international system and to observe international norms on everything from human rights to export of arms-related technologies.

Finally, in Europe, we are striving to fulfill the vision Marshall proclaimed but the Cold War prevented - the vision of a Europe, whole and free, united - as President Clinton said this past week - "not by the force of arms, but by

到正确的道路。

在非洲，贫穷、疾病、混乱和暴政把千百万人隔离于国际体系之外。但是，非洲是一个人力资源和自然资源都很丰富的大陆。今天，非洲新的领导者中，最优秀的那些人正在推行改革，帮助民营企业和民主机构站稳脚跟。在与其他人的合作中，我们必须继续提供援助，鼓励投资，降低债务负担，并努力创造成功的模式，让其他人有学习的榜样。

在拉丁美洲和加勒比地区，推进一体化的步伐更加深入。在我们这个半球上的国家扩大商业关系，打击犯罪，努力提高生活水平并推进合作，以确保经济和政治制度的持续稳定。

在亚洲和太平洋地区，我们看到，这个地区不仅加入了国际体系，而且已成为这个体系背后的驱动力——世界上增长最快的10个经济体中，这个地区占了8个。

我们同盟国一道，努力缓解朝鲜的核计划所构成的威胁，并鼓励该国结束自我孤立的状况。我们鼓励中国扩大在国际体系中的参与，并遵守从人权到出口、与武器相关技术的这些国际规范。

最后，在欧洲，我们正在努力实现马歇尔宣布的愿景，但这个愿景被冷战干扰。愿景描绘了一个完整、自由和团结的欧洲，正如克林顿总统在一周前所说，实现这个愿景的途径，"不是通过武力，而是通过和平"。

半个世纪前，美国的领导作用，帮助西欧加快了繁荣和民主。同样的，今天跨大西洋两岸的国家，都在帮助欧洲的新兴自由国家治理其经济困难，加强法治的管理。

下个月在马德里，北约将邀请来自中欧和东欧的民主国家，作为新成员加入，同时对愿意加入北约的其他国家也敞开大门。这不会像有些人担心的那样，在欧洲制造一个新的分裂。相反，它只是清除掉半个世纪前强加在欧洲的一条不公平和不自然的界线，这将鼓励有关国家解决领土争端、尊重少数族裔的人权，并完成改革的进程。

possibilities of peace."

Where half a century ago, American leadership helped lift Western Europe to prosperity and democracy, so today the entire transatlantic community is helping Europe's newly free nations fix their economies and cement the rule of law.

Next month in Madrid, NATO will invite new members from among the democracies of Central and Eastern Europe, while keeping the door to future membership open to others. This will not, as some fear, create a new source of division within Europe. On the contrary, it is erasing the unfair and unnatural line imposed half a century ago; and it is giving nations an added incentive to settle territorial disputes, respect minority and human rights and complete the process of reform.

NATO is a defensive alliance that harbors no territorial ambitions. It does not regard any state as its adversary, certainly not a democratic and reforming Russia that is intent on integrating with the West, and with which it has forged an historic partnership, signed in Paris just nine days ago.

Today, from Ukraine to the United States, and from Reykjavik to Ankara, we are demonstrating that the quest for European security is no longer a zero-sum game. NATO has new allies and partners. The nations of Central and Eastern Europe are rejoining in practice the community of values they never left in spirit. And the Russian people will have something they have not had in centuries - a genuine and sustainable peace with the nations to their west.

The Cold War's shadow no longer darkens Europe. But one **specter** [n. 幽灵; 恐怖的根源] from the past does remain. History teaches us that there is no natural geographic or political endpoint to conflict in the Balkans, where World War I began and where the worst European violence of the past half-century occurred in this decade. That is why the peaceful integration of Europe will not be complete until the Dayton Peace Accords in Bosnia are fulfilled. (Applause.)

When defending the boldness of the Marshall Plan 50 years ago, Senator Arthur Vandenberg observed that it does little good to extend a 15-foot rope to a man drowning 20 feet away. Similarly, we cannot achieve

北约是一个防御性联盟,不抱有领土野心。它不把任何国家当做对手,当然也不会针对一个民主的、正在改革的俄罗斯。而俄罗斯正想与西方交融,就在 9 天前,俄罗斯与西方在巴黎签署了一个历史性的伙伴关系协议。

今天,从乌克兰到美国,从雷克雅未克到安卡拉,我们正在表明的对欧洲安全的追求,不再是零和游戏。北约有了新的盟友和伙伴,中欧和东欧国家带着它们从未放弃的社会价值观,重新加入北约。而俄罗斯人民将会拥有他们几个世纪来都没能得到的东西:同其西边的国家,实现一个真正和持久的和平。

冷战的阴影不再笼罩欧洲。但是,一个过去留下来的幽灵依然存在。历史告诉我们,巴尔干地区的冲突没有天然的地理或政治终结点,第一次世界大战就是从那里开始的,欧洲过去半个世纪中最糟糕的暴力事件,以发生在近十年的最为残酷。这就是为什么欧洲的和平融合,在波斯尼亚实现"代顿和平协定"之前,将是不完整的。

50 年前,阿瑟·范登堡参议员在褒扬马歇尔计划的气魄时表示,如果有人在 20 英尺以外的距离溺水,你向他扔出一条 15 英尺长的绳子,是没有用处的。同样,我们在波斯尼亚不能仅仅满足于避免一触即发的战争,那样实现不了我们的目标。我们必须竭尽所能,帮助波斯尼亚人民实现永久和平。

几天前,克林顿总统已批准了使和平进程不可逆转的措施,让每一方都明确和平成功和他们自己的利害关系。在过去的这个周末,我亲自去到该地区,向他们阐明,如果当事方希望得到国际社会的接受和我们的援助,他们就必须履行自己的承诺,包括充分配合国际刑事法庭的工作。

该法庭的审判,代表的不仅是波斯尼亚和卢旺达的选择,对世界来说也是一个选择。我们可以接受"暴行的发生是不可避免"的说法,但我们也可以提出更高标准。**我们可以选择忘记那些只有上帝和受害者才有权去原谅的罪行,但我们要牢记本世纪最深刻的教训,那就是:当邪恶没人阻挡时,将会带来更多的邪恶。**

our objectives in Bosnia by doing just enough to avoid immediate war. We must do all we can to help the people of Bosnia to achieve permanent peace.

In recent days, President Clinton has approved steps to make the peace process irreversible, and give each party a clear stake in its success. This past weekend, I went to the region to deliver in person the message that if the parties want international acceptance or our aid, they must meet their commitments - including full cooperation with the international war crimes tribunal. (Applause.)

That tribunal represents a choice not only for Bosnia and Rwanda, but for the world. We can accept atrocities as inevitable, or we can strive for a higher standard. **We can presume to forget what only God and the victims have standing to forgive, or we can heed the most searing lesson of this century which is that evil, when unopposed, will spawn more evil.** (Applause.)

The majority of Bosnia killings occurred not in battle, but in markets, streets and playgrounds, where men and women like you and me, and boys and girls like those we know, were abused or murdered - not because of anything they had done, but simply for who they were.

We all have a stake in establishing a precedent that will deter future atrocities, in helping the tribunal make a lasting peace easier by separating the innocent from the guilty; in holding accountable the perpetrators of ethnic cleansing; and in seeing that those who consider rape just another tactic of war answer for their crimes. (Applause.)

Since George Marshall's time, the United States has played the leading role within the international system - not as sole **arbiter** [n. 仲裁人．主宰者] of right and wrong, for that is a responsibility widely shared, but as pathfinder - as the nation able to show the way when others cannot.

In this decade, America led in defeating Saddam Hussein; encouraging nuclear stability in the Korean Peninsula and in the former Soviet Union; restoring elected leaders to Haiti; negotiating the Dayton Accords; and supporting the peacemakers over the bomb throwers in the Middle East and other strategic regions.

波斯尼亚多数的残杀事件，不是发生在战斗中，而是在市场、街道、游乐场这些地方，像你和我一样的男男女女，像我们所知道的少年儿童，受到虐待或杀害。不是因为他们做了任何事，而仅仅是因为他们的种族归属。

我们有责任去建立这样一个先例，以阻止今后这类暴行的发生，我们要让国际刑事法庭能够更好地给我们带来一个持久和平，而这个法庭的工作就是区分谁有罪、谁无罪，追究实行种族清洗的始作俑者，并将那些把强奸异族妇女当做他们进行战争的一个手段的人，绳之以法。

从乔治·马歇尔时代起，美国就在国际体系内发挥着一个领导作用，不是作为孰对孰错的唯一仲裁者，因为做出这样判决的责任是由大家共享的，而是作为一个探路者——美国要在其他国家做不到的时候，找到正确的方向。

在最近的这十年中，美国带领了打败萨达姆·侯赛因的行动；鼓励在朝鲜半岛和前苏联地区的核武器稳定；恢复海地由民选领导管理；商议了"代顿协议"的达成；并在中东和关键地区，支持和平缔造者，而不是扬威耀武者。

我们担当这种领导作用，按泰迪·罗斯福[8]的话来说，不是因为我们想做"一个国际事物中多管闲事的人"，而是因为我们从经验中知道，我们的利益，以及我们盟友的利益，会受到这样一些情况的影响，比如区域性的或某些国家内部发生战争、还有权力真空让犯罪分子和恐怖分子有机可乘，形成对民主的威胁。

但美国不能独自做这项工作。我们可以指出方向、找到道路，但其他人必须愿意一起上路，并对自己的事情负起责任。他们必须愿意在自身的资源和能力范围内采取行动，参与建立这样一个世界，即大家可以共享经济增长、暴力冲突受到制止，而且那些遵守法律的人会更有安全感。

在萨拉热窝时，我走访了一个一度被称为"狙击手小巷"的游乐场，在那里，曾有不少波斯尼亚人因为种族仇恨而被杀害。但过

We welcome this leadership role, not in Teddy Roosevelt's phrase, because we wish to be "an international Meddlesome Matty," but because we know from experience that our interests and those of our allies may be affected by regional or civil wars, power vacuums that create opportunities for criminals and terrorists and threats to democracy.

But America cannot do the job alone. We can point the way and find the path, but others must be willing to come along and take responsibility for their own affairs. Others must be willing to act within the bounds of their own resources and capabilities to join in building a world in which shared economic growth is possible, violent conflicts are constrained, and those who abide by the law are progressively more secure.

While in Sarajevo, I visited a playground in the area once known as "sniper's alley," where many Bosnians had earlier been killed because of ethnic hate. But this past weekend, the children were playing there without regard to whether the child in the next swing was Muslim, Serb or Croat. They thanked America for helping to fix their swings, and asked me to place in the soil a plant which they promised to nourish and tend.

It struck me then that this was an apt metaphor for America's role 50 years ago, when we planted the seeds of renewed prosperity and true democracy in Europe; and a metaphor as well for America's role during the remaining years of this century and into the next.

As this great university has recognized, in the foreign students it has attracted, the research it conducts, the courses it offers, and the sensibility it conveys, those of you who have graduated today will live global lives. You will compete in a world marketplace; travel further and more often than any previous generation; share ideas, tastes and experiences with counterparts from every culture; and recognize that to have a full and rewarding future, you will have to look outwards.

As you do, and as our country does, we must aspire to set high standards set by Marshall, using means adapted to our time, based on values that endure for all time; and never forgetting that America belongs on the side of freedom. (Applause.)

I say this to you as Secretary of State. I say it also as one of the many

去的这个周末，孩子们在那里玩耍，而不用去区分那些荡秋千的孩子谁是穆斯林、谁是塞尔维亚人或是克罗地亚人。他们感谢美国帮助修好秋千，并请我种下一棵植物，他们保证会好好地浇灌培育它。

我忽然想到，这是 50 年前美国所担任角色的一个贴切比喻，当时我们在欧洲种下了再次繁荣和真正民主的种子；植树的比喻也同样适用于在本世纪剩下的这些年里，以及在下一个世纪里，美国所担负的角色。

就像（哈佛）这所伟大的大学所认识到的，它所吸引的外国学生、进行的研究、提供的课程，以及它传达出的感性，都表明今天毕业的同学将过着一种全球性的生活。你们将在世界市场上竞争，比前辈人旅行得更多更远，和来自各种文化的同行交流思想、爱好和分享经验。你们会认识到，若想有一个完整的和有意义的未来，你必须向外看。

当你们这样做，而且我们的国家也这样做时，我们必须努力达到马歇尔定的高标准，运用适应我们时代的手段，恪守经过时间考验的价值观，并且永远不要忘记，美国是站在自由这一边的。

我作为国务卿对你们说这番话。我的生活受到本世纪中叶欧洲动荡事件的影响，也受益于美国在本世纪起了领导作用，我是生活在其中的一员，我也以这个身份讲话。

我还记得，战争期间我在英国，坐在防空洞里，靠唱歌驱散恐惧，并感谢上帝给我们送来了美国的帮助。我还记得，在战争结束后我来到美国，在这里得到接纳，使我的父母和我的新祖国感到骄傲。

因为我的父母及时逃离，我躲过了希特勒的屠杀，但让我们一直感到哀伤的是，数以百万计的人没能逃过。由于美国的慷慨接纳，我逃脱了斯大林的迫害，但千百万的人没能逃脱。由于杜鲁门和马歇尔那一代人的远见，我有幸生活在自由中，但数以亿计的人还从来没有过这样的机会。由于没有对 50 年前那个时代的印象，这些对你们来说可能很难理解，但你们有必要努力去了解。

people whose lives have been shaped by the turbulence of Europe during the middle of this century, and by the leadership of America throughout this century.

I can still remember in England, during the war, sitting in the bomb shelter, singing away the fear and thanking God for America help. I can still remember, after the war, arriving here in the United States, where I wanted only to be accepted and to make my parents and my new country proud.

Because my parents fled in time, I escaped Hitler. To our shared and constant sorrow, millions did not. Because of America's generosity, I escaped Stalin. Millions did not. Because of the vision of Truman-Marshall generation, I have been privileged to live my life in freedom. Millions have still never had that opportunity. It may be hard for you, who have no memory of that time 50 years ago, to understand. But it is necessary that you try to understand.

Over the years, many have come to think of World War II as the last good war, for if ever a cause was just, that was it. And if ever the future of humanity stood in the balance, it was then.

Two full generations of Americans have grown up since that war - first mine, now yours; two generation of boys and girls, who have seen the veterans at picnics and parades and fireworks saluting with medals and ribbons on their chests; seeing the pride in their bearing and thinking, perhaps, **what a fine thing it must have been - to be tested in a great cause and to have prevailed.**

But today of all days, let us not forget that behind each medal and ribbon, there is a story of heroism yes, but also profound sadness; for World War II was not a good war. From North Africa to Solerno, from Normandy to the Bulge to Berlin, an entire continent lost to Fascism had to be taken back, village by village, hill by hill. And further eastward, from Tarawa to Okinawa, the death struggle for Asia was an assault against dug-in positions, surmounted only by unbelievable courage at unbearable loss.

Today, the greatest danger to America is not some foreign enemy. It is the possibility that we will fail to hear the example of that generation;

多年来，许多人认为二战是最后的一场正义战争，因为如果有什么正义的缘由的话，那就是它了。如果说人类的未来处于紧急关头，它当时就已经是了。

那场战争后，已经有两代美国人成长起来了，我们算一代，现在是你们这一代。这两代人都在野餐会、国庆游行和烟花晚会上，看到过胸前挂着奖章和绶带的退伍军人。看到他们骄傲的模样，我们就会想，也许，**能在一项伟大的事业中经受考验并取得胜利，真是一件足以告慰平生的事情。**

但是，特别在今天，我们不要忘记，每个奖章和绶带的背后都有一个英雄的故事，当然也会有深沉的悲伤，因为第二次世界大战不是一场好的战争。从北非到萨莱诺，从诺曼底到比利时，再到柏林，整个被法西斯占领的大陆，要靠一个村庄接一个村庄、一座山接一座山地收回。在东线，从塔拉瓦到冲绳，为争夺亚洲的殊死战斗，就是向着敌人阵地的冲锋，靠着令人难以置信的勇气和令人难以承受的损失，我们才得到胜利。

今天，美国最大的危险不是外国的敌人，而是听不到二战那一代人的声音，是我们让走向民主的势头停滞不前，是我们将自己自由地赖以依存的机构和原则视为理所当然，而且忘记本世纪历史所提醒我们的，即：国外的问题，如果熟视无睹，往往会波及美国。

从现在开始的一二十年后，我们是将被看做允许暴政和无政府状态重新泛起的"新孤立主义者"，还是被称为巩固民主原则在全球范围胜利的一代？我们是将被看做因为缺乏远见而制造金融危机的"新保护主义者"，还是被称作为世界各地的繁荣奠定了基础的一代？我们是将被看做在新的全球冲突播下种子时袖手旁观的世界级的"犹豫不决者"，还是被称作结成联盟、阻止侵略并维持和平而采取了强有力措施的一代？

无论是某个人，还是某代人，都不会有固定的成功路线图。归根结底，这是一个判断的问题、一个选择的问题。在作出这个抉择时，让我们记住，我们感到自豪的美国历史上的每一页，没有一页

that we will allow the momentum towards democracy to stall; take for granted the institutions and principles upon which our own freedom is based; and forget what the history of this century reminds us - that problems abroad, if left unattended, will all too often come home to America. (Applause.)

A decade or two from now, we will be known as neo-isolationists who allowed tyranny and lawlessness to rise again; or as the generation that solidified the global triumph of democratic principles. We will be known as the neo-protectionists, whose lack of vision produced financial meltdown; or as the generation that laid the groundwork for rising prosperity around the world. We will be known as the world-class ditherers, who stood by while the seeds of renewed global conflict were sown; or as the generation that took strong measures to forge alliances, deter aggression and keep the peace.

There is no certain road map to success, either for individuals or for generations. Ultimately, it is a matter of judgment, a question of choice. In making that choice, let us remember that there is not a page of American history, of which we are proud, that was authored by a chronic complainer or prophet of despair. We are doers. We have a responsibility, as others have had in theirs, not to be prisoners of history, but to shape history; a responsibility to fill the role of pathfinder, and to build with others a global network of purpose and law that will protect our citizens, defend our interests, preserve our values, and bequeath to future generations a legacy as proud as the one we honor today.

To that mission, I pledge my own best efforts and summon yours. Thank you very, very much.

是由那些总爱抱怨的人或绝望的预言者所写下的。我们是实干家。我们有责任,正如其他人有他们的责任一样,不被历史所束缚,而是去改造历史;我们有责任去担当探路者的角色,并与其他人一道,建立一个有目标、有法律的全球体系,以保护我们的公民、捍卫我们的利益、维护我们的价值观,并留给后代一个我们从前辈得到的同样令人骄傲的遗产。

为了这一目标,我保证付出自己最大的努力,我也呼吁你们这样做。非常非常感谢大家!

1 诺曼底(Normandy)登陆是第二次世界大战中盟军在欧洲西线战场发起的一场大规模攻势,战役发生在 1944 年 6 月 6 日早 6 时 30 分。诺曼底战役是目前为止世界上最大的一次海上登陆作战,将近 300 万名盟军士兵渡过英吉利海峡,登上法国诺曼底。诺曼底登陆成功,美英军队重返欧洲大陆,使第二次世界大战的战略态势发生了根本性转变。

2 布痕瓦尔德(Buchenwald)德国西南部的一个村庄,1937 至 1945 年,德国法西斯曾在此设立集中营,残酷屠杀了数万名反法西斯战士。

3 Sailor's kiss in Times Square,著名摄影作品,画面中一名水手忘情地亲吻一位女子,显示出人们在二战结束后的喜悦心情。

4 铁幕(Iron Curtain)指的是冷战时期将欧洲分为两个受不同政治势力影响的区域的界线。当时,东欧属于前苏联的势力范围,而西欧则属于美国的势力范围。这个词出自英国首相丘吉尔在美国密苏里州的威斯敏斯特学院所发表的题为《和平砥柱》的演讲。

5 杰奇·罗宾逊(Jackie Robinson,1919—1972),美国职棒大联盟史上第一位黑人球员。1947 年 4 月 15 日,他穿着 42 号球衣,作为一垒手出场比赛,此前,黑人球员只允许在自己的黑人联盟(Negro Leagues)打球。因此,罗宾逊踏上大联盟舞台的这一天,被公认为美国近代民权运动史上最重要的事件之一。

6 贝文讲话里用的词是"men"(男人),后来随着女权运动的兴起,英语中用词习惯也发生了改变,一般选用中性词,或言必称"男男女女"(men and women)。

7 扬·马萨里克(Jan Masaryk,1886—1948),捷克政治家,曾任驻英大使,二战中担任捷克在英国的流亡政府外交部长,并在捷克独立后继任外长。他曾批评前苏联不允许捷克接受马歇尔计划援助的做法。捷克共产党掌握政权两个星期后,马萨里克在捷克外交部院内坠楼身亡,死因至今仍无定论。

8 西奥多·罗斯福(Theodore Roosevelt,1815—1919),人称老罗斯福,昵称泰迪 Teddy,美国政治家,第 26 任总统。

玛丽·罗宾逊（1944— ）

玛丽·罗宾逊是爱尔兰共和国第一位女总统，卸任后担任过联合国人权事务高级专员。

1944年，玛丽·罗宾逊（本名玛丽·波尔克）出生于爱尔兰梅欧郡巴利纳镇，父母都是医生，信奉爱尔兰圣公会教。波尔克家族从13世纪起就居住在梅欧郡，祖辈中有许多成员积极参政，并且分属不同社团，从支持到反对皇室的都有。

罗宾逊曾在都柏林三一学院学习法律，后在哈佛大学法学院读研究生。1970年她与三一学院法学院的校友尼古拉斯·罗宾逊结婚。尼古拉斯·罗宾逊信奉新教，新教教义与爱尔兰圣公会教相冲突，为此，她的父母甚至没有参加她的婚礼。

罗宾逊的政治生涯始于1979年，先后担任都柏林市参议员及多个部门的法律顾问。1990年前后，罗宾逊作为劳工党的代表参加总统竞选，并于这年12月获胜，成为第7任爱尔兰总统。1997年9月，罗宾逊提前两个月结束她的总统任期，到联合国担任人权事务高级专员。

罗宾逊强调容忍和多元化的价值，被《时代》周刊誉为"爱尔兰的新象征"，代表了该国"重振的自信和自豪"。

罗宾逊还是都柏林大学的第24任校长，也是第一位女校长。她获得过剑桥大学、布朗大学等校的荣誉学位，2009年获得美国总统奥巴马颁发的自由奖章。

1998年适逢《世界人权宣言》发表50周年，在这篇演讲中，罗宾逊陈述了世界上仍然存在的人权问题，呼吁哈佛毕业生们多关注社会，用自己的能力帮助人们，投身到改善社会的活动中去。

1998

All Human Rights for All
让所有人享有一切人权

Mary Robinson 玛丽·罗宾逊

President Rudenstine, faculty, family and friends, and today's graduates:

It is a great honor and pleasure to be invited today to share this happy occasion, not only with the members of the graduating class of 1998, but also with the families and friends who have no doubt supported you along the way with their kind words of advice and encouragement. I do remember sitting where you sat this morning, when I was part of the class of 1968. I still remember how uncertain and insecure I felt but how proud my father was on the day. I called my father recently and told him that I would be coming here today and giving this address and that it would bring back memories. And being a good west-of-Ireland man, he remembered the important part. "It was damn wet," he reminded me. "It poured all day," which was true.

The class of 1998 has been much luckier with the weather--a bit of wind, a bit cool. I put on the gown this afternoon because I thought I'd need it--a bit of frisson in the air. But also I feel reinvigorated, because now, along with eight other very distinguished honorary graduates, I'm a member of the class of 1998, and I can come back in 30 years' time and feel quite young. All in all, it is a very special occasion, and I think it's appropriate that I would salute all of those have returned for your graduation years, particularly the threes and the eights. It was wonderful to see you file past coming in here this afternoon. But I think you can understand if I particularly want to focus on and to address my words to the class of 1998 because you are the future, you are those who take on the particular responsibility for the shaping of our society and of our world. Your families and your professors are rightfully proud of your achievements and they are delighted to see you graduate with futures so bright with promise.

I too am proud. I was very impressed with the three addresses we heard this morning, one in Latin and two in English. And if that's indicative of the class of 1998, then it's good to hear. I'm proud to see so many capable young men and women about to embark on a future career where they can put their years of learning and preparation to good use. Having passed through the rigors of a formal education, you are now ready to assume new responsibilities and tasks, becoming answerable only to yourselves with regards to your performance, your humanity and your soundness of judgement, in a world full of possibilities.

But I would ask you to remember that it's not a world full of possibilities for all. Each of you has been the beneficiary of a rare privilege. You have received an exceptional education at an exceptional place when there are many, in both your

鲁登斯坦校长、各位理事、各位老师、各位家长、各位毕业生们：

我很荣幸获得邀请，能在今天与你们分享这个幸福的时刻，不仅与1998届的毕业生同喜，而且与一路走来、一直用他们的建议和鼓励支持你们的家人和朋友们同贺。我还记得当我作为1968届毕业生的一员时，就坐在你们今天早晨所坐的地方。我仍然记得当时我是多么的忐忑不安，而我父亲在那天是多么的骄傲。

不久前我给父亲打电话，告诉他我今天要来这里发表演讲，并说这会引起我们对往事的一些回忆。他真是一个爱尔兰西部人，他所记得的重要事情是"那天潮湿得很"，他说"下了一整天的雨呢"，这倒是真的。

天气对1998届的同学足够关照，现在有点风，稍稍有点凉。今天下午我穿上学位袍，我需要它——我想体会衣摆在空气中抖动的感觉。但我也觉得振奋，因为现在和其他八位非常杰出的荣誉学位获得者一起，我也是1998届毕业生中的一员了。30年后我重返校园，依然感觉年轻。总之，这是一个非常特别的场合，我要向所有返校参加毕业周年纪念的校友，特别是那些带"3"字和"8"字年份的校友表示敬意，我想这是恰当的。今天下午，看你们列队来到这里，我非常开心。我特别要对1998届的同学讲几句话，因为你们代表着未来，你们的身上承担着塑造我们的社会和世界这样特别的重任。你们的家庭和你们的教授，有理由为你们的成就而自豪，他们也很高兴地看到，毕业时你们前程似锦。

我也很骄傲。我对今天早上听到的三个学生演讲印象非常深刻，一位演讲者用的是拉丁语，另外两位用英语。如果这是1998届学生才华的一种表现方式，那就太好了。看到这么多有能力的年轻人将要在事业上扬帆启航，把自己多年的学习和准备用到实处，我为此而骄傲。通过了这么严格的正规教育后，你们现在已经准备就绪，要在一个充满机遇的世界里接受新的任务，听从自己内心和价值观的评判，几分耕耘就会有几分收获。

但我提请你们记住，这个世界并不都是充满希望。你们每个人都得到格外的眷顾，在一个特别的地方接受特殊教育，与此同时，在你们的国家、我的国家，以及世界上许多地方，有很多像你们一样有天赋、有雄心壮志的人，却永远不会有你们这样的机会。我这样说，不是为了要

country and mine, and in many, many other parts of our world, who are just as innately talented and just as ambitious as you are but will never have such an opportunity. I say this not to make you feel guilty. You should be proud of what you have achieved. But **I do ask that you use your education to pursue only the worthiest of goals; goals that contribute to the betterment of the lives of others; and goals that give you personal satisfaction because of their contribution to the society we live in.**

1998 is an important year for goals and an important year for the Office of the United Nations High Commissioner for Human Rights. It is a year when we mark the fiftieth anniversary of the adoption of the Universal Declaration of Human Rights. You will notice that I do not use the word "celebrate". I think we don't celebrate; we mark in a somber and reflective way the fiftieth anniversary. It is a year when we re-affirm our commitment to work for change and to demonstrate that the principles of the UN Charter and the Universal Declaration are not too theoretical, nor too abstract. We must all set ourselves the goal of giving such principles practical effect and the success of our efforts can only be measured by the improved well being of individuals around the world.

The Universal Declaration was the first international agreement aimed at the improvement of all human rights for all people. It was a document shaped and generated to a large extent by the vision of a truly inspiring woman from the United States. A woman who had committed her life to worthy goals and who, although extremely shy, made herself a powerful voice on behalf of a wide range of social causes, not least the cause of improving the treatment of women. The woman was, of course, Eleanor Roosevelt who, as the US representative to the UN Commission on Human Rights and later as its Chairperson, was largely responsible for the Universal Declaration.

Unlike the other members of the Commission, Mrs. Roosevelt was neither a scholar nor an expert on international law. She wasn't an academic and she wasn't a jurist, but what she did have was an incredible sense of commitment and compassion. She saw herself as an ambassador for the common man and woman, and her enthusiasm for this goal, combined with her humanitarian convictions, resulted in a Declaration that was direct and straight-forward, and a Declaration that has endured as a universally accepted standard of achievement for all people and all nations. It was adopted on the tenth of December, 1948. It is as relevant now as when it was written. It's a living document--it's written in the present tense. It was written by people with vision.

Fifty years ago was of course "no ordinary time," as quite a number of you sitting

让你们感到内疚,你们应该为所取得的成绩骄傲。但我请求你们,**要把受到的教育用在最有价值的目标上,这样的目标应当有助于改善别人的生活,而且因为对我们所处的社会作出了贡献,会让你自己感到欣慰。**

1998年是我们设立目标的重要的一年,对联合国人权事务委员会来说,也是重要的一年。今年我们要纪念《世界人权宣言》[1]发布50周年。你们会注意到我没用"庆祝"这个词。我想我们无法庆祝,我们将用一种沉重的方式反思这个周年。在这一年里,我们要重申致力于变革的努力,并且证明《联合国宪章》和《人权宣言》的原则不仅仅是理论,也不会太抽象。我们必须为自己确定目标,使这些原则在实践中有效,而且只有世界各地的人民福祉得到改善,才是我们的努力是否成功的唯一标准。

《人权宣言》是国际上第一个旨在改善所有人权利的协议。这个文件的形成和产生,很大程度上要归功于一位很能鼓舞人心的美国妇女。这位女性把她的全部生命都献给了有价值的目标。虽然她很内向,但她就范围广泛的很多社会问题,特别是改善妇女的待遇问题,发出了强大的声音。这位女性就是埃莉诺·罗斯福[2],她先是作为美国代表参加联合国人权委员会,后来出任主席,并对《宣言》的发布起了主要作用。

不同于委员会的其他成员,罗斯福夫人不是国际法的学者或专家,也不是学术界人物或法学家,但她却有着令人难以置信的责任感和同情心。她把自己当做普通人的代表,对实现这一目标怀着极大热情,加上她的人道主义信念,使这项宣言简洁明了,该宣言一直被作为衡量所有人和所有国家的普遍标准。它于1948年12月10日获得通过,直到今天,它仍像诞生时一样鲜活实用。这是一个有生命力的文件,它用现在时态写就,出自有远见卓识的人之手。

50年前,当然是一个"非常时刻",就像今天坐在前排的年长者所记得的那样。由于第二次世界大战的浩劫和纳粹大屠杀的恐怖,让许多国家都觉得应当承诺实行普世的人权标准。但在目前这样的困难时刻,在我们担心人们没有足够强的意愿时,我们还应该记住,在整个二战期间,埃莉诺·罗斯福为了保护普通的美国人的人权进行了坚持不懈的努力,她提醒我们,无论时局有多艰难,我们都不能为了其他目标而牺牲人权。

here near the front will recall. The devastation of World War II and the horrors of the Holocaust made nations more willing to commit to a universal standard of human rights protections. But in times such as these, when we've become concerned about a lack of sufficient will, it is also worth remembering that throughout the war period, Eleanor Roosevelt worked tirelessly for the human rights of the ordinary men and women in America, reminding us that no matter how hard the going gets, we must not sacrifice human rights for other goals.

For Mrs. Roosevelt, all human rights were universal since every man, woman, and child sought equal justice, equal opportunity, and equal dignity without discrimination. But if rights didn't have meaning locally, in the factory, farm, or office, Mrs. Roosevelt thought they would have little meaning elsewhere and she warned that: "Without concerned citizen action to uphold them close to home, we shall look in vain at progress in the larger world."

The Declaration's fiftieth anniversary is an ideal time to assess whether we are upholding human rights close to home as well as further afield. As part of the follow-up to the Vienna World Conference on Human Rights of 1993, the United Nations system and its member-states are undergoing a yearlong assessment of its successes and shortcomings with respect to the protection and promotion of human rights. Human Rights organizations and concerned individuals play an important role in that assessment: encouraging discussion and debate on the continuing relevance of the international human rights standards and pointing to areas of imbalance in protection.

One such area is the promotion at the international level of economic, social, and cultural rights and the right to development. Extreme poverty, illiteracy, homelessness, and the vulnerability of children to exploitation are all areas requiring much greater effort. Economic and social rights are in every sense interdependent with civil and political rights. I find it interesting that since I took up my responsibilities as UN High Commissioner for Human Rights last September, because I've placed a lot of emphasis on having a better balance and having more focus and attention on economic and social rights, some people have said, "Is she not strong on civil and political rights? Is she not clear about torture and disappearances and imprisonment and prison conditions and so on?" But in fact it's because I'm so strong on civil and political rights that I recognize you cannot truly advance them unless you're also prepared to advance strongly economic and social rights. And that's a big challenge for this great country, a very big challenge right now.

对罗斯福夫人来说,人权具有普遍性,因为不管男女老幼,都有权利追求公正、机会平等,以及免受歧视的同等尊严。但如果在工厂、农场或办公室这些你自己所处的地方,人权不受到重视,那么,罗斯福夫人认为人权在其他地方也没有意义,她提醒人们说:"如果公民不去维护跟他们身边密切相关的权益,我们在更大的范围内,又如何能看到人权的进步呢?"

《人权宣言》颁布的第50个周年,是评估我们无论在近邻或远方,是否都尊重人权的一个理想的时间。作为1993年在维也纳举行的"世界人权会议"的后续措施,联合国系统及其成员国正在进行一项为期一年的评估,看看我们在促进和保护人权方面有何成功和不足之处。人权组织和有关人士在进行这种评估方面发挥了重要作用:他们鼓励就国际人权标准是否依然相关等问题进行讨论,并指出人权保护在何处有不平衡的情况。

其中一个问题,是如何在国际上促进人们的经济、社会、文化和发展权。消除极端贫困、文盲、无家可归等问题及保护儿童不受剥削等,所有这些领域都需要我们做出更大的努力。经济和社会权利与公民和政治权利密切相关。

有一点让我觉得有趣。自从去年9月我担任联合国人权事务高级专员以来,因为我把工作重点放在争取几方面之间更好的平衡,更重视经济和社会权利,有人就说,"她对公民和政治权利方面不重视了吗?她对世上存在的滥施酷刑、绑架失踪、随意监禁和监狱条件恶劣等情况不想弄清楚吗?"但事实上,正因为更多关注公民和政治权利,我才认识到,除非你大力推动经济和社会权利的发展,否则无法真正推动公民和政治权利的发展。对美国来说,这也是一个巨大的、迫在眉睫的挑战。

作为人权事务高级专员,我从一个成员广泛且令人敬佩的保护人权集体那里汲取力量,这个集体既包括组织,又有个人,并代表了所有的文化、传统和背景等方方面面。我想,我要向1998届的同学发出特别呼吁,同时也呼吁其他回来参加毕业周年纪念的校友,加入到保护人权的活动中来,遵守体现在《人权宣言》里的原则。该宣言的开始几行就写道:"人类大家庭内每一个人固有的尊严和平等,是世界自由、正义与和平的

As High Commissioner for Human Rights, I draw strength from being part of an incredible and broad human rights community, a community which encompasses both organizations and individuals, and which represents all cultures, traditions and backgrounds. And I think I particularly ask the class of 1998, and indeed other years who have come back for their graduation, to join the efforts of the human rights community by committing yourselves to the principles enshrined in the Universal Declaration, the opening lines of which recognize the inherent dignity and equality of all members of the human family as the foundation of freedom, justice, and peace in the world. I also urge you to take part in the human rights debate so that through informed and purposeful discussion we can achieve a greater understanding of how the rights enshrined in the Declaration can be implemented at both the local and international level.

I'd like to draw on the address of President Rudenstine. He was in fact precisely conveying that message -- the importance of using the resources, the intellectual resources that this great University represents, and to bring them to the issues that confront all of our societies and our global village. The motto of the fiftieth anniversary, "All human rights for all," expresses what we must commit ourselves to achieving in the years ahead. It is evident that in many parts of the world, there is little cause for celebration -- far from it.

At the end of January, while in Cambodia, I visited a shelter in Phnom Pen for women who had been victims of trafficking for the sex trade. I sat in a small room and listened to a 15-year-old girl who explained, through an interpreter, that friends of her family had driven her to the city as she thought to take up a job in a clothing factory. Instead, she was forced in the door of a sex brothel where she was beaten until she complied for 16 or 17 hours a day with what was required of her. She managed to escape after three months and she was trying to rebuild her sense of herself. She was ashamed, she felt humiliated. As I looked into her eyes I was aware that she wasn't alone in her misery; that millions of children and women, worldwide, endure a similar fate. There is a trafficking in human persons. It's modern slavery. The rights for far too many remain little more than words on paper. However, I do believe that we should commit ourselves to focusing on the future, reinvigorating the common will and commitment of the international community to ensuring the enjoyment of human rights by people everywhere. We are all the custodians of human rights and we must all find our own way to do what is required.

基础。"我也鼓励你们参与人权辩论，这样，通过熟悉情况并有目的的讨论，我们就可以更加清楚如何在本地和国际社会中，让《宣言》中神圣的人权能够实现。

我想借用鲁登斯坦校长的讲话。他其实准确地传达了那样的信息，即如何使用资源——这所优秀大学所代表的智力资源，来解决我们这个地球村所面临的问题。纪念《人权宣言》颁布50周年的口号是：所有人都享有一切人权，这表明我们在未来必须致力于实现目标。很显然，在世界上许多地区，我们还很难这样庆祝——为时尚早。

今年1月底，我在柬埔寨金边参观了一个庇护所，这里收留着被强迫卖淫的妇女受害者。在一个小房间内，我在翻译的帮助下听一个15岁的女孩讲述。她说家人的朋友开车带她到城里，原以为是去一家服装厂工作。但是她却被骗进妓院，而且遭受毒打，直到她答应每天接客十六七个小时。3个月后，她设法逃离，试图重新找回自信。她感到非常羞辱。当我注视她的眼睛时，我知道不是她一个人在忍受这样的痛苦，在世界范围内，数以百万计像她这样的妇女和儿童，在遭受着同样的命运。拐卖妇女儿童的事正在发生，这是现代的奴隶制。对很多人来说，人权还只是文字上的东西。然而我认为，我们应该面向未来，在国际社会中共同推波助澜，承诺让世界各地的人都享有人权。我们都是人权的守护者，我们必须找到适合自己的方式，为维护人权而努力。

我想引用谢默斯·希尼[3]的诗歌《共和国的良心》中的一些诗句，此时此刻应当恰如其分。在我准备这个演讲时，并不知道谁会与我一起接受荣誉学位，哈佛的保密工作做得非常出色。我不知道谢默斯·希尼今天也会在这里，否则我会设法引用另一位爱尔兰诗人的诗句。但现在一切都太晚了，而且我认为他的诗句的确强化了我想表达的意思，所以，谢默斯，请掩上你的耳朵，我将尽最大努力把你的诗句读好。下面就是《共和国的良心》诗句摘抄：

……你带着全部家产，很快
优越感就消失……

I thought it fitting, somehow, coming here to Harvard, that I should remind you of some lines of Seamus Heaney's poem "From the Republic of Conscience." I didn't know when I was preparing this address who would be honored with me--Harvard kept the secret well. I didn't know that Seamus Heaney was going to be here or I would have found another worthy Irish poet to quote. But it's too late now, and somehow I think his words do enhance what I'm trying to say, so close your ears, Seamus, and I'll do my best. These words are part of the poem, "From the Republic of Conscience."

> *...you carried what you had to and very soon*
> *your symptoms of creeping privilege disappeared...*
> *I came back from that frugal republic*
> *with my two arms the one length, the customs woman*
> *having insisted my allowance was myself.*
> *The old man rose and gazed into my face*
> *and said that was official recognition*
> *that I was now a dual citizen.*
> *Their embassies, he said, were everywhere*
> *but operated independently*
> *and no ambassador would ever be relieved.*

You who graduate today, and you who are recent and not so recent graduates, who return to meet your Harvard friends again, can, I believe, do much to contribute to the betterment of society. You can become interested and involved in the world around you. By virtue of your education, you can offer society the benefit of your focused knowledge, as well as a wider vision and a great sense of purpose. You also have the skills to teach others to be more tolerant, more understanding and more caring, and I'm confident that your recognition of this special responsibility will guide your actions and perhaps one day--and I think I saw some potential candidates -- inspire a future Eleanor Roosevelt.

I wish you much happiness and success in the years ahead. May your memories of Harvard, as mine are, and the friends you have made here be with you always. Congratulations, new graduates, and I am very honored to be linked with the honored graduates up here of 1998 and to be rejuvenated by joining the class of 1998. Thank you very much.

> 我从那个节俭的国度归来
> 身无分文,海关的妇女坚称
> 我的零用钱就是我自己。
> 老人起身,盯着我的脸
> 并说,这就是官方的认可
> 我现在有了双重国籍。
> 他们的大使馆,他说到处都是
> 但都独立运作
> 从来没有大使会松一口气。

你们这些今天毕业的同学,还有最近毕业的和毕业已久回来看望哈佛朋友的校友们,我相信,你们可以做很多事,尽可能地帮助改善社会。你们能对周围的世界产生兴趣,并参与其中。凭借你们的教育,你们可以为社会提供专业知识,以及更广泛的视野和更大的目标。你们也有能力去教导别人,要更宽容、更能理解和关心别人,我相信认识到这一特殊的责任,会引导你们的行动,也许有一天——我想我看到了一些新秀——你们能成为未来的埃莉诺·罗斯福。

祝你们在未来的日子里幸福、成功!也祝你们对哈佛的记忆像我一样常新!在这里结交的朋友友谊长青!祝贺你们,我们的毕业生,我很荣幸与1998届的同学有了联系,能够跻身于1998届的毕业班,我感到活力焕发。非常感谢各位!

---

1 《世界人权宣言》(of the Universal Declaration of Human Rights)是联合国大会于1948年12月10日通过的一份旨在维护人类基本权利的文献(联合国大会第217号决议)。

2 美国总统富兰克林·罗斯福的夫人

3 谢默斯·希尼(Seamus Heaney,1939年出生)爱尔兰诗人。

艾伦·格林斯潘（1926— ）

"格林斯潘一开口，全球投资人都要竖起耳朵。""格林斯潘打个喷嚏，全球投资人都要伤风感冒。"作为美国联邦储备委员会的五朝元老，许多人认为格林斯潘是美国国家经济政策的权威和决定性人物，是"经济学家中的经济学家"，他曾经对美国乃至全球经济起着举足轻重的作用。

艾伦·格林斯潘出生于纽约的一个犹太家庭，父亲是股票经纪人，母亲在零售店工作。他早年喜爱音乐，曾经在最负盛名的朱莉亚特音乐学院学习单簧管，并成为职业演奏家。后来他意识到自己在音乐方面只是"小有出息"，很难再有长进，便放弃音乐进入纽约大学改学经济，1950年获得经济学硕士学位，1977年在担任福特总统任期内的美国经济顾问委员会主席期间，获得纽约大学经济博士学位。

格林斯潘曾任纽约市工业咨询公司董事长兼总裁、总统经济顾问委员会成员等职，1987年8月开始连续5届出任美联储主席，直到2006年卸任，甚至有人说："谁当总统都无所谓，只要让艾伦当美联储主席就行。"

格林斯潘的经济政策主要是控制利率，运用公开市场业务、银行借款贴现率和金融机构法定储备金比率三大杠杆调节经济。他总是对美国经济是否过热保持着一种警觉，一旦出现过热迹象，他便采取措施把温度降下来。他主导着美国经济度过了艰难的20世纪80年代，并在90年代达到了前所未有的经济繁荣。这一点，连苛刻的批评者们也不得不承认，在那25年里，没有谁比格林斯潘更胜任美联储主席这个职位。

1999

Education as an Investment in the Information Age
信息时代的教育投资

Alan Greenspan 艾伦·格林斯潘

President Rudenstine, President Wilson, Harvard alumni, fellow recipients of degrees, your parents and friends:

It is a distinct pleasure to join you in celebrating this milestone in American higher education, the 348th Harvard commencement.

We are here to honor the achievements and the promise of the members of the graduating class of 1999. To them, let me say: You are being bequeathed the tools for achieving a material existence that neither my generation nor any that preceded it could have even remotely imagined as we began our life's work. What you must shape for yourselves are those values that will enable you to thrive in a world that is becoming increasingly competitive and frenetic.

To the parents and friends of the graduating class, let me say: I had planned to offer you some useful investment advice but, in the end, was dissuaded. My staff informed me that those of you who in recent years have been paying Harvard tuition or have contributed to the endowment fund, must by now have little left to invest.

But clearly you have already made the best investment there is: education.

The creative abilities of this graduating class and their contemporaries will determine the future state of our cultural, legal, and economic institutions. The ideas these graduates create, and employ, will influence the degree of American prosperity in the twenty-first century.

The **quintessential** [adj. 精髓的. 典型的] manifestations of America's industrial might earlier this century--large steel mills, auto assembly plants, petrochemical complexes, and skyscrapers--have been replaced by a gross domestic product that has been downsized as ideas have replaced physical bulk and effort as creators of value. Today, economic value is best symbolized by exceedingly complex, miniaturized integrated circuits and the ideas--the software--that utilize them. Most of what we currently perceive as value and wealth is intellectual and **impalpable** [adj. 感触不到的. 无形的].

The American economy, clearly more than most, is in the grip of what the eminent Harvard professor, Joseph Schumpeter, many years ago called "creative destruction," the continuous process by which emerging technologies push out the old. Standards of living rise when incomes created by the productive facilities employing older, increasingly obsolescent, technologies are marshaled to finance the newly

信息时代的教育投资 艾伦·格林斯潘

鲁登斯坦校长、威尔逊校长、哈佛校友们、今天的学位获得者、学生家长和朋友们：

哈佛大学第 348 届毕业典礼，是美国高等教育中具有里程碑意义的大事，能和大家一起庆祝，我感到非常快乐。

我们来这里，是为了庆祝 1999 届毕业生所取得的成就和希望。对毕业生们，我想说：你们获得了追求物质生存的工具。这些物质，是我这一代人以及我们之前的所有人，在开始他们的职业生涯时完全无法想象的。你们必须决定自己的价值观，这个价值观能够让你们从容应对竞争日趋激烈的世界。

对毕业生的父母和朋友们，我想说：我曾计划为你们提供一些有用的投资建议，但最后想想还是算了。我的工作人员告诉我说，由于你们近年来为支付哈佛学费或为学校基金捐款，现在没什么钱可用来投资了。

但是显然，你们已经做了最好的投资——这就是教育。

这届毕业生，还有他们同代人的创造能力，将决定我们的文化、法律、经济未来的发展，他们创造和运用的理念，将影响 21 世纪美国的繁荣程度。

本世纪早期，美国工业力量的典型表现是大型钢厂、汽车装配厂、石化联合体，以及摩天大楼。后来，创意取代了材料的多少和努力的程度，成为创造价值的因素，老一套东西在国民生产总值中的地位也随之降低。今天，经济价值的最好体现，是那些极其复杂的、小型化的集成电路和人们的构思——在集成电路上应用的软件。今天我们认为有价值和属于财富的东西，都是智力方面并且是无形的。比起其他大多数经济体来，美国经济显然隶属于著名的哈佛大学教授约瑟夫·熊彼特[1]在很多年前就形容过的"创造性破坏"，即新兴技术取代旧技术的这样一个持续不断的过程。当我们把采用陈旧的、越来越过时的技术生产设施所创造的收益，投入到那些最新、最尖端技术的生产设施时，我们的生活水平就会提升。

财富的创造过程就是这样，步步为营地逐渐增多。它的前提条

produced capital assets that embody cutting-edge technologies.

This is the process by which wealth is created, incremental step by incremental step. It presupposes a continuous churning of an economy as the new displaces the old. Although this process of productive obsolescence has ancient roots, it appears to have taken on a quickened pace in recent years and changed its character. The remarkable, and partly **fortuitous** [adj. 偶然的，幸运的], coming together of the technologies that make up what we label IT--information technologies--has begun to alter, fundamentally, the manner in which we do business and create economic value, often in ways that were not readily foreseeable even a decade ago.

Before the advent of what has become a **veritable** [adj. 确实的，真正的] avalanche of information technology innovation, most twentieth-century business decisionmaking had been hampered by dated and incomplete information about customer preferences in markets and flows of materials through a company's production systems. Relevant information was hours, days, or even weeks old. Accordingly, business managers had to double up on materials and people to protect against the inevitable misjudgments that were part and parcel of production planning. Ample inventory levels were needed to ensure output schedules, and backup teams of people and machines were required to maintain quality control and respond to unanticipated developments.

Of course, large remnants of imprecision still persist, but the remarkable surge in the availability of real-time information in recent years has sharply reduced the degree of uncertainty confronting business management. This has enabled businesses to remove large swaths of now unnecessary inventory, and dispense with much programmed worker and capital redundancies. As a consequence, growth in output per work hour has accelerated, elevating the standards of living of the average American worker.

Intermediate production and distribution processes, so essential when information and quality control were poor, are being bypassed and eventually eliminated. The proliferation of Internet web sites is promising to alter significantly the way large parts of our distribution system are managed. Moreover, technological innovations have spread far beyond the factory floor and retail and wholesale distribution channels. Biotech, for example, is revolutionizing medicine and agriculture, with far reaching consequences for the quality of life not only in the United States but around the

件是新的东西取代旧的东西,从而推动经济的不断更新。虽然这种淘汰过程自古就有,但近年来,更新的速度似乎加快了,性质也起了变化。新兴技术风起云涌,甚至带有部分偶然性。我们把这个新技术称为IT——信息技术,它已开始从根本上改变我们经商和创造经济价值的方式,这种影响,我们甚至在十年前还无法预见。

在信息技术创新如山呼海啸来临之前,多数商家在客户市场调查和了解材料如何在公司的生产系统中流动等一些情况时,所获信息要么过时,要么不完整,相关资料往往会迟到几小时、几天,甚至几周。因此,在制定生产计划时,企业管理者为避免误判,不得不准备双份材料和两倍人工。为确保计划实施,需要有充足的库存量;为保证质量和应对意外事件,员工与机器也要有所备份。

虽然仍有很多信息不精确的时候,但近年来大量增加的实时信息随手可用,已大大降低了企业管理中面临的不确定性。这使得企业现在可以大量减少不必要的库存,并去掉很多在编人员和重复投资。因此,每个工时的产出增长速度加快,提升了美国上班族的平均生活水平。

当信息和质量不易掌控时,生产半成品和分销过程最为重要。现在这种方式已日渐式微,可能还会被淘汰出局。风生水起的互联网,预示着我们的物流系统管理模式将有很大变化。此外,科技创新已远远超出了工厂车间、零售及批发分销渠道。例如,生物技术就给医药和农业带来了革命,不仅在美国,在世界任何地方,它都将对人们的生活产生深远影响。

许多产品都追求多样设计,具有不同品质,其爆炸式的增长正在满足消费者潜在的需求,这些需求在十年、二十年前都还很难看清。随之而来的收入和财富增长,也同样令人印象深刻。但遗憾的是,这种好处还没有普及到最广泛的民众家庭。

如何保证这部优良的经济机器持续运转?怎样才能让它的好处最大限度地惠及更广泛的人群?

当然,我们必须营造这样一种环境,让技术的不断进步受到鼓

world.

The explosion in the variety of products of many different designs and qualities has opened up the potential for the satisfaction of consumer needs not evident even a decade or two ago. The accompanying expansion of incomes and wealth has been truly impressive, though regrettably the gains have not been as widely spread across households as I would like.

How is this remarkable economic machine to be maintained, and how can we better ensure that its benefits reach the greatest number of people?

Certainly, we must foster an environment in which continued advances in technology are encouraged and welcomed. If the graduates of 1999 are going to be able to build on the accomplishments of their forebears, many of them must push forward to expand our knowledge in science and engineering, and our universities must ready themselves to meet the technical needs of our students yet to come.

But scientific proficiency will not be enough. Skill alone may not be sufficient to move the frontier of technology far enough to meet the many challenges that our nation and educational system will confront in the decades ahead. And technological advances alone will not **buttress** [n. 扶墙, 拱壁; v. 支持] the democratic institutions, supported by a rule of law, which are so essential to our dynamic and vigorous American economy. Each is merely a tool, which, without the enrichment of human wisdom, is of modest value.

A crucial challenge of education is to transform skills and intelligence into wisdom--into a process of thinking capable of forming truly new insights.

An agile young mind has the facility to solve a complex set of equations. But that mind must be broadened if it is to make effective use of that solution to meet human needs. There is little doubt of the relationship between our ability to think creatively and our productiveness as individual members of society.

The roots and nature of how the human mind innovates, however, have always been subject to controversy. Yet, even without indisputable evidence, there has been a remarkable and pervasive assumption that the ability to think abstractly is fostered through exposure to philosophy, literature, music, art, and languages. **A liberal education was presumed in years past to produce a greater understanding of all aspects of living--an essential ingredient for broadening one's world view.** I believe

励和欢迎。如果1999年的毕业生能够在他们前辈成就的基础上更进一步，他们中的许多人就必须努力扩大我们在科学和工程方面的知识。我们的大学也必须做好准备，以满足今后入学新生在技术上的需求。

但光懂科学远远不够。技能本身不一定推动技术向前，不一定能让技术进步到足以帮助我们的国家和教育体系，在未来几十年里迎接即将到来的诸多挑战。仅靠技术进步，还无法支撑一个以法治为基础的民主制度，而这些对我们充满活力的美国经济来说，是至关重要的。这些技术作为独立的存在，仅仅是一个工具，如果没有人类智慧来提炼其精华，其价值将会大打折扣。

教育所面对的一个关键挑战，是将技能和智力转化为智慧，转化成一个能够形成真正崭新见解的思维过程。

年轻敏捷的头脑，有办法解开一个复杂的方程，但如果想要有效地使该方案满足人类的需要，头脑就必须拓宽。创造性地思考问题的能力和我们作为社会一员的生产能力之间的良好关系，是不容质疑的。

然而，人类思维创新的根源及其性质到底如何，一直争议不休。不过，哪怕不举出雄辩的证据，人们也都认同一个普遍的、浅显的观点，那就是，抽象思维能力可以通过接触哲学、文学、音乐、艺术和语言等来培训。人们早就意识到，**人文教育能让人更多地了解生活的方方面面——这是扩大一个人世界观的重要组成部分**。我相信现在依然如此。

欣赏一幅杰出的画作，或聆听一首深刻动人的钢琴协奏曲，会给人带来审美上的愉悦和心灵上的满足。而且欣赏本身能够强化形成概念的过程，这个概括能力对创新来说，非常重要。

具体来说，通过人文教育扩大视野，几乎肯定会有助于人们理解不同领域之间的相互关系。**重要的新知识，往往是这种跨学科的研究结果。在研究问题时，视野越宽，产生创造性见解的可能性就越大，而这些最后都会有助于带来更大的经济效益。**

it still does.

Viewing a great painting or listening to a profoundly moving piano concerto produces a sense of intellectual joy that is satisfying in and of itself. But, arguably, it also enhances and reinforces the conceptual processes so essential to innovation.

Specifically, the broadening of one's world view that is acquired through a liberal education almost surely contributes to an understanding of the interrelationships of different fields of endeavor. **Important new knowledge is very often the result of such interdisciplinary observation. The broader the context that an inquiring mind brings to a problem, the greater will be the potential for creative insights that, in the end, contribute to a more productive economy.**

But learning and knowledge--and even wisdom--are not enough. National well-being, including material prosperity, rests to a substantial extent on the personal qualities of the people who inhabit a nation.

At the risk of sounding a bit uncool, I say to the graduating class of 1999 that your success in life, and the success of our country, is going to depend on the integrity and other qualities of character that you and your contemporaries will continue to develop and demonstrate over the years ahead. A generation from now, as you watch your children graduate, you will want to be able to say that whatever success you achieved was the result of honest and productive work, and that you dealt with people the way you would want them to deal with you.

Civilization, our civilization, rests on that premise. It presupposes the productive interaction of people engaged in the division of labor, driven--I cannot resist the jargon--by economic comparative advantage. This implies mutual exchange to mutual advantage among free people. Coercive societies and coercive relationships among people rarely enhance the state of what we call civilization.

I presume that I could offer all kinds of advice to today's graduates from my half-century in private business and government. I could urge you all to work hard, save, and prosper. And I do. But transcending all else is being principled in how you go about doing those things.

It is decidedly not true that "nice guys finish last," as that highly original American baseball philosopher, Leo Durocher, was once alleged to have said.

I do not deny that many appear to have succeeded in a material way by cutting corners and manipulating associates, both in their professional and in their personal

但是，仅仅学习知识，甚至智慧，都还不够。国家的福祉，包括物质的繁荣，在很大程度上取决于一个国家的人民素质。

听起来也许不够酷，但有些话我还是要对1999届的毕业生们说：个人的成功和我们国家的成就，与你们如何在未来培养和展现正直无私等优良品质密切相关。一代人之后，当看着自己的孩子毕业时，希望你能够说，你取得的所有成就都是诚实和努力工作的结果，而你待人的方式，也是如你所希望别人对待你的那样。

我们的文明就建立在这个前提之下。此前提是：人们从事自己擅长的工作，这种分工——我忍不住要说句行话——是由经济的比较优势驱动的。这意味着人们可以根据各自优势，自主地进行互相交换。在人与人之间建立起强制的社会和强制关系，极不益于我们称之为文明的状态。

我想，基于我在私营企业和政府任职的长达半个世纪的经验，我可以为今天的毕业生提供各种建议。我会鼓励大家努力工作，别忘记存钱，希望各位兴旺发达，我是这样做的。但最重要的一点，是提醒你们在做这些事情时，一定要恪守信念。

"好好先生总是被人抛在最后"，据传这句话是美国棒球界的先哲利奥·杜罗彻[2]说的，但事实决不是这样的。

我不否认，许多人似乎在他们的职业生涯和个人生活中，依靠投机取巧和利用他人，在物质上获得成功。但在这个世界上，不用盘剥他人也能获得物质上的成功，而且这样才更能让自己满意。**衡量一个人职业生涯的真正标准，是你没有伤害别人，而且依靠自己的努力取得成功，惟其如此，你才会感到欣慰，甚至自豪。**

我无法为他人代言，因为他们的心理我不大了解。但在我个人的工作生活中，**让我获益最大的是，诚实的做派及严格遵守这种做派，当你有所收获时，也要让别人受益。无论是私人的还是职业上的，人与人之间的关系不应该是零和游戏。**

除了个人的满足感外，拥有一个公平做事的声誉还会有很大的实际用途，商界称之为"商业信誉"，还把它用到我们的资产平

lives. But material success is possible in this world and far more satisfying when it comes without exploiting others. **The true measure of a career is to be able to be content, even proud, that you succeeded through your own endeavors without leaving a trail of casualties in your wake.**

I cannot speak for others whose psyches I may not be able to comprehend, but, in my working life, **I have found no greater satisfaction than achieving success through honest dealings and strict adherence to the view that for you to gain, those you deal with should gain as well. Human relations--be they personal or professional--should not be zero sum games.**

And beyond the personal sense of satisfaction, having a reputation for fair dealing is a profoundly practical virtue. We call it "good will" in business and add it to our balance sheets.

Trust is at the root of any economic system based on mutually beneficial exchange. In virtually all transactions, we rely on the word of those with whom we do business. Were this not the case, exchange of goods and services could not take place on any reasonable scale. Our commercial codes and contract law presume that only a tiny fraction of contracts, at most, need be **adjudicated** [Adjudicate; v. 判决，充当裁判]. If a significant number of businesspeople violated the trust upon which our interactions are based, our court system and our economy would be swamped into immobility.

It is not by chance that in nineteenth century America, many bankers could effectively issue uncollateralized currency because they were able to develop a reputation that their word was their bond. For these institutions to succeed and prosper, people had to trust their promise of redemption in **specie** [n. 硬币，以同样的方式]. Now, as then, a contractor with a reputation for shoddy work will not prosper long.

In today's world, where ideas are increasingly displacing the physical in the production of economic value, competition for reputation becomes a significant driving force, propelling our economy forward. Manufactured goods often can be evaluated before the completion of a transaction. Service providers, on the other hand, usually can offer only their reputations.

The extraordinarily complex machine that we call the economy of the United States is, in the end, made up of human beings struggling to improve their lives. The

衡表上。

　　信任是任何一个基于互利交往的经济体制的根本。在几乎所有的交易中，我们都要依靠那些与我们有业务往来的人所说的话。若非如此，商品和服务的交换就很难在相当的规模上进行。我们只是假设，商业法规和合同法律只有很小一部分需要诉诸仲裁。如果商业领域很多人在我们以信任为基础的交往中背信弃义，那我们的司法系统和整个经济都会被压垮而无法运作。

　　19世纪的美国，许多银行家能够发行几乎没有担保的货币，绝非偶然，因为他们建立起如此良好的声誉，他们说过的话就是保证。这些机构想要成功和发展，就必须赢得人们的信任，保证他们有办法兑现承诺。和过去一样，现在的承包商如果有一个偷工减料的坏名声，想长久地做下去会非常之难。

　　在当今世界，创意越来越多地取代实体，成为创造经济价值的因素，争相建立良好声誉，成为推动我们的经济向前发展的一个重要推动力。产品在完成交易前就可以进行评估，而服务提供商只能依靠他们的声誉招徕生意。

　　我们称之为美国经济的东西，说到底就是由人们改善自己生活的努力而构成的一个极其复杂的机制。参与其中的每个美国人的价值观，都将影响维持市场交易的结构，这种情况贯穿于我们的整个历史。如果没有相互信任，如果市场参与者不遵守法律规则，那么经济就无法繁荣。

　　我们的体系，从根本上来说，是要靠每个人的公平行事。我们只需要在当今世界四处看看，就会认识到这个东西是多么的稀有和珍贵。

　　虽然我们在这方面已经颇有进步，但仍有许多事情要做。例如，近几十年里，在减少针对种族和其他形式的歧视方面，我们取得了相当大的进展，但这项工作还远未完成。

　　除非在经济中的所有参与者都得到机会，做到自己的最好，否则自由市场的资本主义制度便不能充分有效地运作。如果我们成功

individual values of those Americans will continue to influence the structure of the institutions that support market transactions, as they have throughout our history. Without mutual trust, and market participants abiding by a rule of law, no economy can prosper.

Our system works fundamentally on individual fair dealing. We need only look around today's world to realize how rare and valuable this is.

While we have achieved much in this regard, more remains to be done. Considerable progress, for example, has been evident in recent decades in the reduction of racial and other forms of discrimination. But this job is still far from completion.

A free market capitalist system cannot operate fully effectively unless all participants in the economy are given opportunities to achieve their best. If we succeed in opening up opportunities to everyone, our national affluence will almost surely become more widespread. Of even greater import is that all Americans believe that they are part of a system they perceive as fair and worthy of support.

Our forefathers bestowed upon us a system of government, and a culture of enterprise, that has propelled the United States to the greatest prosperity the world has ever experienced.

Today's graduates from Harvard and other schools are being passed the standard to carry forward our traditions. I know you will improve upon this inheritance in ways that we have yet to imagine.

I offer you all my congratulations and wish you success in your chosen careers. You honor me by listening to the musings of an old, idealistic, central banker.

Thank you and best wishes!

地把机会开放给大家,我们国家的富裕几乎肯定会让更多人分享。但更重要的,是要让所有的美国人都相信,他们是自己认为公平和值得支持的体系的一分子。

我们的先辈传承给我们一个政府管理系统和进取文化,我们依靠这些,把美国推到了史无前例的繁荣高度。

今天从哈佛和其他大学毕业的学生,要继承这些准则,发扬我们的传统。我知道你们会在这种继承的基础上继续提高,你们取得的成就将让我们无法想象。

谨向各位表示我的祝贺,并祝愿你们在自己选择的职业生涯中获得成功。你们愿意听一位年老但还有理想的央行行长的漫谈,让我倍感荣幸。

谢谢大家,并祝你们前程似锦!

---

1 约瑟夫·熊彼特(Joseph Schumpeter,1883—1950),美籍奥地利经济学家,曾任教于哈佛大学。他认为,经济学的全部内容就是变化。他既研究了短期经济波动,又研究了资本主义的长期趋势。熊彼特对现代经济学和政治学的发展都具有重要影响,其主要学说可概括为"景气循环"(也称"商业周期",Business cycle)理论、"创新"(Innovation)理论、"资本主义的创造性破坏"(The creative destruction of capitalism)理论,及"精英民主"(Elitism democracy)理论等。

2 利奥·杜罗彻(Leo Ernest Durocher,1905—1991),美国棒球界名人,曾为著名棒球手和球队主管。

2000's

阿玛蒂亚·森（1933— ）

阿玛蒂亚·森1933年出生于印度孟加拉湾的一个大学校园内，其父在大学教化学，外祖父则教授梵文和古印度文化。阿玛蒂亚·森曾说，他生在校园，长在校园，工作在校园，一生都没有离开过校园。他在泰戈尔创办的学校里完成了初级和中等教育，1959年在英国剑桥大学获得博士学位后，先后在印度德里大学，英国伦敦政治经济学院和牛津大学，美国哈佛、斯坦福、麻省理工等大学任教，教授经济和哲学。1998年离开哈佛大学到英国剑桥三一学院任院长。2003年又重返哈佛校园工作。他曾为联合国开发计划署写过人类发展报告，做过联合国前秘书长加利的经济顾问。因为在福利经济学上的贡献，阿玛蒂亚·森获得1998年诺贝尔经济学奖。

阿玛蒂亚·森年轻时爱好广泛且多才多艺。他曾在《纽约书评》杂志上撰文，评论泰戈尔的诗歌和绘画，获得好评。说起来，森与泰戈尔还有一点特殊关系。森出生时，其外祖父请泰戈尔为外孙起名字，泰戈尔选择了Amartya，意为"不朽的、永生的"，并说"希望这孩子将来成为一个杰出的人"。当阿玛蒂亚·森在1998年获得诺贝尔经济学奖时，印度报纸纷纷报道这一段佳话。

阿玛蒂亚·森曾说，他研究经济学的重要动机之一，是帮助他的祖国印度摆脱经济贫困，走向繁荣。为此，他选择发展经济学作为他的主攻方向之一。他在1971年离开印度，求学工作于欧美众多著名学府，但他始终和印度国内的大学保持着紧密联系，尤其是他曾经学习和工作过的德里大学。他也一直保持着印度国籍，因为那样可以保证他对于印度国内公众事务具有发言权。

2000

Global Doubts
对质疑全球化的回应

Amartya Sen 阿玛蒂亚·森

On behalf of all the honorary graduands, I would like to thank Harvard warmly for making us so splendidly privileged. John Dryden, the English poet, has offered the sobering thought that honour is "but an empty bubble." But we honorary graduands refuse to be put off by old Dryden - especially today. I personally think that Dryden was only trying to rhyme with the previous line of his poem. Having said, "War, he sung, was toil and trouble," it would have been difficult to resist the temptation to rhyme it with "Honor but an empty bubble." We shall take no notice of all this, and opt not for rhyme, but for reason. And so, we are most grateful to Harvard for what it has done for us.

It is also marvelous for us to join, on this occasion, the student graduands who have worked hard for their well-earned degrees. We honorary graduands are, in fact, free riding on the hard work of the students. Since my own research work has always strongly benefited from questions and comments of my students, I am very used to being thoroughly dependent on students. And free riding, as we all know, can be wonderfully pleasant.

There is something extraordinarily exciting about good academic education. Nowhere is this seen more clearly than at Harvard. As teachers here, we all get used to astonishing brightness. Even before you have asked your question, your student proceeds to answer it, explaining modestly that her answer may have left room for doubt, going on to add - perhaps not so modestly - that the question that you chose to ask left even more room for doubt.

Indeed, the cultivation of doubts and the sharpening of questions are an integral part of university education. Its importance lies partly in the close connection between science and doubting. Francis Bacon distinguished between two different contributions that doubt can make, in his essay on "The Advancement of Learning," published in 1605, nearly 400 years ago. "The registering and proposing of doubts has a double use," Bacon said. One use is straightforward: it guards us "against errors." The second use, Bacon argued, involved the role of doubts in initiating and furthering a process of inquiry, which has the effect of enriching our investigations. Issues that "would have been passed by lightly without intervention," Bacon noted, end up being "attentively and carefully observed" precisely because of the intervention of doubts.

The constructive value of doubts applies not only to science and to academic studies in general, but also to the assessment of public policy. Take the current debates

请允许我代表所有荣誉学位的获得者,真诚地感谢哈佛带给我们如此巨大的荣誉。英国诗人约翰·德莱顿[1]曾经提醒人们说,荣誉"不过是个空的泡沫"。但是,我们这些荣誉学位获得者可不想受德莱顿的"干扰",尤其是在今天这个时候。我个人认为,德莱顿只是想让他的诗合辙押韵。前面写了"战争,他唱道,是辛劳困苦",后面也就无可避免地要写下"荣誉不过是个空的泡沫"。我们应当忽略所有这些,不要管韵律,而选择理智。所以,我们非常感谢哈佛为我们所做的一切。

今天的毕业生们为了他们来之不易的学位努力向学,我们能在这个场合加入他们,甚是奇妙。我们这些荣誉学位获得者实际上是借了他们辛勤工作的光。我自己的研究工作,很多是从我的学生提出的问题和评论中受到启迪,所以我很习惯于完全依赖学生。随处可借别人的光,大家都知道,是件多么愉快的事。

优秀的学术环境是令人兴奋的,在哈佛尤其如此。作为这里的教师,我们对令人吃惊的聪明人士早已司空见惯,常常问题还没说完,那些学生就抢先回答,并略带谦虚地解释说,他的回答可能会有值得存疑之处,而且还会加上一句——这句话也许就没那么温和了——说你的问题其实更加令人生疑。

事实上,提出怀疑,并将问题深化,这是大学教育必不可少的一部分。其重要性,一方面在于科学和提出疑问之间的紧密联系。弗朗西斯·培根在1605年,也就是400年前发表的文章《学术的进步》中,辨析了疑问的两种不同作用。培根说:"持有并提出疑问,会有双重用途。"疑问的一个直接作用,是防止我们"犯错误"。疑问的第二个作用,培根认为是在提出疑问与推进探索过程中的作用,它能够强化我们探讨。培根指出,有些"本来会轻易被省略过去"的问题,正是因为有了疑问的介入,才最终得到"用心和仔细的观察"。

疑问的建设性作用,不仅适合于科学和一般的学术研究,也适用于公共政策的评估。例如目前有关全球化问题的辩论,近年来很热烈,不只是在西雅图或华盛顿特区发生了抗议示威,而且在曼谷、雅加达和墨西哥城、阿比让,以及其他地方,也引起了一些不那么有组织的抗议。

on globalization, which have been so active in recent years - not just in Seattle or Washington, D.C., but also in less organized protestations in Bangkok an Jakarta and Mexico City and Abidjan, and elsewhere. The case for global trade and worldwide use of modern technology and finance is strong - very strong. And yet we cannot begin to understand the intellectual content of these disputes without addressing the reasons that inspire the doubts and disputations.

Unfortunately, we frequently encounter a dialogue of the deaf here. Those who blame globalization for all evils are ready to turn their doubts into indictments which propose summary rejection, and which then get translated into over-simple slogans. Those, on the other side, who believe that the anti-globalization rhetoric is ill founded, tend immediately to dismiss it as foolish - or worse. The two sides face each other like ships passing in the night.

We have to question both sides. Opponents of globalization may see it as a new folly, but it is neither particularly new, nor, in general, a folly. It is largely an intensification of the processes of interaction involving travel, trade, migration and dissemination of knowledge that have shaped the progress of the world over millennia. The polar opposite of globalization is persistent separation and relentless **autarky** [n. 自给自足]. There is a worrying image of seclusion that has been **arrestingly** [adj. 醒目的，引人注意的] invoked in many old Sanskrit texts in India (I know of four such texts, beginning about two and a half millennia ago, but there are undoubtedly many more references to the same concern). This is the story of a frog that lives its whole life within a well and is suspicious of everything outside it. This "kupamaduka" - the well-frog - has a world view, but it is a world view that is entirely confined to that well. The scientific, cultural and economic history of the world would have been very limited had we lived like such well-frogs. This is an important issue, since there are plenty of well-frogs around - and also, of course, many attorneys of well-frogs.

The more immediate point, however, is that there is extensive evidence that the global economy has actually brought prosperity to many different areas of the globe. The productive and economic contributions of global integration can scarcely be denied. But we also have to recognize the enormous inequalities that exist across the globe and often within each country. Doubts about global economic relations come from different ends of the globe, and they are in this sense "global doubts" - not just an assortment of local opposition. **We have to examine the manifest inequalities**

全球贸易和在全球范围内使用现代技术和资金,这种做法是有益处的——非常有益。然而,如果不了解激发这些疑虑和争议的原因,我们就无法理解这些争议在知识层面上的含义。

不幸的是,我们经常面临对牛弹琴的谈话。那些指责全球化带来万般罪恶的人,随时会将他们的疑虑变成对全球化全面排斥的判决,然后将这种态度化作简单的口号。另一方面,那些认为反对全球化的论调是毫无根据的人,往往会立即把对方的观点斥之为愚蠢的,或者更糟的东西。彼此无视对方,就像在夜间过往的船只。

我们必须对双方都提出问题。全球化的反对者可能会把它看做一件新的蠢事,但它既不特别新,而且总体来说,也不那么蠢。它主要涉及旅游、贸易、移民和知识传播,这在过去的千百年间,一直推动着世界的进步。全球化的对立面,是持久的分隔和不断地追求自给自足。在许多印度梵文的古老篇章中,都有这样一个令人担忧的与世隔阂的形象,(我知道的就有四篇这样的东西,见于约2500年前的记载。无疑,我们还可以看到更多这类描写。)故事讲的是,一只一生住在井底的青蛙,对井外的一切都表示怀疑。井底之蛙(梵文音为"kupamaduka")有它的世界观,但这是一种完全封闭的世界观。如果我们像井底之蛙那样生活,那么世界的科学、文化和经济的历史,就会非常有限。这是一个重要的问题,因为世界上有许多井底之蛙——当然,也有许多为井底之蛙服务的律师。

然而,更直接的一点是,大量的证据表明,全球性经济事实上已经给地球的许多不同地方带来了繁荣,全球一体化对生产和经济上的贡献是不可磨灭的。但我们也必须认识到,在全球各地,甚至在每个国家,都存在着巨大的不平等,对全球经济关系的疑虑来自世界不同的地方。从这个角度说,我们看到的是"全球性的疑虑",而不只是各地有些反对者。**我们必须审视这些明显的不平等和差异,正是这些因素,让全球性的疑虑成了显然的政坛话题。我们需要的,不是对带来收益和财富的市场机制这种积极的作用进行排斥,而是要有这样的重要认识,即市场机制必须在有多种机构存在的现实条件下运作。我们需要有这些机构的权**

and disparities that give these global doubts the political salience they undoubtedly have. What is needed is not a rejection of the positive role of the market mechanism in generating income and wealth, but the important recognition that the market mechanism has to work in a world of many institutions. We need the power and protection of these institutions, provided by democratic practice, civil and human rights, a free and open media, facilities for basic education and health care, economic safety nets, and, of course, provisions for women's freedom and rights - a neglected area which is only now beginning to receive the attention it deserves.

Let me give a few quick examples. First, a well-functioning market economy does not obviate the need for democracy and civil and political rights. The latter not only give people more freedom to live the way they would like (without being bossed around), they also allow people to have more voice to demand that their interests not be ignored. The fact that no famine has ever occurred in a democratic country with a free press and regular elections is only one rudimentary illustration of this connection. It is not surprising that the demand for democracy and for civil and political rights became much stronger in East and Southeast Asia, as the economic crisis of 1997 developed and spread. Voice as Albert Hirschman has discussed so well, is the alternative to exit. There is, of course, no basic conflict between economic globalization and the fostering of democracies. But quite often global capitalist institutions show distinct preference for orderly autocracies over the adversarial politics of democratic governance and the activist use of human rights.

To take a second issue, the ability to participate in the market economy is radically influenced by social arrangements for education, health care, microcredit, land reform, and other public policies. Furthermore, the sharing of the benefits of the market economy also depends on social institutions. This applies even to very prosperous countries. Take the deprivation of disadvantaged groups in the United States, for example African Americans. It is often claimed that even though African Americans as a group are poorer than American whites, they are typically many times richer than people in the developing world. And so indeed they are in income per head. But in terms of the probability of surviving to mature ages, African Americans in the United States fall behind the population of many third-world regions, including substantial parts of China and India. For this the blame is often exclusively on death from violence, but the higher mortality rate of African Americans continues well

力和保障，而这些机构的基础是推行民主实践、公民权利与人权、自由开放的媒体、基础教育和医疗设施、经济保障的措施，当然还有保障妇女的自由和权利——这是一个被忽视的领域，现在才开始得到应有的重视。

让我举几个简单的例子。首先，一个运作良好的市场经济，并不意味着人们不需要民主以及公民权利和政治权利。后者不仅给人们以更多的自由生活方式（人们不被呼来唤去地受到指使），而且让人们发出更多的声音，他们的利益要求不被忽视。在有新闻自由和定期选举的民主国家里，从来没有发生过饥荒，这样的事实，就是这种联系的最好说明。

在东亚和东南亚，随着1997年经济危机的发生和扩大，要求民主以及公民权利和政治权利的呼声越来越高，这毫不奇怪。阿尔伯特·赫什曼[2]很好地讨论过选择发声，就是相对于选择而退出的好办法。经济全球化和促进民主之间，当然没有根本的矛盾。但全球资本主义的机制，常常显示出偏好于有序独裁，而不是民主治理和积极行使人权活动的那种对抗性政治。

第二个问题，参与市场经济的能力，从根本上说取决于教育、医疗卫生、小额信贷、土地改革，以及其他公共政策的社会统筹安排。此外，市场经济的利益共享也取决于社会制度。对于非常富裕的国家也是如此。可以看看美国对弱势群体，比如非洲裔美国人的剥夺。人们常常声称，即使作为一个群体的非洲裔美国人比美国白人贫困，也比在发展中国家的人强上好多倍，人均收入上也高好几倍。但就活到成熟年龄的概率而言，在美国的非洲裔美国人要落后于许多第三世界国家，包括中国和印度相当一部分地区。对于这个现象，人们往往只是归罪于暴力死亡，但美国黑人的死亡率，即使到了老龄，因暴力死亡不再有任何区别时——依然偏高。缺乏医疗保险，教育和其他社会保障的失败，也是这种现象出现的原因。美国的经济空前繁荣，却并没有解决这些问题。

第三，现在有确凿的证据表明，通过为妇女提供就学、就业机会等加强妇女权益的行动，对所有人（包括男性、妇女和儿童）的生活都产生了深远影响。它降低了儿童死亡率，减少了因出生时体重过低而带来

beyond the ages when this can make any real difference. Lack of medical insurance has a role to play here, and so has the breakdown of inner city education and other social arrangements. The unprecedented economic boom that the American economy has enjoyed has not resolved these problems.

Third, there is now overwhelming evidence that women's empowerment through schooling, employment opportunities, etc., has the most far-reaching effects on the lives of all - men, women and children. It reduces child mortality; it cuts down health hazards of adults arising from low birth weight; it increases the range and effectiveness of public debates; and it is more influential than economic growth in moderating fertility rates. We can see its influence in the halving of the fertility rate of Bangladesh in less than two decades, and in the fact that while some districts of India have high fertility rates, others with more gender equity already have fertility rates lower than the United States and Britain. The reach of social institutions that work for gender equity is astonishingly large. There is also a related point of great importance which John Kenneth Galbraith has made very forcefully. The role of institutions has to be assessed in terms of the "countervailing power" they exercise over one another. Asymmetric power in one domain can be checked by a different configuration of forces in another domain. All this - and more - was discussed in Galbraith's book American Capitalism, first published in 1952. I remember reading it as a college student in Calcutta, in a coffee house, while trying to resist being evicted by the waiter on the not unreasonable ground that I could not hog a chair and finish reading an entire book while consuming only one cup of coffee. On that occasion, I got by through using only the countervailing power of my voice and determined immovability, but in general we need an institutional balance more far-reaching than that. Distribution of power in the world relates closely to institutional plurality.

This applies even to the institutional basis of world trade and finance, which includes, among other arrangements, such institutions as the World Trade Organization, the World Bank, the IMF, and so on. It is necessary to re-examine the balance of power in the running of different institutions that make up the global architecture. The present institutional architecture was largely set up in the middle 1940s, on the basis of the understanding of the needs of the world economy as interpreted in the Bretton Woods conference held just as the Second World War was coming to an end. That framework did help to foster trade and development, but not

的对成年健康的危害；它让公共辩论的范围和效果更加宽泛，而且在延缓生育率方面，比经济增长对生育率的影响更大。孟加拉国的生育率在过去近20年内减半，这让我们看到加强妇女权益的影响力。虽然印度部分地区生育率仍然很高，但在另外一些性别比较平等的地区，出生率已低于美国和英国。

为妇女平等做事的社会机构，涉及范围之广，令人吃惊。约翰·肯尼思·加尔布雷斯[3]雄辩地阐述过一个重要观点，即在评估某些机构的作用时，要看它们彼此之间的"相互抵消能力"。一个领域中的不对称影响，可以通过在另一领域不同势力之间的消长来评估。所有这一切，包括更多的东西，都在加尔布雷斯于1952年首次出版的《美国资本主义》中有所讨论。我记得在加尔各答读大学时，曾在一家咖啡馆读这本书，一边试图抵抗服务员的驱逐。他并非无理，因为我不能只买一杯咖啡，就霸占着椅子读完一整本书。那个场合里，我只是用声音作为相互抵消的能力，以示我绝不挪窝的决心，但在一般情况下，我们需要比这更深远的体制平衡。世界上权力的分配，与体制的多元化密切相关。

这也适用于世界贸易和金融，其中包括世界贸易组织、世界银行、国际货币基金组织等机构的体制基础。我们有必要重新审视搭建全球架构的不同机构之间，它们在运行中是如何取得权力平衡的。目前的体制架构，诞生于20世纪40年代中期、第二次世界大战即将结束之际的布雷顿森林会议上，根据人们对当时世界经济需要的理解而设定。这一框架的确有助于促进贸易和发展，但没有考虑到公平分配问题——无论是经济领域还是政治领域。

这个世界在上世纪40年代非常特别，当时亚洲和非洲的大部分地区仍然受到这样或那样的殖民统治，人民对不安全和贫困的承受能力也更大（就连西方世界，也是才刚刚经历过大衰退和一场极具破坏性的战争），那时，人民对世界上的民主、经济发展和人权在全球发展的前景还知之甚少，布雷顿森林体系的世界，与今天的世界大不相同。

即使在现有的全球体系里，那些重要机构采取哪些实质性的政策，也可以带来很大的区别。例如，最近世界银行制定的政策中，重点强调

much distributional equity - either in the economic or the political sphere. The world was, in fact, very different in the 1940s, when the bulk of Asia and Africa was still under colonial rule of one kind or another, when the tolerance of insecurity and of poverty was much greater (even the West had just emerged from a massive depression and a very destructive war), and when there was little understanding of the huge global prospects of democracy, economic development and human rights in the world. The world of Bretton Woods is not the world of today.

Even within the existing global architecture, the substantive policies followed by the principal institutions can make a big difference. For example, the recent changes in the policy priorities of the World Bank, with a much greater involvement with economic security and social development, has been undoubtedly influential. The existing institutions can address the global doubts more fully, and the United Nations can also play a very big role in forcing attention on these concerns. The U.N. has, of course, been kept in a state of financial precariousness particularly by member countries failing to pay their dues. There has also been a persistent attempt by some politicians to use ill-judged attacks on the functioning of the United Nations, trying their best to make a mole hill out of a real mountain. But the mountain is there, and the U.N. can play a most important part in the institutional balance in global economics and politics, provided it gets the support it deserves.

The real debate on globalization is, ultimately, not about the efficiency of markets, nor about the importance of modern technology. The debate, rather, is about the inequality of power, for which there is much less tolerance now than in the world that emerged at the end of the Second World War. There may or may not be significantly more economic inequality today (the evidence on this is conflicting, depending on the indicators we use), but what is absolutely clear is that people are far less willing to accept massive inequalities now than they were in 1944. The global doubts partly reflect the new mood, and it is, to a great extent, the global equivalent of the within-nation protests with which we have been familiar for quite some time. The global doubts have something in common with the spirit of an old American song - a variant of a defiant verse composed originally by Leadbelly:

In the home of the brave, land of the free,
I will not be put down by no bourgeoisie.

要参与经济安全和社会发展,这无疑是有深远意义的。现有的机构可以更充分地应对全球疑虑,而联合国也能在迫使人们意识到关注这些方面,起到非常大的作用。当然,联合国的资金一直不稳定,特别是有些成员国不缴纳会费。也有一些政客对联合国的运作不断进行不公正的攻击,他们竭力想把一座真正的山说成是个小土丘。但山就在那里,如果得到应有的支持的话,联合国可以在平衡全球经济和政治体制方面,发挥最重要的作用。

关于全球化问题的真正辩论,最终不是讨论市场的效率,也不是评价现代科技的重要性。这个辩论更确切地说是有关权力的不平等,因为与二战结束时相比,现在的人们对权力不均更加无法容忍。今天,经济上的不平等可能更大,也可能没那么突出(要看我们用的是何种指标,这方面的证据是相互矛盾的),但显而易见的是,相比于1944年,人们现在很难接受大规模的不平等现象。全球性的疑虑部分反映了这种新的心情,有点类似于我们已经熟悉了的那种在具体某个国家内部经常会发生的抗争。这种疑虑在某种程度上,与美国一首老歌的精神有共通之处,就像列贝利[4]最初写出的桀骜不驯的诗句:

在勇敢者的家里,在这片自由的土地,
我可不会再受制于资产阶级。

针对全球化的抨击来自不同方面,有着不同风格,出于不同的抱怨。要拒绝这类批评丝毫不难,对于应当反驳的观点予以回应,无可厚非。但尽管全球化经济对全世界的繁荣作出了很大贡献,我们也必须看到,全球面临的不平等现象所产生的严重后果。

许多年前,上世纪50年代,当目前的全球化还处于起步阶段时,一位英国朋友在访问印度之后告诉我,他没有料到,不同的国家,贸易和商业用语是那么不同。他在新德里的一个糖果店给他的孩子买糖果,看到两个装满糖果的玻璃罐被醒目地摆放在店内,一个用粗体字母描述瓶子里的东西,说是"高级",另一个罐子也是粗体字,但写着"低级"。

Attacks on globalization come from different quarters, in dissimilar styles, with disparate grumbles. It is not at all difficult to reject many of the criticisms that have been made, and it is right that rejectable points should be repulsed. But there is a basic need to recognize that despite the big contributions that a global economy can undoubtedly make to global prosperity, we also have to confront the far-reaching manifestations of global inequality.

Many years ago, in the 1950s, when the present phase of globalization was in its infancy, an English friend of mine told me, after visiting India, that he was struck by the fact that the language of trade and commerce was so different in different countries. He had gone to a candy shop in New Delhi to buy sweets for his children and found two glass jars full of candies, prominently displayed in the shop. One described the contents, in bold letters, as "Superior," and the other said, also in bold letters: "Inferior." My English friend was not yet ready for such plain speaking; he would have expected the second jar to be called "regular," or "standard," or something like that.

In the growing intolerance of inequality on which the global doubts draw, there is something of a similar inclination to recognize and react to disparities - not only in terms of affluence but also in terms of power. What may have looked like "regular" or "standard" inequality in 1944 appears more and more as an intolerable imposition of inferiority on hundreds of millions of people. This recognition does not, of course, validate all the slogans on the placards and posters of anti-globalization rhetoric. Nor can it be seen as an invitation to become well-frogs. Nor indeed does it obviate the need for critical examination of institutional reform and policy initiatives.

There can be no holiday from scientific scrutiny in answering questions. But in deciding on what questions to ask, what problems demand attention, we cannot ignore the voices of concern - and of humanity. We cannot, to use Francis Bacon's words, let these broader doubts pass "lightly without intervention." The significance of the global doubts lies in the themes, not in the theses. These doubts may often take a critically destructive form, but their ultimate importance is constructive. We cannot ignore that importance any more than we can neglect the positive contributions of globalization.

Thank you!

我的英国朋友还不习惯于这样直接的表述，他想第二个罐子应该写着"普通等级"或"标准等级"等类似的字眼。

全球性的疑虑表明人们越来越无法容忍不平等，人们对差距的认识和反应，也出现一些类似的倾向，不仅在财富方面，在权力方面也是如此。在 1944 年看起来像是"普通等级"或"标准等级"而被忽视的不平等，现在对亿万人民来说，成了越来越不能容忍的侮辱。当然，这种认识并不表明那些反对全球化的招贴和标语牌上的口号有什么道理，它也不能成为人们退作井底之蛙的借口，而且也确实不能排除我们对体制的改革和政策措施，需要再去进行认真的分析。

在回答问题时，我们不能回避科学性的审视。但在决定问什么问题，决定什么问题需要关注时，我们不能忽略顾虑的声音，也不能忽视人文的关怀。用培根的话来说，就是我们不能让这些更广泛的疑虑"轻易地、没经过思考就蒙混过关"。全球性疑虑的意义，不在于它的论点，而在于它的主题。这些怀疑可能会表现出极具破坏性的形式，但其最终作用是建设性的。我们不能忽略其重要性，就像我们不能忽略全球化的积极贡献一样。

谢谢各位！

---

1 约翰·德莱顿（John Dryden，1631—1700），英国诗人、文学评论家与剧作家，是当时英国最有影响的作家，1667 年被授予"桂冠诗人"称号。

2 阿尔伯特·赫什曼（Albert Hirschman），1915 年出生于德国，政治经济学家，曾在哈佛、耶鲁等大学任教。

3 约翰·肯尼思·加尔布雷斯（John Kenneth Galbraith，1908—2006），加拿大出生的美国经济学家，凯恩斯主义者，是 1950 年代至 1970 年代间，在美国经济问题方面颇有影响力的公共知识分子。

4 列贝利（Leadbelly，原名 Huddie Ledbetter，1885—1949），黑人歌手，美国民谣的传奇人物。

罗伯特·鲁宾（1938— ）

罗伯特·鲁宾是美国银行家。1938年出生于纽约市，1956年考入哈佛大学，4年后获哈佛经济学学士学位，后就读于耶鲁大学法学院，并于1964年获得法学学位。后来，哈佛、耶鲁、哥伦比亚大学，宾夕法尼亚大学、纽约大学和迈阿密大学等，都先后授予鲁宾荣誉博士学位。

1964至1966年，鲁宾在纽约的一家律师事务所任律师，1966年加入高盛公司，历任合伙人、副董事长兼联席运营官、联席高级合伙人兼联席董事长。1993年加入克林顿内阁，在白宫担任总统经济政策助理和首任国家经济委员会主任。1995年1月至1999年7月，出任美国第70任财政部长。鲁宾在任期内，把国家的赤字转为盈余，并在1995年援助解决墨西哥财政危机中发挥了积极的作用。

1999年10月，鲁宾加入花旗集团，任董事、执行委员会主席和董事长办公室成员，并担任美国著名的社区发展援助组织 Local Initiatives Support Corporation（LISC）的理事长。此外，他还是福特汽车公司董事和纽约大学西奈山健康医院（Mount Sinai-NYU Health）理事、哈佛大学理事会（Harvard Corporation）理事。2003年10月，他出任美国对外关系委员会副主席。

鲁宾著有《不确定的世界：从华尔街到华盛顿的艰难选择》(Random House, 2003年出版，与 Jacob Weisberg 合著)，曾列《纽约时报》畅销书榜，并入选《商业周刊》评选的年度十佳商业著作。

有人评论说，鲁宾是自汉密尔顿（Alexander Hamilton）以来美国最了不起的财政部长。

2001

The Critical Function of Decision-making
决策能力决定命运

Robert Rubin 罗伯特·鲁宾

I am deeply honored to be your commencement speaker today. A little over forty years ago, I arrived as a freshman at Harvard College, from a public school in Miami Beach, Florida. I remember the first day of orientation, when the incoming freshman class met together at Memorial Hall, and the acting Dean of Freshman said, as an effort at reassurance, that only 2% of the incoming class would fail out. I felt that I was providing enormous protection to the rest of my incoming classmates, because in my mind I was going to fall short so colossally as to fill that whole 2% all by myself.

However, I remained, and my Harvard experience reshaped the intellectual framework through which I viewed everything that came my way, including the decision-making that has been the critical core of my professional life, both on Wall Street and in government. My views on that critical function of decision-making derived from my life's activities and formatively and powerfully from my Harvard experience, will be the primary focus of my remarks today, because I believe that decision-making will be at the core of your lives, too, no matter what you do. The only question will be how well you make those decisions.

Larry Summers, my former colleague at Treasury and your outstanding incoming President, used to say, when we faced tough situations in Washington, that life is about making choices. And I think that is exactly right. Curiously, though, despite this profoundly important reality, most people give very little serious consideration to how they make decisions. Thus, I would add to Larry's comment, that how thoughtfully you make those choices will critically affect how good those choices will be and how effective you will be.

In addition to discussing decision-making, I'll end my remarks by urging that today's graduates spend at least part of their careers in public service, where so many of our society's most complex decisions - affecting the lives of all of us - must be made.

Sophomore year, in Emerson Hall, I took Philosophy I with Professor Rafael Demos. I still remember the first day of class when a relatively short, white haired, elderly Greek man walked onto the stage in the lecture hall and instead of using a podium, turned a wastebasket upside down on a desk, put his notes on top, and started to speak. That unadorned simplicity - in the best sense - permeated his thinking and his teaching. And Philosophy I was only part of a broader Harvard intellectual experience that provided my most important training for subsequent careers in risk arbitrage investment on Wall Street and in economic policy making in government.

The Critical Function of Decision-making Robert Rubin
决策能力决定命运 罗伯特·鲁宾

作为今天的毕业典礼演讲者，我感到非常荣幸。40多年前，我从佛罗里达州的一所公立学校来到哈佛，成为一名一年级新生。我还记得在开学情况介绍会的第一天，当一年级学生聚在纪念大厅的时候，新生学院院长想要安慰我们，说每年入学的新生里，一般只有百分之二的人会因为学不下去而辍学。我当时很自卑，觉得自己简直要为同年入学的同学垫底儿——我认为自己会彻底失败，我一个人就会把那百分之二的名额占满。

不过，我熬过来了。我的哈佛经验重塑了我的知识体系，在我后来的人生道路上，我就用这种知识架构来看问题，包括构成我职业生涯中的重要核心部分，那些需要作出决策的时候。在华尔街时是这样，在政府决策中也是如此。我对作出决策这种关键能力的看法，来自我的生活经验，并因为我的哈佛经历而定型，这也会是我今天讲话的要点。我认为不管你将来做什么，决策能力都将影响你的生活。唯一的问题是，你如何作出最佳决定。

我在美国财政部曾经的同事拉里·萨默斯[1]——也是你们即将上任的校长——这样说过：当我们在华盛顿面临严峻问题时，其实就是考验你如何作出选择。我完全同意他的说法。奇怪的是，尽管这是生活中很重要的一部分，多数人对此却很少认真考虑。因此，我要对拉里的话作些补充，那就是：经过深思熟虑所作的决定的好坏，取决于你如何决策，决定的好坏会影响到你的效率。

除了谈如何决策，我在讲话的最后还想敦促今天的毕业生们，在你们的职业生涯里至少花上一些时间，任职于政府事务中，因为我们社会中许多最复杂的决定要在那里作出，而这些决定会影响到我们所有人的生活。

大学二年级的时候，我在爱默生教学楼上了拉菲尔·德默斯教授的哲学入门课，我还记得第一天上课的情景。一个身材不高、满头白发的希腊裔老人，走到课堂的台阶上，他没有用讲台，而是把一个垃圾篓倒扣在一张桌子上，接着开始讲话。那种令人心仪的简单淳朴，贯穿着他的思想和教学。哲学入门课只是我在哈佛获得广泛知识经验的一部分，这为我后来的职业生涯，比如在华尔街进行风险套利投资和在政府内作

Professor Demos would lead us through the great philosophical thinkers of the ages, not in the spirit of simply understanding and accepting their views, but rather to use their views as launching points for our own critical thinking, to question how well each thinker's analysis held together and, most importantly, to question how each assertion of truth was proven. And, as I slowly came to realize, the absolute truths that were asserted turned out to be unprovable and, in the final analysis, to be based on belief or assumption. Only later did I learn that many in modern science hold exactly the same view, that is that sophisticated theories can be developed and then proven by experimentation, but that ultimately this whole structure rests on unprovable assumptions.

I also remember that after we had struggled with thinkers whose work was immensely difficult to understand, Professor Demos then assigned another set of thinkers whose work was relatively easy to understand. However, we came to realize that this group lacked the trying but tight rigor and discipline of a Kant or Spinoza, and seemed intellectually loose, and unsatisfying. We then returned to the more difficult philosophers, with a newly developed appreciation for rigorous thinking.

From the guidance of this gentle professor, and from all my other experience at Harvard, I developed in the core of my being the view that **there are no provable absolutes, and that, with the absence of provable certainty, all decisions are about probabilities** - that is, all decisions are about the respective probabilities, of each of a number of possible outcomes actually occurring. Moreover, recognizing that all decisions are about probabilities rather than certainties should lead us to uncover and engage with the full array of complexities around making the best decisions.

Perhaps most importantly, rejecting the idea of certainties and needing to make the best judgments possible about probabilities, should drive you restlessly and rigorously to analyze and question whatever is before you - and to treat assertions as launching pads for analysis, not as accepted truths - in pursuit of better understanding.

Moreover, judging probabilities is far from the only complexity in decision-making. Often, each alternative possible outcome is not a simple, single effect, but the net effect of tradeoffs between competing considerations. I'm not expecting in these remarks to fully discuss these thoughts, but rather to convey my view as to the intellectual complexity inherent in making good decisions.

To exemplify both probabilities and tradeoffs, when the new administration's

出经济决策，提供了最重要的培训。德默斯教授带着我们领略了历史上伟大哲学家们的学说，不是简单地去理解和接受他们的看法，而是把他们的那些看法当做我们自己批判性思考的起点，去探讨每一位思想家的分析是否站得住脚，最重要的是，去研究哲学家们是如何证明自己观点的。同时，正如我逐渐认识到的，有些人信誓旦旦阐述的绝对真理，实际上是无法证明的，说到底，那些绝对真理最终的依据还是信仰或设想。我到后来才知道，现代科学中的许多人也是这样看的，因为人们可以提出很多复杂的理论，并用实验证明，但最终，这一整套东西依然是无法证明的假设。

我还记得，在我们无法读透某些极难理解的思想家的作品时，德默斯教授会指定我们去接触另一些思想家，他们的作品较易读懂。但是我们会认识到，这些作品缺乏康德或斯宾诺莎著作里的那种严谨和训练有素的张力，所以显得思维松散，让人读了不大过瘾。等我们再回过头来阅读那些艰深的哲学家著作时，就对他们的严谨思维有了新的欣赏与理解。

由于这位教授的耐心指导，还有我在哈佛的所有其他经历，我有了自己的处世哲学，即**世上没有什么可验证的绝对事物，由于没有可验证的确定性，我们所有的决定，其实都是对各种可能性的反应，也就是说，所有的决定都要针对各种可能性，针对一系列实际可能出现的结果来做。此外，认识到所有的决定都是针对概率而不是必然，我们在力图作出最佳决策时，就要全方位地发现并把握复杂问题。**

也许最重要的是，拒绝接受"必然性"这种想法，以及需要根据各种可能性而作出最佳判断，这两点认识应当让你无论面临什么问题，都要进行严格分析和提出质疑，并把前人论断作为进一步分析的起点、而不是必须接受的真理，这样我们对事物才能有更好的认识。

此外，概率的评估远不是决策中唯一复杂的东西。每一个可能的替代选择，并非表现为一个简单的、单一的效果，而是利弊取舍、综合权衡之后的考虑。我不指望在这个讲话中充分讨论这些观点，而是希望表达一个看法，即作出好的决策，需要复杂的脑力劳动。

举个例子说明一下概率评估和利弊取舍：1993年，当我们新政府的

economic team opted for deficit reduction to stimulate economic recovery in 1993, we told the President that the likelihood of success was good, but that there were no guarantees, so that he could make a decision on this dramatic change in fiscal policy with full awareness of the economic and political risks. We also said that even if the strategy did work, the result would be a tradeoff between competing considerations - the positive of economic recovery and the negative of being unable to fund some of his desired programs. Again life is about making choices, and that quickly leads you to probabilities and tradeoffs.

With that, let me make one final point about how complex decision-making can be - the point that sometimes all choices are bad, but some are better than others. For example, our administration was greatly criticized for having worked with the International Monetary Fund to extend support to Russia in 1998, when Russia was facing a severe financial and economic crisis. Clearly, there was a substantial risk that additional assistance would not be effective. On the other hand, there was no question that our country had a very substantial national security interest in attempting to help stave off economic crisis in Russia, even if the likelihood of success was relatively low. All choices were probably bad in that case, including doing nothing, but there was still one choice that was least bad. Often, decision-makers faced with a situation where all choices are bad, react by not deciding. That, however, is a decision in itself, and often the wrong decision.

Let me mention one other situation that exemplifies what I've been saying about decision-making.

I often remember an experience early in my own Wall Street career, when I was investing our firm's capital in arbitrage and a friendly competitor at another firm explained his massive investment in what he viewed as a sure thing.

I agreed that it looked certain, but on the theory that **there are no certainties but only probabilities, I made a very large investment, but still at a level where the loss was affordable if the entirely unexpected happened.** And, it did. The investment failed: we took a large loss, and he took a loss beyond reason - and lost his job.

I doubt if Kant or Spinoza viewed themselves as offering the best and more important preparation for risk arbitrage or for intervention in the dollar/yen foreign exchange market or for the many other activities of a finance minister. But, in my view, they did. Looking back on all my years in the private and public sectors, in the most important issues, certainties were almost always illusory and misleading, as were the

经济顾问小组选择减少赤字来刺激经济复苏时，我们告诉总统说，成功的可能性挺高，但无法保证，这样，总统就可以作出导致财政政策发生巨大变化的这一决定，并充分认识到其中的经济和政治风险。我们还说，即使该策略有效，其结果将是不同考虑之间的一个权衡取舍：积极的一面是，经济会复苏；消极的一面是，总统希望推行的一些项目会得不到资助。在这里，生活又意味着作出抉择，那就又回到概率评估和权衡取舍的讨论上了。

我还想谈谈，决策过程有时会是很复杂的。有时候，所有的选择都不好，但两害相权取其轻。例如，1998年，当俄罗斯面临严重的金融和经济危机时，我们的政府与国际货币基金组织一同给俄罗斯提供了帮助，这个做法遭到很多批评。显然，一个很大的风险是，这样做没什么成效。另一方面，试图帮助俄罗斯避免经济危机，哪怕成功的可能性较低，对我们国家来说，也会有非常重大的国家安全影响。所有选择可能都是坏的，包括袖手旁观，但总还有一个最不坏的选择。决策者在面临所有选择都不好的情况下，往往采取无为而治的态度。不过，这样做本身就是一种决策，而且常常是错误的决策。

让我再举一个例子，解释我说的有关决策的讨论。

在我华尔街生涯的早期，一次我用公司的资本进行套利交易投资，这时另一个公司的友好竞争者对我说，他的一笔巨大投资十拿九稳。

我赞同他说的，这看上去比较稳妥，但从理论上说，**没有什么是必然的，只有概率。我也做一笔很大的投资，但其规模是，如果意外的事情发生，我们足以负担得起所带来的损失**。后来，意外真的发生了。该项投资失败，我们损失了一大笔，而他的损失大得不可思议，导致他失去了工作。

我不知道康德或斯宾诺莎是否认为自己能为风险套利，或美元与日元汇率市场进行干预，或对一名财政部长的诸多行动提供最佳和更重要的理论依据，但我认为，他们做到了。回顾我在私营和公共部门的这些年头，在最重要的问题上，绝对必然的东西几乎总是存在于虚无飘渺之间，容易产生误导。在政治讨论或私营部门里，面临复杂的问题时，人们往往习惯于给出简单的答案或发表单纯的意见。现实是复杂的，认识

simple answers or opinions that often were the response to the complicated issues in both political discourse and the private sector. Reality is complex, and recognizing complexity and engaging with complexity was the path to best decision-making.

This, as you leave Harvard to undertake a vast variety of pursuits, I believe that nothing will be as important to you - no experience or professional training - as the ways of thinking and the restless pursuit of understanding you have had the opportunity to develop at this great institution.

An important corollary [n.[数] 系理. 推论] **to recognizing that decisions are about probabilities is that decisions should not be judged by outcomes but by the quality of the decision-making,** though outcomes are certainly one useful input in that evaluation. Any individual decisions can be badly thought through, and yet be successful, or exceedingly well thought through, but be unsuccessful, because the recognized possibility of failure in fact occurs. But over time, more thoughtful decision-making will lead to better overall results, and more thoughtful decision-making can be encouraged by evaluating decisions on how well they were made rather than on outcome. In managing trading rooms, I always focused on evaluating and promoting traders not on their results alone, but also and very importantly, on the thinking that underlay their decisions. Unfortunately, this approach is not widely taken, much to the detriment of decision-making in both the private and public sectors.

In Washington, for example, there is very little tolerance for decisions that don't turn out to be successful, creating a tendency to counter productive risk aversion. In 1995, for example, our administration decided to assist Mexico financially in attempting recovery from an economic crisis, and the program succeeded. Then, three years later, we made a conceptually similar decision with regard to Russia and the effort did not succeed. I believe that the decision on Mexico would have been right even if the program had failed, and that the decision on Russia was right even though it did fail. In both cases, we knew that there were no guarantees of success - and in fact, real chances of failure. But we also felt that the chances of success were good enough, and the consequences of not engaging were a severe enough threat to American economic and national security interests, that involvement was the right decision. We were praised for the Mexican program, and criticized for the Russian program, in both cases because of the outcomes. I think both those reactions were based on looking at the wrong things. And that has real consequences. In the Mexican case, especially,

到这个复杂性，并对付这种复杂，才是取得最佳决策的路径。

当你们即将离开哈佛，各自追求三百六十行的事业时，我认为，对你们而言最重要的一点，不是过去的经验或专业培训，而是你们有机会在这所名校锻炼的思维方式和对事物的不懈探究。

认识到我们作决定时都要评估各种可能性，那么，我们就可以得出一个重要的结论：评价某个决定是否正确，不应只看结果，而要看决策过程的质量。当然结果的好坏也是评估的一个方面。任何一个决定，都有两种可能性：虽然草率，却无心插柳柳成荫；或经过慎重考虑，却无功而废。因为天有不测风云，有时担心的事偏偏发生了。但总的来说，考虑周到的决策能够导致整体较好的结果。如果我们评价一个决定的好坏，不是光看结果如何，而是看决策过程是否够好，这样就能鼓励人们审时度势地作决定。在管理投资交易部门时，对交易员的评估和提拔，我一向着重于不仅看结果，也看他们的决策的思维基础。不幸的是，这种办法并不太流行，这大大损害了私营企业和公共部门的决策能力。

在华盛顿，人们很难容忍事后被证明是不成功的决定，这使得一些人办起事来前怕狼后怕虎。比如 1995 年，我们的政府决定在财政上帮助墨西哥度过经济危机，该项目获得了成功。3 年后，我们作出了一项从概念上来说相类似的决定，去帮助俄罗斯，但却没有成功。我认为，在墨西哥问题上，即使最后方案失败了，也不影响决定的正确性；而有关俄罗斯的决定，虽然它的确失败了，那项决定也是该做的。在那两种情况下，我们知道没有任何成功的保障，事实上，失败的可能性倒是真正存在的。但我们也感觉到，成功的机会还是有的。如果不去做这两件事，对美国经济和国家安全利益的威胁会相当大，所以伸出援手是正确的决定。由于这两个项目的结果不同，我们针对墨西哥的项目受到了赞扬，而对俄罗斯的项目受到了批评。我认为，这些反应都是因为人们看问题的角度错了，那样的后果会是严重的。特别是在墨西哥那件事上，克林顿总统作出决定之时很清楚地知道，如果事与愿违，会对他政治生涯造成很大损害，而且知道，媒体和政坛对此的评价只会看结果好坏。幸运的是，克林顿总统愿意冒这样的风险，但在通常情况下，我们的环境会导致人

President Clinton made the decision well knowing that failure could cause him great political damage, and that the judgment and evaluation of the decision in the media and the political universe would be based solely on the outcome. Fortunately, President Clinton was willing to take that risk, but too often this environment deters optimal decisions where there is a risk of failure.

And that leads me to the thoughts on public service I mentioned at the beginning of my remarks.

When I began in the new administration, a distinguished former cabinet member told me that I would now live off my previously accumulated intellectual capital, because I would be too busy to add to it.

I found just the opposite - that my time in government was an intense learning experience about how our government and our political processes worked and about a vast array of policy issues. I also found that the decisions that had to be made were often amongst the most complex faced anywhere in our society. Public service was a powerful challenge in using all the intellectual qualities that Harvard had sought to develop, towards the objective of furthering the public good.

I believe strongly in a market based, private sector driven economy. But there are a host of critically important functions that markets by their nature cannot or will not perform optimally, from education, programs for the inner city, law enforcement, defense, and environmental protection or defense and foreign policy, and this array of functions becomes greater and more challenging in a world of increasing global interdependence.

Thus we must attract to government a critical mass of people with the intellectual drive, the restless quest for understanding, and the effectiveness at decision-making that we have been discussing this afternoon. There was a terrible period during my time in government when radio talk shows and even important elective officials regularly derogated public service and public servants. The atmosphere around government has substantially improved in the last few years, but simply reducing the level of **disparagement** [n. 轻视. 轻蔑] is not enough. The people I worked with in government were as capable and committed as any I had worked with anywhere. But, to continue to attract the outstanding people to public service that the issues and functions require, I believe we all have the obligation - especially those who have received the benefits conferred by our great universities to reject the **denigration** [n. 诋毁. 损贬] of public service and to help re-establish an environment of honor and respect for

们不去作最佳决定,从而求得自保。

顺着这个思路,回到我在讲话开始时提到的,到政府部门服务这个话题。

当我开始在新政府任职时,一位有名的前内阁成员告诉我说,从现在起,要靠以前积累的经验和知识了,因为我会忙得没时间给自己充电。

我发现情况恰恰相反,我在政府任职的那段时间,是一个紧张的学习过程,去了解政府和我们的政治程序,以及一系列政策性的问题。我也发现,我们必须作出的决定,常常涉及社会中最复杂的问题。公共服务部门能够为在哈佛培养出的所有智慧与才华,向着促进公众利益的目标,提供一个大显身手的舞台。

我对以市场为基础、由私营企业来推动的经济深以为然。但由于市场经济的性质,有一些至关重要的职能无法由市场来决定,从教育、贫困城区的支持项目、执法机构、国防,到环境保护、国防政策和外交政策等等,在全球日益相互依存的环境下,这一系列的政府职能变得更重要,也更具挑战性。

因此,我们必须吸引一定数量的人到政府任职,他们具备我们今天下午讨论的那些素质:有智慧、很强的求知欲,并有决策能力。我在政府工作期间,有一段日子,电台节目、甚至重要的民选官员,都经常抨击公共服务部门以及公务员,那个阶段不那么令人愉快。过去这几年,气氛有所改观,但只是减低了对公共部门轻视的程度,这远远不够。我在政府的同事和我在任何地方一起做过事的人相比,同样有能力,很投入。但是,应当继续吸引优秀人才投入到公共服务部门中来,去处理问题,胜任其职。我认为,我们——特别是那些已经从大学得到收益的人——都有义务不去理会对公共服务的贬损,并携手努力重建一个对公共服务和公职人员心怀尊敬的环境。

请允许我再迅速补充一点。我所说的,一点也不涉及政府到底应该在我们的社会里扮演什么角色,我们的辩论完全适当。这种辩论和美国联邦制的历史一样长,在我们的历史进程中,政府的作用也有很大的变化。不过,有一点是不该成为辩论话题的,那就是:政府的作用大小以及如何才是最好

public service and public servants.

None of this, let me quickly add, has anything to do with the perfectly proper debate about what the role of government should be in our society. This debate is as old as our republic, and the role of government has fluctuated substantially over the course of our history. However, what should not be a matter of debate - no matter what one views may be as to the appropriate role of government - is the respect that we accord public service and public servants.

Beyond urging that all of us contribute to re-establishing that environment of respect, I would also urge that those of you graduating today consider spending at least some time - and hopefully, for some of you, a whole career - in public service.

Public service, at whatever level of seniority, can provide immense challenge to all of your capabilities, as you help make and execute decisions in the most complex of circumstances, to further the well-being of the nation and even the world. And, you can get a very special insight into many of our society's most important policy issues, and a very special insight into how our society works - for example, how policy, politics, and media interact to affect what happens.

Government service, whether for a few years or for a career, can provide enormous challenge and intellectual growth, and the satisfaction of working to directly further the public good.

With that, let me conclude by thanking you for the opportunity to share views that I have thought a great deal about over the years. Important issues are complicated, and many of the most complicated are involved in the immense challenges requiring effective governance in our country and throughout the world. You have been prepared by an outstanding institution - Harvard - to deal with this complexity in whatever you do and to contribute greatly to that governance.

Thus, you have an extraordinary opportunity to develop lives that work for you and to serve your country and all of human kind. That is a wonderful prospect.

And so, I congratulate each of you graduating today on all that you have accomplished and on this momentous occasion in your lives; I wish each of you the best in the years and decades ahead; and I hope you will cherish and advance in the world the great intellectual traditions that Harvard represents as so many of your predecessors have before you.

Thank you.

的——对此无论看法如何，我们都应当对公共服务和公务员给予尊重。

除了敦促我们所有人，都为重新建立起这种表示尊重的环境而作出努力，我也敦请今天毕业的同学们，考虑至少到政府部门工作一段时间，并希望你们中的一些人，终身供职于公共服务部门。

到政府部门服务，不管在任何一个级别做事，都可以考验你所有的才能，因为你要在最复杂的情况下作出决定并去执行，从而促进我们国家，甚至全世界的福祉。而且，你还得以对我们社会中许多最重要的政策问题有深入的了解，知道我们的社会是如何运行的，比方说政策、政治与媒体之间，是如何相互影响，从而导致后来会有什么样的事情发生等等。

在政府部门服务，不论几年，也许一辈子，都会带给你巨大的挑战和智力发展，也因为你直接服务于大众利益，而能从中得到一种满足感。

在即将结束讲话之际，我非常感谢你们给了我这个机会，让我就自己过去多年一直思考的问题与大家一起交流。重要的问题会是复杂的，那些牵涉到巨大挑战的最复杂的问题，很多都需要我们国家和世界范围内提供有效的管理人才。经过哈佛的磨练，不管你们将来做什么事，都能够处理这种复杂性，并为这种管理添砖加瓦。

因此，你们生逢其时，可以让自己的人生更精彩，并为国效力，服务于全人类。那真是一个非常美好的前景。

所以，我祝贺今天毕业的各位，为你们已经取得的成绩，为你们生命中这个重大的时刻。我祝福你们在今后的岁月里前程远大，也希望你们在实际工作中珍惜和推动哈佛所代表的优秀的知识传统，正如你们之前那么多学长所做出的那样。

谢谢各位！

---

1 拉里·萨默斯（Larry Summers），美国经济学家，曾任美国财政部长（1999年7月至2001年1月在任），哈佛大学校长（2001年7月至2006年6月在任）。

Daniel Patrick Moynihan

丹尼尔·帕特里克·"帕特"·莫伊尼汉（1927—2003）

丹尼尔·帕特里克·"帕特"·莫伊尼汉，美国社会学家、政治家，美国民主党成员，曾任美国驻印度大使、美国驻联合国大使和美国参议员，是唯一一位两次应邀在哈佛毕业典礼上发表演讲的人。

莫伊尼汉出生于美国俄克拉荷马州的一个犹太裔家庭，6岁随父母移居纽约，在普通的居民区长大。高中毕业后，他先在纽约城市大学读书一年，随后加入美国海军，得到资助进入塔夫茨大学。获得学士学位后，他于1944至1947年在美国海军服兵役，后来又回到塔夫茨大学，先后获得社会学硕士和博士学位。之后莫伊尼汉获得富尔布莱特奖学金，到伦敦政治经济学院学习。

上世纪50年代，莫伊尼汉在纽约州长办公室任职，就此开始了其政治生涯。1960年，他成为约翰·肯尼迪旗下的民主党全国代表大会的一名代表，先后参与支持肯尼迪、尼克松的总统竞选活动。他还是福特总统的内阁成员。

莫伊尼汉曾担任由哈佛大学和麻省理工学院合办的城市研究中心主任，也曾在威斯里安大学做研究。除了研究美国的城市问题，也非常关注城市中的贫民问题。他总共撰写了19本书，他的一位教授朋友称赞他"写的书比许多参议员读过的书还要多"。由于学术上的成就，美国著名政治评论家迈克尔·巴伦（Michael Barone）评价莫伊尼汉是"自林肯总统以来，全国政治家中最好的思想者，自杰弗逊总统以来，思想者中最好的政治家"。

这篇演讲是莫伊尼汉在哈佛毕业典礼上所作的第二次演讲（第一次演讲在1976年）。由于9·11事件发生不久，莫伊尼汉着重讲了国际关系、文化冲突与并存，以及反恐等问题。

2002

History Summons Us Once More
历史的再次召唤

Daniel Patrick Moynihan 丹尼尔·莫伊尼汉

Mr. President, Dear professors, alumni, and today's graduates:

A while back it came as something of a start to find in The New Yorker a reference to an article I had written, and I quote, "In the middle of the last century." Yet persons my age have been thinking back to those times and how, in the end, things turned out so well and so badly. Millions of us returned from the assorted services to find the economic growth that had come with the Second World War had not ended with the peace. The Depression had not resumed. It is not perhaps remembered, but it was widely thought it would.

It would be difficult indeed to summon up the optimism that came with this great surprise. My beloved colleague Nathan Glazer and the **revered** [Adj. 受尊敬的] David Riesman wrote that America was "the land of the second chance" and so indeed it seemed. We had surmounted the depression; the war. We could realistically think of a world of stability, peace — above all, a world of law.

Looking back, it is clear we were not nearly so fortunate. Great leaders preserved — and in measure extended — democracy. But totalitarianism had not been defeated. To the contrary, by 1948 totalitarians controlled most of Eurasia. As we now learn, 11 days after Nagasaki the Soviets established a special committee to create an equivalent weapon. Their first atomic bomb was acquired through espionage, but their hydrogen bomb was their own doing. Now the Cold War was on. From the summer of 1914, the world had been at war, with interludes no more. It finally seemed to end with the collapse of the Soviet Union and the changes in China.

But now we have to ask if it is once again the summer of 1914.

Small acts of terror in the Middle East, in South Asia, could lead to **cataclysm** [n. 大洪水，(社会政治的) 大变动], as they did in Sarajevo. And for which great powers, mindful or not, have been preparing.

The eras are overlapping.

As the United States reacts to the mass murder of 9/11 and prepares for more, it would do well to consider how much terror India endured in the second half of the last century. And its response. It happens I was our man in New Delhi in 1974 when India detonated its first nuclear device. I was sent in to see Prime Minister Indira Gandhi with a statement as much as anything of

History Summons Us Once More
历史的再次召唤
Daniel Patrick Moynihan 丹尼尔·莫伊尼汉

尊敬的校长,各位老师,各位校友和今天毕业的同学们:

前一阵子,《纽约客》杂志发表的一篇文章引用了我以前的一篇文章,我在这里引述一句:"上个世纪50年代。"我的同龄人时不时就会想起那个时代,没想到后来的情况会变得这么好,也没想到会坏成这样。我们数以百万计的复员军人,看到在实现和平之后,伴随二战而起的经济增长一路持续下去,大萧条没有再现。人们也许不记得这回事了,但都认为它还会发生。

经历了这些大风大浪,的确很难再保持乐观。我的同事内森·格拉泽[1]和广受尊敬的戴维·里斯曼[2]写道,美国是一个"能让人跌倒了再爬起来的地方",看来的确如此。我们克服了大萧条,赢得了战争。我们能够很现实地希望世界和平、稳定,最重要的是,这个世界变得有法可循。

现在回过头来看,很明显我们没那么幸运。伟大的领袖人物能够坚持,并且延续民主。但是极权主义还没有被打败。相反,到了1948年的时候,极权主义控制了欧亚大陆的大部分地区。就像我们现在所知道的,在长崎核爆的11天之后,苏联就成立了一个特别委员会,要研制出相同的武器。他们的第一颗原子弹是通过间谍活动获得的,但他们的氢弹是自己研制出来的,结果冷战持续多年。从1914年夏天起,全世界就战火纷飞,没有停歇。至苏联解体和中国发生变化后,这个情况似乎终于结束了。

但现在我们要问一下,局势是否又如同1914年的夏天?

在中东地区和南亚,小规模的恐怖行为,都可能导致严重灾难,就像萨拉热窝的事件[3]一样。而那些强国,不管是否愿意,都在为此准备。

这两个时代在重叠。

当美国忙于应对9·11这样大规模的屠杀,并时刻防范着新一轮的袭击时,不妨想一下,印度自上世纪后半期经历了多少恐怖事件,也想想他们是如何反应的。1974年,印度第一次引爆核装置,那时我是美国驻新德里的大使。我受命去见英迪拉·甘地总理,并发表了一个类似表示遗憾的声明。因为我们没什么可以做的,该发生的还是要发生。作为地球上人口第二多的国家,印度不想解除自己的武装,让人轻视。因为

regret. For there was nothing to be done; it was going to happen. The second most populous nation on earth was not going to leave itself disarmed and disregarded, as non-nuclear powers appeared to be. But leaving, I asked to speak as a friend of India and not as an official. In twenty years time, I opined, there would be a Moghul general in command in Islamabad, and he would have nuclear weapons and would demand Kashmir back, perhaps the Punjab.

The Prime Minister said nothing; I dare to think she half agreed. In time, she would be murdered in her own garden; next, her son and successor was murdered by a suicide bomber. This, while nuclear weapons accumulated which are now poised.

Standing at Trinity Site at Los Alamos, J. Robert Oppenheimer pondered an ancient Sanskrit text in which Lord Shiva [印度湿婆神．湿婆也称"大自在天"。] declares, "I am become Death, the shatterer of worlds." Was he right?

At the very least we can come to terms with the limits of our capacity to foresee events.

It happens I had been a Senate observer to the START negotiations in Geneva, and was on the Foreign Relations Committee when the treaty, having been signed, was sent to us for ratification. In a moment of mischief I remarked to our superb negotiators that we had sent them to Geneva to negotiate a treaty with the Soviet Union, but the document before us was a treaty with four countries, only two of which I could confidently locate on a map. I was told they had exchanged letters in Lisbon [the Lisbon Protocol, May 23, 1992]. I said that sounded like a Humphrey Bogart movie.

The hard fact is that American intelligence had not the least anticipated the implosion of the Soviet Union. I cite Stansfield Turner, former director of the CIA in Foreign Affairs, 1991. "We should not gloss over the enormity of this failure to forecast the magnitude of the Soviet crisis…The corporate view missed by a mile."

Russia now faces a near-permanent crisis. By mid-century its population could well decline to as few as 80 million persons. Immigrants will press in; one dares not think what will have happened to the nuclear materials scattered across 11 time zones.

Admiral Turner's 1991 article was entitled "Intelligence for a New World

没有核武器的国家,说话就无足轻重。道别之际,我说我想作为印度的一个朋友,而不是带着官方身份再讲几句话。我阐述道,未来20年内,在伊斯兰堡可能会出现一个莫卧儿[4]的将军,他将拥有核武器,并以此要求印度交还克什米尔,或者旁遮普邦。

总理未置可否,我敢说她所见略同。不过后来她在自己的花园里被杀害,接下来,继任她的儿子也被人肉炸弹谋杀。与此同时,核武器不断累积,如今蓄势待发。

置身于洛斯阿拉莫斯的三位一体核试验基地,罗伯特·奥本海默[5]心中默念着古梵文里印度湿婆神所说的"我是死神,是世界的毁灭者……",他这样想对吗?

至少,我们可以原谅自己,在预见突发事件方面,能力有限。

凑巧的是,我曾作为参议院观察员,参加在日内瓦举行的"削减战略武器协议"[6]谈判,并在协议签署后,送到参议院等待批准时,担任对此进行审批的外交关系委员会的成员。我对那些优秀的谈判代表有点恶作剧地说,我们把他们送到日内瓦与苏联谈判,但放在我们面前的文件,却是一项与四个国家的协议,其中只有两个国家我能在地图上轻易找到。有人告诉我,他们在里斯本交换过文本(《里斯本议定书》是1992年5月23日交换的)。我说那听起来简直就像一部亨弗莱·鲍嘉[7]的电影。

严峻的事实是,美国的情报单位根本就没能预测到苏联会崩溃。我可以引用美国中央情报局前局长斯坦斯菲尔德·特纳于1991年在《外交事务》杂志上所写的一篇文章:"我们没能预测到苏联危机的严重性,对这个失职不能敷衍了事……我们的工作失之毫厘,谬以千里。"

俄罗斯现在面临近乎旷日持久的危机。到本世纪中叶,其人口也可能下滑到8000万人。外来移民会蜂拥而至,我们不敢想象,那些核材料分散在宽达11个时区的地方,将会出现什么情况?

海军上将特纳写于1991年的那篇文章,名为《世界新秩序下的情报工作》。两年后,塞缪尔·亨廷顿在同一份杂志上发表了题为《文明的冲突》一文,文中概述了将会出现的新世界秩序——或者无秩序。他随后以相同标题出版专著,这本书是为我们这个时代作出定义的宏篇巨著。

Order." Two years later Samuel Huntington outlined what that new world order — or disorder — would be in an article in the same journal entitled "The Clash of Civilizations." His subsequent book of that title is a defining text of our time.

Huntington perceives a world of seven or eight major conflicting cultures, the West, Russia, China, India, and Islam. Add Japan, South America, Africa. Most incorporate a major nation-state which typically leads its fellows.

The Cold War on balance suppressed conflict. But the end of the Cold War has brought not universal peace but widespread violence. Some of this has been merely residual **proxy** [n. 代理人，委托书] conflicts dating back to the earlier era. Some plain ethnic conflict. But the new horrors occur on the fault lines, as Huntington has it, between the different cultures.

For argument's sake one could propose that Marxism was the last nearly successful effort to Westernize the rest of the world. In 1975, I stood in Tiananmen Square, the center of the Middle Kingdom. In an otherwise empty space, there were two towering masts. At the top of one were giant portraits of two **hirsute** [adj. 多毛的] 19th century German gentlemen, Messrs. Marx and Engels. The other displayed a somewhat Mongol-looking Stalin and Mao. That wasn't going to last, and of course, it didn't.

Hence Huntington: "The central problem in the relations between the West and the rest is ... the discordance between the West's — particularly America's —— efforts to promote universal Western culture and its declining ability to do so."

Again **there seems to be no end of ethnic conflict within civilizations. But it is to the clash of civilizations we must look with a measure of dread.** The Bulletin of the Atomic Scientists recently noted that "The crisis between India and Pakistan, touched off by a December 13th terrorist attack on the Indian Parliament marks the closest two states have come to nuclear war since the Cuban Missile Crisis." By 1991, the minute-hand on their doomsday clock had dropped back to 17 minutes to midnight. It has since been moved forward three times and is again seven minutes to midnight, just where it started in 1947.

The terrorist attacks on the United States of last September 11 were not

亨廷顿描述了这个世界将分为七个或八个主要的互相冲突的文化：西方国家、俄罗斯、中国、印度和伊斯兰教世界，外加日本、南美和非洲。这几大部分主要由某个国家及其追随者组成。

总的来说，冷战制约了冲突，但它的结束并没有带来普遍的和平，而是到处出现的暴力。这些暴力中，有些要追溯到更早时候进行的"代理人战争"所遗留下来的冲突，有些则纯属种族冲突。但正如亨廷顿所言，新的恐怖会发生在不同文化之间的断层面上。

为了方便辩论，我们可以说，马克思主义是最后的几乎成功地把世界进行西化的一次努力。1975年，我来到天安门广场这个"中央之国"的中心，在一片空旷的地方竖着两根旗杆，顶端挂着19世纪两位留着大胡子的德国绅士——马克思先生和恩格斯先生的巨幅画像，另外两幅是斯大林和毛泽东。这不会持续很久的。果然，它当真没有持续太久。

因此，亨廷顿说："西方与其他国家之间的关系，问题的关键……是西方国家——尤其是美国——推行西方文化的努力，以及它们在这方面的能力不断下降所造成的不平衡。"

相同文明内部的民族冲突似乎没有尽头，但不同文明之间的冲突，才真正让我们不寒而栗。《原子能科学家公报》最近指出，"印度和巴基斯坦之间的危机引发了12月13日对印度议会进行的攻击，这是自古巴导弹危机以来，两个国家间最接近爆发核战争的危险行为"。到1991年，由该组织发布的世界末日时钟的分针跌到距离午夜有17分钟的位置，这段时间，分针向前移动了三次，又回到了离午夜只有7分钟的刻度，这跟1947年危险警示钟表开始时的刻度一模一样。

去年的9月11日，恐怖分子对美国发起袭击，没能用上核武器，但他们想这样做。让我再次引用亨廷顿的话："到某一时候……几个恐怖分子就能引发大量的暴力和大规模的破坏。另外，西方之外的弱者，会用恐怖主义和核武器来作为他们的武器。而如果恐怖主义和核武器结合起来，西方之外的弱者就会变得很强。"

这段话写于1996年。恐怖分子的第一次大规模谋杀发生于去年9月。就在上个月，美国副总统在接受蒂姆·拉瑟特[8]的采访时说："未来再次

nuclear, but they will be. Again to cite Huntington, "At some point ... a few terrorists will be able to produce massive violence and massive destruction. Separately, terrorism and nuclear weapons are the weapons of the non-Western weak. If and when they are combined, the non-Western weak will be strong."

This was written in 1996. The first mass murder by terrorists came last September. Just last month the vice president informed Tim Russert that "the prospects of a future attack ... are almost certain. Not a matter of if, but when." Secretary Rumsfeld has added that the attack will be nuclear.

We are indeed at war and we must act accordingly, with equal measures of audacity and precaution.

As regards precaution, note how readily the clash of civilizations could spread to our own homeland. The Bureau of the Census lists some 68 separate ancestries in the American population. (Military gravestones provide for emblems of 36 religions.) All the major civilizations. Not since 1910 have we had so high a proportion of immigrants. As of 2000, one in five school-age children have at least one foreign-born parent.

This, as ever, has had **bounteous** [adj. 慷慨的, 宽裕的] rewards. The problem comes when immigrants and their descendants bring with them — and even intensify — the clashes they left behind. Nothing new, but newly ominous. Last month in Washington an enormous march filled Pennsylvania Avenue on the way to the Capitol grounds. The marchers, in the main, were there to support the Palestinian cause. Fair enough. But every five feet or so there would be a sign proclaiming "Zionism equals Racism" or a placard with a **swastika** [n. 万十字章 (纳粹党所用的十字记号), 万字饰] alongside a Star of David. Which is anything but fair, which is poisonous and has no place in our discourse.

It is a testament to our First Amendment freedoms that we permit such displays, however obnoxious to our fundamental ideals. But in the wake of 9/11, we confront the fear that such **heinous** [adj. 可憎的, 十恶不赦的] speech can be a precursor to violence, not least here at home, that threatens our existence.

To be sure, we must do what is necessary to meet the threat. We need to better understand what the dangers are. We need to explore how better to organize the agencies of government to detect and prevent calamitous action.

But at the same time, **we need to take care that whatever we do is**

发生恐怖袭击的前景……几乎可以确定。不是可能发生与否的问题，而是何时发生的问题。"国防部长拉姆斯·菲尔德则补充说，今后这种袭击，会是核攻击。

我们现在就是身处战时，我们必须采取相应的行动，拥有同样的胆略和防范措施。

至于预防措施，请注意文明之间的冲突，是如何轻而易举地就会蔓延到我们自己的家园。美国人口普查局列出了美国人口中有 68 种不同的祖先谱系（美国军方也为阵亡将士提供 36 种不同宗教的墓碑标志）。我们代表着所有主要的文明，我们人口中移民的比例是 1910 年以来最高的。到 2000 年，美国的学龄儿童，每 5 人中至少有一个孩子的父母是在外国出生的。

这种多样性带给我们很多好处。但当移民者和他们的后人把原来的冲突一并带来，甚至加剧那些冲突时，问题就出现了。这没什么新鲜的，但它是一种新的不祥之兆。

上个月在华盛顿，从（白宫门前）宾夕法尼亚大街通往国会大厦的路上，挤满了游行的人群。那些示威者主要是想表示支持巴勒斯坦的事业，这是可以的。但差不多每隔 5 英尺就有标语牌宣称说"犹太复国主义就是种族主义"，或把（以色列的标记）大卫之盾和纳粹的万字标志排在一起。这是不公平的，这是有毒的东西，不能让这些东西出现在我们的讨论之中。

这表明我们在第一修正案[9]中，阐明的自由得到彰显，我们允许这种意见的表达，无论它与我们的根本理念是多么的背道而驰。但在 9·11 事件之后，我们必须面对这样的担心，那就是，这种令人发指的演讲可能是暴力的前兆，它甚至发生在我们家门口，乃至威胁到我们的存在。

可以肯定的是，我们必须采取必要措施以应付威胁。我们需要更好地了解何为危险，我们需要探讨如何更好地把政府机构组织起来，检测并防止灾难性行动的发生。

但同时必须注意，**我们所做的一切都要符合宪法的基本设计。我们所做的事，必须与威胁的严重程度相称，而不能破坏我们想保护的自由。**

consistent with our basic constitutional design. What we do must be commensurate [adj. 相称的，成比例的] with the threat in ways that do not needlessly undermine the very liberties we seek to protect.

The concern is suspicion and fear within. Does the Park Service really need to photograph every visitor to the Lincoln Memorial? They don't, but they will. It is already done at the Statue of Liberty. In Washington, agencies compete in techniques of intrusion and exclusion. Identity cards and X-ray machines and all the clutter, plus a new life for secrecy. Some necessary; some discouraging. Mary Graham warns of the **stultifying** [vt. 使……显得愚蠢，使……无效] effects of secrecy on inquiry. Secrecy, as George Will writes, "renders societies susceptible to epidemics of suspicion."

We are witnessing such an outbreak in Washington just now. Great clamor as to what the different agencies knew in advance of the 9/11 attack; when the President was briefed; what was he told. These are legitimate questions, but there is a prior issue, which is the disposition of closed systems not to share information. By the late 1940s the Army Signal Corps had decoded enough KGB traffic to have a firm grip on the Soviet espionage in the United States and their American agents. No one needed to know about this more than the President of the United States. But Truman was not told. By order, mind, of Omar Bradley, Chairman of the Joint Chiefs of Staff. Now as then there is police work to be done. But so many forms of secrecy are self-defeating. In 1988, the CIA formally estimated the Gross Domestic Product of East Germany to be higher than West Germany. We should calculate such risks.

The "what-ifs" are intriguing. What if the United States had recognized Soviet weakness earlier and, accordingly, kept its own budget in order, so that upon the breakup of the Soviet Union a momentous economic aid program could have been commenced? What if we had better calculated the forces of the future so that we could have avoided going directly from the "end" of the cold War to a new Balkan war — a classic clash of civilizations — leaving little attention and far fewer resources for the shattered Soviet empire?

Because we have that second chance Riesman and Glazer wrote about. A chance to define our principles and stay true to them. The more then, to keep our system open as much as possible, with our purposes plain and accessible,

人们担心的是从内部引起的怀疑和恐惧。美国的公园管理局真的需要把每个到林肯纪念堂的游客都拍下照片吗？他们不需要，但他们会那样去做。在（纽约的）自由女神像就已经做着这样的事了。在华盛顿，不同的机构在侵犯个人隐私和排斥特定群体方面，你追我赶。身份证和 x 光扫描仪等设施到处都是，官方机构行事隐秘，又有了新的用武之地。这些做法，有些是必要的，有一些则有点牵强。玛丽·格雷厄姆[10]警告说，过分的隐秘会带来僵化保守。乔治·威尔[11]写道，隐秘"使社会滋生一种怀疑的流行病"。

我们眼见着这种情况正在华盛顿到处出现。人们热烈地争执着，在 9·11 袭击发生之前，美国不同的机构都事先知道了什么？当向总统汇报时，都说了些什么情况？这些都是合理的问题。但在提出这些问题前，有一个情况是，我们的封闭系统之间没有分享信息。在 1940 年代后期，美国陆军通讯兵部队已经捕获了许多信息，足以表明前苏联克格勃和他们在美国的间谍之间的活动。美国总统是最需要知道这些情况的人，但没人把这些消息告诉杜鲁门总统。请注意，这是参谋长联席会议主席奥玛尔·布拉德利下的命令。就像那时一样，警察有很多工作要做，但诸多形式的保密却弄巧成拙。在 1988 年，中央情报局还正式地评估说，东德国内生产总值高于西德。我们需要计算这些错误评估的风险。

这些"假设"很有趣。假如美国早一点就认识到苏联的弱点，并相应地做出自己的预算，在苏联解体后，我们是否就能够向它提供重要的经济援助？如果我们能够更好地计算今后的力量，那么我们是否可以避免直接从冷战的"结束"，走向一场新的巴尔干战争？这场战争是文明冲突的一个典型例子，它使人们对四分五裂的苏联帝国几乎没空多加注意，更没精力去提供帮助。

因为我们有里斯曼和格拉泽所写的那种"跌倒再爬起来"的机会，这让我们有了规定我们的原则并遵守它们的借口。只要我们继续理解 20 世纪给我们的教训，所谓开放的社会也会有敌人，这样我们就能够让我们的社会尽可能地开放，让我们的目标显得简单明了。

so long as we continue to understand what the 20th century has surely taught, which is that open societies have enemies, too. Indeed, they are the greatest threat to closed societies, and, accordingly, the first object of their **enmity** [n. 敌意. 憎恨].

We are committed, as the Constitution states, to "the Law of Nations," but that law as properly understood. Many have come to think that international law prohibits the use of force. To the contrary, like domestic law, it legitimates the use of force to uphold law in a manner that is itself proportional and lawful.

Democracy may not prove to be a universal norm. But decency would do. Our present conflict, as the President says over and again, is not with Islam, but with a malignant growth within Islam defying the teaching of the Q'uran that the struggle to the path of God forbids the deliberate killing of noncombatants. Just how and when Islam will rid itself of current heresies is something no one can say. But not soon. Christianity has been through such heresy — and more than once. Other clashes will follow.

Certainly we must not let ourselves be seen as rushing about the world looking for arguments. There are now American armed forces in some 40 countries overseas. Some would say too many. Nor should we let ourselves be seen as ignoring allies, disillusioning friends, thinking only of ourselves in the most narrow terms. That is not how we survived the 20th century.

Nor will it serve in the 21st.

Last February, some 60 academics of the widest range of political persuasion and religious belief, a number from here at Harvard, including Huntington, published a manifesto: "What We're Fighting For: A Letter from America."

It has attracted some attention here; perhaps more abroad, which was our purpose. Our references are wide, Socrates, St. Augustine, Franciscus de Victoria, John Paul II, Martin Luther King, Jr., Alexander Solzhenitsyn, the Universal Declaration of Human Rights.

We affirmed "five fundamental truths that pertain to all people without distinction," beginning "all human beings are born free and equal in dignity and rights."

We allow for our own shortcomings as a nation, sins, arrogance, failings.

事实上，开放的社会对封闭的社会来说是最大的威胁，因此，也是它们表示敌意的第一个对象。

就像宪法里规定的那样，我们承诺要尊重"国家之间的法律"，但要正确理解那项法律。许多人会认为，国际法禁止使用武力。相反，就像国内法一样，它允许用恰当与合法的方式去使用武力，以便维护法律本身。

民主可能无法成为一个普遍的规范，但礼貌得体应该得到人们的遵守。正像我们的总统一遍又一遍说过的那样，我们目前的冲突，不是和伊斯兰教的冲突，而是与伊斯兰教中恶性增长势力的冲突，该势力违背《古兰经》的教义：在追随神的道路上，禁止故意杀害非战斗人员。只是，伊斯兰教如何摆脱、何时摆脱目前这些异端邪说的存在，还很难说清。肯定不会很快。基督教也曾经历过这样的异端邪说，而且不止一次。其他的冲突，也将随之发生。

当然，我们不能被人看做在世界上奔波不停，只是为了给这些冲突寻找论据。现在，美国在约40个国家里有驻军，有人会说这太多了。我们也不应该让自己显得忽略盟友，让朋友失望，只从最狭窄的方面为自己考虑。过去的20世纪我们不是那样做的。

在21世纪也不能那样做。

今年2月，大约60余名带有不同政见和宗教信仰的学者，其中一些来自哈佛，包括亨廷顿，共同发表了一份宣言，题目是《我们为何而战：来自美国的一封信》。

这份宣言引起了一些关注，也许在国外影响更大，而这正是我们的目的。宣言广泛地引用了苏格拉底、圣奥古斯丁、弗朗西斯、约翰·保罗二世、马丁·路德·金、亚历山大·索尔仁尼琴，以及《世界人权宣言》等言论。

我们肯定了"涉及所有人而不会有区别的五个基本事实"，首先就是，"所有的人都天生自由，且享有平等的尊严和权利"。

我们承认，作为一个国家，我们有自己的弱点，有着自己的原罪、傲慢及不足。但我们认为，我们的道德义务并不比别人少，而

But we assert we are no less bound by moral obligation. And finally, ...reason and careful moral reflection ... teach us that there are times when the first and most important reply to evil is to stop it.

But there is more. Forty-seven years ago, on this occasion, General George C. Marshall summoned our nation to restore the countries whose mad regimes had brought the world such horror. It was an act of statesmanship and vision without equal in history. History summons us once more in different ways, but with even greater urgency. Civilization need not die. As we fight the war against evil, we must also wage peace, guided by the lesson of the Marshall Plan -- vision and generosity can help make the world a safer place.

Thank you.

且最后……理性和谨慎的道德反思告诉我们，面对邪恶，首要的回答就是：予以制止。

不过，还应当有更多。47年前，就在这个场合，乔治·马歇尔将军呼吁我们去帮助那些由于其政权的疯狂而给世界带来诸多恐怖的国家，使之恢复正常，这种政治家的胆略和远见前所未有。历史以不同的方式再一次召唤着我们，但这次带有更大的紧迫感。文明不应该死亡。当我们与邪恶对抗时，我们还必须遵循马歇尔计划的教导，去创造和平——那种远见和慷慨，可以帮助世界成为一个更安全的地方。

谢谢大家！

History Summons Us Once More　Daniel Patrick Moynihan
历史的再次召唤　丹尼尔·莫伊尼汉

E 458　C 459

1 内森·格拉泽（Nathan Glazer，1924 年出生），美国社会学家，曾长期担任哈佛教授，对美国种族关系颇有研究。

2 戴维·里斯曼（David Riesman，1909—2002），美国社会学家，曾长期担任哈佛教授，对美国社会及动向的分析很有影响。其代表作为 1950 年出版的《孤独的人群》（"The Lonely Crowd"）。

3 这里是指一次世界大战的导火索——萨拉热窝的刺杀事件。

4 莫卧儿（Moghul），曾经统治印巴地区的一个古代王朝。

5 罗伯特·奥本海默（Robert Oppenheimer，1904—1967），美国犹太物理学家，"曼哈顿计划"的主要领导者之一，被誉为"原子弹之父"。

6 "削减战略武器协议" START (Strategic Arms Reduction Treaty)，美苏在 1990 年代初期达成的一项协议。

7 亨弗莱·鲍嘉（Humphrey Bogart，1899—1957，美国著名演员，1942 年凭借在《卡萨布兰卡》中的出色表演获得奥斯卡最佳男演员奖提名。

8 蒂姆·拉瑟特（Tim Russert），美国著名新闻评论员、全国广播公司（NBC）《与新闻界对话》节目主持人。

9 美国宪法第一修正案（The First Amendment, 简称"第一修正案"）是美国权力法案的一部分。该修正案禁止制定任何法律以确立"国教"、阻碍信仰自由、剥夺言论自由、侵犯出版和集会自由、干涉或禁止人民向政府和平请愿的自由等。

10 美国情报界的一位主管。

11 乔治·威尔（George Will），美国记者和专栏作家，曾获普利策奖。

欧内斯托·塞迪略（1951— ）

欧内斯托·塞迪略出生于墨西哥一个普通家庭，他的父亲是个机械修理师。寒微的家庭背景，使塞迪略发愤努力，珍惜每一个机会。1972年他从墨西哥国家理工学院获得学士学位后留校任教，1973年赴英国布拉德福德大学和美国科罗拉多大学研究经济问题，后于1974年获得墨西哥科学技术委员会提供的奖学金，到耶鲁大学经济学院就读，至1978年毕业，获硕士和博士学位。1978年至1987年间，他供职于墨西哥中央银行，后任墨西哥财政预算部副部长，1992年被任命为教育部长。1994至2000年，出任墨西哥总统。

塞迪略现在耶鲁大学任教，担任"耶鲁国际化研究中心"主任，兼任国际经济与政治教授。此外他还是美国对外关系委员会国际咨询委员会成员。

塞迪略与中国有着多方面的联系，曾多次到中国参加经济研讨活动，接受过多家媒体的专访，并在2006年主持了胡锦涛主席在耶鲁大学的演讲会。

从全球化的视角，塞迪略也对中国进行了相当细致的研究，比如，在为美国《福布斯》杂志2006年5月号撰写的《中国：既是富国，又是穷国》一文里，他说："作为一个低收入国家，中国在发展方面存在严重的不平衡。例如：创造财富繁荣和对环境影响的矛盾；对自然资源的爆炸性需求和相对资源贫乏之间的矛盾；加速采用市场运作方式和缺乏社会安全保障的矛盾；私营经济和国有企业之间的矛盾；贫富收入差距扩大的矛盾；沿海发达地区和欠发达内地之间的矛盾，以及最难处理的，是中国充满活力的自由经济和政治自由度之间的矛盾。"

在哈佛毕业典礼上，塞迪略的演讲强调了多边合作的作用和意义。

2003

The Impact of Multilateralism
多边合作的作用和意义

Ernesto Zedillo 欧内斯托·塞迪略

President Summers, Ladies and Gentlemen:

I am deeply moved and grateful to receive an honorary degree from Harvard and for having the undeserved privilege to speak at this ceremony. This is a very special occasion and I wish to use it, first of all, to pay sincere tribute to Harvard's outstanding achievements in advancing knowledge and in educating men and women from this great country and from all over the world. Harvard -- elder, gracious, and wise sister of my own alma mater -- long life to you!

With pride I acknowledge the links between Harvard and another great nation: my beloved Mexico. For many years, the history, the biodiversity and geography, the arts and culture, and the economic, social, and political life of Mexico have been expertly researched and taught in Harvard's cubicles and classrooms. Significant numbers of my compatriots have had the privilege of a good Harvard education and some have even had the honor of teaching here.

Harvard is an institution that has made a great difference to you, ladies and gentlemen, and indeed it has to all the people of the United States and to humanity at large. You are right to be proud of this great institution.

You also should be proud of many other institutions that the United States has envisioned and nurtured and that have provided great service to this nation and to the world.

I am speaking of those international institutions that, by promoting the causes of peace, prosperity, and human rights, have helped decisively to improve the quality of human life in the last 50 years. The world improved over its **execrable** [adj. 恶劣的，该诅咒的] performance of the first half of the 20th century not solely but significantly because of the international system of rules and institutions that was developed in the period around the end of the Second World War. This afternoon I want to speak for this international system.

Particularly in the present days, let us not forget that this system was to no small extent the product of the political genius of great American leaders. Let us not forget what your admired United States President Franklin Delano Roosevelt meant to do when in 1941 -- just two days after the attack on Pearl Harbor -- he spoke of not only winning the war, but also of winning the peace that would follow. Roosevelt's purpose was to promote the enactment of rules to govern international behavior and the creation of institutions to foster

萨默斯校长，女士们、先生们：

哈佛授予的荣誉学位，使我深受感动并万分感谢，在这个仪式上发言，更是我不敢当的厚爱。这是一个非常特殊的场合。首先，我想借此机会，对哈佛在拓展知识、培养来自这个伟大国家和世界各地的学子方面取得的杰出成就，表示诚挚的敬意。哈佛，你是我母校[1]的长姐，具有优雅、明智的特点，祝你生命之树长青！

我也很骄傲地看到哈佛和另一个伟大国家——我深爱的墨西哥——之间的联系。多年以来，哈佛的学者们很专业地研究并讲授着墨西哥的历史、生物多样性、地理、艺术和文化，以及经济、社会和政治生活。我的许多同胞享受过哈佛良好的教育，有的甚至荣幸地在这里任教。

哈佛改变了你们。其实，它也改变了所有美国人和整个人类。你们有理由为这个伟大的机构感到自豪。

你们也应当为美国设想和培育出的、为这个国家和全世界作出了卓越贡献的其他一些机构感到自豪。

我讲的国际机构，促进和平与繁荣，建立人权大业，并在过去50年里显著地改善了人类的生活质量。正是因为这些二战结束后依据规则成立的国际体系和机构，我们的世界比起悲惨的20世纪前半叶，有了相当大的改变。今天下午，我想就此谈谈这个国际体系。

我们不应忘记——特别是在当下，这个体系在某种程度上是杰出的美国领导人在政治方面的天才产物；我们不应忘记，你们广受尊敬的前总统富兰克林·德拉诺·罗斯福想做的事情。1941年，在珍珠港遇袭两天之后，他谈到不仅要赢得战争，还要赢得战争结束之后的和平。罗斯福的目的是想制定一种共同规则，以便规范国际行为，并建立机构来加强国际合作。他预见到就像联合国那样的机构，用来维护所有国家之间的和平，并促进国家之间为共同的利益而合作。

因此，当时机到来，美国带领着世界创建了旨在恢复稳定和

international cooperation. He foresaw nothing less than the building of the United Nations, as the centerpiece of a system charged with keeping the peace among all nations and making them collaborate for the common good.

And so, when the time came, the United States led the world in creating a system of multilateral institutions to restore stability and security. The United Nations charter was negotiated and ratified in San Francisco, and the organization itself was housed in New York. At a conference not far from here -- in Bretton Woods, N.H. -- the IMF and the World Bank were established, to guide international economic cooperation and invest in reconstruction and development; they were subsequently headquartered in Washington, D.C. The United States led the creation of the General Agreement on Tariffs and Trade to foster international commerce. Eleanor Roosevelt played a key role in drafting the Universal Declaration of Human Rights. In Europe, the United States created NATO and later encouraged the development of the institutions that became the European Union.

General George Marshall stood on these very steps in 1947 and warned of the dangers that "hunger, poverty, desperation, and chaos" posed to the newly freed nations of Europe. By paving the way for post-war reconstruction, those words helped remake the world.

Why did American and other world leaders in the 1940s and '50s devote so much energy and so many resources to building international institutions? Because they had learned the bitter lessons of two world wars and a depression. Because they had seen the destruction that results when nations are divided and pursue only their own self-interest. And so they sought to create a system, anchored in freedom, openness, and the rule of law, that would support the security and prosperity of all its members.

How well has this system worked?

Like any human creation, it has had its shortcomings and even some big failures. But its successes are impressive beyond doubt.

International institutions have fostered a greater convergence of values than ever in human history. For the first time in history, most of the world's governments are democratic. Principles of democracy, individual liberty, and the rule of law are almost universally accepted. Even regimes that routinely violate

安全的一个多边机构——联合国宪章，该宪章在旧金山起草并获通过，其组织机构落户纽约。后来，在距此不远的新罕布什尔州的布雷顿森林的一个会议上，国际货币基金组织和世界银行宣告成立，用以引导国际经济合作，以及在重建和发展方面的投资。这两个机构的总部，均设在华盛顿特区。美国还领导制定了促进国际贸易的"关税和贸易总协定"。埃莉诺·罗斯福[2]在起草"世界人权宣言"中发挥了关键作用。在欧洲，美国发起创立了北约，后又鼓励发展日后成为欧盟的相关机构。

1947年，乔治·马歇尔将军就是站在这个讲台上，向人们发出警告：那些新近获得自由的欧洲国家，正面临"饥饿、贫困、绝望和混乱"而带来的危险。那些话为战后重建铺平了道路，从而改写了世界。

20世纪四五十年代的美国以及世界其他领导人，为什么要费尽心机和如此多的资源，建立起这样一些国际机构呢？因为他们从两次世界大战和大衰退中看到了惨痛的教训。他们认识到：当不同国家分成阵营，只顾追求自身利益时，就会带来破坏。于是他们试图建立一个体系，以自由、开放和法治为基础，从而保证所有成员的安全与繁荣。

那么，这个体系的效果如何呢？

如同人类的所有创造一样，它有缺点，甚至遇到过一些大的失败。但它令人印象深刻的成功，同样是毋庸置疑的。

国际机构已促成了比人类历史上以往任何时候都更多的汇合点。世界上大多数国家的政府都是民主政府，这是前所未有的。民主、个人自由和法治的原则，几乎受到普遍接受。哪怕是经常违反这些原则的政权，也宣称他们支持这些价值观，这证明自由赢得了这场论战！这种权利和价值观所以得到普及，一个主要原因是，浩瀚的联合国文件提供了定义和规定。从"世界人权宣言"开始，联合国已经协调制定了一系列全球性公约，这些公约构成了国际法的主体。我们要记住，这一切都不是预先注定的，它是

these principles proclaim their allegiance to them -- proving that freedom has won the argument! A principal reason for this universality of rights and values is the wide array of United Nations documents that define and prescribe them. Starting with the Universal Declaration of Human Rights, the UN has orchestrated a series of global covenants that together make up the body of international law. Let us remember that none of this was foreordained. It is owed to the patient efforts of committed individuals and governments across the world.

The multilateral order has also presided over the greatest period of wealth creation in human history. The impressive economic expansion achieved by the United States and other industrial countries would not have been possible without the multilateral economic system. The great strides we have seen in technology, health care, and the many other things that enhance the quality of our lives emerge directly from this prosperity. In the developing world, millions of people have been lifted out of poverty, though much more remains to be done. Again, none of this was foreordained. The international economic order has encouraged nations to trade and interact with each other. Without this framework, we would live in a much worse world than we do today. Allow me to emphasize this: international cooperation has not been a useless abstraction. It has been a powerful and tangible force driving global prosperity.

Today, however, the international system may be in crisis. Deep disagreements have emerged about how best to combat new threats to international peace and security and how best to preserve and extend prosperity in the world.

Contempt for the multilateral system can be seen in the marginalization of the UN, the trans-Atlantic rift, the division in NATO and the European Union, and the current resentment among old friends, neighbors, and partners.

Does the record warrant this contempt?

Certainly not, as I have just argued. But that is not the relevant question. What is at stake now is not the interpretation of the past but the building of the future. So the relevant question is: At the beginning of this new century, marked by unquestionable unipolarity, who needs the multilateral system?

My claim (along with many others') is that all nations, even the most

世界各地的人民和政府耐心努力的成果。

多边秩序也带来了人类历史上创造财富的最好时期。假如没有这个多边的经济体系，美国和其他工业化国家取得的令人印象深刻的经济发展是不可能的。我们看到在技术、医疗保健和其他诸多提高我们生活质量的方面的巨大进步，也有赖于这种秩序。在发展中国家，虽然仍有许多工作要做，但已有千百万人摆脱了贫困。同样，这一切都不是天上掉下来的。国际经济秩序鼓励了各国的贸易和互相交流。如果没有这个框架，我们将生活在一个比今天糟得多的世界。请允许我强调这一点：国际间的合作不是一个无用的抽象说法，它是一个强大的有形的力量，推动着全球繁荣。

然而今天，这个国际体系可能处于危机之中。在有关如何最好地应对国际和平与安全遇到的新威胁，以及如何最好地维护和发展世界的繁荣等问题上，人们有着很深的分歧。联合国的被边缘化、大西洋两岸间的裂痕、北约和欧盟的分裂及盟友、邻国和合作伙伴之间出现的不满等现象上，都显露出对多边体系的蔑视。

我们成败得失的记录是否让这种蔑视有了理由？

正如我刚才解释的，当然不应该，但这是不相关的问题。现在重要的不是解释过去，而是建设未来。因此，相关的问题是：在新世纪之初，在一个很明显的单极世界里，谁还需要这个多边体系？

我个人的观点（和许多其他人同样）是，所有国家，即使是最强大的国家，也需要这种多边体系。

当然，国际社会中较弱的成员更愿意根据商定好的国际规则在国际舞台上行事，并更愿意让世界倾听他们的声音，让他们的合法权益得到认可，对多边主义的支持是无需赘言的。

那么美国呢？它是我们这个时代真正的超级强权。对这个国家来说，对多边主义的需要其实同样迫切，尽管这种需要有点微妙。自然，这个国家的领导人必须照顾国家利益，在决定如何与

powerful, need the multilateral system.

Certainly the weaker members of the international community would prefer to navigate in the international arena according to agreed international rules, and by means of institutions in which their voices can be heard and their legitimate interests represented and recognized. This case for multilateralism is too clear to need elaboration.

What about the United States, the true hyper-power of our era? For this country, the case for multilateralism is no less compelling, though it is more subtle. Of course, this country's leaders must look after national interests; in deciding how to interact with the rest of the world, any government must put national interests before global altruism. Perhaps this is why some influential people are tempted to believe that, to protect its national interests, all the United States need do is to exert its unmatched military and economic power -- and no matter if that implies sidelining the multilateral system.

I dare to dissent with this view, however, not only because it can lead to unwarranted adverse consequences for other countries, including my own, but also because as a friend I want to suggest that unilateralism may actually undermine the interests of the United States itself.

The fundamental flaw of the unilateralist way of thinking is to ignore how interdependent all countries -- the United States among them -- have become, for better or for worse. True, the rest of the world depends **perceptibly** [adv. 可知觉的程度．显然地] on what the U.S. does or does not do, but the converse is also true. The world in our time may be unipolar, but it is interdependent, too.

At this hour of global interdependence, even the mightiest power has limits to its influence, to its capacity to control how others react to its actions. For unipolarity to be more than a moment in history, others must perceive it not as a threat but as a true anchor of peace. Peaceful and lasting unipolarity depends on the multilateral system -- as much as the multilateral system depends on the enlightened, not the aggressive, leadership of the sole hyper-power. Aggressive unipolarity sooner rather than later would set the world in search of a different **equilibrium** [n. 平衡．均衡], one in which the military power of the United States could be balanced. This process would prove expensive and tragic. A world with so much poverty cannot afford another arms race. A world

世界上其他地方交往时,任何政府都必须把国家利益放在对外的利他主义之前。也许这就是为什么一些有影响力的人倾向于认为,为了保护自己的国家利益,美国需要做的就是展示其无与伦比的军事和经济力量,哪怕这样做意味着抛开多边体系。

但是,我不敢苟同这种观点,不仅因为它会导致对其他国家(包括我自己的国家)不必要的伤害,而且——作为朋友——我要声明,单边主义可能会损害美国自身的利益。

单边主义的思维方式,其根本缺陷是忽略了这样一个事实,即所有国家(包括美国在内)都是相互依存的,不管这种依存是好是坏。诚然,世界许多地方很明显地依赖于美国,但反过来也如此。我们这个时代的世界也许是单极化的,但它也是相互依存的。

在这个全球相互依存的时刻,即使最强大的政权,其影响力也是有限的,它操纵别人的能力同样有限。单极强权如果不想在历史上昙花一现,就必须让人们不把它看成是一种威胁,而是和平的真正依托。和平与持久的单极强权,要依赖于一个多边体系,就像这个多边体系有赖于傲世独立的超强权的开明领导,而不是做出侵略性姿态一样。过激的单极化行为,迟早会让人们寻找另一个平衡力量,从而抗衡美国的军事力量。这个过程将被证明是昂贵的和悲剧性的。一个还存在着如此多贫困的世界,无法承受另一次军备竞赛。在拥抱民主价值方面取得了这么多进步的世界,理应有更好的局面,而不是重蹈相互毁灭的覆辙。

此外,光靠力量的强大,不能让美国脱身于那些不可避免地需要国际协调讨论对策的事物。美国和许多国家在安全方面最为关切的是跨国恐怖主义。以为美国可以用一举之力打击恐怖主义,这将是危险的天真想法。没有国际合作,能打败恐怖分子吗?如果各国不齐心协力,能制止致命武器的跨国运输,还有狂热主义的蔓延吗?绝无可能!打击恐怖主义需要朋友、盟友,有时甚至是对手的支持。要获得安全,军事实力不是唯一手段。

that has made so much progress in embracing the values of democracy deserves better than to relapse into threats of mutual destruction.

Further, the United States is not exempted, even by the sheer force of its power, from problems that inexorably call for internationally coordinated responses.

Consider for a moment the biggest security concern of this and many other nations: transnational terrorism. It would be dangerously naive to think that terrorism can be fought single handedly. Can terrorists be defeated without international cooperation? Can the international traffic in deadly weapons, or the spread of fanaticism, be stopped if countries do not work together? Never. Combating terrorism requires the support of friends, allies, sometimes even adversaries. To achieve security, military might is not all that counts.

International cooperation advances not only the security but also the military superiority of the United States. It would be cynical not to believe that the multilateral instruments, including the Nuclear Non-proliferation Treaty, adopted to prevent the spread of weapons of mass destruction in fact help to entrench the overwhelming military advantage of the United States.

Other than security there are many problems, faced by the United States and all countries, that respect no national boundaries and therefore require global cooperative solutions. Think of global warming, destruction of biodiversity, fisheries depletion, ocean pollution, infectious diseases, drug trafficking, or human smuggling, just to name a few. Not one of these dire challenges can be met by a nation acting alone. Only through international cooperation can there be any hope of success.

Equally, in the pursuit of prosperity and the prevention of evils such as international financial crises, recessions, and now deflation, international cooperation is vital to success. Economic cooperation is needed now more than ever. There is a danger that the multilateral trading system could become the battleground of unsettled geopolitical disputes, with disastrous consequences. This danger haunts the ongoing WTO Doha round of trade liberalization -- now practically at gridlock -- and fuels numerous trade disputes between old partners. The Doha round must be saved and the neo-protectionist spiral must be checked right now; any later may be too late. International cooperation is

国际合作不仅加强了美国的安全，也对美国的军事优势大为有利。多边协议，包括为防止大规模杀伤性武器扩散的"不扩散核武器条约"等等，事实上强化了美国压倒性的军事优势，对此毋庸置疑。

除了安全议题之外，美国和所有国家还面临着许多问题，这些问题是不分国界的，因此需要全球合作才能解决。全球变暖、生物多样性遭到破坏、渔业资源枯竭、海洋污染、传染病流行、毒品走私成灾、偷运人口猖獗……略举几例就够了。这些严峻的挑战，都不是一个国家单独行事就能对付的，只有通过国际合作才能有成功的希望。

同样，在追求繁荣和防止诸如国际金融危机、经济衰退及现在的通缩等问题方面，国际合作亦是成功的关键。我们比以往任何时候都更需要经济合作。多边贸易体制可能成为尚未解决的地缘政治纷争的战场，从而带来灾难性的后果，这种危险是存在的。这种危险困扰着正在进行的世贸组织多哈回合贸易自由化的协商——这个协商现在几乎瘫痪——并引起许多老伙伴之间的诸多贸易纠纷。我们必须拯救多哈回合谈判，必须现在就制止新保护主义的增加，否则就会为时太晚。我们也需要通过国际合作，以协调的方式来解决困扰世界所有主要经济体的宏观经济严重失衡的问题。不进行合作，就会让以后不可避免的调整更加痛苦，并最终导致国际经济秩序出现更大的难题。

据我所知，一些单边主义阵营中的人知道这些论点。他们也愿意承认，说美国在追求正当的国家利益的时候，必须吞下国际合作的苦果。因此，他们建议依照双重标准。这有点意思，但没有说服力。

国际合作与咄咄逼人的单边主义能够共存吗？几乎不可能。一个有用的多边体系取决于谈判、妥协和协议。在怨愤和不满的土壤里，是不可能培养出这些结果的。从这个土壤里萌发的，是对立、嫉妒和恐惧的杂草，这些杂草会排挤掉我们如今比以

also needed to tackle in a coordinated fashion the very serious macroeconomic imbalances afflicting all the major economies of the world. Failure to coordinate will make the unavoidable adjustment more painful, and could eventually cause a major headache in the international economy.

I am aware that some in the unilateralists' camp are mindful of these arguments. They are ready to concede that the United States must swallow a dose of international cooperation in the pursuit of legitimate national interests. And so they propose to live by double standards.

Interesting but not convincing.

Could international cooperation coexist with aggressive unipolarity? Hardly, if at all. A useful multilateral system depends on negotiations, compromises, and agreements. None of these can be cultivated in a soil of acrimony and resentment. From this soil spring the weeds of antagonism, envy, and fear -- weeds that may crowd out the inclusive globalization and constructive interdependence that are needed more today than ever.

Inclusive globalization is needed, not only by the weak of the world but also by the strong; not only to defeat economic and social polarization but also to alleviate the old and new resentments that threaten the security and stability of our world. Constructive interdependence is needed, not only to share better the benefits of prosperity but also to achieve better mutual understanding -- and, eventually, irreversible mutual respect and tolerance. Interdependence is not always free of transitional tensions. But embracing interdependence is the only way to achieve a truly international regime of toleration -- that is, of the peaceful coexistence of people with different histories, cultures, and identities. I believe it is only through the deliberate building of this interdependence, practical step by practical step, that we can achieve a more prosperous world with lasting security -- a world in which the poor and excluded are released from misery and the privileged are released from fear.

In 1945, the United States saw the wisdom of building an inclusive world order in which every country could have a voice. True, since then much has changed, but much abides. True, the United States now enjoys unprecedented strength, but so it did in 1945. True, we face appalling new dangers today in the form of terrorism. But, in a deeper sense, terrorism feeds on the same forces

往任何时候都更加需要的那种具有包容性的全球化，以及建设性的相互依存。

包容性的全球化，不仅世界上的弱国需要，强国也需要；不仅在战胜经济和社会的两极分化方面需要，在缓解那些威胁着我们世界的安全和稳定方面，在旧的和新的怨恨方面，同样需要。建设性的相互依存关系，不仅在分享经济繁荣的好处时需要，为达到更好的相互理解时也需要，并由此最终给我们带来稳定的相互尊重和容忍。相互依存并不意味着不会出现过渡性的紧张关系。但接受这种相互依存关系，是实现真正意义上的国际间宽容环境的唯一道路。也就是说，有不同历史、文化和身份的人，可以和平共处。我相信，只有通过认真加强这种相互依存关系，一个实际步骤接着一个实际步骤地去实施，我们才能够拥有一个更加繁荣而且持久安全的世界——在这个世界里，被排斥的穷人从苦难中获得解放，拥有特权者可以摆脱恐惧。

早在1945年，美国就看到了建设一个包容性的世界秩序，让每个国家都能发出声音的益处。不错，自那时起，世界变化巨大，但还有许多东西延续下来。是的，美国现在享有前所未有的强大，但它在1945年时也是如此。当然，我们今天面临令人震惊的以恐怖主义形式出现的新的危险，但是，从更深层的意义上说，恐怖主义来源于马歇尔将军在争取重建欧洲计划时所要对付的势力："饥饿、贫穷、绝望和混乱"——那才是我们永远的敌人。

要打败恐怖主义，捍卫民主和自由，人类和它的领导人必须战胜那些永远的敌人，这只能通过多边体系齐心协力才可实现。我要重申一下，这个多边体系是在美国的倡导下建立起来的。

我认为应该停止对多边机构的批评了。他们能做得多好，取决于大国为之投入多少领导人才、有技巧的双边外交，以及资源。正确的方法不是去削弱这些机构，而是在需要的时候改革它们，使这些机构能够更好地服务于人权、安全、和平与繁荣等公益事业。

that General Marshall fought with his plan for rebuilding Europe: the eternal enemies of "hunger, poverty, desperation, and chaos."

To defeat terror, and to defend democracy and freedom, humanity and its leaders must prevail against those eternal enemies. This can only be done by working together through the multilateral system that, I repeat, was built under the impulse of the United States.

I submit that it is time to stop bashing the multilateral institutions. They are no better or worse than what the major powers put into them, in leadership, skillful bilateral diplomacy, and resources. The right way is not to undermine these institutions but, where needed, to reform them so that they can better serve the good causes of human rights, security, peace, and prosperity.

Going forward, this enterprise will require the enlightened, not the aggressive, leadership of the United States. It will require the leadership and constructive power used in Doha in November of 2001, to launch the new round of trade liberalization; in Monterrey, Mexico, in March of 2002, to commit a significant increase in aid to fight poverty and injustice in the world; and in Washington a few days ago, to champion the roadmap for peace in the Middle East and to triple the U.S. support to fight AIDS in the poorest countries in the world.

Going forward, the reform of the international system must certainly accommodate the new political realities and be fit to confront the new challenges of the 21st century.

But the pursuit of this endeavor should assuredly be guided by the same vision that President Roosevelt outlined in 1941: the vision of a world order founded upon " a cooperation of free countries, working together in a friendly, civilized society." Above all, by the vision of a world order founded upon the essential human freedoms.

Thank you very much.

展望未来，这个体系需要开明的、而不是咄咄逼人的美国领导。在 2001 年 11 月的多哈，我们需要美国建设性的领导力量，来启动新的一轮贸易自由化；2002 年 3 月，在墨西哥的蒙特雷，我们需要美国大幅度增加援助的承诺，以对付世界上的贫困和不公正；前几天在华盛顿，美国倡导中东和平路线图，并为在世界上最贫穷国家防治艾滋病，增加了 3 倍的援助。

展望未来，国际体系的改革一定要适应新的政治现实，使之适应 21 世纪的新挑战。

但对这一努力的追求，应当依据罗斯福总统在 1941 年描绘出的愿景为指导："由自由国家合作，在友好和文明的社会里通力协作。"在这个基础上建立起世界秩序。而最重要的，世界秩序应当建立在必不可少的人类自由的基础之上。

非常感谢各位！

---

1 塞迪略于 1974 — 1978 年在耶鲁大学学习经济，先后获得硕士和博士学位。哈佛与耶鲁是美国两所历史最悠久的名校，经常互相竞争，拿对方来相比，故有此"姐妹"说。

2 美国总统罗斯福的夫人

科菲·阿塔·安南（1938— ）

"联合国秘书长安南"，是我们从1996年到2006年间经常从电视节目中听到的名字。多年来，他的名字总是和国际大事联系在一起：从非洲战乱到中东危机；从南亚克什米尔争端到海湾战争；从东帝汶暴乱、阿富汗战争，到其他极度敏感的政治危机……处处可见安南和他的团队穿梭斡旋的身影。

科菲·阿塔·安南，1938年出生于加纳库马西市的一个非洲部落酋长之家，受到过良好的西方教育。早年就读于库马西理工大学，曾到美国和瑞士留学，先后获明尼苏达州麦卡莱斯特学院经济学学士学位和麻省理工学院管理学硕士学位。安南1962年开始了他的联合国生涯，直至退休，可以说他大半生的工作只和联合国有关。

1990年海湾战争爆发，时任助理秘书长的安南负责同伊拉克谈判有关释放联合国以及其他国际组织工作人员的人质问题。后来又率领联合国小组同伊拉克进行"石油换食品"的谈判。1993年安南出任联合国副秘书长，负责维持和平事务，主管联合国在世界各地的维和行动。他还曾作为当时的秘书长特使，前往南斯拉夫协调有关国家的关系。

1996年，第51届联合国大会任命安南为第七任秘书长，到2006年止，连续两届任期。他曾于1998年赴巴格达，化解伊拉克武器核查危机。

鉴于安南为促进世界和平与共同发展，以及巩固联合国在国际多边机制中的核心地位所作出的贡献，他在2001年被授予诺贝尔和平奖。

安南是一位通晓多国语言、经验丰富的外交家，曾多次来中国访问。离开联合国后，安南出任"非洲绿色革命联盟"主席。

2004

Three Crises, and the Need for American Leadership
三个危机呼唤美国的领导作用

Kofi Annan 科菲·安南

President Summers, dear friends:

My wife Nane and I are both extremely happy to be here with you today. I feel truly proud to belong to this extraordinary Class of 2004, and I am pleased that so many parents and family members are here. This day belongs to them, too. Without their constant support, understanding and sacrifice, none of us could have achieved what we have achieved.

For me, to receive a degree from Harvard University is a very great honor indeed. There are few countries in the world whose leaders in public life, business, science and humanities have not had some association with Harvard University — and no country that has not benefited from Harvard's outstanding contributions to human knowledge. Indeed, I am told that Harvard even produces, from time to time, a very successful secretary of the U.S. Treasury.

You have invited me, I know, not as an individual, but as secretary-general of the United Nations. You are saying that the United Nations matters, and that you want to hear what we have to say.

Are you right in believing that the UN matters? I think you are, because the UN offers the best hope of a stable world and a broadly equitable world order, based on generally accepted rules. That statement has been much questioned in the past year. But recent events have reaffirmed, and even strengthened, its validity.

A rule-based system is in the interest of all countries — especially today. Globalization has shrunk the world. The very openness, which is such an important feature of today's successful societies, makes deadly weapons relatively easy to obtain, and terrorists relatively difficult to restrain. Today, the strong feel almost as vulnerable to the weak as the weak feel vulnerable to the strong.

So it is in the interest of every country to have international rules and abide by them. And such a system can only work if, in devising and applying the rules, the legitimate interests of all countries are accommodated, and decisions are reached collectively. That is the essence of multilateralism, and the founding principle of the United Nations.

All great American leaders have understood this. That is one of the things that make this country such a unique world power. America feels the need to frame its policies, and exercise its leadership, not just in light of its own particular interests, but also with an eye to international interests, and universal principles.

萨默斯校长、亲爱的朋友们：

我妻子娜内和我非常愉快和你们相聚在这里，能成为2004届毕业生中的一员，我感到特别自豪[1]。我很高兴看到这么多的学生家长和家人在这里，今天同样也属于他们，没有他们的不断支持、理解和奉献，我们没有谁能得到今天的成绩。

对我来说，获得哈佛大学学位的确是一个极高的荣誉。放眼世界，在绝大多数国家里，在公共领域、商业、科学和人文学科等方面的领军人物，都和哈佛大学或多或少有些关联。而哈佛对人类知识的杰出贡献，更是让所有国家从中受益。有人告诉我说，哈佛还不时培养出非常成功的美国财政部长。

我知道，你们邀请我不是因为我个人，而是因为我的联合国秘书长这个位置。你们的意思是说，联合国重要，而且你们想听听我们有什么可说的。

你们认为联合国有用，对吗？我认为是这样的。因为联合国为维护根据人们普遍接受的规则而建立的一个稳定的世界，和一个大致公平的世界秩序，提供了最好的希望。在过去的一年，这种说法一直备受质疑。但是最近发生的事件，再次证明、甚至加强了它的有效性。

建立一个以规则为基础的体系，符合所有国家的利益，这在今天尤为重要。全球化已让世界变小，这种开放，是今天成功社会的一个重要特征，但这种开放也使致命武器相对容易获得，使恐怖分子较难控制。今天，强者觉得易受弱者的伤害，几乎就像弱者觉得易受强者的伤害一样。

因此，制定并遵守国际规则，符合每个国家的利益。这样的系统要能起作用，只有在制定和实施规则时，考虑所有国家的合法权益，并共同做出决定，这个体系才能有效。这是多边主义的精髓，也是联合国的创始原则。

所有美国杰出的领导人都知道这一点。这是使这个国家成为一个独特的世界强国的因素之一。美国认为在制定其政策并行使其领导作用时，不仅需要考虑它自己的特有利益，也要考虑到国际利益和普世原则。

Among the finest examples of this was the plan for reconstructing Europe after World War II, which General Marshall announced here at Harvard in 1947. That was one part of a larger-scale and truly statesmanlike effort, in which Americans joined with others to build a new international system — a system which worked, by and large, and which survives, in its essentials, nearly 60 years later.

During those 60 years, the United States and its partners developed the United Nations, built an open economy, promoted human rights and decolonization, and supported transformation of Europe into a democratic, cooperative community of states, such that war between them has become unthinkable.

In all these achievements the United States has played a vital role. This country is, **inextricably** [adv. 分不开地. 无法摆脱地] and indispensably, a part of this successful international system, based on the primacy of the rule of law.

American power is an essential ingredient in the mix. But what makes that power effective, as an instrument of progressive change, is the legitimacy it gains from being deployed within a framework of international law and multilateral institutions and in pursuit of the common interest. Once again, in recent weeks, the United States found that it needed the unique legitimacy of the United Nations to bring into being a credible interim government in Iraq.

American leaders have generally recognized that other states, big and small, prefer to cooperate on the great issues of peace and security through multilateral institutions such as the United Nations, which give legitimacy to such cooperation.

They have accepted that others with different views on a specific issue may, on occasion, be right.

They have understood that true leadership is ultimately based on common values and a shared view of the future.

Over 60 years, whenever this approach has been applied consistently, it has proved a winning formula.

But today it is threatened by a triple crisis, which challenges both the United Nations as a system, and the United States as a global leader. It challenges us both to live up to the best in ideals and our best traditions.

What does this crisis consist of?

First, a crisis of collective security.

Second, a crisis of global solidarity.

最好的一个例子是二战结束后的1947年，马歇尔将军就在这里宣布欧洲重建计划。这是一个大规模的计划中的一部分，也是一个真正的政治家的杰作，美国人与其他人一起，建立起一个新的国际体系，这个体系在近60年后还基本有用，其理念也延续至今。

在这60年中，美国和其他伙伴一起创建了联合国，建立起开放的经济，促进了人权和去殖民化，并帮助欧洲演变成一个民主的、各国相互合作的社会，以致这些国家之间若要发生战争，已成为不可思议的事情。

美国在所有这些成就中起到了至关重要的作用，这个国家和我们这个成功的、将法治置于首要地位的国际体系，有着千丝万缕和不可或缺的关系。

美国的力量是这个体系中必不可少的组成部分。但要使这种力量成为带来进步的工具，使这种力量卓有成效，需要在国际法和多边机构的框架内，追求共同的利益，唯其如此，这种力量才具有合法性。就在最近几周，美国再一次发现，它需要联合国独特的合法性，来认可在伊拉克成立的临时政府。

美国的领导人通常都知道，国家不论大小，在和平与安全这些重大问题上，都愿意通过联合国这样的多边机构来进行合作，而这种合作也给了以上所说的行动以合法性。

他们意识到，在某一个特定问题上持不同意见的人，有时也会是正确的。他们明白，真正的领导最终要基于共同的价值观，对未来达成共识。60多年来，每当这种方法得到贯彻应用时，它就是一个成功的模式。

但是今天，它受到三重危机的威胁，这些危机对联合国的体系是个挑战，也对作为全球领袖的美国是个挑战。它促使我们追求最好的理念，保持最好的传统。

这场危机是由什么构成的呢？

首先，这是一场集体安全的危机。

其次，这是一场全球团结的危机。

And third, a crisis of cultural division and distrust.

From here in North America, the security crisis looks the most obvious. We have seen international terrorism emerge as a major threat. We worry about the spread of weapons of mass destruction. And we fear that existing rules governing the use of force might not give us adequate protection, especially if terrorism and weapons of mass destruction were to be combined.

This crisis came to a head last year, in the argument over Iraq. On one side, it was said that force should only be used in the most compelling circumstances of self-defense — when you are already being attacked or when you clearly are just about to be attacked — or otherwise by a decision of the Security Council.

On the other side it was argued, in essence, that in the post-9/11 world preventive use of force has become necessary in some cases, because you can't afford to wait till you are sure that someone has weapons of mass destruction and is going to attack you. By then it may be too late.

Indeed, the combination of global terrorism and possible proliferation of weapons of mass destruction and the existence of rogue and dysfunctional states does face us with a new challenge. The United Nations was never meant to be a suicide pact. But what kind of world would it be, and who would want to live in it, if every country was allowed to use force, without collective agreement, simply because it thought there might be a threat?

I believe the way forward is clear, though far from easy. We cannot abandon our system of rules, but we do need to adapt it to new realities, and to find answers to some difficult questions: When is use of force by the international community, acting collectively to deal with these new threats, justified? Who decides? And how should the decision be taken, in time for it to be effective?

Last year I appointed a panel of **eminent** [adj. 著名的，卓越的] persons to look into those questions, and suggest ways of making our United Nations work better, in an age when humanity needs the Organization more than ever.

I expect their recommendations by the end of this year, and I hope that they will lead to wise decisions by governments. But panels and governments cannot change the world by themselves. They need not only good ideas but also sustained pressure from internationalists in all countries — people who are both visionary and pragmatic: people like you in this audience.

第三，这是一场文化分裂和互不信任的危机。

从北美这个位置来看，安全危机最为明显。我们已经看到国际恐怖主义显现为一个重大威胁。我们担心大规模杀伤性武器的扩散，担心现有的有关使用武力的规则无法给我们以充分的保护，尤其是当恐怖主义和大规模杀伤性武器沆瀣一气之时。

这场危机去年在有关伊拉克问题的争论上达至顶点。一方面，有人说，武力应该只在不得不奋起自卫的情况下——比如当你已经受到进攻或当敌方很明显地将对你发起进攻时，或者是安理会作出了决定的情况下——才能使用。另一方面，也有人认为9·11事件之后，在某些情况下，预防性地使用武力已经成为一种必要。因为你不能等待，等到你确信有人拥有了大规模杀伤性武器，并将向你发动攻击的时候，可能为时已晚。

的确，当全球恐怖主义和大规模杀伤性武器的潜在扩散组合在一起，当流氓国家和无能政权存在的时候，我们就面临着一个新的挑战。联合国从来就不是一个要让人坐以待毙的协定。但是，如果每个国家在没有集体商议的情况下，只是因为它自认为有可能受到了威胁，就要使用武力，那将是一个什么样的世界？又有谁愿意生活在这样的世界里呢？

虽然前途艰险，我相信前进的方向是明确的。我们不能放弃我们的规则体系，但我们确实需要使其适应新的现实，并找到解决一些难题的答案：当国际社会采取集体行动，为处理这些新的威胁而使用武力时，如何做到师出有名？谁来作这个决定？在作这个决定时，如何才能做到及时、有效？

去年，我任命了一个由知名人士组成的小组，来研究这些问题，并为我们联合国的工作如何做得更好提供建议，因为人类比以往任何时候都更需要这个组织。

我预计他们在今年年底会提出建议，我希望这些建议会引导各国政府作出明智的决定。但不能仅靠专门小组和政府来改变世界。他们不仅需要良好的想法，也需要来自所有国家的国际主义者的压

The issues go beyond terrorism and weapons of mass destruction. We also need better criteria for identifying, and clearer rules for dealing with, genocide and crimes against humanity, where the problem often is that the international community reacts too weakly, and too late.

As undersecretary-general for peacekeeping 10 years ago I lived through the traumatic experiences of Bosnia and Rwanda, where UN peacekeeping forces had to witness appalling massacres but could do almost nothing to stop them, because there was no collective will to act.

As secretary-general I have warned the Security Council that it cannot expect to be taken seriously unless it fulfills its responsibility to protect the innocent. National sovereignty was never meant to be a shield behind which massacres are carried out with impunity.

As things stand, today we still face too many cases where governments tolerate, incite, or even themselves perpetrate massacres and other crimes against international humanitarian law. In the Darfur region in western Sudan, for example, thousands of villages have been burnt and more than a million people forced from their homes. In all, about 1.3 million need assistance.

The international community must insist that the Sudanese authorities immediately put their own house in order. They must neutralize and disarm the brutal "**Janjaweed**" [苏丹的伊斯兰民兵组织 "牧民武装部队"] militia, allow humanitarian supplies and equipment to reach the population without further delays, ensure that the displaced people can return home in safety, and pursue the political negotiations on Darfur with a renewed sense of urgency. Further delay could cost hundreds of thousands of lives.

Now I come to the second crisis — the crisis of solidarity.

Whatever our views about the war in Iraq, we should never have let it divert our attention and resources away from the goals of reducing extreme poverty and its worst effects that all nations set themselves four years ago, at the UN Millennium Summit. These, you remember, are goals to be reached by 2015: goals such as halving the proportion of people in the world who don't have drinking water; making sure all girls, as well as boys, receive at least primary education; slashing infant and maternal mortality; and stopping the spread of HIV/AIDS.

Of course, much of that can only be done by governments and peoples in the poor countries themselves. But richer countries, too, have a vital part to play. They

力,这些国际主义者有远见而且务实,就像在座的各位。

时下的问题不仅包括恐怖主义和大规模杀伤性武器,我们还需要更好的识别标准,并制定更加明确的处理规则,来对付种族灭绝罪和危害人类罪。但问题往往是,国际社会在这方面常常反应过弱,且为时过晚。

10年前,作为负责维和的联合国副秘书长,我经历了发生在波斯尼亚和卢旺达的可怕的大屠杀,但由于没有采取集体行动的意志,联合国维和部队几乎只能袖手旁观。

作为秘书长,我曾警告说,除非安理会履行其保护无辜者的职责,否则人们不会对它另眼相看。国家主权从来就不是为肆无忌惮的大屠杀行为提供保护的借口。

据目前情况看,今天,我们仍然看到太多的例子,某些政府容忍、煽动,甚至自己犯下大屠杀和其他违反国际人道主义法则的罪行。例如,在苏丹西部达尔富尔地区,数千个村庄被烧毁,超过百万人被迫离开家园,造成总共约130万人需要援助。

国际社会必须要求苏丹当局立即恢复秩序。他们必须遣散和解除残忍的"贾贾威德"阿拉伯民兵组织的武装,允许人道主义物资和设备不被拖延地送到需要的人们手里,确保流离失所的人们可以安全返回家园,并立刻就达尔富尔问题进行政治谈判。如再推迟,就有可能造成成千上万人丧命。

我再来讲讲第二个危机——团结的危机。

无论我们对伊拉克战争的看法如何,我们绝不能让它转移我们的注意力和资源,而忽略了4年前在联合国千年首脑会议上,所有国家都为自己设定的目标,那就是减少极端贫困和贫困带来的最坏影响。

你们还记得,这些是我们到2015年要达到的目标,比如:将世界上没有饮用水的人口比例减半;确保所有的女孩像男孩一样,能够得到至少小学的教育;削减婴儿和产妇死亡率,以及阻止艾滋病毒和艾滋病的蔓延。

must meet agreed targets on aid, trade and debt relief. American leadership is essential here, too.

Now those are issues and questions I'd like to hear Americans ask candidates about, in this election year!

Unless we make those issues a priority now, we shall soon run out of time to achieve the Millennium Goals by 2015 — which means that millions of people will die, prematurely and unnecessarily, because we failed to act in time.

And we know, from bitter experience in Afghanistan and elsewhere, that our world will not be secure while citizens of whole countries are trapped in oppression and misery.

Finally, the third crisis — the crisis of prejudice and intolerance: We must not allow ourselves, out of fear or anger, to treat people whose faith or culture differs from ours as enemies.

We must not allow ourselves to blame " Islam," or to suspect all Muslims, because a small number of Muslims commit acts of violence and terror.

We must not allow anti-Semitism to disguise itself as a reaction to Israeli government policies — any more than we should allow all questioning of those policies to be silenced with accusations of anti-Semitism.

And we must not allow Christians in the Muslim world to be treated as if their religion somehow made them a fifth column of western imperialism.

It is in times of fear and anger, even more than in times of peace and tranquility, that you need universal human rights, and a spirit of mutual respect.

This is a time when we must adhere to our global rule-book: a time when we must respect each other — as individuals, yes, but individuals who each have the right to define their own identity, and belong to the faith or culture of their choice.

So those are the three great tests that our system faces, in these first years of the new century:

the test of collective security;

the test of solidarity between rich and poor;

and the test of mutual respect between faiths and cultures.

I know that we can pass those tests.

当然，其中许多目标只能由贫穷国家的政府和人民自己去实现，但较富裕的国家也能发挥重要的作用。他们必须在援助、贸易和债务减免等方面，达到商定的目标。美国在这里的领导地位也是必不可少的。

现在，我想听到美国人在今年的选举中，向候选人就这些议题和问题发问！

除非我们把这些问题当成当务之急，否则我们不可能在2015年实现"千年发展目标"，而这就意味着，因为我们未能及时采取行动，数以百万计的人们过早地、或平白无故地死亡。

通过在阿富汗和其他地方的痛苦经历，我们知道，当整个国家的公民都被困在压迫和苦难中时，我们的世界也将不会是安全的。

最后，我想讲一下第三个危机——偏见和不容忍。

我们不能让自己因为恐惧或愤怒，而把与我们信仰或文化不同的人当做敌人。我们决不允许因为穆斯林里的少数人犯有暴力和恐怖行为，而去责怪"伊斯兰"或怀疑所有的穆斯林。决不允许反犹太主义的行为被伪装成是对以色列政府政策的反应——就像我们同样不能用"反犹太主义"的指控，来压制人们对以色列政府政策的质疑。我们也决不允许在穆斯林世界里的基督徒，因为他们的宗教信仰，而在某种程度上被当做是西方帝国主义的第五纵队。

在恐惧和愤怒的情况下，比在和平与安宁的时候，更需要普世人权和相互尊重的精神。

这是一个我们必须恪守全球规则的时候：我们必须相互尊重——没错，尊重个人，而且作为个人，都有权利界定自己的身份，并选择自己的信仰或文化。

因此，这就是在新世纪的头几年里，我们的体系面临的最大考验：

考验我们共同的安全；

考验富国和穷国之间的团结；

考验不同信仰和文化之间的相互尊重。

I know we can preserve and adapt, for the 21st century, a system that served us well in the second half of the 20th.

But we shall need, once again, enlightened American leadership.

And so I say to the American graduates: Live up to your country's best traditions of global commitment and global leadership.

Listen to the arguments of those from other nations, assess them on their merits, and remember that they also want what you want: the chance to live decent lives in dignity and safety. As Americans knew when they strongly supported the founding of the United Nations 60 years ago, we all depend on each other.

To the graduates from other countries, I say: Tell your fellow-citizens back home to look beyond facile stereotypes about this country. Whatever you may think of particular American policies, you have been here long enough to know the dynamism of American society, and the generosity of the American spirit.

To all I say: these are difficult times, but we can rise above them. We have much to be grateful for, much to be proud of, and much that we must keep safe, for future generations' sake.

Now is not the time to abandon our rule-based international system.

Let us preserve it. Let us improve it. And let us pass it on — intact, and even stronger than ever!

To my fellow graduates of 2004, wherever you may be this afternoon, go out to the great big world and make a difference.

Thank you very much.

我知道我们可以经受住这些考验。

我还知道，我们可以把这个在20世纪后半部分行之有效的体系，为面向21世纪而保留和调整。

不过，我们再次需要美国的开明领导。

所以我对美国的毕业生们说：不要辜负贵国对全球负责和在全球起到领导作用的最佳传统。

听听那些来自其他国家的论点，评估其理由，并且要记住，他们也想要你要的东西，有尊严、有安全地过着体面的生活。美国人在60年前，坚定支持联合国成立的时候就知道，我们都互相依赖。

对来自其他国家的毕业生们，我要说：告诉你们的同胞，不要用简单的老一套的东西来看这个国家。不管你对美国的政策评价如何，你在这里已经待了足够长的时间，应该了解美国社会的活力，以及美国精神中的慷慨侠义。

对所有人，我想说：这是艰难时期，但我们可以实现超越。我们有很多值得感恩、值得骄傲，以及很多我们必须为子孙后代好好保留的东西。现在还不是放弃我们以规则为基础的国际体系的时候。让我们维护它，并改进它，将它一代一代传递下去，使之保持完整，甚至比以往任何时候都更为强大！

2004届的毕业生们，不管你今天下午身处何地，走向外边的广阔天地，你们都将会大有作为！

非常感谢各位！

---

1 因为哈佛在当天授予了安南荣誉博士学位

约翰·利特高（1945— ）

约翰·利特高是历届哈佛毕业典礼演讲者中第一位专业演员。他是演员、歌手和诗人，同时也是一位毕业于哈佛本科的校友。

利特高出生于一个艺术世家。父亲是戏剧制作者，母亲是一名演员。在就读于哈佛大学英国历史与文学系时，利特高就活跃于校园舞台。1967年哈佛毕业后，利特高拿到伦敦音乐和戏剧艺术学院的奖学金，到英国继续他的艺术追求。

利特高的职业艺术生涯始于1973年，那一年他登上百老汇的舞台。他曾与梅丽尔·斯特里普等明星合作过，并两次获得托尼奖。1979年，利特高开始了其电影生涯，1983和1984年，因出演电影《加普的世界观》(The World According to Garp) 和《母女情深》(Terms of Endearment)，他连续两年获得奥斯卡最佳男配角奖提名。

利特高在电影界最著名的角色，是广大影迷们熟知的《史瑞克》(Shrek) 系列中的"法夸国王"(Lord Farquaad)。

利特高同时也是著名的电视剧演员，他在NBC的电视剧《外星人报到》(3rd Rock From The Sun) 中扮演主要角色。这部电视剧一共播出了六季，每年利特高都因为在这部剧中的出色表现而获得艾美奖最佳喜剧类男主角奖的提名，并三次夺得这一奖项。此外，利特高在《嗜血判官》(Dexter，又译作《双面法医》) 中饰演的连环杀手也深受观众喜爱，他因出演这个角色而获得了2010年金球奖的最佳男配角奖。

利特高多才多艺，除了表演，他还编写过儿童读物，录过唱片。在这个面对哈佛本科毕业生的演讲中，他的风趣幽默和表演天分得到了充分的展示和发挥。

2005

An Actor's Own Words
一个演员自己的话

John Lithgow 约翰·利特高

Mr. President, faculty, graduates, families, and friends, good afternoon and thank you for the honor of addressing you today.

This speech is a major event in my own personal history but an interesting little footnote in Harvard's history as well: I am the first professional actor to speak at a Harvard Commencement. Notice that I have specified "professional" actor, since I am sure that, as in all walks of life, there has been plenty of play-acting at this **dais** [n. 讲台] over the years.

In choosing me, the thoughtful men and women who selected your Commencement Speaker have shown uncharacteristic recklessness. You see, we actors make our reputations and build our careers by speaking other people's words. Ask us to express our own thoughts and you never know what's going to come out. I barely know myself. My reflexive instinct is simply to entertain you (and in fact, I do intend to offer up a modest performance by the end of my remarks), but I am well aware that this is an occasion of dignity and of gravity, and that a certain amount of Graduation Day wisdom is called for.

But wisdom from an actor? Are you kidding? If I were a wise man I never would have gone into the acting profession. Rather than presuming to pass down wisdom, I have decided to think of my address as a friendly and anecdotal conversation with the Harvard College Class of 2005. Thirty-eight years ago, I was one of you, sitting with my classmates and listening to a speech. I am going to touch on a few episodes in my **picaresque** [adj. 以流氓为题材的] journey from down there to up here, and I leave it to you to root out any wisdom therein.

I bet that word "picaresque" got your attention. I am afraid that is one of the few words that I still remember from my four years of studying English History and Literature at Harvard. As I recall, the word "picaresque" is used to describe a long adventure which teaches its hero a series of lessons to live by - an apt subject for a Commencement Address. Although I hesitate to dub myself a hero, I've stumbled across a few lessons, especially in the last dozen years, and, considering the occasion, this is a good time to share them with you. I'll get to the adventures in a moment, but I'll lead with the lessons. Basically they boil down to four succinct phrases:

Be creative.

Be useful.

Be practical.

尊敬的校长、老师、毕业生以及毕业生的亲友们：

下午好！谢谢你们给我发表演讲这个荣誉。

这个讲话，对我个人来说是件大事，在哈佛的历史上也是一个有趣的小注脚：我是第一个在哈佛毕业典礼上致辞的专业演员。请注意，我强调了"专业"演员，因为我相信，就像在各行各业一样，在这个讲台上，多年来也有不少人演过戏。

在让我来致辞这件事上，为毕业典礼遴选演讲者的负责人表现出了反常的行事草率。[1] 你看，我们演员靠讲别人的话来获得声誉和创建事业。如果让我们表达自己的思想，你可能根本不知道我们会说出什么话来。我都不太了解自己。我的自然反应是要来给你们逗乐（事实上，我打算在发言结束时，给大家来段小小的表演）。但我深知，这是一个庄重和有分量的时刻，所以还得讲一些毕业典礼上该讲的智慧之言。

但一个演员能有箴言吗？您开玩笑吧？如果我是一个聪明的人，就不会投身到演员这个行业里了。[2] 我其实没什么智慧可以在这里传播，而是准备和哈佛 2005 届的毕业生们做一个朋友式的漫谈。38 年前，我就像你们一样，和我的同学们坐在台下一起听演讲。我想谈谈我从这里的台下走到这个台上，这个漫长的云游过程，如果其中能提炼出什么智慧的话，就全凭你们自己去挖掘了。

我相信"云游"这个词抓住了你们的注意力。这恐怕是我在哈佛学了 4 年英国历史与文学后，还记得的为数不多的几个词之一了。我记得"云游"这个词也被用来形容某个长期的探险，往往能教会人们一些人生准则，而这倒是毕业演讲的一个合适话题。

虽然我不敢把自己称作英雄，但在过去的十几年里，我愚者偶得地撷取了一些心得，今天这个场合正是一个适合分享的机会。我会在后面谈到我的经历，但我会先谈谈体会。这些体会基本上可以归结为四句简洁的话：

要有创造力；

要实用；

要脚踏实地；

要待人豪爽。

Be generous.

Simple as that.

And now for the adventures.

I actually had two Harvard Educations. The first one concluded on the day I graduated. Shortly thereafter, I launched myself into the acting game where, for the next twenty years, I virtually kept my Harvard degree a secret. Somehow it never seemed to come in all that handy when I was auditioning for a soap opera or a potato chip commercial. My second Harvard education began when I was invited back into the fold, in 1989. In another example of Harvard recklessness, I was asked to run for the Board of Overseers, presumably to **redress** [vt. 纠正，赔偿] the fact that no one from the world of the Arts had served on the Board since the poet Robert Frost in the 1930's.

Equally reckless, the Harvard Alumni elected me.

In what I eventually learned was a typical pattern, I spent the first half of my six years as an Overseer wondering what in the world I was doing there. Then I recalled my personal agenda. I was presumed to be the Arts Overseer, so I proposed an Overseers' Ad Hoc Committee on the Arts. The Committee was quickly established, mainly because there seemed to be no good reason not to. In 1992, with the support and encouragement of the new University President Neil Rudenstine, the Committee created Arts First, a springtime celebration of undergraduate arts activity at Harvard. We joined forces with Myra Mayman, then Head of the Office of the Arts, and together we applied ourselves to the rare and exhilarating task of inventing traditions. That 1992 festival, with its parade, its Saturday performance fair, its campus barbecue and its big yellow tent, has been replicated a dozen times since, growing bigger and bigger every year. It is now virtually impossible to imagine a school year at Harvard College without it. And without it, I assure you, I would not be delivering your Commencement Address today.

The creation of Arts First was a lesson for me in the power of a simple idea. But the big lessons were yet to come.

In 1995, my last year as an Overseer, I proposed the Harvard Arts Medal, to be awarded every year during Arts First to an alum who had gone into the creative arts. The idea was to highlight the fact that, although the instances are rare, Harvard students do sometimes become artists, and major artists at that. Again, the Board

就这么简单。

现在先来谈谈冒险。

我其实接受过两次哈佛教育。第一次在我毕业那天就算结束了。那之后不久，我投身演艺事业，而在后来的20年里，我几乎从来不提我有个哈佛学位。不知怎的，这个学位对我为演一个肥皂剧而试镜，或是承接一个马铃薯片的商业广告这些事，好像没什么用途。我的第二次哈佛教育开始于1989年，我被邀请回来共襄盛事。作为哈佛行事草率的另一个例子，有人鼓励我参选哈佛的监察委员会，因为自从诗人罗伯特·弗罗斯特在上世纪30年代担任过哈佛董事以来，文艺界还没人担任过此职，这大概是为了矫枉过正。

哈佛校友会同样行事草率，竟然把我选上了。

我后来才知道这是一个典型的过程，那就是我作为哈佛监管会的董事，用了6年时间在想我到底能起什么作用。然后，我想起了我的职责。我是文艺方面的监管会董事，所以我提议监管会成立一个艺术委员会特设小组。特设小组迅速成立，主要是因为没有什么理由说不要成立这样一个组织。在当时新任校长尼尔·鲁登斯坦的支持和鼓励下，委员会在1992年创立了促进哈佛大学本科生艺术活动的"艺术领先节"，这是在春天举行的庆祝活动。我们和当时担任哈佛艺术办公室主任的迈拉·梅曼齐心协力，一起致力于这样一个难得而又令人振奋的工作。1992年的艺术节包括了游行、星期六才艺展示表演、校园烧烤等活动，还有一个大大的黄色帐篷。那以后，这个活动又重复了十几次，而且规模越来越大。现在，几乎难以想象在哈佛学院学习一年而没过上一个艺术节。我可以向你们保证，没有这个艺术节，我绝不会有机会来发表今天这个毕业演讲。

对我个人而言，"艺术领先节"的创立教会了我一个道理，即简单想法也会产生大的能量。不过更大的收获还在后面。

1995年，我在作为监管会董事的最后一年里，提议设立"哈佛艺术奖章"，每年在"艺术领先节"的时候授予一位进入文艺领域的哈佛校友。当时的想法是，虽然数量有限，但毕竟有一些哈佛毕业生成为了艺术家，而且是颇有成就的艺术家。同样的，监管会又接纳了这项建议。那年春天，

agreed to the proposal, and that spring the first Harvard Arts Medal was presented to Jack Lemmon, a delightful, open-hearted honoree. Since then, the award has been presented annually, eleven times in all. This spring was the first time in all these years that I could not be here for Arts First, so sadly I missed the presentation of the Medal to the poet Maxine Kumin.

Every spring, one of the events planned around the presentation of the Arts Medal has been a Question and Answer session that I have conducted with the honoree, for an audience of interested students. The Q&A's have been held under the **auspices** [n. 赞助. 前兆] of the Office of the Arts' splendid "Learning from Performers" series. My yearly conversations with the Medal-winning artists made up the core curriculum of my second Harvard education. For, although none of them was an educator, all of them were dazzling, inspiring teachers. My moments with them, with all those students following every word, are the adventures I was just talking about.

Several of the Medal recipients had something in common. They told us about pet projects they had initiated that went outside and beyond what they were known for. Having achieved success in their fields, they had looked around, spotted problems or challenges, and figured out how they could help. Then they had boldly used their success to make good things happen. They tended to tell their stories without self-**aggrandizement** [n. 增大. 扩大], only after being prodded, and they tended to tell them in a sensible, businesslike manner, as if they were describing good carpentry or a well-run board meeting. **I began to see that many of the qualities that made them great artists were the same qualities that made them good people.** It was through their words that I began formulating my simple lessons to live by. They were creative, God knows. But their actions were also eminently useful, practical, and generous.

Let me give you some examples.

The 1996 Medal recipient was Pete Seeger. He thrilled the students with his story of the Sloop Clearwater. One day in the mid 60's, on a train to New York City from his upstate home, he sat next to an acquaintance from the world of business and finance. Looking out the window at the Hudson River, Seeger daydreamed aloud about building a replica of one of the great sailing vessels that had carried goods along that route to and from the Erie Canal, a hundred and fifty years earlier. Six months after that chance meeting, Seeger was astonished when the same acquaintance approached him on the same train and told him he had raised the money for Pete's

第一枚"哈佛艺术奖章"颁发给了杰克·莱蒙,他是一个令人愉快、心胸开阔的获奖者。自那时起,该奖项每年颁发一次,到现在已是第 11 届了。今年春天,我因故头一次未能参加"艺术领先节",遗憾地错过了给诗人马克辛·库民颁发奖章的机会。

每年春天,艺术奖章颁发的项目之一,就是我与受奖人共同为有兴趣的学生举办一个问答活动,此项活动是学校艺术办公室主持的"与艺术家互动"系列内容的一部分。我每次与获奖艺术家的交谈,构成了我的第二次哈佛教育的核心课程。因为他们虽然不是职业教育工作者,但他们都是了不起的、鼓舞人心的老师。我有幸与他们共聚,台下所有学生也不愿错过艺术家们说的每一个字,这就是我刚才说的经历。

好几位获奖者具有相同的方面。他们介绍自己倾心的项目,而这些项目并不是在他们为人所知的领域和范围之内。他们在各自的领域取得成功,然后环顾四周,发现问题,并想出他们能够提供帮助的法子,接着大胆地运用其影响力,让美事成真。他们不炫耀自己,大多是在被追问的情况下才介绍自己的故事,还常常以一种平常心态和务实的方式缓缓道来,好像他们描述的只是一件不错的木工活,或是一次进展顺利的董事局会议。**我发现,使他们成为伟大艺术家的特质,就是使他们同样成为一个优秀的人的那些品质**。正是通过他们的话,我开始制订自己简单的生活准则。谁都知道,他们很有创意,但他们的行动也明显是有用的、实用的和豪爽大方的。

让我举几个例子。

1996 年的奖章获得者是皮特·西格。他的"清水帆船"故事让学生们激动不已。60 年代中期的一天,他从纽约州北边的家乘火车去纽约市,途中与一位金融界的熟人不期而遇,两人忘情畅谈。看着车窗外的哈得逊河,西格突发奇想:重建一条沿着哈得逊河和伊利运河运送货物的轮船,就像 150 年前的那样。这次旅行过后 6 个月,当这位老相识在同一班列车上告诉西格,他已经为西格白日梦般的幻想拉到了赞助,西格万分惊讶。西格后来回忆说,他当时的反应是:"嗯,看来现在我们必须建这么一条船了!"

短短几年内,西格就让他的"清水帆船"在哈得逊河上顺利通行,在沿岸城镇举办音乐会,并让孩子们沿着历史实地考察,从而使人们对

fanciful pipe dream. Pete's response, he recalled, was "Well, I guess now we're gonna have to build it!"

Within a few years, Seeger was sailing the Hudson on the Sloop Clearwater, giving concerts at cities and towns along the banks, taking children on historical field trips, and raising people's consciousness about the sad state of the polluted Hudson. Using the ship as a potent symbol, he lobbied the Federal Government on behalf of the Clean Water Act. The Act was passed in 1972 and remains one of the most successful environmental laws in history. As for the Hudson River, its level of pollution is drastically lower than it was that first day on the train, a change which came about substantially because of Pete Seeger's whim.

And Pete Seeger, you recall, is a folk singer.

The following year, the Medal winner was Bonnie Raitt. She had a good story, too. At the height of her success, having sold millions of records and having won a slew of Grammy Awards, she was approached by Fender Guitars with a very lucrative offer. They wanted to produce and sell a new model autographed guitar, one suited to her particular style of blues playing. She answered that she had no interest in making money off her autograph on a guitar, but that she would accept their offer on one condition. She would use her share of the proceeds from the sale of this new guitar as seed money to fund guitar lessons for inner city kids all over the country, through the Boys and Girls Clubs of America. Fender, she insisted, would have to lend its support as well.

The program quickly spread to over two hundred venues. Twelve years have passed since Bonnie's bright idea. Now known as the Boys and Girls Club Program for Music Education, it is still going strong.

My entire speech could be devoted to stories like this: David Hays and the National Theatre of the Deaf, Mira Nair and her film school in Uganda, William Christie and his "Jardins des Voix," Yo Yo Ma and his Silk Road Project. These were all marvelous, inspiring tales, but what was especially exciting about them was the fact that they were being told to college students, just at the moment when they most needed to hear them.

Because here is the point:

Many of you are leaving Harvard with lofty, ambitious goals. (Those of you who have no immediate goals, don't worry, you will discover them soon). A lot of you

哈得逊河所受污染的严重性有所认识。他以这艘船作为有力的凭证,向联邦政府进行游说,力主建立"清洁治水法案"。该法案最终于1972年通过,迄今为止,仍然是历史上最成功的环保法律之一。哈得逊河的污染程度与这两位故交在火车巧遇的时候相比,已大大降低。这种水质改善,很大程度上是因为皮特·西格一时的心血来潮。

但是,你们印象中的皮特·西格是一位民谣歌手。

次年的奖章获得者是波妮·莱特。她也有一个动人的故事。在她成功的巅峰时期,已售出数百万张唱片,并赢得了一系列格莱美奖,冯得吉他公司给了她一个非常有利可图的机会。他们希望生产和销售一种新的带有莱特签名的吉他,那种吉他特别适合莱特的蓝调演奏风格。她回答说,她对把她的签名用在吉他上赚钱没有兴趣,但是,她会有条件地接受他们的建议,那就是,用她从这种吉他销售所分得的钱作为种子基金,通过"美国男孩女孩俱乐部",赞助全美各地的贫穷孩子们学习吉他。她坚持要求冯得吉他公司对此事给予支持。

该方案迅速启动,惠及超过两百个地方。现在,波妮的这个好主意已经过去12年了,该项目以"男孩和女孩俱乐部音乐教育计划"闻名全美,它依然强劲有力。

我的整个演讲都可以用来讲述这样的故事:大卫·海斯和他的"全国聋哑人剧团"、米拉·奈尔和她在乌干达办的电影学校、威廉·克里斯蒂和他的"花园之声"、马友友和他的"丝绸之路"项目等等。这些都是了不起的、鼓舞人心的故事。但是,更加振奋人心的是,这些故事是讲给大学生们听的,而大学生们在这种时候最需要听到这样的故事。

这正是我想要说的:

你们将满怀雄心壮志离开哈佛,(那些还没有近期目标的同学,不用担心,你会很快找到自己的目标),很多人都将实现那些目标,而且有的人会大获成功。事实上,我暗自希望你出去好好闯闯,为这个充满危险和痛苦的世界,以及这个深受困扰的国家做些好事。但是,**当你达到自己的目标时,甚至在这种努力的过程中,就该想想还有什么是你也可以做的事。想想我刚才跟你们提到的那些人,他们是如何跨越自己原先的**

will achieve those goals, some with extravagant success. In fact, I'm secretly counting on you to go out and make things right in this perilous, suffering world and in this deeply troubled nation. But **when you get what you're aiming for, or even as you go through the process of getting it, think about what else you can also do. Think about the people I just described to you, how they went beyond their original aspirations, sometimes in wildly unlikely ways. Think about how they made a difference in the world and how much joy and pride they took in what they accomplished. Think about how they mingled art and commerce for the public good.** And then, if you like, take the word "art" out of the equation; because you certainly don't have to be an artist to follow their example. It is sometimes a very simple thing to be creative, to be useful, to be practical, and to be generous.

I followed their example myself. I conducted six of those yearly Arts Medal symposia during my six seasons on the TV sitcom "3rd Rock from the Sun." That show was arguably the most successful job I've ever had -- popular, high-profile, lucrative, and deliriously fun. But its very success gave me the opportunity to branch out from it. In retrospect, I have come to believe that, consciously or unconsciously, my annual visits to Harvard inspired me to create an entire concurrent second career.

Let me explain.

Ever since my own kids were tiny, I always entertained children. I sang songs, played guitar, and told stories to them in classrooms, assemblies and benefits. I got very good at performing for that extremely difficult, distractible audience. And I just loved it. Back from Harvard, sprawled in my dressing room near the 3rd Rock sound stage, I began thinking of what good use I might make of that particular enthusiasm. A hit sitcom is like a magic wand: when you suggest things to people they tend to say yes. So I began making suggestions.

First there was an album of kids' songs for Sony Records. That led to children's concerts at Carnegie Hall and with major symphony orchestras in Baltimore, Pittsburgh, Detroit, and Chicago. I started writing songs and stories for the concerts. One of the stories became a children's book. Then a second, third, fourth. I started being referred to as "Actor and Best-selling Author." I wrote the narration for a new version of "Carnival of the Animals" for the New York City Ballet. I even danced the role of "The Elephant"!

All of these projects had the simple, obvious goal of delighting children, but I had

愿望，做成了不可思议的事情；想想他们如何让世界有所不同，并从自己所做到的事情当中，获得莫大的喜悦和自豪；想想他们如何把艺术和商业融合在一起，从而实现公众利益。

然后，如果你喜欢，也可以把"艺术"这个词从中拿掉，因为你不用去做一个艺术家，也肯定能以他们为榜样。有时要做到勇于创新，对人有益，达到实用，豪爽大方，其实是件非常简单的事情。

我也以他们为自己的榜样。我在艺术奖章座谈会期间所做的电视节目"太阳边的第3块岩石"中，做了6年"哈佛艺术奖章论坛"的演播，我觉得这个节目是我有史以来最成功的：很受欢迎、有知名度、利润丰厚，而且特别有趣。但它的成功本身，也给了我其他的发展机会。回想起来，我认为每年回访哈佛，使我自觉或不自觉地获得灵感，启发我创建职业生涯中的并行发展。

请允许我解释一下。

还在我自己的孩子很小的时候，我就为儿童们提供娱乐。我唱歌、弹吉他，在课堂、集会和慈善福利活动中，给他们讲故事。给这些极难吸引、极容易分心的观众表演，我做得很棒，也乐在其中。从哈佛回来后，坐在"第3块岩石"的化妆室里，我开始思考如何能把我的这些个长处发挥出来。做一个情景喜剧的想法如同一根魔杖紧紧抓着我的心：当你向人们提出建议时，他们往往会说"行"。于是，我开始提建议。

刚开始是索尼唱片公司帮我出版儿童歌曲专辑。这使我得以在卡内基音乐厅举办儿童音乐会，以及和巴尔的摩、匹兹堡、底特律和芝加哥等重要交响乐团的合作。我开始为这些音乐会写演唱的歌曲和故事，其中一个故事成为一本儿童读物。然后是第二本、第三本、第四本。我开始被称为"演员兼畅销书作家"。我为纽约市立芭蕾舞团的"动物狂欢节"表演写了旁白，我甚至扮演了其中的"大象"那个角色。

所有这些项目，都有一个简单而明确的目标，即取悦儿童，但我暗地里还有一个计划。我想激起年轻人对艺术的兴趣，在潜移默化中让他们受到教育。我坚定地认为，艺术对一个健康社会来说不可或缺。但放眼望去，对艺术的支持者寥寥无几，甚至受到打击。我意识到我可以对此做些什么。带着

a secret agenda, too. I was seeking to stir an interest in the Arts in young people, to educate them without their knowing it. I hold the fierce conviction that the Arts are indispensable to a healthy society, but everywhere I see evidence that support for the Arts is **foundering** [founder, v. 摔倒. 失败], even under assault. I realized there was something I could do about it. With Jesuitical zeal, I began to see a personal mission taking shape: I could get them while they're young.

But I was also a busy working actor, and this was getting completely out of hand.

So I joined forces with a consulting firm in Los Angeles. It was made up of three smart, vibrant women who called themselves "Broadthink." Together we devised various publishing and media projects for kids, parents, teachers, and public schools, many of them spun off of what I had already done. We carefully refined our mission, always striving to connect the dots between entertainment, education, the arts, creative play, and family. This was our attempt, however naïve and idealistic, to educate and enliven young minds and to loosen the grip that violent video games hold these days on the imagination of millions of young people. To my surprise, I emerged as a kind of Pied Piper of arts education and literacy for kids. I delighted in this quixotic new role. And I had chosen such expert collaborators that I still had time to, for example, perform eight times a week on Broadway, the sort of thing that is generally expected of me.

Through all of this, Pete Seeger, Bonnie Raitt, and all the others were never far from my thoughts.

Then came that voice on the telephone this past March, asking me to deliver today's Commencement Address. Overwhelmed by the honor but daunted by the task, I went back to basics. In plotting my course, I reminded myself of my four lessons: be creative, be useful, be practical and be generous. And for today, I have added a fifth **dictum** [n. 格言. 名言], tailored to those of you out there who are heading into the world of entertainment: finish big.

As promised, it's now time for my performance.

"What is it?" you ask.

Well, number one, it's creative. A little crackpot, perhaps, but definitely creative. Since college graduation is the clearest possible **demarcation** [n. 划界. 限界] between childhood and adulthood, I have decided to write a brand new children's book and to recite it for you. Think of it as a kind of fond farewell to your young years.

传教士般的热情,我的个人计划初具雏形:趁孩子们年轻时候影响他们。

但我首先是个演员,工作繁忙,少有闲暇,所以事情开始完全失控。

后来我和一家在洛杉矶的咨询公司合作。该公司由三位聪慧且充满活力的女性组成,自称为"Broadthink"。我们一起设计了针对孩子、家长、教师、公立学校不同的出版和媒体项目,其中不少是根据我已经做过的东西而来的。我们精心提炼我们的使命,一直致力在娱乐、教育、艺术、创造性的发挥和家庭之间,建立起连接点。即便天真,未免有点理想化,但却是我们的尝试,给那些幼小的心灵提供教育和启发,并让他们脱离那些操控着成百万年轻人想象力的暴力视频游戏。令我惊讶的是,我成了一个倡导儿童艺术教育和识字的鼓吹手。我很高兴扮演这个唐·吉诃德式的新角色。由于有了这些专家合作,我仍然有时间每周8次在百老汇表演,因为这是我的主业。

在做所有这一切时,皮特·西格和波妮·莱特等人的影子一直在我的脑海里。

今年3月我接到电话,请我为今天的毕业典礼演讲。这个荣誉让我不知所措,要做的事难倒了我,于是我又回到起点。在策划方案时,我想起了自己的四条经验:有创意、有益处、实用、大气。今天,针对那些想要进入娱乐界的同学,我想加入第五个要点:把事情尽量做大。

现在,按照先前的承诺,该是我的表演时间。

"那会是什么?"你们会问。

首要是要有创意,也许有点疯疯癫癫,但肯定有创意。因为大学毕业清晰明确地意味着童年和成年之间的分界线,我决定写一个全新的儿童故事,在这里给你们背诵一下,就把它当成向你们的青春岁月的温情道别吧。

本书讲的是一只名为玛哈莉亚的老鼠上了大学。回到我们的起点,这是一个云游者一样的故事。她去冒险,并从中学到了很多。

它是有益的吗?我当然想做到这一点。我想做的,是让小孩子们对教育,特别是大学教育,感到好奇和兴奋。其实用性也许会扩大到火上浇油的地步:在你们本科的最后一学期里,哈佛校园被激烈的争议搅乱。本书是我对这些动荡作出的一个充满欢乐并有建设性的回应:玛哈莉亚主修的是理科。

它实用吗?哦,当然,否则我将徒劳无功。这份手稿已经通过了西蒙与舒

The book is about a mouse named Mahalia who goes to college. Just to bring things full circle, call it a picaresque tale. She has adventures and she learns a lot.

Is it useful? Well, it's certainly intended to be. It is calculated to make little children curious and excited about the notion of education in general and college in particular. And hopefully its usefulness will extend to pouring oil on troubled waters: your campus was roiled by a bitter, divisive controversy in the last semester of your undergraduate years. The book is my cheerful and constructive response to all the turbulence: Mahalia Mouse, you see, studies science.

Is it practical? Oh yes, I'm nothing if not practical. The manuscript has been reviewed and accepted by my editor at Simon & Schuster, and the long journey to publication is already underway. The book will be out in the spring of 2007.

And generous? Well, I have come to see performing in its purest form as a gift to an audience, so perhaps you can think of my recitation as my graduation gift to you. But beyond that, the book itself, in a sense, is yours. Go into a bookstore about twenty months from now. Find the book, open it up and look at the **verso** [n. 左页．(小钱币或奖章的) 反面]. It will be dedicated to the Harvard College Class of 2005.

And one more thing. The heart of an old Overseer still beats in me. In hopes of inspiring you to be generous to Harvard for all the days of your lives, my advance for the book is my contribution to your Class Gift.

But to my story.

First, some brief author's notes: although it is not mentioned in the text, the illustrations will distinctly show that the setting is Harvard. The first page, in fact, will feature Dunster House in the rain, as seen from across the Charles River. Any mention of news or a newspaper will feature an image of the Harvard Crimson. Finally, my science consultant for the book was none other than Harvard's own Professor Jeremy Knowles. You may want to picture Mahalia as his plucky granddaughter.

Now sit back, savor the sublime absurdity of the moment and listen to the last storybook of your childhood.

The Tale of Mahalia Mouse *(a children's story told in twenty-four stanzas of rhyming verse, recited by the author).*

My gift to the Class of 2005. Congratulations and have a wonderful life!

斯特出版公司的审读，漫漫的出版旅程已经开始，将于 2007 年春天面世。

豪爽大方？在我看来，表演的最本质形式，就是把它当做送给观众的礼物，所以，你们也可以把我的朗诵当做是我给你们的毕业礼物。除此之外，从某种意义上说，这本书本身是属于你们的。再过 20 个月，到书店里去找这本书，你会在封面背后看到：本书献给哈佛学院 2005 届毕业生。

还有一点，我的身上依然跳动着一颗老董事会成员的心。抱着激励你们在今后有生之涯都努力回报哈佛的希望，我把这本书的预付稿酬，捐给你们的"本年级向母校捐款"项目。

现在回头讲书里的故事。

首先做些简单的说明：虽然文中没有提到，书里的插图清楚表明，故事发生在哈佛校园，第一页插图画的就是从查尔斯河对岸看雨中邓斯特楼的景象。提到新闻或报纸的画面时，出现的将是《哈佛深红报》的形象。最后，我写本书时，请教的科学顾问杰里·米诺尔斯先生也是本校的教授，你可以把玛哈莉亚当成是他的一位勇敢的孙女。

现在请放松身心，细细品味一下这个崇高的离奇时刻，听听你的最后一个童话故事。

（演讲者在这里朗诵了他用二十四行诗形式写的童话故事《老鼠玛哈莉亚上学记》）[3]

这就是我给 2005 届同学的礼物。祝贺你们，并预祝一生精彩！

---

[1] 约翰·利特高在此是拿哈佛演讲人甄选委员会开玩笑，表现一个演员的幽默和风趣

[2] 演讲人这里是在表现幽默

[3] 《老鼠玛哈莉亚上学记》故事梗概：老鼠玛哈莉亚一家住在哈佛大学的一间宿舍下面。一次，她出去觅食，不慎掉进一个学生的书包里出不来了，等那个学生在教室里打开书包拉链时，玛哈莉亚才得以脱身，但她却被教授有关空间中的原子的讲座吸引住了，就停下来记笔记。学生们看到老鼠大惊小怪，但教授看出玛哈莉亚的潜力："这只老鼠是个天才！"教授让玛哈莉亚上了 4 年学，去攻读学位。故事的含义是，哪怕再小的生命，如果自己努力，都有成功的可能。书中带着手提电脑的老鼠和头发乱蓬蓬的教授，都令人过目不忘。

吉姆·莱勒（1934— ）

吉姆·莱勒（Jim Lehrer）是美国著名的电视新闻深度分析栏目《新闻一小时》的主持人，也是节目制作公司的总编。吉姆·莱勒曾多次主持美国总统竞选的电视辩论，在美国可说是一位家喻户晓的电视新闻评论家。

现年70多岁的吉姆·莱勒1934年出生于美国中部堪萨斯州的一个普通家庭，父亲是一个长途汽车公司的司机，后来做到经理，母亲是一个银行职员。莱勒的青少年时代在得克萨斯州度过。早年曾做过长途客车公司的检票员。莱勒从密苏里大学新闻学院毕业后，加入美国海军陆战队，驻扎在远东地区。3年的服兵役生活和到外面的旅行，对他日后产生了非常大的影响。莱勒认为，他拓展了自己的眼界，不再只是关注自己。

莱勒的新闻职业生涯开始于《达拉斯晨报》，他曾是1963年肯尼迪遇刺事件的主要报道者。后来参与电视报道，逐渐创立了自己的电视栏目，做深度新闻分析。他也参与了"水门事件"和美国国会讨论弹劾尼克松总统的深度报道。

莱勒曾主持过11场总统辩论会，其中包括2008年的奥巴马和共和党总统候选人约翰·麦克恩的辩论会。在2012年美国总统选举中，他再一次主持了两位总统候选人的辩论会。

2006

All Aboard for Your Departing Bus
长途客车的下一站：
参与服务

Jim Lehrer 吉姆·莱勒

Thank you, thank you. As the single freshest graduate of Harvard University - remember I was the last one to get in ... in fact, I'm so fresh, I still have my robe on ... and that makes me the most recent new member of the Harvard Alumni Association.

I would like to say to Larry Summers that on behalf of everybody in this room and everybody associated with our school, we accept your challenge and we will make it happen, sir.

I don't know about you all, you're probably used to this, but I was really impressed with the rundown on the financial condition. But that aside, on behalf of the nine of us who received honorary degrees today, we as a group would like to pledge, the new group of the Class of 2006, we would as a group like to pledge $127 billion.

Go way beyond Allston, way beyond **Allston**. [奥尔斯顿是波士顿城市西部的一个市区]

This is truly a great day for me personally. In fact, in the words of my 3-year-old granddaughter who is here, Olivia, this is what she would call a hoot and holler day for me.

In the morning I am awarded an honorary degree, and now, as the Commencement speaker, I have the opportunity to cause second thoughts for everybody who had anything to do with what happened this morning. And I thought I would make those folks particularly nervous by beginning with a bus call.

You heard several references this morning to the fact that I have a bus background. And that bus background includes: in the 1950s, I worked as a ticket agent in a Continental Trailways bus depot in a place called Victoria in south Texas. And one of my duties was to do this into a microphone:

"May I have your attention, please. This is your last call for Continental Trailways 8:10 p.m., Silversides air conditioned Thruliner to Houston now leaving from lane one for Inez, Edna, Ganado, Louise, El Campo, Pierce, Wharton, Hungerford, Kendleton, Beazley, Rosenberg, Richmond, Sugarland, Stafford, Missouri City, and Houston. All aboard. Don't forget your baggage, please."

Now you may be asking, "What in the world does that have to do with anything that's happening here today?" First of all, I try very hard to include a bus call in every speech I make for good luck. The second thing: it does serve a real purpose this afternoon ... kind of.

Fifty years ago almost to this very day, I received my undergraduate degree in college. The commencement speaker was a man who wore the gaudiest red tie I had

谢谢！谢谢各位！作为哈佛大学最新的一位毕业生——你们看，我是最后一个进入这个毕业典礼场地的。实际上，我新鲜得毕业袍还穿在身上，这也意味着我是哈佛校友会最新的一名成员。

我想代表在这里的每一个人，以及和与本校相关的所有人，对拉里·萨默斯（校长）说，我们接受你的挑战，并将使之成为现实。

不知道你们怎样想，你们可能已经习惯了这种情况，但我对学校的财务状况真是印象深刻。除此之外，我谨代表今天获得荣誉学位的 9 个人共同承诺：作为 2006 届的新成员，我们将给学校捐献 1270 亿美元。[1]

让我们跨越奥尔斯顿，远远地跨越奥尔斯顿[2]。

这对我个人来说，真是伟大的一天。事实上，用我年仅 3 岁的外孙女（她今天也在场）的话来说，今天是我棒极了的一天。

今天早上，我获得了哈佛荣誉学位，现在，作为毕业典礼的演讲人，我有机会让今天早上给我颁发学位的人心生悔意。我想用车站的发车通知来开始我的演讲，大概这会让那些给我荣誉学位的人紧张。

你们今天上午听到人们几次提到过，我曾有服务于长途客车公司的背景。这个经历包括上世纪 50 年代，我曾在得克萨斯州南部的一个叫做维多利亚的地方，做过"大陆长途客车公司"的检票员，我的职责之一是通过麦克风宣布：

"请注意，这是大陆长途客车晚上 8 点 10 分班次的最后一次发车通知，发往休斯顿的空调班车就要从第一车道开出，班车经停伊内兹、埃德娜、加纳多、路易斯、艾尔坎普、皮尔斯、沃顿、亨格福德、比兹利、罗森伯格、里士满、舒格兰、斯塔福德、密苏里市，最后抵达休斯敦。请各位上车，不要忘记行李。"

现在你可能会问："这和今天的毕业典礼有什么关系吗？"首先，为了求得好运气，我在每一次演讲中，都会尽量讲一遍"发车通知"。其次，它跟我们今天下午的事儿还真有点关系。

50 年前，几乎就是我们今天的这个时候，我拿到了大学本科学位。记得当时发表毕业演讲的是一名男子，他戴着我从来没见过的最花哨粗俗的红色领带，他说，他戴那样的领带，是为了让我们 1956 届的毕业生

ever seen in my life. And he wore it because he said he wanted us, the Class of 1956, to remember him.

He said, "Nobody in their right mind, particularly those graduating, listens to commencement speeches. So you won't remember anything I say. You won't remember my name, or even what I look like, but maybe you will remember this awful red tie."

Well, I've just proven him correct. I remembered the tie. He was also right: I did not remember his name and I did not remember what he looked like, but he was wrong about one very important thing. I did remember what he said, more or less.

I paraphrase from vague memory: "Since you will not remember a word I say, I have chosen to say very little. Good luck in your life from this day forward. Try to be kind to one and to all, and to yourself. Thanks for the honorary degree and have a great afternoon."

He gave us a little nod and then he returned to his seat. As you can imagine, to great and thunderous and thankful applause. And so, "Since you will not remember a word I say, I have cho - No, no, no. No such luck. No thankful applause right now, but in keeping with the man's basic principles of commencement addresses, I promise not to keep you long, and here comes the purpose, and think of the bus call as my equivalent to his red tie. Something to remember me by.

Journalism is my line of work and is at the heart of why I am standing here today. But the kind of broadcast journalism we do on the NewsHour is the ultimate, ultimate collaborative enterprise. As I suggested at a Shorenstein Center/Kennedy School event here a few weeks ago, getting pretty faces like mine on and off the air takes villages of talented professionals.

Thus, whatever honors come to me, including those of today, I accept them always for them as well as me.

Also honored in my case are some guidelines that I also shared with that earlier Harvard audience. They are my personal ones that we use at the NewsHour in our practice of journalism. I wrote them down several years ago at the behest of a seminar being held at the Aspen Institute.

Do nothing I cannot defend

Cover, write and present every story with the care I would want if the story were about me

们记住他。

他说:"没有一个头脑清醒的人,尤其是那些毕业生们,会要听毕业演讲。因此,你们不会记住我说些什么,你们不会记得我的名字,甚至我的长相,但也许你会记住这条难看的红领带。"

瞧,我刚才就证明了他是对的——我想起了他的领带。他还有对的地方:我不记得他的名字,也不记得他的长相如何。但在一件非常重要的事情上他错了,我多多少少记住了一些他说过的话。

我模糊地记得他说:"既然你们不会记住我说的任何话,我就选择言简意赅。祝你们从今天起都是好运。善待他人、善待所有人,也善待自己。谢谢学校授予我的荣誉学位,并祝大家下午愉快!"

他向我们微微点了下头,然后回到自己的座位上。你可以想象,当时他获得了雷鸣般的感激的掌声。因此,"既然你们不会记得我说的任何话,我就选择……"不不不,今天你们没有这样的运气,先别给我感谢的掌声。但根据那位先生毕业演讲的基本原则,我承诺不会讲得太长,这里先讲讲目的,请把我的长途客车发车通知当做那位先生的红领带,当做一件以后你们会用来记起我的东西。

新闻是我从事的工作,也是我今天站在这里的中心话题。但我们在"新闻一小时"所做的电视新闻,是一种最讲究协作的工作。正如几周前,我在索伦斯坦中心和肯尼迪学院举办的活动中所说,让像我这样的漂亮面孔[3]出现在电视上,背后有无数优秀专业人员的努力。

因此,我得到的任何荣誉,包括今天的荣誉,我在接受时既是为自己,也代表他们。

此外,我还荣幸地在今天早些时候,与部分哈佛听众共享过一些指导方针。这些我个人的指导方针,指引着我们"新闻一小时"的实践。几年前,在阿斯平研究会[4]举行的一个研讨会的要求下,我写下了这些:

- 不要做我无法为之辩解的任何事
- 用心采访、编写和发表每一条新闻,就像这条新闻写的是我自己一样
- 要考虑到每一条新闻都会有另外的一面,或不同的说法

Assume there is at least one other side or version to every story

Assume the viewer is as smart and as caring and as good a person as I am # Assume the same about all people on whom I report

Assume personal lives are a private matter until a legitimate turn in the story absolutely mandates otherwise

Carefully separate opinion and analysis from straight news stories and clearly label everything

Do not use anonymous sources or blind quotes except on rare and monumental occasions. No one should ever be allowed to attack another anonymously

And finally, finally I am not in the entertainment business

I have come with only one major commencement-like point to make, you'll be delighted to hear. And let me put it simply and directly. I believe we should consider adopting some form of national service. No, not a return to the military draft, something entirely different, and completely new for us. National service in its fullest meaning.

My reasons have to do mostly with what I see as an urgent need to address the growing state of disconnection we have in our country today. But it is based also on my personal experiences which flow directly from something else I did on my graduation day 50 years ago, besides listen to a man in a red tie speak.

I went with my parents from the commencement ceremony to a building on campus and I raised my right hand and was sworn in as a **second lieutenant** [n. 少 尉] in the United States Marine Corps. I spent the next three years as an infantry officer, mostly in the Far East.

It was between the Korean and Vietnam wars. I saw no combat, fired no rounds in anger, had none fired at me, had no roadside bombs kill fellow Marines of mine. I was spared events that might have triggered losing control, to going over the top of civilized behavior into angry barbarism, as has been charged against a group of Marines these days in Iraq.

My Marine service was a life-changing experience for me. A positive one that had I not had, I most likely would not be standing here today. Because I would not be a person deemed worthy for such honor.

I went into the military because I had to. Join on your own or be drafted was the

- 要把观众假设为和我一样，是一个明智、有爱心和善良的人
- 要把我报道的人，都给予上面这样的假设
- 要假设个人生活是件私人的事，除非故事的转变让这种假设发生完全的变化
- 从纯粹的新闻报道中，仔细区分并明确标出哪些是个人的意见和分析
- 除去极个别特殊情况，不要使用匿名消息来源，或没有出处的引语。不允许任何人匿名攻击别人
- 最后，一定要记住我可不是在娱乐行业

你们会很高兴地听到，我只想讲一些毕业演讲式的要点，简单而直接。我认为我们应该采取一些要求国民为国家服务的措施。不，不是回到征兵制度那种形式，完全不是那么回事，对我们来说是全新的一种东西，真正意义上的为国家服务。

我这样说的理由，主要是觉得我们国家目前日益加剧的混乱状况迫切需要得到解决。这也是基于我个人的经验，这种体验来自我 50 年前毕业时听戴大红领带的人演讲那天。

我和我的父母在毕业典礼之后来到校园中的一座建筑前，在那里我举起右手宣誓入伍，成为美国海军陆战队的少尉。作为一个步兵军官，接下来 3 年的时间里，我大部分时间驻扎在远东。

这段时间处于朝鲜战争和越南战争之间。我没有参加战斗，没有在愤怒中发射炮火，没有人朝我开枪，也没有看到被路边炸弹炸死的海军陆战队同伴。我没有遭遇导致我失去自控的事件，保持着文明行为，没有丧失理智做出野蛮的事情，比如最近在伊拉克的一批海军陆战队员被指控做出的那些事。[5]

对我来说，在海军陆战队服役是一段改变人生的经历。这是一种有益的经历，没有它，我今天很可能不会站在这里，因为我不值得获此殊荣。

我参军是迫不得已。那时可以自愿入伍，不然就得应征入伍[6]，我选择海军陆战队完全出于个人原因。你们可以从我的体型上看出来，反正

choice. I chose the Marines for personal, not heroic or, as you can clearly see, physique reasons.

My Dad had been a Marine and so had my brother, and so I would be a Marine. That required service changed me and the life I have led ever since.

My travels up till then had been restricted pretty much to central Kansas, eastern Oklahoma, and south Texas. My mode of transport was mostly on Trailways buses. But as a Marine I took my first plane ride, to Washington, D.C., and then on eventually to California and to Japan and to Okinawa and to Taiwan and to the Philippines and to essentially the world.

My friends and acquaintances up till then had been mostly people who looked, talked, and thought like me. But now I was eating, drinking, sleeping, sweating, and running up and down hills with, and listening to and depending on people who had little in common with me.

Some spoke and looked different. Most were larger and stronger than me, a few smaller. Some were smarter, others dumber, some were rich, others poorer. Some were wonderful people, others were less so. Some wouldn't hurt a fly, others sometimes deserved to be hurt by flies.

In that diverse company I learned to be responsible for others, I learned to depend on others, and to understand what being depended on by others really meant.

I learned that there was more to the world than me, and my kind. There was more to my life than me, me, me, and me...

I learned there was joy and satisfaction to be had by looking past the mirror. By serving common interests rather than only those of self.

I am grateful my country forced me to serve my country. Not for my country's sake, but for my own. My three years of service connected me to the rest of the world, the world outside myself, and the connection has been permanent.

The experience also left me with a firm conviction that beyond the benefits to individuals, connecting and connections are essential for our democratic society to work.

And speaking now as a journalist whose job it's been to pay attention to such things, I have never seen us more disconnected from each other than we are right now.

We are **splintering** [v. 劈开. 破裂] off into segments, interest groups, lobbies, target audiences, blogs, boxes.

不是因为勇敢。

我父亲曾经是一名海军陆战队员，我哥哥也当过，所以我也得加入海军陆战队。这项必尽的义务从此改变了我的生活。

在那之前，我的旅行主要局限于堪萨斯州中部、俄克拉荷马州东部和得克萨斯南部，我的交通工具是长途客车。但作为一名海军陆战队员，我第一次飞行就去了首都华盛顿，然后去加利福尼亚，再到日本、冲绳、台湾地区、菲律宾，以及世界上很多地方。

在那之前，我的朋友和熟人基本上和我用相同的方式看问题、交谈和思考。但参军后，我和一帮与我没什么共同点的人一起吃喝，一起流汗，并沿着山丘跑上跑下，听他们谈话，互相依赖。

有些人说话难懂，有些人长相和我很不一样。大多数人比我强壮，有的人块头比我小一些。有些人聪明，有些人笨点；有些人富有，也有些人较穷；有些人为人极好，有些人则差点劲儿；有些人连一只苍蝇也不愿伤害，有些人则应该让苍蝇去叮咬他。

在这样一群很不相同的人群里，我学会了对他人负责，学会了互相支持，也了解了什么是别人把你视为后盾的真正含义。

我了解到，世界并不限于我或者和我相同的人，不光只有我的生活和"我、我、我"这样狭隘的观念……

我体会到透过现象看本质的喜悦和满足，知道不应只顾自我，而要服务大家。

我很感谢我的祖国强迫我为她效力，不是为国家之故，而是为我自己。从军的3年，把我和世界其他地方，以及自己外部的世界联系了起来，这样的联系是那样恒久。

我的经历也让我坚定地相信，除了对个人有益之外，人际的交流和连接，对我们的民主社会至关重要。

作为一名记者，就是要关注这些事情。我看到，我们从来没有像现在这样彼此隔膜。

我们分裂成不同的派别、利益团体、游说组织、宣传对象、网上群体、条条块块等等。

Our racial, cultural, and religious differences, always our great strength, have become an instrument in our great disconnection. Our growing economic differences, as Larry put it brilliantly, are feeding this. Our politics at the moment actually seem to be encouraging it, and our otherwise terrific explosion in new media outlets for information and debate are helping facilitate it.

I believe what we need is a new hard real-world dose of shared experience. We had one after 9/11, and it drifted away. We had one after Katrina, and it went away. We have yet to even have one on Iraq.

A show of hands please in this room.

How many of you know someone personally who has served or is now serving in Iraq? How many of you know a person or a relative of a person who has been killed or wounded in Iraq?

Raise your hand if our being at war in Iraq has had any direct effect on your life at all.

What's left, I believe, for us all, the issues of the war in Iraq aside, how do we connect ourselves and then stay connected to the other Americans who do serve in the military and elsewhere in our name, on our behalf, without having to sustain a tremendous man-made or natural disaster.

I would submit one way is service itself. Service in all of its many forms. Service that can mean the Peace Corps, a teacher corps, a conservation corps, a police corps, a hospital aid corps, a tutor corps, a Big Brother/Big Sister corps, a coping corps, a pick up the trash corps as well as the Marine Corps.

I do not have a specific 10- or 12-point proposal to put on the table. I am a journalist, not a proposalist.

But I do have some framing questions for the discussion. In order to be fair, should it be mandatory, no exemptions, no permanent deferments, everyone eventually serves?

Should it apply across the board, men, women, all physical and intellectual sizes and abilities included? What should be the age parameters? Should there be a way to involve not just the young? Should it be constructed around choices, each individual choosing the form of service, military or specific civilian, he or she wishes?

Should it be developed in partnership with private and corporate resources as well as governmental? Should it be tied to a G.I. Bill type program? Service earns

我们在种族、文化和宗教方面的不同,本来是我们强大的实力,但现在已成为制造隔阂的工具。正如拉里[7]所精辟阐释的:我们不断增长的经济差异在强化着这种隔阂。我们目前的政策好像在鼓励隔阂,我们用来获取信息和进行辩论的新媒体爆炸式地增长,这本来是件好事,却也让制造隔阂更加方便。

我认为,现实世界中我们需要一个新的共同体验。我们在9·11事件之后有过,但它飘然而去。我们在"卡特里娜"飓风过后有过,但它也无影无踪了。在伊拉克问题上,我们还没有达成共识。

请在座的各位举手:

你们当中,有多少人直接认识曾在或正在伊拉克服役的人?

你们当中,有多少人认识在伊拉克阵亡或受伤的人,或是他们的亲属?

如果伊拉克战争对你的生活产生过直接影响,请举手。

对剩下的人及我们所有的人来说,先不谈伊拉克战争,我相信我们的问题是如何才能彼此沟通?如何才能关注那些以我们的名义、代表我们而在军队和其他地方服务的人,让他们不用经历人为的或自然的伤害?

我想提出一个办法,就是服务本身。服务可以是多种多样的,可能意味着参加和平队、义务教师团体、保护组织、警察部队、医院援助团、义务辅导团、大哥哥/大姐姐组织、协作团队、垃圾清理小组,以及服务于海军陆战队等等。

我拿不出特定的10条或是12条建议放到桌上,我是一名记者,而不是一个提案专家。

不过,我有一些框架性的建议。为了公平起见,这些服务是否应该是强制性的,不能有例外,不能长期推迟,而且每个人最终都要参与服务?

或者是应该一刀切?无论男女,也无论什么样的体力、智力及能力的人,都要参与服务?年龄大小的依据是什么?用什么方法,可以不仅仅只是让年轻人承担?如果可能的话,每个人是否都可以选择参军或某些平民性质的服务形式?

鼓励这种服务,除了政府之外,是否还应该与私人机构及公司一起

education, home and other benefits. In addition to the benefits of connection, and of the soul.

I know some will argue that such a program would cost too much. I would only ask, compared to what?

Others would argue that it, for it to really work politically, it must be voluntary. I don't do politics, so I'll leave the politics of national service to someone else.

But voluntary service is what we have now. The result, to my observation, at least, it may be cheaper, but it's also causing a serious heightening of our differences and our disconnections. And definitely not just as it involves the military.

My guess is that all of you in this room - alums, students, parents, whatever - have an interest in volunteer public service and that you have no doubt already done some of it and will always continue to do so.

Am I right about that? Yes. Absolutely. No question about it.

But volunteer service, voluntary service - the kinds that you perform and the kinds that I perform - is not an equal opportunity operation. Non-military volunteerism is pretty well confined to the well-educated and the well-off.

The majority of Americans are simply not in a financial position to delay careers, to take no-pay internships, to take off a year or two, or even a few weeks or even a long weekend to do good, to help people rebuild their homes in New Orleans or Indonesia. Do tutoring of low-income kids in Los Angeles or Des Moines, find food and shelter for the devastated of Darfur or Biloxi.

So we have a rather stark division among us. The most fortunate volunteer for the non-military, the less fortunate volunteer for the military. And those in between, the vast majority of Americans, do neither because they can't afford to.

I know for a fact I would not have voluntarily gone into the Marine Corps 50 year ago. I would have gone directly from my commencement ceremony to a job ... to my job that I already had as a newspaper reporter, which is what I did three years later after my service.

Trust me, I was a much better reporter then because of how I spent those intervening three years. And a much better person, and even Commencement speaker now, 50 years later.

The bottom line for me on this is simply this: whatever the ultimate conclusion, I believe passionately that we would all benefit from a full and frank discussion of

共同进行？是否应该把鼓励服务和给退伍军人的福利相结合？让参军服务除了具有建立联系、强化灵魂的好处外，还可获得教育、住房及其他福利的资助？

我知道有些人会认为，这种方案成本太高。那我想问，是相比什么样的成本呢？

另一些人则认为，如果在政治上想让这个做法过关，服务就必须是自愿的。我不搞政治，所以我把为国效力这个政治议题留给别人来谈。

但是根据我的观察，我们现有的志愿服务虽然比较简便，却也造成了我们之间严重的分歧与隔阂，而且绝不是因为这个问题涉及服役。

我想所有在这里的人——校友、学生、家长等等——都对志愿为公众服务感兴趣，毫无疑问，你们已经做了一些并将继续做这些志愿工作，我说得不错吧？

但是，志愿服务、自主服务——你们和我做的那些——并不是一种平等的作为，非军事需要的志愿服务，仅限于受过良好教育和小康人群。大多数美国人的财务状况，根本无法保证他们推迟事业、从事无薪实习，或者拿出一两年、几个星期、甚至只是一个长周末，去做点好事，帮助在新奥尔良或印尼的灾民重建家园，再或者为洛杉矶或德梅因的低收入孩子提供家教，帮助达富尔或比洛克西的难民寻找食物和住房。

因此，我们之间就有了严峻的分工：条件最好的人在非军队领域服务，家境不好的人去参军。绝大多数美国人身处这两者之间，他们什么都没做，因为他们做不起。

我知道如果有可能（如果没有必须服兵役的要求），50年前我也不会自愿去海军陆战队。我会在毕业典礼之后直接参加工作，我当时已经有一份报社记者的工作了，而这也是我服役3年后所从事的职业。

不过相信我，正是因为这3年的经历，我成了一个更好的记者，50年后成了一个更好的人，甚至成为现在的毕业典礼演讲者。

对我来说，无论最终结果如何，**我深信：全面和坦率地讨论我们共同承担服务的责任，会让所有人都从中受益，对此我充满信心。比如，讨论参与这种服务的喜悦和满足感；讨论如何暂时忘掉自己的需要，而**

our mutual responsibilities to serve. Of the joys and satisfactions that come from such service. From lifting ourselves away from our own needs just for a while to pay attention to those of others, and of trying to find a way that involves every one of us.

I am well aware of the collateral debates that would most likely spring from this one. One has to do with going to war. National service, with a military option, would complicate decisions of presidents and congresses about using force.

Parents and spouses and children of the potential combatants would have to be in the loop along with the volunteer experts, the pundits, the politicians and the generals.

Some would argue that's a good thing because it would force more public explanations and justifications and thus harder thinking before rushing off to invade or to bomb.

Others would say that's terrible because the result could be a hand-wringing public referendum on every military use decision our country makes. And back and forth, and back and forth, and so the debate would go.

And I say, let that debate and all others on national service begin. And as they say in other venues, thus ends the rendering of the message.

Thank you very much. Thank you. Thank you.

But let me add very quickly: I am not urging any of you - students, alums, faculty members, members of the administration, parents - to run off and join the Marines.

And I say that because one of the first major commencement addresses I made to a college graduating class, my theme then was risk: **take risks in your personal lives, in your professional lives,** and I went on and on about the joys and satisfactions to be had from a risk-filled life.

A few weeks later the phone rings at our house in Washington after midnight.

A young male voice on the phone says, "Mr. Lehrer? You changed my life."

"Mmmm." I was trying to wake up.

He said, "I was in that graduating class. I heard what you said in your commencement address about taking risks."

"Mmm."

"I was in the class. I had already taken a job on Wall Street. But when you said that about taking risks, I changed my mind and I decided to do what I wanted to do in the first place anyhow. And as soon as the ceremony was over I told my mom and dad, 'No Wall Street.' I was going into the business of making sunglasses frames with

去关注一下其他人的需要；讨论如何才能找到一种让我们每一个人参与其中的方法。

我深知由于这个话题可能引起相关的辩论。一是有关是否应该参与某场战争。当涉及战争时，全国都参与服务的事实，会让总统和国会在是否使用武力的问题上更难决策。

可能参战人员的家长、配偶和子女，与志愿者、专家学者、政治家以及军队将领等，同在一条线上。

有些人会认为这是一件好事，因为这会迫使有关方面在匆匆地决定入侵或轰炸前，必须对公众做出更多的解释和说明，从而三思。

另一些人则会说那样不好，因为其结果可能是国家在做每一个军事决定时，都要缩手缩脚地让公民投票，一来二去，辩论无休无止。

我想说的是，让我们开始那个辩论，以及展开所有有关为国家服务的辩论。像人们说的，这样我们就不用一遍遍地只是发出信息了。

谢谢你们，非常感谢！

但是，我还要加上一句：在座的学生、校友、教职员、校方管理人员、家长们——跑步前进，快速去海军陆战队报名吧。

我说这句话的原因是，在我前几次重要的毕业演讲中，我讲的主题是冒险：**在你的个人生活中要冒险，在你的职业生涯中要冒险**，我谈了许多从充满冒险的生活中你所能得到的快乐和满足。

之后几星期的一个午夜，我在华盛顿家中的电话铃响了。

一位年轻男性的声音说："莱勒先生吗？你改变了我的生活。"

"哦。"我试着让自己清醒一些。

"我那时坐在台下听你的毕业典礼演讲，你说要勇于冒险。"他说。

"嗯。"

"我是毕业生中的一员，我已经得到了一份华尔街的工作。但你说人生应当冒险，这让我改变了主意，决定首先要做点什么。毕业典礼一结束，我就告诉父母不去华尔街了。我自己创办企业，做有透明塑料管的太阳镜镜架，这样你可以随意改变镜架的颜色，可以今天要红色、白色和蓝色，明天换成粉红色……总之，可以任意变换颜色。"

clear plastic tubes where you could change the color with little BB-like things. You want red, white and blue one day ... you want pink the next ... you want whatever."

And he said, "I've done it, Mr. Lehrer. I'm going to be on the CBS morning news tomorrow demonstrating my frames. I figured you'd want to know. Thank you, sir, for changing my life."

Now I was really awake and I was thinking, "Oh my. What had I wrought?" Of course, mostly I was thinking that his parents probably had a hit out on me, on my head.

So ...

In the unlikely event one of you all does decide to join the Marines today, pick up and go and run and go and do it. Fine. **Semper Fi** [拉丁语 "always faithful", 永远忠诚]. But please, just don't tell me about it.

For the record, I do now know about my own commencement speaker 50 years ago.

I went to my university's Web site the other day. He was a popular novelist, screenwriter and playwright at the time.

So what this means for you, 50 years from now, if you want to know about the Commencement speaker, you can go to www.harvard.edu and find out who he was at the time, in addition, of course, to remembering that he began by calling a Continental Trailways bus to Houston.

And now, as the man said, "Good luck in your life. From this day forward, try to be kind to one and to all, and to yourself. Thanks for the honorary degree. And have a great afternoon".

他接着说,"我成功了,莱勒先生,我要在 CBS 明天的早间新闻节目里展示我的镜架,我想让你知道,是你改变了我的生活,谢谢你。"

这时我真的醒过来了,我在想:"噢,都是因为我吗?"当然,我主要在想他的父母可能在我的头上打了一下。

因此,万一你们当中有人决定今天加入海军陆战队,那么赶快去做,"永远忠诚"[8]。但你不用把这消息告诉我。

可以记录在案的是,我现在知道 50 年前在我自己的毕业典礼上演讲的是什么人了。

前些天,我去了我母校的网站,得知那位演讲者是一个在当时挺受欢迎的小说家、编剧和剧作家。

所以,对你们来说,从现在起的 50 年后,如果你想知道谁是你们毕业典礼的演讲者,并知道当时这人是干什么的,你可以点击网站 www.harvard.edu,此外,要记住他开始演讲时念了一通"大陆长途客车"到休斯敦的发车通知。

而现在,就像他说的那样:祝你们生活美满。从今天起,善待他人、善待所有人,也善待自己。谢谢学校授予我的荣誉学位,并祝大家下午愉快!

---

1 莱勒这里是针对哈佛的巨额校友捐赠,讲了句幽默的话。

2 奥尔斯顿是波士顿城市西部的一个市区

3 这里又是一个幽默,1934 年出生的人当时已经 72 岁,并不靠面貌英俊吃饭。

4 阿斯平研究所(The Aspen Institute)于 1950 年创建于美国科罗拉多州的阿斯平,总部现设在美国首都华盛顿。是一个旨在为围绕全球性问题进行广泛深入探讨以及组织信息与学术交流的非营利性组织。阿斯平研究所致力于促进不同文化背景和社会制度的国家、团体间的自由交流,以充分彰显各自的观点、才能、学识和特长,因此成为当今有影响的思想库之一。

5 美国报刊时有对美国军队在伊拉克过度使用暴力以及杀害平民的报道。

6 当时美国规定所有适龄男子都必须服兵役

7 指时任哈佛校长拉里·萨默斯

8 Semper Fi,(拉丁语)"永远忠诚",这是美国海军陆战队的座右铭。

比尔·盖茨（1955— ）

比尔·盖茨出生于美国华盛顿州的西雅图市，父亲是一位著名律师，母亲是银行系统的董事，他的外祖父是一位银行家，他有一个姐姐和一个妹妹。盖茨的父母很重视家庭教育，总是鼓励孩子积极进取、追求卓越，凡事尽力做到最好。比尔与他的母亲感情很深。还在孩童时期，母亲就经常带着他去参加学校或社区的义工活动，尽己所能帮助人们，这对日后他所从事的慈善事业有着深刻的影响。在这篇演讲中，盖茨专门提到他的母亲，以及其母的临终心愿。

盖茨从中学开始就对计算机深感兴趣，13岁开始电脑程序设计，15岁时就与他的中学好友保罗·艾伦合作编了一套监控西雅图交通状况规律的程序，获得了2万美元的利润。1973年考入哈佛大学，比尔本计划像父亲一样学法律，但一年下来，他在计算机实验室里的时间，远远超过他在教室的上课时间。他与保罗·艾伦合作为世界上第一台微型计算机 MITS Altair 开发了一个 BASIC 编程语言的软件。接着他在大学二年级时辍学，于1975年与保罗·艾伦共同创建了微软（微型计算机与软件）公司。比尔·盖茨过人的技术和敏锐的商业头脑使微软很快成为世界上最大的软件王国。他及微软的最大成就之一，是极大地降低了计算机的成本，让计算机进入了寻常百姓家，使复杂的计算机变为普通人都会使用的工具。

2008年，比尔·盖茨宣布离开微软，把580亿美元的个人资产捐给以他和夫人名字命名的比尔与梅琳达·盖茨基金会，全力投身到减少"世界不平等"的慈善事业中。因为认同和赞赏盖茨基金会的方向与工作，世界另一富豪巴菲特把自己的370亿美元资产捐给了盖茨基金会。

2007

From Those to Whom Much Is Given, Much Is Expected
得到越多 责任越重

Bill Gates 比尔·盖茨

President Bok, former President Rudenstine, incoming President Faust, members of the Harvard Corporation and the Board of Overseers, members of the faculty, parents, and especially, the graduates:

I've been waiting more than 30 years to say this: "Dad, I always told you I'd come back and get my degree."

I want to thank Harvard for this timely honor. I'll be changing my job next year ... and it will be nice to finally have a college degree on my resume.

I applaud the graduates today for taking a much more direct route to your degrees. For my part, I'm just happy that the Crimson has called me "Harvard's most successful dropout." I guess that makes me valedictorian of my own special class ... I did the best of everyone who failed.

But I also want to be recognized as the guy who got Steve Ballmer to drop out of business school. I'm a bad influence. That's why I was invited to speak at your graduation. If I had spoken at your orientation, fewer of you might be here today.

Harvard was just a phenomenal experience for me. Academic life was fascinating. I used to sit in on lots of classes I hadn't even signed up for. And dorm life was terrific. I lived up at Radcliffe, in Currier House. There were always lots of people in my dorm room late at night discussing things, because everyone knew I didn't worry about getting up in the morning. That's how I came to be the leader of the anti-social group. We clung to each other as a way of validating our rejection of all those social people.

Radcliffe was a great place to live. There were more women up there, and most of the guys were science-math types. That combination offered me the best odds, if you know what I mean. This is where I learned the sad lesson that improving your odds doesn't guarantee success.

One of my biggest memories of Harvard came in January 1975, when I made a call from Currier House to a company in Albuquerque that had begun making the world's first personal computers. I offered to sell them software.

I worried that they would realize I was just a student in a dorm and hang up on me. Instead they said: "We're not quite ready, come see us in a month," which was a good thing, because we hadn't written the software yet. From that moment, I worked day and night on this little extra credit project that marked

From Those to Whom Much Is Given, Much Is Expected   Bill Gates
得到越多　责任越重　比尔·盖茨

伯克校长、鲁登斯坦前校长、即将上任的福斯特校长、哈佛集团和监管理事会的各位理事、各位老师、家长，特别是今天毕业的同学们：

我等了足足30年，今天终于可以说这句话了："老爸，我一直跟你说，我会回来拿我的学位的！"

我想感谢哈佛大学及时地给我这个荣誉。因为明年我就要换工作了[1]……我终于可以在自己的简历里写上一个大学学位，这真是太好了！

我为今天毕业的同学们叫好，你们通往学位之路可比我直接多了。对我来说，我很高兴哈佛的校报称我为"哈佛大学历史上最成功的辍学生"——我想这个使我有资格代表我这一类学生发言——在所有"失败者"中，我做到了最好。

不仅如此，我还想提醒大家，我还使斯蒂夫·鲍尔默[2]也从哈佛商学院退学了。因此，我是个有着不好影响的人。这就是为什么我被邀请在你们的毕业典礼上演讲。如果我在你们的开学欢迎仪式上演讲，那么坚持到今天在这里毕业的人大概就会少得多。

哈佛对我来说是一段不同寻常的经历，校园生活令人着迷。我经常去旁听一些我并没有注册的课程。哈佛的宿舍生活也很棒，我在拉德克利夫（Radcliffe，哈佛的一个宿舍院）过着逍遥自在的日子。每天我的宿舍里总有很多人聚在一起讨论各种事情，一直待到很晚，因为每个人都知道我从不考虑第二天要早起。这使得我变成了校园里那些不安分学生的头儿，我们整天待在一起，做出一副与所有正常学生不同的样子。

拉德克利夫是个生活的好地方。那里的女生比男生多，而且男生大多数都是理工科的。这种组合状况为我创造了最好的机会——如果你们明白我的意思的话。可正是在这里，我学到了令人叹息的一课：机会大，并不能保证你一定能成功。

哈佛最令我难忘的回忆之一，发生在1975年的1月。当时，我从宿舍楼里给位于阿尔布开克市[3]的一家公司打了一个电话，那家公司已经在着手制造世界上第一台个人电脑。我想向他们出售软件。

我起初担心他们如果发觉我是一个住在宿舍的学生，会挂断我的电话。但结果相反，他们说："我们还没准备好，一个月后你再来找我们吧。"

the end of my college education and the beginning of a remarkable journey with Microsoft.

What I remember above all about Harvard was being in the midst of so much energy and intelligence. It could be exhilarating, intimidating, sometimes even discouraging, but always challenging. It was an amazing privilege – and though I left early, I was transformed by my years at Harvard, the friendships I made, and the ideas I worked on.

But taking a serious look back … I do have one big regret.

I left Harvard with no real awareness of the awful inequities in the world – the appalling disparities of health, and wealth, and opportunity that condemn millions of people to lives of despair.

I learned a lot here at Harvard about new ideas in economics and politics. I got great exposure to the advances being made in the sciences.

But **humanity's greatest advances are not in its discoveries – but in how those discoveries are applied to reduce inequity. Whether through democracy, strong public education, quality health care, or broad economic opportunity – reducing inequity is the highest human achievement.**

I left campus knowing little about the millions of young people cheated out of educational opportunities here in this country. And I knew nothing about the millions of people living in unspeakable poverty and disease in developing countries.

It took me decades to find out.

You graduates came to Harvard at a different time. You know more about the world's inequities than the classes that came before. In your years here, I hope you've had a chance to think about how – in this age of accelerating technology – we can finally take on these inequities, and we can solve them.

Imagine, just for the sake of discussion, that you had a few hours a week and a few dollars a month to donate to a cause – and you wanted to spend that time and money where it would have the greatest impact in saving and improving lives. Where would you spend it?

For Melinda and for me, the challenge is the same: how can we do the most good for the greatest number with the resources we have.

During our discussions on this question, Melinda and I read an article

From Those to Whom Much Is Given, Much Is Expected Bill Gates
得到越多　责任越重 比尔·盖茨

这真是个好消息,因为那时我还根本没把软件写出来呢。从那一刻起,我夜以继日地在这个小课外项目上工作,它使我提早结束了我的大学生涯,开始了通往微软的不平凡之旅。

然而我对哈佛的主要记忆,就是被旺盛的精力和过人的智慧包围着。哈佛的生活是令人振奋的,也是令人生畏的,有时甚至会让人有些气馁,但它永远充满了挑战性。生活在哈佛是一种神奇的特殊待遇——虽然我提前离开了,但是我在这里的经历、在这里建立的友谊、在这里产生的一些想法,都极大地改变了我本人。

不过现在认真地回忆起来,我确实有一个比较大的遗憾。

当年离开哈佛时,我并没有真正认识到这个世界是这么的不平等。人们在健康、财富和机会上的悬殊差距骇人听闻,这种不平等迫使数以千百万计的人们生活在绝望之中。

我在哈佛学到了很多经济学和政治学方面的新思想,我也有很多机会了解到许多科学上的新进展。

但人类最大的进步并不在于这些发现,而在于如何运用这些发现来减少世上的不平等——无论是通过民主制度、强大的公共教育体系、高质量的医疗保健服务,还是广泛的经济机会——减少不平等才是人类最高的成就。

我离开校园的时候,并不知道在我们国家有几百万的年轻人没有得到接受教育的机会。我也完全不知道,在发展中国家,有无数的人生活在难以形容的贫穷和疾病之中。

我花了几十年时间才了解了这些事实。

各位毕业生们,你们在不同的时代来到哈佛。你们比以前的学生,更多地了解世界是怎样的不平等。在你们的哈佛生涯中,我希望你们思考过:在这个科技加速发展的时代,我们最终将如何应对这种不平等,我们将怎样来解决这个问题。

为讨论方便,这里试想一下,如果你每周有几个小时、每个月有些钱可以捐出——你希望这些时间和金钱,能够用在拯救生命和改善人类生活等作用最大的地方。你会选择哪里?

对梅琳达[4]和我来说,面临的问题是一样的:如何能将我们所拥有的

about the millions of children who were dying every year in poor countries from diseases that we had long ago made harmless in this country. Measles, malaria, pneumonia, hepatitis B, yellow fever. One disease I had never even heard of, rotavirus, was killing half a million kids each year – none of them in the United States.

We were shocked. We had just assumed that if millions of children were dying and they could be saved, the world would make it a priority to discover and deliver the medicines to save them. But it did not. For under a dollar, there were interventions that could save lives that just weren't being delivered.

If you believe that every life has equal value, it's revolting to learn that some lives are seen as worth saving and others are not. We said to ourselves: "This can't be true. But if it is true, it deserves to be the priority of our giving."

So we began our work in the same way anyone here would begin it. We asked: "How could the world let these children die?"

The answer is simple, and harsh. The market did not reward saving the lives of these children, and governments did not subsidize it. So the children died because their mothers and their fathers had no power in the market and no voice in the system.

But you and I have both.

We can make market forces work better for the poor if we can develop a more creative capitalism – if we can stretch the reach of market forces so that more people can make a profit, or at least make a living, serving people who are suffering from the worst inequities. We also can press governments around the world to spend taxpayer money in ways that better reflect the values of the people who pay the taxes.

If we can find approaches that meet the needs of the poor in ways that generate profits for business and votes for politicians, we will have found a sustainable way to reduce inequity in the world.

This task is open-ended. It can never be finished. But a conscious effort to answer this challenge will change the world.

I am optimistic that we can do this, but I talk to skeptics who claim there is no hope. They say: "Inequity has been with us since the beginning, and will be with us till the end – because people just … don't … care."

From Those to Whom Much Is Given, Much Is Expected Bill Gates
得到越多　责任越重 比尔·盖茨

资源，发挥出最大的作用。

我们在讨论这个问题时，梅琳达和我读到一篇文章，关于那些贫穷的国家，每年有数百万的儿童死于一些在美国早已不成为问题的疾病：麻疹、疟疾、肺炎、乙型肝炎、黄热病。还有一种以前我从未听说过的小儿肠胃炎病毒——仅这种疾病每年导致 50 万儿童死亡——这些都不会再在美国发生。

我们很震惊。我们在想，如果数百万儿童正在濒临死亡，而他们的生命是有可能被挽救的，那么世界理应将用药物拯救他们作为头等大事。但是事实并非如此。那些价格还不到一美元的救命药剂，还没有送达他们的手中。

如果你相信每个生命都具有同等价值，那么当你发现某些生命被挽救了，而另一些生命则没有，你会觉得无法接受。我们对自己说："这不是真的。如果这是真的，那么它应该是我们必须要努力去做的头等大事。"

因此，我们用任何人都会想到的方式开始工作。我们质问："这个世界怎么能看着孩子这样死去？"

答案很简单，也很冷酷。在市场经济中，拯救这些儿童的生命，是一项没有利润回报的事业，政府也不会提供资助。这些儿童之所以会病死，是因为他们的父母在经济上没有实力，在政治上也没有能力发出自己的声音。

但是你们和我，拥有这两种能力（在经济上有实力，在政治上能够发出自己的声音）。

如果我们能设计出一种更有创新力的资本主义模式，就能让市场经济更好地为穷人服务；如果我们能够最大限度地运用市场力量，让更多的人获得利润，或至少可以维持生活，就可以救助那些正在极端不平等中挣扎的人们。我们还可以推动各国的政府，要求他们把纳税人的钱，用到更符合纳税人价值观的地方。

如果我们能够找到一种方式，既能满足穷人的需要，又可为商业带来利润，还可为政治家带来选票，那么我们就找到了一种减少世上不平等的可持续发展之路。这个任务是永无止境的，它不可能全部完成。但是任何有意识地解决这个问题的努力，都将会使这个世界改观。

对于这个问题，我持乐观态度。但是我也跟那些绝望的怀疑主义者

I completely disagree.

I believe we have more caring than we know what to do with.

All of us here in this Yard, at one time or another, have seen human tragedies that broke our hearts, and yet we did nothing – not because we didn't care, but because we didn't know what to do. If we had known how to help, we would have acted.

The barrier to change is not too little caring; it is too much complexity.

To turn caring into action, we need to see a problem, see a solution, and see the impact. But complexity blocks all three steps.

Even with the advent of the Internet and 24-hour news, it is still a complex enterprise to get people to truly see the problems. When an airplane crashes, officials immediately call a press conference. They promise to investigate, determine the cause, and prevent similar crashes in the future.

But if the officials were brutally honest, they would say: "Of all the people in the world who died today from preventable causes, one half of one percent of them were on this plane. We're determined to do everything possible to solve the problem that took the lives of the one half of one percent."

The bigger problem is not the plane crash, but the millions of preventable deaths.

We don't read much about these deaths. The media covers what's new – and millions of people dying is nothing new. So it stays in the background, where it's easier to ignore. But even when we do see it or read about it, it's difficult to keep our eyes on the problem. It's hard to look at suffering if the situation is so complex that we don't know how to help. And so we look away.

If we can really see a problem, which is the first step, we come to the second step: cutting through the complexity to find a solution.

Finding solutions is essential if we want to make the most of our caring. If we have clear and proven answers anytime an organization or individual asks "How can I help?," then we can get action – and we can make sure that none of the caring in the world is wasted. But complexity makes it hard to mark a path of action for everyone who cares — and that makes it hard for their caring to matter.

Cutting through complexity to find a solution runs through four

谈论过。他们说："不平等从人类一开始就存在，并将存在到最后，因为人类对此根本不在乎。"我完全不同意这种观点。

我相信，问题不在于我们是否在乎这个问题，而在于我们不知道怎么去解决。

在座的所有人，总有这样或那样的时刻，曾经目睹人类令人心碎的悲剧，但是我们什么也没做。并不是因为我们无动于衷，而是因为我们不知道怎么做。如果我们知道该怎样去提供帮助，那么我们就会去行动。

改变世界的障碍，不是人类的漠不关心，而是这个世界太复杂。

把关心转换为行动，我们需要发现问题，找到解决方法，预见它的影响。但是世界的复杂性阻挡了这三个步骤的实施。

哪怕有了互联网和24小时即时直播的新闻，让人们发现真正的问题所在，仍然是十分复杂困难的。当一架飞机坠毁，官员们立刻召开新闻发布会，他们承诺要进行调查，找到原因，防止将来发生类似的事故。

但是如果这些官员足够诚实，他们应该说："今天，全世界所有可以避免的死亡之中，只有百分之零点五的死者来自这次空难。我们决心尽一切可能，来解决这个导致百分之零点五的死亡问题。"

这里更重要的问题不是这次空难，而是其他几百万可以预防的死亡事件。

我们没有很多机会读到关于那些死亡事件的报道。媒体总是报道新闻——而几百万人将要死去不是新闻——所以它们总是在幕后，很容易被忽视。然而即使我们亲眼目睹了事件本身，或者看到了相关报道，我们也很难持续关注这些事件。看着他人受苦是令人痛苦的，尤其是问题又非常复杂，我们不知道如何去帮助他们，所以我们只好把目光转向别处。

假如我们真发现了问题之所在，这只是第一步；接下来第二步，就是要从复杂的情况中找到解决办法。

如果想把我们的关心落到实处，找到解决问题的办法就是必须的。如果我们有一个清晰而准确的答案，那么在任何时候，当某个组织或个人询问"我怎样能提供帮助"时，我们就能采取行动。我们就能保证不浪费世上人类对其他人的关心。但是，世界的复杂性使我们很难找到一

predictable stages: determine a goal, find the highest-leverage approach, discover the ideal technology for that approach, and in the meantime, make the smartest application of the technology that you already have — whether it's something sophisticated, like a drug, or something simpler, like a bednet.

The AIDS epidemic offers an example. The broad goal, of course, is to end the disease. The highest-leverage approach is prevention. The ideal technology would be a vaccine that gives lifetime immunity with a single dose. So governments, drug companies, and foundations fund vaccine research. But their work is likely to take more than a decade, so in the meantime, we have to work with what we have in hand – and the best prevention approach we have now is getting people to avoid risky behavior.

Pursuing that goal starts the four-step cycle again. This is the pattern. **The crucial thing is to never stop thinking and working – and never do what we did with malaria and tuberculosis in the 20th century – which is to surrender to complexity and quit.**

The final step – after seeing the problem and finding an approach – is to measure the impact of your work and share your successes and failures so that others learn from your efforts.

You have to have the statistics, of course. You have to be able to show that a program is vaccinating millions more children. You have to be able to show a decline in the number of children dying from these diseases. This is essential not just to improve the program, but also to help draw more investment from business and government.

But if you want to inspire people to participate, you have to show more than numbers; you have to convey the human impact of the work – so people can feel what saving a life means to the families affected.

I remember going to Davos some years back and sitting on a global health panel that was discussing ways to save millions of lives. Millions! Think of the thrill of saving just one person's life – then multiply that by millions. ... Yet this was the most boring panel I've ever been on – ever. So boring even I couldn't bear it.

What made that experience especially striking was that I had just come from an event where we were introducing version 13 of some piece of software,

种对全世界的善心人都有效的行动方法，因此人类对他人的关心通常很难起到实际作用。

从这个复杂性中找到解决办法，可以通过以下四个步骤：确定目标；找到最高效的方法；发现适用于这个方法的理想技术，同时巧妙地运用现有的技术，不管它是复杂的药物，还是最简单的什么东西，比如蚊帐。

艾滋病就是一个例子。总的终极目标，当然是消灭这种疾病。最有效的方法是预防。最理想的技术是发明一种疫苗，只需注射一次，就可以终生免疫。所以，政府、制药公司、基金会都可资助疫苗研究。但是这样的研究工作，很可能需要十年以上的时间。因此与此同时，我们必须使用手中现有的技术，目前最有效的预防方法，就是使人们避免那些危险的行为。

要实现这个新的目标，可再次采用上述的四步循环。这是一种模式。**最重要的是，永远不要停止思考和行动。永远不能重复我们20世纪在疟疾和肺结核上犯过的错误——那时我们屈服于它们的复杂性，而放弃了战胜它们的努力。**

在发现问题和找到解决方法之后，最后一步是评估你的工作之影响，将你的成功经验或者失败经验传播出去，让其他人从你的努力中有所收获。

当然，你必须有一些统计数字。你必须能向他人展示，你的项目为几百万儿童接种了疫苗。你也必须向他人展示，儿童死于这些疾病的人数下降了多少。这很关键，不仅有利于改善这个项目，也有利于从商界和政府得到更多的资助。

如果你想鼓励人们参与，你就必须拿出比统计数字更多的东西；你必须传达出项目中的人性因素影响，这样人们才能够感受到，拯救一个生命对受影响的家庭意味着什么。

记得几年前我去瑞士达沃斯旁听一个全球健康问题论坛，讨论关于如何拯救几百万人的生命。数以百万计！想想看：拯救一个人的生命已经让人多么激动，现在你要把这种激动再乘上几百万倍——然而，这是我参加过的最最乏味的论坛，枯燥到我无法忍受下去。

这次经历之所以让我难忘，是因为那之前我们刚刚发布了一个软件

and we had people jumping and shouting with excitement. I love getting people excited about software – but why can't we generate even more excitement for saving lives?

You can't get people excited unless you can help them see and feel the impact. And how you do that – is a complex question.

Still, I'm optimistic. Yes, inequity has been with us forever, but the new tools we have to cut through complexity have not been with us forever. They are new – they can help us make the most of our caring – and that's why the future can be different from the past.

The defining and ongoing innovations of this age – biotechnology, the computer, the Internet – give us a chance we've never had before to end extreme poverty and end death from preventable disease.

Sixty years ago, George Marshall came to this commencement and announced a plan to assist the nations of post-war Europe. He said: "I think one difficulty is that the problem is one of such enormous complexity that the very mass of facts presented to the public by press and radio make it exceedingly difficult for the man in the street to reach a clear appraisement of the situation. It is virtually impossible at this distance to grasp at all the real significance of the situation."

Thirty years after Marshall made his address, as my class graduated without me, technology was emerging that would make the world smaller, more open, more visible, less distant.

The emergence of low-cost personal computers gave rise to a powerful network that has transformed opportunities for learning and communicating.

The magical thing about this network is not just that it collapses distance and makes everyone your neighbor. It also dramatically increases the number of brilliant minds we can have working together on the same problem – and that scales up the rate of innovation to a staggering degree.

At the same time, for every person in the world who has access to this technology, five people don't. That means many creative minds are left out of this discussion — smart people with practical intelligence and relevant experience who don't have the technology to hone their talents or contribute their ideas to the world.

From Those to Whom Much Is Given, Much Is Expected   Bill Gates
得到越多　责任越重   比尔·盖茨

的第 13 个版本，我们让观众兴奋得跳起来，喊起来。我喜欢人们因为软件而激动，但我们为什么不能让人们为能够拯救生命而更加激动呢？

你无法让人们激动，除非你能让他们看到或感受到该行动的影响力。如何做到这一点，是一个复杂的问题。

我仍然是乐观的。是的，不平等一直存在，但是那些能够化繁为简的新工具，并不是一直都存在的。这些新工具可以帮助我们，使人类的爱心发挥最大的作用，这就是为什么将来与过去是不一样的。

这个持续不断创新的时代——生物技术、计算机、互联网——给了我们一个前所未有的机会，去结束那些极端的贫穷，避免可预防性疾病的死亡。

60 年前，乔治·马歇尔来到这个（哈佛的）毕业典礼上，宣布了一个计划，帮助欧洲国家战后重建。他说："我认为，我们面临的问题是如此庞大复杂，而报纸和电台向公众提供的报道是如此之多，以至于作为一位普通人，要对这纷繁的情况作出一个明确的分析，是极其困难的。隔着这样的距离，要想把握情况的真正意义，几乎是不可能的。"

马歇尔发表这个演讲之后的 30 年，我们那一届学生毕业（当然我不在其中）。新技术刚刚开始萌芽，它们使这个世界变得更小、更开放、更可见，不那么遥远。

低成本的个人计算机的出现，促进了强大的互联网的诞生，这为学习和交流提供了巨大的便利和机会。

网络的神奇之处，不仅是它缩短了空间距离，使得天涯海角仿佛近在咫尺。它还极大地提高了有共同理想和智慧头脑的人们聚集的机会，我们可以针对同一问题一起工作。这极大地加快了创新的进程，发展速度达到惊人的地步。

但另一方面，世界上有条件接触到这个互联网技术的人，只是人口的六分之一。这意味着还有许多具有创造力的人们，没有加入到我们的讨论中来。那些有实际的操作经验和相关经历的聪明人，因为没有接触到互联网技术，而无法将他们的天赋或想法与全世界分享。

我们要尽可能让更多的人有机会接触新技术，因为这些新技术正在引发一场革新，使人类可以互相帮助。那些新技术正在创造这种可能性：

We need as many people as possible to have access to this technology, because these advances are triggering a revolution in what human beings can do for one another. They are making it possible not just for national governments, but for universities, corporations, smaller organizations, and even individuals to see problems, see approaches, and measure the impact of their efforts to address the hunger, poverty, and desperation George Marshall spoke of 60 years ago.

Members of the Harvard Family: Here in the Yard is one of the great collections of intellectual talent in the world.

What for?

There is no question that the faculty, the alumni, the students, and the benefactors of Harvard have used their power to improve the lives of people here and around the world. But can we do more? Can Harvard dedicate its intellect to improving the lives of people who will never even hear its name?

Let me make a request of the deans and the professors – the intellectual leaders here at Harvard: As you hire new faculty, award tenure, review curriculum, and determine degree requirements, please ask yourselves:

Should our best minds be dedicated to solving our biggest problems?

Should Harvard encourage its faculty to take on the world's worst inequities? Should Harvard students learn about the depth of global poverty … the prevalence of world hunger … the scarcity of clean water …the girls kept out of school … the children who die from diseases we can cure?

Should the world's most privileged people learn about the lives of the world's least privileged?

These are not rhetorical questions – you will answer with your policies.

My mother, who was filled with pride the day I was admitted here – never stopped pressing me to do more for others. A few days before my wedding, she hosted a bridal event, at which she read aloud a letter about marriage that she had written to Melinda. My mother was very ill with cancer at the time, but she saw one more opportunity to deliver her message, and at the close of the letter she said: "From those to whom much is given, much is expected."

When you consider what those of us here in this Yard have been given – in talent, privilege, and opportunity – there is almost no limit to what the world has a right to expect from us.

不仅是政府,还包括大学、公司、小机构,甚至个人,能够发现问题、能够找到解决方法、能够衡量他们的影响力,去改变那些马歇尔60年前就提到过的问题——饥饿、贫穷和绝望。

哈佛大家庭的成员们:哈佛院里在场的人们,是全世界最有智慧的群体之一。

我们能做些什么?

毫无疑问,哈佛的教师、校友、学生和资助者们,已经用他们的能力参与改善了这里和世界各地人们的生活。但我们还能再多做些吗?哈佛人是否能贡献他们的智慧,来帮助那些甚至从来没有听说过"哈佛"这所学校名称的人们?

请允许我向各位院长和教授——哈佛的智力领袖们——提一个请求,当你们雇用新的教师、授予终身教职、评估教学大纲、决定学位要求的时候,请问一下你自己:

我们最出色的人才是否在致力于解决我们面临的最大问题?

哈佛是否应鼓励他们的老师去研究解决世界上最严重的不平等问题?哈佛的学生是否了解深度的全球贫困:世界范围内普遍发生的饥荒、缺乏清洁的水资源、失学的女童、死于非恶性疾病的孩子?

世界上过着最优越生活的人们,是否应该了解那些最贫困的人们的生活状态?

这些都不是语言上的修辞问题,你要用自己的准则来回答它们。

我母亲在我被哈佛录取的那一天感到非常骄傲,她从没停止督促我为他人做更多的事情。在我结婚的前几天,她主持了一个新娘进门仪式。在这个仪式上,她高声朗读了一封她写给梅琳达的关于婚姻的信。当时我母亲因为患癌症已经病入膏肓,但是她还是认为这是又一个好机会来传播她的信念。在那封信的结尾,她说:"当你得到的越多,你被期望的也就越多。"

当你想到我们现在在这个院子里的人被给予过天赋、特权,还有机会,似乎全世界的人都有权力要求我们做出更多贡献。

与这个时代的期望一样,我也想敦促今天毕业的各位同学:选择一个

In line with the promise of this age, I want to exhort each of the graduates here to take on an issue — a complex problem, a deep inequity, and become a specialist on it. If you make it the focus of your career, that would be phenomenal. But you don't have to do that to make an impact. For a few hours every week, you can use the growing power of the Internet to get informed, find others with the same interests, see the barriers, and find ways to cut through them.

Don't let complexity stop you. Be activists. Take on the big inequities. It will be one of the great experiences of your lives.

You graduates are coming of age in an amazing time. As you leave Harvard, you have technology that members of my class never had. You have awareness of global inequity, which we did not have. And with that awareness, you likely also have an informed conscience that will torment you if you abandon these people whose lives you could change with very little effort.

You have more than we had; you must start sooner, and carry on longer.

Knowing what you know, how could you not?

And **I hope you will come back here to Harvard 30 years from now and reflect on what you have done with your talent and your energy. I hope you will judge yourselves not on your professional accomplishments alone, but also on how well you have addressed the world's deepest inequities ... on how well you treated people a world away who have nothing in common with you but their humanity.**

Good luck.

问题，一个复杂的问题，一个关于深层不平等的问题，然后成为这个问题的专家。如果你们能使这个问题成为你们职业的关注点，那就太好了。你们也不一定要去做那些有巨大影响的事。只要每个星期用几个小时，你就可以运用互联网得到信息，找到志同道合的朋友，发现问题，并找到解决它们的方法。

不要让复杂性阻挡了你。做一个行动者，致力于解决人类的不平等问题。这将成为你生命中最重要的经历之一。

各位毕业生们，你们所处的是一个神奇的时代。你们离开哈佛时所拥有的技术，是我们那一届学生从未有过的。你们已经认识到了世界上的不平等，我们那时却还不知道这些。有了这样的了解之后，如果要放弃帮助那些你可以帮助的人们，你就会受到良心的谴责。只需很小的一点努力，你就可以改变那些人的生活。你们比我们拥有更多，你们必须尽早开始，坚持下去更长时间。

知道了你们所知道的一切，你们怎能视若惘闻、不理不睬？

30年后再回到哈佛，回想你们用自己的天赋和精力所做的一切，我希望那时你们评价自己时，不仅仅关注你们在专业上的成就，还包括你们为改变这个世界的严重不平等做出了什么样的努力，以及你们如何善待那些远在天边、与你们毫不相识的人们，他们与你们唯一的共同点，就是同为人类。

祝各位同学好运。

---

1 当时盖茨已经宣布将从微软退休，全职投入慈善事业。

2 斯蒂夫·鲍尔默（Steve Ballmer），微软总经理，在盖茨从微软退休后，继任微软总裁。

3 阿尔布开克（Albuquerque）美国新墨西哥州中部的一个城市

4 盖茨的妻子

乔安妮·凯瑟琳·罗琳（1965— ）

今天，还有谁不知道 J.K. 罗琳和她的《哈利·波特》呢？这部小说的问世发行，可说是当代出版界的一个奇迹。

《哈利·波特》系列一共 7 本，被翻译成 50 多种文字，总共销售了至少 4 亿册，并激发出一个总值 70 亿英镑的附带产业。罗琳由此成为世界上最富有的人之一，个人财富高达数亿英镑，比英国女王还富有。

1965 年 7 月 31 日，J.K. 罗琳生于英国的格温特郡。其父是罗伊斯罗尔飞机制造厂一名退休管理人员，母亲曾是实验室技术人员。正如罗琳在这篇演讲中提到的：她出身贫寒家庭，父母都没有受过高等教育。罗琳在大学时未顺从父母的意愿，选择了法语和古典文学专业，毕业后曾做过短时间的教师和秘书工作。一段短暂的婚姻结束后，她独自带着 5 个月大的女儿从葡萄牙回到英国，住在没有暖气的公寓里，领着微薄的失业救济艰难度日。但是她从未放弃自己的梦想——写作，那是她唯一的兴趣和专长。罗琳的命运终于随着《哈利·波特》第一部的问世而彻底逆转，随后几部续集都引发了一浪高过一浪的世界范围的"哈利·波特"热，销售数量一次次刷新纪录。罗琳的理想终于实现了，事实上已远远超出她当初的预想。

在这次演讲中，罗琳以她的亲身经历，强调了失败的积极意义——任何时候都不要被失败击垮，任何时候都不应放弃理想。

2008

The Power of Imagination
想象的力量

J.K.Rowling J.K. 罗琳

President Faust, members of the Harvard Corporation and the Board of Overseers, members of the faculty, proud parents, and, above all, graduates,

The first thing I would like to say is "thank you." Not only has Harvard given me an extraordinary honour, but the weeks of fear and **nausea** [n. 恶心，反胃，作呕] I've endured at the thought of giving this commencement address have made me lose weight. A win-win situation! Now all I have to do is take deep breaths, **squint** [vi. 眯眼看] at the red banners and convince myself that I am at the world's largest Gryffindors' reunion.

Delivering a commencement address is a great responsibility; or so I thought until I cast my mind back to my own graduation. The commencement speaker that day was the distinguished British philosopher Baroness Mary Warnock. Reflecting on her speech has helped me enormously in writing this one, because it turns out that I can't remember a single word she said. This liberating discovery enables me to proceed without any fear that I might **inadvertently** [adv. 疏忽的，非故意的] influence you to abandon promising careers in business, law or politics for the **giddy** [adj. 轻率的，轻浮的] delights of becoming a gay wizard.

You see? If all you remember in years to come is the 'gay wizard' joke, I've still come out ahead of Baroness Mary Warnock. **Achievable goals - the first step to self-improvement.**

Actually, I have **wracked** [vt. 破坏] my mind and heart for what I ought to say to you today. I have asked myself what I wish I had known at my own graduation, and what important lessons I have learned in the 21 years that has expired between that day and this.

I have come up with two answers. On this wonderful day when we are gathered together to celebrate your academic success, I have decided to talk to you about the benefits of failure. And as you stand on the threshold of what is sometimes called 'real life', I want to extol the crucial importance of imagination.

These may seem **quixotic** [adj. 唐吉诃德式的，狂想家的] or **paradoxical** [adj. 似是而非的，矛盾的] choices, but bear with me.

Looking back at the 21-year-old that I was at graduation, is a slightly uncomfortable experience for the 42-year-old that she has become. Half my lifetime ago, I was striking an uneasy balance between the ambition I had for myself, and what those closest to me expected of me.

福斯特校长、哈佛集团和监管董事会的各位成员、各位老师、自豪的家长们,还有最重要的,各位毕业生们:

首先,我想说一声"谢谢"。哈佛不仅给了我无上的荣誉,也让我减肥瘦身。几个星期以来,一想到要做这个演讲,我就惴惴不安、饮食不宁,导致我体重减轻。这就是所谓的"双赢"吧!现在我要做的就是深深呼吸几下,眯起眼睛看看周围的深红横幅,让自己相信,我正在参加世界上最大的格兰芬多[1]重逢聚会。

对我来说,发表毕业演讲是一个巨大的责任,这让我记起自己当年毕业典礼时的情景——那天做演讲的是英国著名哲学家玛丽·沃诺克男爵夫人。回忆她的演讲,对我今天的演讲有着极大的帮助——因为,我不记得她说过的任何一句话了!这个发现让我松了口气,我不再担心自己可能会无意中影响你们,使你们放弃在商业、法律或政治上的大好前程,而醉心于成为一个快乐的魔法师。

你们看,如果在许多年后,你们对我的演讲只记得"快乐的魔法师"这个笑话,那说明我已略胜玛丽·沃诺克男爵夫人一筹。**设立可达到的目标——这是完善自我的第一步。**

其实,我为今天要和大家说些什么而绞尽脑汁。我曾自问,什么是我希望早在毕业典礼时就该知道的?从毕业那天起到现在的21年间,我又学到了什么重要的经验和启示?

我想到了两个答案。在今天这样美好的日子,当我们一起欢庆你们的学业成就的时刻,我想和你们谈的,却是失败的益处;此外,在你们即将迈向"现实生活"的人生关口,我还想强调一下想象力的重要性。

这两个主题看似不切实际,甚至是自相矛盾,但请耐心听我解释。对于现年42岁的我来说,回忆21岁刚刚毕业时的自己,是一件不那么令人愉快的事情。可以说,我人生的前半部分,一直在自己的雄心壮志和亲人的期望之间找寻平衡。

我始终坚信自己唯一想做的事情就是写小说。不过,由于我的父母都出身贫寒,没有上过大学,所以他们坚持认为,我想入非非的想象力不过是聊以消遣的个人怪癖,既不能支付房贷按揭,也不能靠它来养老。

I was convinced that the only thing I wanted to do, ever, was to write novels. However, my parents, both of whom came from **impoverished** [adj. 贫困的, 赤贫的] backgrounds and neither of whom had been to college, took the view that my overactive imagination was an amusing personal **quirk** [n. 怪癖] that could never pay a mortgage, or secure a pension.

I know the irony strikes like with the force of a cartoon anvil now, but...

They had hoped that I would take a vocational degree; I wanted to study English Literature. A compromise was reached that in retrospect satisfied nobody, and I went up to study Modern Languages. Hardly had my parents' car rounded the corner at the end of the road than I ditched German and **scuttled** [vt. 奔跑] off down the Classics corridor.

I cannot remember telling my parents that I was studying Classics; they might well have found out for the first time on graduation day. Of all the subjects on this planet, I think they would have been hard put to name one less useful than Greek mythology when it came to securing the keys to an executive bathroom.

I would like to make it clear, in parenthesis, that I do not blame my parents for their point of view. There is an expiry date on blaming your parents for steering you in the wrong direction; the moment you are old enough to take the wheel, responsibility lies with you. What is more, I cannot criticise my parents for hoping that I would never experience poverty. They had been poor themselves, and I have since been poor, and I quite agree with them that it is not an ennobling experience. Poverty entails fear, and stress, and sometimes depression; it means a thousand petty humiliations and hardships. Climbing out of poverty by your own efforts, that is indeed something on which to pride yourself, but poverty itself is romanticised only by fools.

What I feared most for myself at your age was not poverty, but failure.

At your age, in spite of a distinct lack of motivation at university, where I had spent far too long in the coffee bar writing stories, and far too little time at lectures, I had a **knack** [n. 技巧, 诀窍] for passing examinations, and that, for years, had been the measure of success in my life and that of my peers.

I am not dull enough to suppose that because you are young, gifted and well-educated, you have never known hardship or heartache. Talent and intelligence never yet **inoculated** [vt. 给……注射疫苗, 灌输] anyone against the caprice of the Fates, and I do not for a moment suppose that everyone here has enjoyed an existence of **unruffled** [adj. 不骚

我现在明白，这种反讽就像老生常谈一样。

我的父母希望我去拿个有实用技能的学位，而我想去攻读英国文学。最后，我们达成了一个双方都不太满意的妥协：我改学现代语言学。可是父母的车刚刚开走，我就丢下德语，改报古典文学了。

我不记得当时是否告诉了父母改学古典文学这件事儿，他们可能直到我毕业典礼那一天才发现。他们或许认为，世界上的所有专业中，再没有比研究希腊神话更没用的专业了，因为它甚至无法给你带来一间独立宽敞的卫生间。

我想特别强调一下，我并不抱怨父母会有这样的看法。埋怨父母给你指错方向是有一个时间范围的。因为当你长大到可以独立驾驭方向的时候，你就应当自己承担责任。尤其是，父母的出发点是希望我不再过穷日子，所以我不怪他们。他们一直贫困，我后来也一度很穷，我自然很理解他们。贫穷不是什么光彩的事，在某种意义上贫穷意味着恐惧、压力、有时甚至让人绝望，贫穷意味着无数的羞辱和艰辛。靠自身的努力摆脱贫穷，非常让人引以为豪，但只有傻瓜才会将贫穷本身浪漫化。

我在你们这个年纪时，其实最害怕的还不是贫穷，而是失败。

我那时缺乏学习的动力，花了太多时间在咖啡吧里写故事，而听课的时间却少得可怜。好在我有对付考试的本领，而应试的本领，是人们长久以来看待我和我的同龄人的成功标准。

我不会笨到认为你们年轻、有天分，并且受过良好的教育，就从来没有遇到困难或感觉心碎的时候。才华和智慧，从来就不能保证让人避开命运的无常；我也绝不会假设说，大家坐在这里，就会平静地满足于自身的优越感。

不过，毕业于哈佛这个事实本身，已意味着你们对失败不会很熟悉。你们也许害怕失败，就像你们渴望成功。说实话，你们眼里的失败，很可能对普通人来说已经是某种成功，毕竟你们在学业上已经达到了相当的高度。

我们所有人都最终必须自己决定什么算作失败，但如果你愿意，现实世界会急于给你提供一套固定的标准。所以我很客观地说，按任何传

privilege and contentment.

However, the fact that you are graduating from Harvard suggests that you are not very well-acquainted with failure. You might be driven by a fear of failure quite as much as a desire for success. Indeed, your conception of failure might not be too far from the average person's idea of success, so high have you already flown academically.

Ultimately, we all have to decide for ourselves what constitutes failure, but the world is quite eager to give you a set of criteria if you let it. So I think it fair to say that by any conventional measure, a mere seven years after my graduation day, I had failed on an epic scale. An exceptionally short-lived marriage had imploded, and I was jobless, a lone parent, and as poor as it is possible to be in modern Britain, without being homeless. The fears my parents had had for me, and that I had had for myself, had both come to pass, and by every usual standard, I was the biggest failure I knew.

Now, I am not going to stand here and tell you that failure is fun. That period of my life was a dark one, and I had no idea that there was going to be what the press has since represented as a kind of fairy tale resolution. I had no idea how far the tunnel extended, and for a long time, any light at the end of it was a hope rather than a reality.

So why do I talk about the benefits of failure? Simply because failure meant a stripping away of the inessential. I stopped pretending to myself that I was anything other than what I was, and began to direct all my energy into finishing the only work that mattered to me. Had I really succeeded at anything else, I might never have found the determination to succeed in the one arena I believed I truly belonged. I was set free, because my greatest fear had been realised, and I was still alive, and I still had a daughter whom I adored, and I had an old typewriter and a big idea. And so rock bottom became the solid foundation on which I rebuilt my life.

You might never fail on the scale I did, but some failure in life is inevitable. It is impossible to live without failing at something, unless you live so cautiously that you might as well not have lived at all – in which case, you fail by default.

Failure gave me an inner security that I had never attained by passing examinations. Failure taught me things about myself that I could have learned no other way. I discovered that I had a strong will, and more discipline than I had suspected; I also found out that I had friends whose value was truly above the price of rubies.

The knowledge that you have emerged wiser and stronger from setbacks means

统的标准，我毕业后 7 年的那些日子里，完完全全是个失败者：一桩短暂的婚姻破裂了，我没有工作，成了一个单身母亲。除了不至于无家可归，我是当代英国最穷的人之一。当年父母和我自己对未来的担忧，都变成了现实。不管按什么标准来看，我都是自己所认识的人里最失败的。

现在，我站在这里，不是想告诉你们失败多么有趣。那段日子是我生命中最黑暗的岁月，后来媒体把它描绘成童话般的磨难故事。我那时不知道黑暗的隧道还有多长。在相当长的时间里，前面留给我的亮光只是希望，而不是现实。

那么，为什么我还要谈论失败的好处呢？这是因为，失败意味着我们必须摆脱那些无关紧要的东西。我因此不用伪装，而能回归自己，从而把所有精力放在对我来说最重要的事情上。如果在其他领域也有所收获，我可能就不会下定决心，在这个我确信自己真正倾心的领域里争取成功。我有了自由，因为最害怕的事已经发生了，但我还活着，而且有一个我深爱的女儿，我还有一台老旧的打字机和大脑中的构思。所以困境的谷底，成为我重建生活的坚实基础。

你们应该不会像我这样摔得那么惨，但人生中有些失败是不可避免的。一个人不可能永远不败，除非你生活得过分小心谨慎，就像从没活过一样。如果是那样的话，无论怎样，不敢冒险本身就是一种失败。

失败反而使我的内心获得一种安全感，这是我以前即使通过了考试也得不到的感觉。失败让我认识自己，这也是无法通过其他方式学到的。我发现自己有一个坚强的意志，比自己想象的更加自律；我发现朋友的友谊，比宝石更加珍贵。

从挫折中获得智慧，贫穷但却坚守，意味着你有了更强的生存能力。只有在逆境中，你才能认清自己，也才了解身边的人。这种经历是真正的财富，虽然它是用痛苦换来的，但比我获得过的任何资格证书都更有价值。

假如时光能够倒流，我会告诉 21 岁的自己，**人的幸福在于知道生活不仅仅是一份罗列成就的清单，你的资格、简历，并不能代表你的生活。**虽然你会碰到很多与我同龄、甚至年龄更大的人，依然还将这两者混淆。

that you are, ever after, secure in your ability to survive. You will never truly know yourself, or the strength of your relationships, until both have been tested by adversity. Such knowledge is a true gift, for all that it is painfully won, and it has been worth more to me than any qualification I ever earned.

So given a Time Turner, I would tell my 21-year-old self that **personal happiness lies in knowing that life is not a check-list of acquisition or achievement. Your qualifications, your CV, are not your life,** though you will meet many people of my age and older who confuse the two. Life is difficult, and complicated, and beyond anyone's total control, and the humility to know that will enable you to survive its **vicissitudes.** [n.（人生的）盛衰, 变迁]

You might think that I chose my second theme, the importance of imagination, because of the part it played in rebuilding my life, but that is not wholly so. Though I will defend the value of bedtime stories to my last gasp, I have learned to value imagination in a much broader sense. **Imagination is not only the uniquely human capacity to envision that which is not, and therefore the fount of all invention and innovation. In its arguably most transformative and revelatory capacity, it is the power that enables us to empathise with humans whose experiences we have never shared.**

One of the greatest formative experiences of my life preceded Harry Potter, though it informed much of what I subsequently wrote in those books. This revelation came in the form of one of my earliest day jobs. Though I was sloping off to write stories during my lunch hours, I paid the rent in my early 20s by working at the African research department at Amnesty International's headquarters in London.

There in my little office I read hastily scribbled letters smuggled out of totalitarian regimes by men and women who were risking imprisonment to inform the outside world of what was happening to them. I saw photographs of those who had disappeared without trace, sent to Amnesty by their desperate families and friends. I read the testimony of torture victims and saw pictures of their injuries. I opened handwritten, eye-witness accounts of **summary** [adj. 立即的, 即决的] trials and executions, of kidnappings and rapes.

Many of my co-workers were ex-political prisoners, people who had been displaced from their homes, or fled into exile, because they had the **temerity** [n. 鲁莽, 大胆] to think independently of their government. Visitors to our office included those who had come to give information, or to try and find out what had happened to those who

生活是艰辛复杂的，超出人的掌控，只有谦卑地认识到这一点，你才能笑对人生沧桑。

对于我选择的第二个主题——想象力的重要性，你们可能会认为，是因为想象力对我重建生活起到了帮助，但事实并非完全如此。虽然我要极力捍卫睡前故事对培养想象力的重要性，我对想象力的珍惜已经有了更广的范畴。**想象力不仅仅是人类幻想虚无缥缈事物的这种独特的能力，从而为所有发明和创新提供源泉，想象力也给人们带来变革性和启示性的力量，它还使我们学会关爱他人，哪怕他人的经历我们从未经受。**

对我一生影响巨大的经历，发生在我写《哈利·波特》之前，这一经历为我后来写书提供了诸多启示。20多岁时，为了交房租，我为总部设在伦敦的大赦国际[4]的非洲研究部工作，并在午餐时间偷偷写点小说。

在我小小的办公室里，我读着从极权统治地区偷偷送出来的信件，写信的人字迹潦草，冒着坐牢的风险，告诉外界自己遭受了何种虐待。我看过那些由绝望的亲友寄来的照片，那照片里的人已经神秘失踪。我看过被严刑拷打的受害者的证词和他们伤痕累累的照片。我打开过目击者的手记，上面记载着关于速决审判并执行死刑，还有关于绑架和强暴等情况的第一手记录。

我的很多同事曾经是政治犯，因为他们敢于独立思考、批判政府，因而流离失所，或因此被迫逃离家园。到我们办公室的访客里，有些人是想提供信息，还有些人前来打探有关他们还在水深火热之中的同伴的消息。

只要我活着，我就不会忘记一个曾经遭受酷刑的非洲受害者，一名当时不会比我大多少的年轻男子，他因在故国受过的折磨而精神失常。在对着摄像机讲述自己被残暴地折磨的时候，他的身体止不住地颤抖。他比我高一英尺，看上去却像孩子一样脆弱。我被安排随后护送他到地铁站，这个人生已遭到残酷摧毁的男子，优雅有礼地握着我的手，为我的未来祝福。

只要我活着，我就会记得，在一个空荡荡的走廊，突然从一扇关着的门里传来我从未听过的痛苦和恐惧的尖叫声。门打开了，一个工作人

they had left behind.

I shall never forget the African torture victim, a young man no older than I was at the time, who had become mentally ill after all he had endured in his homeland. He trembled uncontrollably as he spoke into a video camera about the brutality inflicted upon him. He was a foot taller than I was, and seemed as fragile as a child. I was given the job of escorting him to the Underground Station afterwards, and this man whose life had been shattered by cruelty took my hand with **exquisite** [adj. 精致的，细腻的] courtesy, and wished me future happiness.

And as long as I live I shall remember walking along an empty corridor and suddenly hearing, from behind a closed door, a scream of pain and horror such as I have never heard since. The door opened, and the researcher poked out her head and told me to run and make a hot drink for the young man sitting with her. She had just given him the news that in retaliation for his own outspokenness against his country's regime, his mother had been seized and executed.

Every day of my working week in my early 20s I was reminded how incredibly fortunate I was, to live in a country with a democratically elected government, where legal representation and a public trial were the rights of everyone.

Every day, I saw more evidence about the evils humankind will inflict on their fellow humans, to gain or maintain power. I began to have nightmares, literal nightmares, about some of the things I saw, heard and read.

And yet I also learned more about human goodness at Amnesty International than I had ever known before.

Amnesty mobilises thousands of people who have never been tortured or imprisoned for their beliefs to act on behalf of those who have. The power of human empathy, leading to collective action, saves lives, and frees prisoners. Ordinary people, whose personal well-being and security are assured, join together in huge numbers to save people they do not know, and will never meet. My small participation in that process was one of the most humbling and inspiring experiences of my life.

Unlike any other creature on this planet, human beings can learn and

员探出头来,请我为坐在她旁边的青年男子拿一杯热饮。因为她刚刚告诉那个年轻人一个不幸的消息,由于他公开反对本国的政权,他的母亲被逮捕并已遭杀害了。

在那段日子里,我每天的工作都在提醒着我,让我知道自己是多么幸运:生活在一个由民主选举政府的国家,人人都享有依法申述与公开审理的权利。

而每天我都会看到更多有关人性邪恶的证据,总是有人为了得到或巩固自己的权力,而不惜对同类施暴。我开始做噩梦,那些噩梦和我所见、所闻、所读的东西搅扰在一起。

然而,在大赦国际我也接触到许多展示人类善良的东西,这些也是我以前了解不够的。

大赦国际动员了成千上万的人,他们并没有因为信仰而受到折磨或监禁,但却在为那些遭遇这种不幸的人而奔走。人类同情心的力量,引发集体行动,共同去拯救生命、解救囚徒。那些个人的福祉和安全有幸获得保障的普通人,为了拯救与他们素不相识、也许永远不会谋面的人,心甘情愿地走在一起。尽管我个人的力量微不足道,却有幸参与了这一进程,并从中学会谦卑,也获得了很多启发。

与这个星球上其他的生物不同,人类可以学习和理解自己未曾亲身经历过的东西,他们可以将心比心、设身处地的为他人着想。

当然,这种能力是一种力量,就像在我虚构的魔法世界里一样,它在道德上是中立的。人们可以利用这种能力去操纵或控制他人,也可以用来理解或同情他人。

但很多人却宁愿不去使用他们的想象力。他们选择逗留在自己舒适的固定世界里,从来不愿花力气去想想,如果生为别人,命运会是怎样?他们拒绝倾听别人的哭喊,也不去探视监牢里的状况;他们可以封闭自己的思想和内心,只要痛苦不触及个人,他们可以拒绝去了解。

也许我会妒忌能够那样生活的人,但我不认为他们做的噩梦会

understand, without having experienced. They can think themselves into other people's places.

Of course, this is a power, like my brand of fictional magic, that is morally neutral. One might use such an ability to manipulate, or control, just as much as to understand or sympathise.

And many prefer not to exercise their imaginations at all. They choose to remain comfortably within the bounds of their own experience, never troubling to wonder how it would feel to have been born other than they are. They can refuse to hear screams or to peer inside cages; they can close their minds and hearts to any suffering that does not touch them personally; they can refuse to know.

I might be tempted to envy people who can live that way, except that I do not think they have any fewer nightmares than I do. **Choosing to live in narrow spaces can lead to a form of mental agoraphobia** [n. 广场恐惧症，旷野恐惧症]**, and that brings its own terrors. I think the wilfully unimaginative see more monsters. They are often more afraid.**

What is more, those who choose not to empathise may enable real monsters. For without ever committing an act of outright evil ourselves, we collude with it, through our own apathy.

One of the many things I learned at the end of that Classics corridor down which I ventured at the age of 18, in search of something I could not then define, was this, written by the Greek author **Plutarch** [普鲁塔克 (Plutarch, 46-120 A.D.) 是一位用希腊文写作的罗马传记文学家、散文家、以及柏拉图学派的知识分子。]: **What we achieve inwardly will change outer reality.**

That is an astonishing statement and yet proven a thousand times every day of our lives. It expresses, in part, our inescapable connection with the outside world, the fact that we touch other people's lives simply by existing.

But how much more are you, Harvard graduates of 2008, likely to touch other people's lives? Your intelligence, your capacity for hard work, the education you have earned and received, give you unique status, and unique **responsibilities.** [其命益幸，其责益重。] Even your nationality sets you apart. The great majority of you belong to the world's only remaining superpower. The way you vote, the way you live, the way you protest, the pressure you bring to

比我少。**选择生活在狭隘的空间里，就会害怕面对外边的世界，这同样会给人带来恐惧感**。我认为，那些不愿展开想象的人会看到更多的恶魔怪兽，因而会感到更加害怕。

更糟的是，选择不去同情他人的人，可能会激活真正的恶魔怪兽。因为尽管自己没有直接作恶，但如果对邪恶无动于衷，就等同于与之勾结。

我18岁时开始探寻古典文学的殿堂，从中汲取知识，学到了许多当时并不完全理解的东西。其中就有古希腊传记作家普鲁塔克[5]写的这句：内心世界的改变，也将促使我们改变外在的现实世界。

这是一个震撼人心的论断，然而在我们生活的每一天里，它都被无数次地验证。它在某种程度上指明了我们与外界无法脱离的联系，也就是说，只要我们存在，我们对他人的人生就会产生影响。

那么，哈佛大学2008届的毕业生们，你们又将对他人的生命产生多大的影响？你们的智慧，你们应对艰难工作的能力，以及你们所受到的教育，都赋予你们独特的地位和责任。甚至你们的国籍也让你们与众不同，你们绝大部分来自这个超级大国。你们投票的方式、生活的方式、抗议的方式，以及向政府施加的压力，其影响都会远超出你们的国界。你们是何等幸运！肩负的责任又是何等重要！

如果你选择利用自己的地位和影响，去为那些没有发言权的人呐喊；如果你选择不仅与强者共舞，也能同情和帮扶弱者；如果你一以贯之地为处于劣势的人们着想，那么，你的存在将不仅仅是你家族的荣耀，更是无数因为你的帮助而改变命运的成千上万人的骄傲。我们不需要用魔法来改变世界，因为改变世界的力量已经根植于我们的内心：我们可以梦想，让世界变得更美好！

在讲话即将结束之际，我对你们还有一个愿望，这也是我21岁时就开始有的理想。在毕业典礼那天与我同坐的朋友们，成了我终身的挚交。他们是我孩子的教父和教母，也是在我身陷困境时可以求助的人。我把他们的名字套用在《哈利·波特》中的"食死徒"

bear on your government, has an impact way beyond your borders. That is your privilege, and your burden.

If you choose to use your status and influence to raise your voice on behalf of those who have no voice; if you choose to identify not only with the powerful, but with the powerless; if you retain the ability to imagine yourself into the lives of those who do not have your advantages, then it will not only be your proud families who celebrate your existence, but thousands and millions of people whose reality you have helped to change. We do not need magic to transform the world, we carry all the power we need inside ourselves already: we have the power to imagine better.

I am nearly finished. I have one last hope for you, which is something that I already had at 21. The friends with whom I sat on graduation day have been my friends for life. They are my children's godparents, the people to whom I've been able to turn in times of real trouble, people who have been kind enough not to sue me when I've used their names for Death Eaters. At our graduation we were bound by enormous affection, by our shared experience of a time that could never come again, and, of course, by the knowledge that we held certain photographic evidence that would be exceptionally valuable if any of us ran for Prime Minister.

So today, I can wish you nothing better than similar friendships. And tomorrow, I hope that even if you remember not a single word of mine, you remember those of Seneca, another of those old Romans I met when I fled down the Classics corridor, in retreat from career ladders, in search of ancient wisdom:

As is a tale, so is life: not how long it is, but how good it is, is what matters.

I wish you all very good lives.
Thank you very much.

身上,他们宽宏大量,并没有因此起诉我。在毕业典礼上,深厚的情谊以及我们携手走过、但却一去不复返的时光,将我们紧紧相连。当然,如果我们当中的任何人要竞选首相的话,那些合影就愈加弥足珍贵了。

所以,我今天可以给你们的最好祝福,就是愿你们拥有这样的友情。我希望即使以后你们不记得我说的任何一个字,还能不忘哲学家塞内加的一句至理名言。我当年没有顺着事业的阶梯向上攀爬,转而与这位古罗马先贤在古典文学的殿堂相遇,他的智慧给了我人生的启迪:

人生犹如故事,关键不在于长短,而在于是否精彩。

愿你们都将拥有精彩的人生。
非常感谢大家!

---

1 格兰芬多(Gryffindor),是《哈利·波特》小说中霍格沃茨魔法学校的一部分。

2 玛丽·沃诺克男爵夫人(Baroness Mary Warnock,生于1924年),英国哲学家、存在主义作家

3 英文"gay"有"快乐的"或"同性恋"两种解释

4 大赦国际(Amnesty International),一个保护人犯、人权的国际性非政府组织

5 普鲁塔克(Plutarchus,约公元46—120),罗马帝国时代的希腊作家,以《比较列传》(又称《希腊罗马名人传》或《希腊罗马英豪列传》)一书闻名后世。

朱棣文（1948— ）

朱棣文应该是迄今为止登上哈佛毕业典礼演讲台的第一位、也是唯一一位华裔科学家。他于1997年因为发明了用激光冷却并俘获原子的方法，获得诺贝尔物理学奖，成为第四位获得诺贝尔物理学奖的华人。朱棣文于2008年由美国总统奥巴马提名，出任本届内阁的能源部长。

朱棣文1948年出生于美国密苏里州的圣路易斯市，父母都是来自中国的留美学者。朱棣文于1970年毕业于罗切斯特大学，获数学和物理学学士，1976年获加州大学伯克利分校物理博士学位。留校做了两年博士后研究后，朱棣文加盟贝尔电话实验室。1987年任斯坦福大学物理学教授，1990年出任系主任。2004年开始出任劳伦斯伯克利国家实验室负责人，麾下有4000名员工，研究经费高达数亿美金。

1993年朱棣文被选为美国国家科学院院士，1998年当选为中国科学院外籍院士。

朱棣文的家族可谓书香世家。他的双亲都毕业于清华大学，而后就读并获得美国麻省理工学院的博士学位。其外祖父早年毕业于天津大学，1923年公费留美康奈尔大学，回国后曾任天津大学校长、国民政府教育部长。朱棣文的三位姑妈也都曾留日、留美。他的哥哥是麻省理工学院博士，现任斯坦福大学医学教授；弟弟则是律师。朱棣文的父辈和同辈中至少有12位拥有博士学位或大学教授职位。

成名后，朱棣文很感谢父母对他们的教育和对他们发展个人兴趣爱好的鼓励。在报考大学时，他的父亲认为朱棣文善于绘画，应该学建筑，不过最终还是支持了他的决定。朱棣文目前致力于环保，从事有关替代能源与核能的科学研究。

2009

Play Your Role in Our Future
在未来扮演好你的角色

Steven Chu 朱棣文

Madam President Faust, members of the Harvard Corporation and the Board of Overseers, faculty, family, friends, and, most importantly, today's graduates, thank you for letting me share this wonderful day with you.

I am not sure I can live up to the high standards of Harvard Commencement speakers. Last year, J.K. Rowling, the billionaire novelist, who started as a classics student, graced this podium. The year before, Bill Gates, the mega-billionaire philanthropist and computer nerd stood here. Today, sadly, you have me. I am not wealthy, but at least I am a nerd.

I am grateful to receive an honorary degree from Harvard, an honor that means more to me than you might care to imagine. You see, I was the academic black sheep of my family. My older brother has an M.D./Ph.D. from MIT and Harvard while my younger brother has a law degree from Harvard. When I was awarded a Nobel Prize, I thought my mother would be pleased. Not so. When I called her on the morning of the announcement, she replied, "That's nice, but when are you going to visit me next?" Now, as the last brother with a degree from Harvard, maybe, at last, she will be satisfied.

Another difficulty with giving a Harvard commencement address is that some of you may disapprove of the fact that I have borrowed material from previous speeches. I ask that you forgive me for two reasons.

First, in order to have impact, it is important to deliver the same message more than once. In science, it is important to be the first person to make a discovery, but it is even more important to be the last person to make that discovery.

Second, authors who borrow from others are following in the footsteps of the best. Ralph Waldo Emerson, who graduated from Harvard at the age of 18, noted "All my best thoughts were stolen by the ancients." Picasso declared "Good artists borrow. Great artists steal." Why should commencement speakers be held to a higher standard?

I also want to point out the irony of speaking to graduates of an institution that would have rejected me, had I the **chutzpah** [n. 放肆. 厚颜] to apply. I am married to "Dean Jean," the former dean of admissions at Stanford. She assures me that she would have rejected me, if given the chance. When I showed her a draft of this speech, she objected strongly to my use of the word "rejected." She never rejected applicants; her letters stated that "we are unable to offer you admission." I have difficulty

尊敬的福斯特校长、哈佛集团的各位成员、监管理事会的各位理事、各位老师、各位家长、各位朋友，以及最重要的，今天毕业的各位同学们：

感谢你们让我分享这样一个美妙的日子。

我不敢确定自己是否够得上"哈佛大学毕业典礼演讲人"这样的殊荣。去年是J.K.罗琳——英国拥有亿万财产的小说家，她最早曾是一个专修古典文学的学生——站在这个讲台上。在这之前一年，站在这里的是比尔·盖茨，他是一个超级富豪、慈善家和计算机高手。今天，很可惜你们的演讲人是我，虽然我不是很有钱，但好在我也算一个科技行家。

我很感谢哈佛大学给我的荣誉学位，这个荣誉对我来说比你们想象的还要重要。你们想想看，在学术上，我是我们家的"黑羊"——一个无用之辈。我的哥哥从麻省理工学院和哈佛大学得到了医学博士和哲学博士学位；我的弟弟有哈佛大学的法律学位。当我得到诺贝尔奖的时候，我想我的妈妈该会高兴了，但并非如此。消息公布的那天早上，我给她打电话，她回答道："挺好的，但你什么时候再来看我？"如今在我们兄弟中，我终于也拿到了哈佛的学位，这次，她可能会感到满意了。

在哈佛大学毕业典礼上发表演讲的另一个难处，就是你们中有些人可能会不赞同我借用前人演讲中的东西。我想取得你们的谅解，因为有两个理由：

首先，要想产生影响力，很重要的就是要重复同样的信息。在科学中，作为第一个发现者是重要的，最后一个将这个发现重新挖掘出来的人更为重要。

其次，借鉴他人的经验，只不过是跟随着最优秀的前人所留下的脚印。18岁就从哈佛毕业的诗人拉尔夫·沃尔多·爱默生[1]曾说："古人把我最好的想法都偷走了。"毕加索则宣称："优秀的艺术家借鉴，伟大的艺术家偷窃。"那么为什么毕业典礼的演说者，就该有更高的标准呢？

我还要指出的是，向哈佛毕业生发表演说，对我来说有点讽刺意味，因为如果当年我有胆量向哈佛递交入学申请，一定会被拒绝的。我的妻子简曾当过斯坦福大学的招生办主任，她很肯定地对我说，如果她遇到我这样的申请者，肯定会将我拒之门外。当我把这篇演讲的草稿给她看

understanding the difference. After all, deans of admissions of highly selective schools are in reality, "deans of rejection." Clearly, I have a lot to learn about marketing.

Unsolicited advice

My address will follow the classical **sonata** [n. 奏鸣曲] form of commencement addresses. The first movement, just presented, were light-hearted remarks. This next movement consists of unsolicited advice, which is rarely valued, seldom remembered, never followed. As Oscar Wilde said, "The only thing to do with good advice is to pass it on. It is never of any use to oneself." So, here comes the advice. First, **every time you celebrate an achievement, be thankful to those who made it possible.** Thank your parents and friends who supported you, thank your professors who were inspirational, and especially thank the other professors whose less-than-brilliant lectures forced you to teach yourself. Going forward, the ability to teach yourself is the hallmark of a great liberal arts education and will be the key to your success. To your fellow students who have added immeasurably to your education during those late night discussions, hug them. Also, of course, thank Harvard. Should you forget, there's an alumni association to remind you. Second, **in your future life, cultivate a generous spirit. In all negotiations, don't bargain for the last, little advantage. Leave the change on the table.** In your collaborations, always remember that "credit" is not a conserved quantity. In a successful collaboration, everybody gets 90 percent of the credit.

Jimmy Stewart, as Elwood P. Dowd in the movie "Harvey" got it exactly right. He said: "Years ago my mother used to say to me, 'In this world, Elwood, you must be … she always used to call me Elwood … in this world, Elwood, you must be oh so smart or oh so pleasant.'" Well, for years I was smart. … I recommend pleasant. You may quote me on that.

My third piece of advice is as follows: **As you begin this new stage of your lives, follow your passion. If you don't have a passion, don't be satisfied until you find one. Life is too short to go through it without caring deeply about something.** When I was your age, I was incredibly single-minded in my goal to be a physicist. After college, I spent eight years as a graduate student and postdoc at Berkeley, and then nine years at Bell Labs. During that time, my central focus and professional joy was physics.

Here is my final piece of advice. Pursuing a personal passion is important, but it should not be your only goal. **When you are old and gray, and look back on your life, you will want to be proud of what you have done. The source of that pride won't be the**

时,她强烈反对我使用"拒收"这个词。她从来不拒收任何申请者,在发出拒绝信时,她总是写"我们无法提供你入学的机会。"我无法弄清这两者到底有何不同。说到底,那些入学竞争激烈的学校的招生办主任,与其叫做招生办主任,还不如称为"拒收办主任"。很显然,我还很需要好好学习如何做好营销。

演讲大都按古典奏鸣曲的结构来展开,我的演讲也不例外。第一乐章就是刚才谈的轻松闲话。接下来的第二乐章包括了不请自到的忠告。这种忠告很少有人重视,总是被人遗忘,几乎不会实践,就像王尔德[2]所说:"对于良言忠告,你所能做的唯一一件事,就是把它转送他人,因为它对你自己不会有任何用处。"以下就是我送出的忠告。

第一,每当成功之际,你要感谢那些助过你一臂之力的人。要感谢一直支持你的父母和朋友,要感谢那些启发过你的教授,特别是那些讲课枯燥的教授,因为他们迫使你学会自学。从今以后,拥有自学能力将是优秀的文理教育留给你的印记,也将是你成功的关键。你需要拥抱你的同学,那些同你进行过许多彻夜长谈,从而给你的学业增添了无法衡量的价值的同学。当然,你还要感谢哈佛大学,如果忘了这一点,会有校友会在拉捐款时来提醒你。

其次,**在未来的人生中,你要做到慷慨大度**。在任何谈判中,不要贪求那最后的一点利益,在桌上留点零头给别人。"荣誉"不是一种数量有限的东西,成功的合作中,每一方都只应获得全部荣誉的百分之九十。

吉米·斯图尔特[3]在电影《哈维》中扮演的角色埃尔伍德·道得就完全体现了这一点。他说:"多年前,母亲总是对我说,'埃尔伍德,人生在世,你要么必须聪明过人,要么就要容易相处。'"怎么说呢?多年来我一直觉得自己够聪明……但是,我劝告你们更要做到容易相处,你们不妨引用我这句话。

第三,当你开启新的人生阶段时,请跟随自己的爱好。如果你没有所钟爱的事情,就要去寻找,否则永不言弃。生命太短暂,你必须为某样东西倾注你的深情。我在你们这个年龄时,满脑子想的就是要成为一个物理学家。本科毕业后,我在加州大学伯克利分校又待了8年,读了

things you have acquired or the recognition you have received. **It will be the lives you have touched and the difference you have made.**

After nine years at Bell labs, I decided to leave that warm, cozy ivory tower for what I considered to be the "real world," a university. Bell Labs, to quote what was said about Mary Poppins, was "practically perfect in every way," but I wanted to leave behind something more than scientific articles. I wanted to teach and give birth to my own set of scientific children.

Ted Geballe, a friend and distinguished colleague of mine at Stanford, who also went from Berkeley to Bell Labs to Stanford years earlier, described our motives best:

The best part of working at a university is the students. They come in fresh, enthusiastic, open to ideas, unscarred by the battles of life. They don't realize it, but they're the recipients of the best our society can offer. If a mind is ever free to be creative, that's the time. They come in believing textbooks are authoritative, but eventually they figure out that textbooks and professors don't know everything, and then they start to think on their own. Then, I begin learning from them.

My students, post doctoral fellows, and the young researchers who worked with me at Bell Labs, Stanford, and Berkeley have been extraordinary. Over 30 former group members are now professors, many at the best research institutions in the world, including Harvard. I have learned much from them. Even now, in rare moments on weekends, the remaining members of my biophysics group meet with me in the **ether** [n. 以太，太空] world of cyberspace.

A scientific discovery and a new dilemma

I began teaching with the idea of giving back; I received more than I gave. This brings me to the final movement of this speech. It begins with a story about an extraordinary scientific discovery and a new dilemma that it poses. It's a call to arms and about making a difference.

In the last several decades, our climate has been changing. Climate change is not new: the Earth went through six ice ages in the past 600,000 years. However, recent measurements show that the climate has begun to change rapidly. The size of the North Polar Ice Cap in the month of September is only half the size it was a mere 50 years ago. The sea level has been rising since direct measurements began in

研究生，做完博士后，然后又在贝尔实验室待了9年。在那些年里，我关注的焦点和职业上的全部乐趣，都集中在物理学上。

我还有最后一个忠告，个人的兴趣爱好固然重要，但不应仅止步于此。**当你白发苍苍、韶华已逝、回首人生时，要为自己做过的事情感到骄傲。物质的得失、名声的显赫，都不足以带给你那种自豪感。只有那些被你感动过的生命、因你而改变的事物，才会让你心生自豪。**

在贝尔实验室工作了9年后，我决定离开那个温暖舒适的象牙塔，走进我眼中的"现实世界"——大学。贝尔实验室就像有人形容电影里的玛丽·波宾丝[4]那样，"基本上完美无缺"，但是，我不光想为人们留下科学论文，还有更多的东西。我要去教书，培育出自己在科学上的后人。

我在斯坦福大学的好友、成就卓越的同事泰德·戈巴尔，也是早年从伯克利分校去了贝尔实验室，再从那里到了斯坦福大学，他对我们的动机做出了最好的描述：

大学校园里最吸引人的就是那些学生。他们年轻热情、思想开放，还没有被生活撞击得伤痕累累。他们自己没有意识到，但是他们享受着我们这个社会所能提供的最好的东西。如果一个人的思想能够无拘无束、充满创造力，那么就是在这个阶段了。进校时，学生们对教科书奉若神明，但他们会发现，其实课本和教授并不是无所不知的，于是他们开始独立思考。从那时起，就轮到我向他们学习了。

我在贝尔实验室、斯坦福和伯克利教过的学生、带过的博士后、合作过的年轻同事，都非常优秀。他们中有30多人现在已经成为教授，其中有许多人在包括哈佛在内的世界一流的研究机构工作。我从他们身上学到了很多东西。即使现在，我偶尔周末还会上网，和我生物物理学研究组的其他成员在网上切磋。

我带着回报社会的想法开始教学生涯，结果我得到的却多于我付出的，这就引出了这次演讲的最后一个乐章。首先我要谈谈一个了不起的科学发现，以及由此带来的新挑战。它是一个动员令，号召我们必须做

1870 at a rate that is now five times faster than it was at the beginning of recorded measurements. Here's the remarkable scientific discovery. For the first time in human history, science is now making predictions of how our actions will affect the world 50 and 100 years from now. These changes are due to an increase in carbon dioxide put into the atmosphere since the beginning of the Industrial Revolution. The Earth has warmed up by roughly 0.8 degrees Celsius since the beginning of the Revolution. There is already approximately a 1 degree rise built into the system, even if we stop all greenhouse gas emissions today. Why? It will take decades to warm up the deep oceans before the temperature reaches a new equilibrium.

If the world continues on a business-as-usual path, the Intergovernmental Panel on Climate Change predicts that there is a fifty-fifty chance the temperature will exceed 5 degrees by the end of this century. This increase may not sound like much, but let me remind you that during the last ice age, the world was only 6 degrees colder. During this time, most of Canada and the United States down to Ohio and Pennsylvania were covered year round by a glacier. A world 5 degrees warmer will be very different. The change will be so rapid that many species, including Humans, will have a hard time adapting. I've been told for example, that, in a much warmer world, insects were bigger. I wonder if this thing buzzing around is a precursor.

We also face the specter of nonlinear "tipping points" that may cause much more severe changes. An example of a tipping point is the thawing of the **permafrost** [n. 永久冻土层]. The permafrost contains immense amounts of frozen organic matter that have been accumulating for millennia. If the soil melts, microbes will spring to life and cause this debris to rot. The difference in biological activity below freezing and above freezing is something we are all familiar with. Frozen food remains edible for a very long time in the freezer, but once thawed, it spoils quickly. How much methane and carbon dioxide might be released from the rotting permafrost? If even a fraction of the carbon is released, it could be greater than all the greenhouse gases we have released to since the beginning of the industrial revolution. Once started, a runaway effect could occur.

The climate problem is the unintended consequence of our success. We depend on fossil energy to keep our homes warm in the winter, cool in the summer, and lit at night; we use it to travel across town and across continents. Energy is a fundamental reason for the prosperity we enjoy, and we will not surrender this prosperity. The

出改变。

  在过去几十年中，我们的气候一直在发生变化。气候变化并不是新鲜事，在过去的60万年中，地球就经历过6次冰河期。但是，最近的测量表明，气候变化开始加速。北极冰盖在9月份的面积，只相当于50年前的一半。从1870年起，人们开始测量海平面上升的速度，现在增高的速度是那时的5倍。这就是一个重大的科学发现。在人类历史上，科学第一次预测出我们的行为对50年到100年后的世界会有怎样的影响。这些变化的原因是从工业革命开始，人类排放到大气中的二氧化碳增加了。从工业革命开始到现在，地球的平均气温上升了0.8摄氏度。即使我们今天就停止所有产生温室效应的气体排放，这个测量系统仍然预计气温将比过去上升大约1度。为什么呢？这是因为在气温达到均衡前，深海水温要几十年后才会受热升温。

  如果全世界保持这种"一切正常"的方式，联合国政府间气候变化专门委员会（IPCC）预测，到本世纪末，气温将有百分之五十的可能会至少上升5度。这听起来好像不多，但是请让我提醒诸位，在上一次的冰河期间，地球的气温仅仅降低了6度。那时，加拿大的大部分地区和美国一直到俄亥俄州和宾夕法尼亚州以北的部分，都终年被冰川覆盖。气温升高5度的地球，将会非常不同。由于变化来得太快，包括人类在内的许多生物，都将很难适应。比如，有人告诉我，在温暖得多的环境里，昆虫的块头将变大。不知道现在身边嗡嗡叫的这只大苍蝇，是不是就是那个前兆。

  我们还面临着另一个幽灵，那就是引发严重变化的非线性的"气候引爆点"。这种"气候引爆点"的一个例子，就是永久冻土层的融化。永久冻土层里封冻着巨量的有机物，这是经过千万年的累积所形成的。如果冻土融化，微生物就会苏醒繁殖，冻土层中的堆积物就会腐烂。我们都很熟悉冷冻后的生物和冷冻前的生物，它们在生物活动方面的差异。在冷库中，冷冻食品在很长的保存时间后，依然可以食用，但是一旦解冻，食品很快就腐烂了。永久冻土层腐烂后，将释放出多少甲烷和二氧化碳？即使那里只有一部分的碳被释放出来，也可能比我们从工业革命开始以

United States has 3 percent of the world population, and yet, we consume 25 percent of the energy. By contrast, there are 1.6 billion people who don't have access to electricity. Hundreds of millions of people still cook with twigs or dung. The life we enjoy may not be within the reach of the developing world, but it is within sight, and they want what we have.

Here is the dilemma. How much are we willing to invest, as a world society, to mitigate the consequences of climate change that will not be realized for at least 100 years? Deeply rooted in all cultures, is the notion of generational responsibility. Parents work hard so that their children will have a better life. Climate change will affect the entire world, but our natural focus is on the welfare of our immediate families. Can we, as a world society, meet our responsibility to future generations?

While I am worried, I am hopeful we will solve this problem. I became the director of the Lawrence Berkeley National Laboratory, in part because I wanted to enlist some of the best scientific minds to help battle against climate change. I was there only four and a half years, the shortest serving director in the 78-year history of the Lab, but when I left, a number of very exciting energy institutes at the Berkeley Lab and UC Berkeley had been established.

I am extremely privileged to be part of the Obama administration. If there ever was a time to help steer America and the world towards a path of sustainable energy, now is the time. The message the President is delivering is not one of doom and gloom, but of optimism and opportunity. I share this optimism. The task ahead is daunting, but we can and will succeed.

We know some of the answers already. There are immediate and significant savings in energy efficiency and conservation. Energy efficiency is not just low-hanging fruit; it is fruit lying on the ground. For example, we have the potential to make buildings 80 percent more efficient with investments that will pay for themselves in less than 15 years. Buildings consume 40 percent of the energy we use, and a transition to energy efficient buildings will cut our carbon emissions by one-third.

We are revving up the remarkable American innovation machine that will be the basis of a new American prosperity. We will invent much improved methods to harness the sun, the wind, nuclear power, and capture and **sequester** [vt. 扣押] the carbon dioxide emitted from our power plants. Advanced bio-fuels and the electrification of personal vehicles make us less dependent on foreign oil.

来所制造出的所有温室气体的总和还要多。这种局面一旦发生,极有可能会失控。

气候问题是我们的成功所带来的没有预料到的后果。我们依赖石油能源,用于冬天取暖、夏天制冷、夜间照明,我们依靠它来做长短途旅行。能源是我们所享受的繁荣的基础,我们不可能放弃这种繁荣。美国人口占全世界的3%,但是我们消耗全球25%的能源。相比之下,全世界还有16亿人没有电,还有数亿人依靠燃烧树枝或动物粪便来煮饭。发展中国家的人民可能享受不到我们所过的生活,但是他们都看在眼里,并且也想过我们这种生活。

这就是让我们进退两难的地方。作为一个世界的整体,我们到底愿意投入多少资金,来缓解气候变化的后果?而这种投资至少在100年内都还不会看到效果。代际责任感深深根植于所有文化中。家长努力工作,就是为了让他们的孩子有更好的生活。气候变化将影响整个世界,但是我们的天性使得我们只关心个人家庭的福利。全世界如果作为一个整体,我们能否为后代们负起责任?

虽然我感到焦虑,但我对我们能够解决这个问题抱有希望。我同意担任劳伦斯-伯克利国家实验室主任的部分原因,是想吸引一些世界上最好的科学家,来帮助对付气候变化的问题。我在那里做了4年半的时间,是这个实验室78年历史中任期最短的主任,但是当我离任时,在伯克利实验室和伯克利分校,已经建立起一些非常激动人心的能源研究机构。

我非常荣幸能够成为奥巴马政府团队的一员。如果说有什么恰当时机可以引导美国和全世界走上可持续能源发展道路的话,那么现在正当其时。总统现在传递的信息,不是说我们在劫难逃,而是乐观且有机会,我也抱有这种乐观态度。我们面对的任务令人生畏,但是我们能够并且将会成功。

我们已经知道了一些答案,节约能源和提高能源使用效率,可以带来立竿见影的效益。有效使用能源不仅是挂在低矮枝头容易采摘的水果,而且是已经成熟、掉在地上俯身可拾的东西。例如,我们有可能把楼房的耗电减少80%,而这部分的投资在15年内就可以收回。楼房的耗电占我们

In the coming decades, we will almost certainly face higher oil prices and be in a carbon-constrained economy. We have the opportunity to lead in development of a new, industrial revolution. The great hockey player, Wayne Gretzky, when asked, how he positions himself on the ice, he replied," I skate to where the puck is going to be, not where it's been." America should do the same.

The Obama administration is laying a new foundation for a prosperous and sustainable energy future, but we don't have all of the answers. That's where you come in. In this address, I am asking you, the Harvard graduates, to join us. As our future intellectual leaders, take the time to learn more about what's at stake, and then act on that knowledge. As future scientists and engineers, I ask you to give us better technology solutions. As future economists and political scientists, I ask you to create better policy options. As future business leaders, I ask that you make sustainability an integral part of your business.

Finally, as humanists, I ask that you speak to our common humanity. One of the cruelest ironies about climate change is that the ones who will be hurt the most are the most innocent: the world's poorest and those yet to be born.

The **coda** [n. 乐章结尾部．（小说．戏剧等的）结局部分] to this last movement is borrowed from two humanists.

The first quote is from Martin Luther King. He spoke on ending the war in Vietnam in 1967, but his message seems so fitting for today's climate crisis:

This call for a worldwide fellowship that lifts neighborly concern beyond one's tribe, race, class, and nation is in reality a call for an all-embracing and unconditional love for all mankind. This oft misunderstood, this oft misinterpreted concept, so readily dismissed by the Nietzsches of the world as a weak and cowardly force, has now become an absolute necessity for the survival of man ... We are now faced with the fact, my friends, that tomorrow is today. We are confronted with the fierce urgency of now. In this unfolding conundrum of life and history, there is such a thing as being too late.

The final message is from William Faulkner. On December 10th, 1950, his Nobel Prize banquet speech was about the role of humanists in a world

能源消费的40%，节能楼房的推广将使二氧化碳的排放量减少三分之一。

我们正在促使美国这个非凡的创新机器加速运转，这将是给美国带来新的繁荣的基础。我们将大力改进有效利用太阳能、风能、核能的新方法，以及捕获和隔离从我们的核电站排放出的二氧化碳的方法。先进的生物燃料和用电驱动的汽车将使得我们不那么依赖外国的石油。

在未来的几十年中，我们几乎肯定会面临更高的油价，以及受到二氧化碳限制排放政策影响的经济。我们有机会引领一场全新的工业革命。有人提问出色的冰球运动员韦恩·格雷茨基[5]是如何在冰上抢位时，他回答说："我滑向球下一步的位置，而不是它现在所处的位置。"美国也应该这样做。

奥巴马政府正在为美国的繁荣和可持续能源的未来打下新的基础，但是我们还没有所有的答案，这将是你们可以施展的空间。在这个演讲中，我请求在座的各位——你们这些哈佛的毕业生——加入我们。你们是我们未来的智慧领袖，请多花些时间来了解目前的危险，然后采取相应的行动。你们是未来的科学家和工程师，我请求你们给我们提供更好的技术解决方案。你们是未来的经济学家和政治学家，我请求你们制定出更好的政策。你们是未来的企业领袖，我请求你们将可持续发展作为你们行业中不可分割的一部分。

最后，你们是人道主义者，我请求你们直面全人类。气候变化带来的最残酷的讽刺之一，就是那些最受伤害的人，恰恰就是那些最无辜的人：那些世界上最穷的人和还没有出生的人。

在这个乐章的完结部分，我想要借用两位人道主义者的讲话。

第一段引语来自马丁·路德·金。这是他在1967年呼吁结束越南战争时的评论，但是用于今天的气候危机好像如此切题：

我呼吁全世界的人们互相关爱，超越部落、种族、阶级和国籍的局限，这个呼吁，就是希望人们对全人类有一种包融一切的、无条件的爱。这个概念经常会遭到误解和误读，世上那些信奉尼采哲学的人会认定这是一种软弱和胆怯的表现，但是，现在这已成为人类存活下去的绝对的必

facing potential nuclear holocaust.

I believe that man will not merely endure: he will prevail. He is immortal, not because he alone among creatures has an inexhaustible voice, but because he has a soul, a spirit capable of compassion and sacrifice and endurance. The poet's, the writer's, duty is to write about these things. It is his privilege to help man endure by lifting his heart, by reminding him of the courage and honor and hope and pride and compassion and pity and sacrifice which have been the glory of his past.

Graduates, you have an extraordinary role to play in our future. As you pursue your private passions, I hope you will also develop a passion and a voice to help the world in ways both large and small. Nothing will give you greater satisfaction.

Please accept my warmest congratulations. May you prosper, may you help preserve and save our planet for your children, and all future children of the world.

需条件。……朋友们，眼前的事实是，明天就是今天，此刻我们面临着最紧急的情况。在生活和历史的风云变幻中，有一样东西叫做悔之晚矣。

我最后的引语来自威廉·福克纳。他在1950年12月10日诺贝尔奖获奖晚宴上发表的演说中，谈到在一个受到核战争威胁的世界里，人道主义者所应当扮演的角色：

我相信人类不仅会忍耐，而且会获胜。人类是不朽的，这不是因为万物当中只有他会有永不止息的呐喊，而是因为他有可以展现同情心、牺牲精神和忍耐力的那种灵魂和精神。诗人和作家的责任就是描写这些东西。他们有幸能够通过鼓舞人类，唤醒人类原有的荣耀——勇敢、荣誉、希望、自豪、怜悯之心和牺牲精神，从而帮助人类延续下去。

毕业生们，你们在我们的未来中将要扮演举足轻重的角色。当你们追求个人的志向时，我希望你们也要培育热情、积极发声，以或大或小的方式有助于这个世界，这会给你们带来无与伦比的满足感。

最后，请接受我最热烈的祝贺。预祝你们成功，也希望你们帮助保护和拯救我们这个星球，为了你们的孩子，以及未来世界上所有的孩子。

Play Your Role in Our Future Steven Chu
在未来扮演好你的角色 朱棣文

E 572 C 573

1 拉尔夫·沃尔多·爱默生（Ralph Waldo Emerson，1803—1882），美国思想家，诗人。1836年出版处女作《论自然》。他文学上的贡献主要在散文和诗歌上。

2 奥斯卡·王尔德（Oscar Wilde，1854—1900），英国剧作家、诗人、散文家，19世纪与萧伯纳齐名的英国文坛名人。

3 吉米·斯图尔特（Jimmy Stewart，1908—1997），美国著名演员，曾5次获奥斯卡奖提名，1次奥斯卡奖和一项"终身成就奖"。

4 玛丽·波宾丝（"Mary Poppins"，或译《欢乐满人间》），好莱坞1965年电影，主角是一位仙女保姆Mary Poppins，她来到人间，教导主人家的两位小朋友如何克服生活中的困难，并帮助他们重获欢乐。本片获得5项奥斯卡奖。

5 韦恩·格雷茨基（Wayne Gretzky），生于1961年的加拿大著名冰球运动员，被普遍认为是当代最优秀的冰球运动员，曾创下了一系列冰球联盟比赛的纪录。

2010's

埃伦·约翰逊－瑟利夫（1938— ）

2011年的演讲嘉宾，是正在任期内的非洲第一位女性国家元首——利比里亚总统埃伦·约翰逊－瑟利夫。

瑟利夫1938年出生于利比里亚首都蒙罗维亚，早年在西非学院学习经济。1961年瑟利夫随其前夫来到美国，就读于威斯康辛大学和科罗拉多大学，分别获得会计学和经济学学士学位。1969年至1971年在哈佛大学的肯尼迪政府学院学习，获得公共管理硕士学位。

从哈佛毕业后，瑟利夫回国担任财政部部长助理，于1979年至1980年担任利比里亚的财政部长。她还曾担任利比里亚驻联合国的官员。

瑟利夫政治生涯坎坷多变，她多次因持不同政见流亡海外。更引人注目的是她于1985年开始参与利比里亚副总统竞选，因为发表了对当局不利言辞而被捕入狱。不久当局迫于国际压力释放了她，同一年她赢得了参议员的竞选，不过因为整个国会选举过程的不公，瑟利夫拒绝了这一席位。1995年，瑟利夫曾作为13个总统候选人之一参加总统竞选，因只得到百分之十的选票而落选。

瑟利夫从未放弃过她的政治理想，并为实现这一理想而不懈努力。在2005年再次角逐总统竞选中，瑟利夫成为利比里亚第一位女总统，也是非洲历史上第一位女性国家元首，她获得了一个因14年野蛮内战而遭受重创的国家的政权。2011年10月，瑟利夫与利比里亚另一位"和平斗士"莱伊曼·古博韦及也门"阿拉伯之春"活动家塔瓦库勒·卡曼共同获得诺贝尔和平奖。诺贝尔奖委员会评价说："自2006年就职以来，她为确保利比里亚的和平、促进经济和社会发展以及提高妇女地位作出了贡献。"

2011

Keeping Hope and Not Giving Up
坚守希望　永不言弃

Ellen Johnson Sirleaf 埃伦·约翰逊－瑟利夫

President Drew Gilpin Faust, members of the Harvard Board of Overseers, members of the Harvard Corporation, faculty, staff and students, fellow alumni, members of the graduating Class of 2011, parents, family and friends, distinguished guests, ladies and gentlemen, friends:

I am honored not only to be the 360th Commencement speaker at my alma mater, but to do so in the year Harvard University celebrates 375 years of preparing minds as the oldest institution of higher learning in America. Thank you for the invitation and congratulations to you, Dr. Faust, the first female president of Harvard! It is a great privilege to share in Harvard's distinguished and storied history. Harvard has produced presidents, prime ministers, a United Nations secretary-general, leaders in business, government, and the church. But more than anything, Harvard has produced the men and women on whose talent our societies function — the leaders in law, health, business, government, design, education, spirituality, and thought.

An event four decades ago put me on the path that has led me to where I am today. I participated, as a junior official of Liberia's Department of Treasury, in a national development conference sponsored by our National Planning Council and a team of Harvard advisers working with Liberia. My remarks, which challenged the **status quo** [n. 现 状], landed me in my first political trouble. The head of the Harvard team, recognizing, in a closed society, the potential danger I faced, facilitated the process that enabled me to become a Mason Fellow at the Kennedy School of Government. The Mason Program provided me with the opportunity to study a diversified curriculum for a master's degree in public administration. Perhaps more importantly, in terms of preparation for leadership, the program enabled us to learn and interact with other Fellows and classmates who represented current and potential leaders from all continents.

I engaged, thrilled to be among the world's best minds, yet overwhelmed by the reality of being a part of the world's most prestigious institution of learning. As a result, I did things that I should have done, like studying hard, going to the stacks to do the research for the many papers and for better knowledge of the history of my country. I notice a few blank stares — evidence of the generation gap — so let me explain: the stacks contained books, which people used to write, and other people used to read, before Google Scholar was created. I also did things that I should not have done, like exposing myself to **frostbite** [n. 冻伤. 冻疮] when I joined students much

福斯特校长、哈佛监管会的各位理事、哈佛集团的各位成员、各位老师、各位职工、各位同学、各位校友、各位2011级的毕业生、各位学生家长和亲友、各位贵宾先生们、女士们、朋友们：

我非常荣幸，不仅担任母校第360届毕业典礼的演讲者，而且还赶上了哈佛大学——这个美国最早的高等学府375周年校庆。福斯特博士，您是哈佛历史上第一位女校长，谢谢您邀请我，并向您表示祝贺，祝您成为哈佛大学卓越历史和传奇故事的一部分。对我来说这是一个很大的荣誉。历年来哈佛培养出了总统、首相、联合国秘书长、商界、政界和宗教界的领袖，更重要的是，哈佛培养了维持我们社会运转的各行各业富有才华的领军人物：杰出的律师、医生、商人、公务员、设计师、教育家、宗教神职人员和思想家。

40年前发生的一件事，让我走到了今天的位置。当时，作为利比里亚财政部的一个基层职员，我参加了由"国家规划委员会"和与利比里亚合作的哈佛大学顾问团队举办的一次国家发展讨论会。我在会上针砭现状，这使我遇到了人生的第一次政治麻烦。哈佛顾问团团长意识到，在一个封闭的社会中我可能会遭遇到危险。于是，他设法帮助我成为（哈佛）肯尼迪政府学院的梅森研究员。梅森项目使我有机会学习内容广泛的课程，并获得了哈佛公共管理专业的硕士学位。在培养领导能力方面，梅森项目更重要的作用，是让我们有机会与其他研究员和同学一起学习和互动，而这些人是来自全球各大洲目前或潜在的领袖。

与全世界最有智慧的人在一起，成为世界最负盛名学府的一分子，让我既兴奋又感动。因此，我不仅做那些应该做的事情，比如刻苦学习，为了撰写论文和更好地了解我们国家的历史，而在书堆中苦读。（我注意到有些听众不太理解的样子，我想这就是"代沟"，让我来解释一下。所谓"书堆"，是指在Google学术搜索诞生之前，人们习惯于写书和阅读书籍）我也做了些本不该做的事情，比如大冬天和许多比我年轻很多的学生一起，坐大巴去首都华盛顿游行示威，反对美国卷入越南战争，这使我生了冻疮。

younger than I to travel by bus to Washington, D.C., to demonstrate against U.S. involvement in the Vietnam War.

It is difficult to imagine achieving all that I have, without the opportunity to study at Harvard. It is, therefore, for me a profound honor to be counted as an alumna. I salute my fellow graduates who share that rich heritage of academic excellence and the pursuit of truth.

In preparation for this Address, I was pleasantly surprised to learn how far back Liberia's connection to Harvard goes. The establishment of the Liberia College (now the University of Liberia) in 1862, the second-oldest institution of higher learning in West Africa, was led and funded by the Trustees of Donations for Education in Liberia. Simon Greenleaf, the Harvard College law professor who drafted Liberia's Independence Constitution of 1847, was the founder and president of the Trustees of Donations for Education in Liberia.

The first Liberian graduate of Harvard did so in 1920, and since then there has been a steady trail of Liberians to Cambridge. Most of them returned home to pursue successful careers.

Thank you, Harvard, and thank you to the many Mason Program professors, dead and alive, for the compliments you paid when my papers and interventions were top rate, and for the patience you showed when I struggled with quantitative analysis.

The self-confidence, sometimes called arrogance, that comes from being a Harvard graduate can also lead one down a dangerous path. It did for me. One year after my return from Cambridge, I was at it again, in a Commencement Address at my high school alma mater. I questioned the government's failure to address long-standing inequalities in the society. This forced me into exile and a staff position at the World Bank. Other similar events would follow in a life of in and out of country, in and out of jail, in and out of professional service. **There were times when I thought death was near, and times when the burden of standing tall by one's conviction seemed only to result in failure. But through it all, my experience sends a strong message that failure is just as important as success.**

Today I stand proud, as the first woman president of my country, Liberia. This has allowed me to lead the processes of change, change needed to address a long-standing environment characterized by awesome challenges: a collapsed economy, huge domestic and external debt arrears, dysfunctional institutions, destroyed infrastructure,

如果没有哈佛学习的机会，很难想象我会取得今天的成就。因此，能够成为哈佛校友的一员，对我来说是一种无上的光荣。我向那些一起毕业的同学致敬，他们继承了学术卓越、追求真理的优秀传统。

在准备这篇演讲稿的过程中，我高兴地了解到，利比里亚与哈佛大学的渊源可以追溯到很久以前。利比里亚学院（利比里亚大学的前身）成立于1862年，是西非第二古老的高等教育学府。这所学校是由"利比里亚教育基金会"资助和倡导的，哈佛大学法学教授西蒙·格林里夫是这个基金会的创始人和主席，他在1847年还起草了利比里亚的独立宪章。

1920年，第一个利比里亚留学生从哈佛大学毕业。此后，一直不断有利比里亚人来到波士顿的剑桥[1]求学。他们中的大多数后来都回到利比里亚，追求事业的成功。

感谢你，哈佛！感谢许多已故的和仍然健在的梅森项目教授，感谢你们对我的论文和其他活动的高度评价，感谢你们在我学习数量分析遇到困难时所给予的耐心。

因为毕业于哈佛给人带来的自信有时甚至是自大，也能带人走上一条危险的道路，我就是这样。从哈佛毕业回国一年后，在给高中母校的毕业典礼致辞时，我又"惹祸"了。我质疑政府为何没有改变社会上长期存在的不平等现象。之后我不得不流亡海外，到世界银行担任职员。后来又发生了许多类似的事件，使我回国又出国、入狱又出狱，并在职场进进出出。**有时我觉得离死亡不远，有时觉得张扬自己的信念看来只会导致失败。但是经过所有这一切，我的经历所表达的强烈信息就是：失败同成功一样重要。**

今天，作为我的祖国利比里亚的第一位女总统站在这里，我无比自豪。这个职位让我能够领导变革的进程，我的祖国需要变革，来应对我们面临的许多巨大挑战：崩溃的经济、庞大的国内外逾期债务、运行不灵的各种机构、残败的基础设施、脆弱的地区和国际关系，以及被战火毁坏的社会资源。

poor regional and international relationships, and social capital destroyed by the scourge of war.

After election, I moved quickly in mobilizing our team, sought support from partners, and tackled the challenges. In five years, we formulated the laws and policies and strategies for growth and development. We removed the international sanctions on our primary exports; introduced and made public a cash-based budget; increased revenue by over 400 percent; and mobilized foreign direct investment worth 16 times the size of the economy when I assumed office. We built a small and professional army and coast guard, and moved the economy from negative growth to average around 6 percent. We have virtually eliminated a $4.9 billion external debt, settled a large portion of international institutional debt, as well as domestic arrears and suppliers' credit. We restored electricity and pipe-borne water, lacking in the capital for two decades; reconstructed two modern universities and rural referral hospitals; constructed or reconstructed roads, bridges, schools, training institutions, local government facilities, and courts throughout the country; established and strengthened the institutional pillars of integrity; decentralized education by establishing community colleges; brought back the Peace Corps; and mobilized financial and technical resources from U.S. foundations, sororities, and individuals for support of programs aimed at the education of girls, the empowerment of adolescent youth, and improved working conditions for women.

Nevertheless, the challenges for sustained growth and development remain awesome. Our stability is threatened by the thousands of returnees from U.S. prisons and regional refugee camps, the bulk of whom are lacking in technical skills. Our peace is threatened by the challenging neighborhood where we live: two of our three neighbors have either experienced, or narrowly avoided, civil war in the past year, and we patiently host their refugees, since not even a decade ago it was they who hosted so many of us. Implementation of our economic development agenda is constrained by low implementation and absorptive capacity, which means that we are not constrained by funding alone. Plans to enhance performance in governance move slower than desired due to long-standing institutional decay and a corrupted value system of dishonesty and dependency. The development of infrastructure is constrained by the high capital cost of restoration, brought about by the lack of maintenance and exacerbated by wanton destruction over two decades of conflict.

坚守希望 永不言弃 埃伦·约翰逊－瑟利夫

当选总统后,我迅速推动我们的团队,向支持者寻求支持,来应对各种挑战。在5年的时间里,我们制定了促进增长和发展的法规、政策和战略;清除了对主要出口商品的国际限制;采用并公开了建立在现金基础上的财政预算,财政收入增加的幅度超过400%,吸引的外国投资是我就职时国家经济规模的16倍;我们建立了一支小规模、专业化的军队和海岸护卫队;将经济从负增长扭转到平均年增长6%左右,我们基本消除了49亿美元的外债,解决了大部分的国际机构欠款,以及国内的逾期债务和供应商的贷款;我们修复了在首都过去20年来一直缺乏的电力和自来水系统;我们重建了两所现代化的大学和农村的初级医院;在全国各地修建和重修了道路、桥梁、学校、培训机构、地方政府设施和法院;我们建立和加强一些体制性措施来保证正义;建立社区学院,让教育资源非中心化;让和平队重新回到利比里亚;利用来自美国的基金会、联谊会和个人所提供的资金和技术资源,来支持那些激励女童入学、激励青少年、为女性改进工作条件等项目。

然而,可持续发展所面临的挑战仍然很巨大。从美国监狱和其他地区的难民营回来的成千上万的人员,对我们的稳定构成威胁,他们中的大多数人缺乏技能。我们的和平也受到邻国的威胁。在过去一年里,我们的三个邻国当中,就有两个经历或者险些经历内战。

我们有耐心地接受了他们的难民,因为就在不到10年前,正是他们接受了我们大批的避难者。我们的经济发展规划,受到低水平的执行能力和学习能力的制约。这意味着制约我们的并不仅仅是资金不足。提高政府效率的计划,比我们希望的进展缓慢,因为我们的体制长期衰败,而且还有诚信不足、依赖思想的腐败价值观。基础设施的发展,也因为长期缺乏维修,并且过去20多年的冲突带来了恶意破坏,使得修复成本高昂。

不过,现在让我们骄傲的是,利比里亚的儿童已经重返校园,为建设一个新型的利比里亚社会做好准备。我们的7岁儿童不再听到枪声,也不必逃亡,他们又开始微笑。我们由此可以自信地说,

Yet, today, we are proud that young Liberian children are back in school, preparing themselves to play a productive part in the new Liberian society. Our seven-year-olds do not hear guns and do not have to run. They can smile again. We can thus say with confidence that we have moved our war-torn nation from turmoil to peace, from disaster to development, from dismay to hope. And it was the Liberian women who fought the final battle for peace, who came, their number and conviction the only things greater than their diversity, to demonstrate for the end to our civil war. I am, therefore, proud to stand before you, humbled by the success in representing the aspirations and expectations of Liberian women, African women, and, I dare to say, women worldwide.

Today I stand equally proud, as the first woman president of our African continent, a continent that has embraced the process of change and transformation. I am proud that Liberia became a beacon of hope in Africa. With few notable exceptions, Africa is no longer a continent of countries with corrupt big men who rule with iron fists. It is no longer the Dark Continent in continual economic free fall, **wallowing** [vi. 打滚，沉溺于] in debt, poverty and disease.

When he addressed the Ghanaian Parliament in 2009, President Barack Obama reminded the people of Africa that it would no longer be the great men of the past who would transform the continent. The future of all of our countries is in the hands of the young people, people like you, Obama said, "brimming with talent and energy and hope, who can claim the future that so many in previous generations never realized."

While many challenges persist, times have changed and the world you enter today, graduates of the Class of 2011, is much more accountable than the one we faced. At the beginning of this year, 17 elections were scheduled across our continent. In 1989, there were three democracies in sub-Saharan Africa; by 2008, there were 23. That is progress. This is a significant improvement from the days when violent overthrows were the default means of transition. A clear example stands out in West Africa. Although they did not get as much focus as postelection violence in Côte d'Ivoire, Niger and Guinea proved exemplary where the military oversaw democratic elections, turned power over to the civilian government, and returned to the barracks. In the case of Côte d'Ivoire, the Economic Community of West African States (ECOWAS) and the African Union recognized a nonincumbent as the legitimate

我们的努力已经推动这个饱受战火折磨的国家，从战乱走向和平，从灾难走向发展，从失望走向希望。

利比里亚的妇女，在为和平进行最后的战斗，她们的人数和信念战胜内部的差异，她们示威呼吁结束内战。我因此能够非常骄傲地站在你们面前，为能够代表利比里亚妇女、非洲妇女、甚至我敢说全世界的妇女，为能够代表她们的希望和梦想而感到十分荣幸。

今天，作为非洲大陆第一位女总统站在这里，我感到同样自豪。非洲正在迎来变革和转型的过程。我为利比里亚成为非洲希望之光而感到自豪。除了极少数的例外，非洲不再是腐败的独裁者铁腕治国的大陆。它也不再是经济不断下滑的黑暗大陆，不再挣扎于债务、贫穷和疾病。

2009年，奥巴马总统在加纳议会致辞时提醒非洲人民，非洲大陆的变革不能再指望过去的伟人。我们所有国家的未来，掌握在像你们这样的年轻人手中。奥巴马说："你们充满才华、能量和希望，能够实现过去许多代人无法想象的未来。"

尽管我们依然面临着许多挑战，但是时代已经变了。作为2011届毕业生，你们将要走进的世界远比我们曾经面对的世界更加合理。今年年初，非洲大陆计划中的民主选举有17次。而在1989年，在撒哈拉沙漠以南的那些非洲国家里，这样的选举只有3次，到了2008年，民主选举增加到了23次。这就是进步。

以前在非洲大陆是通过暴力颠覆来实现权力更替的。相比那时，现在已有显著的改善，西部非洲就是一个明显的例子。虽然科特迪瓦选举后的暴力冲突受到了高度关注，但是尼日尔和几内亚的例子才是楷模，它们的军队监督了民主选举，将政权移交到了民选政府手中，然后回到兵营。就科特迪瓦而言，西非国家经济体和非洲联盟承认一个在野的竞选者为当选人，这本身就是一个进步。

我们也看到非洲经济发展的证明，在过去10年里它的增长率超过了5%。非洲发展银行最近的一份报告，量化了非洲中产阶级的崛起，报告说10亿非洲人当中有3.13亿人进入这个阶层。中产阶级

winner. That, again, is progress.

We also see evidence of this progress in the African economy, which has been growing at more than 5 percent over the past decade. A recent African Development Bank report measured the rise of the middle class in Africa, totaling 313 million out of 1 billion Africans. The countries experiencing exceptional growth in their middle class include Ghana, Mozambique, Mali, Tanzania, Cape Verde, Botswana, Burkina Faso, and Rwanda. This middle class is changing the face of Africa. We are moving away from dependence on extractive industries and agriculture. There is a rising consumer class that helped brace Africa during the global economic crisis. This is emblematic not only of the progress in purchasing power in Africa, but in the progress that means you can still put food on the table for your family when the rains fail, that you can engage intelligently in political debates and hold your leaders accountable.

Instability and years of conflict in Liberia have pushed us to the bottom of this table in terms of the size of our middle class. We stubbornly refuse to accept this and are preparing a new development agenda that aims, through proper allocation of our natural resources, to graduate Liberia from development assistance in 10 years, and propels us to a middle-income country by 2030.

As Africa charts its economic path, we are taking advantage of South-South partnerships as China, India, and Brazil, not to mention Nigeria and Ghana, become more significant partners in our economic expansion. Their experience is closer to ours, and our cooperation going forward will be crucial.

Even as the African renaissance appears on course, we must recognize that some of this progress is driven by the same forces of commodity demand that led to temporary gains four decades ago. We are the source of raw materials, now to India and China as well as the Western world, yet we generate the least profits from these exhaustible resources. Moreover, we remain vulnerable to external price shocks and receive very little transfer of technology, or growth in related industries. Until we begin to make products to sell, build better road and rail systems, and improve the easy movement of people and goods across our borders; until we supply the engineers and geologists and marketers of our

的人数在加纳、莫桑比克、马里、坦桑尼亚、佛得角、博茨瓦纳、布基纳法索、卢旺达等国家，都在史无前例地增长。

中产阶级正在改变非洲的面貌。我们正在摆脱对开采业和农业的依赖。我们的消费者阶层正在不断扩大，有助于非洲度过这次全球经济难关。这不仅意味着非洲购买力的进步，也意味着当天有不测风云之时，你还能餐桌上有食物，意味着你还能明智地参与政治辩论，促使领导人负起他们的责任。

以中产阶级的人数来衡量，由于多年的动荡和内乱，利比里亚在这方面排名垫底。我们绝不接受这种地位。我们正着手一个新的发展规划，通过合理地分配我们的自然资源，争取用10年时间结束国际援助，并且到2030年使利比里亚成长为一个中等收入的国家。

随着非洲规划的经济发展起步，我们正在抓住南南合作的机遇，加强与中国、印度、巴西，还有尼日利亚和加纳的合作，这些国家成为我们经济增长的重要伙伴。它们的经历与我们相似，我们之间的进一步合作非常关键。

虽然非洲的复兴看来已经走上正轨，我们依然必须认识到，这个经济发展还是依赖于全球旺盛的商品需求，这种现象在40年前也曾导致了昙花一现的增长。我们现在是中国和印度以及西方国家的原材料供应基地，但是我们从这些不可再生的资源当中，只获得了最微薄的利润。而且，我们受外部价格波动的影响很大，引进的技术或者相关工业的增长寥寥无几。只有当我们生产出可销售的产品，修筑出更好的公路和铁路系统，使人员和物资方便地流动，只有当我们培养出能够开发本地资源的工程师、地质学家和营销人员，我们的中产阶级人数才能得到增加。

即使不考虑这些因素，以及能源采掘业本身的经济规律，我在非洲各地都看到这块大陆复兴的迹象。我们有更多的产品，更多的制造业，更多的贸易和更多的合作。诸如"责任制"、"透明度"、"改革"这类词汇，不再只是外国援助者的口头禅，非洲的各国政府为了重新当选，也必须用这些概念来指导幕后决策。人们在这些问题

resources, our middle class will remain stunted.

In spite of these needs, and the fundamental economics of resource extraction, everywhere I travel in Africa, I see signs of a continent rising. We are producing more, manufacturing more, trading more, and cooperating more. Words like accountability, transparency, and reform are not just the calling card of some foreign donor; they are the words that must **adjudicate** [vt. 判决. 裁定] closed-door decisions for those governments in Africa that seek re-election. There is a growing consensus on these issues, giving me great optimism about the future of Africa's common economy and democratic prospects.

I am excited about Africa's future, and more so about Liberia's future. In a few months, the Liberian people will have the opportunity to select their political leadership. This means that Liberia will know a second peaceful democratic transition in six years: this in a country that was **riven** [adj. 分裂的] by political rivalries, tribalism, and civil war for two decades. It is, nonetheless, with cautious optimism that we approach this event and the future. Anxieties remain because we know that as impressive as Liberia's rebirth has been, our achievements remain fragile and reversible.

I have no personal anxieties, however, for in a decades-long career in public service, I have learned many lessons that I can share with you today. In my journey, I have come to value hope and **resilience** [n. 适应力. 弹性]. As an actor in Liberia's history as it has unfolded over the last 40 years, I have seen these characteristics come full circle. I was there in the early '70s, a decade after the independence movement had swept across Africa. Back then, the future appeared full of endless possibilities. Then across the continent there was a gradual descent into militarism, sectarian violence, and divisive ethnic politics. But I have been blessed with the opportunity to watch and participate as not only my nation but other African countries rise out of the ashes of war. With cautious optimism, it is my hope that I will continue to lead Liberia to consolidate and realize the dividends of peace.

As much as I have lived and experienced, what you graduates will know and do will far exceed it. History, it seems, is speeding up. After graduation, you leave the relative security, predictability, and certainty of these walls for a world full of uncertainties. Across the globe, entire societies are being transformed,

上，有了越来越多的共识，这使我对非洲未来的共同经济发展和民主前景，充满无比乐观的期待。

我对非洲的未来非常激动，对利比里亚的未来更是如此。再过几个月，利比里亚人民将选举新的国家领导人，这将是利比里亚6年来第二次通过民主选举来实现政府的和平过渡。这个国家曾经被各派势力四分五裂，部落林立，内战持续了20年。不过，我们谨慎乐观地估计，我们可以应对这个时刻，迎接未来。担忧依然存在，因为我们知道虽然利比里亚的新生令人印象深刻，但我们已取得的成果依然脆弱，并且随时可能发生逆转。

然而，我个人并无太多担忧。我从政已经几十年了，今天有许多经验可以与你们分享。在我的经历中，我非常看重保持希望和适应能力。作为利比里亚过去40年历史发展中的一个角色，我不断目睹了这些特性。

在上个世纪70年代早期，在横扫非洲的独立运动发生后的10年里，我亲临其境。当时，未来看上去那么捉摸不定，但是接下来的时间里，这块大陆就逐渐沦陷到军国主义、宗教暴力和倡导分裂的种族政治的境地中。我很幸运能够目睹和亲身参与历史进程，看到不仅是我的祖国，还有其他非洲国家，从战争的废墟上浴火重生。依然是出于谨慎的乐观主义，我希望接下来还是由我来领导利比里亚，巩固和平，充分利用和平的环境来发展。

虽然我比你们年长，也经历过很多事情，但是你们这些毕业生的知识和成就将来会远远超过我。因为历史正在加快进程。毕业之后，你们要离开相对安全、可以规划和有着确定性的校园，将进入一个充满未知的世界。在全球各地，整个社会都在转型，新的形态正在形成，国家的历史正被重新改写。全世界像你们这样的青年人，对由谁领导他们和领导的方式，正在越来越多地发出自己的声音。在各国处理有关国民性和国家命运的问题中，旧的控制模式已经被颠覆。不管有没有收到邀请，以前那些没有机会发出声音的人们，正走上发言台，提出自己的主张。

new identities forged, and national stories retold. People your age across the world are becoming increasingly vocal about how they are governed and by whom. Old templates of control have been overturned as States struggle internally with issues about national character and destiny. People who, heretofore, had no say in those conversations are asserting themselves and taking a place at the table, with or without an invitation.

Ten years ago, information about the tragic events of September 11 came to us mainly through traditional media: radio, television, and … cnn.com. There was no Facebook, no YouTube, no Twitter and all the other social networking sites that my grandchildren now take for granted. In the intervening 10 years, young people like yourselves have gone on to use technology to improve the overall quality of life and created wealth. In those 10 years, the world has become smaller and more connected. The complex financial instruments of 10 years ago would seem quaint to the hedge funds and investment banks of today. In those 10 years, our markets and economies have become more connected and adjusted faster.

Just six months ago, the Tunisian revolution began, leading rapidly and **inexorably** [adv. 无情地，不可阻挡地] to fundamental change across North Africa and the Middle East. Could this have happened without digital social media, or without heightened correlation of food prices across time and space? Could this have happened just 10 years ago, with the same preconditions but a different degree of connectivity? Can you imagine what the next 10 years will bring? The next 50?

In the time even before Friendster **succumbed** [v. 屈从，死于] to Facebook, our world went through phases of transformation, and Harvard graduates, students, faculty, and commencement speakers have been key actors, writers, and chroniclers of those changes. In 1947, U.S. Secretary of State George Marshall stood in this very Yard before a graduating class such as this one to announce the plan to **salvage** [vt. 救助，打捞] Europe after the devastation caused by the Second World War:

He began, "I need not tell you, gentlemen, (I don't know where the ladies were) that the world situation is very serious. But to speak more seriously" — Marshall said as he went on to advocate the well-known Marshall Plan. In

10年前,我们主要通过广播、电视,以及cnn.com等传统媒体了解悲剧性的9·11事件。那时没有Facebook,没有YouTube,没有Twitter和其他社交网络这类网站,而我的孙辈现在对这些东西觉得理所当然。在过去的10年里,像你们这样的年轻人通过使用新技术,改变了生活的总体质量,创造出了财富。在这10年中,世界变得更小,联系更加紧密。10年前的复杂金融工具,对于今天的对冲基金和投资银行来说,显得稀松平常。10年里,我们的市场和经济更加融为一体,调节的步伐更为快速。

就在六个月前,突尼斯爆发了革命,并导致在北非和中东发生了迅猛不可阻挡的根本性变革。没有数字化的社交媒体,或者如果不是因为各地食品价格的变动紧紧关联,这一切会发生吗?要是换在10年前,就算具备了其他同样的前提条件,如果人们的沟通没有达到现在的程度,这一切会发生吗?你能想象接下来的10年会带来什么吗?接下来的50年呢?

其实在Facebook取代Friendster之前,我们的世界就已经进入了转型阶段,而哈佛的毕业生、学生、老师和毕业典礼演讲者等人,就是导致这些转变的关键演员、作者和历史记录者。

1947年,美国国务卿乔治·马歇尔就是站在这个院子里,面对像你们一样的毕业生,宣布了一项计划,抢救被二战摧毁的欧洲。

他说:"我不必提醒各位先生(不知那时女士们是否在场),世界形势非常严峻。但是,我还有更重要的话要说。"马歇尔接下去就倡导了后来举世闻名的马歇尔计划。由此,我们看到欧洲复兴了,接着是东亚的崛起,这些都是导致非洲目前进展的催化剂。

哈佛的另一个毕业生肯尼迪总统,当时作为马萨诸塞州年轻的参议员,在他为1956年的毕业典礼演讲中,分析了政治家和知识分子之间的紧张关系。在谈到政治家时,肯尼迪这样说道:"我们需要学者公正的观点和技术性的判断,来防止我们被自己的宣传口号固步自封。"

在新兴的民主社会里,由于许多投票者都还是文盲,所以选票

time, we saw a rebounded Europe, and the subsequent rise of East Asia, have been the catalyzing forces behind Africa's own recent progress.

When President John F. Kennedy, another Harvard graduate, spoke to this audience in 1956 as the junior senator from Massachusetts, he analyzed the tension between politicians and intellectuals. Of the politicians, Kennedy said, "We need both the technical judgment and the disinterested viewpoint of the scholar, to prevent us from becoming imprisoned by our own slogans." In newly democratic societies, where ballots are marked with distinctive icons as well as names since many voters remain illiterate, the danger of sloganeering political populism is only greater, and can lead down the road of war, not just bad policy choices. Kennedy, of course, would go on to launch the Peace Corps, which has impacted the lives of millions throughout the world by bringing Americans across the ocean, teaching students and training teachers, and making our world a smaller place.

Ralph Ellison, speaking at the 1974 Commencement, told the graduates and alumni: "Let us not be dismayed, let us not lose faith simply because the correctives we have set in motion, and you have set in motion, took a long time." Ellison believed that despite the challenge, the chance for national regeneration was there.

In the more recent past, Bill Gates, a famous Harvard attendee, has made our world smaller still by having all of us speak the same dialect, by connecting us electronically and opening doors that just one generation ago seemed to belong to the realm of science fiction. Today, because of him, we are closer to living in a global village.

With the election of Harvard graduate Barack Obama to the presidency of the United States, the face of American politics has been altered for good. In the sea change that his election represents, let me remind you, America, that Liberia has you beat on one score: We elected our first female president, perhaps 11 years before the United States might do so.

Today, I share more than a Harvard background with you. In a way, this is also a commencement year for me. Just as you end one journey today and begin the next, so too do I in November. As my first term as the president of Liberia comes to an end, I will be standing for re-election. The person who claims to be

上在印着候选人的名字时,还不得不标上各种符号,在这种情况下,口号政治和民粹主义的危险性只会更大,而且不仅仅会导致坏的政策选择,还可能导致战争。当然,肯尼迪后来倡导了和平队项目,让美国人跨越大洋,教育学生、训练教师,从而影响了全世界无数人的生命,让我们的世界变得更小。

1974年,拉尔夫·埃利森在哈佛毕业典礼上演讲,他这样告诉毕业生和校友:"不要灰心,不要丧失信念,尽管我们采取的行动以及你们也在采取的行动,可能需要很长的时间才能看到效果。"他相信尽管有种种挑战,国家的复兴机会就在前方。

在更近的过去,著名的哈佛辍学生比尔·盖茨,让我们所有人使用同一种计算机"方言",将我们用电子的方式联系起来,打开就在我们前一代人还认为纯属科幻领域的大门,从而使世界变得更小。今天,多亏了他,我们更加接近于生活在一个地球村里。

随着哈佛毕业生奥巴马当选为美国总统,美国政界的面貌从此改变。虽然他的当选代表美国发生的巨大变化,但是让我提醒你们,提醒美国,有一点利比里亚超过了你们,那就是我们选出了第一位女总统,至少比美国早了11年。

今天,我不仅以"哈佛人"的身份与你们交流,某种意义上,今年也是我的毕业年。正如你们今天结束一段旅途,将要开始下一段征程,我在今年11月也将如此。我担任利比里亚总统的第一个任期即将结束,并将投入连任竞选。我的一个最有力的竞争对手,碰巧也是哈佛毕业生。我想告诉你们,这个哈佛毕业生也一心想要赢得大选。因此,哈佛与利比里亚的关系完全有保障,很可靠!

哈佛的毕业生、2011届的同学们!我敦促你们勇敢地面对未来。有些事还没做成,并不意味着不可能做成。我在竞选总统时,没有因为过去在非洲从无女性当选过总统而畏缩。不能因为利比里亚政府总是男人的天下,就说明这是对的,我没有被吓倒。今天,妇女在利比里亚走上领导岗位的数量,正在前所未有地增加,我们还想在这方面继续努力。

the strongest opposition contender is a Harvard graduate. But I want you to know that the incumbent, who is also a Harvard graduate, is determined to win. The relationship between Harvard and Liberia is thus secured and in good hands!

Harvard Graduates, Class of 2011: I urge you to be fearless about the future. Just because something has not been done yet, doesn't mean it can't be. I was never deterred from running for president just because there had never been any females elected head of state in Africa. Simply because political leadership in Liberia had always been a "boys' club" didn't mean it was right, and I was not deterred. Today, an unprecedented number of women hold leadership positions in our country, and we intend to increase that number.

As you approach your future, there will be ample opportunity to become jaded and cynical, but I urge you to resist cynicism — the world is still a beautiful place and change is possible. As I have noted here today, my path to the presidency was never straightforward or guaranteed. Prison, death threats, and exile provided every reason to quit, to forget about the dream, yet I persisted, convinced that my country and people are so much better than our recent history indicates. **Looking back on my life, I have come to appreciate its difficult moments. I believe I am a better leader, a better person with a richer appreciation for the present because of my past.**

The size of your dreams must always exceed your current capacity to achieve them. If your dreams do not scare you, they are not big enough. If you start off with a small dream, you may not have much left when it is fulfilled because along the way, life will task your dreams and make demands on you. I am, however, bullish about the future of our world because of you. We share one defining characteristic that prepares us to transform our world — we are all Harvard University graduates. When we add to that the traditional quests for excellence for which we are known, there is no telling what we can accomplish.

Go forth and embrace a future that awaits you. I thank you.

当你们进入社会,会有太多的现象让人变得厌倦和愤世嫉俗。但是我希望你们能够抵制这种玩世不恭的心态——这个世界依然是一个美好的地方,改变是会发生的。正如我今天在这里所说,我的总统之路并非坦途,其中充满变数。监狱、死亡、流亡,任何一个理由都能使我退却,放弃自己的梦想。但我坚持下来了,我坚信我的国家和人民绝不应该是那时的样子,而应该好得多。**回顾我的人生,我反而珍惜那些艰难时刻。我相信过去所有的经历,让我成了一个更好的领导人、一个更好的人,并更加珍惜当下。**

你们应当志存高远,把梦想设计得看似高不可及。如果你的梦想没有让你惊讶,那说明它们不够宏大;如果你的梦想很小,当它实现之后,你会觉得无所寄托,因为你的梦想为人生指路,对你提出要求。因为有你们,我对我们的世界充满信心。我们有一个重要的相同点,那就是我们都是哈佛大学的毕业生,这使得我们都必须做好去改变世界的准备。再加上我们早已为人所知的追求卓越的传统,我们能取得的成就将无法预料。

大步向前,去迎接等待你们的未来吧!

谢谢大家!

---

1 哈佛大学所在地,英文与英国的剑桥同为 Cambridge。

法瑞德·扎卡利亚（1964— ）

　　法瑞德·扎卡利亚是美国印度裔著名评论家，因在近年两次采访温家宝总理而为中国人民所熟知。

　　扎卡利亚1964年出生于印度孟买的一个穆斯林家庭。他的父亲曾是印度国大党内的一名知识分子，母亲曾任《印度周日时报》编辑。扎卡利亚从小受家庭影响，大量接受和学习包括基督教在内的西方文化。高中毕业后他被耶鲁大学录取，在耶鲁度过了他的本科生涯，获得文学学士学位。在耶鲁求学期间，他积极参与政治社团活动，曾担任《耶鲁政治月刊》主编。随后他进入哈佛大学继续深造，于1993年获得政治学博士学位。

　　扎卡利亚是近年来美国最走红的评论家。从2000年至2010年，他担任美国《新闻周刊》国际版编辑，主要负责采访外交事务和撰写当周的外交评论文章。

2010年受邀担任《时代》杂志的总编辑，并在CNN主持一档关注度很高的节目。他还曾是《纽约时报》《华尔街日报》《纽约客》等报刊的专栏作家，发表过影响广泛的政治、经济方面的专栏文章。

　　扎卡利亚先后出版的《从财富到权力》(From Wealth to Power)、《自由的未来》(The Future of Freedom)、《后美国的世界》(The Post-American World) 等都被翻译成几十种语言在全球畅销，在国际政治界、经济界影响巨大。《后美国的世界》一书描绘了中国崛起后的世界新秩序，详细分析了几个发展中国家在多个领域对当今世界格局的影响和变化，据说这本书也是现任美国总统奥巴马经常带在身边的读物。

　　2007年，扎卡利亚被《外交》和《前景》杂志评为当今世界100名最具影响力的公共知识分子之一。

2012

We Live in an Age of Progress
生活在一个永远进取的时代

Fareed Zakaria 法瑞德·扎卡利亚

Thank you so much, President Faust, Fellows of the Corporation, Overseers, Ladies and Gentlemen, and graduates.

To the graduates in particular, I have to tell you, you're way ahead of me already. I never made it to my commencement, either from college or graduate school. I went to college south of here, in a small town called New Haven, Connecticut. And, well, I celebrated a bit the night before the ceremony. The honest truth is, I slept through much of my commencement. Then, after I had finally made it to Harvard for graduate school, I took a job before I had finished my Ph.D., and wrote the final chapters while working in New York. I couldn't get away from work for Commencement, and I got my degree in the mail. So, 19 years later, it is a great honor to receive, in person, a Harvard degree.

Harvard was, for me, a revelation. Contrary to the conventional wisdom on this campus, it is possible to receive a fine education at Yale, and I did. But Harvard's great graduate programs have an ambition, energy, and range that, for me, made it a dazzling, electric experience. Getting a Ph.D. involves many hours of grueling work, but, if you do it right, also many hours of goofing off with friends, acquiring new hobbies and interests, and working your way through the great resources here — from the libraries to cafes. I fully availed myself of these opportunities, and the time spent not working (in a formal sense) was as valuable as the hours in seminar rooms. I learned from students, faculty, and visitors. Harvard is really where I learned to think, and I owe this University a deep debt of gratitude, as most of you do as well — something the University will remind you of from time to time.

I have always been wary of making commencement speeches because I don't think of myself as old enough to have any real wisdom to impart on such an august occasion. I'd like to think I'm still vaguely post-graduate. But there's nothing like having kids to remind me of how deeply uncool I am. So I accept this task, with some trepidation.

The best commencement speech I ever read was by the humorist Art Buchwald. He was brief, saying simply, "Remember, we are leaving you a perfect world. Don't screw it up."

You are not going to hear that message much these days. Instead, you're likely to hear that we are living through grim economic times, that the graduates are entering the slowest recovery since the Great Depression. The worries are not just economic.

谢谢你们，福斯特校长、哈佛监管会的各位理事、哈佛集团的各位成员、女士们、先生们、毕业生们：

对于今天的毕业生，我得特别说一句，你们已经走在了我的前头，我还从未参加过大学或研究生院的毕业典礼。

正如你们刚才听到的，我的本科是在位于这儿南面的一座小城——纽黑文[1]的"一所小学校"里读的。也许当时我犯了个错误，在毕业典礼的前一晚庆祝了太长时间，结果在典礼上困得睡着了。后来我到哈佛攻读研究生学位，在毕业之前就找到了一份工作，博士论文的最后几章都是在纽约边工作边写的。因为工作缠身，我无法参加毕业典礼，学位证书是学校邮寄给我的。所以，19年后的今天，我很荣幸能够亲自获颁一个哈佛学位[2]。

哈佛对于我来说是一种启示。与这个校园里流行的看法相反，其实人们在耶鲁大学同样可以得到最好的教育——我就是这样的。然而哈佛研究生课程的视野、能量和博大，对我来说仍是一种令人眼花缭乱的神奇体验。攻读博士意味着漫长而艰苦的工作，但如果你安排得当，也可以和朋友们一起消磨时光，发展新的爱好和兴趣，并好好利用校园内从图书馆到咖啡馆这类美妙的资源。我充分利用了这些机会，那些没花在正事上的时间（我真是这么认为的），和花在学术探讨的时间，同样让我受益甚多，从学生、老师和来访者那里学到了很多。我在哈佛学会了真正的思考，我对母校深怀感激，你们中的大多数人也会有同样的感受，哈佛会不时提醒你认识到这一点。

我一直对在毕业典礼上发表演讲退避三舍。因为我不认为自己具有足够的资格，在这样一个庄重的场合来传授任何真正的智慧。我还把自己当做一个毕业不久的新人。让孩子们来提醒我，说我已经过时无法装酷了，是件令人难堪的事。所以我是诚惶诚恐地接受这个演讲邀请的。

我读过的最好的演讲，是幽默艺术家阿瑟·布赫瓦尔德[3]的。他只是简单地说："记住，我们给你们留下了一个完美的世界，别把它搞砸了。"

这年头，我们不太会听到这样的话了。相反，你可能会听到，我们正在经历严峻的经济时期，你会听人们说，眼下的毕业生们正面临着自从大萧条以来最缓慢的经济复苏。忧虑不只是在经济层面。自从9·11以来，我们生活在一个恐惧的时代，由于担心可能发生的袭击，以及未

Ever since 9/11, we have lived in an age of terror, and our lives remain altered by the fears of future attacks and a future of new threats and dangers. Then there are larger concerns that you hear about: The Earth is warming; we're running out of water and other vital resources; we have a billion people on the globe trapped in terrible poverty.

So, I want to sketch out for you, perhaps with a little bit of historical context, the world as I see it.

The world we live in is, first of all, at peace — profoundly at peace. The richest countries of the world are not in geopolitical competition with one another, fighting wars, proxy wars, or even engaging in arms races or "cold wars." This is a historical rarity. You would have to go back hundreds of years to find a similar period of great power peace. I know that you watch a bomb going off in Afghanistan or hear of a terror plot in this country and think we live in dangerous times. But here is the data. The number of people who have died as a result of war, civil war, and, yes, terrorism, is down 50 percent this decade from the 1990s. It is down 75 percent from the preceding five decades, the decades of the Cold War, and it is, of course, down 99 percent from the decade before that, which is World War II. Steven Pinker says that we are living in the most peaceful times in human history, and he must be right because he is a Harvard professor.

The political stability we have experienced has allowed the creation of a single global economic system, in which countries around the world are participating and flourishing. In 1980, the number of countries that were growing at 4 percent a year — robust growth — was around 60. By 2007, it had doubled. Even now, after the financial crisis, that number is more than 80. Even in the current period of slow growth, keep in mind that the global economy as a whole will grow 10 to 20 percent faster this decade than it did a decade ago, 60 percent faster than it did two decades ago, and five times as fast as it did three decades ago.

The result: The United Nations estimates that poverty has been reduced more in the past 50 years than in the previous 500 years. And much of that reduction has taken place in the last 20 years. The average Chinese person is 10 times richer than he or she was 50 years ago — and lives for 25 years longer. Life expectancy across the world has risen dramatically. We gain five hours of life expectancy every day — without even exercising! A third of all the babies born in the developed world this year will live to be 100.

来会面临什么样的新威胁和新危险,我们的生活大受影响。此外,你们还听到其他更大的问题:地球变暖、水资源和其他资源的短缺、地球上还有10亿多人受困于可怕的贫穷之中。

所以,我想通过一些历史背景,来为你们描绘一下我所认识的世界。

首先,我们生活的世界正处在和平时期——一种深刻的和平。世界上最富有的国家之间,没有地缘政治之争,没有打仗或进行代理战争,甚至没有从事军备竞赛和进行"冷战",这在历史上是非常罕见的。你要追溯到几百年前,才能找到类似的大国之间和平相处的时期。 我知道,你们看到在阿富汗发生爆炸,或听到我们国家有人策划恐怖阴谋,就认为我们生活在危险的时代。但数据显示,自上世纪90年代以来,这10年间,因为战争、内战,还有恐怖主义而死亡的人数,下降了50%。比这之前的50年,即冷战时期,下降了75%,而且当然,又比那之前的10年,即二战时期,下降了99%。史提芬·平科说,我们生活在人类历史上最和平的时代,他说的肯定是正确的,因为他是哈佛大学的教授。

这样的政治稳定,带来一个单一的全球经济体系,世界各国参与其中,共享繁荣。在1980年时期,每年以4%的速度增长(这是相当稳健的增长)的国家有60个左右。到了2007年,这样的国家数量增加了一倍。就是现在,在发生金融危机之后,这一数字还超过80(个国家)。即使是目前这样的缓慢增长时期,请记住,全球经济在这个10年的增长,仍比上一个10年要快10%至20%,比20年前快60%,比30年前要快上5倍。

其结果是,据联合国估计,过去50年内所减少的贫困人数,要比前500年加起来的还要多。贫困人数的减少,大多是在过去的20年中实现的。普通中国人比50年前要富10倍,寿命也延长了25年。世界各地人们的预期寿命在大幅度上升。我们不用锻炼,每天就增加了5小时的预期寿命!今年在发达世界出生的婴儿中,三分之一可以活到100岁。

所有这一切,都是由于生活水平的提高、卫生条件的改善,当然,还有医学的进步。阿图·加旺德是哈佛大学的教授,也是一个外科医生,他还为《纽约客》杂志写过有关医学的文章。他在一篇文章中提到19世纪的一个手术,当时外科医生试图切掉病人的腿。医生成功了,但他也

All this is because of rising standards of living, hygiene, and, of course, medicine. Atul Gawande, a Harvard professor who is also a practicing surgeon, and who also writes about medicine for The New Yorker, writes about a 19th century operation in which the surgeon was trying to amputate his patient's leg. He succeeded — at that — but accidentally amputated his assistant's finger as well. Both died of sepsis, and an onlooker died of shock. It is the only known medical procedure to have a 300 percent fatality rate. We've come a long way.

To understand the astonishing age of progress we are living in, you just look at the cellphones in your pockets. (Many of you have them out and were already looking at them. Don't think I can't see you.) Your cellphones have more computing power than the Apollo space capsule. That capsule couldn't even Tweet! So just imagine the opportunities that lie ahead. Moore's Law — that computing power doubles every 18 months while costs halve — may be slowing down in the world of computers, but it is accelerating in other fields. The human genome is being sequenced at a pace faster than Moore's Law. A "Third Industrial Revolution," involving material science and the customization of manufacturing, is yet in its infancy. And all these fields are beginning to intersect and produce new opportunities that we cannot really foresee.

The good news goes on. Look at the number of college graduates globally. It has risen fourfold in the last four decades for men, but it has risen sevenfold for women. I believe that the empowerment of women, whether in a village in Africa or a boardroom in America, is good for the world. If you are wondering whether women are in fact smarter than men, the evidence now is overwhelming: yes. My favorite example of this is a study done over the last 25 years in which it found that female representatives in the House of Congress were able to bring back $49 million more in federal grants than their male counterparts. So it turns out women are better than men even at pork-barrel spending. We can look forward to a world enriched and ennobled by women's voices.

Now you might listen to me and say "This is all wonderful for the world at large, but what does this mean for America?" Well, for America and for most places, peace and broader prosperity — "the rise of the rest" — means more opportunities. I remind you that this is a country that still has the largest and most dynamic economy in the world, that dominates the age of technology, that hosts hundreds of the world's greatest companies, that houses its largest, deepest capital markets, and that has almost

意外地切掉了他助手的手指。结果病人和助手都死于败血症，另一个旁观者则因为惊吓而死亡。这是已知的医疗手术中，唯一一个发生了300%死亡率的事件。现在我们有了长足的进步。

要想了解当今世界的惊人进步，你只要看看自己口袋里的手机（你们当中有许多人已经掏出手机在看了，别以为我看不到你们）。你的手机比阿波罗号飞船的计算能力还强。那个飞船发不了短信！让我们来想象一下摆在我们面前的机会。穆尔定律说，人们研发出的计算能力，每18个月会增加一倍，而费用却减少了一半，这个定律在计算机领域可能会放缓，但在其他领域却仍在加速。人类基因组测序的速度就超过了穆尔定律。涵盖材料科学和根据小批量定制而制造的"第三次工业革命"，还处于起步阶段。而所有这些领域，都开始交叉渗透，并在这个过程中带来我们尚无法预见的新机会。

这样的好消息还有很多。我们来看看在全球范围内的大学毕业生数量。在过去的40年里，男性大学生增加了4倍，而女性大学生则增加了7倍。我相信，无论是在非洲的某个村庄，还是在美国的某个董事会，赋予妇女权力，对世界来说都会是好事。如果你还在思虑女性是否比男性聪明，现在的证据是不容置疑的：是的。我喜欢的一个例子是，对过去25年的研究发现，美国众议院里的女性国会代表比起她们的男同行来，能够为自己的选区多争取回4900万美元的联邦拨款。所以，与男性比较起来，女性在争取专项拨款方面也更有优势。我们可以期待，我们的世界，会因为妇女的声音而更加丰富多彩。

听到我说了这些，你们可能会问："总体而言，对这个世界都很好，但对于美国来说，这有什么好处呢？"嗯，对美国和大多数地方来说，和平与繁荣——"其他地方的发展"——其实意味着更多的机会。我要提醒大家，我们这个国家仍然有着世界上最大和最具活力的经济体，并在这个科技时代占据着主导地位，拥有数百个世界上最大的公司，有着世界上最大且最有深度的资本市场，世界上最好的大学几乎都在美国。中国或印度没有比得上哈佛的大学，10年之内甚至更久，也还不会有。

美国社会也充满了活力。在工业化的国家里，它是唯一一个在人口

all of the world's greatest universities. There is no equivalent of Harvard in China or India, nor will there be one for decades, perhaps longer.

The United States is also a vital society. It is the only country in the industrialized world that is demographically vibrant. We add 3,000,000 people to the country every year. That itself is a powerful life force, and it is made stronger by the fact that so many of these people are immigrants. They — I should say we — come to this country with aspirations, with hunger, with drive, with determination, and with a fierce love for America. By 2050, America will have a better demographic profile than China. This country has its problems, but I would rather have America's problems than most any other place in the world.

When I tell you that we live in an age of progress, I am not urging complacency — far from it. We have had daunting challenges over the last 100 years: a depression, two world wars, a Cold War, 9/11, and global economic crisis. But we have overcome them by our response. Human action and human achievement have managed to tackle terrible problems.

We forget our successes. In 2009, the H1N1 virus broke out in Mexico. Now, if you looked back at the trajectory of these kinds of viruses, it is quite conceivable this one would have spread like the Asian flu in 1957 or 1968, in which 4,000,000 people died. But this time, the Mexican health authorities identified the problem early, shared the information with the WHO, learned best practices fast, tracked down where the outbreak began, quarantined people, and vaccinated others. The country went on a full-scale alert, banning any large gatherings. In a Catholic country, you couldn't go to church for three Sundays. Perhaps more importantly, you couldn't go to soccer matches either. The result was that the virus was contained, to the point where, three months later, people wondered what the big fuss was and asked if we had all overreacted. We didn't overreact; we reacted, we responded, and we solved the problem.

There are other examples. In the 12 months following the economic peak in 2008, industrial production fell by as much as it did in the first year of the depression. Equity prices and global trade fell more. Yet this time, no Great Depression followed. Why? Because of the coordinated actions of governments around the world. 9/11 did not usher in an age of terrorism, with al-Qaida going from strength to strength. Why? Because countries cooperated in fighting them and other terror groups, with considerable success. When we can come together, when we cooperate, when we put

构成方面趋于合理的国家。我们每年增加 300 万人口,这本身就显示着强大的生命力,而且这些增加的人口中很多是移民。他们——应该说是我们——带着愿望、动力和决心来到这个国家,并对这个国家满怀热爱。到 2050 年,美国的人口构成会比中国更好。这个国家有它的问题,但我宁愿面对美国的问题,而不会想去碰世界上任何其他地方的问题。

当我说我们生活在一个不断进步的时代时,我并不是希望大家自满——远非如此。在过去 100 年间,我们经受了许多严峻的挑战:经济大衰退、两次世界大战、冷战、9·11 事件,还有全球经济危机,但我们克服了这些挑战。人类的行动和所取得的成绩,成功地对付了这些可怕的问题。

我们忘记了自己的成功。2009 年,甲型 H1N 1 流感在墨西哥爆发。如果你回头看看这类病毒的传播轨迹,它很可能会像 1957 年或 1968 年发生的造成 400 万人死亡的亚洲流感那样快速传播。但这一次,墨西哥卫生当局很早就发现问题,并和世界卫生组织共享信息,很快掌握最佳处理方案,找到病毒发生的根源,隔离受感染的人群,并为其他人接种疫苗。该国接着进行了全面警戒,禁止举行任何大型集会。在这个天主教国家里,人们有三个星期的时间不能去教堂。也许还有更重要的,你不能去看足球比赛。结果病毒得到有效控制。三个月后,有人质疑是否有必要这样大做文章,是否反应过度了?我们没有反应过度。我们做出了反应,我们采取了措施,我们解决了这个问题。

还有其他例子。经济在 2008 年达到高峰之后的 12 个月里,工业生产急剧下降,和大衰退第一年的程度差不多。抑郁症、股票价格和全球贸易下跌得更多,然而这一次没有再出现大萧条。为什么?因为世界各地的政府采取了协调行动。9·11 没有带来恐怖主义的大行其道、没有出现基地组织不断壮大的时代。为什么?因为各国合作打击基地组织和其他恐怖组织,并取得了相当大的成功。当我们齐心协力、并肩合作的时候,当我们摒弃微小差异的时候,其结果是惊人的。

所以,让我们再来看看所面临的问题——经济危机、恐怖主义、气候变化、资源稀缺——请记住,这些问题都是现实存在的,但人类对这些问题所作出的反应和应对措施,也是真心实意的。政府、公司、组织和许多人士,

aside petty differences, the results are astounding.

So, when we look at the problems we face — economic crises, terrorism, climate change, resource scarcity — keep in mind that these problems are real, but also that the human reaction and response to them will also be real. We can more easily map out the big problem than the thousands of individual actions governments, firms, organizations, and people will take that will constitute the solution.

In a sense, I'm betting on the graduates in this great audience. I believe that your actions will have consequences. Your efforts will make a difference.

And turning to the graduates, I know I am expected to provide some advice at a commencement. **Should you go into nanotechnology or bioengineering? What are the industries of the future? Honestly, I have no idea. But one thing I do know is that human beings will reward and honor those talents of heart and mind they have always honored for thousands of years: intelligence, hard work, discipline, courage, loyalty and, perhaps above all, love and a generosity of spirit. Those are the qualities that, at the end of the day, make you live a great life, one that is rewarded by the outside world, and a good life, one that is rewarded only by those who know you best.** These are the virtues that people honor, that they built statues for 5,000 years ago. Well, nobody builds statues anymore. They build weird, modernist sculptures with strange pieces of metal falling off of them, but you get my idea. **Trust yourself; you know what you should do. You know the kind of life you should live. You don't need an ethics course to know what you shouldn't do. Just trust in your instincts, be true to them, and you will make for yourself a great and a good life. And, in doing so, you will change the world.**

I said that at my age I don't feel competent to give you much advice, but I will give you one last piece of wisdom that comes with age. For all of you who are graduating students or, really, anyone who is still young, trust me. You cannot possibly understand the love that your parents have for you until you have children of your own. Once you have your own kids, their strange behavior will suddenly make sense. But don't wait that long. On this day of all days, give them a hug, and tell them that you love them.

Thank you, ladies and gentlemen, and to the graduates of Harvard University's Class of 2012, Godspeed.

都采取了成千上万的不同举措，来构建解决方案，我们在此基础上，可以更容易地描绘出问题的症结。

在某种意义上，我对今天听众中的毕业生们寄予厚望。我相信，你们的行动会有成果，你们的努力一定会带来成效。

谈到毕业生，我知道在毕业演讲中应当提供一些忠告。**你应当进入纳米技术行业还是生物工程行业？什么是产业的未来？老实说，我不知道。但我知道的是，人类将像千百年来一样，褒奖并尊重人们一直尊重的心智能力：智慧、努力、纪律、勇气、忠诚，而且也许最重要的，要有博爱和慷慨的精神。说到底，这些品格能够让你体验生命的美妙，赢得外界的尊重；也能够使你从外部获得舒适的物质生活，而从精神上得到你最亲近的人的关爱。**人们推崇这些美德，早在 5000 年前就为之树立雕像。嗯，人们现在不再树立雕像了。他们做的现代雕塑奇形怪状，还有可笑的金属片从雕像上脱落，但你们知道我所要表达的意思。**要相信自己，你才知道应该做什么，知道自己要过什么样的生活。你不用上道德课就知道什么是不该做的。相信你的直觉，听从心灵的召唤，你就能为自己创造一个美妙和美好的生活。而且，在这样做的同时，你将改变世界。**

我刚说过，在我这个年纪，我不觉得自己能给你们提供什么建议，但我要告诉你们一个随着年龄增长而得来的智慧。对今天即将毕业的学生们，其实对所有仍然年轻的人，都请在这一点上相信我：除非你自己有了孩子，否则你不可能懂得父母对你的爱。一旦你有了自己的孩子，父母那些看似奇怪的行为，好像突然都变得容易解释了。但不要等那么久。在这样特别的日子里，给他们一个拥抱，并告诉他们说，你爱他们。

谢谢，女士们先生们，对哈佛大学 2012 届的毕业生们，我想说的是：祝你们一帆风顺！

---

1 纽黑文，耶鲁大学所在地。因为哈佛和耶鲁素有互相竞争、挪揄对方的传统，他在这里跟哈佛学生开了个玩笑，故意称耶鲁是一所"small college"——一所"小学校"。

2 哈佛大学的惯例，会给毕业典礼演讲者颁发荣誉博士学位。

3 阿瑟·布赫瓦尔德（Art Buchwald, 1925—2007），美国政治评论家和讽刺家，曾获普利策奖，被称为"华盛顿的智慧"（"Wit of Washington"）。

本书精选了34篇1947年至2012年间哈佛毕业典礼上的优秀演讲作品。鉴于作品时间跨度大，不可避免地存在部分作品因演讲者去世而无法确定权利人、部分作品因权利人分散而无法取得联系等各种客观原因，致使我方虽多番努力仍无法与合法权利人取得联系。在此我们谨向作者及著作权人致谢，并深表歉意，敬请相关著作权人见书后及时与我们取得联系（联系方式后附），我们将依法承担稿酬支付义务。

　　特此声明！

联系地址：中国北京朝阳区金台西路2号人民日报出版社
联系电话：86-10-65369526　65369517
联 系 人：林薇

图书在版编目（CIP）数据

带着激情与梦想上路：哈佛毕业典礼演讲精选：汉英对照 / 刘海翔，甘露编译．
—北京：人民日报出版社，2013.5
ISBN 978-7-5115-1833-0

Ⅰ．①带… Ⅱ．①刘…②甘… Ⅲ．①英语—汉语—对照读物②演讲—世界—选集 Ⅳ．① H319.4：I

中国版本图书馆 CIP 数据核字（2013）第 109917 号

书　　名	带着激情与梦想上路——哈佛毕业典礼演讲精选
编　　译	刘海翔　甘　露
出 版 人	董　伟
责任编辑	林　薇
装帧设计	视觉共振
出版发行	人民日报出版社
社　　址	北京金台西路 2 号
邮政编码	100733
发行热线	（010）65369527　65369846　65369509　65369510
邮购热线	（010）65369530　65363527
编辑热线	（010）65369526
网　　址	www.peopledailypress.com
经　　销	新华书店
印　　刷	环球印刷（北京）有限公司
开　　本	710mm × 1000mm　1/16
字　　数	600 千
印　　张	39
版　　次	2013 年 7 月第 1 版　2013 年 7 月第 1 次印刷
书　　号	ISBN 978-7-5115-1833-0
定　　价	68.00 元